The Diary of James A. Garfield
Volume IV 1878-1881

The publication of this book was assisted by a grant from the Publications Program of the National Endowment for the Humanities, an independent federal agency.

The Diary of
James A. Garfield

Volume IV 1878-1881

Edited with an Introduction by

Harry James Brown
Frederick D. Williams

MICHIGAN STATE UNIVERSITY PRESS
1981

★
 ★
★
 ★
★

The Editors Dedicate Their Work
to the Memory of
ABRAM GARFIELD (1872–1958)
Whose Help Was Indispensable

Contents

The Diary of James A. Garfield
Volume IV 1878-1881

1878

January

TUESDAY, I. Crete and I called on Sister Hittie and examined the new house. It has cost me a little above $500. I am more than ever repaid by the brighter and happier look which it brings to Sister's face. Leaving Crete to go to Hiram in the evening, I took the one o'clock train for Cleveland. Arrived at Dr. Robison's at half-past three where Messrs. Chisholm and Sickels[1] were awaiting me to state the merits of their wood-screw manufacture and the grounds on which they opposed a reduction of the tariff. Spent several hours with them. At six in the evening Dr. Robison and I called at Mr. J. H. Wade's, where we were met by H. B. Payne. We spent the evening there. An elegant supper was served at eight o'clock and we remained until 11. The Doctor and I returned to his house on Superior Street, where I spent the night.

WEDNESDAY, 2. Took the morning train to Garrettsville and at half-past nine o'clock reached Father Rudolph's. Found Libbie very sick but I think Crete's nursing will bring her up. Went to Hinsdale's at 11 o'clock and after dining with him spent the afternoon in writing letters. I am greatly troubled by the request of Halsey Hall to sign his note in bank as security. I have declined doing so and he seems hurt by my refusal. Supper at Father Rudolph's. In the evening reads [read] Burke's lecture (in manuscript) on the Eastern Question. It was very able but dispropor-

---

[1]Either Henry Chisholm (see Vol. III, pp. 147–148) or his younger brother William, an inventor, manufacturer and shipbuilder. They, along with Amasa Stone, Jr., Andros B. Stone, and Henry B. Payne, established the Union Screw Company, of which Sheldon Sickels was secretary.

3

tioned. The Turkish discussion is too minute in proportion to his treatment of the Russian Question.

THURSDAY, 3. Went to Hinsdale's soon after breakfast and spent most of the day in his library, writing letters and preparing a lecture for this evening. After tea at Father Rudolph's Crete and I went to the Chapel, which was well filled with students and citizens. I spoke an hour on public life and some of its phases. A pretty fair lecture but not satisfactory to myself. Spent the night at Father Rudolph's.

FRIDAY, 4. Drove to Garrettsville in a heavy snow storm. Took the train to Cleveland. Thence by 11 o'clock train to Painesville, where, after transacting some business, I took tea at George Steele's. His man drove me to Mentor in the midst of a bad storm. Dr. Robison was awaiting me and we drove to his house to make some arrangements for the following day. We then returned to my house where we spent the night.

SATURDAY, 5. Arose early and breakfasted at six, the Doctor and I intending to go out and purchase cows. But the Doctor was not feeling well and we concluded to leave the purchase to Northcott, the Doctor's farmer. I have concluded to purchase seven additional cows to eat up my surplus feed. At 9 o'clock, hitched the grays to Doctor's bob sled with the wagon box upon them [it] and took the Doctor, Jones and his daughter and myself to Painesville, where I went to procure irons for two sets of bob sleds I am having made to haul wood. Returned to Mentor at 3 o'clock. I took dinner at the Doctor's and came back to the farm to give final directions to Bancroft and Moses in regard to the farm work, and at 5 o'clock went with the Doctor and his wife to Willoughby where we took the train for Cleveland. The ride to Willoughby was the coldest I have had for many years. Reached Cleveland at half-past seven and spent the night at Dr. Robison's.

SUNDAY, 6. Went with the Doctor to East Cleveland and attended church. Hall[2] preached. Dinner at Dr. Streator's. Re-

---

[2]Jabez Hall was pastor of the Euclid Avenue Church of Christ, 1872–89. On September 26, 1881, he participated in the funeral services for Garfield in the Public Square in Cleveland.

turned in the afternoon to Dr. Robison's. Crete came in the evening. We took the Columbus train at seven o'clock. Reached Shelby at ten and at half-past ten took the Baltimore and Ohio train for Washington. Read several interest[ing] articles in the *North American Review.* Governor Dennison came and joined our train at Newark and we visited with him a good part of the day.

MONDAY, 7.   Reached Washington at half-past nine and found the family well. Rose came soon and we spent nearly all the day in bringing up arrears of correspondence.

I came back to Washington with less willingness than almost ever before. There appears to be little in the immediate future of national politics that is pleasing to the intellect, or comforting to the hope. The financial craze has let down upon America a fog denser that [than] London's, through which I see no signs of an early sun, but many signs of an eclipse of national honor. I am fighting for financial honor against the majority of my own party and state, and I grow weary of the contest. If it were one of logic, reason, sense, I could enjoy it; but it is a fight of interest against honor, the brute force of votes against knowledge.

TUESDAY, 8.   Worked on correspondence nearly all day. My mail is becoming every year a heavier burden and I know of no way to lighten it except by quitting public life, or by neglecting the business it brings. I should have [added that this] morning I received a card from Lawrence Barrett with a note of introduction from W. D. Howells.[3] Called on him at the Arlington and in the evening went with Harry and Jimmy to hear him as Cassius in *Julius Caesar.* He invited us to come into his box. The boys

---

[3]The letter of introduction from William Dean Howells, dated January 4, 1878, reads as follows: "I have the pleasure of introducing my friend Mr. Lawrence Barrett, who has had the courage to connect a name distinguished in the drama with a poor little comedy of mine. He is to be seven days in Washington, and I could not think of a greater pleasure to offer him than your acquaintance." Garfield errs in respect to the date of Barrett's appearance in *Julius Caesar:* the play was performed on the evening of January 9. On the 10th the actor appeared in Howells' "poor little comedy," *A Counterfeit Presentment.* During his week at the National Theater he also appeared in *Richelieu, Hamlet, Merchant of Venice, David Garrick,* and *Richard III.*

were delighted with his attentions and particularly with his Roman dress and armor.

WEDNESDAY, 9.   Continued work on my mail. Went to the Departments and also to the Capitol on business. Multitudes of callers have been flocking in for the last two days and pressing me with their importunities for help of all kinds. I should have mentioned that in the morning I called on Lawrence Barrett at the Arlington and went with him and Mr. Hanna[4] of Cleveland to the Executive Mansion, at which place I introduced them to the President. In the evening Crete, Martha Mays, Mollie and I went to the Theatre and heard Mr. Barrett in his *Counterfeit Presentment,* written by W. D. Howells. There is but little plot in the story, but the dialogue is sparkling and the play really very enjoyable.

THURSDAY, 10.   Attended the meeting of the Committee of Ways and Means, but nothing of any account was accomplished. The House resumed its session at 12 and Mr. Wood resumed his struggle in favor of general investigations.[5] The Democrats had been so slow to return to the City that they were left in a minority and their resolutions were amended so as to make them reasonable and therefore not palatable to them. They were reported back to the House, whereupon Mr. Wood by a majority of two [three] succeeded in adjourning the House.

FRIDAY, 11.   Regular meeting of the Committee on Ways and

---

[4]Marcus A. Hanna (1837–1904), a prominent Cleveland businessman, became in later years a powerful Republican leader. He gave Garfield strong support in 1880. In 1896 he was chiefly responsible for the nomination of William McKinley. He was chairman of the Republican National Committee in 1896 and a member of the U.S. Senate from Ohio, 1897 to his death. Interested in the theater, he had numerous acquaintances among actors; he was a close friend and business adviser of Lawrence Barrett. In the 1880's he became the owner of the Cleveland Opera House.

[5]It was well known in Washington circles that the Democratic majority in the House planned sweeping investigations of recent Republican administrations, as well as the right of Rutherford B. Hayes to the presidential title. Wood's resolution, calling for general investigations and authorizing congressional committees "to send for persons and papers," was opposed by Republicans who claimed that such action was unwarranted, unwise, and expensive.

Means with nothing of importance accomplished. In the House the struggle on Wood's resolution was resumed and as the result of a long session all amendments were defeated, among others that which proposed to investigate the expenditures of Committees of Investigation of the last Congress and Wood's original resolution passed by four majority. House adjourned until Monday.

SATURDAY, 12. Hard at work all day on correspondence and arrear of business. Commenced reading Wood's Explorations of Ancient Ephesus[6] which I found very interesting.

SUNDAY, 13. Attended Church with Crete and Mother. Spent the remainder of the day and far into the evening in completing Wood's *Ephesus.* I have found but few books which have interested me so much.

MONDAY, 14. Correspondence in the morning. House at 12. During the day I very foolishly agreed to write an article for the *North American Review,* by February 5th, on Army Organization.[7] I seem to be fated to take masses of work upon my shoulders. I do not know what drives me to it. I am already over-loaded with work and this additional load may break me down.

TUESDAY, 15. Correspondence in the morning. Went to the Treasury Department on business and rode thence to the Capitol with Secretary Sherman, who went to meet the Committee on Ways and Means in regard to the bill authorizing a popular loan. He was heard before the Committee for an hour. In the House not much was done. Went to the Library and got some books for my lecture on Ephesus which I have been dragooned into promising to make in behalf of the ladies of the Disciple Church. Callers

[6]John T. Wood, *Discoveries at Ephesus, including the Site and Remains of the Great Temple of Diana* (1877).

[7]The article appeared in two parts: James A. Garfield, "The Army of the United States, with Letters of Generals Sherman and Hancock," *The North American Review,* Vol. CXXVI, No. CCLX (January-February, 1878), pp. 193–216; and "The Army of the United States, with Letters of Generals M. F. Force and John Pope, Part II, Vol. CXXVI, No. CCLXII (May–June, 1878), pp. 442–465. The second part of Garfield's article concluded with an argument against reducing either the size of the army or the salaries of officers and men, and for the development of an effective army staff.

in the afternoon and evening made work almost impossible.
WEDNESDAY, 16. Callers came in a constant stream all the morning. Dr. Todd came at an early hour, having broken down in his examination before the Medical Board in New York. He failed on the Common Branches. Went to the Capitol at twelve. Soon after reading of the Journal, I introduced a resolution accepting from Mrs. Elizabeth Thompson,[8] Carpenter's picture of the First Reading of the Emancipation Proclamation and presenting the thanks of Congress therefor. The resolution passed unanimously. House adjourned at four. This being Mollie's birthday she had a large party of little friends to dinner and still more came in the evening. Rockwell and Mr. Sumner were here. Secretary Sherman called. When the house became quieter at half-past ten I worked on my lecture on Ephesus until after midnight.

THURSDAY, 17. Correspondence in the morning. Worked on lecture on Ephesus until noon. John Q. Smith came and had a long conversation in regard to his trouble with the Interior Department.[9] I think he has been badly treated by Secretary Schurz.

---

[8]Elizabeth (Rowell) Thompson, who was born in Vermont in 1821 and had worked as a servant to support herself, visited Boston in 1843 and met Thomas Thompson, a millionaire whom she married the next year. At his death in 1869 she inherited his fortune and soon became widely known for her philanthropy. In return for her gift of the Carpenter picture, which she purchased for $25,000, she was given the freedom of the floor of the House of Representatives, a privilege never before given to a woman. In 1875 the House Appropriations Committee, of which Garfield was chairman, failed to secure House approval for the purchase of the painting for $25,000 (see Vol. III, pp. 26, 27 and 31).

[9]In 1875 Garfield helped to secure for his friend John Q. Smith the office of commissioner of Indian Affairs. In June, 1877, Secretary of Interior Carl Schurz appointed a Board of Inquiry to investigate charges against the chief clerk and concerning irregularities in the Bureau. Before the investigation was completed pressure was brought on Smith to resign. He did so reluctantly and only after assurance that his reputation was secure and that he could have the U.S. consul-generalship in Montreal. On December 31, 1877, the Board of Inquiry submitted a report that was very critical of Bureau personnel and practices. Meanwhile the President had twice nominated Smith to the consul-generalship, but he had not been confirmed. Smith believed that a great injustice had been done him and was critical of the Board of Inquiry and bitter towards Schurz. He was also afraid that the report might adversely affect his nomination. He looked to Garfield for help.

Then went to the Capitol, but little was done in the House. In the evening worked on the Ephesus lecture and made some preparations for speaking on the life and character of Senator Morton,[10] but feel quite unprepared to do the subject justice. Retired at midnight.

FRIDAY, 18. Worked on correspondence in the morning, and then commenced preparing some notes for a brief eulogy on Senator Morton. I find myself working within narrow limitations. While I greatly admired the force of Morton's intellect and will, and his great services as War Governor and party organizer, I did not admire many of his methods, and for many years doubted his personal purity of character, though of late years I have inclined to believe he was slandered in that respect. He boxed the compass on financial questions, repeatedly, and much of the heresy in Indiana on these questions is due to him.

But I was so interrupted by Dr. Todd's troubles that I made no adequate preparation, and went to the House with but two ideas determined upon, on the subject.

I spoke, however, and did fairly well. In the evening, I revised my notes carefully and sent them to the printer. Several friends called in the evening. Todd left at 7.

SATURDAY, 19. Correspondence. Shopping with Crete. Committee on Rules at 12. Drove the Grant mare on my return.[11] Call[ed] on Foster with Crete, and on the whole accomplished

---

William T. Sherman also came to his support, indicating that as far as the army was concerned Smith was the best commissioner of Indian Affairs during the last ten years. The Senate confirmed his appointment on February 14, 1878, and he held the Montreal office until his resignation in 1882.

[10]In his eulogy on Oliver P. Morton, who died on November 1, 1877, Garfield focused on his subject's Civil War service, saying that it had brought his well-deserved recognition as one of the greatest war governors, and on his leading qualities of character, describing them as a clear and forceful intellect, outstanding ability as an organizer, stout-hearted persistency, a strong partisan viewpoint which reflected his own greatness and the greatness of the nation's system of party government, and a noble, genuine patriotism.

[11]In December, 1877, Garfield bought a mare (Josie) from Orville L. Grant, brother of U.S. Grant, and gave him a sixty-day promissory note for three hundred dollars. In the spring Josie was sent to the Mentor farm.

but little during the day, and feel much worn out with the work and worry of the week. At eight P.M. went to the President's with John Q. Smith, and talked very plainly to the President about the course which Sec'y Schurz has pursued towards him. I told him the method had been outrageous and unjust, and the result ought to be atoned for in some effective way. He does not seem to be master of his administration. I fear he has less force and nerve than I had supposed. He spoke with some feeling of the fact that Conkling had procured the copies of telegrams which were sent to Hayes during the Electoral count, and which someone has stolen from the telegraph at Columbus. He says C. is preparing to attack him on the alleged bargain with the South. He then talked quite at length on the Bland Silver Bill.[12] He hopes it will pass without amendment, so that he may have stronger grounds for vetoing it. Home at 11.

Retired at 12.

SUNDAY, 20. Attended church, called on General Schenck on my way home, and then spent the remainder of the day in preparing for my lecture on Ephesus. If I had time to work the subject out to my liking, I believe I could make it an interesting one, but without sufficient work I fear it will be dry.

MONDAY, 21. Correspondence in the morning. Worked until noon preparing for my lecture on Ephesus. Went to the House where but little was done besides an attempt made by the Democrats to pass a bill under a suspension of the rules to allow the payment of customs revenues in greenbacks; vote 154 to 96, not 2/3. Home early and spent the evening reading on Ephesus.

TUESDAY, 22. Worked on correspondence until half-past ten

[12]The bill bearing the name of Richard P. Bland (1835–1899), a Democratic member of the House from Missouri, 1873–95 and 1897 to his death, provided for unlimited and free coinage of silver. It emerged from the Senate with amendments limiting the amount of silver to be coined each month and providing that seigniorage be charged by the government. The Bland-Allison bill had broad popular support, particularly in the West. But President Hayes, a "sound money" man, viewing the measure as a stain on the national credit and a violation of the national faith, vetoed it. Without debate both branches of Congress promptly overrode the veto (February 28, 1878).

when Crete and I went to Saint Aloysius Church to witness the ceremonies occasioned by the death of Victor Emmanuel, King of Italy.[13] The mass was celebrated with great pomp. The Quoir [Choir] performed Mozart's *Requiem* for the dead. Attended the House for a short time, but found the Steamboat Inspection Bill under consideration. Came home early to work on my lecture until evening, when Crete, Martha and I attended the lecture of Mr. Waddell[14] at the Disciple Church. His theme was [Samuel F. B.] Morse and [Matthew F.] Maury, a very good lecture. Came home and worked until 12.

WEDNESDAY, 23. Correspondence in the morning. Worked on lecture until half-past two o'clock, when I went to the House. Returned at four and spent the evening in reading on Ephesus. I have accumulated five times as much material as I can use at the lecture.

THURSDAY, 24. Worked at my desk until 10 o'clock, when Rose came and I went with him to the Treasury in reference to his detail to N. Y. Thence to the War Department and saw General Sherman in regard to the Court Martial of Col. Blunt of the Engineers.[15] The General showed me his private journal relating

[13]The Requiem Mass for Victor Emmanuel II (1820–1878), king of Sardinia, 1849–61, and king of Italy, 1861–78, who died on January 9, was attended by the President, the Vice President, the Chief Justice, and many other dignitaries, American and foreign.

[14]Congressman Alfred M. Waddell of North Carolina was a popular lecturer; on this occasion his address was advertised under the title "Two Americans: Morse and Maury." His writings include *Some Memories of My Life* (1908), in which he tells this story of Garfield: "Speaking of Garfield reminds me that the last time I ever saw him was in the Capitol building when, as both happened to be leaving the House at the same moment, I picked up his hat to try on and it went down nearly to my shoulders. I expressed surprise and asked what size he wore. He said, 'a number 8' and that he had to have them made to order, and then laughing and putting his hand on my shoulder, added, 'my head is the same size as Daniel Webster's and measures twenty-four inches in circumference.' "

[15]Charles E. Blunt (1823–1892), a lieutenant colonel in the Corps of Engineers, was court-martialed on January 16–18, 1878, on a charge of "neglect and violation of duty, to the prejudice of good order and military discipline" in 1876 while he was in charge of the public works of harbor improvement at Buffalo, New York. His specific offense related to the preparation in his office and his certification as

to his journey to Ephesus. Col. Audenried[16] showed me his manuscript on the same trip. Went to the House. At one o'clock, went to the Senate and listened to Senator Lamar, who made a brave and able speech against the Silver Bill. Spent an hour in the Library consulting some authorities. Home at five o'clock in the evening. Rose came and I dictated a large number of letters. Then worked on Ephesus Lecture.

Rose leaves me tonight to go to Long Island to take testimony for the Customs Dep't of the Treasury.

FRIDAY, 25.   Worked on Ephesus until half-past ten, when I went to the Capitol and attended the meeting of the Committee of Ways and Means. Long discussion on a private bill to remit the tax on some distilled spirits burned at Au Sable and Chicago, Illinois.

After 12 M. witness[ed] some interesting experiments before the sub-committee on the Tariff, with the polariscope, in testing the quality of sugar. It prove[s] that sugar of low grade color (the present basis of duty) may possess a much higher grade of saccharine quality than that of high grade color. In the House, the day was spent in discussing Blackburn's resolution for extending the time for allowing distilled spirits to remain in bond.[17] I opposed

---

correct of "irregular, incorrect, unauthorized, and deceptive" payroll vouchers. He pleaded guilty to the charge and to thirty-two of the thirty-three specifications (with modifications of three). The court found him guilty of the charge and of all the specifications or parts thereof to which he had so pleaded. It sentenced him to be suspended from rank and command for two years and to forfeit seventy-five dollars a month during that time. On February 16, 1878, President Hayes changed the sentence to "suspension from rank and command, with forfeiture of one hundred and fifty dollars per month of his pay for one year." Colonel Blunt conferred with Garfield about his trouble in the fall of 1877 and during January, 1878, he wrote two letters to him asking for his help. He was restored to active duty in 1879 and retired in 1887.

[16]Joseph C. Audenried (1839–1880), a graduate of West Point in 1861, was aide-de-camp to General William T. Sherman, 1863–80.

[17]The resolution extended the time for holding distilled spirits in bond and suspended until July 1 the tax on such spirits already manufactured. On that date, if proposed legislation was passed, the tax on whiskey would be reduced. Republicans argued that the resolution favored the manufacturers of fine, high-priced

it, as unequal in its operation on ordinary high-wines as compared with table whiskies. Home at five, and worked on lecture till 7.30 P.M., when I was driven to the Disciple Church on Vt. Avenue, and spoke an hour and ten minutes. Fair audience for a stormy night. At nine, Crete and I went to Senator Thurman's, and attend[ed] his large party. Home at half-past eleven. I should have mentioned that Harry made me a fine map of Ephesus.

SATURDAY, 26. Worked at my desk, writing letters and clearing away the debris of Ephesus until 11.30 A.M., when I went shopping with Crete, and at half-past 12 reached the Capitol and sat for two hours on the Committee on Rules to revise and condense them.

Came back by Pumphries' [James W. Pumphrey's] stables and took out "Josie," the mare I recently bought of Orville Grant. Drove with Crete, stopping on business at the War Dep't, where I warned the Sec'y that there was danger of some scandals growing out of the Post Tradership at Laramie. Then drove mother for half an hour. At seven went [to] the Smithsonian and attended the meeting of the Board of Regents. I reluctantly consented to the acceptance of a portrait of Prof. Henry by the Board. Though painted by a N. Y. artist[18] of some reputation (at $1,500), I don't like it. We had on the whole a very interesting meeting. Dr. Parker[19] objected to a paragraph in the Annual

---

whiskies, located largely in Kentucky, who had six million gallons of their product in bond. Garfield pointed out, for example, that since manufacturers of certain whiskies and of ordinary high wines had to market their products at once, the resolution benefited only "a small and exceptional class of manufacturers."

[18]Thomas Le Clear (1818–1882), a New York portrait and genre painter. According to the *Dictionary of American Biography* "his portraits of men are among the best made in America in the nineteenth century." His sitters included President Grant, George Bancroft and Edwin Booth. His portrait of Joseph Henry is in the National Portrait Gallery.

[19]Peter Parker (1804–1888), a graduate of Yale and an ordained minister, went to China as a medical missionary in the 1830's. He was later associated with the American legation in China. After his final return to the United States in 1857 he lived mostly in Washington, D.C., where he was identified with religious and benevolent work, and with the Smithsonian Institution. For many years he was president of the Washington City Bible Society.

Report, which declared that it was now settled that all nations had come up from a state of savagery. Called at Blaine's who gave me a curious account of his row with Dawes and Hoar, in the eulogies on Gov. King.[20] Home, ten.

SUNDAY, 27. Church at eleven. James Mason of Cleveland took dinner with us. Commenced reading for an article in the next number of the *North American Review* which I have agreed to write, or rather edit, on Army Organization. I must have it ready by the fifth of February, and have but little time for doing it justice. At 7 P.M. Crete and I went to Blaine's to tea. There were present, beside[s] the family (of which Miss Abbie Dodge is a member), John Hay and wife, Col. Rob't Ingersoll and wife, Gen. John A. Logan and wife, and Mr. Powers and wife of Maine. A pleasant and brilliant conversation on a wide range of topics. Home at half-past eleven. The account referred [to] at the foot of the last page was this: Blaine said Mass. had always been down on Maine men, that her opposition to him was in the line of her traditions, though she pretended to place it on high patriotic ground. Now said he, "I prefer to have her oppose me because of a personal row, and this King eulogy furnishes it. I am right in my facts, and as to the taste I can stand it."

This is the method of a very brilliant, agressive, calculating man.

MONDAY, 28. Simkins[21] came and I dictated letters. Worked on

---

[20]The eulogies on William King (1768–1852), who had taken a leading part in the movement for the separation of Maine from Massachusetts, and who was the first governor of Maine, were occasioned by the presentation by Maine to the federal government of a statue of King. The statue, sculpted by Franklin Simmons, was to be placed in the Hall of the old House of Representatives. Blaine, speaking in the Senate after Hamlin, lauded King but made derogatory remarks about the people of Massachusetts and the history of that state in the War of 1812. Dawes and Hoar of Massachusetts responded, saying that they had no wish to detract from what was said about King, but defending the people and historical record of their state. There followed an exchange which reflected intense personal and political animus, especially on the part of Blaine, between him and the two Massachusetts senators.

[21]Francis A. Simkins, a clerk in the Treasury Department, was substituting for Garfield's regular stenographer, George U. Rose, while Rose was on a government assignment in New York City.

article for the *North American Review.* I ought not to have taken this new load upon me.

House at 12. The usual hubbub in the demagogue vein.

Stanley Matthews' silver resolution to pay the public debt in "the dollars of the fathers."[22] The vote stood, ayes 189, noes 79. I stood alone in Ohio voting no. Indeed there were but half a dozen noes in the whole Mississippi Valley.

TUESDAY, 29. Letters in the morning, and work on *Review* article until 10 1/2. House Committee on Ways and Means at which the Tariff Bill was reported by the sub-Committee.[23]

This bill will entail a vast mass [of] material for drudgery. Humdrum in the House.

At seven in the evening, Crete and I went to a state dinner at the President's. Forty persons were present—Vice President Wheeler; from the Cabinet (Schurz, Evarts and Devens); Supreme Court (Swayne and Clifford); Senate (Anthony, Hoar, Blaine, Morgan,[24] Bayard, Matthews and ——— [Oglesby]); from the House (Burchard, Willis,[25]

[22]The resolution of Stanley Matthews, approved by the Senate on January 25 and by the House on January 28, provided that bonds issued by the United States under acts of 1869, 1870, and 1875, were "payable, principal and interest . . . in silver dollars." Throughout the silver debate there was much talk of the Act of 1792 which provided for the minting of both gold and silver. Thus the silver dollar was often referred to as "the dollar of the fathers."

[23]This is an error, the result of Garfield's having made the entry subsequent to the date indicated. The minutes of the committee (in National Archives) do not record Garfield as present at the meeting on January 29 nor do they indicate that the Tariff Bill was reported on that day. The minutes for the meeting of January 31 show that Garfield was present and that the Tariff Bill was reported; Garfield does not mention a committee meeting in his entry for that day.

[24]John T. Morgan (1824–1907), a Confederate officer in the Civil War, was a Democratic member of the Senate from Alabama, 1877 to his death.

[25]Benjamin A. Willis (1840–1886) was a Democratic member of the House from New York, 1875–79. His wife, "the acknowledged beauty among the matrons now in Washington," sat at Garfield's left on this occasion, the first state dinner at the White House since the previous spring. (See "Miss Grundy's" column on Washington society in the *New York Daily Graphic,* January 30 and February 25, 1878.) President Hayes adopted a policy of not serving wine at White House functions, a policy which was much discussed throughout his administration.

Gibson,[26] ——— [Conger and Kelley]) and several temporary members of the President's family. Senator Morgan took Crete to dinner. I took Miss Platt,[27] the President's niece. A very pleasant party. No wine, but coffee in the middle of the menu. Home at eleven.

WEDNESDAY, 30. Correspondence in the morning and worked on article until 12. Maj. Swaim came before I left. House at half-past 12. Day spent on Appropriation Bill for Military Academy.[28]

In the evening, Swaim and I, with Harry and Jimmy, went to the Theatre and heard Sothern in the *Crushed Tragedian.* [29] Had never heard it before; it is one of his best efforts.

Home at eleven, and played casino with Crete and Swaim.

THURSDAY, 31. Worked on *North American Review* article until 12. Then House, where most of the day was spent in doing but little.

A day of fierce villa[i]nous weather. Home in the evening. Bezique and work.

February

FRIDAY, 1. Dictated letters, worked on article, arranged for a dinner at Welcker's tomorrow night.

[26]Randall L. Gibson (1832–1892) was a Democratic member of the U.S. House of Representatives from Louisiana, 1875–83, and of the Senate, 1883 to his death.

[27]Emily Platt was the daughter of President Hayes's deceased sister Frances (Fanny). On June 19, 1878, she was married to Russell Hastings of Willoughby, Ohio. Hastings, who served in Hayes's 23rd Ohio Infantry Regiment, 1861–65, lost a leg as a result of a wound received in battle; he was breveted brigadier general. He later served a term in the Ohio legislature and as U.S. marshal for the Northern District of Ohio.

[28]Late in the day, after a long debate on a proposed tax on distilled spirits, the Appropriation Bill for the Military Academy was introduced. It was debated at length on the following day.

[29]Edward H. Sothern was at the National Theater, January 28-February 2. In addition to *A Crushed Tragedian* (a version of Henry Byron's play, *The Prompter's Box*), he appeared in *David Garrick, A Regular Fix* and *Lord Dundreary.*

In the House, the day was spent in overhauling Door-Keeper Polk for malfeasance in office.[30]

Swaim came to the House and lunched with me. Day[31] of Kent came to see about tariff on Glass.

In the evening, after dinner, superintended the literary exercises of the children in the parlor. All took a part.

At eight, Swaim, Martha, Crete and I went to the Theatre and hear[d] Sothern in *David Garrick* and *A Regular Fix.* Came home at eleven, with sides sore from laughing. Gen. Sherman introduced me to Sothern and DeSere [De Vere][32] between the acts.

SATURDAY, 2.   Spent most of the day at work on the *North American Review* article, and in shopping with Maj. Swaim and Crete. A[t] seven P.M. Swaim and I gave a dinner at Welcker's to the Sec'y of War, Gen. Sherman, Gen. Meigs[33] and Col. Rockwell

[30]Doorkeeper John W. Polk was charged with unlawful practices in employing persons and with having an interest in matters about to be considered in Congress. The majority of the Committee on Reform in the Civil Service, which investigated the charges, found that he had engaged in a number of illegal and questionable acts and recommended that the office be vacated. The House acquiesced on April 4. Since there was much sympathy for Polk and because members knew that he had acted in response to pressures from House Democrats to supply jobs, the House on June 19 resolved that in the investigation "nothing was shown affecting his personal integrity or reflecting upon him as an honorable man," and allowed him two months' extra pay for expenses incurred in connection with the investigation. The *New York Times* made this revealing editorial comment on April 4: "The Door-keeper, humble though his title may be, has an enormous patronage. He should be known as Superintendent of the House of Representatives. He employs a small army of clerks, doorkeepers, pages, laborers, and runners. That is to say, he nominally employs them. In reality, the members of the majority employ them through the Door-keeper. But the law cruelly puts a limit to the number of men paid by the Door-keeper's vouchers. There is no limit to the demands of the Democratic members. Hence Door-keeper Polk broke down while attempting to do all that was required of him. Then the members derided and spitefully used him."

[31]Edward L. Day, of Day, Williams & Co., glassmakers of Kent, Ohio.

[32]George F. De Vere, an actor member of Sothern's company.

[33]Montgomery C. Meigs (1816–1892) graduated at West Point and served in the army until 1882. He was quartermaster general, 1861–82; during the Civil War he performed brilliantly in the face of enormous responsibilities. An outstand-

—a very pleasant company. Gen. Sherman is a most delightful talker. His great and varied experience, and his perfect memory of details gives him a remarkable fund of information; and his racy dashing style makes it a perpetual charm to listen to him. We talked on army matters, history, travels, anecdote[s], etc., until eleven.

Home and at 12 retired.

SUNDAY, 3. At home today working on the Army Article. In the evening, at seven, Sherman, White, Matthews and I met at Hale's, at Sherman's request, to consider the course of events in La. in reference to the trial of the Returning Board.[34]

Matthews drafted a telegram to be sent to Gen. Anderson, but after some discussion, Shellabarger was invited in. He thought it better not be sent, lest it might injure Anderson. Laid over until 10 tomorrow morning. The Democrats of La. are attempting to disturb Hayes's title by indirection, and will try to involve as many Republicans as possible.

Home at eleven. I should have added that Gen. Sherman came

---

ing engineer, his achievements included supervision of the construction of the Washington Aqueduct and the new wings and iron dome of the Capitol, and the design of the Pension Bureau building. He was for some time a member of the board of regents of the Smithsonian Institution.

[34]In June, 1877, Louisiana Democrats obtained an indictment against the Republican Returning Board, now abolished, charging that its members "falsely and feloniously published as true" a report of the result of the presidential election of 1876 in the parish of Vernon. In February, 1878, one member of the Board, Thomas C. Anderson, was found guilty and sentenced to imprisonment at hard labor for two years. All this embarrassed and upset Hayes, for Republican leaders opposed to his conciliatory Southern policy had predicted that Louisiana Republicans would be persecuted as soon as federal troops were withdrawn from the state. It was also disturbing to Republicans like Garfield, Matthews and Sherman who had been active in Louisiana in 1876 and who had undoubtedly given members of the Board assurances of protection. Hayes, with the support of leaders of both parties, urged Governor Francis P. Nicholls to stop the "persecutions." In March, 1878, the Supreme Court of Louisiana, whose members Nicholls had appointed, set aside the Anderson conviction on a technicality, and the cases against the other members of the Board were dropped. See Harry Barnard, *Rutherford B. Hayes and His America* (1954), pp. 439–441.

in and wrote a telegram to Pres. Boyd[35] of Baton Rouge, asking him to go to Gov. Nicholls and ask him to stop the persecution of the Board.

MONDAY, 4.   Letters in the morning. At eleven the same parties as last evening, except Gen. Sherman, and with Senator Kellogg, added.

A new telegram was drawn by Matthews, addressed and sent to Anderson, as follows:

Gen. Thos. C. Anderson:

The undersigned feel it due to you, under present circumstances, to assure you of our unhesitating belief that in the matter wherein you stand charged, you are altogether guiltless of any offence against law; that you are falsely accused and maliciously persecuted; that the proceedings, though in the form of law, is without the substance of justice; that we hereby tender you our earnest sympathies and express the hope that the sense of justice and love of peace of the people of La. will protect you, and will not permit the best interests of the whole country to be disturbed by a revival of Sectional animosities.

In any event, we are confident that the American people will redress any injustice of which you may be made the victim.
                        Signed,
                                John Sherman
                                Stanley Matthews
                                J. A. Garfield
                                Eugene Hale
                                Harry D. White

House at twelve.

Home in the evening and worked on article.

---

[35]David F. Boyd (1834–1899), a native of Virginia, devoted his life to education. In 1860–61 he taught in the Louisiana State Seminary, of which William T. Sherman was then superintendent. After serving in the Confederate army he was superintendent of the Seminary, 1865–70, and when it became Louisiana State University he was named president and served from 1870–80 and 1884–86. He taught there, 1886–88 and 1897–99.

TUESDAY, 5. Letters in the morning. Committee of Ways and Means at 10 1/2. The morning was spent in general discussion on the Tariff Bill.[36]

Dull day in the House. In the evening worked on article for *North American Review* and nearly finished it.

Swaim and I went to Col. Rockwell's but did not find him at home.

WEDNESDAY, 6. Finished *Review* article and sent it to N. Y. by Express.

Letters until twelve, when I went to the House. Pacheco Election case. I spoke a few moments near the close of the day.

In the evening, Crete and I went to a reception at Judge Nott's given to Cyrus W. Field. A brilliant company.

THURSDAY, 7. Letters in the morning; went to Committee of Ways and Means at 10.30 and nearly finished Schedule A of the Tariff Bill. In the House, most of the day was consumed in the Pacheco contest. I spoke a few moments, but could make no break in the Democratic lines. Pacheco was unseated by a solid party vote. Perhaps an impartial outsider would reply that he was defended by a solid Republican vote. But the Democracy are doing the same thing in each case as it arises.

In the evening, Crete and I went to dinner at Gov. Swann's. A very elegant dinner, eighteen covers. Madame Mantilla, wife of the Spanish Minister, was in mourning for the Pope, who died at 4.57 this P.M.[37] Home at 10.

The career of Pius IX has been a very remarkable one. His pontificate alone has exceeded in years that which tradition assigns to Peter. It is said that at his coronation, he replied to the formal *"Non videbis annos Petri* [You will not see the years of Peter],'' "That is not a part of the creed."

FRIDAY, 8. Simkins came, and I dictated letters and worked at my

[36]The Committee on Ways and Means, under the direction of its chairman, Fernando Wood of New York, was undertaking an extensive downward revision of the tariff. The Wood bill was the most serious threat the protectionist forces had faced since the Civil War.

[37]Pius IX (1792–1878), who died on February 7, had been pope since 1846.

desk until eleven, when I went with Swaim to the Land Office on business for him and his friend. I went thence to the Capitol, and attended the session of the House, which was devoted to private bills. I went to the Library to make preparation for a speech I am to make on the 12th inst. (Lincoln's birth-day) on the occasion of presenting Carpenter's painting of the Emancipation Proclamation to the House. In the evening, Crete and I dined at Eugene Hale's.

Called on Mrs. Thompson, the giver of the Carpenter picture, and also on Mr. and Mrs. Carpenter and the poet Stoddard.[38]

Also on S. S. Cox and wife, to make arrangements for senators to take part in the performances tomorrow. We agreed to ask Anthony, and Davis of Illinois to speak.

SATURDAY, 9. Spent the morning in work at my desk. Ways and Means at half-past ten; a long session on the Tariff.

House did nothing but general debate.

In the latter part of the day and evening worked on preparation for speech on Emancipation Proclamation.

The artist, Carpenter, called in the evening to see me. It will be a difficult thing to make a fitting speech under all the circumstances.

SUNDAY, 10. Staid at home and work[ed] on Emancipation speech all day, except that at 10 1/2 went to Hale's to consult with Sherman and Hale in reference to condition of affairs in La.

MONDAY, 11. Worked on speech until two P.M. when I went to the Capitol to learn the programme determined on for tomorrow. Found that none but Mr. Stephens and I are to speak. Home in the evening, and worked till past midnight on speech. I have concluded to write it out in full. Retired half an hour after midnight with a severe headache.

[38]Richard H. Stoddard (1825–1903), a native of Massachusetts, was employed in the New York custom house, 1853–70, and at this time as city librarian of New York. He was literary editor of the *New York Mail* (*Mail and Express* from 1882), 1880 to his death. A collected edition of his poems was published in 1880. His works include *Abraham Lincoln: An Horatian Ode* (1865).

TUESDAY, 12. Worked at my desk until half-past one, when I finished the last page of my speech. Crete, Mother, and some other members of the family had gone to the Capitol in advance to secure seats. I reached the House of Representatives at 5 minutes before two.

At 2 the Senate came in, the galleries and floor being crowded. Vice President Wheeler presided. For the first time, I <u>read</u> a speech in the House. It was very hard to do, and I was not satisfied with its delivery; but it was well received, and I think will read well. When I came to see the picture, it seemed to have grown worse in the ten years since I saw it; or I have grown away from it.[39]

A. H. Stephens followed in a somewhat discursive speech, but impressive, as coming from the Vice President of the Confederacy.

Went to the Riggs House with Swaim and played billiards until dinner time.

Home evening, with a severe headache.

WEDNESDAY, 13. Dictated a large number of letters in the morning. Ways and Means at half-past ten.

At two, took lunch at Gen. Butler's,[40] in company with Foster.

[39]In his address Garfield spoke as follows: "I profess no skill in the subtle mysteries of art criticism. I can only say of a painting what the painting says to me. I know not what this may say to others; but to me it tells the whole story of the scene in the silent and pathetic language of art." Donn Piatt's paper, *The Capital* (January 27), had this to say about the painting: "Mrs. Elizabeth Thompson of New York has purchased and presented to the Government Carpenter's woody painting. . . . Mrs. Thompson meant well. Doubtless her intentions are honorable, and, perhaps, when Carpenter's assortment of sticks gets in contrast with Billy Powell's inspired historical house-painting it won't appear so bad. But we are not filled with enthusiasm over the gift. We cannot say even that we are in a cheerful frame of mind." The *Washington Post* (February 13) was also critical: "There is not a loose joint on the canvass nor a natural position in the picture. Even the portraits are not first class. The general verdict, yesterday, was that it was a dull, disagreeable picture, that ought to be sent down to the basement. . . ."

[40]After four elections to the House of Representatives, Benjamin F. Butler was defeated in 1874; in 1876 he was again a victor and served in the 45th Congress, 1877–79. He lived at the corner of New Jersey Avenue and B Street (now

On our return to the House found a great row in progress over the late Presidential Count, with charges of bargains and sales and all sorts of humbugs.

Made a short speech which called out some dissent and much enthusiasm.[41]

At 7 dined with Senator Hoar, who gave an admirable dinner to Chief Justice Gray of Boston. I sat by Hiester Clymer, who told me many interesting things about his ancestors and the country around Reading. He says there are still many descendants of the Hessians there, and to call a man a d----d Hessian is still good ground for instant assault and battery.

THURSDAY, 14. Went to the Navy Dep't for Gen. Schenck, and thence to the Capitol. Ways and Means for two hours.

In the House we had some echoes of yesterday's row; but it soon fell off into humdrum.

At three went with Maj. Swaim and played billiards till dinner. At 9 P.M. he left us for Leavenworth via New York.

Simkins came and I dictated a large number of letters. Then worked at my desk until near midnight.

My correspondence is almost swamping me.

FRIDAY, 15. Letters in the morning. Ways and Means at half-past

Independence Avenue), S.E., in a granite house he had built on the present site of the Cannon House Office Building.

[41]In the "great row" which developed during debate on the Military Academy Appropriation Bill, Garfield declared that any man who claimed that a corrupt bargain had been made for the presidential title "has been miserably duped or he lies." He invited anyone with knowledge of such a bargain to "exhibit the trade and let the scoundrels who authorized it or made it be lashed naked throughout the world." Referring to the situation in Louisiana he said that federal troops were withdrawn from the state in the interests of conciliation and as a matter of constitutional duty, and that "the truculent spirit" of some Louisiana men was "a poor return for the efforts of our people to restore the spirit of peace and brotherhood in that State." At the end of his speech, which was interrupted three times by applause, Garfield was asked to explain what he meant by "truculent spirit." He replied that he was referring to the outrageous persecution of the Returning Board and of army officers in New Orleans, which was contributing to sectional animosity. His response drew laughter from Democrats and applause from Republicans.

23

ten. Iron was under discussion. I moved an amendment to put wrought scrap iron and steel at $6 per ton instead of $4, which at first was carried; but Sayler[42] moved to reconsider at [and] it was fixed at $5.

In the House, the day was spent on private bills. Worked at my desk at home until half-past eight, when I went to Gen. Schenck's and spent the rest of the evening.

The Senate is sitting out the Silver Bill; will probably sit all night.

The public mind is in a state of craze which is not creditable to our people, and the behavior of public men is still less creditable to them.

Lamar made a brief speech in the Senate today, refusing to obey the instructions of the Mississippi legislature, which speech will, in my judgment, give him a higher title to permanent fame than any other act of his public life. If a representative is not able to instruct his people, he is not fit to represent them.[43]

SATURDAY, 16. No session of House or Committee. Wrote a large number of letters, and at 11 went to the P. O. Dep't on business for my District. Spent the afternoon on my correspondence until 3, when I went with Crete to Mrs. Hayes's reception, and thence to Capt. Patterson's at Brentwood. At seven, dined with Sec'y Evarts, a large dinner party given to Mr. Foster, our Minister to Mexico.[44] I sat by Gibson of La., who, I found, was

[42]Milton Sayler (1831–1892), a Democratic member of the House from Ohio, 1873–79, practiced law in New York City after he left Congress.

[43]The Mississippi legislature instructed the state's two senators "to vote for the acts remonetizing silver and repealing the resumption act, and to use their efforts to secure their passage." Unable to reconcile those instructions with his convictions, Lucius Q. C. Lamar (1825–1893), a Democratic member of the House from Mississippi, 1857–60, 1873–77, and of the Senate, 1877–85, secretary of the Interior, 1885–88, and associate justice of the U.S. Supreme Court, 1888 to his death, declared that duty as he saw it compelled him to vote against the Silver Bill. At about 5:00 A.M. on February 16, the Senate passed the measure, 48–21.

[44]John W. Foster (1836–1917), a native of Indiana, practiced law in Evansville, 1857–61, served as an officer in the Union army, and was U.S. minister to Mexico, 1873–80, to Russia, 1880–81, and to Spain, 1883–85. He was secretary of state, 1892–93, and wrote a number of books, including *A Century of American Diplomacy*

at Chickamauga, and took command of Dan. Adams' Brigade, after that officer was wounded and captured by our troops. The Orton Williams who was executed by us at Franklin in 1863 as a spy, was in Gibson's command.[45] After leaving Evarts', I went to Amos Townsend's room to visit the Ohio delegation. Home at half-past eleven.

SUNDAY, 17. Attended Church with Crete and Mother and listened to a stout, old-fashioned Disciple Sermon from [John S.] Sweeney of Ky. whom I met in Chicago, in 1865. He is holding a protracted meeting here. His subject was Christ's Commission to the Apostles.

Carrie Ransom came to dine with us. On our return from Church, found a telegram from Brother Joseph Rudolph announcing the death of his wife Libbie, a dear sweet woman, who leaves him very desolate, with two little boys, one a baby. I telegraphed to Sister Nellie Rockwell of St. Louis, asking her to go to Hiram now, and Crete would go a few weeks later. She replied assenting and so Crete stays.

In the evening, I read Senator Jones's speech in defence of the Bland Silver Bill.[46] It is much the ablest statement of that side of the subject I have seen. If there were any temper in Congress or the country which would tolerate or listen to discussion, I should be glad to debate this case fully. But it is an epoch of madness.

MONDAY, 18. Worked at my letters until half-past ten, when I went to Ways and Means. The morning was spent on the iron and

---

(1900). He was the grandfather of John Foster Dulles, secretary of state, 1953–59.

[45]On June 8, 1863, Colonel Lawrence W. Orton was captured, tried by a military commission, and hanged the next day. Orton was not in Gibson's command. Prior to his capture he commanded a cavalry brigade in General Leonidas Polk's corps. Gibson was then an infantry officer in General William Hardee's corps. In the *Official Records* Orton appears as William Orton Williams, the name he used as a cavalry officer in the United States Army. In the record of the military commission that sentenced him his name appears as Lawrence Auton, Lawrence Orton Williams, and Lawrence Auton Williams (*Official Records,* Series I, Vol. XXIII, Part II, pp. 424–425).

[46]John P. Jones, a bimetallist, delivered his speech on February 15.

steel section of the Tariff Bill. Kelley has lost all his influence with the Committee by his extremes of opinion. I am trying to make the bill as reasonable as I can.

The day in the House was devoted to the District of Columbia. Privately, the Senate amendments to the Silver Bill were much discussed, and upon the adjournment, a call was made for the meeting of the silver union. It is a strange proceeding to see a lobby organized of members of the House to carry a measure through it; yet this is the character of the silver league or union.

Spent the evening on correspondence, and with callers. I have about resolved to make no general speech on the Silver Bill, but content myself with a statement of my position. Retired at eleven.

TUESDAY, 19.   The morning story is the usual one of letters and tariff work. In the House the contested election case of Darrall vs. Acklen[47] was taken up, and after the opening speech by Harris of Va.,[48] Hale got the floor for a personal explanation and spoke nearly two hours.[49] He reviewed the course of events in Louisiana, and the attitude of the President, and spoke with much force, but his speech aroused a good deal of antagonism and he was somewhat worried by the questions of Elam[50] and others. Gibson followed in a speech of considerable force. Clymer spoke a few minutes, and put a phase on the debate which warranted us in believing that the La. persecutions were a part of a general Democratic policy. I took the floor at 4.15 and spoke till 5.[51] I

[47]Chester B. Darrall (1842–1908) was a Republican member of the House from Louisiana, 1869–78, 1881–83. His election to the 45th Congress was successfully contested by Joseph H. Acklen (1850–1938), a Democratic member of the House from Louisiana, 1878–81. See Garfield's next entry.

[48]John T. Harris, chairman of the Committee on Elections, supported the majority report of the committee in favor of seating Acklen.

[49]Eugene Hale of Maine was severely critical of the Democrats with respect to recent developments in New Orleans—the trial of the Republican Returning Board, and the arrest and imprisonment of Thomas C. Anderson.

[50]Joseph B. Elam (1821–1885) was a Democratic member of the House from Louisiana, 1877–81.

[51]Garfield complimented Hayes for his generous attempt to pacify the country and sustain the principle of local self-government; but he criticized him for sending to New Orleans a commission which influenced the decision as to who would be

was surprised to find that I had made an unusually strong impression upon the House. I criticised the President's course kindly but plainly, and at the close, was congratulated by men of quite opposite opinions. Home in the evening. Dictated letters, and revised the notes of my speech.

WEDNESDAY, 20.   Letters in the morning, and at ten went to the Treasury to get some materials that had been worked out for me on the Silver Bill, by the order of the Comptroller of the Currency. Capitol at 10.30, when the Committee of Ways and Means finished the sections of the Tariff relating to Iron and Steel. In the House, the day was spent on the Darrall-Acklen case with the familiar result—the Republican unseated, and the Democrat admitted. They have done this every time thus far.

Home in the evening. Foster and his wife came and spent the evening. Asst. Secretary J. B. Hawley[52] also called and spent some time.

Signed and prepared for mailing a contract to hire Mattison Glasier to work on my farm at Mentor from March 1st, prox., for $24 per month.

Cardinal Pecci was today elected Pope by adoration, after several indecisive ballots. When asked by what title he would be known, he answered Leo XIII.

THURSDAY, 21.   Letters till 10, when I called on Judge Wylie at the City Hall to ask him to give Simkins as early a trial as possible.[53] Then to Ways and Means where two hours work was done on the Tariff.

In the House, after the morning hour, the Silver Bill was taken up on motion of Mr. Stephens of Georgia, and after a debate of

---

governor of Louisiana. That policy, he said, violated the principle of local self-government. He was also critical of Clymer, whose remarks, said Garfield, showed that he regarded the Louisiana prosecutions not as a local issue, but as a wedge with which to reopen the presidential election of 1876 and stamp it "as the great fraud of the century."

[52]John B. Hawley (1831–1895), a Republican member of the U.S. House of Representatives from Illinois, 1869–75, was assistant secretary of the treasury, 1877–80.

[53]See entry for February 26.

an hour, parcelled out to about 20 persons, the voting began. The extreme silver men like Butler and Ewing resisted the bill as amended by the Senate. It was a curious confounding of opinions and parties. I spoke less than two minutes, stating my belief in bi-metallism, and my regret that this bill, though improved by the Senate, would not bring the two metals into equipoise. I vote[d] for the Senate amendments, and in favor of laying the bill on the table. In this last vote I stood almost alone in the West. Time will show whether I was wise or otherwise.

Home at half-past six. John Q. Smith dined with us. He has just been confirmed Consul General of Canada, and goes to Montreal soon. Dictated letters in the evening. Many friends called. Senator Hoar among them. Eugene Cowles[54] brought me the advance sheets of W. E. Chandler's new attack upon me with others.[55] *Brutum fulmen* [An ineffectual display of force].

---

[54]Eugene Cowles (1855–1892), son of Edwin Cowles, was associated with the *Cleveland Leader* as a young man; he was the paper's Washington correspondent, 1877–80. In 1878 he accompanied and reported on General Nelson Miles's military expedition to the Yellowstone region. After abandoning journalism, he achieved distinction in the field of metallurgy; with his brother Alfred he developed new methods in electric smelting that laid the foundation for the aluminum, carborundum and other modern industries. With their father, who contributed most of the capital, they founded the Cowles Electric Smelting and Aluminum Company (1885).

[55]William E. Chandler (1835–1917), of New Hampshire, had a long career as a Republican leader and office holder. He was a member of the state legislature, 1862–64, and 1881, an assistant secretary of the treasury, 1865–67, secretary of the navy, 1882–85, member of the U.S. Senate, 1887–1901, and member of the Republican National Committee, 1868–84. After the election of 1876 he was one of the visiting statesmen who looked after Hayes's interests in Florida. As the Southern policy of the new administration took shape, however, he was much dissatisfied. On December 26, 1877, he erupted in a long letter "To the Republicans of New Hampshire." In it he charged President Hayes with having violated in his Southern policy Republican pledges and principles with disastrous results for the Republican party both in the South and the North. In 1878 he published this letter and other material in *Letters of Mr. William E. Chandler Relative to the So-called Southern Policy of President Hayes. . . .* Garfield is mentioned a number of times as one of the visiting statesmen and "bargainers" in Louisiana. Chandler, however, was a supporter and frequent advisor of Garfield in the campaign of 1880. At Blaine's urging President Garfield nominated him solicitor general but the Senate did not confirm him.

FRIDAY, 22. Worked at my desk nearly all day bringing up arrears of work.

In the evening about a dozen friends came in to attend the literary exercises of our children, and the two little girls, Mary Irish[56] and Clara Jones, who are attending Miss Mays's school. The performance was very creditable to the children.

At nine, I went to Townsend's room to meet him and Foster.

SATURDAY, 23. Correspondence in the morning. At 11 attended the meeting of the Ways and Means and work[ed] on Tariff Bill three hours.

In the evening, Crete and I attended the Literary Society, which met at Dr. Lincoln's in H. St.[57] Several interesting papers were read, one by Mrs. Long,[58] and a quaint poem by Mr. Nicolay, late private Sec'y to Pres. Lincoln.

At 10 Crete and I went to Blaine's reception. Home at half-past eleven.

SUNDAY, 24. Attended church, and listened to an able discourse on the resurrection and future life by E. J. [J.S.] Sweeney.

Afternoon and evening at home, reading and resting.

[56]Mary Irish, who studied with Mollie Garfield and Clara Jones under the direction of Martha Mays, was the daugher of Orsamus H. Irish, a Nebraskan who was assistant chief of the U.S. Bureau of Statistics, 1877–78, and chief of the Bureau, 1878 to his death in 1883. In 1880 and 1881 Garfield turned over to him seven boxes of his papers for safekeeping; Garfield's secretary subsequently increased the number to twenty-nine. Mary died in 1886 while a student at the University (now College) of Wooster in Ohio. Her older sister Annie B. (1857–1886), was with the family in Europe while her father was consul in Dresden, 1870–72, and later returned for study in Germany and France. She also studied at the Johns Hopkins University. She was at this time librarian and translator in the Interior Department. Her translation of Auerbach's *Landolin* was published in 1878. In 1881 she went to Wooster to lecture and remained as professor of the German language and literature to her death. She received her Ph.D. there in 1882.

[57]Nathan S. Lincoln, a physician. His wife, Jeanie Gould Lincoln (1846–1921), whom he married in 1877, was a writer and a member of the Literary Society. Her books include *Marjorie's Quest* (1872), *Her Washington Season* (1884), *An Unwilling Maid* (1897), and *A Pretty Tory* (1899).

[58]Elizabeth W. Long, widow of Robert Cary Long, an architect, was an original member of the Literary Society.

MONDAY, 25. Letters in the morning, Ways and Means at 10 1/2. Dull day in the House.

TUESDAY, 26. Same for morning and Committee as yesterday. At one P.M. received a Subpoena to attend the Criminal Court of the District as a witness to the good character of F. A. Simkins who is on trial for the rape of a little Negro girl—an outrageous case of attempt at black mail. I arrived too late to testify, but heard a portion of the able argument of Chas. Case.[59] Simkins was acquitted.

In the evening Crete and I dined at Fernando Wood's. The party consisted of the Committee of Ways and Means, and a few other members, and some Senators and their wives. It was a very pleasant party. The wit of Proctor Knott, and anecdotes of J. R. Tucker were very bright.

In the evening I dictated letters and read the proof of one of my recent speeches. I refused to accept the edition of my speech on Carpenter's picture, it was so miserably done.

WEDNESDAY, 27. The same story of routine, work and weariness.

The Tariff men throng my house morning and evening.

THURSDAY, 28. Letters and Tariff, and the House. At 2 P.M. the veto of the Silver Bill came to the House, and without a word of debate the bill was passed over the veto by 196 to 73. I again voted alone among the Ohio delegation, and almost alone in the Mississippi Valley.

The Senate was equally summary and decisive in its proceedings. The vote stood 43 [46] to 19. The President was not only unable to influence a single vote, but lost some in each House. He has pursued a suicidal policy towards Congress and is almost without a friend.

In the evening at half-past nine Crete and I attended Mr. Evarts' reception. A great crowd.

---

[59]Charles Case (1817–1883), a native of Ohio, was a Democratic member of the U.S. House of Representatives from Indiana, 1857–61. After leaving the House he practiced law in Washington, D.C. See entry for March 1. Garfield did not succeed in getting Case appointed to a judgeship.

March

FRIDAY, 1. Dictated many letters, and attended the Ways and Means, where the whole morning was spent on the absurd question of allowing our proceedings to be known or persisting in the futile attempt to keep them secret. It appears that our schedule on Sugar got into the papers and nobody knew how.

Private bills in the House. At home, in the evening, we had our literary exercises again. All went well but Irvin, who did not quite dare to recite "The Charge of the Light Brigade." At 7 I went to Chief Justice Waite's, and thence with him to the President's to commend Chas. Case for a District Judgeship.

The President spoke of the Political Situation, wanted me to go to N. H.,[60] and thought our party could be reunited in opposition to inflation. I told him, if he wished to hold any influence, he must abandon some of his notions of Civil Service. He compared the Situation with Lincoln's unpopularity in Congress! Home at 10.

SATURDAY, 2. Simkins came in the morning, and I dictated a large number of letters. At eleven went to the Ways and Means and worked until 2 P.M. We finished several schedules, and reached Wool and Wollens.

Went to the Riggs House and played Billiards with Col. Rockwell.

At seven P.M. Crete and I dined at Blaine's. Present, Mr. and Mrs. Henderson of Chicago, Mr. and Mrs. Nordoff [Nordhoff], Abby Dodge ("Gail Hamilton") and Emmons Blaine—a very pleasant party. The President was discussed quite fully. It is amazing how completely he has lost his hold upon his party. Home

[60]The New Hampshire state campaign was now in progress (the election was on March 12). One story had it that Garfield was invited to go to the state "to answer Chandler" (see note 56 above) but that he was later advised not to go because such a discussion might injure the party. A Washington dispatch in the *New York Times* (March 10) called this story fiction and stated that Garfield had been invited to speak in New Hampshire, although not to reply to Chandler, and that his only reason for not going was his reluctance to be away from the Committee on Ways and Means while the Tariff Bill was being considered.

at half-past ten. We sat up till Harry came in from the Theatre where he had gone to see Boucicault as Conn in *Shaughraun.* [61]

Ex-Senator B. F. Wade died at 6.30 this morning, at Jefferson, Ohio. He was born Oct. 27, 1800, Springfield [Feeding Hills] Mass., and was almost the last of the old "Liberty Guard"—a sturdy brave fighter, but not an effective builder.

SUNDAY, 3.   Took Crete and Mother to church, where we listened to a rambling sermon on the Kingdom, by Gonzales, a Portugese.

Miss Ransom dined with us. Cowles of Cleveland came, but too late for dinner. He staid to tea. Several friends called during the day, among them Col. R. G. Ingersoll, Chas. Foster, and Nash of La.[62] I spent several hours in clearing up the rubbish that has accumulated, in and around my desk, and making ready for my next article for the *North American Review,* on "The Army." Much of the conversation today has been upon the President. It is surprising with what strength the current of public sentiment is turning against him. I think his vague notions of Civil Service Reform, and his wretched practice upon it, has wrough[t] the chief mischief with his administration. I don't know but I shall be compelled to state fully my dissent from his policy and practice.

I incline to believe that his election has been an almost fatal blow to his party. The new pope Leo XIII is crowned today.

MONDAY, 4.   Simkins came and I dictated letters till half-past 10, when I went to the Committee of Ways and Means. We passed over the wool schedule and took up Schedule M, Sundries, on which we worked two hours. In the House, a bill was passed to pay pensions to all soldiers of 1812 who had served 20 [14] days. Not much else was done, for the House adjourned early to allow

[61]Dion Boucicault appeared at the National Theater in *The Shaughraun* (which he wrote) during the week of February 25.

[62]Charles E. Nash (1844–1913), a Negro and a native of Louisiana, was a bricklayer by trade, a Union soldier in the Civil War (he lost a leg at Fort Blakely, Alabama) and a Republican member of the House from Louisiana, 1875–77.

the Democratic members to hold a caucus. J. D. Cox told me today that the President had utterly failed to accomplish anything in the way of Civil Service reform, and that he had pursued no system that could be defended by any class of politicians.

The impression is deepening that he is not large enough for the place he holds. Home in the evening and work and play filled the time till I retired.

TUESDAY, 5. Letters in the morning. Committee [on] Ways and Means at half-past ten. Just before we went into the House, as I subsequently heard, Judge Kelley told Robbins[63] of North Carolina that he was about to reply to Garfield's speech of last November "in which, while I shall confine myself within the limits of parliamentary propriety, I shall probably make the most rough and caustic speech of my life; it will an[n]ihilate." About half-past two Kelley got the floor and spoke nearly two hours and a half replying to my speech of November 16th. He was offensively personal and exhibited bitter animosity towards [me].[64] It was surprising. Just before adjournment I obtained consent of the House to use an hour to reply. Home in the evening and worked at my desk until 3 hours past midnight preparing materials for reply.

WEDNESDAY, 6. Dictated to Rose and Simkins head notes for reply to Kelley. Went to the Committee on Ways and Means about half-past 11 and sat with them nearly an hour. At two o'clock got the floor and spoke about one hour in reply to Kelley. I have perhaps never made a speech in the House that elicited

---

[63]William M. Robbins (1828–1905) was a Democratic member of the House from North Carolina, 1873–79.

[64]Kelley, a champion of "cheap" money, not only berated Garfield's interpretation of the monetary history of the nation, but made a venomous personal attack, depicting Garfield as a man who "lives in the comforting assurance that 'foreknowledge absolute is his'; that in the embryo he was endowed with omniscience and infallibility, and released from the duty laid on other mortals of collecting, collating, and comparing facts in order to arrive at just conclusions." Kelley's speech (*Congressional Record,* 45 Cong., 2 Sess., pp. 1494–1504) received no applause.

more attention and applause.[65] A company of prominent citizens from Philadelphia were in the gallery, who at the close came to the door and requested to be introduced to me. Several of them thanked me for the speech and said I had done their state a service by making it. Crete and Mother, Miss Mays, Harry, Jimmy and Mollie and Irvin were in the gallery. I drove home with them at four. Did not correct the notes in the evening but sent word to the Public Printer to withhold my speech until Kelley's had appeared.

THURSDAY, 7. Committee of Ways and Means at half-past 10. Several pages of the Tariff Bill were agreed upon. I am surprised at the impression that appears to have been made yesterday by my reply to Kelley. Some of the parties are very extravagant. They praise it more than it deserves. I have always disliked personal debate and believe I have never begun it. Came home at 3 o'clock and commenced revising notes of my speech. At half-past six dined with Chittenden of N. Y. in company with ten or twelve gentlemen. A very pleasant party. Returned at 10 o'clock and Rose and I worked until after midnight in revising

[65]In his opening remarks Garfield told the House how surprised he had been to hear Kelley, with whom he had always associated on terms of friendship, deliver "a speech of two hours and a half, which from the beginning to the end was filled with the spirit of sneering, unkind personality, closing finally with a statement coarsely irreverent, if not profane, branding me as especially arrogant, conceited, and egotistical in my bearing toward my brother-members. To all that," Garfield said, "I shall make no reply, except simply to say this, that to a charge like that from a gentleman whose colossal self-conceit has been the theme of pleasant jocularity among all his associates during the seventeen years of his service, no man on this floor need make a reply." Garfield then attacked point by point his opponent's position on money, demonstrating that Kelley's speech lacked facts, collation, and synthesis. At the conclusion of his speech, which was interrupted several times by applause, Garfield "resumed his seat amid great applause." *Congressional Record,* 45 Cong., 2 Sess., pp. 1525–1529. According to a story told by Harry Garfield in 1939, Kelley retired to the lobby of the House while Garfield was making his speech. Unable to restrain his curiosity, he stopped a messenger and instructed him in these words: "Find out what the damn fool is saying now." Harry Garfield to Francis Garfield, March 13, 1939, typed copy, Harry A. Garfield Papers, L.C. The writer of the letter erred by about a year in dating Garfield's reply to Kelley.

notes of speech, but the Editor of the *Record* failed to send for it and so it goes over for another day.

FRIDAY, 8. Worked at my desk until half-past ten when I attended the Committee on Ways and Means. Much progress was made on the Tariff Bill. Lively day in the House. Confederate records unearthed showing that Reagan had paid out of the Confederate Treasury for anti [ante]-bellum Postal Contracts.[66] In the evening completed the revision of my speech and the Printer called for it at seven. Bowler of Cleveland, also Townsend,[67] Baldwin[68] and Boardman visited with me until 11 o'clock.

SATURDAY, 9. Dictated letters and cleared up my desk after the speech-work of the past week. Ways and Means at 10 and spent an hour on the bill for a popular loan in the form of deposit savings, which I favor as a means of interesting the mass of people of small means in the preservation of the public credit.

Last hour of Committee work on the Tariff. In the House Judge Kelley rose to a question of privilege and commented for nearly three-quarters of an hour upon my reply to his speech. He denied several points, which thereupon I proved from the public records.

It is evident that his egotism protects him from the suffering he would otherwise endure from the punishment he has received. The Editorials in leading Philadelphia papers in praise of my reply and approval of his castigation are of surprising force and boldness.

[66]During the debate over a private bill appropriating funds to pay for the ante-bellum services of Southern mail contractors, two congressmen presented documents showing that the Confederate government had paid most of the claims. John H. Reagan, who had been postmaster general of the Confederacy, was supporting the bill. It was defeated by the House on March 16.

[67]Amos Townsend (1821–1895), a native of Pennsylvania, moved to Mansfield, Ohio, in 1839 and became a merchant. He served as United States marshal during the civil conflict in Kansas. In 1858 he moved to Cleveland, where he engaged in the wholesale grocery business; he served on the city council, 1866–76, and was a Republican member of the U.S. House of Representatives, 1877–83.

[68]Dudley Baldwin (1809–1896), a native of New York, was brought as a boy to Cleveland, where he had a long career in manufacturing, railroads and banking. He was one of the promoters of the Cleveland, Columbus and Cincinnati Railroad.

In the evening, I went to Townsend's room and visited some Cleveland gentlemen. Home midnight.

SUNDAY, 10. Spent four hours in reading the mail which accumulated during the past three days, but has remained unopened in consequence of the debates and Committee work to which I have been compelled to give my attention.

I did not attend Church, but called at Welcker's to see Judge Black, but found he had gone home. At 2 P.M. Gen. Boynton came and drove me to Brightwood and the Soldiers' Home.

I am not feeling well today, for I have been much overworked and have underslept during the past week. But the weather is delightful. Dr. Pope told me today that all the days of February, but four, were bright and sunny, a very unusual thing, and now it is even uncomfortably warm.

Retired early—*videlicet,* ten P.M.

MONDAY, 11. Rose came in the morning and worked on correspondence and the Journal until 10 o'clock, when I went to the Treasury on business and thence to the Committee on Ways and Means. Spoke part of an hour on the Deposit Savings Bank Bill and then took up the Tariff. The Democrats are afraid of the Saving[s] Deposit clause, for fear it enlarges the powers of the Government. In the House Mr. Wood was alarmed for fear of a resolution against his Tariff Bill. After the morning hour, the Diplomatic Appropriation Bill came up and Hewitt made a long speech. I was taken with a severe pain in the stomach. Resulting probably from overwork and indigestion. I got a horse and buggy and drove for an hour or two. Suffered very much. Crete was with me and drove to Dr. Baxter's, who prescribed for me and among other things forbade me to eat anything but milk and stale bread and a small amount of steak. At eight o'clock went to Welcker's to a dinner given by Prof. Horsford[69] to David A.

---

[69]Eben N. Horsford (1818–1893), a graduate of Rensselaer Polytechnic Institute, was a tutor in chemistry at Williams College and a professor of chemistry in the Lawrence Scientific School when David A. Wells attended those institutions. After resigning his professorship in 1863, he became a manufacturing chemist, a

Wells, Tucker, Nordhoff, Hewitt and myself. Sat with them for two hours but did not eat. Home at 11 1/2.

TUESDAY, 12. Worked at desk until half-past ten. Corrected proof of my reply to Kelley and dictated letters. Then went to Committee of Ways and Means and worked on Tariff Bill until half-past twelve.[70]

Dull day in the House except that Cox delivered a long screed against the President.[71] I was feeling so badly that I had gone home, but no one made a general reply.

Home in the evening working at my desk. Retired early.

I should have added that I went to Randall Gibson's at 7, and spent an hour with a committee (Senator Cockerell [Cockrell],[72] Gen. A. S. Williams and I) who have been chosen by the Sec'y of War to estimate the value of the Military papers of Gen. Albert Sidney Johnston.

WEDNESDAY, 13. Desk in the morning. Tariff from 10 1/2 to 12 1/2—and a dull day in the House. Came home early and worked at my desk until 9 in the evening, when I went to the Depot and took the train for New York. I go to effect, if possible, a settlement of my account for legal services with W. B. Duncan, Receiver of the Mobile and Ohio R. R. Read and visited with friends who were on the train until ten o'clock when I retired.

THURSDAY, 14. Reached New York at 7 A.M. and stopped at the Astor House. Found Judge Black just going out to Breakfast with Tilden, David D. Field and others. I took my raw steak and milk

---

field in which he made important contributions and a fortune. A scholar with wide interests, he wrote numerous works on chemistry, history, geography, and archaeology, and published a lexicon of five Indian languages.

[70]The minutes of the committee for March 12 record only the consideration of a House bill to promote the deposit of savings in the Treasury and the refunding of the national debt.

[71]In a speech on the Consular and Diplomatic Appropriation Bill, Samuel S. Cox denounced the policies of the administration on several public issues and excoriated Hayes, calling him a "non-elect, quasi-President."

[72]Francis M. Cockrell (1834–1915), a Confederate general in the Civil War, was a Democratic member of the Senate from Missouri, 1875–1905, and a member of the Interstate Commerce Commission, 1905–10.

at the Astor, and then called at 11 Pine St. to see Duncan, but he was not in. Returned to my room at the Astor and he called at half-past ten.

At half-past eleven, I called on him at his office by appointment, but could come to no understanding in reference to the fee in the Mobile suit, except that I was to forward my bill, and he would either refer it to the court or we would agree to a referee.

At one P.M. Judge Black and I took train for Washington where we arrived at ten P.M.

FRIDAY, 15. Spent two hours reading my mail and went to the Committee of Ways and Means at 11 1/2. Private bills and an election case in the House.[73] At half-past four the Speaker announced the death of Leonard of La., who died in Cuba, yesterday. It is said he went there to see the young Spanish lady with whom he was in love.[74]

Home in the early evening; children's literary exercises at half-past [*sic*]. At half-past seven went to the Capitol and worked on Tariff Bill with Committee until ten o'clock.

Home at eleven. Retired tired.

SATURDAY, 16. Rose did not come, and I worked at my desk

[73]In this case Benjamin Dean (1824–1897), a Democratic member of the House from Massachusetts, 1878–79, successfully contested the election of Walbridge A. Field (1833–1899), a Republican member of the House from Massachusetts, 1877–78 and 1879–81.

[74]John E. Leonard (1845–1878), a native of Pennsylvania, graduated at Harvard in 1867, studied law abroad and at Harvard, and settled in Louisiana in 1870. He was appointed associate justice of the state supreme court in 1876 but lost this position with the overthrow of the Packard government. He was a Republican member of the House, 1877 to his death from yellow fever in Havana on March 15. He had received an indefinite leave of absence from the House on February 26. Although a rumor had it that he had been sent to Cuba to secure the release of some Florida Negroes who had been kidnapped, the American consul general in Havana, in a letter reporting his death (*New York Times,* March 28), indicated that the affairs that had brought the congressman to Cuba had been of "purely personal character." According to the *Times* (March 16), Leonard, a young widower, had fallen in love in New Orleans with a Cuban girl whose parents opposed his suit. He had gone to Cuba, where the parents had taken the girl, to find her and straighten the matter out.

alone until 10 1/2, when I went to Committee. We have nearly completed the rates of the Tariff Bill. Private bills in the House. We killed the bill for paying Southern mail contractors by striking out the enacting clause.

The developements from the rebel archives show that most of these claims were paid by the Confederate Government.

The *Washington Post* has revived the DeGolyer pavement slander upon me, and is doing all it can to injure my reputation.[75] In the evening Crete and I called on Gov. Pound[76] and wife, and her sister Mrs. Gansevoort, née Niel [Maria] Fenn,[77] who was Music teacher at Hiram in 1857. We also called at Gen. Schenck's. Retired 11.30.

SUNDAY, 17. At ten, called at the St. James Hotel to see Isaac Williams of Portage County who is ill, and consulted with him

[75]On March 15 the *Washington Post* (a Democratic paper that had been launched in the fall of 1877) carried an article more than a column in length headed "Gen. Garfield's Price." It was devoted entirely to an unfriendly discussion of Garfield's relation to the DeGolyer pavement affair. An editorial on the same day called attention to the article and made this comment: "The importance of this complete explanation at this time lies in the fact that a new House of Representatives is to be elected in a few months, and as Garfield will undoubtedly be a candidate for re-election it is proper that the people of his district should know exactly whom they are voting for. That they may be mistaken as to the man Mr. Garfield really is may be inferred from a recent editorial eulogy of him in the Cleveland *Leader,* which gives voice to the peculiar Radical sentiment of the Western Reserve of Ohio."

[76]Thaddeus C. Pound (1833–1914), a native of Pennsylvania, became a prominent Wisconsin lumberman and politician. He was a Republican member of the state legislature in the 1860's, lieutenant-governor, 1870–72, and a member of the U.S. House of Representatives 1877–83. Several months before the meeting of the Republican National Convention in 1880, he had concluded that Garfield was likely to be its presidential nominee (see entry for February 11, 1880). He was active at the convention in Garfield's behalf.

[77]Maria ("Niel") C. Fenn, a native of Ohio, and music teacher at the Eclectic, 1857–58, married Conrad Gansevoort, and lived for a time with her husband in Conneaut, Ohio; by 1877 they were settled in Bath, New York, Gansevoort's birthplace. Maria's younger sister Emily was married to Thaddeus C. Pound of Wisconsin. Gansevoort was the brother-in-law of John N. Hungerford (1825–1883), a Republican member of the U.S. House of Representatives, 1877–79.

in reference to saving the *Portage County Democrat* so that Halsey Hall may continue as its editor. I have alread[y] subscribed $500, and now offer $500 more when all the rest but that sum is subscribed.[78] Went to church, arriving late, and found Mother and Crete there. Mrs. Gansevoort, Miss Ransom, Em Reed and Eugene Cowles dined with us at 2 P.M. At 5, called on Secretary Evarts and had a long talk with him on the political situation. He is so full of sense and ability that I am sorry it is so marred by his great self-consciousness.

Home in the evening writing letters and reading Hamerton's *Wenderholme.*[79] Retired early.

MONDAY, 18. Resume the routine of the week. Desk, Committee, House, Desk again. So go the days and nights.

Stale bread and milk, rare steak without butter, no drink but soda water, this is my diet for two weeks—and longer if my indigestion returns.

Rose does not come and I am single-handed in the fight with piles of letters, etc. Home in the evening.

TUESDAY, 19. Desk in the morning and Ways and Means at 10 1/2. Four hours devoted to the tariff, and only a fugitive attention given to the legislation of the House.

Home in the evening, struggling to keep down the mass of unanswered letters, and replying to the numerous calls of visitors.

"Wearily, wearily stretches the sand to the sea and the sea to the cloud land," and wearily stretches the field of work and perplexity.

WEDNESDAY, 20. The story of yesterday repeated with hardly a change.

Work crowds me so much that I can hardly keep up with this hurried journal.

THURSDAY, 21. Desk in the morning. At ten went to the Treasury Dep't on business, and thence to the Capitol.

---

[78]See Vol. I, p. 292, n. 15.

[79]Philip G. Hamerton, *Wenderholme: A Story of Lancashire and Yorkshire,* 3 vols. (1869). A revised edition in one volume was published in 1877; this is the only copy of the book in the Library of Congress.

The Tariff Bill occupied the Committee nearly three hours. This work keeps me out of the House a large share of the time.

I came home early and commenced work on a second article for the *North American Review.* Rose is kept away by Treasury work, and I am swamped by my correspondence, though Crete and Martha are helping me.

I ought not to have taken the extra work of writing magazine articles.

Home all the evening.

FRIDAY, 22. Desk in the morning, and Ways and Means at 10 1/2. During this session we completed the revision of the tariff, and are to meet on Monday next to act upon the bill as a whole. I am in doubt what ought to be done with it, whether to try to kill it at once or better it in the House. In some things it is an improvement, but I cannot vote for it as it stands. Private bills in the House, but the Committee spent most of the day on the Tariff Bill.

Home literary exe[r]cises in the evening. I have kept up the rigid system of diet prescribed by Dr. Baxter two weeks ago, and my digestion has greatly improved.

I made a mistake in saying I went to the Capitol at 10 1/2, for Sec'y Evarts called at half-past 9 A.M. and stayed an hour and a half, talking over the political situation. Then I went to the Committee.

In the evening Gen. Sherman called, and we talked over army matters.

SATURDAY, 23. Worked at my desk until 10, when Crete and I drove to the St. James and called on Isaac Williams who has been ill. Took him with us to the Agricultural Dep't and called on the new Commissioner Le Duc,[80] and made arrangement for garden seeds for Mentor.

[80]William G. Le Duc (1823–1917), a native of Ohio, moved to St. Paul, Minnesota Territory, after graduating from Kenyon College and being admitted to the bar. In Minnesota he practiced law and engaged in activities related to the development of the area. In 1857 he moved to Hastings, where he had a flour mill. Having attained the rank of lieutenant colonel during the Civil War, he was breveted colonel and brigadier general at its close. President Hayes appointed him commis-

During the afternoon, worked on army article, and at 2 drove with Mr. and Mrs. Foster to Kendall Green and Capt. Patterson's.

At eight in the evening, we went to Sec'y Sherman's and spent three hours visiting with a party of Ohio friends. Home at half-past eleven.

SUNDAY, 24. Worked on army article until two P.M., when Isaac Williams of Portage County and Miss Ransom came to dine with us. Worked in the late afternoon, and at six went to Sec'y Evarts', where I dined with him and family, and Whitelaw Reid, and Phelps of N.J. After dinner we had a long talk with Evarts on the political situation, but he was so full of theory and his own cogitations that we could reach no practical conclusions. I fear that his dreamy doctrines have captivated the President and led him into many of his unfortunate ways, that have done so much to alienate his friends.

Home at eleven. The President and his son Webb[81] called in my absence and spent a quarter of an hour in visiting with Crete.

MONDAY, 25. Desk in the morning at [until] half-past ten.[82]

---

sioner of agriculture in July, 1877. As commissioner he was best known for his efforts to raise tea in South Carolina, an experiment that brought him criticism and ridicule. After his resignation (see entry for May 19, 1881), the *New York Times* (May 24) commented: " . . . Instead of addressing himself to the supply of the real needs of the agriculture of the United States and to the development of practicable branches of the science, Mr. Le Duc has devoted himself chiefly to the cultivation of hobbies." In a letter to Garfield (March 10, 1881) David A. Wells, speaking of the Department of Agriculture, said that it had "never been anything but an expensive humbug."

[81]Webb C. Hayes (1856–1934) was born in Cincinnati, Ohio, attended Cornell University, 1872–75, and served as secretary to his father, 1875–81. He was active in various industrial establishments, 1881–1901. He was an army officer in the Spanish-American War, in the fighting in the Philippines, in China during the Boxer Rebellion, on the Mexican border, 1911, 1913, and 1916, and in World War I. He was awarded the Congressional Medal of Honor for heroism in the Philippines.

[82]Garfield is recorded as present at a morning meeting of the Committee on Ways and Means on March 25 at which the chairman was authorized to report the Tariff Bill to the House.

Wash day[83] in the House. After 12 o'clock, went to the Senate and listened to a portion of Senator Howe's attack on the President.[84] It was a trenchant, bitter, useless speech. Helped defeat three inflation schemes in the House. Got the correspondence between Jefferson Davis and General Scott. One of the most bitter and noteworthy literary productions I have ever seen. I shall make use of it in my article.[85] At seven dined with Blaine and Whitelaw Reid. General Gordon gave an interesting account of his part in the battle of Antietam.[86]

TUESDAY, 26.   Desk in the morning. Ways and Means at half-past ten. House during the day. Made some progress on *Review* article, but spent much time in reading for it.

WEDNESDAY, 27.   The same story repeated. The day has been too full of routine to merit special mention.

[83]Under the rules of the House the morning hour on Mondays was regularly reserved for a roll call of the states and territories, during which members might introduce bills for reference to committees, joint resolutions of state and territorial legislatures for reference and printing, and resolutions.

[84]Speaking on a motion to request of President Hayes information on a public official whose behavior in office was being questioned, Timothy Howe, a Republican senator from Wisconsin, delivered a harsh attack on Hayes and his Southern policy.

[85]From 1853 to 1857 Jefferson Davis was secretary of war in the Democratic administration of Franklin Pierce. Winfield S. Scott, who had been the Whig candidate for President in 1852, was then general-in-chief of the U.S. army, with headquarters in New York. During these years many letters passed between the two men concerning Scott's pay, claims and allowances. Some of them were extremely acrimonious and insulting. The Senate in 1857 obtained from the President this correspondence and related correspondence and documents and published the whole as *Senate Executive Documents,* No. 34, 34 Cong., 1 Sess., Serial 880, a document of 254 pages. For the use Garfield made of the Davis-Scott correspondence, see Part II of the article referred to in note 7 above.

[86]In the Battle of Antietam (September 17, 1862) Colonel John B. Gordon commanded the Sixth Alabama Infantry Regiment in General R. E. Rodes's brigade. The Sixth, in position on the brigade's extreme right, was savagely attacked late in the morning, and did most of its fighting in and near the Sunken Road, in the center of the Confederate line. Gordon was praised for his "admirable conduct" in the battle, during which he received five wounds before he left the field. About six weeks after Antietam his promotion to brigadier general was recommended by General Robert E. Lee.

THURSDAY, 28.   Devoted the morning to working on the *Review* article. Attended the session of the House at 12. Skipped the Committee on Ways and Means, in which nothing was done except a report from a sub-Committee of an absurd bill to reduce the tax on Tobacco and secure an income tax.[87] I am terrified when I look at the pile accumulating on my hands and no Rose near me.

FRIDAY, 29.   Worked at my desk until half-past 11, when I went to the Committee on Ways and Means, where I resisted the imposition of an income tax.[88] Remained in the House until two o'clock, when the House went into Committee of the Whole on the Private Calendar and I returned home to work at my desk.

SATURDAY, 30.   House did not meet. Devoted the day to the article for the *Review*. I am embarrassed with [the] mass of material at my command. It should make a volume rather than a magazine article, but I am working under pressure and am limited as to space. In the evening, Mr. and Mrs. Monroe, Governor Cox, Mr. and Mrs. Jones,[89] Mr. and Mrs. Ballou,[90] and Mr. and Mrs. Bassett dined with us. We had a very pleasant dinner party.

SUNDAY, 31.   Attended church with Crete. Worked on *Review* article until a late hour.

April

MONDAY, 1.   Finished article for the *North American Review*. Attended meeting of the House but not of the Committee on Ways

---

[87]The minutes of the committee for March 28 record Garfield as present and as voting against a motion to reduce the tax on tobacco.

[88]The minute book of the committee has no record of a meeting on March 29.

[89]John S. Jones (1836–1903), a lawyer in Delaware, Ohio, was a Union officer in the Civil War (he was breveted brigadier general after the war ended), prosecuting attorney for his county, a Republican member of the U.S. House of Representatives, 1877–79, and of the state legislature, 1879–84. He became a friend and strong supporter of Garfield for the Senate and the Presidency. His daughter Clara was a friend and fellow student of Mollie Garfield in Washington.

[90]Latimer W. Ballou (1812–1900), a businessman of Woonsocket, Rhode Island, was a Republican member of the House, 1875–81.

and Means. Returned home at five. Lieut. Stevenson and wife to dinner.[91] Henry Wyman[92] broke his arm and came into the house and had it set. Rose came at 8 o'clock and [I] dictated letters until 11 o'clock. Preparing to leave for Ohio in the morning.

TUESDAY, 2.   Crete, Mother and I left by the Baltimore and Ohio train at 8.40 A.M. and had a pleasant ride through Maryland and West Virginia. Dined at Cumberland and spent most of the day in reading *The Two Chancellors, Bismarck and Gortchakoff* by a French author.[93] The book, though Frenchy in style, is very interesting, particularly in its details of Bismarck's life. Supper at Grafton. Awoke in the neighborhood of Shelbyville and arrived at that junction just in time to see the Cleveland train go out of sight. Went on to Monroeville and took breakfast at [Continued in next entry.]

WEDNESDAY, 3.   Chicago Junction[94]and made immediate connection for Cleveland, where we arrived at 10.55. Met Dr. Robison's two boys who informed us that the Doctor had been thrown from his horse and seriously injured. Put Mother in a carriage to go to her niece's, Hattie Palmer's, and Crete and I went on to Mentor. Harry Jones and Mrs. Jones met us at the Depot and took us to the farm. After dinner Crete and I called at Dr.

[91]Jonathan D. Stevenson, whose wife, Mary Elizabeth, was the daughter of Garfield's Detroit friend Richard Hawley, was a first lieutenant in the 8th Cavalry Regiment. He had been on disability leave for several months, during part of which he and his wife had been abroad. They soon started for Texas, his regular station, hoping in time with Garfield's help to obtain a better assignment. In 1879 he was promoted to captain. In 1881, during Garfield's presidency, and after another disability leave, he was detailed to Washington, D.C., effective July 1, as secretary and treasurer of the Soldiers' Home. After about one year in this position he was forced to obtain another leave, and died in October, 1882.

[92]Henry F. Wyman was the son of Albert U. Wyman (1833-1915), a Nebraska pioneer who was connected with the office of treasurer of the United States, 1863-85; he was treasurer, 1876-77, and 1883-85. Henry had a long career as a realtor in Omaha.

[93]Juljan Klaczko, *The Two Chancellors, Prince Gortchakof and Prince Bismarck.* Trans. from the French by Mrs. Tait (1877).

[94]Garfield is misleading in respect to his route. After he left Shelby, he went on to Chicago Junction, where he had breakfast, and then on to Monroeville.

Robison's and found him in bed severely jarred but I think not otherwise injured. Spent the remainder of the afternoon in looking over the farm and arranging for a garden. In the evening a number of friends called and took tea.

THURSDAY, 4. Continued farm plans. Visited the Doctor, and after dinner took Crete to the Station where she left for Hiram. Returned to the farm and worked two hours in getting out the large stump from the hill meadow. Then Harry Jones and I drove to the foot of Little Mountain, where I bought 200 second growth ches[t]nut fence posts to be delivered at the farm at ten cents apiece. Home in the evening and visited the Doctor again. Spent the night at the farm.

I should have mentioned that the large field by the barn has been sown to oats and the harrowing-in was finished today. Just eleven months ago today we finished sowing oats. This shows a remarkable difference in the season, for my Journal for 1877 shows that the ground was still cold and wet when they were sowed.

FRIDAY, 5. Overhauled farm affairs. Gave directions about crops and stock and took the one o'clock train for Cleveland. Settled my debt at the Second National Bank and visited with friends. Visited with Smalley of the *Herald.* Took tea and spent the night with Captain Henry in his new house on Cedar Street.[95] Harry Rhodes and his wife took tea with us.

SATURDAY, 6. Took the seven o'clock train for Solon. Spent an hour with Mother and Sister Mary. Took the train to Hiram. Stopped at Jeddo Station and walked up town. Arrived at 11 and spent the afternoon with Burke, and he came down to Father Rudolph's in the evening.

SUNDAY, 7. In the morning called on Cousin Phebe Clapp. Attended Church and listened to a very able sermon from

[95]Charles E. Henry moved to Cleveland from his farm in Bainbridge, Geauga County, in 1877. In February, 1878, he bought for $3,800 a house on Cedar Avenue, where he lived until 1881. On February 28 he wrote to Garfield with reference to the house: "Had it not been for you we never could have owned it. So it is your home whenever you please to come."

Burke. Crete and I, Phebe Clapp and daughter dined at Hinsdale's. At half-past four Crete and I were driven to Garrettsville, where we took the train for Cleveland. Stopped with her Cousin James Mason on Euclid Avenue where we spent the night.

MONDAY, 8.   Took the 6.55 train for Shelby. Capt. Henry joined us at the Station. After waiting forty minutes at Shelby, took the Baltimore and Ohio train for the East. Dinner at Newark where we met Webb Hayes, the President's son. He came into the car and visited us. Captain Henry continued with us until we reached Barnesville. At Hiram I had finished *The Two Chancellors* and this morning commenced to read George Eliot's novel *Silas Marner.* We changed at Benwood, played cassino for a little while and retired.

TUESDAY, 9.   Awoke near Rockville about sixteen miles from Washington. Reached Washington at 7.50. Jimmy met us at the Depot. Breakfasted with the family and found them all well. Spent four hours in reading my mail, which was a bushel in bulk. Attended the meeting of the House but came home early to work at the mail. Finished *Silas Marner.* It is the poorest novel I have read in my life. I am surprised that George Eliot should have given her name to it.

WEDNESDAY, 10.   Rose came in the morning and I dictated a large number of letters. At eleven o'clock attended a meeting of the Committee on Ways and Means when there was a vote had on the Income Tax. I voted against it. It received a majority of one. At eight o'clock in the evening attended the Republican Caucus in the House of Representatives. It is more to be praised for what it did not do, than for what it did do. At the close of the caucus went to Mrs. [Miss] Ransom's room; attended the closing half hour of her reception. Crete, Martha, and Mollie were there and came home at eleven o'clock.

THURSDAY, 11.   Dictated a large number of letters. Went to the House a little before 12. Soon after the reading of the Journal, the House went into Committee of the Whole on the Pension Appropriation Bill. I presided. The debate lasted nearly five hours. Fierce row between Hanna and Sparks.[96] The Democratic plan for abolishing the Pension Agencies was defeated. The bill passed about five o'clock. Home in the evening. Read manuscript sketch of the life of Platt R. Spencer, preparatory to writing an introduction to it.[97] Also commenced reading Heiskel's [Hesekiel's] *Life of Bismarck.*[98]

FRIDAY, 12. Dictated letters in the morning until 11 o'clock, when I went to the Committee on Ways and Means. Some further discussion was had on the Income Tax Bill but nothing was concluded. In the House the day was spent on private bill[s], mainly on the appropriation for the relief of William and Mary's College. On educational grounds I should be glad to vote for the bill. Perhaps if it were put in the form of a donation to the College, I would vote for it, but as a war claim I cannot approve. Home in the evening. Literary exercises of the children at half-past six. Played Pedro with Crete, Martha and the children until a late hour.

SATURDAY, 13. Understanding that the House was to devote itself to the funeral services of the late Judge Leonard, I did not attend but remained at my desk nearly all day working off a large amount of correspondence. In the afternoon went shopping with Crete. In the evening went with Governor Cox to attend the Meeting of the Philosophical Society at the Medical Museum

[96]John Hanna (1827–1882), a Republican member of the House from Indiana, 1877–79, opposed a section of the Pension Bill which provided for the abolition of pension agencies. He contended that such a move would cause delays in payments to pensioners and would not, despite Democratic claims to the contrary, establish a more economical system. When William A. J. Sparks (1828–1904), a Democratic member of the House from Illinois, 1875–83, accused Hanna of trying to protect his law partner, who was pension agent in Indianapolis, a heated debate ensued.

[97]The biography and Garfield's introduction were published in *History of Ashtabula County, Ohio, with Illustrations and Biographical Sketches of its Pioneers and Most Prominent Men* (1878), pp. 107–110. "I have met few men," wrote Garfield, "who so completely won my confidence and affection."

[98]John George Louis Hesekiel, *Das Buch vom Grafen Bismarck . . .* (1869). An English translation by Kenneth R. H. MacKenzie was published in 1870 and in 1877, the latter edition with an introduction by Bayard Taylor.

Buildings on Tenth Street. Listened to a paper by Professor Doolittle[99] on the effect of aerolites upon the motion of planets; also, a suggestion by E. B. Elliott[100] for the invention of an instrument to be called a "telephote," by which a wire from the telephone would carry its electrical current through a tube filled with gas and thus translate sound into color. Then a paper was read by Dr. Antisell[101] on the Temperature and Currents of the Pacific Ocean.

SUNDAY, 14. Attended church with Crete. Carrie Ransom dined with us at half-past one. Spent most of the afternoon in reading Haskell's [Hesekiel's] *Life of Bismarck.* I am deeply interested in the life of the Great Chancellor. In the evening Foster and Mr. Moss[102] of Sandusky called and spent two hours. Then read *Bismarck* until midnight and retired.

MONDAY, 15. Worked at my desk until half-past ten, when I went shopping with Crete. Thence to the Capitol. Went before the Committee on Commerce and presented some papers from the Engineer Department in favor of extending the piers at Ash-

---

[99]Myrick H. Doolittle was long associated with the U.S. Coast and Geodetic Survey. On this occasion, according to the *Proceedings of the Washington Philosophical Society* (founded in 1871), he "continued his communication on 'Aerolithic Disturbance of Planetary Motions.'" Garfield was not a member of the Society.

[100]Ezekiel B. Elliott (1823–1888) had a long career in government service, chiefly as an actuary in the Treasury Department. He published many reports and studies. He was a founder of the Washington Philosophical Society, the American Meteorological Society and the Cosmos Club.

[101]Thomas Antisell (1817–1893), a native of Ireland who was educated in Ireland, Germany and France, came to the United States in 1848 and settled in Washington, D.C. in 1856. During the Civil War he served as a surgeon in the U.S. army. He was chief chemist in the Department of Agriculture, 1866–71, in the service of the Japanese government, 1871–76, and for many years a professor of chemistry at Georgetown University. His many writings include *The Currents of the Pacific Ocean* (1876).

[102]Jay O. Moss (1838–1911), a member of one of Sandusky's most prominent families. His father, Augustus H. Moss (1810–1888), a native of New York, settled in Sandusky in 1837 and from about 1850 to his death engaged in banking there. Jay was associated with the family bank and was also an official of the Sandusky, Mansfield and Newark Rail Road Company. See entries for July 3, 4, and 5, 1879.

tabula and Fairport Harbors. I was glad to find after I had left the room, that the Committee voted to give ten thousand dollars to each harbor. In the House the Maryland resolutions of Montgomery Blair came up and I objected to their reception.[103] A long parliamentary struggle ensued in which I demanded the Ayes and Noes on the question of referring the paper to any Committee, thus substantially leaving it in the power of the House to reject. This debate continued until two o'clock, when the District of Columbia business intervened and the rest of the day was spent on that. The House sat until after six o'clock in

[103]In 1877 the *New York Sun* published a series of articles based on material supplied by James E. (Scamp) Anderson of Louisiana, who had been election supervisor in 1876 in the parish of East Feliciana. Anderson charged that false and fraudulent means had been used to secure for Hayes the electoral votes of his state. Early in 1878 the public learned that Samuel B. McLin, chairman of the Florida Returning Board in 1876, had signed an affidavit that his vote for Hayes electors had been influenced by partisan zeal and promises of reward, and that Tilden, not Hayes, was entitled to the electoral votes of Florida. With these developments the General Assembly of Maryland, under the leadership of Montgomery Blair, adopted a joint resolution directing the attorney general of the state to exhibit a bill, providing Congress cooperated, in the Supreme Court of the United States stating that Maryland's electoral votes of 1876 had not been given due effect by reason of fraudulent returns from other states which the Electoral Commission had approved. It specified that the electoral votes of Florida and Louisiana be given to Tilden and that he be declared President. When on April 15 the resolution was presented to the House of Representatives, Garfield argued that the House should refuse to receive it because it contained a revolutionary proposal to reopen a question already settled by both houses of Congress. On May 13, Clarkson N. Potter, a Democrat of New York, introduced a resolution to investigate the Florida and Louisiana elections, and four days later, after much maneuvering by both parties, it was adopted. As Hayes noted in his diary, the resolution contained charges of "crookedness" against Secretary of the Treasury John Sherman and former governor of Ohio Edward F. Noyes, presently United States minister to France. The investigation, conducted by a committee headed by Potter, was extremely embarrassing to Hayes and other Republican leaders, including Garfield, but nothing was found to warrant a challenge through impeachment or court action of Hayes's right to the presidency. See *Congressional Record,* 45 Cong., 2 Sess., pp. 2522–2527, 3438–3448, 3471–3472, 3483–3484, 3501–3502, and 3521–3530; T. Harry Williams, ed., *Hayes: The Diary of a President, 1875–1881* (1964), p. 142; and Harry Barnard, *Rutherford B. Hayes and His America* (1954), pp. 465–473.

attempting to finish that bill so as to reach the River and Harbor Bill, but did not succeed. An evening session was held for debate on the tariff. After dinner I went to Foster's room and played Euchre with Foster, Judge Poland and G. W. Scofield. Home at twelve.

TUESDAY, 16. Worked at my desk until one-quarter before eleven, when I went to the Treasury with Capt. McLeer [McAleer][104] of Painesville. Thence to the Capitol. In the House, the day was consumed on the Post Office Appropriation Bill. I spoke a short time against cutting down the appropriation for Special Agents. In the evening we had a pleasant dinner party—Foster and wife, McKinley and wife, Hubbell of Mich. and wife, Shellabarger of Ohio and Amos Townsend. Party broke up by half-past ten.

WEDNESDAY, 17. Worked on my letters until half-past ten when I went to the Capitol and attended the Committee on Ways and Means. The Income Tax was under consideration but no conclusion was reached. In the House the day was spent on the Senate resolution for final adjournment on the 10th of June. The majority were in favor of it, but the Democrats fillibustered, fearing that the Resolution would be the death of the Tariff Bill. Fillibustering continued until six when the House adjourned. At eight o'clock in the evening Crete and I attended the meeting of American Academy of Sciences at the Unitarian Church, where we listened to a paper by the venerable Prof. Guyot[105] on the life and labors of Professor Agassiz. Guyot was he [his] co-laborer in Switzerland during the time of Agassiz's investigations of the glaciers, and he spoke with great tenderness and reverence of the

[104]L. F. McAleer, superintendent of the Painesville and Youngstown Railroad. Garfield had received letters introducing him from two Ohioans, one of whom was J. F. Scofield of Painesville.

[105]Arnold H. Guyot (1807–1884), a native of Switzerland, had published largely in the field of glaciology before he came to the United States in 1848 at the urging of Louis Agassiz. He was professor of physical geography and geology at Princeton, 1854–84. He made important contributions to the teaching of geography in American schools. He was also involved, under the direction of the Smithsonian Institution, in the establishment of weather observation stations. His writings include *The Earth and Man* (1849).

eminent abilities of Agassiz. Home at half-past nine. Retired early.

THURSDAY, 18. For the first time since Rose left for New York, I have nearly caught up with my accumulated mail. Committee on Ways and Means at half-past ten. Worked on Income Tax without result. We failed, however, by a tie vote to strike out the Graduated Tax, which I think is unconstitutional and communistic as well. In the House, after the disposition of the Conference report on the Deficiency Bill, the question of final adjournment came up again. The Democratic Caucus had succeeded in whipping in most of their members and they defeated the passage of the resolution for the present. Before the question was concluded, however, the hour of two o'clock arrived, when speeches were made on the death of Judge Leonard. Went to Col. Rockwell's on business and then played billiards with him for two hours. Home in the evening. Began preparing an introduction to the history of the life of P. R. Spencer, which is about to be publish[ed] in a history of Ashtabula County. Read *Bismarck* until 11 o'clock and retired.

FRIDAY, 19. Letters in the morning. At half-past 10 went to the Committee on Ways [and Means] where the consideration of the Income Tax was resumed and no conclusion reached.[106] In the House the morning was devoted to Private Bills. I remained until the House got into Committee of the Whole on the William and Mary College Bill,[107] then went to the President's on business. He invited me to ride. Drove to the Soldiers' Home and had a long talk; first, on the Fitz John Porter case, which he has lately ordered reviewed,[108] and then on general politics. He thinks we

[106]The minutes of the committee do not record Garfield as present at the meeting on April 19. They do indicate that the vote in favor of a graduated tax was reconsidered, that a motion to adopt a uniform rate was passed and that a decision was made to set the rate at two per cent.

[107]The House did not go into a Committee of the Whole to debate the William and Mary College Bill, for supporters of the measure failed to get control of the floor and the House turned to other business.

[108]In 1862 Major General Fitz John Porter (1822–1910), a corps commander in the Union army, was charged with disobeying orders in the Second Battle of

ought to put in our platforms a resolution against any further payment of claims arising from the war. He stated in rapid review the character of his appointments and said they would compare favorably with those made by any preceding administration. He also mentioned the fact that every president of a college and every Protestant religious paper in the United States approved his administration. In the evening at eight o'clock called at Mr. Hale's to meet the Executive Congressional Committee in reference to the opening of the Campaign. Staid until nearly 11 o'clock. Home at eleven.

SATURDAY, 20. Correspondence in the morning. Committee [on] Ways and Means at half-past ten. In the House until two o'clock. Took part in the debate on the Post Office Appropriation Bill. General Sheldon dined with us at six. At eight o'clock went with Sheldon to the President's and spent an hour and a half discussing Louisiana affairs. Sheldon gave a very interesting account of the situation there and expressed the confident belief that the Bourbon Democracy[109] would be beaten. A secret orga-

---

Bull Run. Tried and convicted by a court martial, he was cashiered from the army in 1863. He promptly undertook what became a twenty-three year campaign to clear his name. He amassed new evidence and worked assiduously for a reinvestigation. His case was fraught with politics and personal feelings. Porter, known as a Democratic general during the Civil War, was greatly disliked by many Republican leaders, including Garfield, who had sat on the court martial and voted for conviction. In 1878 Porter's fortunes turned for the better when Hayes ordered a military board to conduct the investigation mentioned by Garfield in this entry. The board held many hearings, heard and examined evidence not available to the court martial, and reported in 1879 that Porter, far from disobeying orders, had been "faithful, subordinate, and intelligent," saving the Union army from disaster on August 29 and from rout on the following day. Hayes, without making a recommendation, referred the report to Congress, where it became the subject of a debate that continued, off and on, for over six years. Vindication for Porter did not come until 1886 when he was reappointed a colonel in the regular army, retroactive but without back pay to May 14, 1861, the date of his promotion to that rank, and placed on the retired list. (See entries for October 17, 1879; January 21, February 5, 6, 8, 13, 16, and 29, and March 1, 4–6, and 8–10, 1880.)

[109]In the decade and a half following the Compromise of 1876–77, white Southerners, having secured home rule, glorified the ante-bellum South and the Confederacy, and elected to top governmental positions former leaders, mostly

nization has been formed in the State, pledged to the defeat of the Democracy, and eight thousand voters are already enrolled in it. They are determined to put down the violence which has hitherto prevailed and say they are sure of success. The President has had the same information from other quarters. At half-past [nine] Sheldon and I called on Townsend and General McCook, where we visited for two or three hours.

SUNDAY, 21. At ten o'clock by appointment went to Secretary Schurz's and consulted with him and General Walker in regard to the next Census.[110] It was agreed that Walker and I should draft a bill and try to secure a Joint Committee to consider the subject during the recess of Congress. Schurz gave me an interesting account of his visit to Bismarck a few years ago. He was kindly received and Bismarck spent several hours in most familiar and interesting conversation. Schurz says Bismarck is much the greatest man that Europe has produced since the first Napoleon. Home at 12 M. Miss Ransom dined with us. Read Hesekiel's *Life of Bismarck* nearly all the remainder of the day. It is in some sense a panegyric upon the great Chancellor. But the letters of Bismarck to his wife and sister are among the most charming and racy I have ever read. Read also in connection Washburne's correspondence with Bismarck, during the Franco-Prussian War.[111]

Confederate army officers, commonly referred to as Confederate Brigadiers, but derisively named Bourbons by the few who opposed them and their new policies, and who likened them to the reactionary Bourbon kings of post-Napoleonic France. Salient features of Bourbon rule were the maintenance of a solidly Democratic South, the relegation of Negroes to a position of complete political, economic, and social inferiority, and, in cooperation with Northern businessmen, an economic conversion which emphasized industrial development and agricultural diversification.

[110]Francis A. Walker, who was breveted brigadier general in the Union army and was now a professor at Yale University, had recently been appointed superintendent of the census of 1880.

[111]On February 6, 1878, the President at the request of the Senate transmitted to that body copies of the correspondence in relation to the Franco-Prussian War of Elihu B. Washburne, U.S. minister to France, 1869–77, with the State Department, Bismarck, and other officials. The correspondence was published by the

MONDAY, 22. Correspondence in the morning. Arrived at the House at 20 minutes after 12 o'clock. The Montgomery Blair resolutions had already been referred, without a division, to the Committee on the Judiciary. This may be as well but I had intended to contest it. The River and Harbor Bill was passed after a stormy but fruitless opposition led by Mr. Cox. The Speaker, as a question of privilege, recognized Cox's right to enter a protest. Pending that, however, and before the protest was read, the House adjourned. Came home at five o'clock and at half-past five Crete and I drove to the Sixth Street Depot to go to Baltimore to hear Booth in *Hamlet.* We arrived at the Station a minute too late. Returned home. Gilfillan and his wife came and spent the evening. Harry, Mollie, and Jimmy attended a children's party at Fernando Wood's. Shakespeare's Birthday.

TUESDAY, 23. Worked on correspondence until half-past ten, when I went to the Committee on Ways and Means. I made a report on bill for the relief of John Henderson, which was adopted.[112] But as I had been counsel for Henderson in the Supreme Court, I asked the Chairman to assign the report to another man. It was given to Sayler. In the House the day was consumed on Cox's pretended question of privilege, namely, his protest against the passage of the River and Harbor Bill. The Speaker decided that the paper should be read, before he was aware whether it was a question of privilege or not. That is, he granted Cox all that he wanted, before he determined whether the request was in order. I appealed from his decision and my

government under the title *Franco-Prussian War and Insurrection of the Commune. Correspondence of E. B. Washburne . . .* (1878).

[112]For the Henderson case see Vol. II, p. 14. The Supreme Court, ruling against Henderson, had directed that a judgment be entered against him and sureties on his bond for five thousand dollars. A bill had been introduced in the House directing the Treasury to refund the money. In its favorable report the Committee on Ways and Means maintained that Henderson himself had been guiltless of any attempt to defraud the revenue. No further action on the bill was taken in this session but an identical Senate bill became law in February, 1879. In a letter (April 22) Ebon C. Ingersoll, a Washington lawyer, urged Garfield to make the report at the earliest day possible.

appeal would have been sustained by the House but for the fact that Reagan and a few others wanted to make a speech in reply to Cox. As it was my appeal was laid on the table by a vote of 120 odd to 103 [131 to 101].

WEDNESDAY, 24.   Letters in the morning. At eleven o'clock went to the Treasury Department to see the Secretary. Thence to the Capitol and spent most of the day on the Pacific Railroad Sinking Fund Bill, which was passed with but two dissenting votes. I made a brief speech to ascertain whether the bill was sufficiently guarded to stand the construction of the Court, but could not vote upon it, being paired with Mr. Tucker. Home in the evening. Mr. Norcross,[113] of Massachusetts, and his daughter called and spent an hour.

THURSDAY, 25.   Correspondence in the forenoon until half-past ten, when I rode to the Capitol with Colonel Ingersoll and attended the Committee on Ways and Means, where Mr. Wood's bill for suspending the operation of the Sinking Fund was discussed until 12 o'clock. In the House the day was consumed on the repeal of the Bankrupt law. I voted against that bill in the Thirty-Ninth Congress, but doubt the propriety of its absolute repeal now. Still, being paired with Tucker and not knowing how he would vote, I withheld my own vote. At seven in the evening we had a Williams College Dinner. There were present Mr. and Mrs. Dawes and daughter, Mr. and Mrs. Townsend of Troy,[114] Mr. Robinson[115] of the Berkshire District, Colonel Rockwell and wife, Gilfillan and wife and Archie Hopkins. Harry, Mollie and Jimmy went to Mrs. Carpenter's upon Capitol Hill. Our company remained until about 11 o'clock. Very pleasant party.

FRIDAY, 26.   Letters in the forenoon. House at twelve. The day

---

[113]Amasa Norcross (1824–1898) was a Republican member of the House from Massachusetts, 1877–83.

[114]Martin I. Townsend (1810–1903), who graduated at Williams College in 1833, was a Republican member of the House from New York, 1875–79.

[115]George D. Robinson (1834–1896), a graduate of Harvard, was a Republican member of the House from Massachusetts, 1877–84, and governor, 1884–87.

was spent on the Post Office Appropriation Bill. I offered an amendment relieving Postal Clerks, Route Agents, and Mail Route Messengers from the necessity of wearing uniforms and spoke upon it a short time.[116] Literary exercises in the evening. Jimmy was so anxious to attend the Circus in company with Mr. Patterson and his son, that I allowed him to go. Harry had failed to prepare an essay and I required him to deliver a brief lecture on the Roman Invasion of Britain, which he did better than I expected. These exercises have increased in interest week by week and the little fellows are storing up a good many gems of literature. At eight o'clock I went to Townsend's and spent the evening with him and Sanford[117] and Sheldon. While there a correspondent came to see me in regard to the so-called confession of Judge McLin of Florida, about which there is a good deal of a stir. The *Tribune* is right when it calls it another Mrs. Tilton confession.[118]

SATURDAY, 27. Correspondence in the morning. Went to the Capitol at 12 o'clock, and the day was devoted to the Indian Appropriation Bill. The Indian Appropriation Bill passed and the

[116]In support of his amendment Garfield held that a uniform was expensive, inconvenient, and burdensome, and that the proposed blue-cloth uniform would be similar to those worn by train men, policemen, and even peanut boys. This similarity, he said, would "make it easier for those who wish to steal to . . . slip in and get a mailbag without detection and carry it off." The amendment was approved, 54–18.

[117]Probably Lorenzo Danford.

[118]In 1870 Elizabeth Tilton confessed to her husband Theodore that she had had intimate relations with the Reverend Henry Ward Beecher. After a call by Beecher she retracted her confession. When, four years later, Tilton brought suit against Beecher for criminal conversation and demanded $100,000 damages, Mrs. Tilton came to Beecher's defense. On April 16, 1878, the *New York Times* published a letter from Mrs. Tilton in which she confessed that her husband's charge of adultery had indeed been true. The *Times* commented that on evidence at the trial it had reached the conclusion that Beecher was guilty, and that Mrs. Tilton's confession did not strengthen the evidence against Beecher. Thus, a "Mrs. Tilton confession" is a superfluous confession, adding nothing to evidence already available and causing no change in opinion. For McLin, see note 103 above.

Legislative Appropriation Bill was taken up and considerable progress made in it. At four o'clock I took the little mare and drove Crete to the Soldiers' Home. At half-past six I dined at Mr. LeDuc's, Commissioner of Agriculture, with his wife, General Hooker,[119] Senator Hill, ex-Senator Ramsey and Dr. Loring[120] and Rodgers [Rogers], the President's Private Secretary. A long conversation at the table on the administration of Southern Affairs. Home at half-past 11.

SUNDAY, 28. Crete and I attended church. After dinner read the *Life of Bismarck* covering the period of the Franco-Prussian War. His letters to his wife are delightful. At half-past six dined at Bancroft Davis' in company with Senator ——— and ——— Van Vliet.[121] Davis related some very pleasant incidents of his acquaintance with Bismarck. He saw him in Berlin in 1872. Bismarck does not invite foreign ministers to dinner. He takes the position that diplomats are spies in uniform and keeps aloof from them. But he invited Davis to dinner because he was then the Agent of the United States in the Geneva Tribunal, and Bismarck did not wish the Tribunal to break up. Davis says Bismarck is a Protectionist and has weeded out the Free Trade elements from the Emperor's Cabinet. Home at half-past ten o'clock. Retired at half-past eleven.

MONDAY, 29. Correspondence in the morning. Went to the Public Printing Office. Thence to the Baltimore Depot to arrange for shipping my mare to Cleveland. Capitol at twelve. The day was

---

[119]Charles E. Hooker (1825–1914), who rose from private to colonel in the Confederate army, was a Democratic member of the House from Mississippi, 1875–83, 1887–95, and 1901–03.

[120]George B. Loring (1817–1891), physician, agriculturist, and politician, was a Republican member of the Massachusetts state legislature for a number of years, member of the U.S. House of Representatives, 1877–81, commissioner of agriculture (appointed by Garfield), 1881–85, and minister to Portugal, 1889–90. His writings include *The Farm-Yard Club of Jotham* (1876).

[121]Stewart Van Vliet (1815–1901), a graduate of West Point, was on duty in Washington, D.C., during this period as assistant quartermaster general. Breveted major general during the Civil War, he was lieutenant colonel in the regular army, 1866–72, and colonel, 1872–81.

spent in work on the Legislative Appropriation Bill and good progress was made. The bill was half finished. There is a better spirit of work in the House than there has been for some time. Home in the evening. Several gentlemen called—Mr. Defrees,[122] First Auditor Reynolds, and General Sheldon.

TUESDAY, 30. Correspondence in the morning until 11 o'clock,[123] when I went to the stable and arranged for having Josie sent to the cars.[124] I then went to the freight depot and provided for her shipment. I then went to the House where the Legislative Appropriation Bill was further debated. In the course of the day the Speaker came down on the floor and assailed the Republican Party for resisting economy. I replied to him and several others followed. I think he got decidedly the worst of it. It was an indelicacy on his part to introduce partisan debate into the House.[125] At four o'clock I went to the depot and attended the shipment of Josie. At half-past seven went with Foster and Sheldon to the Executive Mansion and had an interview of an hour with the President. He had been told that Sheldon was

[122]John D. Defrees (1810–1882), a native of Tennessee, learned printing and studied law in Ohio before settling in 1831 in Indiana, where he was a member of the state legislature and publisher and editor of the *Indiana State Journal.* Appointed superintendent of public printing by President Lincoln in 1861, he held the office until 1869 (his title was changed to Congressional printer in 1867). After an interval of eight years he was restored to the position (the name of which had been changed to public printer in 1874) by President Hayes, and remained in office until a few months before his death. He was the brother of Joseph H. Defrees (1812–1885), a Republican member of the U.S. House of Representatives from Indiana, 1865–67.

[123]The minutes of the Committee on Ways and Means for April 30 record Garfield as present and voting against a resolution to suspend the operation of the Sinking Fund.

[124]See note 11 above.

[125]In the debate Republican speakers advocated larger appropriations than provided in the Legislative Appropriation Bill, a measure that reflected the retrenchment policies of the Democratic majority. Speaker Randall accused the Republicans of opposing economy and promoting extravagance. Garfield replied that the supreme goal of Congress was wise government, not economy, and that if more funds were needed to carry on the government wisely, Congress should have full liberty to appropriate them.

drinking too much and ought not to be appointed for that reason. The matter was discussed fully and I think we left the President feeling all right. Went thence to Foster's room and visited with Sheldon, Townsend and Foster.

May

WEDNESDAY, 1. Worked at my desk in the morning until half-past ten, when I went to the Interior Department with Miss Rose Brainerd,[126] and got a promise that she should be restored. Called also at the Land Office on business. House at eleven o'clock. Debate on the Legislative Bill was resumed in which I took some part until half-past two when Crete called and I drove with her to the Deaf Mute College to witness the exercises of Commencement, or as they call it Presentation Day. At the conclusion of the graduating speeches, Judge Niblack[127] spoke about 20 minutes. I spoke about ten minutes, in what was said to be an effective speech.[128] The President and Mrs. Hayes were there and a large audience. In the evening several friends called, among [them] Col. John McDowell, General Sheldon, Mr. and Mrs. Rockwell, Mr. and Mrs. Gilfillan. Retired at 12 o'clock.

THURSDAY, 2. Worked at my desk until half-past ten o'clock, when I went shopping with Crete. Thence to the Capitol. The day was consumed working on the Legislative Appropriation

[126]Rose Brainerd, niece of Garfield's friends Enos and Jehu Brainerd, studied at Oberlin, 1872–73, had a government clerkship in Washington for a few years, and served for many years as the matron of Lynn Hospital, Lynn, Massachusetts.

[127]William E. Niblack, former member of the House from Indiana. The *Washington Post* (May 2) in reporting the commencement spoke of the "tall, broad, heavy form of the distinguished Judge, with the massive head, the cavernous eyes, the square jaw, the firm double chin and the prominent pugnacious nose. . . ."

[128]The *Washington Post* (May 2) described Garfield as he appeared that evening: "Gen. Garfield is a handsome man, although his magnificent forehead and bald upper head are continual suggestions of a smooth-rind pumpkin. He sat beside Mr. Hayes on the platform, and looked like an elder but better looking brother of the latter. He made a few remarks in a very pleasant voice. . . ."

Bill, and some progress, though the bill is not yet completed. Returned home at four o'clock. At seven we had a dinner party. There were present Mr. and Mrs. Thurman, Mr. and Mrs. Matthews, the Secretary of War (McCrary), General McCook, General Sheldon, Miss Ransom, and Miss Irish.

FRIDAY, 3. Letters in the morning until ten o'clock when I attended a meeting of the Committee on Rules. At my suggestion a rule was adopted to restrict the right of making special orders by a majority vote to those Committees who have authority to report at any time. Also, another rule making it in order for the Committee on Ways and Means to report revenue bills at any time. In the House the day was consumed on the Legislative Appropriation Bill, which was finished in Committee and reported back to the House, but the votes on the amendments were not taken. In the evening General Sherman and several others called. Crete and I were invited to go to Baltimore to hear Booth in *Richard Third* but we were both too tired with late evenings to go, and so retired at 10 o'clock.

SATURDAY, 4. Correspondence in the morning. Capitol at 11 o'clock. The day was consumed in voting on amendments to the Legislative Appropriation Bill, which passed about half-past four o'clock. An unsuccessful attempt was made to bring up the Tariff Bill. The House adjourned at five o'clock. In the evening we had expected to go to Baltimore to hear Booth in *Richard III.* Crete was too ill to go and we retired early. Edwin Cowles of the *Cleveland Leader* called and spent an hour.

SUNDAY, 5. Crete was quite ill this morning and not able to sit up. Sent for Dr. Pope. She has some fever and sore throat. Staid at home all day. Finished Hesekiel's *Bismarck.* Read hurriedly two or three plays of Ben Jonson—*Every Man in His Humour,* [and] *Sejanus.* Then read his *Catiline,* which is thoroughly Roman and not a little Shakespearian. Mr. Cowles and Miss Ransom dined with us. In the evening the children read from Mark Twain's *Roughing It* [*1872*].

MONDAY, 6. Letters in the morning. Went to the Bank to obtain $166.67 for the first installment on subscription to the New Company at Ravenna, for the purchase of the *Republican Demo-*

crat. [129] This purchase will cause me trouble on account of the odium into which Halsey Hall has fallen by his failure and the causes that led to it. But he has been so long my friend that I cannot allow him to suffer while I can help it. In the House an attempt was made to suspend the rules and reduce the tax on tobacco. The proposition received five majority. It was supported mainly by the Democracy of the South. The rest of the day was consumed on the District of Columbia government. I made two short speeches against vesting the House and Senate with the power of electing Commissioners. [130] Home in the evening until eight when I called at the President's. He was at lunch and I called at Thompson's [a] short time. [131] Home at nine. Finished

[129] See Vol. I, p. 292, n. 15, and entry for March 17, 1878.

[130] In 1874 Congress abolished the existing territorial government of the District of Columbia and established a temporary one under which powers formerly exercised by the governor and the Board of Public Works were vested in three commissioners appointed by the President. It was not until 1878 that Congress enacted what it thought of as a permanent act for the government of the District. The bill before the House at this time provided for three commissioners, one of whom was to be chosen by the House, one by the Senate, and one detailed from the Corps of Engineers by the President. It also provided for an elected council. Garfield objected to the choice of commissioners by Congress on the ground that it was clearly unconstitutional. The act which became law on June 11, 1878, provided for the appointment of two commissioners from civil life by the President and the detailing by the President of a third from the Corps of Engineers. Various independent boards were abolished. There was no provision for an elected council. This measure was the organic act for the government of the District of Columbia until 1967.

[131] Richard W. Thompson (1809–1900), a native of Virginia, settled as a young man in Indiana, where he entered politics and law. He was a Whig member of the U.S. House of Representatives, 1847–49; in Washington he became acquainted with Abraham Lincoln, who was in the House at the same time. During the Civil War he was active in the recruitment and organization of troops. In 1876 at the Republican National Convention he made the nominating speech for Oliver P. Morton, Indiana's leading Republican politician. In March, 1877, Hayes appointed him secretary of the navy; he held this office until December, 1880, when his acceptance of the salaried chairmanship of the American Committee of the Panama Canal Company forced his withdrawal. He lived to become the "Grand Old Man" of Indiana. Among his published works is *Recollections of Sixteen Presidents*, 2 vols. (1894). See Charles Roll, *Colonel Dick Thompson, the Persistent Whig* (1947).

Jonson's *Catiline* and glanced over some of his other dramas. Read some of his shorter poems. I am far from well. I am oppressed with the idea that my mind is producing nothing. Since the article on the Army I have done almost nothing.

TUESDAY, 7. Letters in the morning. Committee on Ways and Means at 11. Several private bills were disposed of. In the House most of the day was consumed in debating and passing the District Government Bill. At four o'clock General Banks got the floor and made a speech against Wood's Tariff Bill. During the day I hear[d] for the first time the story that one of the certificates of the Electoral College of Louisiana had two names, Levisee and Joffrion, forged.[132] Whether this is true or not I do not know, but there seems to be some ground for the statement. I looked through the *Record* of the session of Congress and the Commission and found that the two Hayes certificates from Louisiana published in the *Record* are duplicates, and I think

---

[132]When the eight Republican presidential electors in Louisiana (among whom were Aaron B. Levisee, Oscar Joffrion and Garfield's close friend Lionel Sheldon) met in New Orleans on December 6, 1876, they cast their ballots for Rutherford B. Hayes and William A. Wheeler for President and Vice President. Three copies of a certificate were prepared, two of which were to go to the President of the Senate (Thomas W. Ferry of Michigan), one by mail and one by special messenger. The special messenger chosen to make the trip was Thomas C. Anderson, a member of the Louisiana Returning Board. When he presented the certificate to Ferry the latter refused to accept it because a certificate signed by the electors as required by law did not appear on the outside of the sealed envelope. It was subsequently pointed out that the names of the candidates for President and Vice President should have been on separate sheets rather than together. Anderson returned to New Orleans, where new forms were prepared late in December. On January 3, 1877, Charles Hill of New Orleans delivered one set to Senator Ferry in the presence of John Sherman. In the late December proceedings the signatures were not affixed at the same time. Lionel Sheldon testified before the Potter Committee that he and three other electors had been the initial signers and that they had signed together. He said that he had no knowledge of the other signatures (which included those of Levisee and Joffrion). Levisee denied before the Committee that he had signed the revised forms. Another witness named a person who he said had forged the name of Joffrion. If some of the signatures were forged in the absence of electors, the only reason would seem to be the desire to expedite the return trip to Washington. See *House Miscellaneous Documents,* No. 31, 45 Cong., 3 Sess., Serials 1864 and 1865.

are both the original unchanged returns. In the evening I called on the President and looked over the proceedings thoroughly, and gave him such facts as I had collected. Talked with him also in regard to matters of appointment. He took notes of the points I had made in regard to the Electoral Certificates of Louisiana. He thanked me for the information I had given him.

WEDNESDAY, 8.   Letters in the morning. Called at the War and State Departments. At the latter I looked after the question of the Presidential Count. The Secretary of State was not in, but I found in conversation with Mr. Seward that the certificates of the Presidential electors are not lodged with the Secretary of State, but with the Vice President. At the Capitol at 11 o'clock. At the end of the morning hour, after a long and ugly wrangle,[133] the Tariff Bill was taken up and Tucker made a longer [long] and able speech followed by Robbins. A new idea has come to me today and I spent some time during the evening in working it out. It is that the American mode of National defence is not by a standing army, but by providing within our own borders for the means of sustaining and supplying an army in time of war. That is by keeping up those national industries necessary to a state of war.[134] This it seems to me will place the doctrine of protection upon a new basis. My natural conservatism leads me to hesitate to accept this new suggestion but I shall pursue it until I satisfy myself. Home in the evening.

THURSDAY, 9.   Desk in the morning. Callers interrupted me. Capitol at 11 o'clock. Committee on Ways and Means failed to get a quorum. In the House the morning hour was devoted to the Railroad Bill. Then Kelley spoke two hours and a quarter. His speech, though full of himself, was better than usual for him, though marred by his personal vanity. Home in the evening until

---

[133]The issue was whether the House, sitting as a Committee of the Whole, should limit debate on the Tariff Bill. The vote was in favor of unlimited debate.

[134]Garfield's new idea was similar to one of the recommendations in George Washington's statement on a peace establishment, presented to the Continental Congress in 1783, which called for manufactures to produce tools of war.

nine o'clock when I went to Speaker Randall's Reception. Acklen brought me home in his carriage.

FRIDAY, 10.   Worked at my desk until one-quarter before 11. Went to the House. Soon after the reading of the Journal, introduced a report from the Committee on Rules to make the power of the Committee on Ways and Means to report at any time on bills touching revenue and the public debt equal to that of Appropriations and restricting other committees from the same privilege. After some debate the report was printed and laid over. The rest of the day was consumed by private bills. Home in the evening and read tariff history until a late hour.

SATURDAY, 11.   Desk until 11 o'clock when I went to the Surgeon General's Office and to the Treasury, thence to the Capitol. The House devoted the day to the discussion of the Interstate Railway Bill. I made a ten minutes' speech which was somewhat effective.[135] The previous question was sustained so that the bill will go over as unfinished business. The House adjourned at five. The Democrats have passed the Redistricting Bill through the Lower House of the Ohio Legislature and will doubtless pass it through the Senate.[136] In the evening called at Townsend's to meet several of our Ohio members.

---

[135]Speaking in support of the bill, Garfield pointed out that it defined an interstate railway as "a road owned by one company running through more than one State, or a combination of roads owned by several companies, so as to make a continuous line through more than one State." In particular Garfield approved the measure because it conformed to two ideas: (1) that an interstate railway "shall give equal facilities to all its customers, and shall charge the same rate to all for the same service"; and (2) "that an interstate railway company or combination of companies shall never charge a greater rate for a short distance than they charge for the same service for a longer distance."

[136]Both houses of the Ohio legislature that organized in January, 1878, were controlled by the Democrats. One result of this control was the enactment of a congressional redistricting act. Samuel J. Randall, Speaker of the U.S. House of Representatives, was said to have urged Ohio legislators to take this step. Garfield's Nineteenth District lost Portage County and gained Mahoning. In the 45th Congress (1877–79) the Ohio delegation in the House was made up of 12 Republicans and 8 Democrats; in the 46th Congress, elected in the fall of 1878 under the new law, it was made up of 11 Democrats and 9 Republicans.

SUNDAY, 12. At home all day reading on the Tariff question. I am distressed by the conflicting elements of this question, or rather I should say by the curious state of conflict in my own mind upon the various phases of it. To be an extreme man is doubtless comfortable. It is painful to see too many sides to a subject. In the evening Dr. Tachmyntas called.[137] He is a Greek born in Romania. He talked with me a long time and wrote me the following appended letter in Modern Greek.[138] Several friend[s] called in the evening. Read at my desk until half-past eleven.

MONDAY, 13. Worked at the desk until half-past ten, when I went to the Departments and thence to the Capitol. Soon after the morning [hour] Mr. Potter of New York introduced the long-threatened resolution of investigation in the late Presidential Election, confining inquiries to the states of Florida and Louisiana.[139] Several of us insisted that it was not a question of privilege, but the Speaker overruled. Hale then offered an amendment enlarging the scope of the inquiry, but they would neither allow it to be received nor read. I spoke a little while, effectively my friends say. They demanded the previous question and I called upon our side to sit silent and leave them without a quorum. All the Republicans complied with my suggestions

[137]E. J. Tachmyntas, who called himself an "ultra-republican citizen of the United States," and claimed to be a doctor of medicine, believed himself the victim of long persecution. He claimed to have been persecuted by the Greek government for 14 years and robbed of two hundred thousand dollars. In Washington, where he arrived in July, 1877, he found spies of European absolute governments, particularly the Greek government, at work against him. In the Capital he had been ejected from rooming houses and had failed to obtain recognition as a physician although he had sought the help of numerous prominent men. He believed that the object of the persecution was to send him back to Greece. "But," he wrote in a pamphlet (dated February 1, 1878) detailing his woes, "the diplomatic persecutors should know that I am Leonidas Spartiatis, and say, 'My head bowed down but not surrendered.'"

[138]Tachmyntas hails "the most illustrious General Garfield," says he is happy to have met him, and that if Garfield considers carefully and conscientiously what he (Tachmyntas) has said, he will bring him some relief from his troubles. He signs as one who is unjustly harried and still living in distress.

[139]See n. 103 above.

and the Democrats were compelled to adjourned [adjourn]. Prof. Henry died at ten minutes after 12 today. At eight o'clock an informal meeting of the Board of Regents was held to make arrangements for the funeral. On my suggestion the Chancellor, Chief Justice Waite, was authorized to invite the President and Cabinet, Courts and Congress, Diplomatic Corps and Light House Board, and the Scientific Associations with which Prof. Henry was connected, to attend the services, which are to be observed at half-past four o'clock Thursday at the New York Avenue Church. Returned home at half-past nine feeling quite unwell. The President sent word that he thinks we ought to insist on debating the Potter resolution at length. This we will probably do. Mollie is quite sick this evening with fever. Late in the evening I went to Foster's room to consult in reference to the suggestions of the President. Retired at 12.

TUESDAY, 14. Worked at my desk until near 11 o'clock, but was quite unwell. Went to the Capitol. The Democrats insisted on their Florida resolution as it is, and we declined to vote, leaving them without a quorum. The House adjourned at half-past twelve after adopting the concurrent resolution which came from the Senate, that both Houses adjourn on Thursday at four o'clock to attend the funeral of Professor Henry.

WEDNESDAY, 15. Worked at correspondence until 10 o'clock, when I went to the War Department and thence shopping with Crete. Went to the House at 11. The Democrats found themselves still without a quorum and after half a dozen fruitless votes adjourned. Republican House caucus was called. Sat two hours. A Committee was appointed, of which I was a member, to draft resolutions in regard to the pending controversy. Reed[140] of Maine drew the first and I drew the second. They were reported to the Caucus and after some debate adopted. Home at five o'clock. In the evening we gave a dinner party. Speaker Randall and wife, Mr. and Mrs. Blaine and Miss Dodge, Judge Swayne

[140]Thomas B. Reed (1839–1902), a Republican member of the House from Maine, 1877–99, and Speaker of the House, 1889–91, 1895–99. He ranks as one of the ablest and most powerful leaders in the history of the American Congress.

and wife, Scofield and wife, Judge Black and Mr. Sayler. A very pleasant party and successful dinner.

THURSDAY, 16. Worked at my desk until half-past ten, when I went to the Capitol. Deadlock continued. The Democrats have failed to call in a quorum and after three or four votes adjourned. Went to the Executive Mansion and spent two hours with the President. I gave him the results of my examination of the certificate of Electoral votes of Louisiana. The Genuine certificate is in Senator Ferry's Safe, with all the other certificates. We discussed quite at length the probabilities of the investigation fight now going on in the House. The President brought out his Diary and read me the entries relating to visitors to Florida and Louisiana. He said that Noyes was indiscreet, but he did not think he had said or written any such thing as charged in connection with the Florida count.[141] At half-past four attended the funeral of Professor Henry at the New York Avenue Church. It was an occasion long to be remembered. The sermon by Mr. Mitchell, though

---

[141]In the affidavit referred to in note 103 above, Samuel B. McLin, chairman of the Florida Returning Board in the election of 1876, claimed that former Governor Edward F. Noyes of Ohio, who had been one of the Republican visitors to Florida after the election, had promised that he would be rewarded if Hayes became President. Later, before the Potter Committee, he said that Noyes's promise had not been made until after the canvass had been completed. In June, Noyes, U.S. minister to France, 1877–81, returned from Paris to testify before the committee. With reference to the Florida Returning Board he declared flatly: "I never made one of them a promise, nor intimated a promise, nor held out any inducement whatever to have them declare that State for Governor Hayes rather than for Governor Tilden." He readily admitted, however, that after the Florida canvass had been completed he told the depressed and worried McLin that he would take pleasure in telling Hayes of his conduct and in recommending him for a position. In April, 1877, President Hayes appointed McLin an associate justice of the Supreme Court of the Territory of New Mexico. In December, after McLin had been in his new position for six months, the Senate, influenced by Senator Simon Conover of Florida, rejected the nomination. The President was unwilling to nominate McLin for another position unless he could be sure of confirmation. McLin's bitterness is evident in his affidavit, in which he speaks of Hayes as having "basely betrayed and mercilessly destroyed the Republican Party of the South, and crushed the very men who did so much for his election." For McLin's affidavit and for his and Noyes's testimony before the Potter Committee, see *House Miscellaneous Documents,* No. 31, 45 Cong., 3 Sess., Serials 1864 and 1865.

able, was mainly devoted to proving Prof. Henry an orthodox Presbyterian. I do not believe he cared much about church organization. I have no doubt but that the Professor accepted the general doctrine of Christianity, but I think he had little sympathy with the narrow bigotry which afflicts nearly all churches. I did not accompany the Regents to the Cemetary but returned home. In the evening Mr. Stephens sent me a letter requesting me to see him at half-past ten tomorrow morning, and also sent word by messenger that he should do what he could to break the deadlock and left the Republican Resolutions in. Retired at half-past 11.

FRIDAY, 17. Worked at my desk until one-quarter before ten, when I attended a meeting of the Board of Regents at the Smithsonian Institution. Dr. Parker moved to postpone the election of a Secretary until the next annual meeting. This was generally opposed, was finally withdrawn, and we proceeded to the election. Eleven ballots were cast and all for Prof. Spencer F. Baird. After other business, arranged for a Memorial for Prof. Henry. The meeting then adjourned. Reached the Capitol at 11 o'clock. Notwithstanding all the talk of Stephens and others no Democratic opposition was made and at half-past five o'clock, a Democratic quorum being secured, the resolution was passed without amendment or debate. If I am not mistaken this day's business will prove an unfortunate investment for the Democrats. It is revolutionary and unpatriotic and will be so regarded by the country. Home in the evening. A number of gentleman callers.

SATURDAY, 18. Desk in the morning until half-past ten. House at 11; ordinary business resumed. Democrats surprised that we did not offer the Hale resolutions. We prefer to let them stand on their partisan programme without mitigation. House went into Committee of the Whole on the Army Bill and Hewitt of N. Y. made a speech of two hours and a half, in the course of which he complimented me very highly, but criticized my *North American* [*Review*] Article on a few points.[142] McCook followed

---

[142]Garfield, who favored a larger appropriation than the bill proposed (see note 148, May 21, 1878), had written in his article that "during the last three years there has been manifested in Congress a growing spirit of unfriendliness, if not

in a bright, able speech in defense of the army. Home in the evening, made some further study on the tariff. Retired early, at half-past ten.

SUNDAY, 19.   Attended church with Crete, Miss Mays, and George Needham[143] of Cleveland. Home the remainder of the day. Spent an hour in reading my Journal of European Travel to Miss Ransom and family. Read in the evening and retired early.

MONDAY, 20.   Worked at my desk until half-past ten when I went to the Capitol. Introduced a bill for taking the Tenth Census. Its main provisions were drafted by General Francis A. Walker, but I made some additions to his draft. After the morning hour the House went into Committee of the Whole on the State of the Union on the Army Bill. Two speeches were made; one by Kimmel[144] of Maryland and another by Humphrey[145] of our side. At the close of the morning hour [the Chair] announced the Committee to investigate the Presidential Election.[146] I presented to the House a cable dispatch from Minister Noyes asking to be subpoenaed as a witness. From two o'clock the remainder of the day was spent on the District of Columbia Bill. I spent

---

of positive hostility, toward the Army." Hewitt stated that Garfield was actually accusing Democratic congressmen of hostility to the army, denied the validity of the charge and criticized him for making it. He prefaced his criticism with a handsome compliment, saying among other things that Garfield "has no greater admirer in this country than I am. I have read his speeches on financial questions and his budget speeches, so to call them, with great admiration and instruction, and I do not think in our congressional history there have been more able, more profound, and more useful contributions to economy than the gentleman from Ohio has made."

143George E. Needham (1829–1907) was for many years a partner in the Garry Iron Roofing Company in Cleveland.

144William Kimmel (1812–1886) was a Democratic member of the House from Maryland, 1877–81.

145Herman L. Humphrey (1830–1902) was a Republican member of the House from Wisconsin, 1877–83.

146The committee consisted of seven Democrats—Clarkson N. Potter, chairman, William R. Morrison, Eppa Hunton, William S. Stenger, John A. McMahon, Thomas R. Cobb, Joseph C. S. Blackburn—and four Republicans—Jacob D. Cox, Benjamin F. Butler, Thomas B. Reed, and Frank Hiscock.

some time in the Library on the Tariff Question. Found some very striking passages in Madison's works, which overwhelmingly answer Tucker's consti[tu]tional objection to protective tariff.

TUESDAY, 21. Was at the desk until ten o'clock, when I went to the Committee on Ways and Means. A few bills were considered and agreed to. The day in the House was spent on the Army Appropriation Bill. At twelve o'clock I went to Miss Ransom's studio where Crete was sitting for a picture and stayed three-quarters of an hour.[147] Session of the House in the evening. At nine o'clock I got the floor and spoke three-quarters of an hour on the Army Bill, discussing particularly the dangers of reducing the army and necessity of sufficient force to keep the public peace.[148] My friends thought my speech was unusually effective. Home at half-past ten a little hoarse. I should have remarked that in the afternoon Senator Hoar told me he thought we ought to issue an address signed by every Republican member of Congress warning the people against the revolution which the Democrats were threatening. He thought we ought to recommend the organization of military companies and prepare for trouble. I hardly think the danger so imminent, though I recognize the revolutionary spirit of the Democratic Managers.

WEDNESDAY, 22. Worked at my desk until half-past ten when I

---

[147]The portrait of Mrs. Garfield by Caroline Ransom is now at Lawnfield in Mentor, Ohio.

[148]In his speech against the proposed reduction of the army from 25,000 to 20,000 enlisted men, Garfield pointed out that on the question of a standing army military men had for many years supported one of two theories—either the maintenance of a sufficient force "to meet the immediate wants of actual military service," or John C. Calhoun's plan of an expandable army "so organized and disciplined that when a sudden emergency should come upon us it could be expanded by mere enlistment to double or quadruple its size, with nothing in the way of organization to new-model or create." He declared that the nation needed an army to keep alive the practical knowledge of military art and science, to guard against possible trouble with Indians or a foreign power, to protect Alaska, and to defend laborers in their right to work when strikers unlawfully interfered with that right. Calling for a force capable of maintaining liberty ruled by law, he closed with a plea that the army be kept at its present size.

went to the Public Printing Office; thence to the Capitol. In the House, the day was devoted to the Army Bill. After an able speech of an hour by Schleicher of Texas,[149] the bill was taken up by paragraphs under the five minute rule but no vote was taken. I did not attend the evening session but sat up until midnight revising the notes of my speech on the Army Bill. Retired at half-past twelve.

THURSDAY, 23. Worked at my desk until 10 o'clock, when I went to the Capitol and attended the meeting of the Committee on Ways and Means. A few private bills were acted upon, nothing of importance done. In the House after the reading of the Journal, I called up the report of the Committee on Rules, which after three-quarters of an hour's discussion was recommitted to the Committee. Debate on the Army Bill was resumed and the amendment to raise the number of enlisted men from 20 to 25 thousand was adopted by about eight majority. This I hope will save the army from reduction. A very bright speech was made by Maginnis[150] of Montana in defence of the army. My speech was so badly botched that I have requested the reprinting of it tomorrow. Did not attend the evening session. At seven o'clock we had a dinner party. Senator Allison and wife, Senators Anthony and Ingalls, General Schenck and daughter Lillie, Mr. Wood and Mrs. Hickok,[151] Governor Pound and wife and Mrs. Landers

---

[149]Gustave Schleicher (1823–1879), who was born in Germany and was a civil engineer there, migrated to Texas in 1847. During the Civil War he served in the Confederate army. He was a Democratic member of the House from Texas, 1875 to his death. He was one of the largest men who ever sat in that body. On February 17, 1879, Garfield eulogized him in the House. The Ohio Republican's respect for him owed something to the fact that the Texan, like Garfield himself, was a "sound" money man.

[150]Martin Maginnis (1841–1919), a native of New York, was a Democratic delegate to the House from the Territory of Montana, 1873–85.

[151]Mrs. Hickok of New York spent several winters in Washington at the home of Fernando Wood on Fifteenth Street, where she acted as his hostess; she also frequently accompanied him to social events. A society reporter wrote thus of her: "She is a stylish, blonde matron, devoted to her husband and children, the latter of whom are here permanently with her during the winter months." Three times married, Wood was the father of sixteen children, eleven of whom survived him.

[Lander]¹⁵². A very pleasant party. They left us about 11 o'clock. Retired at 12.

FRIDAY, 24. Worked at my desk until 1/4 before 11, when I went to the Capitol. After the morning [hour] devoted to private bills, the House went into Committee of the Whole on the Military Appropriation Bill. We made points of order against several of the sections which changed the law and provided for the muster out of officers, and Springer, Chairman of the Committee of the Whole, ruled in our favor. This so disconcerted the Democracy that at four o'clock they carried a motion that the Committee rise and the House adjourned. They are manifestly lacking in parliamentary skill to manage their own case. Home in the evening. After dinner we had the children's literary exercises which closes the season. These exercises have been profitable to the children and very pleasant to us. On the whole I am better pleased with their progress this winter than I expected. Crete has succeeded admirably as a teacher of Latin and the boys have nearly finished the fifth book of Caesar. Several friends called in the evening. Sherman and Scofield. Sherman is delighted with our fight for the army.

SATURDAY, 25. Worked at my desk until half-past ten when I went to the Capitol. The day was consumed in a debate on the Army Appropriation Bill. The Democrats had rallied in force and carried several of their amendments cutting down the force of officers. I spoke a short time, but my hoarseness made it difficult.¹⁵³ Home in the afternoon early and went with Crete to call at General Myer's. At six o'clock we went to Colonel Rockwell's to dinner and spent the evening. Home at 10.

---

¹⁵²Jean Margaret Davenport Lander (1829–1903), who was born in England, won fame as an actress and public reader under the name of Jean Davenport. She was so successful in the United States that she decided to settle here. In 1860 she married Frederick W. Lander (1821–1862), who participated in a number of transcontinental surveys before the Civil War, and who, at death, was a brigadier general in the Union army. She retired from the stage at the beginning of 1877, and lived thereafter in Washington, D.C., and Lynn, Massachusetts. She and Mrs. Garfield became friends.

¹⁵³Garfield spoke in opposition to proposed salary reductions for army officers.

SUNDAY, 26. Did not attend church. Went to Miss Ransom's studio at 10 o'clock where we remained until half-past one.

Read Shakespeare's *Passionate Pilgrim* [154] for the first time. At four o'clock General Sherman came and drove me to Mr. Hume's at the boundary near the Tennallytown Road. He read me a speech which he had prepared for Decoration Day in New York, and asked for criticism. I suggested a few changes which he made. Home at eight o'clock and found some friends at tea. Read Shakespeare's Sonnets until 11 o'clock and retired.

MONDAY, 27. Desk until one-quarter before 11, when I went to the Interior Department with Mr. Shallenberger and his constituent Senator Morgan, [155] thence to the Capitol. The day was consumed on the Army Appropriation Bill. The amendment transferring the Indian Bureau to the War Department was adopted by a small majority. When the bill was reported from the Committee of the Whole the Democrats had mustered in force and defeated the 25th amendment. I changed my vote for the purpose of moving a reconsideration and then the Speaker refused to recognize me to make the motion. I denounced it as a breach of courtesy and the Speaker showed temper and our side was much incensed at his conduct. [156] Home in the evening until nine

[154] An anthology of poetry by various authors published in 1599 as the work of W. Shakespeare. Shakespeare is known to have written only five of the twenty-one poems in the book.

[155] Elliott S. N. Morgan was a member from Lawrence County of the Pennsylvania house of representatives, 1874–78, and secretary of Wyoming Territory, 1880–87.

[156] The 25th amendment provided that "no money appropriated by this act shall be paid for recruiting the Army beyond the number of twenty-five thousand enlisted men." After the roll call Garfield tried twice to change his vote from nay to aye, and twice Speaker Randall refused to recognize him, saying on the second attempt that "if the gentleman from Ohio gave an insincere vote it is not the fault of the Chair." Garfield replied that he had cast a sincere vote "for a purpose which under the rulings of the House I have never before known the Speaker to decline to recognize." He demanded the yeas and nays on the motion to reconsider the vote and to lay the motion on the table. On that he voted nay. He then asked for unanimous approval to have an aye vote on the amendment recorded for him to

o'clock, when we went to Mr. Riddle's with the children and spent an hour.

TUESDAY, 28. Desk until ten o'clock when I went to the Committee on Ways and Means. Some private bills were considered and some reports adopted. In the House the day was consumed on the Army Bill which finally resulted in the Democrats rallying and beating all the amendments we had made. The power of caucus is an overwhelming one with them. I have never seen so little personal independence of party as is exhibited by them this Congress.

WEDNESDAY, 29. After correspondence went to the Treasury Department for Mr. Sumner. Also, for consultation with Secretary Sherman. Thence to the Capitol where most of the day was consumed in a struggle over the adjournment question, where the power of caucus was again exhibit[ed] in the compulsion of leading Democrats of Pennsylvania to vote squarely against their wishes. The House, however, agreed to an adjournment on the 17th June. If the Senate will concur, I think we can get away at that time. In the evening several friends called, among them Foster and wife and two daughters and Mr. Townsend. Harry has a serious attack of rheumatism which has postponed his visit to Boston for the present.

THURSDAY, 30. I am feeling miserable, unwell and unfit for work. Remained at home nearly all day. In the evening went to Secretary Sherman's to meet the Republicans of the Investigating Committee who are about to go to Louisiana or Florida. Arranged some resolutions to be offered in the Potter Committee. Returned home at half-past ten.

FRIDAY, 31. Worked at my desk until 10, when I went to the Navy Department with Captain Weaver. Thence to the Capitol. The day was spent on Private bills. Swaim came and we went to Miss Ransom's studio at two o'clock. Then played billiards for an hour or two. Home in the evening feeling quite unwell.

---

show that no one other than the Speaker would think his vote insincere. The House so voted.

June

SATURDAY, 1. Worked at my desk until half-past ten, when I went to the Capitol. After the morning hour, the House took up Burchard's bill to revise the machinery of Internal Revenue collection. I was feeling too ill to remain in the House and went out with Swaim and exercised. During the day the Potter Committee commenced its investigation and heard the testimony of Anderson, who was supervisor of Registration in the East Feliciana Parish. He offered a pretended copy of a letter from John Sherman which Sherman pronounces a forgery.[157] The only thing of note in his testimony was an alleged contract between himself and Webber [Weber] of West Feliciana reciting that although the election was fair and without intimidation, they agreed to certify that it was unfair and thus aid in the election of Hayes. This contract in March 1877 was placed in the hands of Stanley Matthews and it appears that afterwards he wrote a letter recommending Anderson for office. This makes a singular showing for

[157]James E. Anderson and D. A. Weber, supervisors of registration in 1876 in the Louisiana parishes of East and West Feliciana respectively, signed affidavits after the election stating that intimidation of voters had occurred in their parishes. Anderson told the Potter Committee on June 1, 1878, that the two men had then prepared another affidavit declaring that the election had been the most peaceable and orderly ever witnessed by either but that to save the state for Hayes they had consented to protest the counting of the votes as cast in their parishes. Then Anderson, having heard that his original affidavit had been altered, let it be known that the document as it stood was a forgery to which he did not propose to submit. A few days later he and Weber had a brief interview with Sherman, who intimated his desire that they let their protests stand as they then were. Next they received a letter from Sherman promising that both men would be "provided for." When hastily summoned before the Potter Committee on June 1 and shown a copy of the alleged letter (an original was never produced by anyone), Sherman said that he believed that he had never written such a letter. On July 25, after Anderson's credibility had been damaged and after a woman had testified that she had written the letter, Sherman, with memory refreshed, declared: ". . . I now say, most emphatically, that I never did write that letter." See Harry Barnard, *Rutherford B. Hayes and His America* (1954), pp. 465–473, and *House Miscellaneous Documents,* No. 31, 45 Cong., 3 Sess., Serials 1864 and 1865.

Matthews, but his testimony may clear it up. At nine o'clock
Swaim and I called upon the President, who went over the
ground of the situation and thinks every thing is coming out
right.

SUNDAY, 2. Crete and I attended church. Miss Ransom and
Major Swaim came to dinner at two. Read from my notes of
travel in Europe for an hour or two and at seven dined with the
President. All his Cabinet except Evarts were at dinner. Gen'l
Keifer and Major McKinley of the House, also, Miss Bates[158]
and another lady. Mrs. Hayes was still away. We had a trout for
dinner weighing fifteen pounds, caught on Lake Saranac by Mrs.
Hayes and sent by express. Lengthy conversation on the pending
investigation. Matthews' letters to Anderson are the only things
thus far that cause annoyance.[159]

MONDAY, 3. Worked at my desk until 10 o'clock when I went
to the Capitol. After the morning hour the day was consumed on
the Internal Revenue Bill. I staid until about three o'clock, then
went to the Bureau of Statistics to get some materials and then
with Swaim. Home in the evening and worked on Tariff speech
until a late hour.[160]

[158]In his diary for June 3, 1878, President Hayes writes of the dinner party of
June 2. He refers to the presence of Miss Emily Platt and Miss Ellen Kent but
makes no reference to a Miss Bates.

[159]In the course of James E. Anderson's appearance before the Potter Committee on June 1 a number of letters (some originals and some copies) from Stanley
Matthews to or about Anderson were introduced into the record. They made clear
that in 1877 Matthews was trying to help Anderson secure a government position.
In a letter dated May 14, 1877, which Anderson identified as a copy of one
addressed to Secretary of State Evarts, Matthews wrote thus: "The circumstances
in which Mr. Anderson has been placed, and in which he has been compelled to
act a very difficult part, are such as to give him very strong claims upon the
administration in the public interests, and I do most earnestly urge that some
satisfactory public employment may be found for him at once." *House Miscellaneous
Documents,* No. 31, 45 Cong., 3 Sess., Serial 1864, pp. 20–23.

[160]Garfield opened his speech, delivered on June 4, with a refutation of John
R. Tucker's contention in a speech of May 8 that a tariff was unconstitutional. He
then declared that the existing tariff provided adequate revenues, strengthened the
nation's economy, protected her security, and promoted the general welfare.
Insisting that a proper tariff policy lay between prohibitory duties and no protec-

TUESDAY, 4. Crete suffered a good deal during the night with an attack of erysipelas which has involved one of her ears and a portion of the neck. The Doctor says she cannot leave for Ohio tomorrow as she expected to do. I am very anxious in consequence. Went to the Capitol at half-past ten o'clock to attend a meeting of the Committee on Rules. They had, however, adjourned. Sat in Committee on Ways and Means until 11. At 2 o'clock Mr. Wood moved to go into Committee of the Whole on the Tariff Bill. I moved to limit the debate to four hours. Mr. Conger moved to make it two hours and that was adopted by a heavy vote. When the amended motion was about to be put Mr. Hooker of Mississippi moved to lay it on the table, a motion I have never before heard made. I argued that it was not in order, being a motion about the order of business and not a motion on proposition of legislation. After some debate the Speaker submitted it to the House and it was almost unanimously voted out of order. When it was decided, we went into Committee of the Whole.

WEDNESDAY, 5. I am glad to see that Crete is better this morning and if she continues to improve it will be possible to leave for Ohio. Worked at my desk until 11 o'clock when I went to the

---

tion at all, he called for "a rate so high that foreign producers cannot flood our markets and break down our home manufacturers, but not so high as to keep them altogether out, enabling our manufacturers to combine and raise prices, nor so high as to stimulate an unnatural and unhealthy growth of manufactures." The present law, he believed, came close to doing this and could be perfected with minor revisions. He then assailed the bill before the House, saying that it attacked the entire tariff structure, abolishing the free list which in fact should be expanded, increasing without justification the duties on raw sugar, raising duties on refined sugar to levels that would make absolute the monopoly of the refining interests, and proposing many reductions, notably in textiles and metals, that would be fatal to those industries, to labor, and indeed to the national economy. The bill, he said, should be defeated at once, for it was "a very Polyphemus which stalks through the land," and even the threat that it would be passed menaced the health of the economy. He asserted in closing that he intended to present a motion to strike the enacting clause, and on the following day the House used that tactic to kill the measure. To bring this about a number of protectionist Democrats joined the Republicans.

Capitol. Came home early and made preparations for leaving in the morning.

Harry and Major Swaim left at 1.30 today for Boston. Harry goes to spend a few weeks with his young friend Bentley Warren.[161]

THURSDAY, 6.   At half-past eight the whole family, including Miss Mays, Mary McGrath, Johanna the new girl, took the Baltimore and Ohio train for the West. I spent a portion of the day revising my Tariff speech, as much as I could do in the cars. Read a few chapters of Scott's ——— . The journey does not seem to injure Crete and I think her ear is getting better. We retired among the Allegheny Mountains.

FRIDAY, 7.   Reached Monroeville at half-past eight o'clock. Change of time has broken connection with the Lake Shore Road and we were compelled to wait at Monroeville until 12 o'clock. Took the train for Cleveland, arrived at half-past two. Crete and I went up town and did some shopping, then return[ed] to the depot and took the 4 1/2 train to Mentor. Dr. Robison met us with his omnibus and Moses with our two teams. Found supper awaiting us which had been prepared for [by] Mrs. Glasier. The beds being damp I did not dare to risk Crete's health so she and I went to Dr. Robison's and spent the night.

SATURDAY, 8.   Spent the day in going over the farm and examining into the condition of the fields, crops and stock. It rained nearly all day, but I accomplished considerable work. Spent the night at home.

---

[161]Bentley Warren (1864–1947), son of William Wirt Warren (1834–1880), a Boston lawyer who was a Democratic member of the House from Massachusetts, 1875–77. During the father's term in Congress the Warrens lived only a block from the Garfields, and Harry and Bentley became friends. Bentley attended St. Paul's School with Harry and James, graduated with them at Williams College in 1885, studied law and was admitted to the bar in 1889. Thereafter he practiced law in Boston. For many years he and Irvin McDowell Garfield were partners in a law firm. He was a member of the state legislature, 1891–92, the legal adviser of the U.S. Fuel Administration (of which Harry Garfield was head) during World War I, a member of the state Civil Service Commission, 1903–05, and long a trustee of Williams College.

SUNDAY, 9.   Drove to the lower fields of Dr. Robison and thence went to church. Listened to a sermon by A. B. Green. At one o'clock took Crete, the children and Miss Mays to Dr. Robison's where we dined. The Doctor and I drove to Willoughby and took the train to Cleveland. Called on Mr. Cowles, Editor of the *Leader.* Spent the night at Dr. Robison's.

MONDAY, 10.   Took the 7 o'clock train for Shelby, thence by the Baltimore and Ohio Road eastward. Worked on the revision of my tariff speech as much as I could until nine o'clock. Retired in the neighborhood of Grafton.

TUESDAY, 11.   Arrived in Washington at half-past seven. Found a great mass of mail awaiting me. Rose came soon after breakfast and we continued work on the revision of the Tariff speech. At half-past 11 went to the Capitol and attended the session of the House. The day was devoted to a discussion of the Sundry Civil Bill. In the evening Rose and I completed the revision of the Tariff speech. Swaim is here, having returned from Boston before I reached Washington.

WEDNESDAY, 12.   Tariff speech appeared in the *Record* this morning in fair shape. Worked at my desk until ten, when I went to the Committee on Ways and Means, a special meeting having been called in regard to the sugar tests. A quorum was not present until near 11. The subject was set for a special meeting tomorrow morning. In the House debate was continued on the Sundry Civil Bill. The greenback men attempted to fasten an amendment upon one of the bills, to repeal the Resumption Act. I made a rather effective five minutes' speech, denouncing the amendment as an attempt to bolster up the despairing fortunes of the greenback men. The amendment in four different forms was beaten by a majority ranging from 15 to 20. It is a great triumph considering the strength of the soft money men in the House. Home in the evening. Swaim and Rockwell dined with me. Rose came after dinner and I dictated a large number of letters.

THURSDAY, 13.   Worked at the desk in the morning. Half-past ten at the Departments. Capitol at 12. A long struggle over the Sundry Civil Bill. More amendments offered than I have ever seen on a bill. I made the point on 40 sections of the bill which were stri[c]ken out.[162] After a long struggle the bill was taken out of Committee and reported to the House.

FRIDAY, 14. Worked at my desk until ten o'clock when Bright[163] came and we spent 3/4 of an hour in considering the plans for repairs of the house. Capitol at half-past 11. A long weary session.[164] Home in the evening. Dictated large number of letters.

SATURDAY, 15. Worked at my desk until 10 o'clock, when I spent an hour with Bright and Swaim in regard to repairs of the house. Called at the different departments. Went thence to the Capitol. A dreary day of work on the Internal Revenue Bill. Took a recess until evening. Went to the evening session little after nine o'clock and remained until near midnight. Swaim and Rockwell had dined with me and they went to the Capitol and returned when I did.

SUNDAY, 16. Remained at home all day clearing up my desk and bookcases preparatory to leaving for the summer. Swaim and I dined alone at two o'clock. At half-past four General S. C. Boynton came and drove us to ———— . On our return we called at Rapley's,[165] where we saw the actress Lotta.[166] We call[ed], also, at General Sprigg Carroll's. On our return General Boynton surprised me by telling the story of his early life. He ran away

[162]The *Congressional Record* has nothing that supports this statement.

[163]John G. Bright, a member of Bright, Humphrey, & Co., carpenters, builders, and contractors. During 1878 the company enlarged the home of the Garfields on the corner of 13th and I streets, N.W., which it had built in 1869. Among the additions was a room about twenty-five by fourteen feet on the second floor to which Garfield moved his growing library from the sitting room on the first floor.

[164]In this session the House approved by a vote of 215 to 21 a resolution stating that no subsequent Congress and neither the House nor the Senate had jurisdiction to revise the decision that put Hayes in the White House.

[165]William W. Rapley was long associated with the National Theater as proprietor and manager.

[166]Lotta Crabtree (1847–1924), a native of New York City, first appeared on the stage in California during the 1850's, and subsequently became nationally known as "Lotta." She retired from the stage in 1891. Her leading characteristic as an actress is said to have been "a bouyant, joyous, not to say childlike manner." A wealthy woman who never married, she left her fortune to charity.

from home at 14 and joined the circus. He was with them two years and a half, rising to the next highest grade in the profession.

He was subsequently appointed a cadet at West Point, and declined in favor of McPherson,[167] and about twenty-five years ago came to Washington as a clerk.

MONDAY, 17. Letters and Departments in the morning. House at eleven. A long weary session. In the evening Swaim left me, and I went to the Capitol and attended the long evening session. The Appropriation Bill (Sundry Civil) has detained us many days, and has compelled the postponement of adjournment until Wednesday next. Evening session which continued until three hours past midnight. Home at 3.30 and retired at four.

TUESDAY, 18. Slept until eight. Miss Ransom came and breakfasted with me.

House at eleven, and another long weary session, day and night. We adjourned an hour past midnight. Just about midnight[168] the Sundry Civil Bill was brought in by Conference Report. The Speaker requested me to defend the appropriation of five and a half millions for the Halifax Award, which, he said, was to be savagely attacked by Gen. Butler and others. It occurred to me that I could treat it as the closing act of our war diplomacy. I made some hasty notes, and spoke ten minutes, very effectively. Our friends thought my speech saved the measure.

Home very tired.

The above entry about the Halifax Award should have been on the next page [under Wednesday, June 19], which see.

WEDNESDAY, 19. A noisy disgraceful session, which lasted until three o'clock in the morning when we adjourned.[169] Came home

---

[167]James B. McPherson entered West Point in 1849, and graduated at the head of his class in 1853. See Vol. III, p. 365, n. 359.

[168]On June 18 the House adjourned at 9:48 P.M., shortly after voting to nonconcur with Senate amendments to the Sundry Civil Appropriations Bill.

[169]The session of June 19 lasted throughout the night, with final adjournment, after two brief recesses, at 7:00 A.M. on June 20. At about 11:00 P.M. the House received the conference report on the Sundry Civil Bill, and Garfield spoke in favor of appropriating $5,500,000 to be paid to Great Britain, an award (Garfield called it the Halifax award) made by the Geneva Tribunal which ruled on the

in the midst of a pouring rain and retired at half-past three. Slept until nearly eight. After breakfast did some work in arranging for leaving. Went to the House at eleven and sat in continuous session through the day and night. Several extensions of the time for adjournment were agreed upon. About midnight the Sundry Civil Bill came in. The Speaker informed me that Butler was going to make a speech assailing the Halifax Award and wished me to reply. I made some hasty preparation. Hale followed Butler. I then spoke ten minutes. I think it was more effective than any ten minute speech I ever made. The Award was carried and the Conference Report.

THURSDAY, 20. House remained in continuous session interrupted only by an occasional bright speech. Several members were disgracefully drunk and scenes of confusion continued the whole night and up to seven, the hour of adjournment; disgraceful in the extreme.[170] The delay in adjournment was caused by the labor of enrolling and comparing the amendments to the Sundry Civil Bill. When the hammer fell at seven, I came home and slept two hours and a half. Spent the day in clearing the rooms of the east wing of the house, preparatory to repairs. Called at the Treasury on Departmental business. Home in the evening. Rose came and I dictated letters.

Alabama claims. Although Garfield believed personally that the sum was unreasonable and exorbitant, he argued that the United States had accepted the award of the tribunal when the decision favored her, and that Britain had paid; now in all fairness the United States must pay the sum awarded to Britain by the same tribunal.

[170]Donn Piatt's Washington *Capital* (June 23) had this to say about the closing scenes: "Confusion was worse than confounded; brains were muddled and tongues were thick, and the atmosphere wild with maudlin music. The scene might be termed a mental pandemonium, except that such a term would presuppose a brain, and we know our Congress too well to attribute it with such an accomplishment." On June 21 Harry Garfield wrote thus to his mother: "I ought to write to Papa, but I saw by the papers that Congress adjourned yesterday morning at 7 o'clock, and that over half the members were drunk, and when the sargent of arms [*sic*] walked around they fired 'spit balls' at him just like little boys, so I suppose that by the time this reaches you Papa will be with you." See also entry for June 28, 1878.

FRIDAY, 21.   Soon after breakfast went to Mr. Riddle's on business, and then worked at my desk for an hour; then went to the Navy Department and back and found Bright awaiting me. Arranged details for house repairs. Then went to pay bills. Called at the Agricultural Department, Capitol, Republican Office, Republican Committee Rooms. Home again, dictated letters. Closed arrangements with Bright. Spent an hour in preparing for departure. At 7.47 took the train by the Pennsylvania line for the West.

Continued dictating letters and arranging affairs till fifteen minutes before train time, when I left and reach[ed] the Depot just as the bell struck for departure.

Spent two hours visiting with friends on board, and retired at 10 P.M.

SATURDAY, 22.   Awoke a short time before we arrived at Pittsburgh.

After breakfast, which occupied most of the 30 minutes' delay, took the train for Cleveland, where I arrived at 3.15 P.M. At Newburgh, Captain Henry and Jimmy came on board.

Found Crete and Abe at Dr. Robison's. Did some shopping, and took the 4.50 train to Mentor, arriving at 5.57. Myron Canfield, the new man, met us with Josie and Kit in the spring wagon. Found supper awaiting us. Heavy rain falling. Happy to be at home but jaded to the bone.

I have fallen off in weight the last few months, being the first time for many years a little below 200 pounds.

SUNDAY, 23.   After breakfast, went to Dr. Robison's and set in order the Farmer's Indicator which I obtained at the Signal Office in Washington.[171]

---

[171]The Weather Case or Farmer's Weather Indicator, consisting of a barometer and two thermometers, had recently been prepared for issue by the Signal Corps. It was designed largely to supplement with local signs and indications the general indications in weather bulletins. In a set of instructions accompanying the indicator was this admonition: "It must never be forgotten that the weather case is only to aid, sometimes, in making up one's mind as to what the weather of the next day will be. While it will often be very useful, there will be many instances in which everything will be left in doubt." References to it disappear from the Annual Report of the Chief Signal Officer within two or three years.

The Doctor and his wife came home with me, took dinner and spent the day. It has rained heavily nearly all day.

In the evening wrote and read. As I look over the work of the late session so far as my own part in it is concerned, I incline to think I have done more effective service than in any other session. I attribute some of its effectiveness to the five months I spent on the farm last season. It gave me robust health, and let my mind lie fallow for a while. From the first day of the October session I felt my intellectual atmosphere to be clearer, and vigorous thinking was easier for me than usual. I come home, now, a good deal jaded, but I hope the touch of the earth will give me renewed strength, as is related in the Greek fable.

MONDAY, 24. Breakfast at 7. Took hold of farm affairs. The ground being too wet to cultivate corn, set the men to grading the lane and filling up the low places in the lane yard. In the afternoon the sun was out enough so that they got in two loads of hay. The carpenters were at work on the new barn. Dr. Robison and I went to the lower fields. I found that the big red Ky. cow had gone to the woods and dropped a calf. Got it up to the barn. After dinner drove my two mares to Willoughby, and thence down the west bank of the Chagrin to the lake to Mr. Harkness' to arrange for getting gravel for our walks. Home at 4. Lillie Steele[172] and Irene Baumgras came and took tea with us. Played a game of croquet after tea. Several neighbors called in the evening. Read and wrote, and retired early.

TUESDAY, 25. Busy day on the farm, and in the library. Drove to the Blacksmith's and Harness-maker's to get repairing done; to Henry Clapp's for cabbage plants.

Put my library in order. Had the harness room in the horse barn enlarged to a sleeping room for hands. Drove horse rake two hours.

A Committee from Painesville came to invite me to deliver an address on the 4th prox. I had declined by telegraph from Washington, but concluded, reluctantly, to go.

---

[172]Lydia ("Lillie") C. Steele was the youngest daughter of Garfield's friend George W. Steele (1824–1881) of Painesville. In November, 1881, she married Frank C. Moodey of Brooklyn, New York.

In the evening, drove to Willoughby with Dr. Robison and called on Mr. and Mrs. Andrews.[173] Their new house is very fine. Home at ten and retired.

WEDNESDAY, 26. Men getting in hay from orchard lot. In the afternoon, the barn frame was raised. Crete gave the men a lunch, bread and butter, cake and cheese and coffee.

The day has been very hot, and I have felt the heat more by the contrast with the late cool weather.

Made some headway in setting my library in order. Also read a little on a theme for the address which I am to deliver July 10th before the Ohio Editorial Association. I am not in a good condition for intellectual work. Retired at 9 1/2 P.M.

THURSDAY, 27. Overhauled the pipes leading to the kitchen, and found that a joint had been bursted by the frost. Sent to Painesville for a new one, and before sunset had water from the tank again in the house.

Finished getting in hay from the orchard meadow and put up a temporary fence between the young apple trees and the remainder of the meadow.

Hot, growing weather. Upper timbers got in place on new barn. Several friends called in the afternoon and evening. Men have been hoeing corn in the Ram Lot, where an interesting struggle is going forward between nature and civilization. The first is represented by ferns and wild grass, the second by the hoe.

---

[173]Wallace C. Andrews (1833–1899) was a businessman for a number of years in Cleveland, where he was one of the original directors of the Standard Oil Company, several of his companies having entered the combination. In 1877 he and his wife, Margaret St. John Andrews (1846–1899), moved to Willoughby, where they lived in the renovated house that had belonged to Orson St. John, the father of Mrs. Andrews. In 1879 Andrews entered business in New York City, where he became president of the New York Steam Heating and Power Company. In 1899, Wallace and Margaret, four of their relatives and six servants died in a fire in the New York home. The wills of both husband and wife provided that most of their estate should be used to found The Andrews Institute for Girls in Willoughby; after years of litigation the wills were upheld, and about $4,600,000 ultimately made available for the school. It opened in 1910 in the house mentioned in this entry. The greatly expanded institution is now known as The Andrews School.

FRIDAY, 28. Andrew Barless is making farm gates. Has completed the enlargement of a room in the Horse barn for Moses and Myron, and is doing a variety of carpenter work about the premises. F. Thorp and Capt. Burridge[174] called this morning. Spent three hours with my correspondence, which is very burdensome without Rose. Two Congressmen who took too much stock in John Barleycorn during the last night of the session, have appealed to me to help them out of the public consequences of their cups. I can do them but little good, for the facts will not warrant a very complete defense.[175]

SATURDAY, 29. Crete and I went to Cleveland to do shopping, and also to enable me to attend the meeting of the directors of the Citizen's Saving and Loan Association. I was chosen a member some time last winter, but have not accepted or qualified until today. A full meeting of the Board.

Went with Crete to many shops in her circuit of purchasing. Home on the 4.50 P.M. train.

In the evening Mr. and Mrs. Reevson of Painesville called.

In my absence the boards have been put on the barn, with the

---

[174]Eleazer Burridge served in the Union army, 1861–63; he entered as a private and rose to the rank of captain.

[175]There are two letters in the Garfield Papers bearing on this matter. One (dated June 23) is from William H. Calkins (1842–1894), a Republican member of the House from Indiana, 1877–84. According to him the *Chicago Times* had reported that he was intoxicated in the House during the last night of the session. He said that he was conscious of his innocence and asked for a supporting letter from Garfield. The other letter (dated July 3) was from Thomas M. Browne (1829–1891), a Republican member of the House from Indiana, 1877–91. He quoted a despatch in the *Boston Herald* that he said was being circulated in his district to his injury. According to the *Herald* Browne "had absolutely to be pulled down into his seat when the House was voting on the question of extending the time of adjournment." Browne went on to say that if this was true, he had disgraced himself and should retire to private life. He asked Garfield to state what he knew in respect to his condition and behavior on the night in question. He added that he thought the *Herald* correspondent had the names of the Indiana members confused. If Browne's appeal is one of those referred to in this entry, the entry itself was written several days late. Both congressmen were reelected in the fall of 1878.

rough side out, or faced side in. Dr. Robison wanted them so, to be followed with whitewash. I prefer paint, and shall have them torn off and turned.

SUNDAY, 30. A very hot day. Family went to church and listened to a sermon from Amzi Atwater, whom I have not heard before, since he declaimed to me as my student at Hiram.

The day was so oppressively hot that he could hardly do himself justice; but he spoke fairly well.

After dinner Dr. Robison and I drove via the Kirtland road to Martin Carroll's and took tea. Home at seven, and found Geo. A. Baker and wife awaiting us. The day has been very hot, and we had a smart shower about one P.M. Crops are looking remarkably well. Some fly on the wheat, and opinions differ in reference to the probable yield.

July

MONDAY, 1. A busy day. Ordered the boards torn off the new barn and turned face side out. Contracted with Barnes for a cupola 5 × 8 and six feet high on new barn.

Determined to move my long shed so as to place it north and south in line with the old barn.

Drove to Willoughby and thence to Kirtland with Dr. Robison and engaged a Mr. Randall to move shed on Wednesday next.

Had half of meadow north of Ram Lot mowed and had small orchard plowed.

W. E. Chandler has given before the Potter Committee his version of the Wormley Conference.[176] Reports my opinions and sayings. I presume I shall be summoned.

[176]William E. Chandler made his second appearance before the Potter Committee on June 29, 1878. He testified that he had been in the habit of calling on Garfield (in the period before the inauguration of Hayes) and that on one occasion, in a conversation at Garfield's home, Garfield had told him about the Wormley conference, mentioning some of those present. When Chandler asked about its object Garfield had said that it "was to see if some arrangement could not be

Telegram from Mr. Warren that Hal and Bentley leave Boston at six this evening for Mentor.

TUESDAY, 2.   Got hay in cock before heavy rain which came at half-past four. I raked three hours with Dave. Had timber and plank hauled from Dr. Robison's for moving barn. Two men worked half a day clearing away manure from rear of shed. Crete had trouble with new washerwoman, one of those small miseries which become great ones in the difficult questions they raise. I lost my temper over the fact that a girl we have brought from Washington, and who does less work than Crete, should be impertinent and unjust to the best woman whom I know, and that we are so far in her power, that we must suffer her paltry ways or go without any help for an indefinite time.

Got two ideas in line for the 4th, but am not pl[e]ased with them after they are paraded.

Hal and Bent arrived at 7.30 P.M. Irvin fled to the Barn.

WEDNESDAY, 3.   Busy with affairs of the farm. But towards evening, I made some notes for speech tomorrow in which I summarized six groups of perils through which Americans have passed in achieving what we now are. 1. Struggle against a wild unknown nature. 2. Wild Tribes of men. 3. International struggle of France, Spain and England for supremacy in America. 4. Independence of England. 5. Equality on the sea. 6. Unity and equality among ourselves (War vs. Rebellion). This historical resumé is basis for 7. Struggle for law and order against the Commune and its politica[l] atheism.

If I had the time to develope these points I could make an effective speech, *mais je n'ai pas le temps,* and must shoot on the wing.

---

made by which the Packard government could be abandoned, or surrendered, or given up." When pressed by Chandler, Garfield had admitted that "Sherman seemed to be looking for some way to arrange so that Packard should voluntarily withdraw as governor and get out." Chandler said that he had not asked Garfield about his entering into an agreement because he did not dream that it was possible Garfield would do so. He added: "I have since become satisfied that he did, and have so said." *House Miscellaneous Documents,* No. 31, 45 Cong., 3 Sess., Serial 1864, p. 536.

THURSDAY, 4. Moses, Myron and the three older boys drove with the grays. Crete and I went in the buggy after Josie, to Painesville.

Spoke 45 minutes to about 3,000 people on the public square, and satisfied myself fairly well considering my hasty preparation.[177] Two Cleveland reporters there, but no competent stenographer.

Dinner at Horace Steele's. Home at 2 1/2 P.M. No hoarseness. Heavy rain in the morning, rain again the evening.

FRIDAY, 5. Spent the day overlooking farm affairs. I find myself greatly disinclined to write, and so my letters are greatly behind. I wish I could strike a truce with the mass of my correspondents. They are too much for me, especially during the hot weather, when I want to see the developement of farm affairs.

We have commenced cutting our Clawson Wheat on the south side of the road. The east half of the field of 12 acres is good and heavy for it was summer fallowed; but the west half which has been in wheat three successive seasons is not nearly so. The land cannot be cheated. She will honor drafts only when and in proportion as depos[i]ts have been made.

SATURDAY, 6. Busy day at the farm. South wheat cut and in shock by eight P.M.

At eight I went to Dr. Robison's where I met Mr. J. H. Wade and Mr. Everett[178] of Cleveland, who had come out to spend the

[177]In dealing with point seven as indicated in the entry for July 3, Garfield spoke of "the so-called war between labor and capital," the dangerous element of which derived from the French commune of 1871. "If Christianity and right are to prevail against this danger," he went on to say, "it must be confronted by three things: First, intelligence, disseminated by the light of our schools; second, by giving all the play and force to Christian morality that it is capable of receiving; and third, by using all our powers to enforce the laws." *New York Times,* July 7.

[178]Sylvester T. Everett (1838–1922), Cleveland banker, railroad executive and city treasurer, was active in politics. In 1880 he was a delegate to the Republican National Convention. On his way back from this convention Garfield stayed in the Everett home. In 1881 Garfield appointed him United States director of the Union Pacific Railroad. In 1879 he married as his second wife Alice Louisa Wade, daughter of Randall P. Wade and granddaughter of Jeptha H. Wade.

night. We visited and played eucher until 11.50, when I came home.

SUNDAY, 7. Drove to the Doctor's at 10 A.M. and took him and Messrs. Wade and Everett out to drive. Went near to the foot of Little Mt. and back to our house. Drove them back to the farm, and then to the Doctor's. In the evening Maj. Clapp came and spent an hour or two. The day has been excessively hot and uncomfortable. Read in the evening.

MONDAY, 8. Spent nearly all the day running about on farm affairs. Drove over the two farms in the forenoon.

Devoted part of the afternoon in reading up the history of the press, and its struggle for freedom.

Callers in the evening.

TUESDAY, 9. Worked on my address, or rather on the materials for an address before the Editorial Association of Ohio, until noon, when I took train for Cleveland, and took rooms at the Forest City House. Got Pomerene, shorthand writer, to aid me and dictated about 20 letters to him, and then commenced dictating my address. Worked until eleven P.M. Staid at Forest City House over night.

WEDNESDAY, 10. Crete and the boys came at 9 A.M. Worked at the materials for my address before the Editors, until noon. Went to Pomerene's. Worked on speech until eight o'clock. I feel but little enthusiasm on the subject, and do not expect to make a very effective speech. I ought not to have agreed to make it. Many friends called towards evening. At eight o'clock, went to the Tabernacle, and after a speech by the Mayor, and a reply by Mr. Mack[179] of the *Sandusky Register,* I was introduced to about 2,000 people and delivered my address, not effectively. It will read better than it sounded.[180] Crete, Jim and I staid at the Forest

---

[179]Isaac F. Mack was president of the Editorial Association of Ohio.

[180]Hinsdale, ed., *Works of Garfield,* II, pp. 575–585. Garfield discussed the struggle for freedom of the press and what the community now demanded of the press. He called for "a veritable and intelligible record of important current events," assistance to readers in understanding the significance of the news, and the advocacy by newspapers of their own opinions while representing fairly the opinions of antagonists. Praising the *Cincinnati Inquirer* (a Democratic paper) for

City House. Hal and Bentley when [went] to Mentor at 5.

THURSDAY, 11.   Shopped with Crete, and went to lumber-yard to buy fencing, etc.

At 11.15 took train for Mentor, having declined to go on the Press excursion on the lake.

In the afternoon we completed the harrowing and drilling in of sowed corn in the young orchard.

Finding that the man at hand did not know how to drive oxen, I drove them three hours and came in much heated. Overdid the work a little for my soft muscle.

Bathed and changed. New barn rapidly approaching completion. Ready for the Hay.

FRIDAY, 12.   Put all hands into the meadow below the Ram Lot, and by holding them until half-past eight, got it all in cock.

At 6 P.M. drove to the station to meet E. V. Smalley who came to spend the night.

Sat on the porch and talked politics till half-past ten P.M. I gave him my ideas of the philosophy of the Greeley movement, and of the present reaction against it.[181]

SATURDAY, 13.   Dr. Robison and I drove to Painesville where I did some shopping. Home at one. Dined with the Doctor. At three, I went to the meadow north of the Ram Lot and helped

---

its fairness to Republicans in the campaign of 1877, he uttered one of his most famous sentiments: "The few flowers that grow over the wall of party are among the most graceful and beautiful that bloom in the gardens of the world."

[181]The *Herald* article (July 15) which resulted from Smalley's visit has this description of Garfield:

In the midst of these sylvan possessions General Garfield goes about in a broadbrimmed chip hat, with his pantaloons tucked in a pair of stout cowhide boots, giving directions to his hired men, and lending a hand at the haying and harvesting. None of his Washington friends, had they seen him yesterday driving a yoke of oxen in the broiling sun and emphasizing with a gad the stentorian shouts of "Gee," "Haw," and "Whoa, Back!" without which no oxen seem able to do a proper amount of work, would have suspected that the broad-shouldered, sun-burned farmer under the chip hat was the famous Republican chief, fresh from parliamentary victories on the floor of Congress.

with the Hay until 7 P.M. Got it all in after the stalling and dividing of one load, the last.

Lamed myself pitching and loading, which last was not well done. I have not loaded before for at least 25 years.

SUNDAY, 14. No services in our church today. Drove with Maj. Clapp to the Mountain, and dined at the Club House with a number of old friends. Home at 3 P.M. At half-past five drove the family to the Lake at Hopkins' Point, and Hal, Jim, Bentley and I went in bathing. Home by moonlight.

MONDAY, 15. Crete went to Cleveland to get a cook. Men commenced mowing the lower meadow. Barnes finished the new barn. Harry drove to the Depot expecting to meet Crete on the noon train. She did not come, but he brought a Mr. M. P. Jones who came to get materials for a sketch of my life, for Cleave's Cyclopedia of Ohio. I spent an hour with him, giving him the main facts, but declined to subscribe for the book.[182]

Then got up two loads of hay from lower meadow (north of R. R.) It has been a fine day for curing hay. At 5.44 went to the Depot and brought Crete, who came without a girl; but one is promised for tomorrow noon.

In the evening, read *The Wreck of the Grosvenor,*[183] a nautical tale written with fine power, and, it is said, with technical correctness in reference to its seamanship. Retired at eleven.

TUESDAY, 16. Men finished cutting hay at 9 1/2 A.M. Put reaper into the oat field near the barns. One man cradling around the field, and then cradling the north end, among the peach trees. Other men, with oxen and gray horses, hauling hay from lower meadow.

---

[182]Work on "Cleave's Cyclopedia" was begun by Egbert Cleave in 1873. In 1878 the material accumulated by Cleave was acquired by John C. Yorston & Co., which added to it and published this volume: J. Fletcher Brennan, ed., *A Biographical Cyclopedia and Portrait Gallery of Distinguished Men, with an Historical Sketch, of the State of Ohio* (Cincinnati, 1879). A biographical sketch of Garfield appears on pp. 130–131.

[183]William C. Russell, *The Wreck of the Grosvenor: An Account of the Mutiny of the Crew and the Loss of the Ship When Trying to Make the Bermudas* (1876). This very popular novel was reprinted as late as 1959.

At noon, Hal drove to the Depot for the new cook.

I spent the whole forenoon in fussing about the farm; neglected my growing pile of unanswered letters.

Made a contract with Jas. Doty to furnish materials and paint the new barn for $35 (two coats, white lead and oil).

WEDNESDAY, 17. Major Clapp came and joined me in hauling hay from lower meadow. At noon, sent Moses and Devereaux to Dr. Robison's to help him thrash. Rest of us were getting in hay and preparing for threshing. Fine but hot weather and a very busy day on the farm. Some of the Doctor's men "bucked," being overcome with the heat.

Cook, Mary P[owers] came by evening train.

THURSDAY, 18. Went with Wallace Hammond[184] and the oxen to Dr. Robison's south woods for 40 ft. poles for straw stack. Lifted too hard in loading them and came home very weary.

At three o'clock thunder and lightning to the south and rain threatened. At half-past three, put my teams into south wheat field. At 4 1/2 the threshing machine had come, and at 8 P.M. the whole south field, 12 acres, was threshed and in the barn. We gave the men a lunch at 5. Maj. Clapp helped very efficiently.

FRIDAY, 19. The threat of rain which happily passed yesterday was renewed this morning, but we escaped it and at noon had all the wheat (18 acres) threshed, except seven or eight loads which were put into the barn yesterday. We threshed 173 bushels Clawson wheat from south field (seven loads yet to thresh); 145 bush[els] red wheat north of R. R. (6 acres); and 25 bushels of oats. Maj. Clapp has helped valiantly.

In the afternoon got in balance of hay, two loads, and finished cutting oats. Some progress also made in binding and shocking. Towards evening, Lt. G. B. Harber of the Navy came to make us a visit. He is a noble fellow, my first cadet at the Naval Academy.

SATURDAY, 20. Washed, and dressed like a gentleman, and spent the day mainly visiting with friends. Hon. A. G. Riddle of Wash-

---

[184]Wallace Hammond, of Mentor, a farm laborer in his early thirties, died in 1882.

ington came and spent the day with us. He is to write a sketch of my life for the history of Lake County.[185] We went quite fully over the history of my father and mother, and of my own early life. Lt. Harber was with us and appeared to enjoy it very much.

The men worked on the oats, and nearly finished binding them.

I ought to have added that in the morning, I drove to Kirtland with the Doctor to see about selling our wheat. He sold his at 90 cents per bushel. I concluded to hold mine for the present.

Riddle staid until dark when he went to Painesville.

Finished *The Wreck of the Grosvenor,* a charming story.

SUNDAY, 21. Spent most of the day in answering letters. Crete, Martha and Lt. Harber aiding me. At four P.M., in company with Dr. Robison and his family, took my two teams and drove all our family to the lake at Hopkins' Point. Harber and the boys and I had a fine swim in the breakers.

Home at half-past six, after a fine drive. Spent the evening in adjusting farm affairs with Northcott, preparing to leave home to meet the Potter Committee.

MONDAY, 22. Was awakened at half-past three, and at four left for the Depot. Took the 4.15 train to Cleveland, arrived about 5, slept an hour and a half in Bro. Joseph's bunk in the mail room,

---

[185]"General James A. Garfield. A Study" is in *History of Geauga and Lake Counties, Ohio, with Illustrative and Biographical Sketches of its Pioneers and Most Prominent Men* (1878), pp. 64–73. This is a perceptive article. Riddle, who knew his subject very well indeed, raised the question of what was lacking in Garfield: "Some little thing wanting to completeness; a lack felt, not seen, hard to define, yet a coming short of the perfection demanded of him." Pointing to a seeming lack of design in Garfield's life, he reached the conclusion that egoism was the missing quality. "That setting of oneself above all others is not much in his nature, no vestige of arrogance. Courage of the chivalrous order—spirit abundant, but to set himself up, claim for himself, which this involves—is certainly not much in him." Declaring that growth had always been a phenomenon attending Garfield's career, he foresaw but one danger—"the peril of being named by some superservicable friend, or ingenious enemy, for an unnamed place prematurely." Riddle's advice was: "Let the future provide for him as it has in the past. He may leave himself in the hands of the fates or forces which have been so kind to him."

and after breakfast took the 7 A.M. train for Shelby. En route, read Victor Hugo's *History of a Crime.* [186]

Arrived at Newark at one P.M. and was met by A. B. Clark,[187] who drove me to the Fair ground (old Mound Builders' Circle), w[h]ere Gen. Keifer was addressing the soldiers' reunion, about 15,000 people present.[188] After him, the President, Gen. Sherman, Att'y Gen. Devens, and Gov. Fletcher[189] of Mo. spoke, and last I spoke about ten minutes. I noticed that the President omitted all notice of the rightness of our cause, and I emphasized it. Dinner on the grounds. Went to Clark's where many called on me. After tea went to the Hotel, where general reception was held. At ten we sat down to a banquet. At 12 I responded to "Our Country," the first toast, and immediately took the eastern train, President's special car, and retired.

TUESDAY, 23.   Awoke about 20 miles east of Belle Air [Bellaire] and about eight o'clock had a good breakfast served on board. The party are Pres. Hayes, Sec'y Devens, Gen. E. B. Tyler,[190] and a gentleman from Fremont—President of a bank. The day was hot and uncomfortable. I divided between conversation, Victor Hugo and sleep. During the day the President said to me

[186]Hugo's *Histoire d'un Crime,* written in 1852, was published in two volumes in 1877. English translations had appeared by 1878.

[187]A. B. Clark was editor and a proprietor of the *Newark Weekly American,* a Republican paper.

[188]The reunion was in memory of Major General James B. McPherson, who was killed on July 22, 1864, when he was commander of the Army of the Tennessee.

[189]Thomas C. Fletcher (1827–1899), lawyer, supporter of Lincoln in the Republican National Convention of 1860, and Union officer in the Civil War, was governor of Missouri, 1865–69; he afterwards practiced law in St. Louis and Washington, D.C.

[190]Erastus B. Tyler (1822–1891), a native of New York, was brought to Portage County, Ohio, as a boy. In 1861 he defeated Garfield for the colonelcy of the 7th Ohio Infantry Regiment. His service in the army, 1861–65, brought him a brevet major generalship. After the war he settled in Maryland, living on a farm outside Baltimore and engaging in business in the city. In 1877 President Hayes, who had served under him during the war, appointed him postmaster of Baltimore, a position he held until 1881 when President Garfield requested his resignation after a jury had awarded $5,000 to a woman, a former employee in the Baltimore post office, who had brought suit against him. At the time of his death he was employed in the custom house in Baltimore.

that the chief political mistake of my life was in refusing the governorship in 1867, and he thought I ought yet to take it. He intimated that it was the surest road to the Presidency. At Cumberland, the President was met by the Mayor and a large concourse of people, who tendered us a dinner and a welcome. After dinner the President introduced me to the crowd, and I spoke three minutes; then Devens, and then we went on the train. Washington at eight P.M. Devens drove me home. Mary and Daniel had tea ready for me in the sitting room. Rose came and I dictated twenty letters and retired.

WEDNESDAY, 24.   Inspected the new wing of our house, which is up and roofed. Miss Ransom came and took breakfast with me, also Em Reed who is well nigh crazy over her dismissal from the Treasury. Went to the Treasury on Dep't business, especially to aid Em and other friends. Spent some time with Col. Rockwell. Home at lunch, and made further arrangements about repairs on house. Treasury again in the afternoon for Em. Dined with Gilfillan at 5 1/2 and returned home at 7. Rose and Young came. I dictated letters and arranged affairs. At 9 P.M. Col. Rockwell's man came and drove me to the Baltimore & Ohio Depot, where I took the train for Philadelphia. After a chapter of Victor Hugo, retired.

THURSDAY, 25.   The train arrived at West Philadelphia at 3 A.M., but I slept until 5.30 when I was awakened. I dressed and took a carriage to the Camden Ferry, and at Camden took the 6.30 train for Atlantic City, arriving at 9 A.M. Stopped at the United States Hotel and took breakfast. At ten attended the meeting of Potter's Committee, and heard Sherman (John) for more than two hours. Then I was called and was examined until 4 P.M. After adjournment Potter told me my testimony was in better shape than any of the visitors who had yet appeared before the Committee.[191] Took a long walk with Potter on the beach, and talked

[191]Garfield was questioned at length concerning his visit to Louisiana in November, 1876, and his activities there. Benjamin F. Butler pursued a line of questioning about the Packard government which was obviously intended to bring out a relationship between its collapse and a pre-inaugural bargain. He did not succeed in reaching his objective. As reported in the *New York Tribune,* the session ended with Butler's saying "I propose to find the missing link in the chain of con-

de omnibus et singulis [about everything and anything]. Potter is much too good a man to be in this business.

Talked with Sherman a short time before he left for Washington. Wrote to Crete and a short note to Sherman for Em Reed, and retired at 9 1/2 not feeling very well.

FRIDAY, 26.   Arose at seven A.M. to take a sea bath. Went in beside a wreck in company with Springer, Hiscock[192] and two or three others. The water was cold and I neglected to dive when I first went in. I did not stay long, and on my way back to the bath house I grew dizzy, and finally unconscious. The first I knew, I felt my feet in hot water and my limbs being rubbed. I was brought to the Hotel in a carriage and carried to a room on the second floor. Dr. Erwin[193] of Philadelphia and Dr. Pugh,[194] a New Jersey member of the House of Representatives, were with me nearly all day. They were disturbed by a fluttering motion about my heart, which is something entirely new to me. I was kept in bed all day, and felt singularly weak and unsteady.

The Doctor gave me a purgative, and I find I was very bilious. Perhaps that may have been the cause. I went into the water thinking of the old wreck and comparing it with the *Wreck of the Grosvenor,* and neglected the proper precautions.

SATURDAY, 27.   Slept well during the past night and feel much better this morning, though I am somewhat weak and the circulation about my heart is not yet regular. At ten A.M. went before the Committee for a few moments, but they asked me to postpone the further examination until their next session, which will be held in N. Y. about the 12th August.[195] Took the 11 A.M.

---

spiracy." These words do not appear in the official printed document (Serial 1864).

[192]Frank Hiscock (1834–1914) was a Republican member of the House from New York, 1877–87, and of the U.S. Senate, 1887–93.

[193]Neither the name Erwin nor a variation of it appears in a list of more than one thousand physicians in *Boyd's Philadelphia City Business Directory* (1879).

[194]John H. Pugh (1827–1905), a physician, was a Republican member of the House from New Jersey, 1877–79.

[195]Garfield was on the stand only a few minutes during which he was asked a few questions by the chairman. Although the committee met in New York City

train to Philadelphia and remained there, not feeling very well, until eight P.M. when I took the Lehigh Valley R. R. for Buffalo. Read Victor Hugo till dark.

SUNDAY, 28.   Awoke at Hornellsville where I took breakfast. Reached Buffalo at 11.15 A.M. At 12.30 took Lake Shore train for the West. Col. Thomas[196] of Nicaragua fame was on the train, and we had a long talk about the relations of the United States to Mexico and Central America. Arrived at Painesville at six P.M. and found Harry awaiting me at the Depot. The newspapers have been full of accounts of my illness at Atlantic City. Found affairs at the farm in good shape. The oats are in the barn, and part of the rye. Men have made some progress in the corn.

Harry Jones spent the night with us.

MONDAY, 29.   Spent most of the day reading my accumulated mail, and overhauling farm affairs. In the evening Capt. Henry, Pres. Hinsdale and his wife and daughter Millie, came to visit us. For want of room our boys slept on the hay.

Harry Jones remained until noon, when he went to the train.

TUESDAY, 30.   In the afternoon I drove to Painesville and Fairport with Hinsdale and Capt. Henry. I went to see Capt. Ottinger,[197] of the U. S. Revenue Cutter *Commodore Perry,* which

---

in August, Garfield was notified by Potter that Butler did not wish to question him at that time. Garfield never appeared before the committee again and was never at any time questioned about the Wormley conference.

[196]William Walker (1824–1860), a native of Tennessee, gained fame in the 1850's by his filibustering expeditions against Nicaragua. On his third expedition he was executed in Honduras before reaching his destination. For a reference to Thomas that associates him with Walker, see Vol. II, pp. 328–329.

[197]Douglass Ottinger, a native of Maine, had a long career as an officer in the United States Revenue Marine Service. Following an appropriation for the purpose by Congress in 1848, he was assigned to build and equip a number of life saving stations along a portion of the New Jersey coast. The equipment of the stations included "life cars," waterproof containers of corrugated iron, capable of holding about four persons, which could be drawn on hawsers between the shore and ships in distress. Joseph Francis (1801–1893), who devoted his life to the building of boats and life saving equipment, is credited with the invention of the life car. Ottinger, however, claimed that he was the inventor, and during the 1850's he made unsuccessful efforts to secure from Congress compensation and

has been sent to Fair[port] by the Treasury Department, with a request that I go on her to see the Life Saving Stations along this shore of the lake. Agreed to go tomorrow.

Home at five P.M. Several friends called in the early evening. At seven drove to Willoughby with Crete, Burke and wife and my mother, and attended the Sunday School Convention. Robt. Moffett[198] spoke. At the close a [I] spoke 20 minutes on the relation of Church to State.

WEDNESDAY, 31. Busy with letters and farm affairs in the forenoon. At 10 sent Burke to Willoughby, where he is to make an address and go thence by train to Painesville.

At half-past 12, Myron drove us (Harry, Jim, Bentley Warren and me) to Painesville, where Burke joined us, and thence to Fairport. The *Perry* had steam up, and at 2 P.M. we were steaming down the lake. We inspected the Cutter and heard from Capt. Ottinger the story of his invention of the life car in 1848–9. He is a genial old man, 72 years of age, and in a fine state of preservation.

At eight P.M. we steamed into Erie Harbor. Went up town and were called [on] by several prominent citizens.

At midnight we steamed out of Erie and turned eastward.

August

THURSDAY, 1. Awoke in sight of Buffalo, and at 9 A.M. were in the Harbor. After breakfast Burke and I and the boys went up

---

additional money to enable him to test the practicality of the life car at sea. See next entry.

[198]Robert Moffett (1835–1900), of Cleveland, was a well-known Disciple preacher. He was born in Indiana, lived in Illinois, where his father was a pioneer Disciple preacher, attended the Western Reserve Eclectic Institute in 1854, and graduated at Bethany College in 1859. He was for many years corresponding secretary of the Ohio Christian Missionary Association and of the American Christian Missionary Association. He was the author of *Seeking the Old Paths and Other Sermons* (1899). His wife was the daughter of Almon B. Green, who is mentioned a number of times in the diary.

town, and at noon took the train to Niagara where we spent the day until six-thirty, looking at the points of interest on both sides the river and falls. Boys were greatly delighted with the trip. At 6.35 we took train and reached Buffalo in an hour. The Captain's Cutter was waiting for us at the foot of main street and took us to the *Perry* where we spent the night.

FRIDAY, 2. Jim was up before the rest of us, and managed to fall into the river from the dock, and get himself out and dried in time for breakfast.

Several citizens called during the forenoon. At 12.50 went with the boys to the Depot to meet Mr. Warren of Boston, who comes to get his son. We asked him to go on board the Cutter with us, but he could not. We parted with him and Bentley and returned to the *Perry* for dinner. At two we went down to the mouth of the harbor to witness the experimental use of the life saving apparatus. It was poorly handled; but the result was otherwise very satisfactory. At eight we were about leaving Buffalo, when the ding[h]y with three men was upset, and one of the men came near drowning. At nine we were outside and steaming up the lake.

SATURDAY, 3. Spent a delightful forenoon on the lake steaming up in sight of shore. At one P.M. we put into Ashtabula Harbor, and spent an hour and a half.

Telegraphed home to have the team meet us at Fairport at 5 P.M.

We made fine speed from Ashtabula, and reached Fairport soon after 5.

Myron and Irvin were awaiting us. Drove to Painesville and after a little shopping and horse-shoeing, we came on home and found all well, and Cousin Phebe Clapp and daughter, and Mrs. Dr. Boynton awaiting us. They and Burke spent the night with us. Late in the evening Cousin Dr. Boynton came and spent the night.

SUNDAY, 4. Burke went to church at Willoughby with Dr. Robison. I remained at home with the other visitors.

In the afternoon we drove to Little Mountain and spent an hour or two among our acquaintances who are sojourning there.

Crete, Mother and our guests made up our party. Except Burke, who went to visit his relatives, the Loomises.

All at home in the evening.

MONDAY, 5.   Dr. Boynton and wife left for Cleveland by carriage at 5 A.M. At 7.30 sent Burke to the Mentor train. At noon, Mrs. Clapp and Lizzie remained.

Men hauled rye until the rain stopped them.

TUESDAY, 6.   Busy with farm matters. At noon Cousin Phebe and Lizzie left us. In the afternoon H. H. Mason[199] and N. N. Bartlett[200] of Niles came to see me in reference to the appointment of a route agent on the new R. R. from Pittsburgh to Youngstown.[201]

Men getting in turnips and hoeing corn.

In the evening Crete and I made some calls.

WEDNESDAY, 7.   Spent the forenoon in answering letters, by the help of Crete and Martha. At noon Judge Kinsman and Harmon Austin of Warren came to visit us, and I spent the P.M. with them going over the farm and visiting Dr. Robison's. I got several valuable suggestions from them in reference to farm management.

They spent the night with us.

THURSDAY, 8.   Judge Kinsman and Mr. Austin left by the 7.44 train.

I spent the forenoon in farm affairs and in writing about 20 letters by the help of Crete and Martha. Went to Cleveland by the noon train. Spent the afternoon in shopping. Dined with Mr. Everett on Prospect Street. After dinner he drove me on Wilson Avenue, behind his fast team. At 7 1/2, Messrs. Payne, Wade,

[199]Henry H. Mason, cashier of the savings and loan association in Niles, and a prominent Republican. He was first mayor of Niles, postmaster, 1880–89, and president of a national bank, 1890–93.

[200]Nelson N. Bartlett (1840–1882), who attended the Western Reserve Eclectic Institute during Garfield's time, became a Disciple preacher, and, for a time, editor of the Niles *Independent,* a weekly paper. Early in 1880 he became pastor of the Disciple church in Painesville; he died of typhoid fever.

[201]The main line of the Pittsburgh & Erie Railroad, between Pittsburgh and Youngstown, a distance of 68 miles, was begun in May, 1877, and went into operation on February 12, 1879.

Robison, and several other gentlemen came and spent the evening with him. I remained until near midnight when I went home with Dr. Robison and spent the night.

I should have added above that I dictated about 30 letters to Pomerene, a short-hand writer.

FRIDAY, 9.   Spent the forenoon in shopping, dictating more letters, and arranging for the sale of my wheat.

Took the 11.15 train for home. In the P.M. arranged for threshing my grain tomorrow or Monday. The men got in three acres of buckwheat, to be plowed under for manure, and also completed sowing turnips.

In the afternoon Judge Taft of Cincinnati called and spent an hour or two. He had been at Little Mountain for a day.

SATURDAY, 10.   Men commenced plowing oat lot by the barn to make room for some manure (top-dressing) which must be cleared away before threshing the remainder of our grain. They hauled out 13 loads. In the P.M. Moses helped Dickey haul oats. My Cousin Amasa Garfield came and spent part of the day. Sent him to Willoughby to evening train. At 7 P.M., W. J. Ford and family and Miss Lottie Sackett[202] came and spent the night. I spent the day in picking up and setting the grounds in order. At 8 1/2 P.M. George W. Steele and the Smith family of Painesville came and serenaded us.[203]

SUNDAY, 11.   Ford took his team, and I mine, both full, to Willoughby and attended church. A quiet good sermon by A. B. Green. We called a few moments at Mr. Hanscom's to let Lottie Sackett see Miss Alice H., an old friend.[204]

[202]Charlotte Sackett (1830–1919), sister-in-law of Harmon Austin, was a school teacher; she was in charge of the Ladies' Department of Hiram College, 1867–68.

[203]The Smith family began singing publicly in 1853, when Ashbel G. Smith (1829–1928) organized a family quartet and arranged the music for a program in Painesville which featured a Fourth of July oration by Henry Ward Beecher. In 1886 Estelle J. Smith, a daughter, married Frank P. Pratt, and the group became known as the Smith-Pratt singers. During its long career the Painesville group sang at hundreds of funerals.

[204]Alva Hanscom was a farmer in Willoughby. His daughter Alice (1848–1932) taught school in Ohio, New York and Kentucky. During the school year 1878–79 she and Martha Mays, governess of the Garfield children, taught together in Dayton. She spent her last years in Willoughby. The Alice Hanscom House at The

Home to dinner. In the afternoon drove Crete, Mother, and the children and our visitors to the lake at the mouth of the Chagrin River, a pleasant drive. Home in the evening. Dr. Robison's people went also.

MONDAY, 12. The threshers came early in the morning and began work. The remainder of the white wheat reached 138 bushels, making 311 bushels of Clawson wheat (white) on the 12 acres south of the road. The rye (six and a half acres next to the woods on the Geo. Dickey place) yielded 163 bushels. They had not completed threshing the oats when the day closed. The Fords left before noon. At 8 1/2 P.M. Crete and I, Mary McGrath, Irvin and Abram started in the spring wagon for Hiram. We arrived at Burton at eleven P.M. and spent the night at Wallace Ford's.

I should have added that before leaving home, I sold my wheat to Mr. Storm,[205] the Kirtland Miller, for 96 cents per bushel.

TUESDAY, 13. After breakfast we resumed our journey, had a pleasant drive to Hiram. Stopped at Father Rudolph's. After dinner, went to Hinsdale's and spent most of the afternoon, and wrote some letters. Spent the night at Father Rudolph's.

WEDNESDAY, 14. Spent the forenoon in calling with Crete. We called on Aunt Emeline Raymond, John Rider's [Ryder's],[206] Clark Norton's,[207] and also went to the Graveyard where our little ones are buried.

In the afternoon, Hinsdale came down to Father Rudolph's and spent a part of the evening.

Spent the night at Father Rudolph's.

Andrews School commemorates her friendship with Margaret St. John Wallace (see note 173 above). She was the author of *Perennia,* a volume of prose and poetry published privately in Cleveland in 1898. Her sister Blanche is also mentioned in the diary.

[205]S. T. Storm and R. Y. Carroll operated the Kirtland Flouring Mills.

[206]John F. Ryder, son of Jason Ryder, was a fellow student of Garfield at the Western Reserve Eclectic Institute. He was a farmer in Hiram, where he lived all his life. He married Emily Mason and was the father of several children. He was a trustee of Hiram College, 1872–92.

[207]Clark Norton was a farmer in Hiram for many years.

THURSDAY, 15.   Arose at 5 and at 6 staterd [started] for Mentor, taking Mother Rudolph and little Max Rudolph.

At 9 A.M. we stopped at a Mr. Robbins' in Russell, and let the team eat. Mr. R. occupies the House which I helped Jedediah Hubbell to build in 1851, 27 years ago.

After half an hour we resumed our journey. Near the Chester line while Irvin was driving, the wheel struck a stone and the shock broke a spring. Tied it up, and went on through Kirtland and reached home at eleven o'clock.

Found the men hoeing corn and hauling away wheat.

FRIDAY, 16.   Spent the day in overhauling farm affairs. Moses finished hauling the wheat to Kirtland, where I sold 400 bushels, reserving about 70 bushels for seed and for family use.

Bought of the miller, two tons of Shorts at $15 per ton to feed the stock.

Have begun feeding the cows. Sowed corn at noon. Found the second crop of sowed corn in the young orchard doing very finely. The straw has been well cared for, and on the whole, the plentiful grain harvest has been well secured.

SATURDAY, 17.   Spent the day in farm affairs, and shopping in Mentor for Crete.

Drove to Kirtland with Mother and settled the wheat account at 96 cents per bushel. A number of friends called in the P.M. and evening.

Tonight the primary meetings are held in all the townships and wards of this 19th District for choosing delegates to the Congressional Convention, to be held in Warren, next Tuesday. Nothing portends any contest, unless it be the silence and apparance [apparent] absence of any opposition to me.

SUNDAY, 18.   No church today. Heard that the caucus at Mentor was well attended, about 80 voters being in attendance, and no opposition to me. Similar news in the Sunday *Leader* from Ashtabula. Dr. Robison and his wife came and spent the evening. I am not feeling very well.

Retired early.

MONDAY, 19.   I have tried to give some time this forenoon to the plan of a speech at the Warren Convention, but find myself singularly averse to continuous thought. The nearest I have come to any plan has been the idea of analysing the characteristics of this district, and for its recent history, inject my own notions of public policy into the sketch. I tried Hal's mind on the question, and was glad to find he had the notion of representative independence. At noon Crete and Jim and I went to Cleveland, did a little shopping and took the 4.25 train for Warren. Stopped at the Austin House, where we were given a fine supper and a party of about 20 friends. Delegates arriving. Crete, Jim and I spent the night at Harmon Austin's.

TUESDAY, 20. After breakfast at Austin's went to the hotel and received my friends who came in great numbers, among them several from Portage County, who have always stood by me, and still come, though that county has been separated from the old 19th District. The Convention organized at 11 to 12, adjourned for dinner and to await the narrow gauge train with delegates from Lake and Geauga. At half-past one a Committee came to wait on me and inform me of my unanimous nomination, and invited me to attend and address the convention, which I did. Harry had come and was in the hall. I followed the plan mention[ed] on yesterday, and made a more than usually effective speech.

Crete and I took the 2.30 narrow gauge train for Painesville, leaving the boys at Austin's. Myron met us, at Geo. Steele's, whence, after we had taken tea, he drove us home.

WEDNESDAY, 21. Looked after farm affairs and began reading up for my opening campaign speech at Massillon, Saturday next. Am receiving a great many pleasant congratulations on my Convention speech of yesterday at Warren.

Have concluded to omit Hayes from the discussion almost entirely, insist upon the equality before the law—required by the war and the Constitutional amendments—as an aim to be fully and actually reached, and then reviewing Thurman,[208]

[208]The platform of Ohio Democrats in 1878 called for the repeal of the Resumption Act of 1875, which was to become effective on January 1, 1879. In his Massillon speech on August 24, Garfield quoted from earlier speeches of

make a renewed plea for the public faith and honest money.
Smalley came out on the evening train and spent the night.

THURSDAY, 22. Sent the team to take Smalley, Miss Mays, Clara
Jones and Mollie to Little Mt., while I spent most of the forenoon
looking up materials for campaign speech.

At noon Pomerene came from Cleveland to help me in short-
hand. Dictated about 30 letters, for I cannot do much on a speech
until my table is cleared, and late in the P.M. commenced dictating the speech. It is surprising how difficult it is for me to begin
a speech. If I get the first paragraph started to suit me, I feel that
a prime difficulty is got over. After much struggle and halting
made a fair start, and worked until 10 1/2 at night.

I had been interrupted during the afternoon by a number of
callers, among others a pleasant party, an omnibus load from the
Mountain.

FRIDAY, 23. Resumed work early, mixing the forenoon with farm
affairs and work on speech. Got about 2/3 of speech done by
noon, when I took the train to Cleveland and stopped at the
Forest City House. Sent the manuscript, as far as we had gone,
to the *Herald* office, and dictated the balance, getting it all in type
by 6 P.M.

Spent the night at the Forest City House. The speech lacks fire,
but is a succinct and careful statement of the issues as I conceive
them. I am curious to know how its tone and scope will be like
those of others who are to speak the same evening. Spent the
night at the Forest City House.

SATURDAY, 24. Took the 7 A.M. train for Massillon, where I
arrived at 10 A.M. Capt. Ricks met me at the Depot and took me
to his house where I took a bath, dined and slept three hours.
Toward evening many gentlemen called to see me, among them
Geo. Harsh who served in the Senate with me 18 years ago.[209]

Democratic Senator Thurman of Ohio to support his arguments in behalf of
resumption, and charged Thurman with inconsistency in his current stand
against it.

[209]George Harsh, a native of New York whose family settled near Massillon in
1813, was a member of the state house of representatives in 1846 and of the

At 7 1/2 in the evening, the opera house was crowded to the utmost, and I spoke an hour an[d] a quarter, following in the main the line of my printed speech. The spoken speech was more effective than the written one. McKinley followed 40 minutes.

After the close received many citizens at the hotel, and then drove with McKinley to his home in Canton, arriving at midnight. Retired tired.

SUNDAY, 25. Arose at eight o'clock and after breakfast went down to McKinley's office and to the office of the *Canton Repository,* and looked over the old files of the paper from early in 1815 down to 1840.

Back to McKinley's to dinner w[h]ere quite a large company of gentlemen had assembled.

After dinner we drove through the suburbs of the town, and through the principal streets. Retired early.

MONDAY, 26. Arose at five, and after taking breakfast, McKinley drove me to Massillon, ten miles, where I took the 7 A.M. train for Cleveland, arriving at ten and a half. Called at the bank, and wrote a letter to Hon. Amos Townsend. Took the 11.15 train to Mentor where Harry met me. Home to dinner. Spent the afternoon in farm affairs and writing letters.

Mrs. Riddle of Washington is visiting us. Towards evening drove her and Crete and our two mothers to the lower end of the farm.

Dr. Robison and wife spent the evening with us.

TUESDAY, 27. Busy with farm, new well at the tenant house south of the road, and correspondence until noon, when Mrs. Riddle, Mother Rudolph and Max, and Crete and I took the 12.31 train to Cleveland. After shopping and visiting, Mother R. took train for Hiram, and Crete and I to La Grange, where Gen. Sheldon met us and drove us to his farm. Townsend, Foster and McKinley, together with many officers of the 42nd were there. We had a pleasant evening there and in town, and Crete and I spent the night at Gen. Sheldon's farm home.

senate, 1860–63. He became an extensive property holder in and around Massillon.

WEDNESDAY, 28. At 10 A.M. went to La Grange where were about 150 members of the dear old Regiment assembled in reunion, and about 4,000 citizens to greet us. Capt. Jones [Mitchell][210], a preacher, late Captain in the 32 O.V.I. made the address of welcome to which I responded. After a fine dinner in the grove, we had speeches from Foster, Townsend, McKinley, Maj. Clapp and others.

The soldier feeling is much revived this year. It is the reaction against the President's policy. On the whole, this is the happiest reunion our Regiment have ever had. Adjourned at 4. Supper at Sheldon's at 6. Crete and I took the cars at La Grange at 7 and reached Cleveland at half-past eight. At 10.30 P.M. took the train to Painesville, arriving 11.20, where Myron and Jimmie met us. Home an hour past midnight.

THURSDAY, 29. Spent the forenoon on farm affairs, and in bringing up arrears of correspondence, and putting my affairs in shape to be left. At two P.M. started in the buggy with Harry for Painesville, and after some business in town, took the 3.36 P.M. train for the East. To escape the crowd of visitors, rode in the mail car which was in charge of John Hofste, late of the 42nd.[211] Passed Buffalo at 8.45, and spent the night in the Postal Car.

FRIDAY, 30. Was awakened at Schenectady, and changed cars for Troy where I took breakfast at half-past seven, and then took train for Boston, going via Eagle Bridge and Hoosac Falls on the old track I first passed over 24 years ago on my way to college. Caught a glimpse of Pownal, where I taught penmanship (alsas [alas]! now a lost art!) and saw the spires of dear old Williams which seemed so grand and aweful in 1854. Then through N. Adams, the Hoosac Tunnel, 4 3/4 miles longs [long], thence across the Conn. River, through Fitchburg and Weston (in which

[210]The Reverend John Mitchell, formerly 1st lieutenant in the 32nd Ohio Infantry Regiment, delivered the welcoming address.

[211]John W. Hofste, a native of Holland, was a member of the 42nd Ohio Infantry Regiment from September, 1861, until his company was mustered out in December, 1864. He was now a railway mail clerk between Toledo and Buffalo.

latter place my great-grandfather was born), and reached Boston at 2.40 (1.50 Ohio time) and in half an hour was on the Eastern R. R. and reached Portland, Maine, 8 P.M. of Ohio time. Stopped at the Falmouth House. Tea, Bath, bed.

SATURDAY, 31. In the forenoon received many visitors, wrote seven letters, and at 1.30 P.M. Mr. Dow,[212] son of General Neal Dow, drove me ten miles to the old town of Yarmouth where I spoke an hour and a half to an open air meeting.[213] Visited the ship yards, and returned along the bay road to Portland.

In the evening attended the theatre in company with Mr.

[212]Frederick Neal Dow (1840–1934), businessman and politician, was a member of the executive council of Maine during the early 1870's, the state house of representatives, 1887–90, the Republican state committee, 1876–92, and collector of the port of Portland, 1883–85 and 1890–95.

[213]In a letter to his wife from Lewiston on September 2, Garfield described the political climate of the state in a way that helps to explain his presence there and why his major theme on this trip was "sound money":

The political situation here is full of peril and uncertainty. Within the last year, and notably within the last six months, the greenback craze has broken out with the force and spirit of an epidemic. While we were battling with it in the West, New England was free from its ravages; but now, when we have almost reached specie payments, the pest has burst upon Maine, like a thief in the night, and no one can foretell the result. I shall not be surprised if it defeats Powers and Reed, and perhaps Hale. Even Frye is thought to be in danger. It spreads among the staid citizens like a midsummer madness. You can hardly imagine the welcome which has met me here by our friends. All other issues are swallowed up in the absorbing question of what money is and what it ought to be. The old questions which I have been discussing during the last ten years are as fresh and new here as the telephone.

The mysteries of this intellectual epidemic will never cease to be a wonder to me. It is comfortable to feel that in such a fight, I can look back over 12 years of public discussion, and challeng[e] my opponents to find a speech or a vote of mine in conflict with the positions now held by our sound money men.

The fears of Maine Republicans were not without foundation. In the 45th Congress (1877–79) Maine was represented in the House by five Republicans; in the 46th Congress (1879–81) she was represented by three Republicans and two Greenbackers. The Republican casualties in 1878 were Eugene Hale and Llewellyn Powers.

Pullen of the *Press,* [214] and heard Kate Claxton in *The Two Orphans.* [215] It was well rendered.

Visited with Pullen and Hon. T. B. Reed until 12.30 when I retired. A little hoarse from the speech and ride.

September

SUNDAY, 1. Slept till nearly nine, in the cool rainy morning. Attended the Unitarian Church with Pullen in the forenoon, and heard an able discussion of the causes of the decay of religious observances. Stopped at the club on my return and spent an hour. Falmouth House to dinner. I suspect that Kate Claxton is the daughter to Spencer H[W]. Cone of the Bible Union.

At 3 P.M. went to 62 Gray St., a private residence, where 20 Disciples were met to break the loaf. It seemed like the days of my very early life. They had no preacher, but each bore a part in mutual encouragement. I spoke two or three minutes, enough to excuse the intrusion of a stranger.

At 5 went to the *Press* Office and revised the notes of my Yarmouth speech. In the evening wrote to Crete, and read another chapter of the manuscript copy of Gen. Upton's book on the Military History of the U. S.[216]

[214]Stanley T. Pullen (1843–1910) was editor of the *Portland Daily Press,* 1872–83, a member of the state legislature, 1875, and surveyor of customs in Portland, 1883–85.

[215]Kate Claxton (1848–1927), a native of New Jersey, was the daughter of Spencer Wallace Cone, a lawyer with literary interests, and Margaret Martinez. Throughout her career on the stage she was most prominently identified with the role of Louise, the blind girl in *The Two Orphans,* a melodrama from the French.

[216]In the latter 1870's the U.S. army was far different from that of the Civil War period. Limited by law to 25,000, it commanded small public interest or support. For its members promotions were frequently long delayed, pay not always prompt, and service generally unattractive. Garfield was one of those interested in army reorganization, discussions of which were somewhat related to the growth of labor disorders. Another was Emory Upton (1839–1881), a graduate of West Point in 1861, who had distinguished himself during the Civil War, achieving the rank of major general. After the war he continued his military career as a lieutenant colonel and colonel (1880). His *Infantry Tactics,* first published in 1875, became a standard manual. In 1875–76 he toured Europe and Asia as an army observer,

MONDAY, 2. After breakfast went with Mr. Dow to visit his father, General Neal Dow, who has done so much to repress the liquor traffic in Maine. He is now a well preserved man of about 74 years. On my return to the hotel, Mr. Pullen of the [*Press*] drove me to several points of interest in the city, and at 12.50 took [me] to the station where I took the Grand Trunk train for Lewiston. Was driven to the residence of Hon. W. P. Frye, by his son-in-law Mr. White.[217] Wrote and visited with the family and with Dr. Garcelon, the Democratic candidate for Governor.[218] After tea, went to the city hall and addressed for two hours an audience of 2,500. Made a more effective speech than at Yarmouth. Passed the night at Mr. Frye's, who was away from home, on the stump.

TUESDAY, 3. Arose at half-past six, and at seven took the train for

and in 1878 published *The Armies of Europe and Asia.* He was now at work on a historical study of the military policy of the United States. He himself was persuaded that only a regular army was capable of national defense. History, he thought, demonstrated the inadequacy of reliance upon civilians—he maintained that 20,000 regular troops at Bull Run would have ended the Civil War. Garfield read chapters of the work in progress and offered comments and criticisms. It was also read by Upton's friends General W. T. Sherman and Henry A. Dupont. Before the work was completed Upton committed suicide. His manuscript, somewhat revised, was published by the War Department in 1904 as *The Military Policy of the United States.* A number of letters of Upton to Garfield are in the Garfield Papers. Five letters of Garfield to Upton are in Peter S. Michie, *The Life and Letters of Emory Upton* (1885). For a modern study of Upton and his influence that contains numerous references to Garfield, see Stephen E. Burnside, *Upton and the Army* (1964).

[217]Wallace H. White (1848–1920), of Lewiston, was the attorney for Androscoggin County at this time. His son, Wallace H. White, Jr. (1877–1952), was a Republican member of the U.S. House of Representatives from Maine, 1917–31, and of the U.S. Senate, 1931–49.

[218]Alonzo Garcelon (1813–1906) returned to Lewiston, his birthplace, to practice medicine after receiving his degree at the Medical College of Ohio in Cincinnati in 1839. During the Civil War he was a hospital surgeon. He was a member of the state legislature in the 1850's, mayor of Lewiston, 1871, and governor, 1879. In the 1878 election, since no candidate for governor had a majority, the choice fell to the legislature. Although the Republican and Greenback candidates were in first and second place respectively in the general election, the Senate chose Garcelon after the House had narrowed the choice to him and the Greenbacker.

Portland, where I arrived at 9 A.M. and took breakfast with Pullen at the Falmouth Hotel. We then drove along the beach and took a tug to one of the islands where the fishermen were curing cod fish, taken on the banks of New Foundland. At 12.50, Pullen and I took the train at [to] Old Orchard Beach, and stopped at the Ocean House. We took a bath in the surf; and though I wet my head, took all the usual precautions, and remained in the water not more than ten minutes, yet while dressing I became very faint, and came near repeating my experience at Atlantic City. I fear I must abandon surf-bathing. Dinner at the Ocean House, where a Committee met us and took us to Biddeford, where I addressed a large audience for an hour and ten minutes. After which we took train to Portland. Retired at 11.

WEDNESDAY, 4. Arose at half-past 5 and at 6.15 took train for the East, and at nine A.M. arrived at Damariscotta. Ex-Congressman Flye[219] (Blaine's successor for the short term) met me at the station and took me to the hotel, where I read and slept an hour. Mr. Flye then drove me to the new 2,000 ton ship he is building, where I passed an hour and a half very pleasantly. Dinner at the Hotel. At 2 1/2 I spoke to a fine audience in the hall for an hour and a half. My best speech thus far. Mr. Flye then drove me to the famous oyster beds above the town, a peninsula covered 10 to 15 feet deep with oyster shells, evidently placed there in the pre-historic times by human hands, a wonderful aggregation greater than the Monte Testac[c]io at Rome. Spent the evening in writing and in reading the ancient history of the Dominion of Maine. Letter from Crete. Tired and homesick.

THURSDAY, 5. After breakfast, took the 9 A.M. train to Rockland, in company with Mr. Flye. After stopping a few minutes at the hotel, called on Mr. Farwell[220] who was, for a few months,

[219]Edwin Flye (1817–1886), a shipbuilder and banker, was a paymaster in the army during the Civil War, a delegate to the Republican National Convention in 1876, and a member of the U.S. House of Representatives, 1876–77.

[220]Nathan A. Farwell (1812–1893), an insurance executive in Rockland, served a number of terms in the state legislature during the 1850's and 1860's and was a Republican member of the U.S. Senate, 1864–65.

senator while Pitt Fessenden was Sec'y of the Treasury. Took dinner at his house. The Committee came to say that no hall could hold the people, and I must speak out of doors. Reluctantly consented, and addressed a large audience on the green beside the Custom House. Think I made a better impression than in any previous speech. At the close an earnest appeal was made to me to speak at Camden. Finding Hale in so much danger I consented. Mr. Crockett[221] drove to Camden, eight miles, in a heavy sea fog which, however, gave me occasional glimpses of the beauties of Penobscot Bay. At 7.30 P.M. found the hall at Camden nearly full, and spoke nearly an hour and a half. Great enthusiasm, though this is the center of the Greenback movement in this District. Hotel over night.

FRIDAY, 6.   After breakfast, Paul Stevens,[222] whom I have known in Washington, drove me through the town, a fine village in a very beautiful valley—the blue Camden Mts. in the rear, and a lovely bay filled with islands in front. At 9.30 A.M. Hon. Seth Milliken[223] came from Rockland and drove me 18 miles to Belfast. We took the river road, and, at one point, about five miles from Belfast, we clim[b]ed a height from which we could see a water view covering 3/4 [of] the horizon, with several hundred islands in sight. It strongly resembles the pictures of Naples. Spoke an hour and a half at Belfast to a fair audience in the hall. Telegram from Crete that Sammie Robison was killed yesterday.[224] Found I could not reach Cleveland in time for the funeral.

[221]A. F. Crockett, a Rockport businessman, was chairman of the Knox County Republican Committee.

[222]Paul Stevens (1826–1884) was employed for a number of years during the 1860's and 1870's as an assistant librarian in the library of the U.S. House of Representatives. After leaving this post, he was a claim agent in Washington before returning to live in Camden, Maine.

[223]Seth L. Milliken (1831–1897), a Belfast lawyer, was a member of the state legislature in the 1850's, clerk of the state supreme judicial court, 1859–71, and a Republican member of the U.S. House of Representatives, 1883–97.

[224]Samuel Robison (1843–1878), son of John P. Robison, was killed by a horse falling upon him at an agricultural fair near Paris, Kentucky. He owned a farm near that place.

Great audience in the evening. Seth Milliken spoke. At the close I spoke ten minutes and aroused more enthusiasm than any where yet. Ferguson[225] and Milliken stayed at my room until one o'clock. Many compliments.

SATURDAY, 7. Arose at 7 and after breakfast and several calls made upon me by the citizens, I took the steamer for Bangor. The weather was so chilly that, fearing to increase my hoarseness, I stayed in the cabin and read *The Sun Maid,*[226] and caught but few glimpses of the fine scenery along the Penobscot. Arrived at Bangor at one P.M. where I was met by Gen. Hamlin and taken to the Senator's (Hannibal Hamlin's). I find myself very hoarse as the result of speaking four times during the last two days. In the evening addressed an immense audience which filled Norombega Hall to overflowing. Spoke with difficulty on account of hoarseness. Less satisfied with my speech than any I have yet made. My mind seemed choked as well as my throat. Spent the night at Senator Hamlin's.

SUNDAY, 8. Very hoarse and tired. Rested most of the day. Senator Hamlin drove me over the city and to his farm a mile outside. Made a pleasant call on the Senator's son, Gen. Hamlin.[227] Judge John A. Peters,[228] and Mr. Boutelle[229] dined with us. Senator H.

[225]George B. Ferguson (1832–1893), a Belfast businessman who was later collector of customs for the Belfast district.

[226]Maria M. Grant, *The Sun-Maid. A Romance* (1878).

[227]Charles Hamlin (1837–1911), a Belfast lawyer who graduated at Bowdoin College and was breveted brigadier general during the Civil War, was at this time a U.S. register in bankruptcy and a U.S. commissioner. For twenty years he reported the decisions of the supreme judicial court of Maine. His publications include *The Insolvent Law of Maine . . .* (1878).

[228]John A. Peters (1822–1904), a graduate of Yale, began the practice of law in Bangor in 1844. He was a Republican member of the state legislature in the early 1860's, of the U.S. House of Representatives, 1867–73, associate justice of the supreme judicial court of Maine, 1873–83, and chief justice, 1883–1900. He had a reputation as a very effective speaker.

[229]Charles A. Boutelle (1839–1901), who was an officer in the U.S. Navy during the Civil War, was at this time editor and part owner of the *Bangor Whig and Courier,* and a member of the Republican state committee. He was a member of the U.S. House of Representatives, 1883–1901.

sums up the situation by saying that the Greenbackers and Democrats will sweep the state like a whirl-wind.

It seems to be a regular mania, an intellectual epidemic.

After dinner slipt off to my room and read *The Sun Maid.* Kept
up the reading of the story until an hour after midnight. I am very
hoarse and apprehensive of my unfitness to speak at Boston.

MONDAY, 9. Early breakfast at Senator Hamlin's and took the
7.30 A.M. train to Augusta. On the way finished *The Sun Maid.*
It is a powerful story, in which are strikingly grouped and contrasted the fierce beauty of a Russian winter, and the soft loveli-
ness of the Pyrenees, in the neighborhood of Pau. The author
delights too much in the pompous nothings of society talk. At
Augusta, Blaine's son Walker[230] met me and drove me to their
house. Visited and rode with J. G. Blaine for two hours. He does
not wholly share Hamlin's fears of defeat. After dinner took the
train to Boston. En route received indications from many towns
of the vote. Democrats losing heavily. Republicans considerable.
Greenback vote large. T. B. Reed came to see me at the Portland
Station. Reached Boston at 9.30 and stopped at the Parker
House. Very hoarse, and apprehensive of hard time for tomorrow night.

Bathed and retired, expecting disaster in Maine.

TUESDAY, 10. Maine has been struck with the greenback tor-
nado. Powers and Hale defeated. The Democratic party below
both others. The Governorship in doubt, probably anti-Republi-
can. My throat some better, but still rough. Nearly the whole day
consumed in receiving calls, and consulting on the situation here.
I have determined to do what I can to keep the party in Mass.
from wasting its strength on anything but the financial peril. The

[230]Walker Blaine (1855–1890), eldest son of James G. Blaine, graduated at
Yale University and Columbia School of Law before beginning the practice of law
in St. Paul. President Garfield appointed him third assistant secretary of state (see
entry for July 1, 1881). His father, then secretary of state, soon sent him to Latin
America, where he served for a time as chargé d'affaires in the U.S. legation in
Chile. He was assistant counsel for the United States Court of Commissioners of
Alabama Claims, 1882–85. After practicing law in Chicago, he became in 1889
solicitor of the State Department, of which his father was again head.

Young Men's Committee gave me a dinner at 3 P.M. My class-mate Hill, and many prominent citizens present. A drive to Brighton and Cambridge, and at eight in Faneuil Hall. It was packed to its utmost capacity. Turbulence from roughs was apprehended.[231] I spoke two hours, and have rarely controlled and carried an audience better. Lunch at the Club. Retired an hour past midnight.

Many extravagant things were said of the speech by Senator Hoar, Adin Thayer[232] and others. But my hoarseness was a drawback.

WEDNESDAY, 11.   I got but three hours of sleep out of last night, probably due to the fact that I drank a cup of strong tea before retiring. Took breakfast at half-past seven. Many friends called, and Johnson[233] went with me to the train. Left in company with Col. Nichols [Nichol][234] of Chicago at 8.30. The Boston papers

[231]The nomination of Benjamin F. Butler for governor by Greenbackers and Democrats had generated some political excitement in Massachusetts. Butler's partisans were responsible for several interruptions at Garfield's meeting. Most of Garfield's speech, which was devoted to the theme of "Honest Money," is in Hinsdale, ed., *Works of Garfield,* II, pp. 586–608.

[232]Adin Thayer (1828–1888), a Worcester lawyer, was chairman of the Republican state committee. In the fall of 1878 he was appointed judge of probate and insolvency for Worcester County, a position he held until his death.

[233]Robert M. Thompson (1849–1930), a Boston lawyer, was chairman of the Young Men's Republican Committee under whose auspices Garfield spoke in Boston. He later moved to New Jersey, where he was prominent in the fields of smelting and mining, becoming chairman of the board of International Nickel.

[234]Thomas M. Nichol's origins are obscure. He is said to have published a weekly newspaper in Kansas before going to Racine, Wisconsin, in 1877. He quickly joined in the fight for resumption, becoming secretary of the Honest Money League of the Northwest—"the chief soul" of the organization, Garfield called him. At this time he was in New England in support of his cause. On October 5 he delivered an address in Faneuil Hall on "Fiat Money or Resumption for Workingmen. . . ." He was instrumental in getting Garfield to deliver an address to the Honest Money League in Chicago on January 2, 1879. A year later he was writing Garfield from Columbus during the senatorial contest. Having become friendly with John Sherman, he supported him for the presidential nomination but helped to pave the way for the switch to Garfield; he was a busy alternate delegate from Wisconsin at the Chicago convention in June, 1880. During the campaign he aided Garfield at Mentor and reported to him from

are full of my speech. It seems to have made a much greater impression that [than] I expected.

Mr. Thayer accompanied me as far as Worcester. At Albany stopped at the Delavan House for dinner. At Utica took tea. A hot uncomfortable day. Late in the night it rained heavily.

THURSDAY, 12. Awoke at Geneva, and at 5.40 A.M. reached Painesville where Myron met me, and drove me home in a heavy rain. The earth is afloat with a three days' rain. Breakfast with all the dear ones at 7 A.M. Mrs. Smalley is here. Spent three hours on my mail, and in the afternoon worked on the revision of the *Boston Journal's* report of my Faneuil Hall Speech. One hundred thousand copies have been ordered by the Mass. Central Republican Committee.

Retired at ten.

FRIDAY, 13. Spent two-thirds of the day in revising my Faneuil Hall Speech, and towards evening sent it to Boston by Express.

The rain has been unprecedented. The R.R. is broken and but few trains have run since yesterday morning. At 7 P.M. Maj. Swaim and his wife and daughter came to visit us. They report great damage done by the flood.

SATURDAY, 14. Swaim and I took the 7.45 train for Cleveland and thence by the Atlantic & Great Western R. R. to Mantua Station. The Cuyahoga was up much higher than I ever saw it before.

At 12 Maj. McKinley came and at 2 P.M. we had a fine meeting in Atwater's Grove. McKinley spoke an hour, and I followed him about 3/4 of an hour. Austin Beecher[235] then drove us across the

---

Indiana, New York and elsewhere. When he visited Washington after the election, Blaine introduced him jokingly as "the ambassador from Mentor." On March 23, 1881, Garfield nominated him commissioner of Indian Affairs but shortly withdrew the nomination as a result of western dissatisfaction with it. After leaving politics he was for a time a member of a New York banking firm. He is said to have died insane. There are more than one hundred letters of Nichol to Garfield in the Garfield Papers.

[235]Austin S. Beecher, a hardware merchant and local office holder in Mantua, was a member of the committee on arrangements for the meeting in Atwater's Grove.

Cuyahoga Bridge and the overflowed road—the water came over his hind wheels. Thence to Ravenna. Aetna House. In the evening I addressed the [largest?] audience I ever saw in the Opera House. I spoke an hour and a half. McKinley followed 3/4 of an hour.

Many old friends called. We spent the night at the Aetna House.

SUNDAY, 15. Arose at five and after taking a cup of coffee with McKinley, Mr. Menary[236] took Swaim and me in a carriage and after fording the overflowed Cuyahoga, in Streetsboro, we reached R. P. Cannon's in Aurora and took breakfast, waiting an hour. Then drove home to Mentor, having had a stirring adventure at Kirtland, getting through the river. Pleasant afternoon on the farm.

Dr. Robison called in the evening. He is greatly broken down by the sudden death of his son Samuel.

MONDAY, 16. Letters and farm affairs in the forenoon. After dinner Swaim and wife, Crete and I went to Painesville shopping. Called at Geo. Steele's, where Mother (whom Harry drove down in the buggy) visited with Mr[s]. Palmer.[237]

Home in the evening. Finished reading aloud Warner's *My Summer in a Garden.*[238] Retired at 10 P.M.

TUESDAY, 17. Wrote letters and attended farm matters until eleven A.M. when I took the mares, with Dr. Robison's hack, and with Swaim and wife, Grandma, Martha, Harry, Irvin and Crete, drove to Willoughby and stopped at G. W. Clement's, whence Swaim and I drove to the Depot to receive the President and his party who came to attend the reunion of the 23rd O.V.I. Several thousand people were at the Depot, but there was no cheering when the President alighted. Procession through the principal

[236]J. C. Menary wrote an account of his trip with Garfield and Swaim that was published in the *Republican-Democrat* (Ravenna), October 2, 1878.

[237]Candace (Adams) Palmer (1800–1880) was the widow of Benjamin Palmer (1795–1873), a native of New Hampshire who practiced medicine for many years in Ohio, first in Bloomfield and later in Painesville. Their daughter Sarah was the wife of George W. Steele.

[238]Charles Dudley Warner, *My Summer in a Garden* (1871).

streets and to the public square in front of the college. Welcome address by Mayor Ellen,[239] response by Pres. Hayes. Dinner in the College Hall, at which Maj. Swaim and wife, Mother and Harry, Martha and Irvin, Crete and I were present. After dinner, assembled on the stand; speech by J. C. Cowin,[240] and other members of the regiment. The President presided, and I was much embarrassed by the fact that the audience began to call for me before the President was ready to do so. There were signs of feeling in the audience that he was reluctant, but I think he was not. I spoke a few minutes. Called on him and Mrs. Hayes at Gen. Hastings' and drove home at six. Spent three hours at Dr. Robison's, drawing a new contract between him and Dr. Streator.

WEDNESDAY, 18.   Completed preparations for sowing wheat on barn lot, and men commenced drilling it P.M. I have had it plowed 10 to 11 inches deep, narrow furrows, and have brought up soil that does not appear to have been disturbed before. Put on 175 loads barn yard manure, plowed it in with cultivator, and then harrowed. Picked up eight loads small stone, and put in 2 bushel Clawson wheat with drill, and six quarts timothy grass seed to the acre. The field will be little more than seven acres.

Spent the afternoon in answering letters and visiting. The day is very beautiful. Nature seems to have sounded a truce with the farmer, and the earth and sky is full of restfulness and peace. More and more I long for leisure to enjoy these sweet days. Major Swaim drove Mamie and Mollie to Painesville.

In the evening several young people came in and sang and played and danced with the children.

Retired at 10.30, hardly yet rested from my Eastern trip.

THURSDAY, 19.   Men finished drilling wheat today. I spent the

---

[239]John S. Ellen, a native of England, was brought to Willoughby as a boy. During the Civil War he attained the rank of captain in Hayes's regiment. After the war he was a merchant in Willoughby for many years. President Cleveland appointed him postmaster.

[240]John C. Cowin (1846–1918), a native of Warrensville, Ohio, attended the Western Reserve Eclectic Institute, served as a private in the 23rd Ohio Volunteer Infantry Regiment, 1861–64, and in 1867 moved to Omaha, Nebraska, where he became a prominent lawyer.

forenoon writing letters and arranging to have drainage from kitchen to old barn yard well. At noon Swaim and wife and Mamie and I left by 12.31 train for Cleveland, where we parted; they for Chicago and Leavenworth and I via Cleveland and Pittsburgh R.R. to Wellsville, where I waited two hours for the train on the River Division. Had a long visit with Gen. Reily [Reilly].[241] Arrived at Steubenville at 9.45 where a very large audience was awaiting me. Spoke an hour and a half and satisfied myself fairly well. By carelessness, left my overcoat either in the wagon at Mentor or in the car at Cleveland. This will probably cost me a cold and make the trip end more hoarsely than usual. Several citizens called after the meeting. Retired at 11 P.M.

FRIDAY, 20. At half-past eight was invited to visit the High School. Spoke half an hour to the young people. At 11 went to the Depot and found the train nearly two hours late. Returned to the hotel and wrote several letters. Train came at near one, and left for Zanesville. Reached Dresden Junction at 4.30. All trains gone. In an hour a special train was sent for me, and we reached Zanesville at 7.30. Addressed a large audience in the hall, speaking an hour and a half. Then went home with Cousin Orrin Ballou and spent the night. He is the county sherriff. Twenty-seven years ago, he was my pupil in the school I taught in Back Run, Harrison Township, Muskingum County. He is a strong Democrat, inheriting his politics from his father, my Uncle Henry Ballou.

SATURDAY, 21. After taking breakfast with Cousin Orrin, went to the hotel and found that Capt. Farrar had gone. Took the train at 7.40 A.M. and through a cold rainy morning rode to Lancaster, arriving at 9.45. Found Hon. V. B. Horton[242] awaiting me.

---

[241]James W. Reilly (1828–1896), who attained the rank of brigadier general in the Union army during the war, was a lawyer and bank president in Wellsville, Ohio; he was a member of the state legislature, 1862.

[242]Valentine B. Horton (1802–1888), a native of Vermont, was trained as a lawyer but became wealthy by exploiting the bituminous coal and salt deposits in Meigs County, Ohio; he lived in the county seat, Pomeroy, which he named for his father-in-law, a Boston merchant. He was a member of the U.S. House of Representatives, 1855–59, and 1861–63. His daughter Clara was the wife of

Many friend[s] called at the hotel. The Pendleton debate here, last year, was still spoken of with enthusiasm. Called on Prof. E. B. Andrews, Geologist and late Col. of the 36th O.V.I. At one P.M. went to the hall which was crowded. Mr. Horton spoke three-quarters of an hour. I have never heard him before. He has some of the feebleness and rambling of an old man; but has strong sound sense, and makes a good impression upon his hearers. I followed an hour and a half, and had the close, and finally the very enthusiastic, attention of my audience.

In half an hour after closing I was on the train for Athens, and in twenty minutes after arriving was addressing a hall full of people. Spoke an hour and a half. Spent the night at the Warren House.

SUNDAY, 22. Slept until eight, and arose feeling much better than I had a right to expect after so severe a day as yesterday. My voice holds up well. I give it no spirits or medication. Capt. Jo. Kisslinger [Joseph L. Kissinger], late quartermaster of the 40th O.V.I. and my comrade in the Sandy Valley Campaign, came soon after breakfast and we took a long walk. Then attended the Presbyterian Church and heard a sermon rededicating the newly repaired building.

After church Hon. Van Voorhees [VanVorhes],[243] M.C. of this District, called. Wrote letters and read Walker's *History of Athens County.* [244]

MONDAY, 23. Early breakfast, and took six A.M. train to Logan. Read Walker's *History* on the way. Was met at depot by Committee and taken to hotel. Soon afterwards Hon. V. B. Horton came. At 1.30 P.M. Horton spoke in the hall to a large audience. He

---

General John Pope, and his daughter Frances the wife of Manning F. Force; his son, Samuel Dana Horton, was a distinguished economist and advocate of bimetallism.

[243]Nelson VanVorhes (1822–1882), a native of Pennsylvania, moved to Ohio as a boy. Trained as a printer, he owned and edited a newspaper in Athens for a number of years, served several terms in the state legislature, was a Union officer in the Civil War, and a Republican member of the U.S. House of Representatives, 1875–79. He was an unsuccessful candidate to succeed himself in 1878.

[244]Charles M. Walker, *History of Athens County, Ohio* (1869).

is 76 years old, [a] finely preserved, clear-headed man. I followed an hour and a half. Great enthusiasm was manifested in the audience.

At half-past 5 P.M. Mr. H. and I took the train for Athens. I borrowed an overcoat from Mr. Remple [Rempel][245] before leaving. We spent the night at Athens.

TUESDAY, 24. At half-past six Mr. [J.S.] Blackaller of Pomeroy took us in his carriage and drove to Pomeroy via Rutland, 30 miles. A mile out from Middleport we were met by a large escort of cavalry, which accompanied us to Pomeroy, leaving us at Mr. Horton's residence. After dinner we met a great audience fronting the high cliff. Mr. H. spoke half an hour. I followed an hour and a half. Quick and hearty responses from the hearers. Spent remainder of the afternoon at Horton's. After tea Mr. Horton, Judge Force[246] and I drove to Middleport, where an immense meeting filled one of the streets. We both spoke. More enthusiasm here than even in Pomeroy. Back to Horton's. Took a bath, read Emerson's "Over-Soul" and slept.

WEDNESDAY, 25. After an elegant breakfast at Mr. Horton's in company with Mr. and Mrs. H. and Mr. and Mrs. Force, Mr. Blackaller took us in the carriage and drove us 18 miles, over the hills to Porter, Gallia County, where we addressed 2,000 in an orchard. A very successful meeting. Then drove over very wild hills, 13 miles, to Wilkesville. Two miles out were met by a large cavalry escort and a band. The town was illuminated, many tor-

---

[245]Ferdinand F. Rempel, a native of Prussia, was a merchant, the owner of the Opera House and postmaster in Logan, Hocking County. An officer in the Union army, he first met Garfield in the South during the war.

[246]Manning F. Force (1824–1899), a native of Washington, D.C., was the son of Peter Force (1790–1868), archivist and historian. A graduate of Harvard College and the Harvard Law School, he was admitted to the bar in Cincinnati, 1850. He was judge of the court of common pleas, 1867–77, judge of the superior court of Cincinnati, 1877–87, and professor in the Cincinnati Law School. A Union officer during the Civil War, he was the author of *From Fort Henry to Corinth* (1881) and *General Sherman* (1899). His wife was Frances Horton, daughter of Valentine B. Horton.

ches and transparencies in procession. We addressed 1,500 people in the street.

The long ride, the damp night air, and much speaking have at last roughened my throat, and tonight for the first time I speak with difficulty. Slept at a wretched hotel in a very mean feather bed.

THURSDAY, 26.   Started at half-past seven and rode in the rain 15 miles over horrible hilly roads to McArthur. Three miles out, a large escort met us, joining the Wilkesville troop that came with us. Judge Lawrence spoke an hour to the 2,000 assembled in the open air. I followed an hour and a half, and then Mr. Horton spoke half an hour. His endurance is remarkable. At 4.45 I took a freight train at McArthur, and slept away part of the slow time to Chillicothe, arriving at 8.15. Committee met me. Mr. Townsend[247] of Athens was speaking to a court-house full when I arrived. I followed an hour and a half. My voice behaved well and I made the best speech of the week thus far. Many enthusiastic friends called on me at the hotel.

Lawrence Barrett was playing at the Opera House while I was speaking.

FRIDAY, 27.   Took six and a quarter train for Columbus. Rode most of the way with Lawrence Barrett and his company. Gen. Robinson met me at Columbus Depot and took me to the Neil House and the Committee rooms. Answered several telegrams and took the 10 A.M. train north. Reached Gilead at 11.30 where Committee met me, among them my second Cousin O[scar] L. R. French, and drove me to Mt. Gilead. At 2 P.M. spoke to the new Opera House full of people, and closed at 4, a fair speech but with a hoarse voice.

Took 4.45 train and arrived at Cleveland 8.30. Had arranged by telegraph to have the night express stop at Mentor. Spent an hour at the *Leader* Office, among Eastern papers, and at 10.40

[247]Charles Townsend was born in Harrisonville, Ohio, in 1834, attended Ohio University, was a Union officer in the Civil War, and graduated at the Cincinnati School of Law in 1866. He was prosecuting attorney for Athens County for six consecutive years, a Republican member of the Ohio house of representatives, 1878–81, of the Ohio senate, 1888–89, and secretary of state of Ohio, 1881–83.

took train east; reached Mentor 11.35, where Harry met me and drove me home. All well.

SATURDAY, 28. Worked on letters, telegrams, and farm until noon, when I drove Crete, Harry and Jimmie to Painesville, and at 2 P.M. addressed a large audience in Childs' Hall. Spoke two hours, my voice holding out well. We took tea at Horace Steele's and drove home at seven.

This makes my tenth speech during the week, five of them in the open air.

Hon. F. Thorp spoke at the Town Hall in Mentor, but I was too tired to go.

SUNDAY, 29. At home resting and looking over the fields. Wrote a little and made arrangements for another week's absence. In the evening we drove to church and heard a good sermon by John Encell, who was my school mate at Hiram 27 years ago. His wife (née Jennie Gardner) was a member of the Greek class which recited to me nearly two years.

Retired at 10 P.M.

MONDAY, 30. Worked on farm matters and on mail until noon, when Crete and I went to Cleveland and did a considerable shopping. Came home on the 4.50 train, leaving Crete at Mentor, and went on to Ashtabula, where I spoke nearly two hours at the Opera House to a large audience. Good feeling among the people. Spent the night at Mr. Henry Fassett's. Several friends called before the meeting.

October

TUESDAY, 1. Took the 8 A.M. train to Rock Creek and stopped at the Hotel. Many friends called, some for consultation and some for questions on finance.

At half-past one, met a large outdoor audience, and spoke an hour and a half, effectively.

A Mr. Ensign[248] came from Warren and at half-past three we

[248]Erastus H. Ensign, a native of Connecticut, settled in 1844 in Trumbull County, Ohio, where he became a lawyer; he was prosecuting attorney of the

125

started in a carriage for Warren; stopped at Bloomfield for tea, and reached Warren (29 miles) at 7 P.M. Took a cup of tea at the Clifford House, and at eight met a fine audience in the City Hall and addressed them an hour and a half. Speech well received. Spent the night at Harmon Austin's.

WEDNESDAY, 2. Spent the forenoon in writing letters and visiting. Several gentlemen were at dinner at Austin's, among them a Mr. Harmon of San Francisco, chief of the Odd Fellows of the world.[249]

At 2 P.M. Judge E. B. Taylor, Harmon Austin and [I] drove to Youngstown and stopped at the Tod House. Many friends called, and not a few violent Greenbackers also.

In the evening (after taking tea at the Widow Wick's)[250] I spoke nearly two hours to the Opera House full of people—the largest indoor audience ever there, they say. I was conscious of a hostile element in the crowd and made special effort to capture their understandings. The antagonism helped me, and I think I made the most effective speech I have yet made in Ohio. Many callers at Hotel. Spent the night at Mrs. Wick's.

THURSDAY, 3. Spent the forenoon visiting friends, and among

---

county, 1861–65. From 1862 he resided in Warren, where, for a short period, he edited the Warren *Constitution.*

[249]John B. Harmon (1822–1899), a native of Ohio and a graduate of Yale, arrived in California by the Panama route in 1853, and established himself as a lawyer, with a practice largely confined to mining cases. Long active among California Odd Fellows, in 1876 he was elected deputy grand sire of the Grand Lodge of the United States; while holding that office he visited Australia and New Zealand during the spring and summer of 1878 and established the Grand Lodge of Australasia. On September 21, 1878, he was installed as grand sire, a position, as Garfield notes, that made him the chief of the Odd Fellows of the world.

[250]Maria (Griffith) Wick (1812–1887) was the widow of Caleb Wick (1795–1865), a prominent businessman in Youngstown, where Wick Avenue was named for him. Maria, his second wife, was the mother of a number of children, including Henry K. (1840–1916), known as "Nunky," who was associated with the development of the coal and iron industries in Youngstown, and Rachel, who married Robert W. Tayler (1812–1878), a prosecuting attorney, a member of the Ohio state legislature, state auditor, and from 1863–78, first comptroller of the U.S. Treasury.

others called on Stewart [Stuart] and Frank Siles [Stiles][251] and their sisters Eleanor and Laura, old Hiram friends.

Took dinner at the Tod House and then drove with Judge Taylor to Hubbard, thence to Coalburg and back to Hubbard. A long and interesting talk with Taylor on the way. In the evening, addressed a large out-door meeting, and after many calls of friends retired at 11; poor bed and insomnia.

FRIDAY, 4. Judge Taylor and I took the 7.40 A.M. train for Warren, where was a great parade of Odd-Fellows. At 10.30 D. C. Thompson, and W. T. Spear[252] drove with me to Bristol, 13 miles. We took dinner at Mr. Sager's[253] with a large company of friends, among them E. B. Wakefield and W. J. Ford and wife. At 2 address[ed] an audience of 2,500 people on the public square, then drove to Warren, and after tea at the Clifford House, Messrs. Ritezel and Wells drove me to Mineral Ridge (8 miles) where I spoke nearly two hours to a large audience. Denounced Tuttle's pretentions to debate with me, and answered sharply some stupid questions. Drove back to Warren, arriving at the Clifford at eleven, and spent the night.

SATURDAY, 5. Took the 8 A.M. train on the narrow gauge R.R. and reached Chardon at 11 A.M. Was taken to the house of J. O. Converse, where several friends met me at dinner. Soon a cold heavy rain began to fall, but at 2 P.M. the Opera House was filled and I spoke nearly two hours.

At five, took the train to Painesville, where Capt. C. E. Henry met me, and I went with him by the six P.M. train to Cleveland. Took tea at the Forest City House and after introduction by Judge Burke,[254] and a short speech by lawyer McKenny [McKin-

---

[251]During the 1850's these members of the Jairus Stiles family of Medina, Ohio, attended the Western Reserve Eclectic Institute. In the 1870's all four moved to Youngstown, where Stuart became an engineer and Frank a bookkeeper.

[252]William T. Spear, a Warren lawyer, was elected judge of the court of common pleas for the Fourth District in October, 1878, and served until 1886.

[253]William Sager, a Bristol farmer and local office-holder who was described as "a firm Republican."

[254]Stevenson Burke (1826–1904), a native of New York, was admitted to the bar in 1848. From 1862 to 1869 he was a judge of the court of common pleas

ney]²⁵⁵, I spoke an hour and a half in the Globe Theatre to a crowded house, very effectively.

After meeting, many friends called on me at the hotel.

Spent the night at Forest City House.

SUNDAY, 6. Took the 7.30 A.M. train to Mentor where I was met by Myron. Found Sister Hitty and Sister Mary and her husband at our house. Spent the day in visiting and resting. Read Manton Marble's History of the Presidential Fraud of 1876. A curious piece of stilted pamphleteering.²⁵⁶

I have made 19 speeches during the last fortnight and have not let down the standard of sound finance at any place. I am sure we have been gaining all the time. I cannot be mistaken that weakness on the rugged issues is weakness before the people.

Whether we have gained enough to carry the state remains to be seen. Our side have been forced, by stress of political weather, to stand up nearer to the perpendicular than usual. Retired early.

MONDAY, 7. Spent the day visiting with my sisters and attending to farm matters. Feel the weariness of the campaign far more than when I was speaking twice a day. In the evening the Disciple Church was crowded to overflowing and I spoke nearly two hours on the financial issues, closing the campaign. The speech was well received.

And now for the verdict. We shall not be able to recover from the Democratic Gerrymander all the districts they have taken

---

of the Fourth District. After leaving the court he moved to Cleveland and became one of the most prominent lawyers in Ohio, particularly as counsel for railroads. He also gained prominence as an organizer and owner of railroads. For nearly a quarter of a century he was president of the Cleveland and Mahoning Railroad.

²⁵⁵Henry McKinney (1828–1910), a native of Canfield, Ohio, was admitted to the bar in 1850 and practiced law for many years in Akron. Moving to Cleveland, he practiced law, 1873–80, was judge of the court of common pleas, 1880–88, and returned to the practice of law as a partner in the firm of Ranney and McKinney.

²⁵⁶*A Secret Chapter of Political History,* a pamphlet of 24 pages, contains a letter addressed by Manton Marble to the editor of the *New York Sun* on August 3, 1878. It was intended to counteract a belief or suspicion sometimes expressed "that the rightful President might have become the President in fact, except for some act or omission of his own."

from us; but we shall recover some, and make good gains on the state ticket. This is my hope and belief.

Visited an hour with sisters and mother, and retired at 11 P.M.

TUESDAY, 8.   Spent the forenoon in hurried work on farm affairs. Sent Myron to Solon with sisters and Marenus. Maj. Swaim came early and spent the forenoon with us, and at noon, he and Mother and Crete and I went to the Depot. I thence ran down to the town hall and voted, and then we took train to Cleveland. Shopped for an hour or two, got Mother on Atlantic train for Solon, and the rest of us went to Dr. Robison's to supper.

At 7.20, took Swaim to the train for Chicago. Spent an hour or two at Brainard's Hall to hear the Election returns. It comes in well and looks as though we have carried the state.

Crete and I spent the night at Dr. Robison's.

WEDNESDAY, 9.   Spent the forenoon in shopping and looking into the question of chopping my coarse fodder and cooking it by steam, mixing ground feed with it. Nothing but the cost prevents me trying the experiment, and I may yet conclude to do so.

At noon we went to James Mason's and took dinner. At 2 P.M. Crete and I took the Pittsburgh train at the Euclid St. Station en route for Washington to look after the repairs of our Washington home. The returns show we have carried the state ticket and at least nine Congressmen.

Greenbackery and Democratic apostasy on the question have received a staggering blow. I think it has ruined Senator Thurman's Presidential hopes.

Supper at Wellsville. Sleeping car at Pittsburgh.

THURSDAY, 10.   Arrived in Washington at 8.50 A.M. and found our house in the midst of confusion with two weeks' work yet to be done. Bathed and dressed while Mary White got us breakfast. We spent the day in directing further improvements and selecting paper for the Dining Room and Library. Considerable additional expense is necessary to put it in good order. Several friends called. We retired early, sleeping in Mother's room, after taking tea in the parlor.

FRIDAY, 11.   Spent a very busy day in house affairs. Agreed

129

to have several floors stained and shellac[k]ed, the two upper halls painted, and the ceilings of papered rooms kalsomined. Visited the Departments on business, made a few calls, and received many during the day and evening. Daniel and Mary are keeping us. Late in the evening determined to paper lower hall, and bay window room on second story, and selected the paper.

Prices: paper for Dining Room, dado and frieze and paper and frieze for library, $55. Paper and frieze for lower hall, $14. Ditto for bay room second story, $9. Picture moulding, all put on, 12 cents per foot.

Painting as per mem., by Spalding, $71, including shellac[k]-ing floors.

Called at Mr. Riddle's and got copy of *History of Geauga and Lake Counties.*

Retired at 10 1/2.

SATURDAY, 12. Riddle's sketch of my live [life] in the *History* referred to is the best that has yet been written. His criticisms of my character are revelations of myself to myself, and I think in the main are correct.[257]

Spent three hours in errands for friends, and completing further details of repairs of house. At five Rose came and I dictated a large number of letters.

Crete spent part of the evening reading *The Sun Maid,* which delights her very much. Riddle called while I was out, and she said not a word about his sketch; but when he had gone, she wrote him a beautiful note in regard to it.

Retired at half-past ten.

SUNDAY, 13. After breakfast Col. Rockwell called. At ten, went by appointment to Senator Matthews' to see Washington McLain [McLean] of Cincinnati in reference to the promotion of Gen. Hazen.[258] Returned and found Rose awaiting me. Signed the

---

[257]See n. 186 above.

[258]After the Civil War, in which he attained the rank of major general, William B. Hazen became a colonel in the regular army. During the following years he served mostly on the frontier and without promotion. His failure to be promoted

letters he had written out and dictated 30 more. Rose took dinner with us, a pleasant time in the parlor. Gen. Schenck and Judge James called. At 3 Washington McLean came and we took in Senator Matthews and drove to the Soldiers' Home and called on the President and Mrs. Hayes. A full talk in reference to Gen. Hazen. Home at 5. Tea with Crete. Riddle called and spoke enthusiastically of Crete's letter about his sketch.

In the evening, I called on Hale and Scofield, on H. St. (Chandler's).

Home at 9.30. Wrote and visited with Crete. She has finished *The Sun Maid* and is delighted with it.

MONDAY, 14.   More last words in getting ready to leave. Rose came, and I dictated some letters and gave final orders in reference to repairs. At 10.10 A.M. Crete and I took the train for Harrisburg. On the way read in second volume of *Life and Letters of George Ticknor.* Reached H. at 2.30 P.M. and were met by Senator Cameron and wife, and taken to their residence on the river bank. At 3.30, we (Senator C. and wife and Crete and I) drove to his farm about three miles out of town and spent an hour amid its fine views and pleasant grounds. Returning, took dinner and at 7.30 addressed a very large audience in the City Court House.

A large party followed us home to Senator Cameron's, where I was called out by a Serenade. At 11 P.M. the Senator drove us to the Depot, where we took the train for the West.

TUESDAY, 15.   Awoke on the western slope of the mountains, and at 8.10 reached Pittsburgh. At Senator Cameron's request, the train on the Erie and Pittsburgh train [Railroad] had been held forty minutes for us, and we at once went on board and at 3.30, arrived in Erie and stopped at the Reed House. Many prominent

---

is in part attributable to his outspoken criticisms of army administration and of the abuses of post traderships. Not until late 1880 did President Hayes, at Garfield's urging and against the wish of General Sherman, appoint Hazen chief signal officer with the rank of brigadier general. Hazen attended the Western Reserve Eclectic Institute briefly before entering West Point in 1851. His wife was the daughter of Washington McLean, editor of the *Cincinnati Enquirer.*

citizens called. In the evening I spoke at the Court House an hour and a half to a very large audience, who appeared to receive my speech with interest and enthusiasm.

After a hot bath, at eleven P.M. we retired.

WEDNESDAY, 16. Friends called, and we had several pleasant interviews until 10 A.M., when we took the Lake Shore train for home, reaching Mentor at 12.31, and were met at the Depot by Myron and Jimmie. Found all well, but the usual heavy burden of mail and telegrams awaiting me. A very large number of requests for speaking.

I ought to have mentioned that during last week and this, the famous cipher dispatches of the Tilden Managers in Florida and South Carolina have been published and translated by the N. Y. *Tribune,* and have marked an era in the very curious history of American politics in 1876. It seems to end the career of several prominent Democrats. I suppose the dispatches were those obtained by Senator Morton's Committee, but have been neglected since his death.[259]

---

[259]In January, 1877, the Western Union Telegraph Company, in response to subpoenas, turned over to congressional committees a large mass of dispatches relating to the election of 1876, the great bulk of them going to the Senate Committee on Privileges and Elections, whose chairman was Oliver P. Morton. In due course most of the telegrams were returned to the company. Some, however, were withheld, and copies of about 400, about half of them in cipher, came into the Republican hands of Whitelaw Reid, editor of the *New York Tribune.* The *Tribune* succeeded in translating most of the cipher letters and on October 8, 1878, published a large number that had been sent by Democrats relative to the post-election situation in Florida, and on October 16 another series related to South Carolina. Many of the messages were to and from William Pelton, the nephew of Samuel J. Tilden, who at the time was living with Tilden. It was clear from the dispatches that bribery of officials in the two states was contemplated by Democrats as a means of securing the electoral votes for Tilden—although their evil designs did not come to fruition. The publication of the telegrams produced a sensation, coming as it did in the midst of the political campaign. In a statement published in the papers on October 18, Tilden disclaimed any prior knowledge of the missives. In January, 1879, the House directed the Potter Committee to look into the matter. At about the same time the *Tribune* published its story and telegrams related to South Carolina, Florida and Oregon in a forty-four page pamphlet entitled *The Cipher Dispatches.* The Democratic majority on the Potter Committee

THURSDAY, 17. A very cold rainy day, in contrast with the charming weather we have had for the last fortnight. Answered many letters and telegrams and ran over farm affairs. In the evening E. V. Smalley, Editor *Cleveland Herald,* [260] came and spent the night. He thinks I have made the most effective speeches of any Republican in the country. Dr. Robison came and spent part of the evening.

FRIDAY, 18. Smalley staid until noon. Spent most of the time visiting, and giving him an outline of the comparison between the present epoch, and that which followed the panic of 1837, showing that the Republicans now occupy ground similar to that of the Democracy of 1837 to [18]44, and the present Democracy similar to that of the Whigs of the former period. In the afternoon, Dr. Robison, Jimmie, Crete and I, went to Painesville shopping and came back in the rain. Examined the language of the deeds given by Geo. and Jas. Dickey granting land to the Cleveland and Painesville R.R. Company, so far as it relates to the maintenance of a fence, and found it as follows: "The grantor also agrees to build and sustain a good fence on both sides of said strip, the entire length of said land" and then proceeds to bind the grantor, his heirs and assigns to warrant and defend the title to the land sold. This clearly made the maintenance of the fence binding only upon the Dickeys. It now falls upon the R. R. Company, not upon me.

---

condemned the actions of the Democrats involved in the wrong-doing but could find no evidence of the involvement of Tilden or the Democratic national committee in the exchanges. The Republicans viewed the disclosures as offsetting any political capital accruing to the Democrats as a result of the Potter Committee's investigation of Republican activities in Louisiana and South Carolina. When the committee majority, in March, 1879, reported its conclusion that Tilden and Hendricks had been the real choices of a majority of presidential electors in 1876, the country received it calmly. In addition to the *Tribune* publications, see *House Miscellaneous Documents,* No. 31, Part 4, 45 Cong., 3 Sess., Serial 1865, *House Reports,* No. 140, 45 Cong., 3 Sess., Serial 1866, and Harry Barnard, *Rutherford B. Hayes and His America,* pp. 474–478.

[260]Eugene V. Smalley was briefly associated with the *Cleveland Herald* during this period. The Cleveland directory, 1878–79, lists him as secretary of the Herald Publishing Company; he does not appear in later directories.

Home evening.

SATURDAY, 19. Spent nearly the whole day in answering letters and telegrams and preparing to leave for Michigan early Monday morning. Many people called.

I spent some time with farm affairs, and also consulted Mr. [Oscar L.] Loomis (carpenter) in reference to some enlargement and repairs of our house here. I greatly desire to improve it, but fear it will incur an expense beyond my means.

The storm of yesterday reached over into today, but died out before night.

SUNDAY, 20. A bright day. We went to church and heard a very long, dry and profitless sermon by E. H. Hawley of Cleveland. Geo. W. Steele and family drove out and spent the afternoon.

In the evening, after tea, talked with the children half an hour on the origin of the earth and developement of life. I tried to give them such a view as children can understand, and as well give them some largeness of thought.

Wrote letters until 9 P.M. and retired.

MONDAY, 21. Arose at half-past 3 A.M., awakened Jimmie. Myron drove us to the Depot, and at 4.15 we took the train to Cleveland. Went to the Forest City House and took breakfast, and at seven o'clock we took the western train. On the way I read two manuscript chapters of Gen. Upton's forthcoming military history of the U. S. His citations of authorities to prove the state sovereignty and disloyal spirit of Mass. and Conn. surprise me by their completeness.[261] I have never seen them before. Reached Toledo at 10.45 A.M. and at 11 took the Flint and Père Marquette R. R. Found Prof. Monroe and Gen. Warner[262] on board. At Monroe Junction we were joined by W. N. Hudson,[263] Editor

[261]Reference is to the War of 1812.

[262]Sidney S. Warner (1829–1908), for many years president of the First National Bank in Wellington, Ohio, and a member of one of the largest cheese companies in the state, was a Republican member of the state legislature, 1862–65, and state treasurer, 1866–72. Although he was called "General" he had had no military connections. See entry for August 25, 1879.

[263]William N. Hudson, a native of Ohio, where Garfield had known him, was on the staff of the *Cleveland Leader* before joining the *Detroit Advertiser and Tribune*

of Detroit *Post and Tribune,* who with his stenographer were going to attend my meeting. Reached Flint at 3.30. Many calls. In the evening spoke an hour and a half at Fenton Hall. Speech reported in full. Made some new points. Asa Cole[264] of Port Huron came to see me. Jimmie and I passed the night at the hotel.

TUESDAY, 22. In the morning many friends called, and Mr. Bostwick, late of Geauga County, drove me through the town. We called on Col. Thompson, who has a remarkable Shakespearean library.[265] This place was the home of Gov. Crapo,[266] father of the present Representative from Mass. of that name.

At 10 we took the train via Lansing to Charlotte, and thence, after 40 minutes' delay, took the Grand River Valley R. R. and arrived at Grand Rapids at 4.10 P.M. L. W. Heath,[267] (formerly

---

(later *Post and Tribune*). His brother, James F. (1846–1915), was an Ohio journalist and author. The *Post and Tribune* (October 23) printed Garfield's Flint speech in full in a one page supplement, which it offered for distribution singly or for newspaper supplements at seventy-five cents a hundred.

[264]Asa Cole, son of Garfield's friend, Edmond Cole, was U.S. inspector of steamboat boilers in Port Huron.

[265]Edward H. Thomson (1810–1886), a native of New England, was brought to the United States as a child and became a lawyer, practicing for several years in Buffalo, New York. In 1837 he moved to Michigan and in the following year settled and began practicing law in Flint. He was prosecuting attorney of Genesee County, 1845–46, a member of the Michigan senate, 1848–49, and of the house of representatives, 1859–60, and held several other public offices, including the mayoralty of Flint. During the Civil War he was on the state military board. In 1880 he was the Democratic candidate for lieutenant governor. He had, it was claimed, "the largest private Shakespearean library on this continent." After his death the collection was purchased for the University of Michigan.

[266]Henry H. Crapo (1804–1869), a native of Massachusetts, moved to Flint in 1856, where he became a lumber manufacturer and dealer. He was mayor of Flint, a member of the state legislature, and governor, 1865–69. Garfield has a reference to his son in the entry for March 2, 1876.

[267]Lewis W. Heath (1837–1911), a native of Ashtabula County, Ohio, and a student at the Western Reserve Eclectic Institute during Garfield's time, went to Michigan in 1857, where he taught school until the outbreak of the Civil War. He served in the Union army, 1861–63, attaining the rank of captain. In 1867 he settled in Grand Rapids, where, at the time of Garfield's visit, he was a hatter and furrier. It is said that he made the hat that Garfield wore at his inauguration and

a Hiram student) and several other friends met me at the station and took me to the Morton House. Judge Williams,[268] Judge Stone,[269] and many others called. In the evening the Opera House was crowded, and I spoke 2 1/2 hours. I would not have so far exceeded the bounds of reason, but for the demands of the audience to go on. Several old friends called at the close. Brother Thomas came and his son. I did not dare drive 12 miles in the sharp air, after speaking, and so remained at the hotel.

WEDNESDAY, 23. After breakfast L. W. Heath and Judge Stone drove me around the town, and at 10 A.M. Heath drove Jimmie and me via Grandville to my Brother Thomas' in Jamestown, Ottawa County. Arrived at half-past twelve. Spent two hours and a half visiting with Thomas and his family. Went over his farm and looked into his affairs. At three he and his wife and son James drove us to Byron Station.[270] Called on Aunt Calista on the

---

on the morning he was shot. He was long a member of the Republican state committee of Michigan, and was elected to fill the vacancy on the national committee created by the death of Zachariah Chandler in 1879. On October 5, 1880, he spoke briefly at a campaign rally in Painesville, Ohio, on the character of Garfield. In 1881 he was appointed a postal inspector, a position he held for several years.

[268]William B. Williams (1826–1905), a native of New York, moved to Allegan, Michigan, in 1855, where he practiced law. He was a judge of probate, a member of the state legislature, a Republican member of the U.S. House of Representatives, 1873–77, and state railroad commissioner, 1877–83. It was he, and not Alpheus Williams, to whom Garfield referred in the entry for December 11, 1876.

[269]John W. Stone (1838–1922), a native of Ohio who settled in Michigan in 1856, was a state circuit judge, 1873–74, and 1890–1909, a Republican member of the U.S. House of Representatives, 1877–81, and justice of the state supreme court, 1909–22.

[270]Thomas Garfield and his wife were living in Jamestown Township, Ottawa County, about sixteen miles from Grand Rapids, on an eighty acre farm that they had acquired in 1867. Their two surviving children, James A. and Florence, were now grown; James A. was said to resemble his uncle strongly. Many years after Garfield's visit Thomas recalled it to a visitor: "Only three years before he was killed he came to spend the day with me here, coming down from Grand Rapids, where he made a speech in Powers' Opera House, and he was just the same old 'Jim' as ever. He sat in the doorway there, beside you, munching maple sugar, petting the cat and talking over old times." *Grand Rapids Herald,* August 20, 1910.

way.[271] Jimmie and I took the train at 5 P.M. Visited with several persons on the cars, among them Gen. Pritchard,[272] and reached Elkhart at 9.30. In 40 minutes were on the through train East.

THURSDAY, 24.   Awoke early, and finished M. L. Scudder's little book *Almost an Englishman* [1878]. It is a charming story and gives a new and wise impulse to patriotism. It makes me want to deliver a lecture on the absurd tendency of some Americans to ape foreign manners.

Reached Cleveland at 7 A.M. Breakfast at Forest City House. Calls and business until 11.15 when we took the train to Mentor. Walked home and found all the family away except Abe, who was delighted to see us. Very lonesome until the light of the household returned at five.

Mail and farm affairs until evening. Father Rudolph came home with Crete.

FRIDAY, 25.   Spent the day in overlooking the farm and planning repairs to the farm house to be made during the winter. I am brought near to the verge of my financial ability to meet expenditure, but I think it better to use rather than accumulate until the day for enjoyment is past, and so if I can, I shall make the little cottage better fitted to its sweet mistress and light. In the evening wrote letters, and made ready to start for New York tomorrow morning.

I often wonder how long this power to do muscular work in the field of public life will remain to me. I have frequently a rheumatic reminder that I am not a very young man any longer.

SATURDAY, 26.   After an early breakfast, Myron drove me to

[271]Calista Boynton, half sister of Garfield's father and sister of Amos Boynton, moved from Ohio to Byron, Michigan, with her first husband, Joseph Skinner, in 1854.

[272]Benjamin D. Pritchard (1835–1907), a native of Portage County, Ohio, attended the Western Reserve Eclectic Institute before settling in Michigan in 1856, where he became a lawyer. He became widely known at the close of the Civil War, when, as commander of the 4th Michigan Cavalry Regiment, he participated in the capture of Jefferson Davis and his party, for which he was breveted brigadier general. In 1870 he organized the First National Bank of Allegan and was its president for many years. He was elected state treasurer in 1878.

Painesville where I took the 8.20 A.M. train east. On the way, read Hinsdale's new book on *The Jewish Christian Church.* [273] It exhibits his usual style and habit of thorough scholarship and strong thinking. At 4 P.M. reached Rochester N.Y., where I was met by Chas. E. Fitch and J. T. Pingree[274] (Williams College friends) who took me to Fitch's house. At 6, he gave a dinner to twelve prominent gentlemen who were invited to meet me. At half-past seven I went to the Mayor's office where many citizens were introduced. At 8 P.M. addressed a large audience in the City Hall. I spoke nearly two hours effectively except that I was annoyed by an echo in the hall which made articulation difficult and brought on hoarseness. Spent the night at Fitch's. He is the Editor of the *Rochester Democrat and Chronicle.* [275]

SUNDAY, 27. Spent the morning pleasantly at Fitch's, who has a very bright family.

At 10 Judge Danforth[276] came and drove us to the Water Works and various parts of the city. It is singular, how universal the feeling is that a public man wants to be driven around interminable streets, in order to be entertained. I enjoy it in a moderate degree when the weather is fair, but today I am tired and the are [air] is raw, and though I had pleasant companions and saw fine places, I would have preferred to rest and lounge in Fitch's fine library.

At two, my classmate John T. Pingree and wife came and dined with us and we had a pleasant college reunion. At 5 1/4 P.M. I took the train and at 8 reached Syracuse, where I was met by Hon. Frank Hiscock and driven to his fine residence, where I passed a restful night.

---

[273]See Vol. II, p. 199, n. 116.

[274]John T. Pingree (1835–1883), a native of Salem, Massachusetts, graduated at Williams College in 1856, and practiced law, mostly in Auburn, New York, for twenty-five years.

[275]The paper welcomed Garfield in a laudatory editorial on October 26 and reported his complete speech on October 28.

[276]George F. Danforth (1819–1899), a Rochester lawyer, was elected in 1878 associate justice of the state court of appeals and served, 1879–89. His son, Henry G. Danforth (1854–1918), was a Republican member of the U.S. House of Representatives, from New York, 1911–17.

MONDAY, 28. Spent the forenoon in reading and sketching the outline of a new plan of speech for tonight. I tire of following the old line so long. Read a large portion of Curtis' life of Webster,[277] especially that which relates to the period between 1837 and 1843, while the Whig party was behaving as the Democracy now are on finance.

In the afternoon drove two or three hours and came back to dinner at 4 with a large party at Hiscock's.

In the evening spoke at the Opera House to a crowded audience. My new plan of speech suited me quite well; and will in time work itself into a fine speech. It is as yet a little raw. There was much enthusiasm. Spent the night at Hiscock's.

TUESDAY, 29. Spent the forenoon driving with Gen. Leavenworth,[278] late M.C., and in making calls. The speech of last night seems to have made a good impression. Lunch at Hiscock's, and at 1 P.M. took train via Cortland to Ithaca, where I was met by Pres. A. D. White of Cornell University and driven to his house. After tea, he drove me to the hotel in the city, where many citizens called. On the way to the hall I met Brown, my Sandy Valley Scout, whom I had not seen for years.[279] Hall very much crowded. Spoke two hours and a half. Extravagant compliments. Very strong approval from Pres. White. Went back to his house, and we talked till an hour past midnight.[280] His recent journey

[277]George Ticknor Curtis, *Life of Daniel Webster,* 2 vols. (1870).

[278]Elias W. Leavenworth (1803–1887), a Syracuse businessman, was mayor of Syracuse, a member of the state legislature and secretary of state of New York before serving as a Republican member of the U.S. House of Representatives, 1875–77. His military title was earned in the state militia.

[279]Henry S. Brown ("Harry") was associated with Garfield on the canalboat *Evening Star* in 1848. During Garfield's campaign in eastern Kentucky, 1861–62, Brown appeared in camp, offered his services, and proved useful. In Ithaca Garfield found him impoverished; he died in Buffalo a few months later. Garfield, who received information about him from acquaintances in Buffalo and Ithaca, made some contribution to the alleviation of his wants. He appears as Bradley Brown in Edmund Kirke (James R. Gilmore), *On the Border,* and in Gilmore's campaign biography of Garfield, where he is identified as "Harry Brown—baptismal name, Henry S. Brown." See Vol. III, pp. 233–234, n. 35.

[280]In his *Autobiography* (1905), I, p. 188, Andrew D. White remembered the talk by the fire:

of two years in Europe has been rich in results of scholar[ly] work. His account of the method of religious instruction at Cornell strikes me as a good solution of that question for a college.

WEDNESDAY, 30. In the morning, a large number of students called on me. I was sorry I could not have spent the day at the University, but was compelled to leave on the 8.45 A.M. train. Reached Elmira at noon, where I met Senator Conkling and talked half an hour. He believes Hayes will be unseated by the Democrats if they get both houses of Congress. I do not. Conkling is very strong, a great fighter, inspired more by his hates than his loves; desires and has followers rather than friends. He will be of more service in a minority than a majority. In his long service he has done but little constructive work. He will be re-elected.

Reached Bath at 2.30 and was met by Conrad Gansevoort, who drove me to his house. His wife was Niel Fenn, once a music teacher at Hiram.

At six P.M. we went to dinner at Mr. Hull's, Editor of the

Having settled down in front of the fire in my library, we began to discuss the political situation, and his talk remains to me among the most interesting things of my life. He said much regarding the history of the currency question and his relations to it, and from this ran rapidly and suggestively through a multitude of other questions and the relations of public men to them. One thing which struck me was his judicially fair and even kindly estimates of men who differed from him. Very rarely did he speak harshly or sharply of any one, differing in this greatly from Mr. Conkling, who, in all his conversations, and especially in one at that same house not long before, seemed to consider men who differed from him as enemies of the human race.

On the right side of the front panel of the mantelpiece in the living room of the Andrew D. White house on the Cornell University campus is a bronze plaque engraved with this inscription:

AT THE SOUTH CORNER OF THE CHIMNEY
BEFORE THE FIRE UPON THIS HEARTH
SAT LATE INTO THE NIGHT OF
OCTOBER 29, 1878
JAMES A. GARFIELD
AFTERWARD
PRESIDENT OF THE UNITED STATES

Republican paper of Bath.[281] In the evening I spoke two and a half hours at the Court House, making the new speech more effective than ever before. Spent the night at Gansevoort's.

THURSDAY, 31. During the forenoon, Mr. and Mrs. G. drove me to several points where the view of the valley is very beautiful, also to the new Soldiers' Home not yet finished. At 11.45 I took the train for the East; and finished the reading of Gen. Upton's manuscript on the Military History of the War of 1812. The behavior of New England—especially of Mass., Vt., and Conn. —was very bad, almost rebellious.

On the way, formed the acquaintance of Miss Frances E. Willard of Illinois, who is a conspicuous public lecturer on temperance.[282]

Arrived at New York at 10.30 P.M. and stopped at the Brevoort House. Weary with work, and glad to have reached the end of campaign speaking for this year.

---

[281]H.S. Hull was editor of the *Steuben Courier,* which his father, Henry H. Hull (1816–1876) had founded and edited to his death.

[282]Frances E. Willard (1839–1898), a native of New York who lived for a time in Ohio as a girl, was a school teacher and administrator before she joined the temperance crusade in 1874. She soon embraced also the related cause of woman suffrage. In 1879 she was elected president of the National Women's Christian Temperance Union. In a letter to Garfield (June 10, 1880) she recalled their meeting in October, 1878, and appealed to him not to patronize the products of the vineyard, brewery and still during the campaign. Although she hailed his nomination and election and attended his inauguration, she was soon disappointed. On March 8, 1881, she visited the White House with a group of temperance women to present to Garfield a portrait of Lucy Webb Hayes and to express the hope that he would follow in the footsteps of that friend of temperance. "His manner," she wrote, "seemed to us constrained. He was not the brotherly Disciple preacher of old, but the adroit politician 'in the hands of his friends' and perfectly aware that the liquor camp held the balance of power." The ladies, "surprised and pained by his language," adjourned to a hotel where they held a prayer meeting in which they prayed "that total abstinence might be enthroned in the White House, that a chief magistrate might come unto the kingdom who would respond to the plea of the nation's home-people seeking protection for their tempted loved ones." See Frances E. Willard, *Glimpses of Fifty Years; the Autobiography of an American Woman* (1889), pp. 371–372.

November

FRIDAY, 1. Spent the day in shopping and calling on friends. Made some explorations of questions relating to furnishing our house in Washington. Had a long and very interesting visit with Hurlbert, Editor of the *New York World,* who has just returned from Europe. He is distressed at the aspect of the Caucasian race, because of the decay of religion and social order, and because of the accumulating signs of military migrations from China. His suggestions are very striking.

Dined with Senator Allison at the Brevoort, and at 9 P.M. in company with Blaine, took the train for Washington. Sat up till midnight with B. until he left the train at Philadelphia, when I retired.

SATURDAY, 2. Reached Washington at half-past six and found the house repairs badly delayed. Spent the day in hurrying up the workmen and sett[l]ing some unsettled questions about the finishing. Dined with Col. Rockwell, and at 7.15 P.M. took the Baltimore & Ohio train for the West, hoping to reach home tomorrow evening.

I believe I have done essential service to the cause of honest money and the public faith in this campaign. On the whole, I think my work has been more highly appreciated than ever before.

SUNDAY, 3. Awoke on the western slope of the mountains, train an hour and a half late. Breakfast at Benwood. Read Black's new novel, *McLeod of Dare,* [283] during the day.

At Newark, Ohio, dined, and met Archibald Campbell[284] of

[283]William Black, *Macleod of Dare,* 3 vols. (1878).

[284]Archibald W. Campbell (1833–1899), a native of Ohio, was taken to West Virginia as a boy. After graduating at Bethany College in 1852 and studying law, he began a long association with the *Wheeling Intelligencer,* a Republican paper of which he became editor and part owner. He also entered the iron manufacture, becoming president of the Benwood Iron Works. He was for a time chairman of the state Republican committee and in 1860 and 1880 a delegate to the party's national convention. In the latter year he received national attention when he (with two other West Virginia delegates) voted against a resolution of Roscoe Conkling that would have bound delegates in advance to support the nominee of the convention, and then defended his vote when Conkling sought to have the trio expelled. Garfield also won favorable comment by his defense of the West Virginians.

Wheeling, who rode with me to Shelby. Talked of the Caucasian and Chinese question. He speaks with enthusiasm of my work in the campaign.

Finding there is no train on the Lake Shore R. R. that will take me home tonight, I stopped at Shelby and finished Burke's new book, and read many chapters [of] *McLeod of Dare,* and spent the night.

MONDAY, 4.   Took the train at 4.45 and reached Cleveland at 7.10, and Painesville at 8.20, where Myron met me, and we reached home at 9.15, never so glad to get home again, and to feel that I was not to hurry away to speak.

Spent the day in reading my mail and enjoying home. Family all well and happy to see me. I can not do justice to the gratitude I feel for this love, rest and peace.

TUESDAY, 5.   Took up farm affairs a little, wrote some letters, went to Willoughby, and in the evening spent some time in discussing with Mr. Loomis plans for repairing the house here during the coming winter. The house is too small for our wants and ought to be enlarged. I am troubled about my ability to bear the expense of it now. I must take account of my means and see if I can carry the load.

Capt. Henry came on the evening train and spent the night.

I wrote a long letter to Gen. Grosvenor making suggestions in reference to the preparations for next year's campaign.[285]

Elections in most of the states today. We shall see the fruits of our work and I expect good results.

WEDNESDAY, 6.   The morning papers bring news of great Republican victories almost everywhere in the North, and a nearly solid Democratic South. The result in the North is even better than I hoped. It answers the solid South by a vote which would give us the Presidency. This election changes the face of the political sky and gives an immense impulse to business

---

[285]Charles H. Grosvenor (1833–1917), a Union officer in the Civil War, 1861–65, was breveted brigadier general in 1865. He was a Republican presidential elector in 1860 and served as speaker of the Ohio house of representatives, 1876–78. As a member of the Republican state committee he had asked Garfield to put in writing, for presentation to the committee, his "views and ideas" of what Ohio Republicans ought to do to win the next election.

by adding confidence to the sanctity of the public faith.

Spent the forenoon with Capt. Henry and the farm, and at noon went to Cleveland. Settled bills and shopped until 4.50, when I returned home. Myron met me at the Depot. A raw cold night, reminding me of Black's description of the winter climate of north Scotland about Mull.

THURSDAY, 7. Election news even better than yesterday's indication. The vote this year would have given the Republicans 57 majority of electoral votes.

Letters and farm affairs. Still suffering from rheumatism in my right shoulder, which attacked me a fortnight ago. It is difficult for me to realize that my best physical days are past.

Am housing apples and roots, and preparing to put the farm into winter quarters. Loomis came in the evening and discussed plans and cost of house repairs. After he left Crete and I continued the discussion and drafting until midnight.

FRIDAY, 8. Went with Dr. Robison to Kirtland and Willoughby to look after mill feed for our stock.

In the afternoon wrote and read, and what is unusual for me, slept an hour.

In the evening Mr. and Mrs. Aldrich[286] and Mr. Drake[287] called and made us a very pleasant visit.

---

[286]Edmund T. C. Aldrich (1827–1904), whose farm was adjacent to and east of Garfield's, moved to Mentor from New York State in 1866 with his wife, children and father (his father died in 1876). In addition to farming, he sold fire insurance. He was active in local and regional affairs as a leader of the Grange, mayor of Mentor, 1870–72, member of the town council, president of the board of education, member of the Republican central committee of the nineteenth congressional district, and in other ways. He did not succeed in winning his party's nomination for the legislature in 1879. A neighbor whom Garfield held in high regard, he helped during the campaign of 1880 to look after the many visitors at Lawnfield. His wife, Emily Fisher, died in 1897. In 1900 he sold his farm to Mrs. James Mason as a home for her daughter Belle and son-in-law Harry Garfield. At present (1980) the house, enlarged by architect Abram Garfield, is the property of Faith Lutheran Church of Mentor. For a sketch of Aldrich's life with excerpts from his diary, see Louise Aldrich Windecker, "Diary of E.T.C. Aldrich," *The Historical Society Quarterly* (Lake County, Ohio), Vol. 16, No. 4 (November, 1974), pp. 309–313.

[287]M.J. Drake, a farm hand.

Am in much doubt about house repairs on the ground of cost.

SATURDAY, 9. Soon after breakfast, in company with Mr. Aldrich, drove to Painesville and nearly to Fairport in search of cows. I wish to buy a few to eat my surplus fodder. I desire to buy those that are just beginning to give milk, thinking it may be more profitable than summer cows.

Home again at noon, and spent the afternoon and evening [bringing] up my arrears of correspondence, which is still heavy.

SUNDAY, 10. Attended church and heard a very suggestive discourse by Dr. Robison. At two P.M. the Doctor and wife took dinner with us and after dinner visited with us several hours.

Commenced reading for the first time, Dickens' *Hard Times.* The sense of restfulness which home brings is most grateful and I am enjoying it to the full.

MONDAY, 11. Busy with farm affairs and letters. In the forenoon Hon. F. Thorp came and visited me until noon. A rainy, raw day. Spent the day and evening at home, and with the family celebrated the 20th anniversary of our marriage, an event that has brought more and higher happiness into my life than any other human event. The eventful years which have since passed, have deepened, strengthened and sweetened the ties solemnized amidst some doubts and hesitations which surrounded Crete and me on the 11th November 1858.

TUESDAY, 12. Letters and farm affairs in the forenoon, and in the afternoon went to Willoughby to settle some accounts and look after cows. A cold raw day.

Men began to grade south-west corner of barnyard. I am determined to make it a dryer and better drained yard than it has yet been.

Corn husking is going forward satisfactorily. The price of farm products is steadily falling, and I must reduce my expenses to the lowest practical point.

In the evening read aloud to the children Carlyle's Life of Frederick the Great,[288] which I am glad to find Harry has taken up with much zeal. Fi[ni]shed the first volume.

---

[288]Thomas Carlyle, *History of Friedrich II of Prussia, Called Frederick the Great,* 6 vols. (1858–1865).

WEDNESDAY, 13. Drove with Dr. Robison during the forenoon looking after cows. Went to Geo. Blish's[289] and called at several other places. Spent the afternoon in looking after the grading of the barnyard and the construction of the two sheds in the southwest and northwest corners of barnyard. Also wrote some letters, and with Crete and Mother went to Aldrich's to tea. A pleasant party. Home at 8 and wrote and read until bed time.

THURSDAY, 14. Went to Cleveland on the morning train and spent the day among the steam engines and feed cutters. Settled some bills and made some progress towards perfecting arrangements for cutting and steaming food for cattle. Home on the evening train. One shed was finished today, and I am at last in a fair way to realize my purpose to house my manure.

Letters and reading in the evening. Have abandoned for the present my purpose to overhaul and enlarge farm house.

FRIDAY, 15. Soon after breakfast Mr. Hawks[290] of Painesville came with his bird dogs, and he and Dr. Robison and I spent the day hunting. At 2 P.M. Crete, Mother and Martha and all our children took dinner at the Doctor's. The hunting continued until dark. On the whole a good deal of travel, and no great amount of luck—8 quails, one rabbit and an owl.

Home evening very tired.

SATURDAY, 16. The day has given us uncertain weather and catching work on the farm. Barnyard grading was completed, work on second shed begun, field east of lane on the hill nearly finished plowing. Five loads corn hauled from ram lot, and the husking nearly finished.

---

[289]George Blish, who was at the Western Reserve Eclectic Institute for a year during Garfield's time there, was now living on the farm where his father had been a pioneer. His wife was a member of the Dickey family from whom Garfield bought his farm. He later moved into Mentor, where he became mayor.

[290]James D. Hawks was assistant engineer, Lake Shore Division, Lake Shore and Michigan Southern Railroad.

I have not been very well; have written some, gone over farm some and finished Dickens' *Hard Times.* A powerful story in which he gets at some of the serious difficulties of the labor problem, but does little in the way of solving it.

The Gradgrind school of teachers is finely touched off, Sissy [Cissy] Jupe showing more real power of human sympathy and influence that [than] all the nabobs of the book.

Writing in the evening.

SUNDAY, 17.   Home in the forenoon. At one P.M. Mother and I attended the funeral of old Mr. Marshall, formerly of Solon, but for several recent years a resident of this place. A. B. Green preached the sermon. Wrote and read in the evening.

MONDAY, 18.   Barnes came and moved the hog pen from its place in the old orchard to the new orchard, across the lane from the new cow barn, where I shall convert it into a building for cutting fodder and grinding corn by steam. I have engaged an engine from Dec. 1st to April 1st at $6 per month.

In the afternoon, Dr. Robison and I went to Willoughby shopping.

Letters in the evening.

TUESDAY, 19.   Busy with farm affairs during the forenoon. At noon Dr. Streator and wife came to visit us. At 2 P.M. they and Dr. and Mrs. Robison dined with us, and celebrated my 47th birth day. At last, it is a clear case of middle life, a little past, as my rheumatic shoulder reminds me. The day and evening have been too full of engagements to enable me to note those reflections which the occasion brought. In the evening Crete and I went to Dr. Robison's and visited with them and the Streators until 10.30, when we came home.

WEDNESDAY, 20.   In the forenoon I drove to Painesville and bought more lumber to finish off my engine house and hog-pen. Paid taxes and insurance, and hurried back to find Mr. and Mrs. A. B. Green, Mr. and Mrs. W. A. Lillie, and Mr., Mrs. and Miss Encell at dinner. Spent the afternoon with them.

Barless building hog-pen, and men hauling sand from the brow of the hill in the lane, both to grade the hill and fill lane yard.

Letters in the evening.

THURSDAY, 21. Crete and I went to Painesville shopping, and closing up accounts with people for the season. Also made some calls.

On my return several people called. In the evening the children had the closing meeting of their debating club—quite a spirited affair with a dozen older people present. Jimmie presided, and the young ones did well. We made it also the occasion to celebrate Abe's birthday. He is six years old, and appeared in his first pants.[291]

FRIDAY, 22. Spent the day in writing letters and pushing farm affairs. Tore out the inside of the old building and commenced converting it into an Engine House. Men still hauling sand to fill up the lane yard.

Wrote letters till late in the evening.

SATURDAY, 23. Crete, Mother, Abe, Irvin and I, took the 7.44 train to Cleveland. Left Mother at Dr. Boynton's, and the rest of us went to Solon and spent the day and night with Sisters Mary and Hittie. On the train out from Cleveland we found Phebe and Lizzie Clapp, and the former staid with us at Mary's.

During the afternoon, Crete and I and the boys went to Hittie's.

SUNDAY, 24. Took the 8 A.M. train for Garrettsville in company with Crete, Phebe and Lizzie. Reached Father Rudolph's at 9.30. Attended church and listened to a very small sized sermon.

Called at Hinsdale['s] and found he had just returned from Wadsworth. He and his wife went with me to Father Rudolph's and took dinner.

A very significant visit with Burke. The struggle of faith with reason is going on within him.

At 5.30, Gilbert [Rudolph] having driven us to Garrettsville, we took the train for Cleveland. At Solon the two boys came on,

---

[291]Noting this entry in the diary long after the event, Abram Garfield wrote this comment: "I remember the evening, was embarrassed when stood upon a chair in the dining room where the farm hands were eating supper."

and we all went to Dr. Boynton's on Euclid Avenue where, with the family, we spent the evening and night.

MONDAY, 25. Spent the forenoon shopping and settling accounts in Cleveland, and at 11.15 Crete and I with the two little boys, Abe and Irvin, took the train for Mentor where Myron met us. Spent the afternoon reading my mail and inspecting the progress of farm affairs, especially of the Engine House, which is now nearly ready for the engine and cutter and grinder.

TUESDAY, 26. Soon after breakfast Crete and I drove to Painesville and did some shopping, and settled a number of bills preparatory to leaving home. Took dinner at Horace Steele's and on the way home stopped at Mr. Bateham's.[292] Spent the evening in overhauling my papers and putting them in shape for leaving for Washington. Wallace Ford and his wife came and spent the night. Worked on farm affairs until 11 o'clock, when I went to Mr. Aldrich's to visit the village school and spoke a short time.

WEDNESDAY, 27. Spent the forenoon in settling with Northrup

---

[292]Michael B. Bateham (1813–1880), a native of England, came to the United States in 1825. After twenty years in Rochester, New York, during part of which he edited an agricultural paper, he moved to Columbus, where he founded, and for a decade edited, *The Ohio Cultivator.* He helped organize and was first secretary of the Ohio state board of agriculture. In 1863 he moved to Painesville, where he operated a small fruit farm, conducted a column, "Field and Garden," in the *Painesville Telegraph,* wrote for agricultural journals, and carried on his duties as secretary of the Ohio Horticultural Society. Just before the call mentioned in this entry Garfield had read a prize essay of Bateham's, "The Deterioration of Soils in Ohio," (*Annual Report of the Ohio State Board of Agriculture for . . . 1877* (1878). In the *Painesville Telegraph* (December 5, 1878) Bateham had this to say of Garfield: "He was desirous of learning by what means he could best increase the productiveness of his farm, the soil of which is of fair quality, but, like most others was somewhat deteriorated. We found the General quite intelligent in regard to the scientific principles of improved farming, and he is determined to be something more than a routine farmer." In the course of their conversation Garfield suggested that a committee of the local Grange devise and superintend a set of agricultural experiments, and indicated his willingness to do his share in respect to their cost and performance. Bateham's wife Josephine, who had conducted the "Ladies' Department" in *The Ohio Cultivator,* was interested in various reform movements, including temperance.

[Northcott] and closing up farm affairs, putting the library and house in order, shipping trunks to the depot, and at half-past twelve took the train for Cleveland. At one forty-five Mother and Harry joined us and we all took the train for Washington, by the way of Pittsburgh. Took supper at Wellsville and sleeping car at Pittsburgh. Ten of us on board. Mother and Martha, Mary McGrath, Crete and I and five children.

THURSDAY, 28.   Arrived at Washington at 9 o'clock. Found the house warm and breakfast ready. The repairs have been completed very slowly, but on the whole quite satisfactorily. Spent the day in unpacking and putting the house in order. A number of people called in the evening, among others the President and his wife and their son Rutherford.[293] He thinks Butler will be likely to force the Democrats to accept him as their candidate for the Presidency.

FRIDAY, 29.   Crete and I spent a large part of the day in selecting carpets and making the necessary purchases for the winter. Called at the Capitol and got a large mail. Arranged for having newspapers sent to me. People begin to call in considerable numbers. I am surprised to find that I have hardly given thought to public affairs for the last three weeks, but I must turn to such questions as soon as I get the house in order. Home in evening.

SATURDAY, 30.   Crete and I spent an hour in the morning in arranging assessments on my house and paying taxes for the year; also spent several hours in completing our purchases of furniture for the new rooms made in the wing by the addition. Rose came in the evening and I dictated a number of letters. Several persons called.

---

[293]Rutherford Platt Hayes (1858–1927) was born in Cincinnati, Ohio, attended the University of Michigan, graduated at Cornell University in 1880, and from 1882 devoted his career largely to library work, banking, and scientific farming. The latter he carried on in Asheville, North Carolina, where he acquired large land holdings and devoted much time to the development of Asheville as a resort and business center.

December

SUNDAY, 1. Spent most of the day in putting my books in their cases and getting the library in order. In the afternoon Lieut. Harber came and took dinner with us. My shoulder is still troublesome.

MONDAY, 2. Worked at my desk and in setting the house in order until half-past 11, when I went to the Capitol. The formal proceedings were the same as usual, except that Fernando Wood attacked the President's reference in his message to the Southern elections. As soon as the attack was made, I replied and the result was a lively debate which elicited a good deal of interest. It was a great mistake on Wood's part and showed unfavorably the animus of his party.[294] Home in the evening and continued work on house affairs.

TUESDAY, 3. Committee on Ways and Means in the morning. Nothing but formal work done. A short session of the House. In the evening dined with Hale of Maine at Wormley's. There were present Senators Blaine, Anthony, Burnside[295] and two or three other gentlemen. My shoulder still gives me much discomfort.

WEDNESDAY, 4. Worked at my desk until half-past ten, when I went to the Capitol to attend the meeting of the Committee on

---

[294]In a brief passage on the 13th, 14th, and 15th amendments, Hayes stated that throughout Louisiana and South Carolina, and in some congressional districts in other Southern states, the election record compelled one to conclude that Negroes had been deprived of their political rights. Wood denied the charge, saying that he failed to see "any disposition in the South to void or to annul in any regard the recent amendments to the Constitution," or any indication that Southerners were not as law-abiding as citizens elsewhere in the country. He interpreted Hayes's statement as an indication of vacillation in the administration's Southern policy and as evidence that the ultra wing of the Republican party controlled the President. Garfield criticized Wood for debating any portion of the President's message, said that the chief executive had a duty to call the attention of Congress to any irregularities, and expressed the hope that Democratic representatives would not stifle investigations of elections.

[295]Ambrose E. Burnside (1824–1881), a Union general in the Civil War and onetime commander of the Army of the Potomac, was a Republican member of the Senate from Rhode Island, 1875 to his death.

Rules to consider some resolutions in reference to the Yellow Fever.[296] Short session of the House. Returned home at two o'clock and spent the afternoon shopping with Crete. At 8 o'clock in the evening attended an assembly of members of the House at Foster's to make arrangements for transferring the Honest Money League from Chicago to this city and make it national. A curious phenomenon is presented in the fact that [the] Greenback Party shows more signs of activity since the election than before and seems to be bent on proselyting the people and increasing its strength. I should have added that in the morning I called on Dr. Baxter. He thinks my trouble is not rheumatism but irritation of the spine at the point where the nerves branch out to the right arm. He ordered a porous plaster on my back. Suffered much pain during the evening and night.

THURSDAY, 5.   Spent the morning in overhauling my correspondence with Duncan in regard to my Mobile and Ohio fee and wrote a full statement of the case to my classmate Knox of New York, requesting him to effect a settlement with Duncan, if possible.[297] Went to the House soon after 12. At one o'clock made a report from the Committee on Rules in reference to the Yellow Fever. Made a short speech and the resolution was adopted and the House adjourned.[298] Exercised for an hour or two until

[296]Louisiana, Tennessee and Mississippi were the worst sufferers from the great yellow fever epidemic of 1878. In New Orleans, where it began, more than four thousand persons died. In Memphis, where the suffering was most severe, more than half the population fled the city; nearly eighty percent of those remaining contracted the disease, and more than five thousand died. One of the Memphis victims was Jefferson Davis, Jr., only son of the former president of the Confederacy.

[297]Henry W. Knox recommended that Garfield accept a fee of $5,000 offered by William B. Duncan. Garfield did so and his check was forwarded by Duncan before the end of the month. See Vol. III, pp. 482–483, n. 124, in which the following should have appeared as the first line on page 483: pay interest due on first mortgage bonds, Duncan, Sherman and Company paid.

[298]On December 4, 1878, the Senate provided for a select committee of seven senators "to investigate and report the best means of preventing the introduction and spread of epidemic diseases, especially yellow fever and cholera, in the United States," and authorized it to sit with a similar House committee. On

dinner. In the evening Rose came and I dictated a large number of letters. During the day the carpet was put down in my library and the house begins to look in order.

FRIDAY, 6.   Spent the forenoon in hanging pictures in the library, and at one o'clock went with Crete to Mrs. Fassett's Art Gallery, where she sat for her picture in the large picture of the Electoral Commission. The Artist has made an excellent likeness of Crete and at the conclusion of the sitting, I sat for her a short time. I think the picture will prove to be a really wonderful work. Spent some time in settling bills. In the evening Smalley of the *Cleveland Herald* dined with us. Rose came and I dictated a number of letters. My shoulder is not troubling me so much, but the rheumatic pains wander about in my limbs seeking rest but finding none.

SATURDAY, 7.   A day full of miscellany, mainly devoted to house affairs.

SUNDAY, 8.   Crete, Mother and I attended church and listened to a sermon which had little juice in it.

Capt. Henry was here still. Wrote letters, and did more work in putting papers in order.

MONDAY, 9.   Short session of the House, and but little done. I am still a good deal troubled with rheumatism. The day has been full of miscellany. I see increasing signs of good feeling towards me. Many who doubted the soundness of my financial views are now heartily with me.

December 5, Garfield introduced the resolution mentioned in his entry for that day, providing for a joint committee of five representatives and four senators. Although this resolution was passed by the House, it was not adopted by the Senate. On December 9, the House established a committee similar to that of the Senate. Garfield was appointed a member. At the House committee's first meeting, subcommittees were appointed and a motion adopted to inform the Senate committee of "the willingness and readiness" of the House committee to meet with it. Between December 12, 1878, and February 12, 1879, Garfield refers to several "yellow fever" meetings; the "joint committee" meetings referred to are those of the two committees sitting together. On March 3, 1879, "an act to prevent the introduction of infectious or contagious diseases into the United States, and to establish a National Board of Health" became law—the result of the work of these committees.

Dined at John Jay Knox's, in 12th St., with Mr. Wheelock[299] of St. Paul and Messrs. White and Wight of the press.

TUESDAY, 10. The House has not yet got itself in order for much work, except on the appropriation bills. In the discussion of the Consular and Diplomatic Appropriation Bill, I took occasion to give an opening in the direction of political thought, to the effect that we cannot repeat the recent old issues in the old forms.[300] While I am in favor of debating the election outrages in the South, it should be on the new basis of affairs—i.e., after the tender of local self-government.

House repairs drag slowly. I have been the victim of tardy trades people, which appears to be a greater vice here than in Northern cities.

WEDNESDAY, 11. Desk at home until near noon, when I went to the Capitol. At one P.M. went to the Senate and heard Blaine on the Southern Elections.[301] It was a strong, carefull speech, so brief that it can all go by telegraph and will be more widely read than if it were longer. He ought to have strengthened his speech by contrasting the present conduct of the South with their profes-

[299]Joseph A. Wheelock (1831–1906), a native of Nova Scotia, was editor of the influential *St. Paul Daily Pioneer-Press.*

[300]The Consular and Diplomatic Appropriation Bill contained a proposal to reduce salaries of envoys and ministers to Great Britain, France, Germany, and Russia. In a speech opposing such reductions, Garfield said that "the man who attempts to get up a political excitement in this country on the old sectional issues will find himself without a party and without support. The man who wants to serve his country must put himself in the line of its leading thought, and this is the restoration of business, trade, commerce, industry, sound political economy, honest money, and honest payment of all obligations. . . . Now, among the most important things that lie in this direction is our foreign trade." He then spoke of the nation's expanding foreign trade, of the need for strong consulates to keep it expanding, and declared that the proposal before the House "cuts down deeply, strongly, savagely, unwisely" from the current salary levels set by the last Congress after extended debate.

[301]In support of his resolution calling for an investigation of recent elections, Blaine stressed the need "to place on record, in a definite and authentic form, the frauds and outrages by which some recent elections were carried by the Democratic party in the Southern States," and "to find if there be any method by which a repetition of these crimes against a free ballot may be prevented."

sions to Hayes, that if let alone, the Negro would be fully protected.

The House passed the Transportation Bill of Reagan, which I voted for with some hesitation.[302]

Home in the evening. Rockwell and Gilfillan and their wives spent the evening with us.

THURSDAY, 12. Departments in the morning. Committee of Ways and Means at 11. Resolution for adjournment over Holiday recess agreed upon. Plan of investigation of sugar tariff also agreed upon. In the House, the day was spent in discussing the Geneva Award.

Came home early and worked at my desk. Called on Clinton Rice who has had severe hemorrhage.

At 7 1/2 attended meeting of the House Committee on Yellow Fever. Home at 8 1/2. Crete and I called on the President and Mrs. Hayes, also at Gen. Schenck's.

Retired late, near 12.

FRIDAY, 13. Usual morning work. In the House the day was spent on the Geneva Award.[303]

In the evening I dined at Sec'y Evarts' with a large company —among them Gen. Sherman and Admiral Porter,[304] Senators Thurman and Blaine, Judge Hunt[305] of the Court of Claims, and

---

[302]Reagan's bill to regulate interstate commerce and to prohibit discriminatory practices by common carriers passed the House, 139–104, but died in the Senate. It was the forerunner of the Interstate Commerce Act of 1887.

[303]This is an error. The House acted on miscellaneous matters, then went into Committee of the Whole on the Private Calendar and discussed a bill to reimburse the College of William and Mary for property destroyed during the Civil War.

[304]David D. Porter (1813–1891) had a career in the U.S. Navy extending from 1829 to his death. During the Civil War he was advanced from commander to rear admiral without having been either captain or commodore. After the death of David Farragut in 1870, Porter succeeded him as admiral, thus becoming the highest ranking officer in the service. From 1877 he was head of the naval Board of Inspection. He was the author of a number of books, including *The Naval History of the Civil War* (1886). His home on H Street, N.W., was known for its hospitality.

[305]William H. Hunt (1823–1884), a native of South Carolina who received most of his education in New England, practiced law in New Orleans from the

Glenni W. Scofield. Blaine assailed the veracity of Julius Caesar as a Commentator. I defended. Evarts and Gen. Sherman concurred with me. Blaine thinks the numbers, etc., are greatly exaggerated.

SATURDAY, 14. At desk until 11 o'clock, when I went to the Treasury Department and went thence with Crete to the carpet store, thence to the Capitol and met with the Committee on Ways and Means to discuss a modification of the Revenue laws. In the House the day was consumed on the Geneva Award Bill. A great deal of passion is exhibited in the attacks on Insurance Companies but I believe the law is in their favor and shall so hope.[306]

At 7 P.M. Crete and I dined at Senator Allison's. Present, John Sherman and wife, Senator Morrill of Vt. and Miss Swan, ex-Senator Morrill of Maine, and Mrs. Grimes;[307] a pleasant party. At 10 we went to Mrs. Dahlgren's and attended the Literary Club. Home at 11 P.M.

SUNDAY, 15. A dreary day. At home. Wrote a sketch of the life

---

1840's to 1878. In 1876 he was elected attorney general of Louisiana but lost his position when the Democrats gained control of the state. In May, 1878, President Hayes appointed him associate justice of the U.S. Court of Claims. He served as justice until President Garfield appointed him secretary of the navy on March 5, 1881. In 1882 President Arthur appointed him minister to Russia, where he remained until his death. His son Gaillard (1862–1924), who became an intimate of the older Garfield boys, had a long career as U.S. civil servant and historian. He was chief of the Division of Manuscripts of the Library of Congress, 1909–17.

[306]The issue was whether the award money paid by Great Britain and now in the Treasury was in possession of the United States or in trust to insurance companies or private claimants. A majority of the Judiciary Committee submitted a bill which, its defenders argued, did not provide for distribution of the money to anyone, but established a procedure whereby claimants could sue in the Court of Claims, whose decisions could be appealed to the Supreme Court. Opponents of the bill held that it would give relief, not to the uninsured individuals whose property was destroyed by British-built cruisers, but only to the companies, for they alone, by their power to invoke the doctrine of subrogation, had a legal standing in court.

[307]Elizabeth Nealley Grimes, widow of James W. Grimes (1816–1872), a Republican member of the Senate from Iowa, 1859–69. Mary Nealley, her niece and the adopted daughter of Senator Grimes, married William Boyd Allison in 1873. The Allisons and Mrs. Grimes lived together in Washington. She died in 1890.

of Mrs. Hattie Drake Swensburg [Swensberg][308], who recently committed suicide at Grand Rapids.

Wrote letters and brought up my journal. Miss Ransom dined with us at two.

MONDAY, 16.   Attended the joint Committee on Yellow Fever at half-past ten o'clock. Some progress was made in getting the sub-committee in order and providing for the joint action of the House and Senate Committees. In the House the day was spent on the Geneva Award Bill.[309] In the evening Brother Joe Rudolph and Dr. Yeates came to visit us. Dictated letters. Went with the family to visit the new Skating Rink on New York Avenue.

TUESDAY, 17.   Very interesting meeting of the Committee on Ways and Means in relation to the duties on sugar. Sec'y Sherman, Solicitor French,[310] and Mr. James[311] of the Customs Dep't were before the Committee. The history of the Dutch Standard was given to the Committee; also the progress of the manufacture by the centrifugal process and the vacuum pan process; also, the frauds that had been committed on the Revenue by over-coloring

[308]Hattie (Drake) Swensberg (1845–1878), a native of Ohio, attended the Western Reserve Eclectic Institute and Oberlin College and taught a number of years in Michigan, New York and Ohio (she was at Central High School in Cleveland several years prior to her marriage in 1875). In a letter to Garfield, October 22, 1878, she invited him to stay at her home during his impending visit to Grand Rapids, Michigan, and made this comment: "The memory of my school days at Hiram and the interest in study which you awakened in me have been the sources of much happiness and profit all my life, and I can hardly realize that my faithful teacher and the successful statesman are the same."

[309]This is an error. After a morning hour the House devoted the entire day to business relating to the District of Columbia.

[310]Henry F. French (1813–1885) studied law at Harvard and practiced it in his native New Hampshire and in Boston. He was president of the Massachusetts Agricultural College for two years before its opening in 1867. He was assistant secretary of the treasury, 1876–85; one of his duties was the supervision of all work assigned to the Division of Customs. He was the father of sculptor Daniel Chester French (1850–1931), who had a studio in Washington at this time, and whose bust of Garfield was unveiled at Gallaudet College in 1883.

[311]Henry B. James, a native of England, was chief of the Customs Division of the Treasury Department.

sugar. Proposed correction of these abuses by the Polariscope was discussed. In the House further progress was made on the Geneva Award Bill. A bill for the deficiency in Postal Car service was before the House. I ought to make a speech on the Geneva Award vindicating my vote, which will be in favor of the majority bill, but there are so many personal interests that I dislike to join in the wrangle and ill-feeling that the discussion causes. Home in the evening, dictated letters. Called on Foster.

WEDNESDAY, 18. Meeting of the Yellow Fever Committee. I fear we are in danger of making ourselves ridiculous. It is a question of science to be handled by a town meeting. Even that can be done if the town meeting, bravely acknowled[g]ing its own ignorance, calls to its aid men who know. But in getting experts to aid us, our Committee seem bent on getting each a special friend appointed. Cases like this makes one doubt the town-meeting plan of government.

In the House the day was devoted to the Indian Appropriation Bill. Home in the evening.

THURSDAY, 19. Went to the President's with Bro. Joseph and Dr. Yeates who are still with us. Thence to the House, where the day was devoted to the Indian Appropriation Bill, which was passed. Home in the evening. Rose came and I dictated letters. Retired at eleven, not feeling very well.

FRIDAY, 20. Went to the Departments and thence to the House, where a bare quorum met. A morning hour was had, I believe the first during the session.[312] The Committee on Claims reported a number of bills, and some other Committees were called. At about three o'clock adjourned to meet again on the 7th of January. Finished some Department work and spent the evening at home. Rose came in the evening and I dictated a number of letters.

SATURDAY, 21. Prof. Powell sent me a young man, Mr. Brown,[313] a shorthand writer, who came at nine o'clock. I dic-

---

[312]See note 309 above.

[313]Joseph Stanley Brown (1858–1941) was the grandson of Nathaniel Stanley, a Scottish immigrant who took the name James Brown in the United States. Joseph

tated about 25 letters. The day was very unpleasant. A heavy fall of snow during the past night and in the early morning was succeeded by a heavy rain, which flooded the streets and melted the snow. In the afternoon I went to the Smithsonian, settled up bills at shops, and called on Mr. Clinton Rice in Q. Street. He is quite ill. Called at Foster's. Home at 11 o'clock.

SUNDAY, 22. We attended church in the forenoon. Lieut. Harber dined with us at 2 o'clock. I spent most of the afternoon in looking over materials for a speech that I am called upon to make in Chicago in celebration of the resumption of specie payments. I find it difficult to make a satisfactory speech without running the risk of being immodest, for the fact is I am the only person in public life who has steadily and all the while resisted all schemes against resumption. In the evening Mr. Nichol came as representative of the Honest Money League and after some consultation, I agreed to accept their invitation and fixed the evening of January 2d for the address I am to deliver in Chicago.

MONDAY, 23. Worked on matter for the Chicago speech. At nine o'clock Mr. Brown came and I dictated about 20 letters. In the

---

Brown, who was born in Washington, D.C., adopted the name Stanley-Brown in the 1880's. At the time of his appearance in Garfield's life he was secretary to John Wesley Powell, who arranged to have him help Garfield with his correspondence to enable the congressman to work for the passage of the bill to establish the United States Geological Survey. He continued his part-time assistance after the passage of the bill and in June, 1880, Garfield arranged with Powell to employ him full time. During the campaign of 1880 and the months after the election he was an indispensable aid at Mentor, and in March, 1881, moved into the White House as presidential secretary. He resigned his position in November despite President Arthur's desire to retain him. Mrs. Garfield employed him for a considerable period to arrange her husband's papers, a project on which he did much work. In 1888 he graduated at the Sheffield Scientific School at Yale (where he was assisted financially by Mrs. Garfield) and shortly thereafter married Mary (Mollie) Garfield in the library at Mentor. During his subsequent career he was engaged in a number of activities, including investment banking. For many years as a labor of love he edited the proceedings of the National Geological Society. The Stanley-Browns were the parents of Rudolph, Ruth, who married Herbert Feis, and Margaret, who became a surgeon. There is a small collection of Joseph Stanley-Brown Papers in the Library of Congress.

afternoon did some shopping. In the evening Rose came and worked awhile with me. Crete and I went to Rockwell's.

TUESDAY, 24. Wrote the introduction to the Chicago speech. I do not know how it is, but the few introductory pages of an address always give me great trouble. I know of no man who works as slowly as I do on some things, while on others I work with great rapidity. I try a half dozen introductions before I satisfy myself. I cannot understand why I write with such difficulty while I speak so easily.

WEDNESDAY, 25. Worked on Chicago speech until two o'clock, when Mrs. [Miss] Ransom, Mrs. Reed, Lieut. Harber and Mr. Nichol of Chicago took Christmas Dinner with us and stayed during the afternoon. We had a very pleasant and enjoyable time, though I was all the while distressed by the thought of the unfinished Chicago speech. I am compelled to abandon my purpose of attending the Viaduct Celebration[314] at Cleveland on the 27th and have so written.

THURSDAY, 26. Spent the day on Chicago speech. I find it exceedingly slow work, even slower than usual. The general subject is very familiar, but I dislike to repeat what I have frequently been over, and I find myself struggling to get either new facts, or new methods of presenting old facts. Hence the difficulty is great. Rose came in the evening and I continued work on the speech. After he left I continued at the desk until nearly one o'clock.

FRIDAY, 27. Spent the day working on my Chicago speech until three o'clock, when I played billiards until dinner. Rose came in the evening and I dictated some letters and continued work on speech.

SATURDAY, 28. Spent the day working on my Chicago speech. Wrote to Mr. Clapp to arrange for printing it Sunday night and during the day Monday, but late in the afternoon received a telegram from Nichol tendering me an invitation from the Chicago Club to dine with them on Tuesday, and so I concluded to

---

[314]Cleveland's first high level bridge across the Cuyahoga River, connecting the East and West sides of the city, was completed in 1878 after four-and-a-half years of construction. An all day celebration marked its dedication on December 27.

go to Chicago on Sunday night and finish the speech there. I have satisfied myself pretty well with the work today.

SUNDAY, 29. Staid at home all day revising and completing the speech as far as I had gone with it. Took the Baltimore and Ohio train at 7.30 and before retiring read Goldwin Smith's article in the January *Atlantic* entitled "Is Universal Suffrage a Failure."

MONDAY, 30. Awakened on the western slope of the Alleghenies and at half-past eight o'clock took breakfast at Benwood. There was no snow when I left Washington and none in sight until we reached the mountains. There is a beautiful coat of snow in Ohio and sleighs are running in all directions. I worked on my speech all day, but it was difficult to write on the cars. I did, however, sketch out a few pages. Took supper at Chicago Junction in Ohio.

TUESDAY, 31. Arrived at Chicago at half-past six and when [went] to the Grand Pacific Hotel. The snow is much heavier than in Ohio and air colder. After breakfast went to the office of the Honest Money League and wrote out rapidly the concluding pages of my address. As I wrote them, they were copied by Nichol's clerk and as fast as copied passed over to the printer to be set up. By four o'clock in the evening the speech was in type. At half-past six o'clock I went to the Union Club where a dinner was given me by Mr. Fairbank.[315] There were present about 18 prominent citizens, merchants, lawyers and bankers, also Dr. Swing, the famous Chicago Preacher.[316] My opinion was asked on the silver question and I gave it somewhat at length.

---

[315]Nathaniel K. Fairbank (1829–1903), a native of New York, established himself in Chicago in 1855 and became one of the city's wealthiest and most prominent businessmen. His name was primarily associated with the building up of a large oil, lard and soap company with far-flung branches. In his later years he was also active in the grain market and stock exchange and in a number of financial institutions.

[316]David Swing (1830–1894), a native of Cincinnati, was Chicago's best known preacher. In 1875, after being tried for heresy, he resigned his Presbyterian pulpit and became the nucleus of Central Church, which held its services in Central Music Hall. During the rest of his life he preached there to two or three thousand people a week. "For years," says the *Dictionary of American Biography,* "he was one of the institutions of Chicago, beloved by its inhabitants and sought out by visitors from near and far." One of his strong and helpful supporters was Nathaniel K. Fairbank.

1879

January

WEDNESDAY, 1.   A stream of callers from ten in the morning until late in the afternoon. I stole a little time from visits, however, to write a synopsis of the points of my address to have before me as a memoranda while I speak. I have not the courage to read but will speak extemporaneously following the line of thought as well as I can. At half-past five Nichol and I took the train for Racine. Arrived at half-past seven. We were met at the depot by Senator Baker,[1] a prominent manufacturer at Racine, and were taken to his pleasant house where we were delightfully entertained. Some thirty or forty people called during the evening.

THURSDAY, 2.   When I left Chicago the thermometer stood twenty-eight degrees above zero; when I arrived here it was twenty-eight degrees below, a change of forty-eight [fifty-six] degrees in one night. Nichol and I took the train and arrived at Chicago about 11 o'clock. It is the coldest weather I have ever seen. Nearly a hundred people called on me during the day at the Grand Pacific Hotel, among them ten members of Congress. I am pleased to find so strong a feeling of friendship for me among the people of the West. Swaim came from Leavenworth at seven and at half-past [I] went to Farwell Hall and delivered

[1]Robert H. Baker (1839–1882), a partner in the J.I. Case Company of Racine, Wisconsin, was described in 1879 when he became chairman of the Republican state committee as "a young politician of much energy." He was the Republican candidate for governor, 1873, a member of the state senate, 1873, 1875–76, and an alternate delegate to the Republican National Convention, 1880.

my address to a fair audience.[2] The intense cold kept many away. I spoke with fair effect. Senator Howe complimented me very highly and spoke briefly at the conclusion of my address. Spent the night with Swaim at the [Grand] Pacific Hotel.

FRIDAY, 3.   I intended to take the early train for Cleveland, but the storm has so delayed the trains and the cold is still so intense, that my friends insisted that it was not safe to go. A number of friends called during the day. Among others my old classmate Wilber came a long distance to see me. Also ex-Governor Merrill[3] of Iowa, who came from Des Moines to attend the meeting. At half-past five I took the Lake Shore train for Cleveland. Read *Romola*[4] until a late hour. At a late hour took supper at La Porte, Indiana, where I found the best potatoes I have seen this season. I enquired of the Landlord and learned that they were peachblows raised on new land. This accords with my impressions that our light soils have exhausted the potato element in them. Engaged four bushels of them to plant at Mentor next Spring.

SATURDAY, 4.   Reached Cleveland at half-past seven and drove to Dr. Robison's. He has been very sick but is recovering. Found the roads blocked up to the east of Cleveland and if I go today will be uncertain when I can get a train to Warren. I very reluctantly abandon my purpose to visit the farm and conclude to leave for Washington on the 1.45 P.M. train. After all it is partly a boyish wish to see the farm, more than a real necessity for going and so I wrote to Northcott my orders about the farm, settling up some debts in Cleveland and took the train as mentioned above.

SUNDAY, 5.   The train was two hours late, reaching Washington about half-past ten. I found the family all well but shut in by the cold. Spent most of the day in reading my large mail and getting my desk in order.

---

[2]Garfield's speech, "Suspension and Resumption of Specie Payments," is in Hinsdale, ed., *Works of Garfield,* II, pp. 609–626.

[3]Samuel Merrill (1822–1899), a native of Maine, moved in 1856 from New Hampshire to Iowa, where he was a merchant and banker. A Republican, he was governor, 1869–72. The last decade of his life was spent in California.

[4]George Eliot, *Romola,* 3 vols. (1863).

MONDAY, 6.   Soon after breakfast young Brown came and I dictated letters until after 12 o'clock, getting my desk pretty nearly cleared. A portion of the afternoon I played billiards with Rockwell. In the evening Rose came and I dictated Journal and letters.

TUESDAY, 7.   Worked at my desk until half-past eleven o'clock, dictating letters to Brown. Then went to the Capitol where the House met and resumed its duties after the Holidays. The intense cold weather has so obstructed the trains that the House was not very full. The day was devoted mainly to private bills. I returned home early to continue the overhauling of my mail. Rose came in the evening and I dictated letters and the Journal.

WEDNESDAY, 8.   Letters in the morning. At half-past ten met with the Committee on Ways and Means and we listened to the arguments of the sugar men, about 70 of whom were present, to present their views on the subject of the sugar tariff. There are three distinct parties before the Committee—Baltimore men who want but one rate of duty on all unrefined sugar and a higher rate on all refined. The Boston men desire the polarascope test applied to all sugar No. 16 Dutch Standard to be paid at a rate adjusted by the per cent of sac[c]harine matter. The New York parties are favorable to the use of the polarascope, but applied to a smaller number of grades of sugar. We heard five hours of argument.[5]

[5]Duties on sugar accounted for about one-sixth of the revenue of the United States government. Under the law imported sugar was divided into seven classes according to color, the darkest being the crudest product and the lightest being the product of highest quality. The lowest duty, in *ad valorem* terms, was levied on the lowest class and the highest on the highest class. Recently, however, foreign producers had been sending to the United States high quality sugar with a dark color; under the color system of classification this was admitted at a low rate. The Treasury Department favored a change in the law that would allow it to measure the crystallizable content of sugar by use of the polariscope or by other means and to apply higher rates to some sugar now subjected to lower rates because of its dark color. The Treasury's proposal had the support of a minority of the Committee on Ways and Means, including Garfield. The majority proposed to consolidate into one classification the four lowest grades. The duty proposed for the new class would be higher in terms of percentage of value than for the sugar of better quality

THURSDAY, 9. Letters in the morning. At half-past ten attended the Committee on Ways and Means and we listened for five hours to the sugar men of Boston and Baltimore on their several propositions for amending the tariff. House met at 12 o'clock and the death of Representative Hartridge of Ga. was announced, whereupon the House immediately adjourned.[6] Committee on Ways and Means immediately continued its hearing.

FRIDAY, 10. Letters in the morning. Committee on Ways and Means at half-past ten, when Messrs. Havemeyer,[7] Booth[8] and Wells[9] and several other gentlemen addressed the Committee on

---

—a reversal of the schedules then in effect. This was favored by Southerners as a means of encouraging the Louisiana sugar industry, but was opposed by refining interests wishing to import their raw material at low rates. Some refineries, however, were willing to have the majority bill pass, expecting to profit from the refining of the higher grades of imported sugar. On February 26 Garfield gave a very able presentation of the whole question. His speech is in Hinsdale, ed., *Works of Garfield,* II, pp. 637–654. The majority bill was withdrawn a few days after Garfield's speech, and nothing further was done with respect to the sugar question before the end of the session.

[6]The adjournment to honor the memory of Julian Hartridge (1829–1879), a Democratic member of the House from Georgia, 1875 to his death, occurred on January 8, and the adjournment for the funeral services, mentioned in the entry for January 10, took place on January 9.

[7]Theodore A. Havemeyer (1834–1897), of New York, was a member of a family prominent in the sugar refining industry. The Havemeyers later organized the American Sugar Refining Company (known as the Sugar Trust), against which the federal government brought (unsuccessfully) the first suit under the Sherman Anti-Trust Act of 1890. At the time of Theodore's death the *New York Times* (April 27, 1897) said that he "was less aggressive than his brother Henry, and in the various encounters with legislative committees, in Washington, as well as in Albany and New York, Theodore won the reputation of being the diplomatist of the family. He was invariably frank, as well as agreeable, in his statements to legislative investigators." The Havemeyers favored the lowering of tariff rates on imported raw sugar and the protection of refined sugar.

[8]William T. Booth, a member of the firm of Booth and Edgar, sugar refiners in New York City (under the name of the Sugar Refining Company).

[9]David A. Wells, who addressed the committee at length, had been investigating the sugar tariff at the request of four importers and one refiner of sugar. He defended the polariscope as a reliable device for determining the saccharine content of sugar.

the sugar question. Four hours of the day were consumed in hearing arguments. House met at 12 o'clock and adjourned immediately to meet at 3 o'clock to attend the funeral of Representative Hartridge of Ga.[10] Home in the evening. Sugar men chasing me at every street corner to argue their case.

SATURDAY, 11. Brown came in the morning. I dictated a large number of letters. Committee on Ways and Means at half-past ten. Four hours were spent in discussing the various phases of the sugar question. At twelve the House met and the death of Representative Schleicher[11] of Texas was announced and the House adjourned. Home in evening.

SUNDAY, 12. Snow fell heavily all day and I remained home. Wells came, and I had a long conversation on economic questions and in reference to the sugar question. Lieut. Harber and Miss Ransom dined with us. Spent the evening in reading up the history of the early struggles over the Smithsonian bequest, with a view of preparing remarks on Professor Henry.[12] The funeral

[10]The House debated a bill to reimburse the College of William and Mary for property destroyed during the Civil War, and a majority that included Garfield defeated the measure. See January 9, 1879, n. 6.

[11]Gustave Schleicher (1823–1879), a native of Germany, studied at the University of Geissen, became a civil engineer and was employed in the building of European railroads before emigrating to Texas in 1847; he settled in San Antonio in 1850. During the 1850's he was in the state legislature, and was a Democratic member of the U.S. House of Representatives, 1875 to his death. "He was a man of splendid physique, weighing 425 pounds," according to one obituary. His funeral was held on January 13, not on January 12 as indicated by Garfield. When he was eulogized in the House on February 17, Garfield was one of the speakers; in his address he described Schleicher as "the sturdy supporter and able advocate of a currency based on coin of real value and full weight," and a man who possessed "the habit of close, earnest, hard work" and "a noteworthy independence of character."

[12]James Smithson (1765–1829), an English student of chemistry and mineralogy, willed most of his fortune to the United States for the purpose of founding at Washington, D.C., "under the name of the Smithsonian Institution, an establishment for the increase and diffusion of knowledge among men." The United States received more than half a million dollars under this bequest. There were many suggestions for the disposition of the money, some even favoring its return to England. In 1846 Congress established the Institution and Joseph Henry became

of Mr. Schleicher of Texas took place in the House at 3 o'clock today.

MONDAY, 13. Worked at my desk. Dictated letters until half-past ten o'clock, when I went to the Treasury Department and consulted in reference to the tariff on sugar. Went to the Committee at 11 and we had a long conference which lasted until two o'clock. I offered the Treasury proposition but a specific rate was offered by Messrs. Robbins[13] and Tucker, which finally prevailed after an exciting debate. I announced to the Committee that I should resist the bill they had adopted. In the evening Rose came and I dictated letters. Fernando Wood called and I went with him to Sherman's, to consult about the sugar bill. Continued preparations for the address on Prof. Henry.

TUESDAY, 14. Letters in the morning and spent some time reading sketches and memoranda of Professor Henry's life. Committee on Ways and Means at half-past [ten], preparing bills for reporting tomorrow. House at twelve. Proceedings of no special moment. Home in the evening.

WEDNESDAY, 15. Letters in the morning. Committee on Ways and Means at half-past ten and reports from the same Committee in the House during the day. The Treasury Bill authorizing certificates of deposits of ten dollars and upward, to be funded into four per cents when the amount reached $50.00 was discussed.[14] Wood made a long opening speech, and the House got

---

its first secretary. He favored research and the dissemination of knowledge and did not look with favor on the use of the legacy to develop a library and a museum, both of which Congress insisted upon. In 1866, however, Congress provided for the transfer of the library to the Library of Congress, thus removing a large burden from the Institution. In his address Garfield made this comment: "When Congress shall have taken the other incumbrance, the National Museum, off the hands of the Institution, by making fit provision for the care of the great collection, they will have done still more to realize the ideas of Professor Henry." Garfield's address is in Hinsdale, ed., *Works of Garfield,* II, pp. 627–631.

[13]William M. Robbins (1828–1905) was a Democratic member of the House from North Carolina, 1873–79.

[14]The money thus obtained by the government was to be used to retire Civil War bonds bearing six percent interest. Garfield contended that the proposed refunding procedure would save money and enable people of small means to

muddled on the subject. Morrison sought to break down Wood as Chairman of the Committee.[15] I made a speech of ten minutes, which, it was agreed to on all hands, saved the bill from defeat. Evening session was held which lasted until 11 o'clock and during the session of which some other bills were passed. I resisted the bill to make greenbacks receivable for customs dues unless my amendment was adopted to make it applicable only while they were at par with coin. I was beaten, only had 42 votes with me.[16]

THURSDAY, 16. Spent some time in the morning preparing an address in reference to the life and services of Professor Henry to be delivered at the memorial services tonight before the Senate and House of Representatives. I ought to have prepared this address long ago, but have been so much crowded that I am at last compelled to abandoned [abandon] the purpose of writing it, so I shall speak extemporaneously. Attended the meeting of the House at 12 o'clock, when another of the bills of the Ways and Means Committee was passed.[17] Not much of other business was done. In the evening Harber came to go with us to the Capitol. I have never felt such forebodings of failure in any

---

participate; that the federal government, by issuing four percent bonds, would cease competing with business and industry for private loans; and that no contraction of the currency would result because every dollar acquired from the sale of certificates would be used to purchase six percent bonds. In the evening session the House approved the bill.

[15]It was William M. Springer, Democrat from Illinois, rather than William R. Morrison, another Democrat from the same state, who "sought to break down Wood," the Democratic chairman of the Committee on Ways and Means. Springer put as many obstacles as he could in the way of the bill and when it finally came to a vote in the evening session, he voted against it.

[16]Garfield's amendment was defeated, 122–76, and the bill passed, 153–43, with Garfield on the losing side.

[17]The bill authorized the secretary of the treasury to exchange at par outstanding and uncalled six percent bonds for four percent bonds, and when all such bonds had been redeemed, to exchange four percent bonds for bonds bearing five percent or more. The measure, which also permitted the government to pay interest on the bonds redeemed for a period of three months, passed without a roll call.

speech of my life, as I did on the way to the Capitol. The Senate and House assembled with the President, Cabinet and Supreme Court in the area. The Vice-President presided, assisted by the Speaker. Mr. Hamlin's address was read by Mr. Wheeler, Withers[18] followed in a brief address, Dr. Asa Gray[19] of Boston read an address of nearly an hour. It was very interesting but delivered in too low a tone of voice. The venerable Professor Rodgers [Rogers][20] nearly 80 years of age spoke with great force. I followed, speaking not quite fifteen minutes. In spite of all my forebodings, I made a more than usually effective speech for which I was warmly congratulated. Mr. [Samuel S.] Cox spoke and after him General Sherman.

FRIDAY, 17. Dictated letters to Brown in the morning. House at 12. The day was spent on private bills. Home in the evening.

SATURDAY, 18. Worked at my desk dictating letters to Brown, when I went to the War Department with B. W. Summy and thence to the President's on business. To the Capitol at 12. The day was devoted to the Geneva Award. I voted for the bill of the majority to allow the Court of Claims and the Supreme Court to determine who shall receive payments under the award. Any settlement that does not strictly pursue the terms of the Treaty is indefensible and dishonorable to the nation. The bill of the majority was, however, beaten, and the award will be scattered unwisely and disgracefully. I ought to have made a speech on the subject.[21]

---

[18]Robert E. Withers (1821–1907), although normally a Democrat, was elected as a Conservative to the U.S. Senate from Virginia and served one term, 1875–81. He was a member of the Board of Regents of the Smithsonian.

[19]Asa Gray (1810–1888), a botanist, was one of the greatest scientists of the nineteenth century, and the leading scientific defender of Darwinism in the United States. He was professor of natural science at Harvard, 1842–88, and a member of the Board of Regents of the Smithsonian, 1874–88. For a comment by him on Garfield see Vol. II, p. 36, n. 132.

[20]William Barton Rogers (1804–1882), geologist and educator, was president of the Massachusetts Institute of Technology, 1862–70, 1878–81.

[21]After debating and defeating a bill reported by a majority of the Committee on the Judiciary, the House approved a substitute bill (Garfield voted against it) which provided for the revival of the Court of Commissioners of *Alabama* Claims.

SUNDAY, 19.   Attended church in the forenoon. In the afternoon commenced preparing for a short article which I have agreed to write for the *North American Review* as a part of symposium on the question, "Ought the Negro to be disfranchised and ought he to have been enfranchised?"[22]

MONDAY, 20.   Spent the morning in gathering materials for my *Review* article. House at twelve. Nothing accomplished. Home in the evening.

TUESDAY, 21.   Worked on my article for the *Review* until half-past ten when I attended the meeting of the Committee on Ways and Means. In the House Potter moved a resolution appropriating money for the investigation of the cypher dispatches.[23] Some sharp speeches were made on both sides, Hewitt closing the debate with an ugly and ungenerous fling at the President.[24] I

The court was to consist of three judges (a decision required the agreement of at least two), and claimants were obligated to file within six months of the date that the court convened. Although the bill died in the Senate, a similar one became law in June, 1882.

[22]The published symposium, "Ought the Negro to be Disfranchised? Ought He to Have Been Enfranchised?," *North American Review,* Vol. CXXVIII, No. CCLXVIII (March, 1879), pp. 225–283, is organized according to the original plan. The introduction and conclusion are by Blaine. In between are statements by L.Q.C. Lamar, Wade Hampton, James A. Garfield, Alexander H. Stephens, Wendell Phillips, Montgomery Blair, and Thomas A. Hendricks. Garfield's statement, pp. 244–250, ends as follows:

> In conclusion, I answer these questions by saying that on every ground of private right, of public justice, and national safety, the Negro ought to have been enfranchised. For the same reasons, strengthened and confirmed by our experience, he ought not to be disfranchised. Reviewing the elements of the larger problem, I do not doubt that enfranchisement will, in the long run, greatly promote the intellectual, moral, and industrial welfare of the Negro race in America; and, instead of imperiling the safety of our institutions, will remove from them the greatest danger which has ever threatened them.

[23]The resolution authorized the special committee, of which Potter was chairman, to investigate the cipher telegrams and any other matter relative to the presidential election of 1876 that the committee considered proper, and authorized $10,000 for that endeavor. See October 16, 1878, and n. 258.

[24]Hewitt called for an investigation in which Tilden would take the witness stand, if need be, "to satisfy the American people and the world that at least one of the candidates of the two great parties . . . is not a miserable trickster, willing

sought the floor but the time was exhausted. I moved to reconsider the vote by which the previous question was ordered, but the Democrats beat the motion by three [four] votes. In the evening Crete and I dined at Colonel Robert Ingersoll's. There were present Mr. and Mrs. Blaine, Mrs. [Miss] Dodge, Clark Ingersoll and his wife. Very pleasant party. Home at half-past eleven.

WEDNESDAY, 22.   For the first time in many years, I remained at home all day when the House was in session. I spent the day in completing my article for the *North American Review*. I finished it just before dinner. It makes seventeen pages of legal [cap]. Dr. Streator and Mr. Chamberlain from Cleveland dined with us and spent part of the evening. Several friends called. Rose came and wrote up my Journal. I spent some time in revising my *Review* article.

THURSDAY, 23.   Spent the morning in revising the whole and recasting a portion of the article for the *North American Review*, and a little before 12 o'clock sent it to Mr. Blaine's house in order that he might sum up the case after having seen all the other papers. Went to the House at 12 and found there was a stirring and significant debate yesterday between Northern and Southern Democrats involving a first class quarrel on the question of Southern Claims.[25] On my return home in the evening Mr. Barron[26] of the *North American Review* called on a curious errand. He said he was sent to me by Mr. Blaine to say that my paper for the symposium had taken the ground from under his feet by making all the strong points which he had expected to make in his summing up; that if my article went in, he could make no effective

---

to make bargains for the highest office in the gift of the people, every hour's wrongful occupation of which only intensifies the dishonor of its acquisition and the humiliation of its possession."

[25]The debate concerned claims established under an act of March 3, 1871, which authorized every man in the Confederacy who had remained loyal to the Union and furnished supplies to, or whose property was used by, the Union army or navy, to file a claim. Every claim, found to be valid, was to be paid by the federal government.

[26]John W. Barron was secretary of the *North American Review*.

concluding reply to the papers presented by the Democrats. This seemed to me altogether childish for I had seen none of the papers written by the gentlemen on the other side, and my short article of 18 pages has certainly not exhausted the subject. It is apparent to me that Blaine cares more about the glory of replying to these men, than about having the cause of Negro enfranchisement defended. At first I was disposed to say I would withdraw my article, but on reflection I thought, it is a demand which Blaine has no right to make, and so I told Barron to say that I had written the paper for the Editors of the *Review* and they could reject it if they chose, either for being not good enough, or too good, and they must take the responsibility. At half-past 8 o'clock attended the session until 11.

FRIDAY, 24. Brown came in the morning and I dictated a large number of letters. Went to the Capitol at 11 and attended the meeting of the Committee on Ways and Means. In the House the day was spent on Private Bills.

About 12 o'clock, I received a letter from Blaine, saying that Barron of the *North American Review* had proposed that I withhold my article and that Judge Black and I write a Critique on the symposium for the next number of the *Review.* Blaine writes, he was entirely willing I should do so if I choose; "or", said he, "let your reply go in as an answer to all the rest, and I" (Blaine) "will write no more, for your article substantially covers the ground I intended to take in my conclusion." In answer to this letter I wrote him that the symposium would squeeze the whole juice out of the subject and make an article in the next number dull and profitless; besides I had no time to write another paper. I said also that the Editors could leave out my article if they chose, but whether it went in or not he ought to write a conclusion, that my article [could] not possibly be a sufficient reply to the Democratic arguments which I had not seen. On coming home this evening Barron called again to say that my letter had arrived at Blaine's but had not relieved him of his dilemma. I then read Blaine's letter to him and he said at once that he did not suggest to Blaine that I should withdraw from this number and write on the subject in the next; that Blaine made that suggestion and he (Barron) replied that that was inadmissible for the *Review* would not want a second article on the subject, and he was sure Garfield could not write it for the reason that he had promised them an article on another subject. I thereupon told Barron that I should leave the whole subject with the *Review,* that the article was theirs and they must do what they chose about it; that I would make no arrangement with Mr. Blaine about it. On the whole this little incident is a singular indication of the childishness and selfishness of Mr. Blaine. I regret it for his sake. I would withdraw my paper altogether but for the fact that I have already done too much complacent yielding to the demands of ambitious and aggressive friends and I think that Blaine will respect me more for refusing to comply with his childish request in this matter.

SATURDAY, 25. Swaim came in the morning. I dictated letters until 11 o'clock, when I went to the War Department and to the President's on business. House at 11 o'clock and remained until the adjournment near five. The day was spent on private bills. In the evening Crete and I attended the Literary Society at Mrs. Dahlgren's and heard a very striking story of the *Latin Quartier* of Paris, read by Mrs. Burnett, the author of *That Lass of Lowrie's.* [27] Home at 11 o'clock.

SUNDAY, 26. Crete and Mother and I attended church and heard a pretty fair sermon, which is unusual. Home during the after-

---

[27]Frances Hodgson Burnett (1849–1924), one of the most popular novelists of her time, was a native of England, migrating to the United States in 1865. Her first literary work to receive wide attention and acclaim was *That Lass o'Lowrie's,* serialized in *Scribner's* during 1876 and 1877 and published as a book in 1877. Her many later works include *Louisiana* (1880), mentioned by Garfield, *Little Lord Fauntleroy* (1886) and *T. Tembarom* (1913). In 1873 she married Swan Moses Burnett (1847–1906), of Tennessee, who became a distinguished eye and ear specialist in Washington. At this time and for a number of years thereafter the Burnetts lived at 1215 I Street, N.W., thus being close neighbors of the Garfields, who lived at 1227 I Street. The two Burnett children, Lionel and Vivian (the inspiration of *Little Lord Fauntleroy*) sometimes played with Abram and Irvin Garfield. Mrs. Burnett read a poem, "By-the-Sea, September 19, 1881," at a meeting of the Literary Society held in memory of Garfield on November 19, 1881. In a biography of his mother (*Romantick Lady,* 1927) Vivian makes this statement: ". . . When Garfield was assassinated, it was a real tragedy to the entire Burnett family, and the nation's loss, as well as her personal loss, moved Mrs. Burnett greatly."

noon. In the evening at six dined at Secretary Evarts' with his family, Sam Ward and another gentleman from New York. Had a long talk with the Secretary on the Chinese Question[28] and on current political topics.

MONDAY, 27. Dictated an unusually large number of letters and commenced revising my eulogy on Professor Henry. Went to the Capitol at 12 o'clock. Usual Monday work until a logrolling bill, appropriating considerable sums of money for about fifteen public buildings in various parts of the country, came up. We then adjourned the House as the only effective means of resisting it.[29] Swaim was taken quite ill last night with a sore throat and this morning felt some symptoms of diphtheria.[30] Dr. Baxter has

[28]Under the Burlingame Treaty (1869) between China and the United States Chinese subjects were free to come to the United States "for purposes of curiosity, of trade, or as permanent residents." During the 1870's opposition to the migration of Chinese laborers mounted in the United States, the chief opposition coming from the West Coast, where the Chinese were most numerous. On January 29, 1879, the House passed a bill limiting to fifteen the number of Chinese passengers that a ship could bring to the United States at one time. Garfield, considering this bill "a palpable and flat violation" of the treaty, sought unsuccessfully to introduce an amendment to suspend the taking effect of the measure until China had been properly notified of the termination of the treaty. He did not cast a vote on the passage of the bill. The bill presented to the President included a Senate amendment that was designed to bring about the abrogation of two articles of the Burlingame Treaty. Garfield voted against the amended bill and advised the President to veto it (see entry for February 23). The veto was sustained in the House. During 1880 the administration negotiated a treaty with China under which the Burlingame Treaty was modified to allow the United States to regulate, limit or suspend the admission of Chinese laborers to the United States, with the proviso that it would not absolutely prohibit their immigration and that any limitation or suspension would be reasonable. President Hayes submitted this treaty to the Senate in January, 1881, and it was ratified on May 5 of the same year (during Garfield's Presidency). Garfield's views and actions in respect to the admission of Chinese laborers into the United States are of special interest in view of the furor aroused by the "Morey forgery" during the campaign of 1880.

[29]The bill proposed an appropriation of not more than $1,100,000 for the purchase of sites and the erection of ten public buildings in ten different states.

[30]David G. Swaim, who was stationed at Fort Leavenworth, had come East to serve as judge advocate of a court martial in New York scheduled for early February.

been in three times today and thinks he is much better. Worked at my desk.

TUESDAY, 28.   Letters at the desk in the morning. Before I left for the Capitol Dr. Baxter came and found Swaim much better. He says he saw signs of diphtheria and thought the chances were two to one against his recovery. Committee on Ways and Means at 11 o'clock. In the House the day was spent on the Post Office Appropriation Bill. For several days the Democrats have prevented a morning hour for the purpose of avoiding further discussion between themselves on the controversy raised by General Bragg about Southern Claims.[31] Home in the evening and found Swaim improving though he is quite weak. Worked at my desk revising the notes of my speech on Professor Henry.

WEDNESDAY, 29.   Dictated a large number of letters in the morning. Went to the Departments and thence to the Capitol. Another day was spent on the Post Office Appropriation Bill, after a struggle, preventing a morning hour, which the Democrats did not desire to have. Swaim is still mending but keeps his bed most of the time. Mr. and Mrs. Foster and their two daughters came and spent the evening with us. Colonel Rockwell was also with us two hours. It was after midnight when we retired.

THURSDAY, 30.   Dictated letters at my desk in the morning. At ten o'clock attended the Joint Committee on Yellow Fever. Received reports from the Committee of Experts.[32] All but one of

[31]On January 22, Edward S. Bragg (1827–1912), a Democratic member of the House from Wisconsin, 1877–83, 1885–87, reported that a Mississippi Democrat had said that Southerners would become Republicans unless Northern Democrats supported larger appropriations for the South. Bragg expressed the wish that all Southern Democrats with such feelings would join the Republicans, and the sooner the better. Democrats who wished to reply to Bragg could do so under the rules only in the morning hour.

[32]The Board of Experts, appointed to assist the committees on epidemic diseases, had been investigating areas in the South that had been infected with yellow fever. On this day they reported to the joint meeting of the House and Senate committees through their chairman, Dr. John M. Woodworth, surgeon general of the United States Marine Hospital Service. Garfield introduced the resolution directing the chairmen of the two committees to draft a bill embodying suggestions made by the experts.

them, a Homeopathic Doctor, from Savannah, Georgia, held that the disease is not indigenous, but is imported from tropical countries, particularly from the West India Islands, and recommended a partial quarantine as the best mode of preventing its spread in this country. A good deal of interesting conversation was had with the experts and the Chairmen of the two Committees was ordered to prepare a bill embodying their views. At half-past eleven o'clock went to the Committee on Ways and Means and sat with them until half-past twelve. The Post Office Appropriation Bill was passed and then an hour and a half was wasted in the House to prevent a morning hour. At two o'clock the Committee on the District of Columbia had the floor and consumed the remainder of the day. Home in the evening. Rose came and I dictated the Journal and some letters. Swaim is getting better.

FRIDAY, 31. Letters in the morning, Departments at eleven, Capitol at twelve. Private bills occupied most of the day. In the evening at six o'clock dined at Colonel Rockwell's in company with Generals Drum and McKinney[33] of the Army. At nine, they in company with Mr. and Mrs. Rockwell came home with me and sat for an hour or two with a number of friends who had called. Crete is making her Friday evenings very pleasant.

February

SATURDAY, 1. Dictated a large number of letters and finished the revision of my address on Prof. Henry. Went to the House at 12. A dull day and but little accomplished. Home in the evening.

SUNDAY, 2. Did not attend church but went by invitation of Senator Harris[34] to his room—at ten o'clock—and then spent

[33]Probably David B. McKibbin (see n. 94, March 15, 1880).

[34]Isham G. Harris (1818–1897), a Memphis lawyer and Democrat, was a member of the U.S. House of Representatives, 1849–53, governor of Tennessee, 1858–63, and a member of the U.S. Senate, 1877–97.

three hours with him, Senator Matthews and Casey Young in drafting a bill in regard to the Yellow Fever. At two o'clock Miss Ransom and Lieut. Harber dined with us.

MONDAY, 3.   Letters in the morning. Departments and then to the House. A struggle was made to set special days for the Committee on Ways and Means, one day for sugar and the other for general reports. The proposition failed to get a two-thirds vote.[35]

TUESDAY, 4.   A large number of letters in the morning. Departments at half-past ten and attended the Committee on Ways and Means at 11. During the day Blaine sent for me to revise the proof sheets of my article for the *North American Review* and also to determine about some points in the article, to prevent overlapping his own. Home in the evening. Swaim was quite ill again.

WEDNESDAY, 5.   Letters in the morning. Attended meeting of the Committee on Ways and Means.[36] In the House the day was spent in the usual manner. General Sheldon came and spent some time with me in the morning and, also, again at the Capitol. He is very earnest in the opinion that I ought to run for Governor. Insisted that my chances for the Presidency are better than any other man's except Grant, and possibly may be better than his. I ought to notice in this place that I am receiving a large number of letters from various parts of the country in regard to the Presidency. While I am not indifferent to the good opinion of men who think me fit for that high place, I still am wholly disinclined to believe that any result will come out of it other than some general talk. I have so long and so often seen the evil effects of the presidential fever upon my associates and friends that I am determined it shall not seize me, for in almost ever[y] case it impairs if it does not destroy the usefulness of its victim. At eight

---

[35]The proposal was to suspend the rules and set aside February 8 for the Sugar Bill, to debate it each day thereafter until it was disposed of, and to set aside February 12 for general reports from the Committee on Ways and Means.

[36]The minutes of the committee do not record a meeting on February 5. Garfield was recorded as present at a meeting on February 6, which he does not mention in his entry for that date.

o'clock in the evening I called at Foster's room and visited with him and Sheldon until nine o'clock. Returned home and at half-past nine Crete and I went to Senator Matthews', who gave a large party. His rooms were crowded although the Senate was in session and many Senators were kept away. The Senate passed by a strict party vote Senator Edmunds' resolution[s] affirming the validity of the three amendments to the Constitution.[37] Crete and I returned from Matthews' at 11 o'clock.

THURSDAY, 6. Letters in the morning. At half-past ten attended the joint meeting of the Committee on Yellow Fever. Senator Harris laid before us the draft of a bill and report of the Senate branch of the Committee adopted after some modifications, but the House members requested a separate meeting for tomorrow morning to consider the bill. In the House the Army Appropriation Bill was taken up and the Burnside bill offered as an amendment. Debate on it was restricted to thirty minutes. It was ruled in order under the nefarious rule of retrenchment, which is loading appropriation bills with all sorts of general legislation. I spoke for five minutes—all the time I could get. The amendment was then ruled in order.[38] An amendment was also offered to transfer

[37]In addition to affirming the validity of the 13th, 14th and 15th amendments, Edmunds' two resolutions also stated that Congress had the duty to provide and enforce legislation protecting all legally qualified citizens in their right to vote for representatives in Congress, and they directed the Committee on the Judiciary to prepare a bill "for the protection of such rights, and the punishment of infractions thereof."

[38]In December, 1878, Ambrose E. Burnside reported from a joint committee to the Senate a bill "to reduce and reorganize the Army . . . and to make rules for its government and regulation." When the House took up the Army Appropriation Bill, Harry White of Pennsylvania offered a sixteen-page amendment which embodied substantially the proposals of the joint committee. In debate Garfield conceded that it had some merit, but he labelled it "a firebrand of discontent," a proposal for revolutionary changes that had already created enormous bad feeling and controversy within the grades and departments of the army. As an example he singled out provisions for transferring personnel of the line to staff and staff to line, insisting that such transfers would be wasteful, inefficient, and extremely demoralizing to servicemen. He called for a full and careful discussion and declared that he did not believe that the House could, in good conscience, approve the amendment after a thirty-minute debate. Two days later the House passed it.

the Indian Bureau to the War Department. I resisted it as out of order and the Speaker took part in the debate, defending the 120th Rule as a wise Democratic measure. It was the occasion of a sharp collision between him and me. At seven in the evening Crete and I dined at Judge Field's. The Judge's brother Henry M. Field and wife, Senator Blaine and wife and Miss Dodge, also President Welling of Columbian College.[39] Pleasant party. Home at 11 o'clock.

FRIDAY, 7. Letters in the morning. At half-past ten attended the meeting of the House Committee on Yellow Fever. The bill prepared by Senator Harris was vigorously assailed by Mr. Goode of Virginia and Hooker of Virginia [Mississippi], as an unconstitutional interference of the rights of the States. I defended it, stating my constitutional grounds for supporting it. In the House after the morning hour the day was spent on private bills. A large number of friends called on us to spend the evening, but word was sent to me that an attempt was to be made at the evening session of the House to disturb the currency question. I went to the Capitol and arrived just in time to find Muldrow of Mississippi demanding the previous question on Burchard's bill to make all coins exchangeable for paper at the Treasury at the will of the holder.[40] I resisted the previous question, got control of the floor for an hour, discussed the bill, prevented its passage and at ten o'clock we adjourned the House. Came home and found most of our friend[s] still remaining. Had a pleasant visit until two after midnight.

[39]James C. Welling (1825–1894), a native of New Jersey, was associated with the *National Intelligencer* in Washington, D.C., 1850–65, and president of Columbian College (chartered as a university in 1873), 1871–1894. During his presidency the institution (now known as George Washington University) moved from the suburbs into the city, opened a school of graduate studies and made other advances. Active outside the university in the intellectual life of the city, he was a member of the Board of Regents of the Smithsonian, 1884–94.

[40]Henry L. Muldrow (1837–1905), a Democratic member of the House from Mississippi, 1877–85, presented a bill from the Committee on Coinage, Weights, and Measures that precipitated the debate described by Garfield. The motion to table the bill, mentioned in the next entry, was made by Robbins in the evening session of February 7, but lack of a quorum delayed final action until February 8, when the motion was adopted.

SATURDAY, 8.   Dictated a large number of letters and at half-past ten o'clock went to the State Department, thence to the President's and then to the Capitol. The bill to resume paper payments came up immediately after the reading of the Journal and I got Robbins of North Carolina to move to lay it on the table. After rallying all our forces, we succeeded in beating it by about twenty-seven majority. Remembering that this is the same House of Representatives that gave nearly two-thirds majority in favor of repealing the Resumption Act altogether, the result of the vote this morning is very gratifying. It shows at last that men are beginning to recognize the force and pressure of public opinion and the course of events. The House then went into Committee of the Whole on the Army Bill and spent the remainder of the day in fighting over the various amendments. We succeeded in defeating the amendment to transfer the Indian Bureau to the War Department, but the amendment to reorganize the army prevailed. Home at half-past five. James Mason of Cleveland dined with us. Rose came in the evening and I dictated Journal and other things.

SUNDAY, 9.   In company with James Mason attended the Foundry Church and listened to a very able sermon from Bishop Simpson. He made a point which I have not heard before in proof that men after death were conscious of affairs, instancing persons arising from death and being restored to relatives, but especially instancing the cases of Moses and Elias in ——— [Matthew 17:3] one who had passed away from the earth 900 years before, the other 1,400 years before. Yet on their return, they talked of Jerusalem and decease [deeds?] which Christ should accomplish there, in language intelligible to the apostles. The Bishop said it was fortunate they had not forgotten the Hebrew language after a lapse of so many centuries. Lieut. Harber and Miss Ransom took dinner with us. Just as we were concluding the two o'clock dinner, I received a note from the President inviting Crete and I to dinner with Bishop Simpson and wife. We accepted and had a very pleasant dinner with a number of friends. Crete remained until 8 o'clock, but I left at seven to dine again with Mr. Wells and a company of Senators and members.

MONDAY, 10. Dictated letters in the morning. Went to the departments and thence to the Capitol. The day was spent in the usual Monday way with nothing very special accomplished, except that a day was set for the sugar question, and another for the Committee on Ways and Means to make reports. Spent two hours at Colonel Carter's on F Street.

TUESDAY, 11. Dictated letters and then attended three Committees; first, the Committee on Commerce, to secure an increased appropriation for Ashtabula Harbor; second, Committee on Yellow Fever,[41] where I found the Southern members troubled with Constitutional objections to a national quarantine law. I made a speech defending the constitutionality of Senator Harris' bill; and third, attended for a short time the Committee on Ways and Means, where arrangements were made for a debate on the sugar question. During the day in the House, I made a speech on the subject of geological surveys, in which I took occasion to discuss the division of power in our American System into three classes, national, state and the reserved power of the people. I think I made more impression on the thoughtful men of the House than I usually do.[42] Spent the

[41]According to its minutes, the House Committee on Epidemic Diseases met on February 10 and 12, but not on February 11; Garfield was present at both meetings. The Harris bill was taken up on February 12.

[42]Garfield's speech was a call for economy and limited government in science. He opened it with a plea for less discussion of state sovereignty and national supremacy, and more about the reserved rights of the people in such matters as religion and science, which the founding fathers had carefully protected. Although he opposed in principle government intervention in the sciences, he excepted scientific inquiries essential to the exercise of the government's own functions (he cited as an example study of light and sound for the purpose of building light houses and fog signals); any great popular interest requiring scientific investigation which private enterprise could not undertake, but which government could accomplish under the Constitution (he took as a case at point the study of yellow fever); and, perhaps, inquiries so large and costly that they could not be successfully made by individuals. He opposed continuing the rectangular system of survey, saying that its application to unsurveyed land would be worthless. He argued that scientific explorations and surveys should be united and treated in special legislation, not in appropriation bills, and that the federal government had gone too far in competing with, and crippling in the process, private scientific organizations.

evening until midnight revising the notes of my speech.

WEDNESDAY, 12. Dictated a large number of letters in the morning. Called at the Departments and thence to the Capitol. Work continued on the Appropriation Bill in the House until three o'clock when eulogies were delivered on the life of the late Mr. Hartridge of Georgia.[43] In the evening met the Committee on Yellow Fever at the Riggs House but did not remain long. Returned home very weary and retired early.

THURSDAY, 13. Dictated some 35 letters in the morning. Visited the Departments and thence to the Capitol at eleven. The House has been meeting at eleven since Monday. We are preparing for a struggle with the Democrats in their attempt to repeal the national election laws. At 7 o'clock dined at Welcker's with Ingersoll[44] at a dinner given to a number of gentlemen who were Members of the Thirty-eighth Congress, among them Senators Voorhees and Blaine, Dwight Townsend[45] and myself. There were present, also, Robert Ingersoll, Capt. Stevenson and a Mr. Clarke of California. Returned home at nine o'clock and worked at my desk until half-past ten.

FRIDAY, 14. Dictated a number of letters in the morning. Then went to the Printing Office to express my indignation at the Printers for having struck off 6,000 copies of my speech on Prof. Henry with my name on the title page as John A. Garfield. Ordered the edition suppressed and a new one substituted. Went to the House at twelve. The day was consumed on Private Bills. Home in the evening. Number of ladies and gentlemen called. Rose came and I dictated the Journal for several recent days.

SATURDAY, 15. When I awoke in the morning, I found Swaim had returned from New York to remain over until Monday

---

Garfield's guarded language in this speech did not adequately reflect his deep commitment to the proposed Geological Survey.

[43]The House worked on the Appropriation Bill until shortly after 4:00 P.M., when it adjourned. The eulogies on Hartridge were delivered on February 13.

[44]Ebon C. Ingersoll was a member of the 38th Congress.

[45]Dwight Townsend (1826–1899) was a Democratic member of the House from New York, 1864–65, 1871–73.

evening. Brown came and I dictated letters in the morning and went to the Departments and to the Capitol at twelve.[46] The day was spent on the Legislative Appropriation Bill. A considerable progress was made, but the political sections proposed to be offered by the Democrats were not reached. Home in the evening.

SUNDAY, 16. Mother, Crete and I attended church at eleven o'clock with Lieut. Harber, General Sheldon and wife, who dined with us. In the evening Swaim and I called at the President's and spent three-quarters of an hour very agreeably. We then called on Secretary McCrary a short time. Home at ten and retired at eleven.

MONDAY, 17. The Committee on Ways and Means met, but I did not get there until near the close of the meeting and the quorum was gone. Mr. Wood has offered a proposition to use the coin reserve, provided for resumption purposes, to pay the arrears of pension. I have denounced this and resisted it as an act against resumption. In the House, the River and Harbor Bill was passed. The Deficiency Bill was also passed, and from two o'clock onward until half-past four the day was devoted to reports from the Committee on the District of Columbia. In the evening Swaim returned from [to] New York. The House held an evening session devoted to eulogies on Mr. Schleicher of Texas. A large number of speeches were delivered, one by myself. At half-past eight went to Mr. Foster's where, with General Sheldon, I spent the rest of the evening.

TUESDAY, 18. Dictated letters until 10 o'clock. Then attended the Committee on Ways and Means until eleven. The day in the House had been set for the Committee on Ways and Means, but S. S. Cox called up the Census Bill, which threw the Ways and

[46]According to the minutes of the Committee on Ways and Means Garfield was present on this day at a special meeting called by the chairman. The committee considered a letter from the secretary of the treasury concerning deficiencies that would be caused by arrearages in pensions. Garfield moved that the secretary be authorized to buy the amount required in four percent bonds, but no vote was taken on his motion.

Means Committee out of the day. Cox made a long speech on his bill. I followed in a speech of three-quarters of an hour, defining the general provisions of the bill as it came from the Senate but attacking the House amendment giving to the Governors of the states the power of nominating Supervisors. This led to a lengthy debate upon the conclusion of which the Democrats voted solidly for the provision. Home in the evening. Rose came and helped me. Revised the notes of my speech on Mr. Schleicher.

WEDNESDAY, 19. Dictated letters in the morning. Went to the President's and Secretary of State's, thence to the Capitol. The Chairman of the Committee last night ruled in order an amendment to the Legislative Appropriation Bill repealing the Election Laws which provide for supervisors to witness the proceedings at national elections.[47] Very vigorous speeches were made during the day on both sides. Towards the close of the day I spoke denouncing the caucus dictation under which the Democracy were acting as a kind of moral duress which governed both the Chairman and members of the Committee and made this House not a legislative body, but one to register the dictates of a caucus. This created quite an explosion. Sayler moved that my words be taken down, but the Chairman (Blackburn) preferred to come down to the floor and repel my attack. This he attempted to do. I reiterated my statement only saying that it was not personal to him, but governed ever[y] other member, including him, that it applied to the Democratic Party. Home in the evening; several friends called.

THURSDAY, 20. Desk until ten o'clock, when I went to the Senate Wing to meet the Joint Committee on Yellow Fever. It is manifest that the two Committees cannot agree and each Committee will introduce a difference [different] bill and the consequence will be that both will fail. The Democrats are so fearful of inter-

---

[47]The amendment was read during the evening session of February 18, but no point of order was made until the Committee of the Whole took it up the next day. After debate the chairman overruled the point of order on the ground that the tendency of the amendment was to retrench expenditures.

fering with State Rights that they are unwilling that the General Government shall help protect them from Yellow Fever, unless they can degrade the nation in comparison with states. This they shall not do with my consent. At seven o'clock dined at Secretary Evarts'. There were present, Prof. Goldwin Smith, Senators Edmunds, Lamar, Ransom,[48] [and] Matthews, [and] George Bancroft, Robt. C. Winthrop,[49] and Henry Adams. We had a very pleasant time. At half-past nine o'clock, I drove to Marini's Hall to attend a Fancy Dress Ball, which was held at the close of the children's dancing lessons for the Winter. Remained until 11 o'clock when I returned home.

FRIDAY, 21. Worked at my desk until 10 o'clock, when I called at Mr. Merrick's in reference to General Hazen's troubles,[50] and found he was not in. Stopped on the way to the Capitol and paid some bills. Reached the Capitol at 11. We tried to get up the Legislative Appropriation Bill, but under the pretence of trying to take up private bills the Democracy beat us and got a morning hour, by the aid of a few of our men who hoped to reach certain private bills. As soon as the morning hour was over, it was in order to move to go to business on the Speaker's table, which motion Tucker made with a view to reaching the tobacco tax bill as it came back from the Senate Committee. This was the real purpose of the day's work. Thereupon I made the point of order that it required a two-thirds vote to lay aside private bills and take up public bills except in Committee of the Whole. I[51] then move[d] to go into Committee of the Whole on the Private Calendar which was agreed to. This defeated for a time the effort to

[48]Matt W. Ransom (1826–1904) was a Democratic member of the Senate from North Carolina, 1872–95.

[49]Robert C. Winthrop (1809–1894) was a Whig member of the U.S. House of Representatives from Massachusetts, 1842–50 (he was Speaker, 1847–49), and a member of the U.S. Senate, 1850–51, as the successor of Daniel Webster. He was chairman of the Peabody Education Fund for the improvement of education in the South.

[50]See Vol. III, pp. 500–501, n. 156.

[51]The motion was made by John M. Bright of Tennessee. While taking dictation, Garfield's stenographer apparently mistook "Bright" for "I."

reduce the Tobacco tax. Home in the evening. Rose came and
I dictated a short time.

SATURDAY, 22. Dictated letters until 11, when I went to the
Capitol. The Democracy made a struggle to have a morning
hour, for the purpose after it of moving to go to the Speaker's
table to pass the Senate amendments to the Internal Revenue Bill
which reduce[s] the Tobacco tax. We sought to go on with the
appropriation bills, but the Democrats succeeded by a small majority in having a morning hour and after that went to the
Speaker's Table. To the surprise of almost everybody, we found
on the Table the old bill that passed the House nearly 15 months
ago repealing the Resumption Act. It had come back to us with
the Senate amendments, and being rendered useless by time, had
never been taken up. The Greenbackers under Ewing's lead took
it up and sought to pass it. It was so amended as to substantially
destroy the Resumption Act. I replied to Ewing in a speech of
twenty minutes and again in one of ten minutes, and at the
conclusion of the debate moved to lay the bill and amendments
on the table. This was done by 31 majority, in the same House
that a little over a year ago, passed the bill by nearly two-thirds
majority.[52] Home in the evening until half-past 8 o'clock, when
I went with Crete and Major Swaim to Mrs. Dahlgren's. The
President and his wife were there and a large company of literary
people. After a brief paper by Chief Justice Drake and another
by Mrs. Mohun, a recitation of "The Star Spangled Banner" by
Mrs. ——— [Lander] I made a speech of some 25 minutes on the
character of George Washington. It was well-received. At 10
o'clock we went to Senator Blaine's reception and returned
home at midnight. On my return I found the Reporter's notes of
my speech in the House today awaiting me, and revised it, and
waited until half-past 2 o'clock for the messenger. Retired a little
before 3 in the morning very weary.

SUNDAY, 23. Awoke very tired, not having had enough sleep.
Remained at home to read and rest. Read Henry Adams' *New*

---

[52]For material that should have been recorded in this entry, see the entry for
February 24.

England Federalism. [53] Gen. Hazen, Lts. Harber and Wilson,[54] and Miss Ransom came to dinner. Swaim was also with us.

At 6.45 went to Henry Adams' and dined with his family, Mrs. Lawrence and Miss Appleton of Boston, and Mr. Robinson of New York—a very pleasant dinner. During the day, I had received a note from the President asking me to call on him this evening; and so at 9.30 I called. He asked me about the Chinese Bill,[55] and we had a full conversation. I advised him to veto the bill, and point[ed] out, fully, the iniquity of its provision. Sec'y Evarts was there and joined in the discussion. I am sure the bill will be vetoed. The President also told me he would veto the Legislative Appropriation Bill if the clauses were added repealing the election law. He says he has recently had conversations with the Greenbackers who are elected to the next Congress, and believes that they will vote against the Democrats and with us. This is another case of the President's optimism.

MONDAY, 24. Awoke tired. Dictated a large number of letters. Went to the Capitol at eleven. A large part of the day in the House was consumed on the Tobacco Bill, which I should have added on Saturday was reached before adjournment. I ought also to have added on Saturday the Chinese Bill was reached and I voted in company with 94 others to lay it on the table. The sentiment against that bill is growing very strong. I am satisfied that Senator Blaine has made a great mistake in his advocacy of it. At the same time I am anxious to see some legislation that shall prevent the overflow of Chinese in this country. In the evening Swaim, Crete and I dined at Mrs. Johnson's,[56] 1721 H. Street,

[53]Henry Adams, ed., *Documents Relating to New-England Federalism. 1800–1815* (1877).

[54]John C. Wilson (1849–1923), a native of New York, was a classmate of Garfield's appointee Giles B. Harber at the United States Naval Academy, at which both graduated in 1869. Both men were now ordnance instructors at the Navy Yard in Washington. In December, 1879, both were assigned to duty on the *Tennessee*. Wilson retired as captain in 1907.

[55]See January 26, 1879, n. 28.

[56]Ellen (Roche) Johnson, widow of Simeon M. Johnson, Washington journalist and lawyer, who is mentioned in Vol. II, pp. 24 and 25.

in company with Colonel Rockwell and his wife and Miss Hood of Georgia. A very pleasant evening. At ten we visited Miss Ransom's studio, w[h]ere there was a party of callers. Home at eleven o'clock.

TUESDAY, 25.   Dictated letters in the morning until 11 o'clock when I went to the Capitol. After a few preliminary motions the discussion on the Election Clauses of the Legislative Bill was resumed. Mr. Banning of Cincinnati read a prepared speech, attacking me for what I had said in my last Saturday's [Wednesday's] remarks about the Congressional vote in Cincinnati. I replied to him giving the grounds of the position I had taken, and, I think, did so effectively.[57] It is my impression that I made a mistake in not noticing his personal insinuations against me. I think there is danger that I [am] getting too spiritless in regard to personalities but the fact is I thoroughly despise all mere personal debate. I never feel that to slap a man in the face is any real gain to the truth. I was feeling very dull and stupid about three o'clock and left the House after pairing with Mr. Tucker of Virginia. Hale is taking charge of the resistance to the repeal of the Election Laws, and thinks he will push the resistance until tomorrow.[58] I think it not wise to resist until the Senate has acted by striking out the amending clauses.

[57]In his speech of February 19 Garfield argued that repeal of the election laws would produce great fraud at the polls, and that the purpose of the Democrats in seeking repeal was victory in 1880. With Banning in mind, he said that "already enough men from . . . Cincinnati have been sent to the penitentiary for fraud to take away the majority by which one of the members on this floor was declared elected to his seat." Banning, who was not present to hear the statement, replied on February 25, denouncing it as untrue and its author as a falsifier. He declared that he could gather up all the well known charges of slander against Garfield and "pour them out on this floor," but he scorned to do so for he had no personal knowledge as to their truth or falsehood. In response Garfield stated that an individual had been convicted for fraudulent voting after testifying in court that in 1876 he had voted nineteen times and secured about three hundred other fraudulent votes for Banning, whose majority in that election was only seventy-five votes.

[58]Before adjourning the House passed the Legislative Appropriation Bill with the amendments repealing the election laws.

WEDNESDAY, 26. Dictated letters in the morning until half-past ten, when I went to the Capitol. I hear that Mr. Banning intends to attack me for revising the notes of my reply to him yesterday. I have made up my mind that if he does, I will characterize him as he deserves and make him remember me for the rest of his life. I feel too ill this morning to attend the sessions of the House, but so much business of importance is pending that I go. We were hardly started in the day, before the sugar question came up unexpectedly. Mr. Robbins made a speech of an hour and a half in favor of his bill. I took the floor to reply although I was hardly able, having an attack of indigestion and malaria. After having spoken five minutes I felt better, and spoke nearly an hour. I think I made one of the best, most compact and consecutive speeches on a complicated question that I have ever made. I had very close attention, and am satisfied I made many converts to my views, which was not to make any change in the tariff, but to correct the under-valuation now practiced.[59] Mr. Banning was on the floor, but thought best not to put in his appearance on the subject of attack on me. In the evening revised my notes. Retired at nine.

THURSDAY, 27. Dictated a number of letters in the morning. Went early to the Capitol where the approaching end of the session crowded business at every point. Our records show that more than seven thousand bills were introduced during this Congress, four-fifths of them being House bills. The House sat until six o'clock in the struggle on the appropriation bills,[60] six of which are yet pending in one or the other House. An evening

[59]Robbins presented the report of the majority of the Committee on Ways and Means, and Garfield that of the minority. Declaring that all customs bills should be considered in relation to four great interests—the revenues, home industries, foreign trade, and the consumers—Garfield discussed those interests at length and concluded that they would be served best by making no changes in the current tariff. But he did urge an amendment authorizing the secretary of the treasury to use a polariscope or such other means as he might find effective for judging accurately the quality of imported sugar. See January 8, 1879, n. 5.

[60]Almost the entire afternoon session was devoted to miscellaneous items, with considerable debate on the subject of ventilating the Hall of the House.

session was held at eight o'clock for reports from the Committee on Ways and Means. I attended and reported three or four bills which were passed.[61] Harry and Jimmy went with me to the Capitol and we walked home at the end of the session about half-past ten o'clock.

FRIDAY, 28. Devoted only a few moments to dictating letters and was compelled to go back to the House. It seems almost certain that we shall have an extra session. The followers of Blackburn, who desire to elevate him to the Speakership, have come to the conclusion that an extra session will be of service to their cause and so are using all the means in their power to force one upon the country. This they can do only by defeating appropriation bills. We were distressed during the day by a rumor that two Senators, Conover[62] and Patterson, were about to vote with the Democrats on the election clause in the appropriation bills. If this is so, it would be an act of betrayal which would seriously complicate our trouble with the Democracy. I can hardly believe that the rumor is correct.

March

SATURDAY, 1. Dictated some letters in the morning. This is probably the last batch I will be able to do until after adjournment. Went to the Capitol early. In the intervals of the arrival of the appropriation bills from the Senate a struggle ensued on the subject of sugar and Burchard got in a speech in favor of the Robbins bill. At the end of his speech, it was manifest from the temper of the House that the bill would fail, when Mr. Robbins withdrew it. An evening session was held last night on pension bills, but I did not attend, I was too much exhausted to go for

[61]Garfield reported four bills from the Committee on Ways and Means; three passed and one was referred to the Committee of the Whole on the Private Calendar.

[62]Simon B. Conover (1840–1908) was a Republican member of the Senate from Florida, 1873–79.

business wholly of a private character. I have been called upon for a pamphlet edition of my speech on the sugar question and it will be published after the hurry of the session is over. I got home in time for a late dinner, hurried back to the Capitol and sat until past midnight. Home very tired, got to bed at half-past three o'clock.

SUNDAY, 2.   Started to the Capitol at 9 o'clock, but arrived a little late when I found the House had adjourned to allow the Conference Committees time to work on the bills. I came home and got a little sleep. Mrs. [Miss] Ransom, Lieut. Harber and Captain Kellogg[63] of the Army dined with us. At eight in the evening, Crete, Major Swaim, Lieuts. Harber and Wilson, and Miss Mays went with me to the National Theatre to hear Colonel Ingersoll's lecture on the liberty of men, women and children. It was very brilliant and had many important truths in it, but I think he is the victim of intellectual prejudice against the Christian religion, to a degree that he is entirely unaware of. Immediate[ly] after the lecture I went to the House, where the session was resumed and continued until two hours and a half after midnight.[64] Came home and got to bed at three in the morning.

MONDAY, 3.   Congress sat all night and until near seven o'clock in the morning.[65] After the midnight hours we were in a continuous struggle to prevent the impeachment of Minister Seward[66] —in which we were successful—and to secure if possible an

[63]Either Sanford C. Kellogg of the 5th U.S. Cavalry Regiment or W. L. Kellogg of the 10th U.S. Infantry Regiment, both of whom were captains and had corresponded with Garfield.

[64]The evening session adjourned at 10:57.

[65]On March 3 the House convened at 11:00 A.M. and an impeachment debate (see the following note) began immediately after the reading of the Journal. It continued, with interruptions for debate and voting on appropriations bills, throughout the daytime session, which recessed at 6:35 P.M., and well into the evening session, which commenced at 9:00 P.M. and continued until 11:00 the following morning, when the Forty-fifth Congress expired.

[66]George F. Seward (1840–1910), United States minister to China, was accused of high crimes and misdemeanors in his official capacity as consul and consul-general at Shanghai, China, between January 1, 1864 and December 31, 1875, and as minister to China, 1876–78. The charges were made by the Committee on Expenditures in the State Department which, after a year-long investigation,

agreement on the appropriation bills. All have been agreed to except the Legislative and Army bill[s]. Walked home and found the family just sitting down to breakfast.[67] After breakfast revised the notes of my speech last night on the position of the two parties in reference to the appropriation bills. Returned to the House at nine. The struggle for the passage of the Pension and other private bills was kept up until 11, when a final disagreement on the Legislative Bill came, causing a debate which lasted until the moment of adjournment. I think we placed the responsibility for the extra session, now made inevitable, upon the revolutionary element of the Democratic Party.[68] Went with Swaim and Rockwell and played billiards. Came home, retired at three and slept until 6. At seven, Crete and I went to Gov. Swann's to dinner. A very brilliant party. Randolph Tucker and wife, Mr. Goode and wife of Va., Fernando Wood and Mrs. Hickok, General Butler and wife of South Carolina, Speaker Randall and wife and other Philadelphia people were present. We returned home at half-past 11, and retired at 12. Late this afternoon the President has issued his proclamation calling an extra session of Congress to meet on March 18th.

TUESDAY, 4. Hurried to the House immediately after breakfast, where the struggle over the Appropriation Bill was resumed and continued until the adjournment at eleven which ended the legislative Saturday, and immediately the House assembled for Monday. The day was consumed in a long weary struggle on our part

---

recommended impeachment on the date of this entry. As a witness before the Committee, Seward had refused to produce certain books and on February 28 he was brought before the bar of the House and arrested for contempt of Congress. Although Seward was not impeached, his resignation was requested by the State Department in December, 1879, and his successor appointed in March, 1880.

[67]This sentence and the rest of the entry belong in the entry for March 4, portions of which are repetitious.

[68]Democrats blamed Republicans for making an extra session necessary. They accused the Republican-controlled Senate of trying to dictate to the Democratic House, and they charged that Republican representatives used delaying tactics to prevent the impeachment of Seward. They also claimed that Republicans opposed free elections and sought to control voting by using the army at the polls.

to bring some agreement on the appropriation bills. We sat until six o'clock taking a recess until 9, and from 9 o'clock sat through all night. About two hours after midnight I made a speech of fifteen minutes setting forth the stand of the two parties and the conditions under which the bills could be agreed to and passed. If an extra session is caused, it will be in consequence of the three political amendments saddled upon the appropriation bills by the Democrats. First, the repeal of the Juror's Test Oath.[69] Second, forbidding the use of the Army to keep the peace at the poles [polls], and Third, the repeal of the election laws to protect national elections from fraud. I proposed to give up the first two of these if the Democrats would give up the third. This they clamorously refused to do. I told them we would not surrender this just protection to the purity of the elective franchise. The Republicans in the House have followed me with great unanimity in all these days of struggle.

WEDNESDAY, 5.   Rose about 8 o'clock after getting about seven hours' sleep, which still leaves me largely in arrears and feeling a good deal exhausted. Dictated a large number of letters during the forenoon. My mail has accumulated to frightful proportions during the last few days. At half-past twelve o'clock Major Woodworth of Youngstown, took lunch with us. I then went with him and Major McKinley to the President, to commend to his favorable consideration Walter Campbell of Youngstown.[70] Woodworth suggested his appointment as Governor of a Territory, but

---

[69]An oath by which a prospective juror swore that he had not given aid, comfort, or countenance to the Southern Confederacy. Since it could be used by the Republican marshals and their deputies to secure jurors likely to convict men arrested for disturbing the peace at the polls, the oath was a powerful instrument of Republican control.

[70]Walter L. Campbell (1842–1905), a native of Salem, Ohio, was blind from the age of five. Despite his handicap he graduated at Western Reserve College, attended the Harvard Law School for a year and was admitted to the bar. In 1869 he went to the new Territory of Wyoming, where his brother John had been appointed governor (see Vol. II, pp. 86–87). In 1873 he returned to Ohio, where he soon became editor of the *Mahoning Register* in Youngstown. He continued with this paper and its successors until 1882, when he returned to the practice of law. He was mayor of Youngstown, 1884–86.

I think the President was quite right in saying it was wholly out of question that a totally blind man should be a Governor. Went thence to the Post Office Department with Woodworth on Department business. Played billiards with Swaim a portion of the afternoon. Home in the evening. Large number of people called. Rose came and I dictated the Journal.

THURSDAY, 6. Dictated letters in the morning until 10 o'clock, then made preparations for leaving tonight for Ohio. Went to the Public Printing Office and arranged for publishing my speeches [speech] on the Sugar Tariff; then to the Baltimore and Ohio Depot to arrange for sleeping berth; then to the Capitol, War Dep't and the President's. Had a full conversation with the President on the future of our struggle with the Democracy on the subject of the election laws. I told him I had heard rumors that he had expressed himself as willing to give up the election laws, that I could not believe it to be true, and that it was due to the Republicans to be informed first if any such course was intended on his part. He answered by assuring me in the most positive terms that he was heartily with us, that perhaps it was not proper for him to have said that he would veto a bill not yet before him, but that he had said to not less than 20 that he would not hesitate to veto any appropriation bill that had the repeal of the election laws upon it. This was altogether satisfactory. Saw several of our Republican Members of the House, and told them to say to everybody for me that we would make no trade with either Greenbackers or Democrats on the subject of the Speakership, that I would regard it as a calamity to the Republican party to have me or any other Republican elected as speaker of the next House, it being really Democratic, that we could serve more effectively by being a compact independent minority, wielding a free lance and discussing measures without compromise. The political pot in the city is boiling fiercely over the organization of the House.[71] I am glad to go to Ohio for a week and get out

[71]The uncertainty about the Speakership arose largely from the fact that the new House would include more than a dozen Greenbackers, who hoped to be the controlling group in its organization. Another factor causing worry among the

of it. Swaim left us at half-past seven for Leavenworth. At 9 1/2 o'clock Mother, Crete, and I started for the Ohio and Pittsburgh depot to take the western train.

FRIDAY, 7.   Awoke in the Valley of the Monongahela, near Braddock's Field. Reached Pittsburgh at 8.24. Crossed the Monongahela Bridge in the omnibus to the New Depot. In a few moments took the new Lake Erie and Pittsburgh Road, going down the left bank of the Ohio, about thirty miles, to Beaver, thence across the River, up the Valley of the Beaver, reaching Youngstown at noon, and Garrettsville at half-past one, where Crete left us to go to Hiram. I went with Mother to Solon where Alva [Alton Trowbridge] met us and took us to Sister Mary's. Both my sisters were there and I spent the afternoon with Marenus looking over the farm and arranging for fencing. Spent the night at Sister Mary's.

SATURDAY, 8.   Took the 7.51 A.M. train to Garrettsville. Read Douda's [Daudet's] *Nabob*[72] on the way. Heavy thunder storm with rain. Hack to Hiram. This is the first time I have visited Hiram as a citizen for sixteen years.[73] I have been the Representative of this County continuously, until last Tuesday, since 1862 [1863]. Dinner at Father Rudolph's. Mother Rudolph very feeble. In the afternoon went to Hinsdale's where I wrote some letters and read his lecture on "The Division of Labor," which he is to deliver at the Homeopathic College at Cleveland next Monday noon. Read *The Nabob* in the evening and retired early, still weary from want of sleep.

SUNDAY, 9.   Attended church. Being College Vacation, but few were present. No Preacher. A social meeting. At 5, Brother Joe

---

Democrats was their internecine struggle for the Speakership, Joseph C. S. Blackburn having strong support against Samuel J. Randall. Whether the Democratic majority could be held together behind their caucus choice for Speaker was an unanswered question. As it turned out, the Democrats supported their caucus candidate and the Greenbackers voted for one of their own. Even if the Greenbackers had supported Garfield, he would not have won.

[72]Alphonse Daudet, *Le Nabab. Moeurs Parisiennes* (1877) was published in the United States in an English translation as *The Nabob* (1878).

[73]See May 11, 1878, n. 136.

drove me to the train at Garrettsville, whence I went to Cleveland. Arrived at half-past seven and spent the night at Captain Henry's on Cedar Avenue.

MONDAY, 10. After breakfast went to Dr. Robison's and thence to the Bank and to Hubbell's lumber yard where I ordered a thousand feet of fencing to be sent to my Solon Farm.[74] Took the 11.15 train for Mentor arriving at 12.19. Moses met me with the "Grays" and drove me to Mr. Aldrich's where I took dinner. Thence to the farm where I spent the afternoon in examining the stock, barns, feed, etc. My machinery for cutting, grinding and steaming feed is working well and I believe has saved as much as one ton of hay to each head of stock. Last year twenty-five acres of cornstalks were consumed by six less cattle than have been thus far kept through Winter on eighteen acres of stalks and three or four stacks left—more than enough to carry us through. Towards evening Mr. Swift,[75] Reporter of the *Cleveland Herald,* came to interview me. I spent the night at Mr. Aldrich's. Retired at 9 o'clock, needing rest. About midnight I was awakened by a loud knocking at the door and thought it foreboded bad news from Mother Rudolph. It turned out to be Robertson of the *Cleveland [Leader].* He heard that the *Herald* had been down to interview me in the afternoon and he had gotten the Night Express to let him off at Mentor. He sat for three-quarters of an hour at my bedside interviewing me and went thence to the Telegraph

[74]On November 25, 1873, Garfield's sister Mary and her husband, Marenus Larabee, for a consideration of two thousand dollars, deeded about 25 1/2 acres of their farm in Solon to Garfield. On December 4, 1873, Garfield and his wife, for a consideration of eight hundred dollars, deeded about 6 1/2 acres of this land to Mary; this step was taken with the acquiesence of Marenus. In a letter to Mary, written on the same day, Garfield said that he thought he could arrange to let Marenus use his land for five or six years before he had need to raise the money on it. The deeds were recorded in Vol. 221, pp. 600–601, and Vol. 227, p. 81, of the Cuyahoga County deed records in Cleveland. See Vol. II, pp. 236, 242 and 254.

[75]Between 1876 and 1880 William F. Swift was successively city editor of these Cleveland newspapers: *Herald, Sunday Post, Herald,* and *Leader.* For several years thereafter he was associated with the Brush Electric Company in Cleveland, most of the time as secretary.

Office and sent 1,200 words by telegraph, such is the professional
rage of Reporters for surpassing each other.

TUESDAY, 11. Breakfasted at Aldrich's. Spent the forenoon on
the farm overhauling accounts with Northcott, and examining
the grinding, cutting and steaming apparatus. Dined at Mr.
Tyler's.[76] Returned to the farm until three when Mr. Aldrich
drove me to Painesville, where I called upon a few friends to
transact business. Took tea at George Steele's. Went to Cleveland by the 1/2 past 6 o'clock train. Dr. Robison's carriage was
awaiting me and he took me to his house. At eight o'clock attended a party given me at the Hon. Henry B. Payne's, on Euclid
Avenue. A number of prominent citizens were present. Remained until midnight, when I returned home with Dr. Robison.

WEDNESDAY, 12. Spent some time in the morning purchasing
seed for the farm and visiting friends. At eleven o'clock went to
the Atlantic Depot where I met Crete, but the train was a little
late. By the courtesy of the Lake Shore authorities their train was
held until we could reach their depot and about half-past eleven
o'clock Dr. Robison and wife and Crete and I were on the road
for Mentor. Moses met us at the Station and drove us to the
Doctor's where we had dinner. Spent the afternoon with Crete
in planning her garden and making further arrangements for the
Spring. We spent the night at Dr. Robison's. About nine days ago
there was excellent sleighing on all the roads on the Lake Shore.
Today, hardly a handful of snow is left in sight. The blue birds
are singing, the air is balmy and it seems as though Spring is here,
though I presume March storms await us. I can hardly endure the
prospect of returning to Washington and losing the farm life
which I have anticipated in the coming months.

THURSDAY, 13. Soon after breakfast Moses came and drove us to
Capt. Burgess' [Burridge's], where we ate warm sugar, and made
arrangements for molasses for the family. Returned to the farm
and completed our work there, and, after an early dinner at the
Doctor's, Moses drove us to Willoughby where we took the
12.40 train for Cleveland, arriving at half-past one. At 1.45 we

---

[76]John C. Tyler and his wife were farm neighbors of the Garfields.

took the Pittsburgh train and at Euclid Street Station Miss Josie Mason,[77] daughter of Cousin James Mason, came on board to accompany us to Washington. Supper at Wellsville. Reached Pittsburgh at 8.15. Drove rapidly across the City to the Connellsville Depot. Arrived just as the bell was ringing for our train to leave.

FRIDAY, 14. Awoke at Martinsburg, West Va., train two hours late, delayed in the night by a land slide this side of Cumberland. Read *Nabob* for two or three hours. Reached Washington at half-past ten. Found the family in excellent health and spirits. Tired and dirty but glad to get home again. Spent the afternoon in reading the enormous mail which had accumulated in my absence.

SATURDAY, 15. Brown came and I dictated some 40 letters. The Democratic Party is in a great ferment of excitement over the organization of the House. The struggle between Randall and Blackburn is very bitter and is likely to leave its dregs in the cup of their victory. Large number of friends called in the evening.

SUNDAY, 16. A bright, balmy morning. Crete, Josy [Josie], Jimmy and I attended the New York Avenue Church and we heard a very interesting and sensible sermon from the Pastor, Mr. Paxton.[78] At 2 o'clock Lieuts. Harber and Wilson came to dinner. Gen'l Hazen and several other friends called in the afternoon. I spent some time in reading the history of the veto, and beginning my preparation for a thorough study of the relation of the appropriation bills to other legislation, and the English and American precedents. Retired early. In the evening several members called to consult about the Republican organization in the House. Went with Amos Townsend to Frye's at the corner of New York Avenue and 13th Street, where we agreed upon a

---

[77]Josephine Mason, oldest daughter of James Mason and sister of Belle, who married Harry Garfield. She was long an intimate of the Garfield family.

[78]John R. Paxton (1843–1923), a native of Pennsylvania, was pastor of the New York Avenue Presbyterian Church in Washington, D.C., 1878–82. From 1882–98 he held pastorates in New York City, where he retired in the latter year and resided to his death.

caucus at 4 o'clock on Monday in the Hall of the House of Representatives. Frye agreed to accept the Chairmanship of the Caucus. An Executive Committee of Nine was also agreed upon to act with the Chairman of the Caucus in calling caucuses.

MONDAY, 17.   Brown came and I dictated letters until eleven o'clock, when I went by appointment to meet Mr. Merrick, General Hazen's lawyer, called to consult over the pending Court Martial between Generals Hazen and Stanley. Then went to the Pension Office to see if Sister Hittie is entitled to a pension and I am delighted to find that she is, and hope I shall succeed in getting one allowed her. Lunch at half-past twelve. Dictated some 20 more letters and at three o'clock went to the Caucus at the Capitol. At four o'clock, Frye, Chairman, on motion of Hubbell, of Michigan, I was unanimously nominated for Speaker, and being called on for a speech, I spoke a moment, declaring it to be our policy to make no trades or combinations with any party or faction, or accept any official favors at the hands of this Congress, but to act together as an independent united fighting minority, remembering that the stake for which we fight is 1880. I suggested that we remember our colored friends by nominating Rainey[79] for [of] North [South] Carolina for Clerk. This was done unanimously. Remaining nominations made with great harmony. On my motion an Executive Committee of Nine were appointed. I suggested that we introduce no bills and resist all legislation except such as related to appropriation bills. After some debate this view was unanimously adopted. Caucus adjourned at half-past five. Only 100 members were present. Sturdy good-looking fellows. Home in the evening. Rose came and wrote up the Journal. Number of friends called.

TUESDAY, 18.   Brown came in the morning. I dictated a large number of letters. Several friends called. At quarter-past eleven

[79]Joseph H. Rainey's service in the House ended on March 4, 1879. In May, 1879, the President appointed him an internal revenue agent in South Carolina, a position he held until 1881.

Senator Bruce[80] came in company with Mr. French,[81] late of Mississippi, now of Damascoville, Ohio, and I went with them to see the Commissioner of Internal Revenue and if possible secure a place for French. Mr. French then drove me to the Capitol. At twelve o'clock Clerk Adams[82] called the new House to order and read the Roll of Members. Nominations were made for Speaker. Mr. Randall received 144 votes. I received 125. Hendrick B. Wright[83] the Greenback Candidate received 13. One vote was thrown for Judge Kelley. On the first reading of the Roll but 143 votes were thrown for Randall, which was not a majority of the members to elect. Mr. Conger raised the point of order that it was not an election, and while making his objection an additional member arrived—O'Reilly[84] of Brooklyn— and cast his vote for Randall, which gave him a majority of one.[85] As I expected, the boast of any strength in the New Organization calling itself the Greenback party amounted to but little. It has no effect on the organization of the House. In violation of the principal [principle] decided in former cases, the Clerk left off the name of Mr. Bisbee of Florida, and inserted that of his Democratic competitor. We objected to swearing in Mr. Hull and got an order to have the papers in the case printed in the

[80]Blanche K. Bruce (1841–1898), a former slave, was a Republican member of the Senate from Mississippi, 1875–81. In the latter year Garfield appointed him register of the Treasury.

[81]O. C. French was a farmer in Damascoville, Mahoning County. He did not at this time receive a federal appointment. In the fall of 1879 he sold some business interests in Columbus and left for Colorado, where, by 1880, he was a member of the Denver firm of Ware, French & Co., which operated a mining exchange and real estate office. He continued, however, to maintain his farm; in July, 1880, he sent Garfield a bill of sale and a pedigree for a Jersey heifer.

[82]George M. Adams (1837–1920), an officer in the Union army during the Civil War, was a Democratic member of the House from Kentucky, 1867–75, and clerk of the House, 1875–81.

[83]Hendrick B. Wright (1808–1881) was a Democratic member of the House from Pennsylvania, 1853–55, 1861–63, and 1877–81.

[84]Daniel O'Reilly (1838–1911) was a Democratic member of the House from New York, 1879–81.

[85]Although the full complement of members in the House was 293, there were six vacancies. A majority would thus be 144; 283 votes were cast.

Record and set the subject for debate tomorrow.[86] McMahon of Ohio attempted to have read and printed a memorial against two of the Cincinnati members.[87] We resisted and pending action the House adjourned. In the evening Messrs. Frye, Hiscock, Calkins[88] and Bisbee called to consult about the conduct of Bisbee's case tomorrow. Several other Members called during the evening. At nine o'clock the President and his son called and we had considerable conversation on the coming struggle over the repeal of the election laws. The President seems firm and determined in his purpose of resistance. Among other things the President said that Taft would finally be rejected as a candidate for Governor and the Convention would insist on my accepting the nomination. He thought I ought not to refuse. He believed it would not interfere with my Senatorial prospects and perhaps would be the opening to a still higher place. I note this here because usually the President's political judgment of Ohio affairs

---

[86]Horatio Bisbee, Jr. (1839–1916) was a Republican member of the House from Florida, 1877-February 20, 1879, when his election was successfully contested by Jesse J. Finley; he successfully contested the election of Noble A. Hull (1827–1907), a Democratic member of the House from Florida, 1879–January 22, 1881, and served from the latter date to March 3, 1881; he later successfully contested the election of Finley and served from June 1, 1882–85.

[87]John A. McMahon (1833–1923) was a Democratic member of the House from Ohio, 1875–81. His memorial, signed by twenty-three citizens of Cincinnati, charged that corrupt practices of deputy marshals had enabled organized gangs to vote more than once in the recent elections in the first and second congressional districts of Ohio, and that Benjamin Butterworth (1837–1898), a Republican member of the House from Ohio, 1879–83, 1885–91, and Thomas L. Young (1832–1888), a Republican member of the House from Ohio, 1879–83, were not legally elected to the United States House of Representatives. To counter that charge, House Republicans presented telegrams from citizens of Cincinnati declaring that the election had been fair, and that some of the signatures on the memorial to McMahon had been secured through misrepresentation. On March 28 Young told the House that at his request a grand jury whose foreman was a Democrat had investigated the October election and reported that no evidence was discovered to warrant action regarding the election of Young and Butterworth. Both men retained their seats.

[88]William H. Calkins (1842–1894) was a Republican member of the House from Indiana, 1877–84.

has been good.[89] But, while I think there are serious objections to Taft as a candidate which will probably produce some murmuring, I hazard the opinion against the President's that Taft will be nominated. Retired at midnight.

WEDNESDAY, 19.   Brown came and I dictated a large number of letters and received numerous visitors. The Secretary of State [called] and set about an hour to discuss the political situation. He wants a consultation between a few leading members of the House and Cabinet to put our programme of resistance in the best shape. This is wise. The Secretary rather hinted, though he did not state it definitely as his opinion, we had better give up the sections in relation to the Marshals on condition that the sections in reference to the Supervisors were retained in the law. He made this point: that the theory of American Suffrage is that voting is not to be obstructed, but that fraudulent voting is to be punished and it is doubtful whether the power given to the Marshals to prevent people from voting fraudulently is wise. Possibly he may be correct as a matter of theory, but I hardly think our people are in a temper to give up any part of the election laws in this struggle and to do so would probably weaken us in the fight. At the Capitol at 12, thence with the Joint Committee of the two Houses to wait on the President. On my return found Frye in the midst of the Florida debate. After the other side had spoken half an hour, I spoke some twenty minutes, proposing that neither Hull nor Bisbee be sworn in, but that the *prima facie* case as well as the case on its merits be referred to the Committee on Elections. On this motion all the Greenbackers voted with us, but we were beaten by 140 to 137 [136], showing that party lines are sharply drawn at an unusually early period. House adjourned at half-past four. Home in the evening. Rose came and wrote up the Journal. Many callers.

At 9.15 P.M. I went with Crete, Josie Mason, Martha Mays and Harry to call on Mrs. Hayes and the President. Leaving them below I went up to the President's Library and discussed with him the suggestion of Evarts. He (the President) agreed with me

[89]Charles Foster won the Republican nomination for governor of Ohio.

that we could not even go into the merits of the election laws on the Appropriation Bill. The question there would be the effort of Congress to coerce the President. Home at 10.30.

THURSDAY, 20. Letters in the morning. Departments at a later hour. Capitol at twelve. McMahon called up the memorial in reference to the Cincinnati Election and introduced his resolution to have it printed and referred to the Committee on Elections, with power to act upon the case. I resisted the printing of the affidavits and also its reference to the Committee on Elections. Had several telegrams from Cincinnati read. Proposed a Special Committee to investigate the Cincinnati Election and report on the workings of the Supervisor and Marshal Law in that City. After some discussion and a brilliant speech by Butterworth —exceptionally so for a new Member—my resolution prevailed and soon after the House adjourned. Several gentlemen called in the afternoon. At six o'clock the President sent for me to take a family dinner with him in company with Mr. Hiscock. A pleasant party. After dinner we discussed the political situation. I suggested to the President that he had taken a wrong course in reference to the trial of Generals Hazen and Stanley. Went from the President's to Hiscock's Room and talked with him on the organization of Committees. Thence to the Ebbitt House to see Captain Frank Mason, who was quite determined that I ought to be the candidate for Governor. Got him to agree that he would not mention such a contingency in the *Leader.* Home at 10 o'clock.

FRIDAY, 21. Brown came and I dictated letters as usual. Thorp came and spent an hour in talking over Ohio affairs. He thinks Taft will be nominated. I went to the Capitol and found the House had adjourned immediately after meeting.[90] Met in room of the Committee on the Judiciary with the Executive Committee of the Republican Caucus and discussed our policy. Agreed not to hold a general caucus at present, but resolved to introduce a resolution into the House restricting legislation for the present session to appropriation bills. Home at lunch. Thence to the

[90]The House adjourned until March 25.

Sec'y of War in regard to Hazen's troubles. In the evening thirty-five Republican Members met in my parlor to discuss the propriety of maintaining the Honest Money League during the coming campaign. Frye was appointed Chairman and the conference lasted for two hours. There was a general consent that it was important to continue the Honest Money League in its work of distributing sound financial literature. A few members were however disinclined to the movement. The result was the appointment of a Committee of Five to solicit a fund of four or five thousand dollars for the purpose of distributing documents.

SATURDAY, 22. Dictated a large number of letters. I have arranged with the Secretary of the Treasury to have some statistics prepared for my article in the *North American.*[91] James Mason came this morning from New York, and will spend a day or two with us. In the evening the Literary Society met at our house. About forty members were present. Chief Justice Drake presided. Dr. Cox[92] read a paper on Latin Hymns of the Middle Ages, at the conclusion of which a general discussion of the paper was had. I was called on first and made the point that there were three epochs in the history of the Latin language. First, It was the language of law and empire. Second, It was the language of Pagan poetry, epic and lyric. Third, and later the language of religion. These were the three piers that sustained the noble language of Rome and still made it so powerful an instrument among men. I quoted a little Latin poem, the Prayer of Mary Queen of Scots, as an addition to Dr. Cox's topic, and concluded with the suggestion that rhyme was a comparatively late inven-

[91]"National Appropriations and Misappropriations," *North American Review,* Vol. CXXVIII, No. CCLXXII (June, 1879), pp. 572–586.

[92]Christopher C. Cox (1816–1881), a native of Maryland, graduated at Yale, 1835, studied medicine and practiced in Baltimore. He was surgeon general of Maryland during the Civil War, was elected lieutenant governor, 1864, and served as U.S. commissioner of pensions, 1868–69. In 1869 he began the practice of medicine in Washington, D.C., where he also became a professor in the medical department of Georgetown College. He was an organizer of the American Health Association, a member of the Board of Health of the District of Columbia and a contributor to medical and scientific journals.

tion and did not belong to the highest types of poetry. This was controverted by some members but on the whole I think my position was good.

SUNDAY, 23.   Received thirty letters by the morning mail. James Mason, Crete and I attended the Disciple Church on Vermont Avenue. The children, Miss Mays and Josie went to the Epiphany. Miss Ransom dined with us at two. A large number of people called in the evening. Rumors are in the air of a compromise between the President and the Democrats on the election laws. I do [not] believe the rumors. It appears that the Democrats in caucus last night agreed to a modified form of repeal. Saving part of the sections in regard to the Supervisors, but striking out the portion in relation to the Marshals. This will not do.

MONDAY, 24.   Brown came and I dictated a large number of letters, very nearly clearing the desk. On invitation of Mr. Wilson,[93] Member from West Virginia, I called at the National Hotel at half-past two to consult with some gentlemen who were proposing to purchase and [an] interest in a gold mine in North Carolina; I am not sure about the feasibility of their plan. At half-past seven Mr. Mason and I called at Judge Cartter['s], who went with us to the President's, where we had a confidential conversation on the political situation. In spite of all rumors to the contrary, I am perfectly satisfied that he will firmly stand with us in the struggle now preparing. Returned at half-past eight. At one-quarter past nine Mr. Mason and Josie left us to take the Baltimore train to Cleveland. A number of gentlemen called— among them Secretary Sherman—and spent an hour in discussing the political and financial situation.

TUESDAY, 25.   Dictated letters to Mr. Brown. Rose came and I dictated the beginning of the *North American Review* article. Called at the Treasury and thence to the Capitol at 12 o'clock. The House immediately adjourned to give the Democrats time for further consultation. Spent some time in consultation with Republican members on the political situation. In the evening

[93]Benjamin Wilson (1825–1901) was a Democratic member of the House from West Virginia, 1875–83.

Rose came and I dictated a further instalment of the *North American Review* article.

WEDNESDAY, 26. Letters to Brown in the morning. So many people called in the morning that I was unable to make further progress with the *Review* article. Departments at half-past 11. Capitol at 12. The House again adjourned without doing anything. Spent some time in the Library getting materials for the debate on the Election Laws. Home in the evening. Rose came and we made further progress on the magazine article.

THURSDAY, 27. Letters to Brown. Further dictation to Rose. At quarter-past eleven, went to the War Department to see General Sherman on business connected with the new museum building.[94] Thence to the Capitol. Mr. Sparks of Illinois introduced the Army Appropriation Bill and the House went into Committee of the Whole and spent the day until four o'clock agreeing to nearly all the bill except the disputed sections in reference to the use of the Army at the polls.[95] During the day the Republican Executive Committee met in the room of the Committee on the Judiciary and agreed upon a program of resistance to the rider on the Army Appropriation Bill, as follows:

First. To rule it out on a point of order, and if possible argue the proposition.

Second. Amend it by making it apply, also, to the use of state or volunteer troops at elections, with such other amendments as our friends choose to offer.

[94]The National Museum, provided for in the act of Congress creating the Smithsonian Institution, and housed in the original Smithsonian building, had outgrown its quarters as more and more collections came under its management. This was particularly true after the close of the Centennial Exposition in Philadelphia when many exhibitors presented their collections to the government. The Sundry Civil Appropriations Act of March 3, 1879, appropriated $250,000 for the erection of a building for the use of the National Museum east of the Smithsonian Institution. Garfield's inaugural ball and reception took place in the nearly completed building on the night of March 4, 1881.

[95]Section six of the Army Appropriation Bill provided "that no money appropriated in this act is appropriated or shall be paid for the subsistence, equipment, transportation, or compensation of any portion of the Army of the United States to be used as a police force to keep the peace at the polls at any election held within any State."

Third. Vote against the bill if the rider is kept on.

Fourth. No fillibustering except to procure sufficient time for debate.

Immediately on the adjournment of the House a Republican Caucus was held and continued for an hour and a half. I made the above report from the Executive Committee which was adopted almost if not quite unanimously. A resolution was passed recommending Republican Members not to pair during the present struggle. Home in the evening. Rose came but I was so crowded with callers that I could not do any further work. After the visitors were gone worked for two hours on the history of the clause of the Constitution relating to elections.

FRIDAY, 28. While I was at breakfast the President called and read me the rough draft of his Veto Message of the Army Appropriation Bill, stating briefly the grounds of opposition and asking my advice on several points. I made the suggestion that Keifer made in Caucus yesterday, that the clause inserted in the Army Bill goes beyond a prohibition of the use of the Army at the polls. It forbids any cival [civil] officer of the United States having an armed force at the polls; that is, it substantially forbids Marshals having armed force at hand in case of riot. This is a serious matter which had not before been observed. Dictated letters to Brown and to Rose a further instalment of the *Review* article. House at 12 o'clock. Struggle on the point of order continued and a number of speeches were made. Toward the close of the day, I tried to get the floor on the point of order, but finally concluded to let the ruling be made and then make the first speech on the opening of the debate on the sixth section. Home in the evening. Dictated a considerable portion of the *Review* article and work[ed] on the preparation for the debate tomorrow, running through the history of the military interference law of 1865, and late in the evening discovered that all the Democrats voted for it on its passage. Retired an hour after midnight, but could not sleep, finding myself too much interested in the topic of tomorrow's speeches. Did not get to sleep until nearly morning.

SATURDAY, 29. Dictated on *Review* article to Rose and made further preparations for the debate. Went to the House at 12 o'clock. After an hour's debate, the point of order was decided and at half-past one I took the floor to open the debate on the sixth section. I spoke fifty minutes, confining my discussion to the revolution[ary] method proposed by the Democrats for coercing the President. I spoke without any notes and I think more effectively than I have before done in the House. That part of the discussion relating to the voluntary powers of the Government was new, I believe, to all my hearers, and the disclosure that the Democrats themselves voted for the law they are now denouncing took them by surprise. I had better attention than perhaps ever before and many more evidences of approval.[96] Home in

[96]In his opening remarks Garfield accused the Democrats of embarking upon a revolutionary program. He supported his charge by analyzing what he called the voluntary powers of the government, by which he meant powers exercised by the people (voting) and by government officials (congressmen conducting the business of government) on a voluntary basis rather than under a legal or constitutional mandate. The threat of impeachment, he reasoned, restrained judges and executives in their exercise of power, but oath and honor were the only restraints on legislators. He then declared that for the first time in the nation's history congressmen were using those voluntary powers to adopt a course of action that would, unless stopped, destroy the government. Contrary to the American theory of law based on free consent, House Democrats, he said, proposed to stop the government unless the Senate and the President consented to their program. Such a method of legislation was, in his judgment, coercive, revolutionary to the core, and "destructive of the fundamental element of American liberty, the free consent of all the powers that unite to make laws." This, he said, was "the great, the paramount issue."

In a passage that riled opponents he argued that the election laws, which the Democrats now sought to repeal, had been introduced during the Civil War by Democrats who insisted that interference with the proper freedom of elections in the border states made such legislation necessary. He also said that such Democratic "magnates" as Speaker Samuel Randall, Fernando Wood, George Pendleton, Samuel Cox, and William Morrison had supported those laws.

He then accused the Democrats of using a new tactic to subvert the government. In 1861, he said, the Democrats took to the battlefield to shoot the government to death, having failed, by threats, to prevent the election of Lincoln; now they had chosen a new field of conflict for destroying the government, and now, as in 1861, the Republicans were appealing to the people to determine whether the Democrats "shall be permitted to destroy the principle of free consent in legislation under the threat of starving the Government to death."

In replies to Garfield Democratic speakers challenged the accuracy of his history

the evening very weary from overwork and loss of sleep. Went to Secretary Sherman's at seven o'clock to meet the Ohio Delegation. At eight returned home and went with Crete to Mrs. Dahlgren's to a little party. Supper at nine. Very pleasant company. Home at 12 o'clock and found Major Swaim, who had come in my absence.

SUNDAY, 30. At home. Rose came and we spent the day in revising the notes of my speech. I am making less changes than in almost any other speech I have ever delivered. The style is more condensed and satisfactory than usual. Sunday evening. At half-past one [*sic*] went to Speaker Randall's by appointment, to consult on the formation of Committees. Worked with him until 11 o'clock. He is grateful to me for keeping our people aloof from the Greenbackers and is disposed to do whatever I suggest in regard to the Republican cast of Committees.

MONDAY, 31. Remained at home in the forenoon and finished the revision of my speech. The New York Sunday papers treat it as a decided sensation. At 12, went to the Capitol to attend a meeting of the Committee on Rules, where I spent an hour and a half. Returned home at two and read the proof sheets of my speech, which had been set up in the meantime. Dictated further to Rose on the *Review* article and also dictated letters to Brown.

April

TUESDAY, 1. In the morning dictated to Rose on the *Review* article, and on letters to Brown. Meeting of the House at 12. Debate was continued, the Democrats attacking me with great fury, but entirely mistated my position and overshot the mark.

---

of the election laws, held that those laws had been used to intimidate voters and control elections, and insisted that the central issue was whether the nation would have free elections or a military despotism.

The *New York Times* (March 30, 1879) reported that Garfield's speech was "admitted to have been one of the best ever heard in the House."

Chalmers made a fiery and intemperate speech in defence of the Rebellion.[97] Frye replied in a powerful denunciatory speech. I have received 68 letters during the day, nearly all of them full of congratulations and approval.

WEDNESDAY, 2. Received a telegram from the publishers of the *North American Review,* that Randall will not have his article ready for the next number and suggesting that both be laid over until next month. This relieves me of great present pressure.

THURSDAY, 3. Dictated further on *Review* article to Rose, and letters to Brown. Went to the Capitol at eleven o'clock to meet the Committee on Rules, but a quorum was not present. In the House the debate continued, the chief speech on our side being Robeson's who made a very clear and powerful legal argument. On the other side Blackburn made a brilliant speech wholly devoted to me, but based mainly on the false assumption that I denounced the rider to an appropriation bill as revolutionary. This I had not done. I am keeping still until the debate ends, intending then to make a short speech in conclusion. Home in the evening, when at 8 o'clock I went to Randall's and worked with him three hours on the Republican cast of Committees.

FRIDAY, 4. Dictated a large number of letters to Brown and at half-past ten o'clock went to the Capitol to meet the Committee

[97]James R. Chalmers (1831–1898), a Democratic member of the House from Mississippi, 1877–82, and an Independent member, 1884–85, commanded a division in General Nathan Bedford Forrest's cavalry in the Confederate attack on Fort Pillow (April 12, 1864). Reports of Confederate atrocities prompted an investigation by a congressional committee which reported that after capturing the fort the Confederates had murdered in cold blood 300 Union men, mostly Negroes, who had thrown down their arms in surrender. On April 10, 1879, the *Cincinnati Gazette* published an article naming Chalmers as "one of the notorious and bloodyhanded butchers of the forever infamous Fort Pillow Massacre." Five days later Chalmers, offended by the article, moved that the Speaker of the House appoint a committee of seven members "who were officers in the Union army during the Civil War, and a majority of whom shall not belong to the democratic party," to investigate all accusations against him and to determine whether his conduct at Fort Pillow should disqualify him for service in the House. Chalmers vehemently denied that he acted in any way unbecoming an officer and gentleman, but on May 7 his motion was tabled. See entries for April 15 and May 7, 1879.

on Rules. Another failure in consequence of the illness of Mr. Stephens of Ga. In the House the debate continued. The chief speech on our side being that of Hawley of Connecticut. A very prudent and effective speech. The closing speech on the other side by Mr. Tucker was, by all odds, the ablest and most pertinent speech of any that have been made. After we got into debate, under the five minute rule, I got the floor and was allowed to speak fifteen minutes, reviewing briefly the grounds of attack on my speech and vindicating my argument from the assaults which had been made upon it. I do not think I am mistaken in believing that the logic of my position has not been successfully assailed by any of them.[98] The House adjourned at five o'clock after agreeing that all debate should close at two o'clock tomorrow. Home in the evening. Rose came and I dictated the Journal and revised the notes of my speech today.

SATURDAY, 5. Dictated letters in the morning and at 12 o'clock went to the Capitol. Debate under the five minute rule closed at two o'clock and the House proceeded to vote on the several amendments which had been offered to the Army Bill. That of Mr. New of Indiana, providing that the section should not interfere with the duties of the President to protect the States when called on by the Governor or Legislature, was adopted. In order to test the proposition I had made in my speech yesterday—that the Republicans were willing to repeal the two sections of the Revised Statutes relating to the use of the Army—I called the Executive Committee of our Caucus together and proposed that

---

[98]Garfield stated that although fifteen or twenty men had criticized his speech, none had responded to his central point that the Democrats, in declaring that they would compel the repeal of certain laws by refusing essential support to the government, were using revolutionary and unconstitutional procedures to do what they were unable to do "by ordinary and constitutional methods of repeal." He said that if the Democrats would offer "a naked proposition" to repeal the laws mentioned in section six, he would vote with them; but, he argued, the Democrats sought not simply to repeal the election laws, but to strike a negative clause and thereby make new and affirmative legislation of a most sweeping and dangerous character—a modification of the law which affected not the army alone, but the whole civil power of the United States.

Conger should offer such an amendment. It was unanimously agreed to and he did offer it providing that if they would take this section out of the bill, and report a simple repeal of the two sections of the law, we would vote for it. This was refused. He then offered an amendment of similar import to the bill itself. One hundred and nine Republicans voted for it. A few refused to vote. Nearly all the Democrats voted against it. The Committee rose and reported the bill to the House and it was passed by a strict party vote. All the Republicans voted against [it].[99] Home in the evening very tired.

SUNDAY, 6.   I was too tired to go to church and remained at home clearing up the debris of the last week's work and putting my desk in order. Several friends called. Miss Ransom and Lieuts. Harber and Wilson took dinner with [us]. At six o'clock Crete and I went to General Schenck's to take tea. Returned at eight. Major Swaim left us at night to serve as Judge-Advocate on the Hazen-Stanley Court Martial. At eight o'clock went to Speaker Randall's in company with Mr. Frye and worked on the Republican cast of Committees until 11 o'clock.

MONDAY, 7.   Rose and Brown came and I worked at my correspondence until nearly two o'clock. Dictated nearly 70 letters. At two o'clock went to the Pension Office with several cases and then to the other Departments. Found myself so much worn out that I was unable to go to Mr. Randall's in accordance with the appointment and wrote him so. Crete and I went to Gilfillan's and spent an hour in the evening.

TUESDAY, 8.   Dictated letters until half-past 10 o'clock, when I went to the Capitol and met with the Committee on Rules. A report was agreed upon which I in the main concurred in. In the House the Legislative Bill was taken up and about sixty pages of it gone over. By agreement, general debate was reserved for the political sections[100] and so the bill was considered under the five

[99]The House, with over ninety percent of its members voting, passed the Army Appropriations Bill by a vote of 148–122.

[100]The sections dealing with supervisors of elections, deputy marshals, and the test oath.

minute rule. Home in the evening. At half-past seven Gilfillan, Rockwell and our Classmate, Reverend G. B. Newcomb[101] of New Haven—who has recently been appointed Professor in the University—came and Crete and I joined them in going to Judge Nott's to call on Dr. Hopkins and his wife. After my return, continued work on my correspondence until half-past ten, when I retired.

WEDNESDAY, 9. My mail continues to be unusually heavy. I received forty-five letters yesterday and about thirty in this morning's mail. Dictated a large number of replies and then went to the Capitol at twelve. The Committee on Rules made its report, the debate on which consumed the day. I spoke against the amendment made to Rule 126 [120], and the construction which has been given it.[102] The Speaker came down from the Chair to reply to me. The Report of the Committee was adopted with several amendments. It is one of the most dangerous innovations upon the Rules of the House which has ever been made. It adds four or five Committees to those which may report at any time for action, including the Committee on Banking and Currency, and this will allow the opening up of the financial question, in all its forms, at any time. At six o'clock in the evening Crete and I

---

[101]George B. Newcomb (1836–1895), a native of Pennsylvania, studied at the Union Theological Seminary after graduating at Williams. He held pastorates in Connecticut before being appointed professor of philosophy in the College of the City of New York in 1879, a position he held to his death.

[102]Believing that the Committee Report, if adopted, would damage seriously the work of the Appropriations Committee and establish a dangerous procedure regarding financial legislation, Garfield presented a motion to amend Rule 120 as follows: "nor shall any provision in any such [legislative appropriation] bill or amendments thereto changing existing law be in order." In support of his proposal he defended the Appropriations Committee against critics who claimed that it had "been grasping power and getting control of all the business of Congress." He said that such charges stemmed from "the unfortunate extension which has been given to the meaning of the last clause of Rule 120, namely, that all germane propositions which can be construed in any way . . . to retrench expenditures may be put upon appropriations bills." Randall opposed Garfield's amendment, saying that "the object of legislating on appropriation bills . . . should be directed exclusively to the saving of money."

dined at Judge Nott's in company with Dr. Hopkins, his wife and daughter. Home at 11 o'clock and retired early.

THURSDAY, 10. Dictated some thirty-five letters to Brown. At eleven o'clock went to the War and Treasury Departments on business. Thence to the Capitol. Debate on the Legislative Bill was resumed. An amendment was offered by McMahon of Ohio, to appropriate ten millions of dollars for the payment of arrears of pensions by legal tender notes now reserved for the redemption of fractional currency. I resisted it, both on the grounds of order and on the merits of the amendment, which threatens the stability of resumption. McMahon made a personal reference to me, in connection with my currency opinions to which I replied with some severity.[103] Home in the evening. Brown came and worked on correspondence. Rose came and wrote up the Journal.

FRIDAY, 11. Dictated a large number of letters in the morning. Went to the Capitol at half-past 11 and had a final interview with the Speaker, in company with Mr. Frye, as to the Republican makeup of the Committees. In the House, the consideration of the Legislative Appropriation Bill was resumed and continued until half-past three o'clock, when the Committees were announced[104] and the House adjourned. We have now nearly reached the field of battle marked out in the political legislation, added by way of a rider to the Legislative Bill. In the evening dictated further on the *Review* article and at eight o'clock Crete

---

[103]In the exchange McMahon said in effect that Garfield owed more allegiance to the soldier than perhaps any other class, but that he appeared to act as though he owed chief allegiance to Wall Street. In reply Garfield said that McMahon had no more right to say or infer such a thing "than I would have a right to say he owes his chief allegiance to the groggeries and whiskey-shops of Dayton; and as I would not say that I do not think he was entitled to say the other." After considerable debate the point of order was overruled.

[104]Garfield was assigned to the Committee on Ways and Means and the Committee on Rules. In an item headed "Washington News" in the *Painesville Telegraph* (April 17, 1879) this sentence appears: "There is a general feeling that Randall has treated Ohio Republicans in the make-up of the committees, better than their Democratic colleagues."

and I went with Rockwell and his wife to Miss Ransom's. Twenty-five or thirty people were present, and Judge Waite[105] of Chicago read a paper giving a sketch of the life and character of Apollonius of Tyana. A very interesting paper. At the close I made some remarks criticising some of the received opinions concerning Apollonius and combating the notion that his miracles were entitled to credence on the same grounds that Christ's were. Returned home at 11. Retired at 12.

SATURDAY, 12.   Dictated letters in the morning. Departments at eleven. House at 12. The day was spent on the details of the Legislative and Executive Appropriation Bill. An attempt was made to adjourn over until Tuesday to avoid Monday's bills, but it failed by a small majority. Went to the Treasury at half-past three o'clock to get some further facts for my *Review* article. Home in the evening and read a large mail. Went to General Schenck's with Crete at half-past eight o'clock, and staid two hours.

SUNDAY, 13.   Crete and I attended church at 11 o'clock. At two Miss Ransom and Lieut. Harber dined with us. At four they, Crete and I went to Lincoln Hall to hear a sermon by Dr. Mark Hopkins, my Old President. While he has failed some in strength of voice and general vigor, his intellect is still strong and clear and he made an able sermon. On our return Crete and I read the first half of Hinsdale's book on *The Genuineness and Authenticity of the Gospels.* The reading was suggested by some queries that Judge Waite has raised in reference to the genuin[en]ess of the New Testament readings. Retired at 11 o'clock but was unable to sleep until an hour after midnight.

MONDAY, 14.   Brown came and I dictated a large number of letters, and also several pages more of the *Review* article. Went to the House at twelve. When the state of Maine was called for

---

[105]Charles B. Waite (1824–1909), a native of New York and a Chicago lawyer, was associate justice of the supreme court of the Territory of Utah, 1862–64. He was the author of a number of books including *History of the Christian Religion, to the Year Two Hundred* (1881), during the research on which he spent two years in the Library of Congress.

the introduction of bills, Mr. Ladd,[106] Greenback Democrat, offered a bill in reference to silver coinage, when Mr. Conger raised the point of order that the Rule only permitted the introduction of bills on leave and he (Conger) having objected, Mr. Ladd could not introduce it without leave. This seems to be the letter of the Rule, but the practice for at least a quarter of a century, has been otherwise. Considerable debate arose on the point of order, which the Chair finally overruled. Conger took an appeal which was further debated. A motion was made by Mr. Cox, of New York, to lay the appeal on the table. On this the Ayes and Noes were called and before the result was announced the morning hour expired. So up to this time, the other side have not been able to introduce any bill except by unanimous consent. At half-past one, I went over to the Senate and heard the last two-thirds of Blaine's speech on the Army Bill. It was very forcible and aggressive and will read well as a popular presentation of the case, but I do not see that he has added any new points to the discussion already had in the House. At 1/4 before three o'clock the House adjourned. In the evening Rose came and I dictated the Journal and worked on the *Review* article.

TUESDAY, 15. Dictated letters to Brown until eleven o'clock. Also, finished and sent by express the article for the *North American Review*. At 11 started for the Capitol to attend the meeting of the Committee on Ways and Means and found on arriving that I had mistaken the day. The Committee do not meet until tomorrow. In the House, General Chalmers of Mississippi rose to a question of privilege and had read at the Clerk's desk an article in the *Cincinnati Gazette* which quoted a considerable portion of the testimony against him taken before the Committee on the Fort Pillow Massacre. He asked for a Committee of Investigation to examine these charges. I asked the House to lay the matter over for further consideration. The debate on the Legislative Bill was resumed. Bragg of Wisconsin attempted to carry an amendment to abolish the Southern Claims Commission, when Young

[106]George W. Ladd (1818–1892) was a Democratic-Greenback member of the House from Maine, 1879–83.

of Tennessee offered an amendment to transfer its duties to the Court of Claims under the rules of that Court. I made a short speech in opposition to both these measures, in which I took occasion to show the number of loyal white men, amounting to over 50,000, who served in our Army from the seceded States.[107] The two amendments were defeated. The House passed the Senate Bill to provide for a refrigerating ship to combat the yellow fever.[108] Home in the evening. Revised the notes of my speech and dictated to Rose. Capt. Henry came in the morning and will stay with us some days.

WEDNESDAY, 16. Dictated letters until 11 o'clock, when I went to the Treasury Department. Called on the Commissioner of Internal Revenue, also at the Revenue Marine Office and the Office of the Comptroller of the Currency. Thence to Mr. Cluss[109] the Architect, to commend Mr. Bright for employment

---

[107]Garfield argued that the Southern Claims Commission was established to hear the claims of persons in the seceded states who had remained loyal to the Union and could prove it. The function of the Commission was to hear such claims and advise Congress as to the facts. Congress then had to decide what claims to pay. He contended that transferring the duties of the Commission to the Court of Claims would open the latter to claims from all persons who had been pardoned. Strictly speaking, he said, the Commission was not a court, for it performed no judicial functions except "to administer oaths, take testimony, examine claims, and report to Congress the facts found." But the Court of Claims, he continued, was a court, and since congressional and presidential pardons had annihilated the distinctions in law between loyalty and disloyalty, if the transfer motion was adopted virtually all of the 8,000 claims before the Commission would go to the Court of Claims "needing no proof whatever of loyalty."

[108]The bill appropriated $200,000 for the purchase or construction of a refrigerator ship, providing the National Board of Health so recommended, "to disinfect vessels and cargoes from ports suspected of infection with yellow fever or other contagious diseases." What Congress had in mind was a ship to be stationed at a port where contagious diseases had been introduced into the United States and equipped with refrigerating machinery capable of lowering the temperature of cargo ships entering the harbor to the point where germs causing diseases would be destroyed. Numerous plans and specifications for such a ship were submitted to the National Board of Health and referred by it to a board of experts appointed by the secretary of the navy. Considerable controversy resulted.

[109]Adolf Cluss (1825–1905), architect and civil engineer, was a native of Germany who moved to the United States in 1848. He was for many years a partner in the firm of Cluss and Schulze, architects of many public buildings in the District

on the Public Buildings. Thence to the Capitol. During the morning hour a struggle was made by Stephens of Georgia to make a report on Coinage.[110] This was resisted by Conger in a series of brilliant speeches on points of order and the morning hour was consumed without getting the bill even to its second reading. A motion is now pending to refer it to another Committee. House then went into Committee of the Whole on the Legislative Bill and thus consumed the remainder of the day. In the Senate Mr. Beck made a speech in which he quoted largely from the history of England, but in conclusion he manifested signs of weakening on his original proposition to stop the supplies if the President vetoed the bill.[111] Mr. Hoar pushed him in a brilliant dialogue of half an hour, following which Mr. Dawes made a strong speech on the Army Bill. Home in the evening. Rose came. I dictated the Journal and a few letters. Commenced my preparation for a speech on the repeal of the election laws.

THURSDAY, 17. Dictated letters in the morning. At eleven went to the Capitol and attended the first meeting of the Committee on Ways and Means. The names of the Members were called in order and a Clerk and Messenger elected. It was agreed to order a meeting a week from today, at which, on my motion, it was to be determined whether the Committee would undertake any legislation the present session. In the House Mr. Stephens continued his discussion of the bill for the redemption of fractional silver. I spoke a little while, approving generally the objects of

---

of Columbia, including the National Museum (see March 27, 1879, and n. 94). He was inspector of work on federal buildings in Washington, 1890–95.

[110]Alexander Stephens reported for the Committee on Coinage, Weights, and Measures a bill "to provide for the interchange of subsidiary coins for legal-tender money under certain circumstances, and to make such coins a legal tender in all sums not exceeding $20."

[111]Toward the end of Beck's speech on the Army Appropriation Bill, George F. Hoar asked him whether, in the event the President vetoed the measure, he would refuse to grant the supplies necessary to carry on the government. Beck replied that if such a situation developed he would consult with the best men in his party and with good men everywhere to determine the best course of action for the country, and that the President and his patrons would be responsible for the consequences.

the bill, but offered some minor amendments.[112] The morning hour closed without finishing the bill. The rest of the day was occupied in speeches—none very notable.

FRIDAY, 18. Letters as usual in the morning. Departments at 11, House at 12. The morning hour was dispensed with, being Private Bill Day, and the House went into Committee of the Whole, McKinley making the first speech. He made a very clear and effective argument.[113] After an indifferent speech by House[114] of Tennessee, Burrows of Michigan read a very powerful and effective speech. The closing was especially fine, though perhaps a little too ornate. I should have added that at the close of McKinley's speech, Blackburn came down from the Chair and attacked McKinley for not quoting the full paragraph, and thus, as he said, garbling his speech. McKinley replied very prudently. It was Ohio's day in the House. At eight o'clock seven of my family, including Captain Henry, and five of Rockwell's family, attended the National Theatre, and listened to *Pinafore,* [115] which is quite the rage now. I enjoyed it very much.

[112]No amendment was introduced for debate, but Garfield did suggest a number of changes and two other representatives read amendments that they intended to present for the consideration of the House before debate on the measure was closed.

[113]Speaking on the election laws, McKinley charged that the Democrats, bent on accomplishing in Congress what they had failed to accomplish on the battlefield, intended "to usurp all governmental powers," and "to absorb all of the constitutional functions of the President by threat and coercion." He quoted from a speech of April 3 by Joseph C. S. Blackburn, who had said that for the first time in eighteen years the Democratic party was back in power and that it proposed to celebrate by destroying corrupt and partisan legislation: "We do not intend to stop until we have stricken the last vestige of your war measures from the statute-book, which like these [election laws] were born of passions incident to civil strife and looked to the abridgement of the liberty of the citizen." McKinley had quoted this sentence as far as the comma when Blackburn complained that his words had been taken out of context. McKinley then offered to read the entire speech.

[114]John F. House (1827–1904) was a Democratic member of the House from Tennessee, 1875–83.

[115]*H. M. S. Pinafore,* which had its premiere in London on May 25, 1878, was first presented in the United States in Boston on November 25, 1878. In both countries it had an enormous success. It was performed by Ford's Philadelphia

SATURDAY, 19. Dictated letters in the morning. Swaim arrived early. Went to the War Department, also to the President's. Capitol at twelve. The morning hour was spent on the Fractional Silver Coinage Bill, which was not completed. The House then went into debate on the Legislative Appropriation Bill. At one-quarter past three o'clock went to Col. Rockwell's Office, and he, Major Swaim and I played billiards for two hours. In the evening we had a dinner party in honor of Crete's Birthday. There were present, Miss Ransom, Mrs. Lander, Lieut. Harber, Major Swaim, Captain Henry and Mr. Montague.[116] A very pleasant party.

SUNDAY, 20. Remained at home. Several friends called. Miss Ransom came to dinner. Early in the evening Swaim and I called on the Secretary of War. Made arrangements with Swaim for going over to New York as a witness in the Hazen-Stanley Court Martial. At 7 1/2 o'clock Captain Henry left for Ohio, and at half-past nine Major Swaim left for New York.

MONDAY, 21. Dictated a large number of letters in the morning. Went to the Treasury Department at 11. The Capitol at 12. The day was consumed in the introduction of bills. I ought to have added that during the last week, we called the Executive Committee of the Republican Caucus together and the[y] agreed to no longer resist the introduction of bills. Nearly 1,000 were introduced today. At half-past four o'clock I went with Colonel Rockwell to witness the game of baseball between the Nationals of this City and the Holyoke Nine of Massachusetts, the first professional game of baseball I have seen.[117] In the evening Rose came

---

Company in the National Theater in Washington during the week of April 14, 1879. It became a favorite of Garfield; he attended three performances between April 18 and May 24, 1879.

[116]Andrew P. Montague (1854–1928), a native of Virginia, and a teacher of Latin at Columbian (now George Washington) University, tutored Hal and Jim for several months during 1878 and 1879. In 1888 he received one of the first two Ph.D. degrees awarded by Columbian. From 1897 to his death he was associated, chiefly as president, with four southern colleges.

[117]The professionalization of baseball made considerable progress during the 1870's—see Harold Seymour, *Baseball, the Early Years* (1960). In 1879 the

and I dictated the Journal. I also made preparations for a speech on the Election Laws.

TUESDAY, 22.   Letters in the morning. Capitol at twelve. The day was consumed in debate on the election laws. An evening session was also held, where speeches were made. During the afternoon and evening made further preparations for a speech on the election laws. During the day received a telegram from Merrick and another from Swaim, asking me to come to New York to testify before the Hazen Court Martial. In the evening at eight o'clock Crete and I called on ex-Secretary Fish and wife at Bancroft Davis'. Also saw Governor Newells [Newell].[118] Stopped at the Arlington and saw Mr. Pendleton and wife.[119] At ten o'clock took the train for New York.

WEDNESDAY, 23.   Arrived at New York and went to the Saint Nicholas Hotel where Swaim is. At ten o'clock met General Hazen at the Army Building and consulted with him on the situation of his case. Attended on the Court during the day and towards the close was called as a witness to identify the letters that passed between General Hazen and myself in 1872 on the Post tradership business. At five o'clock called at the *Tribune* Office on Whitelaw Reid. Had a brief interview with him and also with

---

National Club of Washington, D.C. (organized in 1859), joined a short-lived organization, the National Association of Base Ball Clubs. Other clubs in the association during the season of 1879 were those of Albany (both the Albany Club and the Capital City Club), Rochester and Utica in New York, Holyoke, New Bedford, Springfield, and Worcester in Massachusetts, and Manchester in New Hampshire. The game witnessed by Garfield was the opening association game of the season. About 2,000 spectators attended, "a large proportion of whom were ladies." Admission was twenty-five cents for men and ten cents extra for a seat on the new stand. Ladies were admitted free. The game started at 4:30. On this occasion only seven innings were played, the Nationals winning, 12–5. The *Washington Post* (April 22) carried a full account of the game.

118William A. Newell (1817–1901), a native of Ohio, became a New Jersey physician and politician. He was a Whig member of the U.S. House of Representatives, 1847–51, a Republican member, 1865–67, governor of New Jersey, 1857–60, and governor of the Territory of Washington, 1880–84.

119William K. Pendleton, president of Bethany College, and his wife, Catherine.

Reverend Mr. Bartholomew. At ten o'clock took the train for Washington.

THURSDAY, 24.   Reached home at half-past six in the morning. Found a very large mail awaiting me. Dictated letters in the forenoon. At eleven went to the Capitol to attend the meeting of the Committee on Ways and Means, where was discussed my resolution that we would not enter upon financial legislation. This view prevailed but we concluded not to pass a formal vote on the subject. Went to the Capitol [House] at twelve. Debate on the Legislative Bill continued during the day. The interest has manifestly flagged and but few are listening to the speeches. At one o'clock went to the Senate and listened to Senator Conkling's speech which took three hours for delivery.[120] It was a very strong and complete presentation of our views and entirely in accord with the position I took in my first speech. The Senator's self-consciousness is always apparent and I think it marred the effectiveness of his speech. He spoke from notes without reading and when he completed the sheet of notes, he tore it up into small bits and threw them on the floor—taking some time to do it. He also held considerable *sot*[*t*]*o voce* conference with those around him. These little touches of self-consciousness detract from the effectiveness of his speaking. The more a man loses himself in his work, the better for the work. But notwithstanding these minor defects his speech was very powerful and valuable. There were some extraordinarily strong passages. The House met in the evening for debate but I did not attend. Worked at my desk.

FRIDAY, 25.   Letters in the morning. Departments at half-past eleven. Capitol at twelve. General debate continued until five o'clock, Ewing closing. I sought the floor under the five minute rule, but Ewing held the floor and the House adjourned. In the evening made some preparations for a brief speech reviewing some general points of the debate. In the evening Crete, Miss Mays and I went to Miss Ransom's and listened to a lecture by Major Powell on Indian Mythology. At the conclusion of his lecture, I spoke from ten to fifteen minutes, comparing the points

[120]Roscoe Conkling spoke on the Army Appropriation Bill.

of his lecture with recent mythology and referred to Coulanges'
book on *The Ancient City State* [*The Ancient City*].

SATURDAY, 26.   Worked at my desk until half-past eleven o'clock,
when I went to the Capitol. Ewing spoke fifteen minutes on the
opening of the debate. I moved to amend by striking out the
political sections. By two extensions, I got in a fifteen minute
speech, reviewing the leading points of the debate and I think
with some effectiveness. At two o'clock the voting commenced
and my amendment was defeated by a vote of 125 [124] yeas to
138 nays. At twenty minutes past two, the bill was passed by a
strict party vote. At four o'clock the House adjourned. Called on
the President and had a full conference on the subject. He gave
me an advance copy of his Veto Message, to enable me to prepare
for its defence, as I have been appointed for that purpose by the
Republican Caucus Committee of the House. Spent the evening
in reading up veto literature.

SUNDAY, 27.   Received large mail. Read on it until eleven
o'clock, when Crete and I attended church. After church read
Belford's speech on the history of vetoes from Roman days until
now. Harber, Miss Ransom and Mrs. Reed came to dinner. At
half-past four o'clock Crete, the children and I walked to Capitol
Hill and called on Mrs. Reed. From there I called on Mrs. Mary
Clemmer[121] on Pennsylvania Avenue between First and Second
streets and showed her a letter which I had received from Mr.
Chaplin[122] of Massachusetts quoting a paragraph from her letter

---

[121]Mary Clemmer (1839–1884), author whose books included *Ten Years in
Washington* (1874), for many years wrote "A Woman's Letter from Washington,"
in the New York *Independent*. In the issue of March 27, 1879, she said of Garfield:
"In mental capacity, in fine, wide, intellectual culture, no Republican for the last
decade has equaled, much less surpassed him. . . . Were it possible to honor his
moral purity as one must his intellectual acumen, he would be as grand in personal
and political strength, that no whim of man, no passion of the hour, no mutation
of party could depress, much less overthrow." From 1866 until her death she lived
on Capitol Hill. An early marriage to Daniel Ames ended in divorce; the year
before her death she married Edmund Hudson, editor of the *Army and Navy
Register*.

[122]Jeremiah Chaplin (1813–1886), a Boston writer whose books included biographies of Henry Dunster, Benjamin Franklin and Charles Sumner, was perturbed
by Mary Clemmer's reflection on Garfield's character in view of his prominent

to the *Independent* which criticises me in a vague, unjust, and indefinite way. I left the letter with her to read at leisure and to let me know what she meant by her language. She asked me to call on Wednesday evening to see her about it. I am curious to know what she will say. Spent the evening in reading further on the subject of vetoes and read carefully the President's paper which he gave me yesterday. Retired at eleven o'clock.

MONDAY, 28. Worked on letters in the morning. Went to the Departments at 11 o'clock. Capitol at 12. The President's veto message came in on the opening of the House, but immediately after the reading of the Journal the death of Rush Clarke [Clark][123] of Iowa was announced and the House adjourned.[124] A good deal of speculation is indulged in as to the behavior of the Democracy. Nothing is yet positively known. At four o'clock I went with Colonel Rockwell to witness the game of baseball between the Capital City Club of Albany, N.Y., and the Nationals of this City. A very closely contested and manful game in which the Nationals were beaten by one.[125] Home in the evening and read up state Constitutions on the subject of veto.

TUESDAY, 29. Letters in the morning. Went to the Riggs House to see Mr. Flagg[126] on business. Thence to the Riggs Bank. At

---

position in the Republican party and "the possibility, not to say probability," that he might be nominated for a higher position. Chaplin to Garfield, April 24, 1879. See April 29, 1879.

[123]Rush Clark (1834–1879) was a Republican member of the House from Iowa, 1877–79.

[124]The House did not meet on Monday, April 28. The House proceedings mentioned in this entry occurred on April 29.

[125]Garfield saw this game on April 29. The Nationals lost their first game of the season, 5–4.

[126]John H. Flagg, a lawyer, was principal clerk of the U.S. Senate, 1869–78; during 1879 he had a law office in the Riggs House. The business referred to was connected with a proposal to organize a company to mine gold in North Carolina in which both he and Garfield were interested. The company, whose incorporation papers were filed on May 21 (see entry for that date), was organized under the laws of Virginia in June as the Beaver Dam Gold Mining Co. There are ten certificates bearing Garfield's name, each for 100 shares in the company, dated August 15, 1881, in the Garfield Papers.

the Capitol a little before twelve. The Veto Message was read and a resolution was passed to postpone the discussion until tomorrow.[127] The morning hour was had, after which an attempt was made to introduce a bill for unlimited coinage of silver and to make fractional silver legal tender.[128] I resisted the resolution for making it a special order and the vote by tellers disclosed a tie and the Speaker voted with the Democrats and Greenbackers, thus putting himself on the Soft Money side. I then demanded the Ayes and Noes on ordering the main question, pending which the House adjourned. At seven o'clock in the evening called on Mrs. Mary Clemmer on Capitol Hill in reference to a letter I have received quoting a paragraph from her recent article in the *Independent,* which reflected on me. I had a long conversation with her on the subject. At home at half-past ten and found Lieut[s]. Harber and Wilson here. They remained half an hour. I retired at twelve.

WEDNESDAY, 30. Letters in the morning. Received from Publishers of the *North American Review* proof sheets of my article on Appropriations. Read them carefully and at half-past eleven took them to the Treasury and requested Upton[129] and

[127]The House proceedings mentioned in this entry occurred on Wednesday, April 30. Garfield probably called on Mrs. Clemmer that evening, as suggested in the entry for April 27.

[128]On April 30, Adoniram J. Warner (1834–1910), a Democratic member of the House from Ohio, 1879–81, 1883–87, introduced from the Committee on Coinage, Weights and Measures a bill that provided for the free coinage of silver, and he moved that it be made a special order for debate on May 3 and every day thereafter until disposed of. The House approved the motion on May 1 and after more than three weeks of debate passed the bill on May 24. In the Senate, however, the Finance Committee refused to report the bill, and Democratic efforts to get it before the Senate were unsuccessful. Warner guided his free coinage bill through the House in the second and third sessions of the Forty-sixth Congress, but in each instance the Senate defeated the measure.

[129]Jacob K. Upton (1837–1902), a native of New Hampshire, was chief clerk in the office of the secretary of the treasury, 1877–80, and assistant secretary of the treasury, 1880–85. After leaving office, he practiced law and engaged in banking in Washington, D.C. He was the author of articles on financial matters and of a book, *Money in Politics* (1884).

Maclennan[130] to revise them and see if the statistics were all right. Capitol at twelve o'clock. The Democrats had the Message read but voted to postpone its consideration until tomorrow and then adjourned. Crete is anxious to get home and I will try if I can to get action on the veto message tomorrow so as to go with her tomorrow evening. Home in the evening. Dictated journal and began to put matters in order for temporarily leaving the City.

May

THURSDAY, 1.   Dictated letters in the morning. Went to the Departments at half-past ten. Committee on Ways and Means at 11. House met at 12, and after the morning hour proceeded to consider the veto. The Democrats determined to allow no debate, by calling the Ayes and Noes on the bill, and at half-past two o'clock the vote was taken, which stood 120 Ayes to 110 Noes on the passage of the bill over the veto. This substantially closes the first stage of the controversy. I made two reports from the Committee on Rules; one to revise the mode of calling the Roll, by leaving off the first name of Members, except where there are two men of the same name. Also, the resolution to increase the Membership of the Committee on the Mississippi Levees. Came home at half-past four o'clock and helped Crete get ready for leaving for Ohio. Rose and Brown came and I dictated a number of letters. At 7.40 Crete, Martha Mays, Mollie, Irvin, Abram and I took the Baltimore and Potomac train for the West.

FRIDAY, 2.   Awoke in the mountains. Heavy frost on the ground. Spring very backward. Breakfast at Pittsburgh [at] 8.20. In half an hour after reaching the City left on the Cleveland and Pittsburgh road, reaching Cleveland at 3.15 P.M. Crete and I went up town and transacted a little business. Visited Brother Joe at the Post Office. Returned to the Depot and took the 4.50 train for

[130]William F. Maclennan was assistant chief of the division of warrants, estimates, and appropriations in the office of the secretary of the treasury.

Mentor, where we arrived at six o'clock. Moses, Northcott and Dr. Robison, met us with teams. Found the two hired girls at the farm with supper awaiting us. House had been put in good order and we began farm life again.

SATURDAY, 3.   Spent the forenoon in overhauling farm affairs. Directed the opening of a new gate to the front, also the building of some new fences, and some changes in the water works. In the afternoon Dr. Robison and I drove to Willoughby to get some plaster for refitting the kitchen. We then drove to Painesville where I did some shopping for the family and farm. Home at supper. At six in the evening Crete and I went to Dr. Robison's and spent two hours visiting. The Spring is very backward but my crops are looking better than any I have seen on the road from Washington here.

SUNDAY, 4.   At 11 o'clock attended church. Dr. Robison spoke 3/4 of an hour. He and his wife dined with us at one. During the afternoon two or three carriage loads of friends came from Painesville to see us. Also Hon. A. M. Pratt, from Bryan, Ohio, who is temporarily stopping at Painesville, called.

MONDAY, 5.   Arose at half-past six. Spent an hour in arranging farm matters to leave for Washington and settling accounts, etc., and at 7.47 Crete and I took the train at Mentor for Cleveland. Spent some time shopping and took dinner at Dr. Robison's at one o'clock. At one-forty-five I took the Pittsburgh train for the East—Crete to go to Hiram in the afternoon to see her mother. Supper at Wellsville, Capt. Henry having joined me on the train thus far. Reached Pittsburgh a few minutes before eight. Drove across the city to the Connellsville Depot, leaving there at 8.21. Retired at half-past nine.

TUESDAY, 6.   Awoke in the neighborhood of the Point of Rocks. Reached Washington at 7.20 and found Jimmy awaiting me at the Baltimore and Ohio Depot. All were well at home. There were one hundred letters awaiting me and about a bushel of paper mail. Worked at my mail and dictated letters until half-past 11 o'clock when I went to the Capitol. The Democrats during my absence have framed a new stump speech bill on the Army, which was this morning introduced from the Committee on the Judiciary as a separate measure. Republicans held a general caucus last night and resolved to oppose the bill. I found it necessary to state that I doubted the wisdom of any strenuous opposition. I suggested to my friends not to make any speeches on the subject so that we might not be unpleasantly committed against it, for when the time came they could vote against it. At three o'clock the bill passed by a strictly party vote.[131] Home in the evening. Dictated Journal. Swaim came in the afternoon from New York and Rockwell called in the evening.

WEDNESDAY, 7. Dictated letters in the morning. Went to the Capitol about twelve and when I arrived found Gen'l Chalmers making a personal explanation in regard to the part he took in the Fort Pillow Massacre. I followed him expressing my gratification at any success he may have had in disconnecting his name from any responsibility for that horror, but stating the general grounds on which the atrocity was believed to have occurred as shown by the report of Senator Wade and opposed reopening the case. I yielded to Mr. Burrows of Michigan, who made a very strong summation of the testimony in Wade's Report. The House then went into a discussion of the Silver Bill. The bill which passed the House yesterday forbidding military interference at elections is more like the resolution of a political convention than an act of Congress. In itself, it is not seriously bad, except that the repealing clause leaves the laws vague and uncertain, making it difficult to say what laws are repealed and what are not. Considering the measure as a part of the political programme of the Democratic Party, the President ought to veto it, but after his commitments on the general subject of his former veto he will find himself embarrassed.

---

[131]The Military Interference Bill provided "that it shall not be lawful to bring to, or employ at, any place where a general or special election is being held in a State any part of the Army or Navy of the United States, unless such force be necessary to repel the armed enemies of the United States or to enforce section 4, article 4 of the Constitution . . . and the laws made in pursuance thereof upon the application of the Legislature or the Executive of the State where such force is to be used; and so much of all laws as is inconsistent herewith is hereby repealed." Hayes vetoed the bill (see entries for May 10 and 12), and on May 13, the House failed to override the veto.

THURSDAY, 8. Worked at the desk until quarter before eleven o'clock, and came nearer reaching the bottom of the letter pile than I have done before for two months. At half-past ten called on Colonel Irish at the Treasury Department and asked him to give employment to Mary McGrath during the summer. This he thinks he can do. Went to the Capitol to meet the Committee on Rules, but a quorum had failed to attend. A dull day in the House except that the silver debate was enlivened by a stirring and effective speech from Mr. Chittenden of New York. Left the House early and stopped at Burchell's to settle the Grocery bill. At six o'clock dined at Mrs. Johnson's on H Street. The company consisted of Secretaries Evarts and daughter, Schurz and daughter and Miss Charlier of New York, Baron Schlözer,[132] the German Minister, the Austrian Minister[133] and a German Baron, whose name I do not recall. A very pleasant party and a fine dinner. I left at nine o'clock to see Swaim before he started for New York. He left us at one-quarter before ten. Played Casino a little while with Jimmy. The boys retired about half-past eleven, but I did not get to sleep until after one.

FRIDAY, 9. Dictated letters until half-past eleven o'clock when I went to the Capitol. The morning hour was consumed on Reports and private bills from Committees and nothing special was accomplished. At two o'clock the House took up the Silver Bill and the debate droned on in the usual way without special interest. I left the Capitol about three o'clock and stopped at Mr. Bell's, the Photographer's, who has requested me to call and sit for a negative. Played billiards for a little while with Colonel Rockwell. Home at half-past five. Felt dull and stupid during the day, perhaps because of lack of sleep last night. Dined at one-quarter before six with Hal and Jim. In the evening Mr. Rose

[132]Kurd von Schlözer (1822–1894), career diplomat and writer, was German minister to Mexico, 1869–71, and to the United States, 1871–81. *Amerikanische Briefe* (1927) is a collection of letters written by him during his years in North America.

[133]Garfield is referring to Chevalier Ernest von Tavera, chargé d'affaires of the Austrian legation in Washington at this time.

came and I dictated the Journal. Also made some studies preparatory to the speech on the Silver Bill. I find it will be necessary
to fight again the battle of honest money at this session. I feel too
weary to go over the old hackneyed question, but it seems to be
necessary. This evening Mary McGrath received her letter of
appointment from Mr. Irish.

SATURDAY, 10. Dictated letters until eleven o'clock when I went
to the Departments. Thence to the Capitol at twelve. The
Speaker signed the bill in reference to military interference in
elections. Several reports were made from the Committee on
Revision of the Laws, which I successfully resisted as not properly
in their charge. At two o'clock I went to the President's and had
a long conversation with him in regard to the Military Interference Bill which has just passed, but which has not yet reached
him. I stated the grounds of my opposition to the bill, that while
it pretends to prevent the use of the troops in conducting an
election, it really prevents the use of the Army in any part of the
United States at any place where an election is being held. I was
glad to find the President in full accord with this view. He read
me a sketch of the points he had already made and I came away
satisfied that we should have a veto very soon. He has a grand
opportunity to make a plea for nationalism against extreme states
rights. Went to Rockwell's at three o'clock and thence went with
him and Jimmy to the Base Ball Ground and saw a fine match
game between the Nationals and the New Bedfords. The Nationals won. Home at half-past six. Harry did not go to the Base
Ball Ground but went to Marini's to prepare for the May Ball.
Home in the evening.

SUNDAY, 11. Spent the most of the day reading Dr. Lieber's
letters to me, which are very numerous and very interesting. His
widow desires to use them in preparing his biography.[134] Col.
Rockwell came and staid with me two or three hours. At two
o'clock Lieuts. Harber and Wilson and Miss Ransom dined with
us. At six o'clock in the evening I called at the office of the *New*

---

[134]Excerpts from a number of Lieber's letters to Garfield, 1868–71, are in
Thomas Sergeant Perry, ed., *The Life and Letters of Francis Lieber* (1882).

York Tribune and dictated to White's shorthand man my reasons why the bill should not be passed. It will be printed in the *Tribune* tomorrow.[135]

MONDAY, 12.   Dictated letters until two o'clock, when I went to the War Department and thence to the Capitol. The day was a peculiar one. After the morning hour a Democrat introduced a proposition to impose an income tax, and this though it did not get a two-thirds vote received a majority. At this point the veto message came in. It was by far the ablest paper which President Hayes has ever produced so far as I know, and it created a profound impression upon the House. I immediately wrote him a letter expressing my high opinion of the Message. Fernando Wood thereupon introduced a joint resolution to adjourn the two House[s] *sine die.* This was referred to the Committee on Ways and Means. Thereupon at my suggestion, Mr. Deering[136] of Iowa, who had the floor for a motion to suspend the rules, offered the Army Appropriation Bill without the rider and called for a vote upon it. The Democrats moved to adjourn the House, but failed by a small number. This brought us to a vote upon the Army Bill direct and the vote stood 109 to 101. Two Democrats voted with us. I should have added that Swaim came from New York this morning. In the evening at eight o'clock, Mr. Brown, the two boys and I attended the National Theatre and heard the Standard Company's rendering of *Pinafore,* a very enjoyable piece.

TUESDAY, 13.   Dictated letters at the desk until half-past ten

[135]The *Tribune* of May 12, 1879, devoted more than a double column on page one to an explanation of why the Military Interference Bill was objectionable. Although Garfield's name does not appear there is no doubt that it is his work. Objections to the bill other than that mentioned in the entry for May 10 were: (1) that it recognized greater sovereignty of the states than of the national government by providing that if a state wanted troops at the polls the United States could go there with the army and serve the state; (2) that it contained a vague expression that laws inconsistent with it were repealed, thus leaving in doubt the validity of numerous laws empowering the President to use the army to enforce the laws.

[136]Nathaniel C. Deering (1827–1887) was a Republican member of the House from Iowa, 1877–83.

o'clock, when I went to the Pension Office to look after Sister Hittie's pension. Thence to the Capitol. Two hours were consumed in disgraceful altercation under the cover of personal explanations of three members. The privilege of personal explanation has been enlarged until it has degenerated into a great abuse. At half-past three o'clock, went to Col. Rockwell's and he and Swaim and I played billiards for an hour. My Classmates Rockwell, Gilfillan and J. K. Hazen,[137] now of Richmond, Va., dined with me and we had a pleasant visit. Rose came in the evening and I dictated Journal.

WEDNESDAY, 14. Worked at my desk dictating letters until eleven o'clock, during which time a number of people called. At eleven o'clock went to the State Department with Mr. Scudder[138] of Chicago, and had a long interview with the Secretary and requested him to write some letters introducing Mr. Scudder to the leading members of the Union League Club of New York with a view to raising money for the publications of the Honest Money League. Evarts was very entertaining in his talk, giving reminiscences of his interviews with Lord Brougham and several leading Englishmen in 1862.[139] Went to the Capitol at twelve; an hour or more was spent on business by unanimous consent. An hour or more was devoted to a bill from the Committee on Revision of the Laws preventing the transfer of cases from the State Courts to the Courts of the United States. At half-past two

[137]James K. Hazen (1833–1902), a native of Massachusetts, engaged in business in Alabama before becoming a Presbyterian pastor there. From 1877 to his death he lived near Richmond, Virginia, where he was secretary of the publication board of the church.

[138]Moses L. Scudder (1843–1917), a native of Massachusetts and a graduate in 1863 of Wesleyan University (Connecticut), was a businessman in Chicago and chairman of the executive committee of the Honest Money League of the Northwest. He later returned to the East, where he became prominent in the world of finance. At his death he was president of the St. Joseph, South Bend and Southern Railway. His writings include *Almost an Englishman* (1878), which Garfield refers to in the entry for October 24, 1878, and *Brief Honors; a Romance of the Great Dividable* (1879), which Garfield refers to in the entry for February 1, 1880.

[139]During the Civil War, William M. Evarts went to England on two diplomatic missions: April–July, 1863, and December, 1863-June, 1864.

discussion on the Silver Bill was resumed. A very sensible speech was made by Mr. Fort of Illinois, who was followed by Ewing in one of his usual financial speeches. At four o'clock I went with Rockwell and Swaim to see a match game of ball between the Nationals and Woosters. The score stood three for the Woosters; one for the Nationals.[140] Rockwell dined with us in the evening. Mr. Burchard,[141] Director of the Mint, came to consult with me in regard to the Silver Bill now pending. In the evening Rose came and I dictated Journal.

THURSDAY, 15. Desk in the morning and letters until eleven when I went to the Secretary of War on business. Thence to the Capitol, where the day was consumed on the Silver Bill. The morning hour was devoted to the Towns[h]end bill for repealing the law for transferring cases to the United States Supreme Court.[142] Swaim has nearly recovered from his throat troubles but is still not well.

FRIDAY, 16. Dictated letters until half-past ten o'clock, when I went to the Treasury to consult the Secretary and the Director of the Mint in regard to the pending Silver Bill and to collect some statistics for the debate. Went to the Capitol at twelve. The morning hour of yesterday was devoted to the Towns[h]end bill repealing the law for transferring cases to the United States Courts. After the morning hour which was mainly devoted to private bills, the Silver Bill was taken up and debate continued. At three I paired for the remainder of the day with Mr. Ewing, and then went with Col. Rockwell and Major Swaim to witness the match game of ball between the Springfields and the Nationals, which was handsomely won by the latter. The pitching of

[140]The Worcesters defeated the Nationals, 3–2, the latter making their second run in the last inning.

[141]Horatio C. Burchard, a Republican from Illinois, who failed to win renomination to the House in 1878, had recently been appointed director of the Bureau of the Mint, a position he held until 1885.

[142]The debate was over a bill introduced by Richard W. Townshend (1840–1889), a Democratic member of the House from Illinois, 1877 to his death, which provided for the repeal of legislation under which certain causes could be transferred from state to federal courts.

Lynch[143] of the Nationals was something wonderful, not only in the strength with which he pitched the ball, but in the skill with which he deceived the batsmen. At half-past eight o'clock Swaim and I called on Mr. Townsend and spent two or three hours at his room in company with Governor Hawley, Mr. Newberry[144] and others. Home at eleven.

SATURDAY, 17. Dictated letters until half-past eleven o'clock. Went to the Capitol. The morning hour was consumed in debate on the bill to remove causes from the State Courts to Federal. Mr. Urner,[145] of Frederick, Maryland, a new member, made a very good speech. This bill is another indication of the tendency of the Democracy to swing back to the extreme doctrine of State rights. They are constantly trying to weaken the National authority and strengthen that of the States. After the morning hour, the Silver Bill was taken up under the five minute rule and several votes were taken. I spoke five minutes quite effectively. The Speaker threw the casting vote in favor of an amendment by Mr. Ewing, which substantially converts the Treasury into a bank, to issue currency on forty percent reserve of silver. Though the amendment was adopted as an amendment to Springer's amendment, fortunately the whole and his amendment was defeated. The House adjourned at half-past four. Swaim was with us at dinner, but left for Leavenworth at half-past seven.

SUNDAY, 18. Thomas Phillips of New Castle came to visit me. Colonel Rockwell and several other friends called. At two o'clock Lieut. Harber, Miss Ransom, Mrs. Lander and her two boys, and Mrs. Reed took dinner with us. I excused myself from

---

[143]John Lynch, a native of New York who joined the Nationals during the season of 1878, was described as "the graceful and deceptive curvist." It was said of him that his principal peculiarity was "a conviction that nothing good can come out of Brooklyn." See the *Washington Post,* April 3, 1880, and March 8, 1879.

[144]John S. Newberry (1826–1887), a wealthy Detroit businessman, was a Republican member of the House from Michigan, 1879–81. He was the father of Truman H. Newberry (1864–1945), a Republican member of the Senate from Michigan, 1919–22.

[145]Milton G. Urner (1839–1926), was a Republican member of the House from Maryland, 1877–83.

the company at three and went to the President's and dined with his family. There were present besides General Wright,[146] of Indianapolis, Mrs. Herron[147] and Mr. Anderson[148] of Cincinnati, Major McKinley and wife and myself. After [dinner] we sat for nearly two hours on the South Portico. Secretary Sherman came and we had a general conversation on the political situation. Home at six. Miss Ransom, Miss Reed and Mr. Phillips took tea with us. I suffered during the evening with headache and took six grains of quinine. Retired at eleven o'clock.

MONDAY, 19.   Dictated letters in the morning, among others a long letter to Burke on his criticism in regard to my speech of March 29th.[149] After lunch went with Jimmy to the clothing store

[146]George B. Wright (1815–1903) was at this time receiver of the Indianapolis, Bloomington and Western Railroad. See Vol. I, pp. 456–457.

[147]Harriet Herron, wife of John W. Herron (1827–1912), a prominent lawyer of Cincinnati. He and Rutherford B. Hayes had been close friends since they shared an office in Cincinnati, 1850–51. He was United States attorney for the southern district of Ohio during the Benjamin Harrison administration. On December 5, 1885, Hayes attended the wedding of the Herrons' daughter Nellie to William Howard Taft.

[148]Larz Anderson (1845–1902), wealthy businessman of Cincinnati, was a guest at the White House, May 15–18. He was the grandson of Nicholas Longworth (1782–1863), Cincinnati lawyer, realtor and horticulturist, who amassed a large fortune.

[149]Hinsdale criticized Garfield (April 27) for representing a "rider" as a revolutionary method of law-making, for using immoderate language in his unwarranted assertion that Democrats were instigating a "revolution" (Hinsdale could find no evidence that a new rebellion was going to break out), and for delivering in the House speeches that were more suited for the campaign circuit. Garfield responded in a letter (May 20) in which he denied saying that it was revolutionary to put a rider on an appropriation bill, and insisted that he was "discussing the refusal [of the Democrats] to vote supplies, if the ridered bill should be vetoed." He defended his use of the term "revolution," pointing out that he was talking, not about revolution in the country, but about revolution in Congress, which was the title of his speech. Disturbing to Hinsdale also was the flagrant partisanship of Republican members of Congress, particularly of men like Blaine and Conkling. Garfield conceded that there was truth in Hinsdale's contention, but he defended Republican behavior as necessary to resist "the wicked spirit of the Democratic party, especially the Southern wing of it." See Mary L. Hinsdale, ed., *Garfield-Hinsdale Letters,* pp. 405–417.

and made some purchases for him. Thence to the Capitol and listened for an hour to Senator Blaine, who made a very strong speech on the Legislative Bill, or rather in reply to some speeches that had been made by Democratic Senators on the subject.[150] At half-past three o'clock we went to Col. Rockwell's and we played billiards for some time. After dinner Rose came and I dictated Journal.

TUESDAY, 20.   Worked at desk until 1/4 before eleven o'clock, when I went to Devlin's to look after some Summer clothes. Thence to the Capitol to attend the meeting of the Committee on Ways and Means. A resolution was adopted that the Committee would not consider at the present session any bills relating to a general change in the revenues. We then debated the resolution of Mr. Wood to provide for a *sine die* adjournment of Congress. In the House the morning hour was spent on Towns-[h]end's bill in reference to the transfer of causes to the United States Courts. After considerable discussion Mr. Wood's resolution was laid on the table by order of the Committee on Ways and Means. After the morning hour in the House, the Silver Bill came up. Many votes were taken on various amendments until finally a proposition offered by Mr. Marsh[151] of Illinois, that the seignorage on silver should be equal to the difference between the normal value of the standard dollar and the market value of the bullion. This we succeeded in carrying by a small majority, to the great dismay of the silver men. They attempted to reconsider, but we succeeded in laying that motion on the table and thus clinched the amendment. Thereupon they adjourned to gain time and take counsel. The adjournment occurred at half-past four. I then took the street car and went to the base ball grounds, arriving at half-past five, and found a very brilliant and close

[150]Blaine declared that despite threats from Democratic colleagues, Republican senators would not abandon their position on the Legislative Appropriation Bill. Subsequently the Senate passed and the President vetoed the bill. The veto message was read to the House on May 29 (while Garfield was in Ohio), after which the House voted to sustain the veto.

[151]Benjamin F. Marsh (1839–1905) was a Republican member of the House from Illinois, 1877–83, 1893–1901, and 1903 to his death.

contest in progress between the Nationals and Albanys. The ninth inning closed with one run for each club. The tenth and eleventh followed with no added run, but on the twelfth inning, the Nationals won a run by a very handsome play. It was much the most skilful and exciting game of base ball I have ever seen.[152] Col. Rockwell came home with me to dinner. We found Miss Ransom at the house who also dined with us. Casino and Greek in the evening. Hal attended the May Ball, returning an hour after midnight. I may add in my own voice, a little [later?] than he intended to return.

WEDNESDAY, 21. Worked at my desk until nine o'clock, when I went to the Riggs House to attend the meeting of the company which is organizing to develop the Beaver Dam property in North Carolina. We discussed quite fully the relative merits of the statutes of West Va. and Conn. for organizing joint stock companies. Returned home at eleven o'clock and worked at my desk until ten minutes before twelve, when I went to the Capitol. The morning hour was consumed in a struggle on the part of the Democrats to order the previous question on Towns[h]end's bill in reference to the Courts. We resisted the previous question and demanded further debate. The Democrats opposed and we prevented action until the morning hour ended. Warner's bill then came up and consumed the remainder of the day. The silver men gained some advantage in the voting today, although they failed to strike out the section as amended by Marsh of Illinois. At two o'clock an adjourned meeting of the stockholders referred to above was held in the room of the Committee on Ways and Means and it was resolved to organize under the statutes of Virginia. At five o'clock Messrs. Flagg of this City, Wilson, M. C. of W. Va., Judge Jackson[153] of Parkersburg, and Mr.

---

[152]The Nationals won 4–1, with three runs in the last inning. The *Washington Post* (May 21) said that the game "was the best played and most brilliant exhibition ever given in this city, and the audience of fully four thousand who watched with intense interest its entire progress through the twelve innings . . . were more than satisfied."

[153]John J. Jackson (1824–1907), the federal district judge in West Virginia for over forty years.

Phelps[154] of Elizabeth, New Jersey, and I took the train for Alexandria and filed our articles of incorporation in the Court. Returned on the 7 o'clock train. Dinner at home at eight o'clock. Rose came and I dictated Journal and worked on my mail.

THURSDAY, 22. Dictated letters in the morning. Went to the Treasury at eleven and thence to the Capitol. The day was consumed in a long struggle over the Silver Bill and no conclusion reached. On the adjournment at five o'clock, I went out to the Base Ball Grounds and saw the second match game between the Nationals and the Capital Citys of Albany. A very brilliant game, which the Nationals won. Home in the evening and commenced the preparation of a speech on the bill to repeal the laws for transferring causes from State Courts to United States Courts.

FRIDAY, 23. Dictated letters in the morning until half-past eleven, when I went to the Capitol. The morning hour was taken up on private bills. I made a short speech in defence of the bill for extending a patent on a new mode of condensing and purifying sugar, but the bill went over without being concluded. After the morning hour the Silver Bill came up and it was considered by sections until half-past five o'clock. A motion was made to adjourn. I voted in favor of it, and supposing the House would adjourn, I went to the Base Ball Grounds to witness an exhibition game between the Nationals and Albanys. Dinner at seven o'clock. Several people called, among others Judge Black. While he was here, Mr. Hill[155] from the Sergeant-at-Arms [came], informing me that there was a call of the House. He did not serve a paper on me. I told him I would go to the House immediately. Judge Black drove me there and I went to the Sergeant-at-Arms's room and I was informed after going to the door that they were not ready for me. Finding they were badgering absent members, I concluded not to go in. Went into the Reporter's Room and remained half an hour or twenty minutes, then stepped out on

---

[154]Phelps has not been identified. Efforts to locate the papers filed in Alexandria by inquiries addressed to the Archives and Records Division of the Virginia State Library and the Alexandria City Circuit Court have been fruitless.
[155]Isaac R. Hill, an Ohioan.

the South Balcony and remained an hour and a half until the proceedings under the call were dispensed with. They made a special point of trying to find me, but of course failed. About half-past eleven o'clock I went in and we remained in session all night, refusing to allow the previous question to be taken unless the Democrats would consent to allow a vote on Mr. Ryan's substitute for the whole bill. We remained in session until nine o'clock in the morning.

SATURDAY, 24. Came home shortly after nine o'clock to breakfast. At eleven o'clock went to the clothing store and purchased a summer suit. Capitol at twelve. The morning hour was called and we prevented the previous question being called on Mr. Towns[h]end's bill. At the end of the morning hour Mr. Warner again demanded the previous question. I suggested that he had better not enter upon the useless struggle that had kept the House in continuous session for 19 hours, but that if he would consent to allow the amendment of Mr. Ryan[156] to be voted on opposition would be withdrawn. After some skirmishing the arrangement was agreed to by unanimous consent, and at half-past one a vote was taken on Ryan's amendment, which failed, and then on the bill, which passed by seventeen majority. The House then adjourned until Tuesday. Having had no sleep for twenty-four hours, I am very much worn out. In the evening Judge Black called, and I drove out with him for three-quarters of an hour. Then went to the Theatre with the boys and heard *Pinafore.* Home at eleven and retired.

SUNDAY, 25. Large mail in the morning. Letter from Crete and also one from Mentor. At ten o'clock Mr. McKinley came and insisted that I should go to Cincinnati. Went with him to Townsend['s] and to Governor Young's. I also called on Dr. Updegraff[157] and all of them agreed to go to Cincinnati. McKinley, Townsend and I then called on the President and consulted him

---

[156]Thomas Ryan (1837–1914) was a Republican member of the House from Kansas, 1877–89.

[157]Jonathan T. Updegraff practiced medicine earlier in his career. He served for a time as a surgeon in the Union army.

on the situation of the Legislative Appropriation Bill. He will [be] ready to send in his veto early next week. We suggested to him to delay his veto until Thursday so that his Ohio friends could return from the Convention. He said he would at least delay it until Wednesday and possibly until Thursday. Home in the evening and read over the history of the great debate of 1833 on the Force Bill. The discussion we are now having on the Towns[h]end bill is a singular reproduction of that controversy. Retired at eleven.

MONDAY, 26. Dictated letters in the forenoon. Secretary Sherman called in the morning to see me in reference to the Cincinnati Convention. There is now a rumor that Senator Thurman has consented to run on the Gubernatorial Ticket. I suggested to Sherman that he find out through McCormick[158] whether this rumor was based on truth and that I would call on him at 12 o'clock for the purpose of knowing the result of his inquiry. At half-past eleven o'clock went to the Treasury, and requested Lamphere[159] to transfer Rose to his office. This was agreed to. Then had a conference with Sherman. He thinks the effort to nominate Thurman is to compel our people to nominate him or me, that in either case the Ohio campaign will be understood to be a race for the Presidency. He thinks that neither of us should be a candidate, in which opinion I agree. He says that such a contest at this time would encounter the opposition of the Grant men in Ohio, which he thinks would be unfortunate. Went to the Capitol and also to the Bank to transact some business. At half-past four went with Colonel Rockwell to the Base Ball Ground and saw a very strong game between the Nationals and the Troys, a Club belonging to the League.[160] The Nationals won the game on eleven innings. Home in the evening. Rose came and I dictated Journal and made preparations for leaving for Cincin-

[158]Richard C. McCormick (see Vol. II, p. 32, n. 116) married Elizabeth, daughter of Allen G. Thurman, in 1873.

[159]George N. Lamphere, of Connecticut, was chief of the appointment division of the office of the secretary of the treasury.

[160]The National League of Professional Base Ball Players, organized in 1876.

nati by the 11 o'clock Baltimore and Ohio train. Left at eleven in company with Townsend and Updegraff of Ohio.

TUESDAY, 27. Took breakfast at Grafton, where I posted a letter to Crete. Thence by the Pittsburgh, crossing the Ohio River at eleven o'clock.[161] Took dinner at Chillicothe at 12. They have had a great deal of rain in this quarter of the state recently, but I understand that Northern Ohio is very dry. Arrived in Cincinnati at half-past six in the evening. Ben Butterworth[162] and Col. Bullock[163] met me and took me to Col. Bullock's house on Walnut Hill, where I took a bath and after supper we drove down to the Gibson House, where I called on Foster and Taft and many delegates who had arrived in large numbers. The contest between Taft and Foster is very close, but Foster's popular manners are in his favor and I think he is likely to succeed. I favor Foster though I think I ought not to take an active part between the two candidates. Returned to Walnut Hill at half-past eleven o'clock, and spent the night at Bullock's house, which is very spacious and elegant.

WEDNESDAY, 28. At eight o'clock Major Butterworth and Crowell,[164] of Ashtabula County, took breakfast with us, after which we went down to the City. I went to the Hotel to attend the meeting of the Nineteenth District Delegation and found they had just chosen me as a member of the Committee on Resolu-

[161]The Baltimore and Ohio Railroad ran from Grafton to Parkersburg, West Virginia, where Garfield crossed the Ohio River and completed his trip on the Cincinnati and Marietta Railroad.

[162]Benjamin Butterworth (1837–1898), a Union officer in the Civil War, was a Republican member of the House from Ohio, 1879–83, and 1885–91. He was a delegate to the Republican National Convention in 1880.

[163]Anthony D. Bullock (1824–1890), a native of Pennsylvania, became one of the most prominent businessmen in Cincinnati. The honorary title of colonel was conferred on him by Governor Dennison in recognition of his wartime services.

[164]William H. Crowell, a delegate to the Republican state convention, had long been auditor of Ashtabula County. In 1880 he entered the Treasury Department in Washington, where he was employed for many years. "A Republican, of the unequivocal kind," he supported Garfield for the Senate. His brother Dwight was deputy auditor of Ashtabula County for many years and later auditor; he was also an active Republican. See December 17, 1879.

tions. I asked the Committee to excuse me serving either as a Delegate or Committeeman, on the ground that I did not wish to take so active a part in the Convention. At eleven o'clock went to Music Hall, which was crowded to its utmost capacity. I was received with a good deal of enthusiasm on reaching the stage. It was the largest and most enthusiastic convention I have ever attended. On the adjournment at nine [noon] I dined with George W. Steele and his new wife, at [of] Painesville, [and] with Mr. and Mrs. Robinson of Marysville.[165] Returned to the Convention at two o'clock. Foster was nominated on the first ballot, by a majority of four. The Convention conducted its business with great harmony, but did not conclude its deliberations until half-past eight o'clock, when I made an address of about 35 minutes, giving in a condensed form a few leading points of the campaign, which I think I did quite effectively.[166] I was immediately driven to the Little Miami Depot, where I had been invited to join Dr. Streator in his Directors' Car. Our company consisted of Drs. Streator and Robison, Charlie Foster, Tinker of Painesville and myself. Several friends called and spent part of the evening with us. Retired at twelve.

THURSDAY, 29. Reached Cleveland at seven o'clock. I had arranged by telegraph to have the Lake Shore Express train stop to let me off at my farm, but on reaching the depot Brother Joe met me with a note from Crete that she would arrive from Hiram on the eleven o'clock train to go with me to Mentor. So I remained over in Cleveland and called on some friends in the meantime. Mr. Sherwin drove over to the Atlantic Depot at 11 o'clock and brought Crete across to the Lake Shore Depot where I was waiting to meet her. She arrived in time and we went together out to Mentor and found Moses at the cars awaiting us.

[165]Aaron B. Robinson, a businessman of Marysville, was a member of the Ohio state legislature, 1880–83.

[166]On May 29, 1879, the *Cincinnati Enquirer* commented: "General Garfield was the central figure of the Convention which met at Music Hall yesterday. He is, in fact, the central figure in the Republican party of to-day, not of Ohio, but of the United States. If that party is to retain its existence, he is in it the man of the future. If a new one is to be formed in its stead, he is the man to form it."

When we arrived at the farm dinner was awaiting us. Affairs are going on well at the farm, but the long continued dry weather has nearly ruined vegetation. Spent the afternoon and evening in overhauling farm matters and receiving calls of friends.

FRIDAY, 30.   Northcott came and we settled our farm accounts for the past two months. I was compelled to shoot my dog in consequence of his having chased sheep. Gave general directions for the management of the farm, and Crete and I took the train for Cleveland. Went shopping and visited Dr. Boynton and wife. At four o'clock and twenty minutes took the train for Hiram. Spent the night at Father Rudolph's. Mother Rudolph is very low, greatly emaciated and growing constantly feebler in mind and body. It rained heavily during the night and I hope it will revive the drooping vegetation.

SATURDAY, 31.   Called at Cousin Phebe's and President Hinsdale's late in the afternoon. Dinner at Father Rudolph's. At two o'clock went to the College Chapel where the students listened to my address for half an hour. At three o'clock left Crete with her Mother. Went to Garrettsville, where I took the train for Pittsburgh, arriving in time for the Connellsville train eastward. Mr. Rogers, the President's Private Secretary, was the only passenger besides myself on the Pullman car. We spent the evening in conversation on the Democratic revival of the doctrine of states rights.

June

SUNDAY, 1.   Awoke between the Point of Rocks and Washington. Arrived at eight o'clock. Jimmy met me at the Depot. Breakfasted with the boys at nine. Thence a bath and change of clothing. I spent the remainder of the day in reading the enormous mail which has accumulated in my absence. Mrs. [Miss] Ransom and Mrs. Reed dined with us at two o'clock. In the evening I called on the President and discussed the political situation here and in Ohio.

MONDAY, 2.   At eleven o'clock called at the War Department and the Treasury Department. Thence to the Capitol. But little business was done and the House adjourned at three o'clock. The Democrats held a caucus which ran far into the night, for the purpose of determining their next move. After dinner heard the boys in their Greek Grammar and the *Anabasis.* I had long before read it and I am gratified to find how readily it comes back to me.

TUESDAY, 3.   Dictated letters until eleven o'clock when I went to the Treasury to look after the appointment of Eugene Cowles. Thence to the Capitol to attend a meeting of the Committee on Ways and Means, and found no quorum present. In the morning hour the time was consumed by Mr. Cox, in a speech on the Juror's Test Oath. Thereupon the House was immediately adjourned, to enable the Democrats to reassemble their Caucus. At four o'clock I attended the funeral of Ebon C. Ingersoll, who was with me in Congress several terms. I append to this page the remarkable address read by his brother Rob't G. Ingersoll as he stood beside the coffin.[167] I was deeply impressed with the utter breakdown of atheistical philosophy in the presence of death. After hearing the boys' recitation in the evening, I commenced to study for a speech on the Democratic doctrine of State rights. I read with great interest the opinions of the Justices of the Supreme Court in the case of *Chisholm versus the State of Georgia* in Second Dallas. It is a remarkable exhibition of the nationality

[167]The widely publicized funeral oration (set forth in the newspaper clipping appended by Garfield) delivered at the home of the deceased on June 2, includes this passage: "Life is a narrow vale between the cold and barren peaks of two eternities. We strive in vain to look beyond the heights. We cry aloud, and the only answer is the echo of our wailing cry. From the voiceless lips of the unreplying dead there comes no word; but in the night of death Hope sees a star, and, listening, Love can hear the rustle of a wing." On the day after the funeral Garfield sent to his wife (June 3) "the paper containing Bob's speech in which I think he hints at a hope for a future life. It was a great trial to him," Garfield explained, "to read his address. The family exhibited more signs of agony than I have ever seen before. One of the adopted daughters tried to jump into the grave, and Bob ordered the coffin opened for her, even after it was partially lowered into the grave. She shouted to the sexton who was laying flat stones across the top of the coffin, 'Take those stones away, you bad man.' On the whole, it was the most painful scene I have ever witnessed and I hope to be spared another."

of the General Government as opposed to State Sovereignty. Retired at twelve o'clock.

WEDNESDAY, 4. Dictated some letters in the morning. Spent most of the forenoon in examining the speeches that have been made in favor of States' rights, at the present session. Call[ed] at the Treasury on my way to the Capitol. I have been suffering this morning from diar[r]hea and did not feel well enough to speak as I was not quite prepared so I let the occasion pass. The Chairman of the Committee on Appropriations introduced a sort of substitute for the Legislative Appropriation Bill,[168] in which he proposed to re-enact the law of last year except some clauses and adding others. At home at five o'clock and heard the boys' recitation in the Greek Grammar and *Anabasis*, but did not conclude until after dinner. Some callers came in the evening. I did not make much progress in my States' rights speech.

THURSDAY, 5. Dictated letters in the morning. Treasury Department. Thence to the Capitol at twelve, having forgotten to attend the meeting of the Committee on Rules. In the House but little was done. The Democrats have resolved upon their plan with the appropriation bills, but have not yet perfected their measures. Came home at four to hear the recitation of the boys, partly before [dinner] and the remainder after. I was detained from work by callers until nearly 10 o'clock. Rose came. I dictated journal and worked on speech.

FRIDAY, 6. Dictated a few letters in the morning, but spent most of the time in reading Calhoun's disquisition on the Constitution and Government of the United States. He denounces the 25th Section of the Judiciary Act of 1879 [1789] as unconstitutional and says it was a restriction upon the independent sovereignty of the States, in that it brought the decision of the State courts by appeal before the Supreme Court of the United States. At half-past eleven went to the Interior and Post Office Departments on business. Thence to the Capitol. The day was spent partly on private bills, but mainly on the bill in relation to the pay of letter carriers. Left the Capitol at half-past three. Played billiards with

[168]This measure was introduced on June 5.

Rockwell for half an hour when I came home. After dinner heard the boys' recitation in Greek. At eight o'clock went to Mr. Townsend's.

SATURDAY, 7.   Dictated letters in the forenoon and worked till nearly [noon?] on the question of state rights, as developed in the history of the country. At twelve went to the Capitol. The day was spent in miscellaneous work, mainly in passing a bill for the pay of letter carriers. At four o'clock went with Colonel Rockwell and played billiards until one-quarter of five, when I went to his house and took dinner in company with his family and Mrs. Johnson. Home at half-past ten.

SUNDAY, 8.   Troubled on account of receiving no letter from Crete. Received a letter from Irvin and Abe saying that Mama had not come home from Hiram. A number of people called during the day. I remained home until after dinner. Mrs. Lander, her two boys and Miss Ransom dined with us. At six o'clock the boys and I drove for an hour. Spent the evening in reading Calhoun and the debates in the first Congress on the power of the General Government over elections of Representatives in Congress.

MONDAY, 9.   Dictated letters until eleven o'clock, when I went to the War Department, and thence drove with Captain Corbin[169] to Sax's [Saks'] on Seventh Street and ordered some clothes. Capitol little after twelve. The Legislative Bill was passed under a suspension of the rules, after a brief statement by Mr. Atkins and another by Mr. Hawley. It is a singular botch of a bill in which the appropriation law of last year is re-enacted in a single clause, followed by a large number of exceptions and additions. If the law passes in that shape, it will need to be codified before it can be executed. Ryan of Kansas offered a resolution to suspend the rules and pass the Army Appropriation

[169]Henry C. Corbin (1842–1909), a native of Ohio, had a long career in the army, during which he attained the rank of major general. At the time of his death the *New York Times* described him as "one of the best known figures in the military life of this country." In March, 1877, he accompanied President-elect Hayes to Washington and after the inauguration was assigned to the Executive Mansion. In 1881 he was secretary of the committee in charge of the inauguration of Garfield, and in September of that year accompanied the dying President to Elberon.

Bill as reported by Mr. Clymer. The Democrats took fright at this and moved to adjourn, which motion was carried by five majority. After dinner I heard the boys' recitation in Xenophon and Greek. Rose came and I dictated Journal.

TUESDAY, 10. [No entry]

WEDNESDAY, 11. Dictated letters in the forenoon until 11 o'clock, when I called at the Departments and thence went to the Capitol at twelve. The day has been a most important one in the management of a contest in the House. The efforts of Senators to create a division among us in regard to the Army Bill had so far succeeded that some Republicans in the House were determined to fight against the Army Bill and many were uncertain how they would vote. We arranged to have all [other] parts of the bill finished before the contested section, the sixth, was taken up—and on that there should be an hour's debate between the two parties. Baker and Hawley of the Committee on Appropriations used up ten minutes and surrendered the balance of the time to me. I recounted the progress of the contest on the Army Bill up to the present time and showed the attempts of the Democracy in the first bill to refuse all civil authority to use force to keep the peace at the polls and [in] the second bill to prevent the President enforcing any of the national laws on election days.[170] I showed that in this bill all attempts were abandoned and that the [end of entry]

THURSDAY, 12. Worked at my desk until 11 o'clock, when I called on the President and discussed the situation in Congress. He was pleased with the result of the contest yesterday and agreed with me in the necessity of vetoing the Judiciary Appropriation Bill, which passed day before yesterday.[171] I talked with

[170]In his speech Garfield reviewed the history of the Army Appropriation Bill and declared that section six repealed no law of the United States and did not apply "to any law or to any practice known." That section, he argued, contained only party literature and was "merely and only a stump speech." He said that he would vote for the bill and did so on the following day, when it passed the House, 172–31. See March 27, 1879, n. 95.

[171]In the debate of June 10 on the Judiciary Appropriation Bill, in which Garfield participated, the Republicans argued that the appropriations were totally inadequate. They charged that limited appropriations would make impossible

him in reference to the appointment of Mr. Tinker to the Chief Justiceship of Utah Territory, but the name of ex-Senator Corbin had not yet been withdrawn.[172] Went to the Capitol and spent the day until after four in a useless wrangle over a number of extreme measures which the Democrats sought to pass.[173] Played billiards with Colonel Rockwell. Then at home and heard the boys' recitation in *Anabasis.* Rose came, when I dictated the Journal.

FRIDAY, 13. Dictated letters in the morning. Went to the Departments at eleven. Capitol at twelve, where the day was spent without much result in any direction. Many members of the House are absent and others constantly going. It will not take long at the present rate to leave us without a quorum. Home in the evening, heard the boys' lessons after dinner. Then Mr. P. H. Watson of Ashtabula came to retain me in a Patent Case. I agreed to give him tomorrow all the time I could spare from my duties in the House.

SATURDAY, 14. Dictated letters in the forenoon. Went to the Capitol, where but little was done. I left at half-past two, went

---

enforcement of laws that the Democrats opposed but had been unable to repeal in Congress, and they objected to restrictions which forbade the federal government to incur a liability for any reason. The bill passed, 102–84. See entry for June 19.

[172]Garfield's friend Alvin L. Tinker, a Painesville lawyer, wished to obtain a federal appointment in the West for reasons of health, and Garfield promised to help him. On June 9, 1879, Tinker wrote Garfield that he understood that the person nominated for chief justice of Utah Territory would not be confirmed, and asked Garfield to take up the matter with the President. David T. Corbin, a state senator and U.S. attorney in South Carolina during reconstruction, who had been elected to the U.S. Senate by one of two contending state legislatures in 1876 but not seated, was rejected by the Senate for the Utah post on June 30. Tinker was not nominated for the chief justiceship nor for any other position by President Hayes.

[173]The most controversial measures were one dealing with the pay, qualifications, selection, tenure, and duties of jurors in United States courts, and another prohibiting federal officeholders and persons with claims against or contracts with the United States from making any contribution of property, money or other valuables for political purposes.

to the Ebbitt House and spent nearly four hours with Mr. Watson, hearing the details of his case. The patent is one of great value and yet consists of a very simple idea—the splitting of a feather so as to remove [the stem], so as to make a duster similar to that now known to commerce as an ostrich feather duster.[174] At seven o'clock dined with Senator Allison in company with Minister Kasson, Secretaries Evarts and McCrary and a number of Senators. A very pleasant party. Home at ten o'clock. Retired at eleven.

SUNDAY, 15.   Letters from Mentor and also one from Crete who is in Hiram. The farm is prospering under the influence of the late rains. At eleven o'clock Jimmy and I attended Church on Vermont Ave. At half-past one Miss Ransom and Mrs. Dean [Reed?] dined with us. Spent the evening at home. Several people called.

MONDAY, 16.   Dictated letters in the forenoon, and at ten o'clock went to the Ebbitt House to consult further with Mr. Watson on the Patent Case. At eleven o'clock Lieut. Hubbard came and I went with him to the War Department to recommend him for appointment as Quartermaster with the rank of Captain.[175] Called also on the President. Then went to the Capitol. The usual Monday work went on with no valuable result. At three o'clock went to the Ebbitt House and worked until six with Mr. Watson on the Patent Case. Home in the evening. Greek lesson after dinner.

TUESDAY, 17.   Brown came in the morning and I dictated letters. Reached the Capitol at half-past eleven o'clock to meet with the Committee on Ways and Means, where a few private bills were

[174]Garfield assisted in this case in its preliminary stages. When it came before the commissioner of patents for decision, Peter H. Watson and Walter Davidge were listed as counsel for Gilbert M. Richmond, who had been denied a patent on a new type of feather duster on the ground that another person had prior claim.

[175]Edward B. Hubbard, a nephew of Garfield's Ashtabula friend Henry Hubbard, served in the Union army during the Civil War and was now a 1st lieutenant in the 2nd U.S. Artillery Regiment. Although Garfield failed in his mission at this time, on March 21, 1881, he appointed Hubbard assistant quartermaster with the rank of captain. Hubbard was dismissed from the army in 1883.

ordered to be reported. In the morning hour Mr. Hostetler[176] of Indiana called up his bill to prevent persons holding office under the Federal Government from making contributions even voluntarily for the expenses of any election. Mr. McLain [McLane] of Maryland made a rambling two hours' speech attacking the Republican Party violently.[177] I sought the floor to reply, but other business intervened. After dinner heard the boys' recitation. In the evening I called on Mr. Watson and concluded our preliminary examination of the case, for which I had drawn a full petition for reopening the interference. I returned home at eight and worked until eleven preparing a speech on the recent Democratic tendency towards the doctrine of extreme states' rights.

WEDNESDAY, 18. Worked at my desk. Left the house at a quarter before twelve, taking my notes and books with me. The morning hour came and I sought the floor, but the other side refused to allow me to speak and demanded the previous question. The Conference report on the Legislative Bill was adopted. A conference was ordered on the Little Judiciary Bill.[178] The Democrats, having given away on some points of difference, now hope to secure the President's signature to the bill. The Senate debated today the Army Appropriation Bill, Conkling and others taking the ground that the sixth section restrained the President from the use of the army for the ordinary enforcement of the laws. In this view I do not concur. Only a little more than a quorum of

176Abraham J. Hostetler (1818–1899) was a Democratic member of the House from Indiana, 1879–81.

177Robert M. McLane (1815–1898), a Democratic member of the House from Maryland, 1847–51, 1879–83, favored passage of a bill "to prohibit Federal officers, claimants and contractors from making contributions for political purposes." His principal antagonist was Omar D. Conger of Michigan who characterized the bill as an infamous caucus measure and made remarks extremely derogatory of the South. Offended by Conger's statements, McLane proceeded to denounce the Republican party and the Grant administrations, charging that only "a corrupt political motive" prevented Republicans from supporting the bill under consideration. The Republicans failed in an attempt to force McLane to sit down because of his "unparliamentary language," and he completed his tirade.

178The Judiciary Appropriation Bill.

members are now present in the House and there are symptoms of a break up. The Speaker told me today that the House would adjourn this week. Home in the evening and after dinner heard the boys' recitation.

THURSDAY, 19. The usual story. Letters in the morning. Capitol at twelve. *Anabasis* with the boys after dinner and work in the evening until a late hour preparing for a speech which I may not have an opportunity to deliver.

But I should add that Mr. McMahon brought in a Conference report on the Judicial Appropriation Bill, and I spoke against it about fifteen minutes showing that it was an attempt to nullify laws that they could not repeal. I think I made the argument against it effective. It passed by a strict party vote, all the Republicans voted against it.

FRIDAY, 20. Letters in the morning. Departments at eleven. Capitol at twelve. But little was done in the House. The bitter contest in the Senate attracted nearly all the members of that body. The Senate continued in session all night last night and until five minutes before twelve this morning. The Republicans in order to compel the majority to allow them to speak, resorted, I think for the first time in the history of the Senate, to breaking the quorum by refusing to vote. The Senate met again at twelve, and after two hours' further wrangle to [the] Republicans carried their point against the Democrats, by their agreeing that after a recess when they met in [the] evening all parties should have time for debate. At six o'clock Harry, Jimmy and I joined in an excursion on the *Mary Washington* [179] down the river to Marshall Hall. Returned at eleven o'clock, when I went to the Capitol and listened to the speeches of Conkling and Blaine until two. All the Republican Senators except Burnside voted against the Army Bill. I think this was a great mistake. It was antagonizing the position taken in the House by the Republicans, and it remains to be seen which side was wisest. Came home and retired at half-past two.

[179] An excursion steamer that was making two trips daily to Marshall Hall and Mount Vernon Spring at a charge of twenty-five cents for the round trip.

SATURDAY, 21. Dictated letters until half-past ten, when I went to the Departments and thence to the Capitol. The day was spent after the morning hour in considering bills on the Speaker's table. One for making an appropriation for a Board of Survey, composed of Officers, to report upon the improvement of the Mississippi, was resisted by Mr. Baker of Indiana. I took occasion to make a speech of ten minutes, advocating the nationality of the subject. I received the cordial congratulations of several leading Southerners. The bill was passed with but eleven dissenting votes, four of those being Democrats. After dinner, I went to Mr. Townsend's room and played Casino with him, McKinley, Hiscock, and McCook until eleven o'clock when I came home and retired.

SUNDAY, 22. Read a large mail in the morning. Went to Church at eleven. On my return found Colonel Rockwell and Henry E. Knox of New York, my two Classmates, awaiting me. They, in company with Miss Ransom and Mrs. Reed, dined with us. After dinner Knox, Rockwell, and I went to the Arlington and consulted for two hours with Knox on the subject matter of his visit to Washington, which was to get me to aid him in a patent suit relating to a combination of driven wells to one general pump, for the purpose of supplying cities with pure water. Home at half-past ten and retired.

MONDAY, 23. Worked at my desk until eleven o'clock, when I went with General Gibson of Louisiana to call on the President in reference to the make up of the Mississippi River Commission authorized by the act passed on Saturday last. Thence went to the Navy Department to secure for Orville Grant an interview with the Secretary. Grant seems to be a man of very loose-jointed mind from the character of his interview. Thence I went to the Pension Office to see about Sister Hittie's pension. Thence to the Capitol where, immediately after prayer, the President sent a message informing the House that he had signed the Army Bill, and, also, another message returning the Judiciary Bill with his veto. His Private Secretary brought me the only printed copy. This signing of the Military Bill is for me a signal triumph over those who would have kept up a harmful warfare which would have implied our willingness to use the Army as an ordinary instrument for running elections. In the long run, I have no doubt my position on this question will receive general approval, although I ran some risk in assuming it. Immediately after the message was read the House was brought to a vote upon the [Judiciary] Bill and, of course, it failed to pass. Thereupon the Democrats adjourned, threatening that they would pass no more appropriation bills and would adjourn *sine die.* We shall see. At 1/4 past five my Classmate Knox and I held a further consultation in regard to his patent case. In the evening Rose came, and I dictated Journal.

TUESDAY, 24. Letters in the morning. Departments at eleven. Capitol at twelve. The Democrats have been thrown into so much confusion by the last veto of the President, that they are quite undecided what they will do. They attempted to adjourn *sine die,* but were defeated by a vote of 102 to 80 [82], and after a profitless session of three hours the House adjourned. After dinner, heard the boys in their Algebra and Virgil. I find that they are not as well up in Latin as in Greek, but need thorough drilling to give them precision. Letter from Crete which gives good news from home and makes me long to be in my fields.

WEDNESDAY, 25. Dictated letters in the morning. At eleven o'clock went with Benj. Summy[180] to the Secretary of War to see about his appointment, but did not complete the work. Went thence to the Capitol. The Democrats having been in a wrangle last night and come to no conclusion, resolved to hold a Joint Caucus at three this afternoon, so after a session of two hours and a half, in which no good work was done, the House adjourned.

THURSDAY, 26. Worked at my desk until ten o'clock, when Benj. Summy came and took me to the War Department, where I got him a position as Messenger in the Archive Office. Thence to the Pension Office where I completed the papers for Sister Hittie's

[180]Benjamin W. Summy, son of the Benjamin W. Summy in Vol. III, pp. 269–270, n. 165, was a clerk in the War Department for many years. On occasion he practiced medicine. Other members of the Summy family also held government positions.

pension and got it promised. Thence to the Public Printing Office to arrange for printing my speeches of the Session. Thence to the Capitol. At two o'clock Mr. Atkins reported the first of the Caucus appropriation bills, appropriating two millions one hundred thousand dollars for the expenses of the courts, covering, indeed, all the appropriations except those for marshals. The second section of the late vetoed bill was left off. The bill was the same as before. After debate in Committee of the Whole on the State of the Union under the five minute rule, the bill was passed by a strict party vote, several implacable Democrats refusing to vote. The Republicans voted against it, because it injects into the Jury law partisan politics.[181] The President I believe will sign this bill for he thinks on the whole that the jury system will be improved by this measure.

FRIDAY, 27. Spent the morning at my desk in condensing my notes so as to make an hour's speech in half an hour. At half-past ten went to the President with Major Holliday [Holladay][182] and thence to the Capitol, attended the meeting of the Committee on Ways and Means. At half-past twelve I got the floor and spoke for half an hour on the doctrine of States' Rights as exhibited by the Democracy in the debates of the present session. While I was

[181]The Judicial Expenditures Bill provided in part that jurors in any federal court be selected in a public drawing from a box containing the names of at least 300 qualified persons placed therein by the clerk of the court and a commissioner appointed by the judge of the district. The commissioner was to be a resident of the district in good standing and "a well-known member of the principal political party in the district in which the court is held opposing that to which the clerk may belong. . . ." He and the clerk were to place "one name of a potential juror in the box alternately, without reference to party affiliations," until the required number should be placed therein.

[182]Ben Holladay, Sr., went to Washington, D.C., from Oregon in 1876 and maintained his residence there until his return to Oregon in 1884. He tried for many years to collect from the government for damages done his stage coach and freighting enterprises in the West by Indians. On July 1, 1879, he wrote Garfield thus: "It does my *heart good* to *lighten* your *political load* with enclosed check for 100$ to *scatter broadcast* your words of *wisdom.*" At the time the letter was written Garfield was seeing through the press an edition of his speeches in the special session.

too much crowded for time to do full justice to the subject, I think my speech is in a more condensed and effective shape as a campaign document than it would have been had it been longer.[183] Hurd of Ohio followed me, but made very few points in direct reply to anything I stated. The two principal points which he mentioned, I replied to in a five minutes' speech, quoting an important historical record of the first Congress on the subject of an amendment to curtail the powers of Congress over the election of Representatives.[184] Home in the evening. Mr.

[183]Using excerpts from speeches delivered by seven Democrats in the present Congress, Garfield said that their declarations "set forth what may be fairly regarded as the doctrines of the democracy as represented in this Capitol. They are, in brief: First, there are no national elections; second, the United States has no voters; third, the States have the exclusive right to control all elections of members of Congress; fourth, the Senators and Representatives in Congress are State officers, or, as they have been called during the present session, 'embassadors,' or 'agents' of the State; fifth, the United States has no authority to keep the peace anywhere within a State, and in fact, has no peace to keep; sixth, the United States is not a nation endowed with sovereign power, but is a confederacy of States; seventh, the States are sovereignties possessing inherent supreme powers. They are older than the Union, and as independent sovereignties the State governments created the Union and determined and limited the power of the General Government."

Garfield argued that these declarations formed a doctrine of states rights "more extreme than was ever before held on this subject, except perhaps at the very crisis of secession and rebellion." The Democrats, he said, had not regarded these doctrines "as abstract theories of government"; they had "sought to put them in practice by affirmative acts of legislation." He condemned such behavior and declared that the Constitution of the United States was created not by the states but by the people; that the United States is a nation with a government whose authority operates upon all the people; and that "by its legislative, executive, and judicial authority the nation is armed with adequate power to enforce all the provisions of the Constitution against all opposition of individuals or of States at all times and all places within the Union." To support his position Garfield presented an historical brief showing to what extent the so-called "sovereignty" of a state was limited by the Constitution.

[184]The two points made by Hurd were that the United States had no voters, and that the states, so long as they did not "neglect or refuse to act," or were not "prevented by rebellion or war from acting," had the exclusive right to determine the time, place, and manner of holding elections. In his response Garfield reaffirmed the nationalistic philosophy expounded in his speech.

Brown came in the evening and we sat until an hour after midnight revising the notes of my two speeches. Retired at one o'clock exceedingly weary.

SATURDAY, 28.   Did not get enough sleep last night to overcome the fatigue. This sultry weather makes it a burden to live. Dictated letters in the forenoon. Called at the Departments. Thence to the Capitol. The day was spent in miscellaneous work and not much accomplished. The Senate passed the Little Marshals Appropriation Bill late in the afternoon.[185] Home in the evening and retired early.

SUNDAY, 29.   After reading my mail, I took an open carriage and with the two boys drove across the Aqueduct Bridge to Arlington and thence across the road leading south of Long Bridge on the road to Alexandria to Mr. ———— who has rented the farm belonging to Judge Black and myself. We returned over the Long Bridge, reaching home a little after one o'clock. Miss Ransom, Mrs. Reed and Henry Wyman dined with us. In the evening I commenced reading the proof of the pamphlet copy of my speech. At half-past nine o'clock Mr. Amos Townsend and I went to the President's and had a conversation with him in regard to the propriety of calling an extra session. I opposed it as profitless either to the Government or to the Republican Party. I was satisfied that the Democrats had resolved not to make an appropriation for Marshals, and if they were called together, there was danger they would go into general financial legislation and do the country much harm. The President read me the draft of his message vetoing the Marshals Bill. I suggested a certain point for his message, which was this sentence. "These marshals are in fact

---

[185]The bill appropriated $600,000 for the payment of United States marshals and their deputies through the fiscal year ending June 30, 1880. The Senate passed it on June 28, 1879, but two days later Hayes vetoed it and the House sustained the veto. His objection was the inclusion of a rider prohibiting payments to marshals and their deputies "for service in connection with elections or on election day" until a sum sufficient to pay for such service had been appropriated by law. Hayes acknowledged that the marshals and their deputies performed an essential function, but pointed out that the rider was identical to legislation he had vetoed on June 23 and that the House had sustained the veto.

the only police force of the Government of the United States.'' He immediately wrote it in.[186] My object in recommending this sentence was that the marshals, not the army, formed the national police. Home at half-past ten and retired.

MONDAY, 30. Dictated letters in the morning and at half-past eleven went to the War Department on business. Thence to the Capitol. Immediately after the reading of the Journal the President sent in his message vetoing the Marshals Appropriation Bill and also notified the House that [he] had signed the Judicial Bill. Thus, at last, our controversy is now down to $600,000. In the Senate the joint resolution to adjourn *sine die* today was called up and Senator Windom objected and the matter was compelled to lie over for a day. He did this for the purpose of giving Congress time if it desired to make the appropriation before adjournment. At half-past two o'clock the President sent in a short message reminding Congress that the appropriations for the support of the Marshals and Deputy Marshals expired today and urged them to give him the proper supplies before the final adjournment. The message came soon after the House had voted on the vetoed bill.[187] I secured an opportunity for Cannon[188] of Illinois to offer the Marshals Appropriation Bill, without a rider, for passage under a suspension of the rules. The vote was a strict party division. The House continued in session until quarter-past five. After dinner I dictated a number of letters to Brown. Rose came and I dictated the Journal and then spent the evening in reading the proof of the pamphlet which I am getting out, embracing the leading speeches I have made during the present session.

[186]The sentence suggested by Garfield appears in the veto message as follows: ''They [United States marshals] are in effect the only police of the United States Government.''

[187]The House sustained the veto.

[188]Joseph G. Cannon (1836–1926) was a Republican member of the House from Illinois, 1873–91, 1893–1913, and 1915–23. He was Speaker of the House, 1903–11.

July

TUESDAY, 1.   Dictated letters in the morning. Read proof slips of the edition of all my late speeches of the present session, until eleven o'clock, when I went to the War Department and thence to the Capitol. At half-past one the Senate sent back our resolution, amended that both Houses adjourn at five o'clock. The resolution, as amended, passed both Houses. In order to prevent the getting through of several jobs we carried recesses—one until four o'clock and still another until near five o'clock. At five o'clock this weary and useless session, damaging as I think to the Democratic Party, came to a close. I should have added that when the hour of recess was taken, I came home and finished reading the proof sheets of my speeches. At half-past five dined with Secretary Sherman and then drove with him far out into Maryland. He talked very freely of the political situation and his prospects for the Presidency. I think he is deeply committed to hope of being nominated. He said he was not a candidate for the Ohio Senatorship and had no doubt I would be chosen by a large majority in case we carried the Legislature. On our return we stopped at the Schuetzenfest and remained until ten. We took part in the Banquet and Sherman and I each made a short address.[189] Home at half-past ten. Brown came and went for me to the Government Printing Office to look after the proof slips. Retired at twelve.

WEDNESDAY, 2.   This has been a very busy day. Brown has been here all day writing letters and settling up affairs. Went to the

---

[189]This was the second day of the annual feast of the Schuetzen Verein of Washington. A prominent feature of the event was a shooting match, the winner of which was crowned king. The King's Banquet (at which Sherman, Garfield, and other notables were guests) followed the coronation. A toast, "The Ladies. We never fail to love them. What, never? Well, hardly ever," was responded to by Garfield. He paid "a rare tribute to women, saying that all over the world the trinity, mother, wife and daughter, were respected and venerated, and that no man is fit to call himself such until he has legally and loyally allied himself to the love of one true woman, and when he has done that, he is a king, indeed." *Washington Post,* July 2, 1879.

Riggs House to meet the stockholders of the Beaver Dam Company. Went to the Interior Department, then to the Printing Office and finished the final reading of the proof sheets of my speeches at the Capitol. Then to the Riggs Bank and various other places of business in closing up the day's work. Afternoon Miss Ransom, Warren Young, and Mr. Brown dined with us. After dinner Rose came and I dictated the Journal. At half-past seven Col. Rockwell sent his spring wagon and baggage express to take us to the Baltimore and Ohio R.R. Company's Depot where we took the train for the West at one quarter-past nine.

We had on board, Mark Brewer[190] and wife of Michigan, Greenbury Fort of Illinois, and Amos Townsend of Cleveland. The evening was cool and pleasant. Harry and I retired at eleven; but Jimmy, who is always wakeful on the cars, preferred to sit up and enjoy the mountain scenery.

THURSDAY, 3.   Arrived in Pittsburgh half-past six in the morning. We drove across from the Connellsville to the Union Depot, and after a good breakfast, took the 8.30 train via Wellsville to Cleveland where we arrived at 2.45 and found Crete and Irvin awaiting us at the Forest City House.

We shopped and visited until 4.50 P.M. when the three boys left for Mentor; and at 5.10, Crete and I took the train for Sandusky where we arrived at 7.30. Mr. J. O. Moss, in company with Chas. Foster, met us and took us to his house. After supper had a long visit with Foster on the state of his campaign for the Governorship.

We (F. and I) went down to the West House and called on Gov. Bishop,[191] and were called upon by a large number of citizens.

Retired a little before midnight. I have come here without any special preparation for tomorrow; but I will draw upon my gen-

---

[190]Mark S. Brewer (1837–1901) was a Republican member of the House from Michigan, 1877–81, 1887–91; he was appointed consul general to Berlin by Garfield and served 1881–85.

[191]Richard M. Bishop (1812–1893), a Democrat and well known member of the Disciples of Christ, was governor of Ohio, 1878–80.

eral fund. This is not a wise thing to do. There is danger that I shall not do as much intellectual work as I ought, if I thus get the habit of relying upon former work.

FRIDAY, 4.   Awoke early, and resolved upon a line of thought for my speech. It lies in the near neighborhood of some pending political discussions, but should not alarm partisans. At ten I joined the procession in the Governor['s] (Bishop's) carriage, and at half-past 12 reached the Fair Grounds, a beautiful grove, overlooking the lake. After the usual preliminaries, I spoke 3/4 of an hour and I think with good effect. Gov. Bishop and Gen. Ewing followed, and then Foster, so we had all the elements of chief political difference represented. After lunch on the grounds, we returned to Mr. Moss's and spent the afternoon and evening with visitors. Moss and I played billiards an hour in his fine basement room.

Later in the evening Foster and I went to the West House where we held an informal reception. A cool summer night for sleep, which I greatly need.

SATURDAY, 5.   After a pleasant breakfast at Mr. Moss's with Foster and his wife and two daughters, Crete and I took the eastward train at 8.15 and at 12 M. were in Mentor where Harry and Jerry[192] met us and brought us to the farm.

It is a great joy to be once more at home and feel the assurance that I can be measurably let alone, for even a few weeks.

I spent the afternoon in going over the farm, and getting the run of affairs, renewing my acquaintance with the cattle, which are quite indifferent to me.

Before evening, an applicant for a post-route agency arrived. In the evening one side of a Post Office fight sent a representative here, and two hours past midnight the representative of the other side came. So the farm and politics must be mingled as of old.

---

[192]Following a visit to Hiram where she attended her dying mother, Mrs. Garfield went to the Mentor farm and was delighted by the work Jerry had done. "Our yard and garden," she informed her husband, "are a delight, so thrifty and tidy. Jerry is a capital gardener and keeps everything about the yard as clean as a good housewife keeps her kitchen."

Retired early.

SUNDAY, 6.   The reaction of the spring and summer work has come upon me, and I am very heavy with weariness.

The Doctor came, and at eleven we went to church. A very small congregation out, to whom the Doctor spoke well for about twenty minutes.

After dinner, I took Crete and Mother and the little boys up to the Doctor's to see Mrs. Robison and her grandchildren. I drove out into his south pasture to see my Jersey calves which are feeding there. The bull, a gift from Hon. A. S. Hewitt of N. Y., and the two heifers, the gift of Gen. E. B. Tyler of Baltimore, are very beautiful creatures, and I hope I may grow a herd that will be worth the having.

Home in the evening. Read Froude's *Caesar,* [193] and retired early.

MONDAY, 7.   Gave the day to a pretty thorough inspection of the farm. It is gradually coming up towards my notions of what it ought to be, but each step discloses new wants, and increases my interest in it.

Evening *Caesar* and rest.

TUESDAY, 8.   Soon after breakfast Dr. Robison came, and we drove to Dr. Streator's farm in Perry, expecting to meet its owner there; but he had not come. Home via Casement's, where we stopped to look at his barns and stock. He has manifestly changed his opinions of me during recent years, or his earlier ones were matters of political convenience. Home evening.

WEDNESDAY, 9.   Crete, Mollie and I went to Cleveland to make some purchases. Among other things, I bought the 12 volumes of John Q. Adams' Diary,[194] and Von Holst's Commentaries on the Constitution of the U. S., 2 vols.[195]

---

[193]James Anthony Froude, *Caesar: A Sketch* (1879). In 1899 an edition was published with the title *Julius Caesar* and an introduction by Burke A. Hinsdale.

[194]Charles Francis Adams, ed., *Memoirs of John Quincy Adams, Comprising Portions of His Diary from 1795 to 1848,* 12 vols. (1874–77).

[195]The second volume of Hermann Eduard von Holst, *The Constitutional and Political History of the United States,* 8 vols. (1876–92), was published in 1879.

Home in the evening.

Men hauled in the wheat.

THURSDAY, 10. At last, mustered up courage to attack my correspondence, which has lain in accumulating weight, a menace to my rest.

In the evening Henry M. James[196] and B. A. Hinsdale, my pupils of former years, came to make us a visit.

A very heavy rain came on towards evening, and lasted nearly all night. It will do much good, though it comes too late to save us from short crops. A pleasant evening with the family and visitors.

FRIDAY, 11. Spent the day with our two friends. At 4 P.M. there was a heavy wind storm which threw down a great many trees, and destroyed some corn. It prostrated about 100 rods of my fences, and killed one of my Durham yearlings by a falling tree.

A pleasant evening of reminiscence and visit with our friends.

Late in the evening rec'd a dispatch from Brother Joseph, that Mother Rudolph is dying. Poor, dear woman, she has had a long wasting sickness.

SATURDAY, 12. After breakfast drove James and Hinsdale to the Mormon temple.[197] After dinner took the train to Cleveland, Crete with me. Shopped until the 4.25 train, when went eastward, Crete to Hiram, I to Solon. Stopped at Sister Mary's, went to Hitty's and then with her to John Rodger's to get her pension papers completed. It is a matter of great satisfaction that I have

---

[196]Henry M. James was a supervising principal in Cleveland. In the early 1880's he moved to Omaha, where he was superintendent of schools for a number of years. He wrote to Garfield on July 7 indicating that he and Burke Hinsdale had been discussing the propriety of their going to Mentor to help for a day on the farm. "He [Hinsdale] used to be a good man with a cradle," he wrote, "and I could once 'rake and bind' with credit to myself, and we talked the matter up. We are not in practice just now, but we have improved our theories since we left off work. We may be of some service to you in the theory of farming."

[197]The temple, built in 1833–34 by Joseph Smith and his followers, is about three miles from Lawnfield. At the time of Garfield's visit it was "deserted and crumbling to decay," but it has since been restored. As a result of a legal battle, it is the property of the Reorganized Church of Jesus Christ of Latter Day Saints.

succeeded in getting her a pension for her son Melvin who died in the army in 1864. This gives her about $1,500.[198]

Drove to Orange and spent the night at Henry Boynton's. Spent some time in working up materials for a sketch of Uncle Amos Boynton's life to be written by Hinsdale for the History of Cuyahoga Co.[199]

SUNDAY, 13.   Breakfast at 6 1/2, and then drove to Solon in time for the 7.46 train to Garrettsville. Bro. Joseph met me at the Station and drove me to Hiram.

Mother Rudolph knew me, but was evidently nearing the end. She asked [me] to put her in a chair and draw her into the parlor, which I did. We watched over her till near evening, when with great difficulty she made us understand that she wished us to take [her] out of doors. We placed her in a rocking chair and drew her out in the eastern shadow of the house, where she sat for half an hour. She looked with great apparent satisfaction over the eastern landscape—doubtless thinking of her first home with her young husband 49 years ago, which lay within the prospect. She closed her eyes and rested with peaceful quiet some time, and then signalled us to take her in. At half-past six she said "I am dying" and in a few moments quietly passed away. All her family were with her, and [she] left to each the perpetual memory of [a] dear, sweet, noble life, which had blessed and elevated all who knew her.

[198]Melvin Trowbridge (1845–1864) enlisted in the First Michigan Regiment of Engineers and Mechanics in the fall of 1863 and died of typhoid fever in a field hospital in Bridgeport, Alabama, the following March. In 1879 his mother was living in Solon in a small house that Garfield had had built for her; she owned eighteen acres of land, "much run down," two cows and a few other animals. Her husband left in 1862 and since then had paid only occasional visits. At the outset she received nearly fifteen hundred dollars—eight dollars a month for the more than fifteen years from Melvin's death until she began to receive a monthly payment. In 1886 the monthly rate was increased to twelve dollars. In all she received for the period from 1864 to 1911 a little more than five thousand dollars. The initial lump sum payment she turned over to Garfield to protect it from her husband, but by 1881 she had spent it, largely on home improvements.

[199]Crisfield Johnson, comp., *History of Cuyahoga County, Ohio* (1879), pp. 495–497.

Crete and I slept in the little bedroom near her while she slept the deeper sleep that awaits us all.

MONDAY, 14. Spent the day in preparations for the funeral. I went to Aunt Emeline Raymond's and took memoranda of the line of Mother Rudolph and her family (father and mother) and gave them to Hinsdale for a sketch to be read at the funeral. Sent letters and telegrams to friends. Went to Garrettsville to make purchases. In the evening Harry and Jimmie came in answer to my telegram.

Having obtained the consent of the family, at two P.M. Drs. Warren and Tiddall [Tidball][200] came and made a post mortem examination. I witnessed it throughout. The left lung was wholly useless, and partly decayed. The liver was torpid and the mesentery gland full of tubercles, so as to be nearly useless for the work of nutrition. All the vital organs were much wasted and the heart had suffered fatty degeneration. Contrary to our expectations, the stomach was sound and healthy.

Crete and I slept at Martha Rudolph's—so did Hal and Jim.

TUESDAY, 15. At half-past ten A.M. President Hinsdale offered a prayer at the house, and we went thence to the grave yard and buried Mother near where our two children lie. At half-past eleven, went to the Church where Burke preached from two verses of John, on the resurrection of Lazarus—texts selected by Mother Rudolph 4 years ago when we expected her to die. He also read a sketch prepared from the materials I gave him yesterday.

The six grandchildren, Gilbert, Lewis, and Ernest Rudolph, Harry and Jimmie, and Arthur Rockwell,[201] acted as pall-bearers. At 5 P.M. the two boys, Crete, and I went to Garrettsville and thence to Cleveland. I arranged with Mr. Stone,[202] the train dispatcher, to let us off the Express at Mentor at eleven. Supper

---

[200]A. H. Tidball, who attended the Cleveland Medical College, located in Garrettsville in 1871.

[201]Arthur Rockwell, son of Camden and Nellie Rudolph Rockwell (sister of Lucretia Garfield) was about the same age as Harry Garfield.

[202]George B. Stone, a resident of Painesville, was dispatcher of the Lake Shore and Southern Michigan Railroad in Cleveland.

at the Forest City House and a call on Edwin Cowles. Home at half-past eleven.

WEDNESDAY, 16. Commenced writing letters in earnest and made a good beginning on my accumulated mail. The men are cutting rye. Weather fine but getting dry again.

THURSDAY, 17. Wrote about 35 letters, and looked after farm matters. Lower rye done and upper field begun.

Numerous callers. Row in the Cortland, Trumbull Co., Post Office, and Mr. Holcomb[203] came to see about it. At noon Thos. M. Nichol, Sec'y of the Honest Money League, came and spent the afternoon and night with us. He and I put up a rod across my library and hung up curtains to convert the west end of it into a sleeping room for the boys.

Croquet and music in the evening. Our children are a great joy to us. Their growth in body and mind is becoming almost visible.

In the evening I drove Crete and Nichol to Dr. Robison's where we visited an hour.

FRIDAY, 18. Martha helped me part of the day, and between us we got off 45 letters, and several hundred speeches (my speeches at the Extra Session, 54 pages).

In the evening croquet and music with the children.

SATURDAY, 19. Worked on correspondence until ten A.M. when I took Crete, Martha and all the children to Mrs. Greer's farm,[204] the old Gov. Huntington place, on the lake shore below Paines-ville, where the [children?] bathed and had a little pleasant pic-nic. Home at half-past six. In the evening went to Dr. Robison's to meet Judge Ranney and Wm. Robison,[205] who came out

[203]The row was over the postmaster, whom many Cortland Republicans, includ-ing H. D. Holcomb, regarded as a weak party man, and the location of the office on Railroad Street, which displeased "the church, school, business, and temper-ance interests" of the town. In response to the protest the office was promptly moved to Main Street and later the postmaster was replaced.

[204]Cornelia Rogers Huntington Greer, widow of William Franklin Greer (1835–1875), was the adopted daughter of Colbert Huntington (1797–1884), son of Samuel Huntington, one of Ohio's most prominent early settlers and governor of the state, 1809–11. The Greers settled on a part of the Samuel Huntington farm, where the widow continued to live after her husband's death.

[205]William Robison, a Cleveland lawyer, was the brother of Dr. John P. Robi-son.

from Cleveland to visit and spend Sunday. Home at eleven.

SUNDAY, 20. With Dr. Robison's team and my new carriage Thomas Northcott drove Judge Ranney, Wm. Robison, the Doctor and me to Bass Lake in Munson, where we took dinner, and visited with a large number of friends whom we found there. Drove back by way of Peck's Corners and Kirtland, reaching home at half-past six. In the evening went with the whole family to church and heard an effective sermon by John Encell. Retired early.

MONDAY, 21. Spent the day in farm affairs and in closing up business for a few days' ab[sence]. Dr. Eames[206] of Ashtabula came to see me at noon, and stayed until the evening train. I had but little time to think of my address at Madison, and must go quite unprepared. At 6 P.M. left for Willoughby, where I took the train for the West. Found W. Neeley Thompson on board en route to California.

Retired at nine.

TUESDAY, 22. Awoke in Chicago, having slept over ten hours. Took breakfast at the Grand Pacific, where I found Senator Zach. Chandler, with whom I took the 9 A.M. train, North Western R. R., to Madison, Wisconsin, arriving at 5 P.M. Was met at the Depot by Hon. Horace Rublee[207] and several Wisconsin members of Congress, and taken to the Park Hotel. After supper Mr. Rublee drove me around the University grounds and along the lake—a beautiful drive and a still more beautiful prospect. Pres. Bascom, my old College tutor, is away for his summer vacation. Hotel in the evening. Many citizens called on me, among them

---

[206]William M. Eames farmed and practiced medicine for many years in Ashtabula County. He was a surgeon in the 21st Ohio Volunteer Infantry Regiment, 1861–62.

[207]Horace Rublee (1829–1896), a native of Vermont, became a Wisconsin newspaperman prominently identified with politics. During the 1850's and 1860's he was editor of the *Wisconsin State Journal.* On July 13, 1854, he was secretary of the mass meeting at Madison, one of the events marking the emergence of the Republican party. He was state chairman of the party, 1859–69, and 1877–79, and U.S. minister to Switzerland, 1869–77. He edited the *Wisconsin Sentinel* from the early 1880's to his death.

Dan. Campbell,[208] my classmate at Williams, whom I have not seen since our graduation.

Retired at eleven, not feeling well.

WEDNESDAY, 23. After breakfast Gen. Cadwallader Washburn took Mr. Chandler and me on a long drive. At eleven I made some notes for a speech. At two P.M. a great audience assembled on the Capitol front, and the State Convention having concluded its work, the 25th anniversary of the Republican party of Wisconsin, was celebrated. The Rev. Mr. Walworth[209] presided—who also presided at the first Convention of the party in 1854. A Mr. Sleeper[210] of Chicago, who was Chairman of the Committee on Resolutions 25 years ago, read the same today. A fine poem[211] was read and Senator Chandler made a speech, after a half hour's address by Hon. C. G. Williams of Painesville [Janesville]. I followed Chandler and spoke an hour quite effectively.[212] I

[208]Daniel Campbell (1836–1893), a non-graduating member of the Williams class of 1856, was a Madison clothier and realtor.

[209]John Walworth (1804–1895), newspaperman and politician, moved from his native state of New York in 1846 and settled in Monroe, Wisconsin. He edited the *Monroe Sentinel,* 1851–54, presided in Madison over one of the first state meetings of the Republican party (July, 1854), edited the *Richland County Observer,* 1858–63, served briefly as a chaplain in the Union army, was a member of the Wisconsin legislature, 1863–64, and after the Civil War edited newspapers in Richland Center, Boscobel, and Monroe.

[210]Joseph A. Sleeper, a lawyer in Chicago for many years.

[211]"The Silver Wedding; a 'Stalwart' Poem," was read by its author, Major S. S. Rockwood, a professor in the Normal School at Whitewater, Wisconsin. It deals with the Republican party and its heroic leaders both living and dead. An excerpt:

Here on this platform shall stand to day
Champions of liberty worthy as they—

. . . .

Garfield wielding the law's keen blade,
Scorning the tricks of a demagogue's trade,
Swift to cut every Gordian knot made;
Chandler, who never has turned his back,
Mightiest hunter on Jeff. Davis' track,
Bitterest foe of the whole rebel pack,
Michigan's chieftain, the warrior, Old Zach.

[212]The *Chicago Tribune,* July 24, 1879, carried the full texts of the speeches of Garfield and Chandler.

sketche[d] the early Republican Party of Jefferson, its rise and fall, and then the new Republican Party of 1854 as the revival from the apostasy of slavery and the resumption of the old Republican Party.

In the evening J. C. Burrows of Mich. spoke in the Hall of the House of Representatives, a fine speech and a good audience. On the whole the Celebration has been impressive and successful.

At 10.30 P.M. I took the train for Chicago via Milwaukee.

THURSDAY, 24.   Awoke in Chicago. Breakfast at the Grand Pacific—train east at 9 1/2 A.M. Reached Cleveland at 10 P.M. and took the train at 10.30 for Painesville. Half an hour late, and reached Painesville at 12.20, where Jerry met me and drove me home, arriving at 1.20 A.M.

Very tired and hoarse.

FRIDAY, 25.   Feeling badly. I cannot stand with impunity the strain of such excessive work as I could a few years ago. I must begin to husband my fuel.

Encountered a great mail and spent the forenoon reading it. At noon T. M. Nichol, Sec'y of the Honest Money League of the North West, came to insist that I should go to Cleveland and address the League tomorrow evening—to which I reluctantly gave consent. [He] helped me with my mail during the afternoon, and we got off about 45 letters, amids[t] numerous interruptions.

I can hardly endure the thought of bracing up to prepare a speech for tomorrow evening.

SATURDAY, 26.   Worked on my mail with Nichol and got off about 40 more letters. At ten o'clock my Uncle Thomas Garfield and wife of Newburgh came to visit us. I divided my time between him and my mail, and other callers. At 3 went to the Town Hall to vote for delegates to the County Convention, in aid of Mr. Aldrich as a candidate for Representative.

At 6 P.M. Uncle Thomas drove Nichol and me to Willoughby, where we took the train at 6.22 P.M. for Cleveland. Supper at the Kennard House. At eight went to the Tabernacle and found an audience of not less than 2,000 people. Kline made a brief bright speech, Stafford [M. W. Safford] and William[s],[213] two other Democrats, then Nichol, and at half-past 9 I took the floor and spoke an hour, keeping clear of party politics, but advocating the doctrines of honest money—a fair speech for a very tired man.[214]

Spent the night at the Kennard.

SUNDAY, 27. The League arranged to have the morning express train stop at Mentor, and so after an early breakfast I was off at 7.30, and in 45 minutes was at Mentor, where Jerry met me and I was soon at home. Mother had not come.

Spent the day visiting with Uncle Thomas. He was 30 years old the day I was born, and is the sole survivor of the Garfield family of his generation. In the afternoon drove him and Aunt Sophy, with Crete and two of the children to Kirtland—Mormon temple and home via the Willoughby road.

Did not attend church.

Bought of Uncle Thomas for $400 the mortgage on my brother Thomas' place in Michigan, which I shall hold both to protect my family from want in case of disaster, and to protect Thomas from being raided on by his children, who I fear are imposing upon his generosity.

MONDAY, 28. Breakfast at 7, when Uncle Thomas and Aunt Sophy left us and the week's work was begun. Hal and Jim recited to me in *Anabasis* and Virgil, and I worked on my endless task of correspondence. Many friends called during the day and I did not accomplish very much. The Cleveland papers of today print a verbatim report of my speech before the Honest Money League and it reads better than I supposed it would. On the whole I am very much pleased with the plain effective way of presenting the case.

[213]Andrew J. Williams (1829–1901), a native of New York, practiced law in Painesville before the Civil War. After the war, in which he served in the Union army, he lived in Georgia for a dozen years before returning to Ohio. In 1879 he settled in Cleveland, where he practiced law. In 1883 he was elected to the state senate, the first Democratic senator Cuyahoga County had had in thirty years. The "sound money" meeting in Cleveland was non-partisan.

[214]In a letter (July 27) with which he enclosed twenty-five dollars for Garfield's expenses John Hay made this comment: "You made a grand speech and one that cannot fail to do a great deal of good, and we all feel very much encouraged."

TUESDAY, 29. Worked at my correspondence and looked after farm affairs. After dinner Crete and I drove to Painesville and spent the afternoon in making calls. We have sadly neglected our social duties since we came to Mentor, and have never called on many friends who called on us soon after we came to town. We took tea with Colonel J. F. Myers [Morse][215] and wife, at his new house. The Colonel has been a staunch friend of mine during my public life. He was a brother member of the Ohio Senate in 1860–1861. Home in the evening.

WEDNESDAY, 30. Worked on correspondence and the farm until three o'clock, when Crete and I drove to Willoughby and made some calls. I also had the wheel of the buggy reset. Took tea at Mr. Andrews'. Home in the evening.

THURSDAY, 31. I intended to go to Cleveland today with Dr. Robison, but found I could not. Worked at my desk and about the farm during the day. Made a study of what I would do with the fields for the coming season and reached several conclusions satisfactory to myself, but have left some portions yet in abeyance. The dry weather has made the farm look badly and I feel uncertain what its real value is as an enduring farm until I have tried it during a rainy season. Several friends called during the day and evening.

August

FRIDAY, 1. Revised Hinsdale's sketch of the life of Uncle Amos Boynton, making several corrections and additions on Wednesday. Also, revised on Thursday a paper sent me by Major Swaim on the power of Courts Martial to summon civilians as witnesses.

---

[215]John F. Morse (1801–1884) spent his boyhood in Kirtland, studied architecture, and settled in Painesville. Strongly antislavery, he joined the Free Soil party, served in the Ohio house of representatives, 1843–44, 1848–49, 1850–51, was a trustee of Painesville, 1857, and a Republican member of the Ohio senate, 1860–61. He was known as "Colonel" before the Civil War. See Vol. III, p. 364, n. 356.

The paper is a reply to a report by Proctor Knott of the Judiciary Committee of the House, during the last session.[216] Also read Ewing's speech made in Cleveland on Tuesday last and found it full of specious and illogical reasoning.[217] At six o'clock drove to the station to meet Mr. Rose, Mr. Sumner and wife, and Mrs. Smalley to come and visit us. Greek with the boys in the evening and, later, music in the parlor. The weather has been very hot and oppressive. Heard the boys recite in Latin and Greek. Spent the forenoon in visiting and dictating.

[216]On April 16, 1879, the adjutant general of the army transmitted to the Speaker of the House of Representatives a subpoena signed by David G. Swaim, judge advocate in the Colonel D. S. Stanley court martial then sitting in New York City; the subpoena, addressed to a file clerk of the House, commanded the clerk to appear before the court martial, bringing with him the manuscript of testimony given before a House committee in 1872 by Colonel W. B. Hazen. The matter was referred to the House Judiciary Committee, of which Proctor Knott was chairman. The committee was inclined to the view that under the law the judge advocate of a court martial had no power to subpoena witnesses beyond the limits of the state, territory or district in which the court was sitting. The two resolutions it submitted to the House, however, were concerned only with House records. The first held that no officer or employee of the House had the right to produce before any court or officer any paper, document or book belonging to House files or any copy of such records (except those authorized by statute or made public by the House) without the prior consent of the House. The second resolution granted the consent of the House to allow either party in the Stanley court martial to have made and proven copies of the testimony mentioned in the subpoena. When the Knott report came before the House on April 22 Garfield indicated that he concurred with the resolutions but not with the notion that a court martial could not issue a summons or enforce it outside the state in which the court was sitting. He also thought that it was going too far to say that the House would not permit the taking of papers from its files under any circumstances. The resolutions were agreed to without a roll call. For the Knott report see *House Reports,* No. 1, 46 Cong., 1 Sess., Serial 1934.

[217]Congressman Thomas Ewing, of Lancaster, who had recently been nominated as the Democratic candidate for governor, was running on a platform that denounced interference with elections by the military power, condemned Republicans in Congress for their stand on the use of the army at the polls, the election laws and the vetoes of the President, advocated the substitution of Treasury notes for bank notes, denounced the demonetization of silver, and demanded its restoration as a money metal.

SATURDAY, 2.   After breakfast, the boys and Mr. Rose and I went
to the pasture below the ditch that runs through Mr. Rose's
farm[218] and made a dam, to see if we could irrigate the pasture,
which is very much burned up with the heat. During the day I
dictated a number of letters to Mr. Rose and superintended farm
affairs. Nichol came and in the afternoon he went with me to the
pasture to examine the dam. I found I had made it too low down
the stream and we made another to the east end of the field. In
the evening I drove the Sumners and Mrs. Smalley to Painesville
and left them with Mr. Howe.[219] Came home by moonlight.
Soon after our return Addie and Louis [Lewis] Rudolph arrived,
having travelled across the country from Hiram.

SUNDAY, 3.   Spent the day at home visiting with our guests. Went
to the pasture with Mr. Nichol to see the progress of the irrigation begun yesterday. In the afternoon Moses drove the Grays
in the new carriage to Painesville, taking all the children and
friends with him. Nichol and I spent some time in overhauling
the history of the Warner Silver Bill.

MONDAY, 4.   Dictated letters. Spent some time in superintending
the irrigation of the pasture below the railroad. I think it possible
to irrigate all the farm below the Ram Lot, and if the seasons
continue to be as dry as they have in recent years, I think it will
be possible and profitable to irrigate.

TUESDAY, 5.   Dictated letters in the morning. Early this morning
sent Harry and Jerry to Painesville to bring home the carriage
which had been repaired. At ten o'clock Crete, Addie, Miss
Mays, Rose and I drove to Willoughby and thence three miles

---

[218]George Rose, who lived on a farm adjacent to Garfield's, is not to be confused with George U. Rose, Garfield's stenographer, who was then visiting the
Garfields.

[219]Eber D. Howe (1798–1885), a native of New York, went in 1818 to Cleveland, where, already an experienced printer, he was a founder of the *Cleveland
Herald* (1819). In 1822 he settled in Painesville, where he founded the *Painesville
Telegraph* in the same year. From 1835 he was engaged in commercial printing and
the wool manufacture. He is the author of *Mormonism Unvailed . . .* (1834), and
Autobiography and Recollections of a Pioneer Printer (1878). Eugene V. Smalley was
his nephew.

to the Southwest to attend a picnic, under the management of Mrs. Andrews. About twenty people were present and we had a very enjoyable time. Home in the evening. At half-past seven went to Dr. Robison's to settle our accounts which had been running for the last eight months.[220]

WEDNESDAY, 6. Spent the day on my correspondence and in dictating portions of a speech to be delivered at Elyria. Read carefully the record of the action of the House of Representatives on the Warner Silver Bill and made it a part of my notes. Telegrams are constantly coming asking for meetings.

THURSDAY, 7. Spent most of the day dictating points for my speech at Elyria. Also dictated letters. Went to the lower fields to superintend the irrigation of the pasture. At noon Hon. Amos Townsend, N. B. Sherwin, and Capt. F. H. Mason of Cleveland came to visit us. Spent the afternoon with them in looking over the farm and having general conversation. At five o'clock we visited Dr. Robison and then I drove them to Willoughby where they took the train. Miss Mays and Addie Rudolph went with us. We called on Blanche Hanscom on our way home. Spent the evening at home.

FRIDAY, 8. Dictated letters in the morning. Worked at farm affairs. Made further notes for my Elyria speech. At twelve o'clock Harry, Addie and I took the train for Cleveland. Spent the afternoon in shopping and towards evening Harry went to the West Side to see his cousin Harry [Hattie] Palmer and spend the night. I went to Dr. Robison's. He and I spent the evening at Mr. Henry B. Payne's until near midnight. Returned to the Doctor's, where I spent the night.

SATURDAY, 9. Took the seven o'clock train for Elyria, Lorain County, where I arrived a little after eight o'clock. I was met at the Depot by several friends. Went to the Hotel and visited and made notes until after dinner and at one o'clock went to the Opera House, which was densely packed. Spoke an hour and a half. My speech was reported by Pomerene of Cleveland. After the meeting visited for an hour with Mr. and Mrs. Sheldon and

[220]In Garfield's absence John P. Robison often acted for him on farm matters.

other friends. Spent the remainder of the afternoon in revising my notes as they were written out by Pomerene, continued at that work until 9 o'clock, when we took the train for Cleveland. He had written out two-thirds of the speech and on the train he read the remainder of his notes and I made sundry corrections. Visited with Kline and J. M. Atwater on the train. Found Crete and the two boys, Harry and Jimmy, awaiting me at the Cleveland Depot and at half-past ten we took the train for home. Arrived at Mentor a little after eleven, where Jerry met us and brought us home.

SUNDAY, 10.   Crete, Mother and I went to church, and Mr. Wallace,[221] who was Pastor of the Mentor Church many years ago, preached. In the evening dictated a number of letters to Rose preparatory to leaving for Long Branch.[222]

MONDAY, 11.   At seven A.M. Mr. Aldrich came and drove me to Painesville, where I took the narrow gauge train for Warren. On the way read my Elyria speech of Saturday, as reported in the *Cleveland Leader* of this morning. Arrived at Warren at 11.20 A.M. and was met at the depot by Harmon Austin, Jr., and driven to his father's and thence to the public square, where Chas. Foster was addressing a large audience. At the close I was called for, but excused myself until evening. Went with Foster to the National Hotel and dined and spent the afternoon. Crowds of people called. The County [Convention] continued until seven P.M. At eight the City Hall was crowded and Foster spoke half an hour. I followed him an hour and a half and was well received. At the close of the meeting, Foster and I went to Harmon Austin's, where we were serenaded by the band and by a colored glee club, to which we responded. Lunch at Austin's, and left there at midnight for the Hotel. At ten minutes before one was driven

[221]H. Wallace was the pastor of the Disciples of Christ church in Mentor, 1872–74.

[222]On June 25, 1879, the House of Representatives authorized the Rules Committee to sit during the recess "for the purpose of revising, codifying, and simplifying the rules of the House." As a result of accretions over the years the House had 166 rules, many of which were obsolete. Garfield was preparing to leave for Long Branch, New Jersey, to meet with other members of the committee.

to the Atlantic and Great Western Depot, and at 1.15 to[ok] the train for New York.

TUESDAY, 12.   Awoke near Hornellsville, New York, where I took breakfast at 10.30 A.M. A hot, weary day's ride. Too unwell to read so heavy a book as Von Holst's History of the Constitution of the United States, and so read the newspapers and endured the day. Arrived at the Brevoort House at 10.45, bathed, read the daily papers, and retired about midnight.

WEDNESDAY, 13.   Arose at nine and found in the breakfast room Baron Schlözer, of the German Legation, who has just arrived from Europe. Also General Francis Walker and Clarence King. The latter I have never met before though I took an active part in securing his appointment by the President as Chief of the Geological and Survey Department. After breakfast went with General Walker to the Windsor Hotel to call on Thomas Bayley Potter,[223] M.P., who had just landed from the *Scythia*. Unfortunately he was not in. Went to Tiffany's and Stewart's shopping. Called on Hon. L. P. Morton,[224] but found him out of town. On my return to the Brevoort, at one P.M., found I was too late for the first afternoon boat to Long Branch, and so spent two hours in my room reading and writing. I should have mentioned that I had a long conversation with General Walker on his new views of paper currency, as developed in his book on money and his later volume of lectures at the John[s] Hopkins University.[225] He is firm in the conviction that he has made an important

[223]Sir Thomas Bayley Potter (1817–1898), a prominent English Liberal, was a member of the House of Commons, 1865–95. He was a founder of and a leading influence in the Cobden Club, which was dedicated to the promotion of free trade. Garfield's election to membership in the Club in 1869 was the source of later political embarrassment to him. Sir Thomas was in the United States in 1879 to further the cause of free trade in this country.

[224]Levi P. Morton (1824–1920) was a Republican member of the U.S. House of Representatives from New York, 1879–81; U.S. minister to France, 1881–85; vice president of the United States, 1889–93; and governor of New York, 1895–97.

[225]Francis A. Walker, *Money and Its Relations to Trade and Industry* (1879), consisted of lectures given at the Lowell Institute early in 1879. His earlier book, *Money* (1878), consisted of lectures given at Johns Hopkins University in 1877.

discovery in monetary science. Took the three P.M. boat for Sandy Hook and thence by rail to Long Branch. General Horace Porter drove me to the Elberon, where I found Mr. and Mrs. Randall, A. H. Stephens, Mr. Blackburn and daughter, and the Clerk Harry [Henry] Smith and family. Mrs. Pelton and her son, Colonel P. of cypher fame, are here.[226] Retired at eleven, sleeping in a cottage with no occupant but myself.

THURSDAY, 14. Soon after breakfast I wrote to Crete and answered some business letters and telegrams. At ten A.M. the Committee met and worked two hours on the codification and amendment of the House Rules. So far as we have gone, we have greatly condensed and simplified them. They are the aggregation of 90 years of parliamentary practice, and, like all such growths, are in irregular and illogical order. Several subjects were referred to sub-committees, for special reports. Rule 155, in reference to the use of the Hall of the House, was referred to me. At one P.M. I went to the beach intending to bathe in the surf, but my head and stomach were not in good condition, and remembering my experience at Atlantic City and Old Orchard Beach, last year, and Crete's present anxiety on my account, I abandoned the purpose of going in. The Committee met again at three and were in session two hours. At eight in the evening Mr. Stephens and I played a rubber of whist with Messrs. Randall and Frye. I returned at eleven. My quarters have been removed from the cottage to Room 21 in the Hotel.

FRIDAY, 15. Held a session of the Committee at ten o'clock and worked until one, making good progress. Blackburn and I were appointed a sub-committee to report upon the several motions and their order of precedence. I spent some time in determining the precise difference between privileged questions and questions of privilege. I came to the conclusion that privileged questions are questions relating to the privileges of the House and the

---

[226]Mary B. Pelton was the sister of Samuel J. Tilden and the mother of William T. Pelton. This was the first time Garfield had seen Pelton since they were students together at Williams College. For Pelton's relation to the cipher letters see October 16, 1878, n. 259.

rank of priority which such questions hold, but question[s] of privilege are questions affecting the rights of members. In short the first class are public questions, the others are personal questions relating to the rights of membership. The Speaker, Mr. Frye, and Mr. Stephens were appointed a sub-committee to report on another group of questions. In the afternoon rolled tenpins and visited. Concluded not to go into the surf, mainly out of regard to Crete's feelings.

SATURDAY, 16.   Another long and interesting session of the Committee from ten to one, and another designation of subjects to be considered by sub-committees. At seven in the evening dined at General Horace Porter's in company with all the members of the Committee except Mr. Stephens and also with General McClellan,[227] George W. Childs[228] and Mr. Pullman.[229] We had an excellent dinner and pleasant conversation. The sad news came to us today of the death of Mrs. Nellie Grant Sartoris.[230] Great sympathy is felt for the General and his family. At nine o'clock we drove to the West End Hotel where the ladies attended a hop, but the Speaker, Harry [Henry] Smith and I played billiards for an hour and a half. Returned to the Elberon at half-past eleven.

SUNDAY, 17.   A heavy rain began last night and continued during the whole of today. It was one of the most powerful and continuous rains I have ever seen. Spent the day in reading and writing. I am reading Von Holst's History of the Constitution of the United States, a fine example of the German method of thorough

[227]George B. McClellan (1826–1885), general in chief of the Union army, 1861–62, and Democratic candidate for President in 1864, was governor of New Jersey, 1878–81.

[228]George W. Childs (1829–1894), of Philadelphia, philanthropist and proprietor-editor of the *Public Ledger,* 1864–94. He was the author of *Recollections of General Grant* (1885) and *Recollections by George W. Childs* (1890). George Augustus Sala, an English journalist who was entertained by Childs in 1879, made this comment about his host: "His activity is indefatigable, his public spirit indomitable, and his hospitality inexhaustible."

[229]George M. Pullman (1831–1897), industrialist and inventor, organized and headed the Pullman Palace Car Company. General Horace Porter became a representative and vice president of the company in 1873.

[230]See Vol. II, p. 319, n. 90 and August 18, 1879.

study. I wrote, also, a portion of the report on the group of rules submitted to me. I am not feeling well. Change of climate and food, as usual, affects my suggestion [digestion]. A weary, dreary day and I long to be at home. I intended to leave this evening, but the storm so delayed the boat that I could not make the connection. The Committee were, also, urgent that I should remain over another day.

MONDAY, 18.   Got the sub-committee together and completed our report from Rule 42 to Rule 50. The Committee met at ten o'clock and sat until one, making good progress. I offered a resolution, which was adopted, that when the session at Long Branch closed, the Committee should adjourn to meet at Washington on the tenth of November next to re-revise the whole work. This will prevent any action by the Democrats without our presence. Mr. Frye will remain until Thursday next. At 2.17 I took the train for New York, in the midst of a continuous and tremendous shower. The cable today brings the gratifying news that Nellie Grant is not dead—that Mrs. Adelaide Kemble Sartoris, a relative of Nellie's husband, was the person who died. Reached New York at 4 o'clock. At six took the Erie train for the West. Retired at nine o'clock, not feeling well.

TUESDAY, 19.   Awoke at Hornellsville, but did not get up until we were entering Buffalo about eight o'clock. At eight-forty-five took the Lake Shore train for the West. The Train Dispatcher telegraphed to Mr. Couch[231] of Cleveland and an order was sent to our Conductor to stop the train at Mentor. Found Judges Hamilton[232] and Cadwell on the train. At Ashtabula Charles Foster got on the train and stopped with me at Mentor. Harry met us and Foster went home with me and spent the afternoon. Found the family all well. He left at 6.15. I dictated a number of letters and partly overhauled my accumulated mail. Retired early with a severe headache.

---

[231]Charles B. Couch, superintendent of the Erie Division of the Lake Shore and Michigan Southern Railway, had his office in Cleveland.

[232]Edwin T. Hamilton, of Cleveland, was judge of the court of common pleas for the Fourth District of Ohio, 1875–95.

WEDNESDAY, 20.   Finished reading my mail. Also sent some campaign telegrams. Dictated a large number of letters. We had heavy rains while I was gone and the crops are looking better than when I went away. Brought up a large share of my back work and will be able before many days to clear my decks for campaign work.

THURSDAY, 21.   Dictated letters in the forenoon and pretty fully closed up my mail. Rose left by the noon train for Washington. Spent the afternoon looking over farm affairs, among other things, discussing the site for our future farm home. If I can buy a portion of Mrs. Alvord's grove, I have determined to build there, and if I am able, will build next spring.[233]

Drove with Father to Dr. Robison's and then with Crete to the lower fields. Rec'd telegram from Gen. Robinson, that I need not go to Noble County this week.

FRIDAY, 22.   Wrote letters and worked on farm affairs until noon, when Crete, Father Rudolph, Jimmy and I went to Cleveland. Took Jimmy to the Dentist's, helped Crete to make purchases of boys' outfit for school, and then took the 2.40 P.M. train to Solon to see Sister Hitty. She has received her arrears of pension, and wants me to take charge of it in order to save it from the raids of her husband. I helped her plan a barn, an addition to her house, and some general repairs on the place. Supper at Sister Mary's, and then took the train to Cleveland where Albert Mason[234] met me and drove me to his father's, James Mason's, where Crete and Jimmy had already gone and where we spent the night.

Before retiring, Frank Mason of the *Leader,* and Jerome B. Stil[l]son of the N. Y. *Herald* came to see me.[235] Stil[l]son had

---

[233]Julia Alvord, a widow, was the next neighbor of the Garfields on the west. The new house, the subject of considerable planning and discussion during the summer of 1879, never materialized for Garfield. In the 1890's James R. Garfield built a house in "Alvord's grove."

[234]Albert Mason, who was about eighteen at this time, was ill for several years before his death in 1886.

[235]On August 29, 1879, the *New York Herald* devoted more than two columns to the interview with Garfield, dispatched from Cleveland on August 25. Accord-

been to Mentor to see me—for an interview for his chief, J. G. Bennett.[236]

SATURDAY, 23. After breakfast we went down town and found Harry at the Dentist's. Went shopping with Crete till half-past ten, when I went to the *Leader* Office, where I had an interview of an hour and a half with Stil[l]son of the N. Y. *Herald.*

Dinner at James Mason's. Shopping until 4.50, when we all took the train to Mentor and were met by Jerry. Mail and accounts in the evening. Read the curious history of Jackson's opposition to the U. S. Bank. It appears to have originated in a personal and political quarrel, and not as a matter of financial conviction. Retired at 10 P.M.

SUNDAY, 24. Spent the forenoon and most of the afternoon at home, reading, and writing, and putting my affairs in order for the absence which must begin tomorrow. At 6 P.M. drove the mares and the carriage to Painesville and back, taking Nellie, Martha, Mother, Crete, Mollie and Abram. On our return, attended evening church and listened to a good sermon by John Encell. After meeting, wrote until ten.

MONDAY, 25. Wrote letters and looked after farm affairs until noon, when, with Jerry, Jimmie and his cousin Archie, I drove to Willoughby. After engaging some new collars for the mares, I took the train to Cleveland.

Spent two hours in shopping and visiting and, at 3.45 P.M., took the train to Wellington. On arriving, was driven to Gen. Warner's. Many called.

At 7 1/2 P.M. went to the old Congregational Church, which was filled to the utmost, and large numbers were standing outside at each window.

The memories of the Oberlin-Wellington rescue,[237] and also

---

ing to the dispatch, the interview, which dealt largely with state and national politics, had taken place that day.

[236]James Gordon Bennett, Jr. (1841–1918) was the owner and chief executive officer of the *New York Herald,* which had been founded by his father in 1835. From 1877 Bennett spent most of his time abroad, managing the *Herald* by cable.

[237]In September, 1858, a Negro who had fled from slavery in Kentucky was legally seized near Oberlin, taken to Wellington and lodged in a hotel, from which

of my first visit here, gave me a new line of thought and I spoke an hour and a half, quite effectively.

After sending off some telegrams in order to get released from Toledo, and so attend the 42nd reunion at Chippewa Lake, I went to the parlor of the village hotel where a large crowd of people called.

Spent the night at Gen. Warner's.

TUESDAY, 26. Took the 8.30 A.M. train for Shelby, and thence went by the Baltimore and Ohio Railroad to Cambridge. On the way read a hundred pages of Von Holst's Constitutional History of the United States. His analysis of Jackson's character, and of his and Van Buren's administration is one of the most thorough and just views of the subject I have ever seen. The train fell behind its time, but I was a good deal interrupted by calls from passengers who knew me.

At 4.50 P.M. arrived at Cambridge and was met by the Mayor, Capt. W. M. Farrar, who was my aide-de-camp during the war.

Was driven to the pine grounds for the reunion, and thence to Capt. F.'s where I took tea. Received a telegram from Foster releasing me from Toledo for tomorrow.

At eight P.M. addressed several thousand people on the public square. I learned, on arriving here, that this reunion is the continuation of the "Blue and Gray" reunions of recent years, which have been attended by a great deal of meaningless gush. So, while I respected the reasonable proprieties of the occasion I spoke plainly on the two issues on which the war was fought, slavery and state sovereignty. I used the suggestion of Von Holst, that state rights in its excessive form, was born of the habit that the fathers fell into of considering the general government (of England) their only source of oppression.

At 10 P.M., I took an engine on the Cleveland and Pittsburgh

---

he was rescued by a crowd made up in part of students from Oberlin College. Thirty-seven men were indicted and in the subsequent court proceedings John Mercer Langston and Albert Gallatin Riddle were both involved, the former as a defendant and the latter as a defense lawyer.

R.R. and arrived at Newcomerstown about midnight. Stopped at
the R.R. hotel.

WEDNESDAY, 27. Was awakened at half-past three, and took the
train for U[h]richsville, where I waited an hour, and took the
5.20 train on the Cleveland and Tuscarawas Valley road, and at
8 A.M. arrived at Chippewa Lake, Medina County.

A very large gathering, six or seven thousand, to see the 42nd.
After dinner by the lake, I spoke an hour, developing more fully
the points made at Cambridge. An excellent reunion—about 150
old comrades present.

At 5 P.M. took the train to U[h]richsville, and retired at 9 P.M.
Cards were sent from several callers, but I had already retired.
Very weary.

THURSDAY, 28. Was awakened at 3.40 and driven to the Depot
at Dennison, where I took the train and arrived at Steubenville
at 7 A.M. Was met by the Committee of Reception and driven
to the central hotel in company with Gen. J. S. Robinson and
Gen. Andrew Hickenlooper.[238] The city is overflowing with
people. At 11 A.M. went to the reviewing stand in company with
Gov. Bishop, Gen. Thos. Ewing and others and saw a column of
veteran soldiers of Ohio, Pa. and West Va. nearly a mile in length
march by. We then went to the grove near the female Seminary,
where a great stand had been built in the jaws of a broad and
deep ravine. Not less than 15,000 people assemble[d] on its sides
and in the valley between. After an address of welcome by Hon.
J. T. Updegraff, and music, Gen. Ewing read a long address,
devoted wholly to the technichs of soldiering, but not a word in
reference to the cause for which our soldiers fought. It was
evidently so written as to be equally welcome to Blue and Gray
—and equally tasteless to both. It seemed to me a stupid avoid-
ance of all the meaning and spirit of the war. When I was called
the old soldier spirit greeted me with the greatest enthusiasm. I

---

[238]Andrew Hickenlooper (1837–1904), engineer and Union officer who was
breveted brigadier general, was a prominent business and political figure in Cincinnati. In 1877 he became president of the Cincinnati Gas Light and Coke
Company. He was lieutenant governor of Ohio, 1880–82.

took for the key of my speech the thought that wild beasts fight, but do not make war nor hold reunions in memory of their combats. Men hold reunions in memory of the cause they defended, etc. I have never been received with more applause.

After dinner at the hotel, took the train to Rochester, Pa., and retired at 10 P.M., ordering the boy to wake me at one o'clock to take the Cleveland train.

FRIDAY, 29.   Awoke and found it five A.M. and the train gone four hours. The boy alleged that he awoke me at one and I answered. I could not dispute him, but did not believe him. I could only chew my disappointment and wait till 9 A.M., when I crossed the Ohio and took the Lake Erie and Pittsburgh train at 9.15, and reached Cleveland via Youngstown, at two P.M. Read Von Holst on the way, nearly completing Van Buren's administration. From Leavittsburgh, I telegraphed to Crete to send a team for me to Painesville to meet the 3.30 P.M. Express. James T. Robison[239] met me, at [and] at 4.15 I was at home—very hoarse and tired. Read a very large mail.

In the evening James Mason came to spend the night. Two of his daughters were already here.

Visited, wrote letters and made preparations for starting to Maine in the morning.

Retired at eleven.

SATURDAY, 30.   Breakfast at 6.30. Hurried preparation for leaving home. At 7.15 Jerry drove Mr. Mason and me to the Mentor station, and then took me to Painesville, where at 8.20 A.M. I took the Eastern Express. My head was too full of inflammation and my heart too full of sadness to endure the gabble of the drawing-room visitors on the route, and so I went into the mail

---

[239]James T. Robison (1858–1905), youngest child of Dr. John P. Robison, graduated at Hiram College and the University of Michigan Law School. Admitted to the bar in 1879, he abandoned the law for business, first in his father's firm and later in his own manufacturing plant, the Robison Basket Company, in Painesville. During the campaign of 1880 he was an aide to Garfield at Lawnfield. His principal duty was to examine the scores of newspapers received there daily, and to cut out and put into scrapbooks items of interest to Garfield. He married Lillian Warner, and was the father of two children, Hortense and Warner.

car, and the clerks kindly gave me a bed on the mail bags, and left me alone.

The cause of the sadness—not usual to me—is the fact that my two boys, Hal and Jim, are to leave home before I return, to enter Dr. Coit's school at Concord, N.H.[240] It is the dawn of independent life for them. I hail it for their sake. But the greater their joy and success, the more certain their separation from home. Till now home has been to them the main fact of life, absence the exception and temporary incident. Henceforward, if they are successful, home will be the exceptional incident. It will require no little self-sacrifice on my part, to see and aid them in the work of separating these precious home ties. I begin to see how it is that parents come to regard children as their own decorations, given for their own selfish comfort. The severe lesson must be learned, that they are given to go alone, to leave the parent nest, and fly to trees of their own seeking. Between sleep and heartache the day wore on. Dinner at East Buffalo, supper at Syracuse, ending with headache, sleep and dreams.

SUNDAY, 31. Awoke at Troy at 3 A.M. with an addition to my head cold. Left the Railway Postal Car, and took a berth in the sleeping car. Lay awake nearly an hour, reviewing, and comparing with the present, my state of mind when I left Troy 23 years ago, just after my graduation at Williams. Fell asleep, but the genius of the Hoosac Valley awoke me on the way from Williamstown to North Adams. I slept again just as we entered the Hoosac Tunnel. I was wide awake a quarter of a century ago, when I rode over this mountain in a stage coach. It is fitting that with these years and this mountain above me I should sleep along the same line.

Awoke and slept at intervals, and dressed at Fitchburg. Caught glimpses of Acton, Concord, Lincoln and Waltham, where six generations of Garfields sleep.

---

[240]Henry A. Coit (1830–1895), an Episcopal clergyman, became the first rector of St. Paul's School for boys in 1856, continuing in the position to his death. Bentley Warren and Don Rockwell also attended the school. Late in 1880 Jim, Hal and Don persuaded their fathers to permit them to leave St. Paul's and study in Washington under a private tutor.

At half-past ten reached Boston, belated by a collision on the Albany line, which sent all the Boston cars by the Hoosac Route.

Went to the Parker House and found Dr. Updegraff awaiting me. (We had agreed at Steubenville to meet here.) Took a hot bath, read, wrote and rested, and at 2 took dinner.

The quiet of the day is most welcome, lacking only Crete. I have fallen into a feeling in the Boston silence, that I have cheated the crowds of visited [visitors] and got a chance [to] be with myself a little, which is a rare but necessary treat—most welcome.

At six called on my classmate Hon. C. H. Hill and dined with him at the Club. Was introduced to several young lawyers. Retired at 10.30.

September

MONDAY, 1. Breakfast at the Parker with Dr. Updegraff and at 8.30 took the train for Portland, arriving at one P.M. After dressing and dining, called on the Committee of which Mr. Dow is Chairman, found my list of appointments and read and wrote until half-past five, at my room at the Yarmouth [Falmouth] House. Suffered and snuffled with headache until 6 P.M. when I went by rail to Biddeford. Many called at the hotel to see me. At eight I met a great audience—the large hall crowded. I spoke with great effort and think I made the most dismal failure of my life. It must have been, in the main, the result of my head and throat cold. Every sentence was forced as sound is forced from a wheezy organ. The failure may not have appeared so bad to the audience as it did to me. The worst phenomenon, and an entirely new one to me, was the fact that I did not seem to care much about making a failure. I knew I should feel desperately after it was over, but for the time being was quite indifferent, only so I finished the talk. I wonder if I shall recover while in Maine. It seems to me not. To be conscious of ability to capture an audience, and almost always to have done it, and always to have care[d] greatly about success, and then have this experience is strange. Closed a little after nine, rejected an invitation to Old

Orchard Beach, and came back to Portland to feel sick, stupid and sad, and write this confession and go to bed sick, at eleven.
TUESDAY, 2. Slept until nine A.M. a troubled dreamful sleep, and was awakened by Clarence Hale,[241] feeling still miserably bad in the head and throat. Spent the day in reading, writing, visiting and moping—thinking much of Crete and the boys who are on their way to New Hampshire.

Read with the surprise which ought not to be felt at anything said by the unveracious press that "Gen. Garfield made a very able and eloquent speech at Biddeford last evening." I know better. Made some careful preparations to redeem my reputation here tonight. Received no letters nor dispatches, and felt not a little isolation and homesickness.

I think the Maine Election is to be very close. It seems to me more likely to go against us than for us. At eight P.M. met a very large audience in the city hall, and spoke an hour and a half. Did much better than I expected considering the state of my head and throat. After the meeting went to Clarence Hale's room, and played whist with him, and Mr. Clark[242] and Mr. Cushing.[243] Worked off the heat and weariness of the meeting and retired at midnight, with some hopes of a better day tomorrow.
WEDNESDAY, 3. Arose at half-past eight still feeling badly in head and throat. Read, wrote and rested during the forenoon, and thought much of the dear wife and boys while they were reaching Concord, and getting their first sight of the new school and temporary home of the young pioneers of our family. At eleven o'clock Clarence Hale drove me to Westbrook Junction, three miles out of Portland, where I met Senators Blaine and Allison for a few moments, and then took the train for the North. Frye came on board and rode with me to Waterville, where I

[241]Clarence Hale (1848–1934), a Portland lawyer, was elected city solicitor in 1879. A brother of Eugene Hale, he was active for many years in Republican campaigns.

[242]Probably Jacob Clark, a resident of Gray who was a member of the Court of County Commissioners, the office of which was in Portland.

[243]John S. Cushing, treasurer of the Maine Central Railroad, was living at the Falmouth Hotel.

changed cars, and at 5 P.M. reached Skowhegan, where I was met by Gen. Shepherd,[244] and driven to his house. At 8 P.M. went to the hall, which was densely packed. The students of Waterville College came down by special train. The Republicans of Skowhegan had a torchlight procession, and manifested great enthusiasm. I spoke nearly two hours. Made the best speech thus far in my Maine engagements. Spent the night at Gen. Shepherd's. He appears to be a most excellent man.

THURSDAY, 4. Breakfast at 8 and at 9.20 started by carriage across the country to Farmington 28 miles distant. The country is very beautiful, and the farmers make more of it than I should suppose was possible, with such climate and such rocky soil. Passed through Norridgewock, the home of Mr. Lindsey,[245] the M.C. for this district. At Mercer it began to rain, and continued in fitful showers until we reached Farming[ton] at 12.40.

There had been a soldiers' reunion in the forenoon, and our friends were expecting 5,000 people. But rainy as it was, nearly 3,000 assembled on the Common. Col. Moore[246] of Nashua, N.H., spoke very effectively for one hour and I followed nearly an hour, meanwhile a constant rain was drizzling, sometimes pouring down. The meeting was more enthusiastic than any I have attended this year in Maine. When I closed, there was a

[244]Russell B. Shepherd (1829–1901), who was breveted brigadier general in the Civil War, raised cotton in Georgia for several years after the war before returning to Maine to settle in Skowhegan, where he became a prominent businessman and a strong supporter of public education. A Republican, he served in the state legislature and on the executive council.

[245]Stephen D. Lindsey (1828–1884), a Norridgewock lawyer, was a member of the state legislature and of the executive council before serving as a Republican member of the U.S. House of Representatives from Maine, 1877–83.

[246]Orren C. Moore (1839–1893) was editor of the *Nashua Telegraph* from the late 1860's to his death and long one of the most prominent Republicans in the state. He was a member of the legislature on numerous occasions (he was a state senator when Garfield met him), chairman of the state railroad commission in the 1880's, and a member of the U.S. House of Representatives from New Hampshire, 1889–91. He participated in every political campaign from 1872, when he became chairman of the state Republican committee. Although he never attended college, Dartmouth awarded him an honorary master's degree.

vigorous call for me to go on, but it was too hard work, and too risky to my voice. I however agreed to speak in the evening. At 7.30 I met a hall full and made the most effective speech yet. Speaking two hours, I found my voice good and had excellent control of the audience. After the meeting, wrote up my Journal, read the Boston papers and Froude's *Caesar,* and slept.

FRIDAY, 5. Took the early train and passed through a fresh, healthful country to Lewiston. After dinner visited a large cotton mill, called on Mrs. Frye, received many callers, and at 8, addressed a very large audience. Hall crowded. Got full freedom of speech, and found enthusiastic responses. In company with Dr. Updegraff of Ohio, took the 10.35 train for the South. No sleeping car.

SATURDAY, 6. Arrived at Portsmouth, N.H., the home of Jeremiah Mason, at 3.45 A.M. Went to the Rockingham House and slept until 7.15, when I took breakfast, and at 7.55 took the train for Concord. Hon. John Wentworth[247] of Chicago, Illinois, rode with me 20 miles for a visit on national affairs.

Arrived at Concord 10.38 A.M. and went to the Eagle Hotel, where I found Crete awaiting me. After making some purchase[s] for the boys, we drove to St. Paul's School, three miles from town, and found Harry and Jimmy started in the 4th form, and full of pluck and the spirit of work. Had an interview of half an hour with Dr. Coit and studied him anxiously and carefully.

I was greatly disappointed in him. I had expected to meet a muscular Christian of the Rugby type. Instead of that I found a man who appeared to be full of transcendental piety, closely resembling cant if not hypocrisy, self-conscious pride which re-

---

[247]John Wentworth (1815–1888), a native of New Hampshire, graduated at Dartmouth in 1836 and in the same year settled in Chicago, where he became one of the best known men in the city's history. He edited a newspaper for a time, became a lawyer, acquired a large amount of real estate, and was a Democratic member of the U.S. House of Representatives from Illinois, 1843–51, 1853–55. After the passage of the Kansas-Nebraska Act he left the Democratic party and became a Republican. He was mayor of Chicago, 1857–63 and a member of the U.S. House of Representatives, 1865–67. The great Chicago fire destroyed his papers, including a diary. Known as "Long John," he was six feet six inches in height and weighed three hundred pounds.

joiced in excessive humility, an ethereal goodness which found the world too bad to be looked at. Add to this much culture, apparent disregard of wealth and persons and pay, with a probable strong interior spirit of tuft hunting, and this is my crude first impression—possibly altogether unjust. I hope it is but fear it is not. Milnor Coit[248] and the other teachers I like very much, and with them I leave my boys with confidence. I hope they may not imitate Dr. C. nor be greatly influenced by him. I shall watch the further developement with anxious interest. Dined with the boys. Left at 2.30. Left Concord at 3.45 and Ayer Junction at 7 for Ohio.

SUNDAY, 7.   Crete and I awoke in Eastern N.Y. and took breakfast at Syracuse.

We beguiled the time for a hundred miles in solving the following problem, which I had found recently in a newspaper. An army, on the march, occupies 25 miles of road. An officer rides from the rear to the front of the marching column, and back again to the rear, which he reaches at the point occupied by the head of the column at the time he started.

This is our solution.[249]

Let X = distance between the head of the column at time officer started, and point where he overtook it.

Then $25 + 2X$ = length of his whole trip.

$25 + X : X :: X : 25 - X$

$\therefore X^2 = \dfrac{}{25^2} - X^2 \therefore 2X^2 = \dfrac{}{25^2} \therefore X = \dfrac{25}{\sqrt{2}}$

$X = 17.68+$ and $25 + 2X = 60.32+$

We dined at East Buffalo. I read Froude's *Caesar,* talked of the

---

[248]James Milnor Coit (1846–1922), brother of Henry A. Coit, was associated with St. Paul's for many years as student, teacher and administrator. After serving as acting headmaster from 1896 to 1906 he spent the rest of his life as headmaster of the Coit School for American boys in Munich.

[249]Dr. Fritz Herzog, Professor Emeritus of Mathematics, Michigan State University, observes that the solution of "this somewhat sophisticated problem" is essentially correct. In the final step the Garfields should have found that $25 + 2X = 60.36$.

boys, compared views of Dr. Coit and found Crete and I agree except that her charity sees self-delusion where I see design. She may be right—probably is—but I fear she is not.

Reached Painesville at six, and were met by Jerry, and were home, with the narrowed circle, at seven. Miss Mays left us yesterday, after living in our family as teacher and friend for nearly three years. She goes to Dayton, O., to teach French and German in Miss Westfall's school.[250] Read part of my mail, and retired at 9.

MONDAY, 8.   Arose early and drove to Dr. Robison's to engage a ton of Bone Dust for my wheat ground. I also wrote to Mr. Capron[251] of Conneaut, O., for 8 tons of ground Limestone. I have read of a recent experiment which shows the relative value of these and other fertilizers. I am sure my soil needs lime in some form.

Read my large mail. Went over the farm to look after the cattle, and the irrigation. The pasture looks finely. Hereafter I shall try to begin earlier to fight the drouth. Several people called, and I spent the remainder of the day on my mail, and making preparations for another long absence on the campaign.

TUESDAY, 9.   After a good night's rest, went to Dr. Robison's to see the trial of a stump machine—a system of cogs and pullies by which one man lifts out the strongest stump.

Mr. Capron of Conneaut called—also Hon. F. Thorp of Geneva. Returned home at 10 and wrote a large number of letters. Gave directions to have 3/4 ton to the acre of ground limestone on the wheat. At 4 P.M. Moses, with the Grays in the large carriage, took Mother, the children, Crete and me by way of Willoughby, Mayfield and Orange, to Cousin Henry Boynton's where we spent the evening and night. I still feel, on revisiting the old home place, the strength of its early associations, and recall vividly the sensations and experiences connected with

[250]Mary Belle Westfall (her name sometimes appears as Belle M. Westfall) was for many years a district school principal in Dayton.
[251]Marshall Capron (1816–1884), Conneaut boat builder and lake captain.

every hill and tree. The farther I grow away from those scenes, the more I and [am] attracted by their memories.

WEDNESDAY, 10.   Breakfast at seven, when Moses drove me to Solon, where I took the train for Niles. Harmon Austin joined me at Warren. Reached Leetonia at 10, and at 11.40 took the train to Salem, where we were met by the Republican Committee. After dinner at the hotel, we were driven eight miles to Goshen, where I spoke an hour and three-quarters to 2,000 people in a grove—where I spoke about 10 years ago. My voice was not in good condition, and I did not satisfy myself. In fact did not speak easily nor very effectively. Returned to Salem, and took supper at the hotel. At half-past 7 went to the hall with Judge West and [he] addressed the very large audience fully two hours. I followed an hour and ten minutes much more effectively than at Goshen. Several hundred people came who could not get into the hall. Meeting closed at eleven. Visited with callers and with Judge West until after midnight. Spent the night at the hotel.

THURSDAY, 11.   After breakfast called at Capt. Jacob Heaton's, who was my Commissary in the Sandy Valley campaign.[252]

Hon. J. A. Ambler drove me for an hour, and we visited the engine works, which have turned out some very finished engines.

Judge Ambler warned me against building a house with an air chamber in the wall, but rather a double wall united by mortar. At 10 A.M. took the train to Alliance and thence to Bayard and via Oneida to Carrollton, having been joined on the way by Hon. J. T. Updegraff, M.C. for this District. At two o'clock met in the grove, on the Fair Grounds, about 2,500 people to whom I spoke nearly two hours.

I spoke more easily and effectively than yesterday, but less so than last evening. Made a few calls in company with Updegraff,

[252]Jacob Heaton (1809–1888), a native of Pennsylvania, settled in Salem in 1830, where he became a merchant and an early advocate of abolition. In his home, which was known as the Quaker Tavern, he entertained many of the notable men of his time. During the war he served in the army as commissary of subsistence. After the war he conducted an insurance business for many years.

wrote and rode for an hour, and retired, spending the night at the hotel.

FRIDAY, 12. Early breakfast, and at 7 A.M. Dr. Updegraff and I started in a carriage, and drove across the country 28 miles to Cadiz, arriving at noon. The town was decorated with flags and five bands were parading the streets. At 2 P.M. I addressed not less than 3,000 people in the Fair Grounds. Spoke an hour and a half, and got an unusual grip on the audience. Dr. Updegraff followed half an hour.

After supper Maj. McIntyre started with us for St. Clairsville, 16 miles distant. Before we had made half the journey, we were overtaken by the night and a heavy rain storm. We felt our way slowly in the darkness, and arrived at St. Clairsville between nine and ten at night. After drying ourselves we spent the night at the Hotel. This has been a hard day of effective work. My chief memories that connect themselves with St. Clairsville are "The Gospel Proclamation" and *Universalism vs. Itself* by Alexander Hall,[253] who lived here when I was a boy reader of his writings.

SATURDAY, 13. Took the early narrow gauge train to Quincy, where we were compelled to wait two hours for our belated train to Quaker City. But we arrived a little after noon, and stopped at a private house. Capt. J[ames] H. Riggs and eight other 42nd boys called to see me. At 2 we met 2,000 people in the grove. Dr. Updegraff spoke an hour and then I an hour. I did only moderately well. Voice bad, mind sluggish. At 4.25 we took the train for Bellaire, where at 7 P.M. we were met by Dr. [John M.] Todd and driven 5 miles to his home in Bridgeport, and took tea. At 8 I was driven to Aetnaville, where for an hour and a half I addressed fully 5,000 people. Many were over from Wheeling. A very good meeting and a much better speech than at Quaker City.

Spent the night at Dr. Todd's.

---

[253]Alexander W. Hall (1819–1902), editor, author, and philosopher, became well known for his attacks against Universalism and the theory of evolution. *Universalism Against Itself* (1843) reached a sale of 50,000 copies.

SUNDAY, 14. Took breakfast at Dr. Todd's, and at 8.30 were driven by Dr. Updegraff to his home at Mt. Pleasant, Jefferson Co., 9 miles from Bridgeport. A pleasant hill country settled at the beginning of the century, by Quakers. Here, Benjamin Lundy[254] made his early efforts to establish an abolition Journal.

Spent the day writing, reading and resting—until 2 P.M., when Dr. Updegraff and I rode on horseback a few miles out to his farms and examined his fine stock. We were in the saddle about three hours, and had a pleasant time.

After tea a large number of people called to see me.

Retired a little before nine.

MONDAY, 15. Breakfast at 5.30, and then Dr. Updegraff drove us to Bellaire, 14 miles. His beautiful Lady Thorn was one of the team, a charming mare. At 8.40 we took the train for Quaker City, where we arrived at 11. A carriage was waiting, and we were driven across Noble County 27 miles to Caldwell, taking one relay of horses at ———— and arriving at half-past two. Five thousand people were in waiting. One procession, consisting of 613 wagons, had come in, and Col. Pond[255] and Private Dalzell had been speaking an hour and a half. I spoke an hour and a half. Saw Capt. C. E. Henry and a dozen members of the 42nd O.V.I. and was driven by Mr. Smiley[256] 12 miles to Reinersville, where a crowd of 75 people had collected to see me and I yielded

[254]Benjamin Lundy (1789–1839), abolitionist leader, organized the Union Humane Society in St. Clairsville, Ohio (1815), one of the first antislavery societies in the country. In 1821 he began publishing *The Genius of Universal Emancipation* at Mount Pleasant.

[255]Francis B. Pond (1825–1883) graduated at Oberlin College (1846) and became a lawyer. He served in the Union army, 1861–64, rising from the rank of private to colonel and commander of the 170th Ohio Volunteer Infantry. He was breveted brigadier general. After leaving the army he resumed the practice of law, served briefly in the Ohio house of representatives, was attorney general of Ohio for two terms, and was a member of the Ohio senate, 1880–81, 1882–83. He was chairman of the Republican legislative caucus that unanimously nominated Garfield for the United States Senate in 1880.

[256]William C. Smiley of McConnellsville was, during this period, treasurer of Morgan County, chairman of the Morgan County Republican Committee and a member of the state Republican Central Committee.

to their urgency and went into a school house and spoke nearly an hour. Retired at ten—having ridden 53 miles in a carriage and 35 miles by rail since morning.

TUESDAY, 16. Awoke at six, took breakfast, and at half-past six started for McConnellsville, 13 miles distant. Arrived at 8.30. Wrote a little, but devoted most of the forenoon to receiving calls. Many old friends who knew me when I taught school near Gaysport 13 miles above here, called and revived old memories.[257] The general rush of strangers to look at me, and shake hands, is and has always been one of the singular mysteries. From my childhood, I have shrunk away from the appearance of tuft-hunting. But this is not that. It seems to be a desire to say "I have seen," etc. I feel when thus beset, as I imagine the ox felt, of which was written the "Ode to the big Ox, written within three feet of him, and a touching of him now and then."

At half-past one addressed an audience of 2,000—an enthusiastic assembly. At the close, Gen. Duvall [Devol][258] of Beverly took me in his carriage and drove 16 miles to Beverly, arriving at 6.30. Supper at Capt. Stull's.[259] Spoke an hour and a half to 700 people in the new Masonic hall, which was crowded to its utmost capacity. A quarter-past nine Mr. Alderman,[260] editor of the Republican paper at Marietta, took me in his carriage and we drove 20 miles to Marietta, arriving half an hour after midnight. This makes 102 miles I have ridden in carriages and 35 miles by rail yesterday and today and spoken four times. Drank a cup of coffee and retired [at] half-past one, spending the night and [at] Mr. Alderman's.

---

[257]See Vol. I, pp. 72–83.

[258]Henry F. Devol, of Waterford, Ohio, returned home from New Orleans in the spring of 1861 to enter the Union army. After four years of service, he was breveted brigadier general. After the war he became a prosperous merchant in Waterford.

[259]C. R. Stull, a proprietor of Stull & Clark Flouring Mills in Beverly, Washington County.

[260]Eli R. Alderman (1839–1901) was editor of the *Marietta Register* (a weekly until 1883) from 1872 to his death. President Harrison appointed him postmaster at Marietta in 1890.

WEDNESDAY, 17. Slept until eight o'clock. After breakfast, wrote, read and rested until dinner, when President Andrews[261] and Prof. Rossiter [Rosseter][262] came, and dined and visited. A committee of students of the Delta Epsilon [Upsilon] Society (Anti-Secret) came and presented me a beautiful bouquet.

After dinner, Col. Moore,[263] the candidate for the Legislature, came and drove me to Belpre, 12 miles, where I found an audience of 2,500 awaiting me. Spoke an hour and a half effectively. Capt. Henry was there, and I invited him to go with me the remainder of the week. We returned by rail to Marietta. Supper at Alderman's. In the evening addressed a large audience. Hall crowded. Made a more complete discussion than any yet, though not more effective.

At 9.40 Capt. Henry and I took train to Parkersburg, West Va., thence to Hamden, O., arriving at one hour after midnight, and stopped at a new hotel near the Depot.

THURSDAY, 18. We took the train at six A.M. for the south, passed Jackson, and later, Oak Hill, where the 42nd O.V.I. was encamped for a short time on its return from Cumberland Gap. At 10.30 arrived at Scioto Furnace, where I found a large package of letters awaiting me. Stopped at the house of a Mr. Williams[264] near the Depot. Capt. Henry answered several letters for me. Half a dozen citizens dined with us, among them, Hon. H. S. Bundy. At 1.30 addressed 1,500 people in the grove. James

[261]Israel W. Andrews (1815–1888), a native of Connecticut, graduated at Williams College in 1837 and the following year began his association with Marietta College that ended with his death. He was president of the college, 1855–88. He was the brother of Ebenezer B. Andrews (see Vol. III, p. 520, n. 183).

[262]George R. Rosseter was professor of mathematics and astronomy at Marietta College, 1868 to his death in 1882.

[263]Thomas W. Moore, a prominent businessman living on the banks of the Ohio near Marietta and a member of the Ohio Republican Central Committee, was a member of the state legislature, 1880–83.

[264]George S. Williams (1821–1881), a resident of Scioto Furnace from 1857 to his death, had a long career in the iron business, the last twenty years of which were in Scioto where he was a member of L. C. Robinson and Company, manufacturers of charcoal and pig iron.

Pinkerton,[265] son of the late L. L. P., came from Greenupsburg, Ky., to hear me.

At 5 we took train to Portsmouth, where posters were out for a meeting. But fortunately for me the steamer came, and we went on board at 7, and an hour after midnight were at Manchester, where S. P. Ellison met us, and took us to the hotel.

FRIDAY, 19. At 9 A.M. Mr. Ellison drove us on the pike to the north, and at half-past ten we reached West Union, Adams Co., having driven part of the way along the pike over which Henry Clay rode on his way to Washington. Stopped at Mr. Grimes's,[266] and received a large number of people. At half-past one o'clock went to the grove, where were not less than 5,000 people, much the largest political gathering Adams Co. has had.

I think I made the best speech I have yet made this season.

At the conclusion we drove back to Manchester, arriving ten minutes too late for the *Bonanza,* the river steamer for Cincinnati. Waited until long past midnight for a boat.

An attempt was made to get up a joint discussion between me and Gen. Rice.[267] I consented, but the other side did not.

SATURDAY, 20. It was three o'clock in the morning before the steamer *Buckeye State* arrived, and in a few moments we were on board and asleep.

We slept until 10, when we dressed and took breakfast which the Captain had kindly ordered for us.

At 12 we reached Cincinnati, where we were met by the Campaign Committee and driven to the Gibson House, and

---

[265]James L. Pinkerton, son of Garfield's old friend Lewis L. Pinkerton and a graduate at Bethany College in 1865, was for many years the Disciple pastor in Greenupsburg, Kentucky, which was about forty miles from Scioto Furnace.

[266]Probably Smith Grimes, who was for several years a banker in West Union.

[267]Americus Vespucius Rice (1835–1904), a native of Ohio and a graduate in 1860 at Union College (New York), was breveted brigadier general in the Union army during the Civil War. After the war he engaged in private banking in Ottawa, Ohio. He was a Democratic member of the U.S. House of Representatives, 1875–79, his party's candidate for lieutenant governor in 1879, and U.S. pension agent for Ohio, 1894–98. He spent his last years in Washington, where he was employed in the Census Bureau.

thence to Carthage, ten miles, where an audience of 10,000 awaited me. I spoke an hour and ten minutes hoarsely but quite effectively. I foresee that this excessive hard work will end in stopping up my voice altogether.

Returned to Cincinnati, stopping at Gen. Thomas L. Young's by the way. Supper at the Gibson. Letters from home. At 7.30 spoke for half an hour to a large audience in the street.[268] Then visited the Exposition for two hours.[269]

Night at the Gibson.

SUNDAY, 21. Slept until 10. At 11 attended Disciple Church, Richmond St., and heard an able discourse by Mr. Hobbs of Ill. Went with him to Dr. Williams' to dinner, in the suburbs of Cincinnati. Isaac Errett was there; and I had a pleasant visit until half-past five, when I returned to the Gibson House. Dr. Updegraff came, and brought good news from the localities where he has spoken.

Wrote to Crete and retired at 10.30.

MONDAY, 22. In company with Hon. D. C. Haskell[270] of Kansas, took the 7 A.M. train, he for Dayton, and I for London. Had a long and very interesting talk with Haskell. The story of his life as a Vermont boy, a Kansas youth, a Yale student, a first class member of a racing boat club, a lawyer, a Kansas patriot, and an M.C. is full of romance.

Arrived at London at 10.30, was driven to the Fair Grounds and attending [*sic*] the celebration of the [Preliminary] Procla-

---

[268]This was a gathering of German Republicans. According to the *Cincinnati Gazette* (September 22) Garfield "delivered one of his earnest addresses, dealing briefly but tersely with the questions of honest money, honest elections, and the supremacy of the nation."

[269]The Seventh Cincinnati Industrial Exposition opened on September 10 and closed October 11. Among the first day visitors were President Hayes and General Sherman.

[270]Dudley C. Haskell (1842–1883), a native of Vermont who moved to Lawrence, Kansas, in 1855, participated in the Pike's Peak gold rush in 1859, served in the Union army during the first years of the war, and attended the Sheffield Scientific School at Yale, 1864–66. He returned to Kansas and after service in the state legislature was a Republican member of the U.S. House of Representatives, 1877 to his death.

mation of Emancipation. Back to town and dinner at Hotel. At 1.30 I spoke to 1,500 people for an hour and 40 minutes. Spoke with great difficulty. The converging lines that mark the limits of my voice have at last touched each other, and I must haul off for repairs. I will not try to speak again for two or three days.

At 8.10 went to train, and thence in company with Maj. Watson[271] of the 40th O.V.I. went to Columbus. Visited the State Central Committee, arranged to have two or three of my appointments filled and went to Neil House to sleep.

TUESDAY, 23. Breakfast at eight. Ordered the withdrawal of my appointments for the next three days, including today, in order to regain my voice. Took the 9 A.M. train for Cleveland. Gen. Leggett and N. B. Sherwin met me at the Depot. Went up town with Sherwin. Business at Bank. Took 4.50 P.M. train to Mentor, where Jerry met me and brought me home. In the last eleven working days I have spoken 17 times, and have travelled unduly far in wagons. 13 of my meetings have been in the open air.

Found all well. Aunt Alpha Boynton here, and Anna Boynton, the Doctor's wife.

Read letters from the boys, and found they are doing well. Hope they will hold out as they begin in Deportment.

Retired at 8.30 but was too tired to sleep. Continued until a late hour to read Gen. John Beatty's book entitled *The Citizen Soldier.* It is his Diary of the late war.

The General writes with great clearness and force, and has made a very readable book, especially for the men who served with him in the Army of the Cumberland. It must have been 2 o'clock Wednesday A.M. before I slept.

WEDNESDAY, 24. Spent the day resting and enjoying the healthful quiet of the farm. I am so hoarse that I feel perfectly justified for being away from the Campaign; and almost rejoice in the illness that gives me this sweet touch of idyllic life. I went over the farm, examined the condition of the newly sown wheat field on which, by way of experiment, I have sowed 1,100 pounds of ground limestone to the acre—except upon a portion where I have put about 300 lbs. of ground bone per acre. I long for time

[271]James Watson, a Union officer, 1861–64, was a Columbus attorney.

to study agricultural chemistry, and make experiment with soils and forces.

Several friends called.

Read my large mail, and wrote some letters. Finished reading Gen. Beatty's book, *The Citizen Soldier,* which I have greatly enjoyed.

THURSDAY, 25. Another red letter day at home. I miss the dear old boys; but there is a tender hush at the table with Mollie and the two little fellows, which shows a constant memory of the absent two. Yet this feeling is manifestly mingled with pride that they are bravely bearing the burdens of the new life, and developing character, which we all feel is the common inheritance of the whole family.

At noon, Aunt Alpha, Cousin Annie, and Mother left us, the latter en route to Zanesville to make a visit to the Ballous, our relatives. In the afternoon, I wrote many letters and received considerable company. My throat is recovering rapidly. I almost wish it would keep me here longer. A large number of telegrams came today from various part[s] of the contested field. Among them, one from Foster asking to dispatch Blaine not to fail us, as rumor says he is likely to. Blaine is inclined to be a little reckless of his promises, and a little selfish withal. He agreed to speak in Ohio last year, but went by to Iowa—after I had helped him in Maine. I telegraphed him strongly—to Washington. I think he will come.

FRIDAY, 26. Wrote many letters this forenoon, and spent two hours with Northcott, going over the farm and inspecting the cattle. I have invited Mollie to go with me to Delaware, O., and visit her little school mate, Clara Jones, and so, at noon we took the train, Crete going with us as far as Cleveland. After shopping a short time with Crete, Mollie and I took to [the] train for the south. I left her in charge of the conductor, having telegraphed Gen. Jones to meet her, while I stopped at Cardington, the former home of Gen. John Beatty. His brother, Maj. Beatty,[272] presided at my meeting, which filled a large hall, and I spoke an

---

[272]William G. Beatty, an officer in the Union army, 1864–65, was associated with the family banking business in Cardington.

hour and a half, without serious difficulty. Mr. Perkins[273] of Medina followed me on state issues; but he emptied the hall rapidly. I was sorry for him. Indeed it was hardly fair to him to put him on the bill.

Spent the night at the hotel.

SATURDAY, 27. At 6.30 took the train for Delaware where I was met by Gen. J. S. Jones, late member of Congress from this place. Found Mollie well and breakfast waiting. At eight went to the College Chapel,[274] and was called on for a speech. Spoke about twenty minutes on the training period of life. Gen. Jones, and Mr. Carper,[275] a lawyer of Delaware, a wit, followed.

Judge T. C. Jones,[276] with whom I served in the Ohio Senate in 1860, drove me to his farm three miles out of Delaware to see his herd of Short-horns. I enjoyed the visit very much. I think his stock is of a better milking breed than most of the Durhams I have seen.

Back at noon. Dinner at Gen. Jones's. Opera House at 2. Spoke nearly two hours to a large audience. Did much better than last night.

At 4 held a reception at the hotel. At five, dine[d] at the Loan Exhibition with several friends. At six Mollie and I took the cars, and arrived in Cleveland at 10.10 P.M. Our train for the east was belated two hours, and we did not reach home until nearly two hours after midnight. Found Crete awaiting us.

SUNDAY, 28. Slept late, and breakfasted at nine with Crete and

[273]Edward S. Perkins, a farmer in Medina, was a local office holder and Republican member of the state legislature, 1876–79. He sought but failed to win his party's nomination for state school commissioner in 1880.

[274]At Ohio Wesleyan.

[275]Homer M. Carper (1826–1895), a graduate of Ohio Wesleyan, studied law under Thomas Ewing, and practiced in Delaware thereafter.

[276]Thomas C. Jones (1816–1892), a native of Wales, was brought to Delaware, Ohio, as a boy. He was a law partner of Homer M. Carper for several years before serving as judge of the court of common pleas of the sixth district, 1862–72. He was a member of the state senate, 1860–61. He was also prominently associated with the advancement of agriculture in the state.

the three children alone, a sweet restful breakfast but with two great lacks—Hal and Jim. Spend [*sic*] the day at home writing and visiting with the family. We took a long walk over the farm, and, in the afternoon, drove to Dr. Robison's. Wrote letters in the evening, and retired early.

MONDAY, 29. Awoke at half-past three, and at 4.15 was at the station, where I took the train to Cleveland. Arrived at 5.20, and went into the Cincinnati mail car and slept about two hours and a half. Awoke at La Grange, and left the train at Wellington. Breakfast at the Hotel. Wrote letters, and at noon Warner—and Congressman Horr,[277] of Mich.—drove me to Sullivan, ten miles, where I had not been since 1861, when I was raising recruits for the 42nd O.V.I.

A large audience was awaiting, and I spoke an hour and a half, not easily, but under the constraint of a bad voice.

Drove back to Wellington and spent the night at Mr. Warner's.

TUESDAY, 30. Awoke at 5 and took the 5.40 train to Cleveland, where I breakfasted and took the 7.30 train for the east. I crossed our farm, Crete, Mollie and Abe stood on the brow of the ridge waving me good morning as I hurried by. Ashtabula at 9.30 and after half an hour, train to Jefferson, where a large crowd were waiting at the Depot. Blaine had not come, nor had he been heard from. I sent five telegrams in various directions, but the noon, and an hour after, came and no response. Went to the Fair Ground where there were nearly 7,000 people in waiting. I spoke nearly two hours, pretty effectively. When I was half through, a dispatch came that Blaine was unable to reach us. I

---

[277]Roswell G. Horr (1830–1896), a native of Vermont, was brought to Lorain County, Ohio, in 1834. After practicing law in Ohio he moved to Missouri, and then, in 1872, to Michigan. He was a Republican member of the U.S. House of Representatives from that state, 1879–85. His twin brother, Roland A. Horr, was cashier of the First National Bank (of which S. S. Warner was president), Wellington, Ohio, and a member of the state senate, 1880–83. Roland was a strong supporter of Garfield for the U.S. senatorship and the recipient of a well publicized letter from Garfield concerning the course Ohio Republicans should pursue in regard to the presidential nomination in 1880 (see January 25, 1880).

made the best of it; but I am indignant at B. for throwing the whole weight of the meeting upon me.

I closed just in time to reach the train for Ashtabula, and there found the Lake Shore train for the west an hour and a half late. Went to Maj. Henry Hubbard's to tea, talked Harbor matters over, got train at 6.20, and at 7.20 found Jerry and the little mares at the Painesville depot. Home at 8.15. Large mail, and retired.

October

WEDNESDAY, 1. Worked on mail and farm affairs until half-past ten o'clock, when we shut up the house, and took the whole family, workmen and girls to Painesville. A very long procession went from this end of the county.

At 12.40 Hon. W. P. Frye came, and we dined at the Stockwell House. At 1.30 P.M. Frye addressed not less than 5,000 people on the public square. He made a very powerful and effective speech. I followed in a speech of about one hour, just a fair speech. On the whole, the meeting has been very effective and satisfactory.

At 5.30 Jerry drove me with Crete and the children home where I spent the night.

Very tired.

THURSDAY, 2. Arose at 4 1/2 A.M. and at 5 was driven by Jerry to Painesville, arriving in time for the 5.40 train to Cleveland, where I took breakfast, and at 7.10 left for Elmore, arriving at 11. Was met by J. B. Luckey,[278] who drove me nine miles to Oak Harbor. At 2 P.M. addressed an audience of about 2,000. Spoke quite effectively for nearly two hours. At 4.45 took the train (Northern Division) for Toledo. Was met at the Depot by Maj. A. L. Hopkins, V.P. [of the] Wabash R.R. (son of Dr. Mark Hopkins) and driven to his house, and, after supper, we went to the Sangerfest Hall, where was the banquet to the soldier prison-

[278]James B. Luckey, a realtor in Elmore, Ottawa County.

ers. About 1,500 men who had been in rebel prisons were there, and the remaining seats crowded to the utmost with ladies and gentlemen. After listening to the speeches for half an hour, I spoke about 20 minutes, and struck a key which evoked very great enthusiasm. I have rarely, if ever, done so well in so short a speech.

After visiting with Col. Streight and other comrades, went home with Maj. Hopkins, bathed and retired.

FRIDAY, 3. Long morning rest. Read Sterne's *Uncle Toby*[279] an hour in bed. Breakfast at half-past eight. Greatly enjoyed the society of the Major and his charming wife. He reminded me that I taught him to swim, by letting him ride on my shoulders while I swam the Hoosac River at Williamstown.

After writing a few letters and visiting friends until eleven, I took the train for Norwalk, whence, after taking dinner, Col. Wickham[280] drove me nine miles to Berlin Heights, where I spoke two hours and a half to 2,500 people.

I met several members of the Ransom family who were pupils of mine, when I taught district school in Warrensville, 29 years ago.

Mr. Pearl,[281] the Republican candidate for the Legislature in Erie Co., drove me to Ceylon Station where I took the train to Cleveland, arriving at 10.10 P.M. Spent the night at the Forest City House.

SATURDAY, 4. Breakfast at Forest City House. Atlantic train at 7.10. Reached Warren at 9.30. At 11 was driven in a procession fully 3 miles long, and not a tenth of the assembly were in it.

At 1.30 P.M. I spoke a few minutes, as President of the day,

[279]Selections from Laurence Sterne's *The Life and Opinions of Tristam Shandy, Gentleman,* 9 vols. (1759–67), were published in New York in 1871 under the title *The Story of My Uncle Toby, &c.*

[280]Charles P. Wickham (1836–1925), a Norwalk lawyer who attained the rank of lieutenant colonel in the Civil War, was judge of the court of common pleas of the fourth district, 1881–86, and a Republican member of the U.S. House of Representatives, 1887–91.

[281]Ancil H. Pearl, of Berlin, Erie County, was a member of the Ohio house of representatives, 1880–81.

and introduced Senator Zach Chandler. Then we organized another meeting on the west side of the Court House, which was addressed by Gen'ls Myer [Meyer][282] and John Beatty. After Chandler had closed I introduced Gen. Kilpatrick, who made a brilliant speech.

I think this is the largest political meeting I have ever seen in Ohio. It is undoubtedly the largest this year.

At 5.20 I took the narrow gauge R.R. and at 9 P.M. was in Painesville. Jerry met me, and at 10 P.M. I was at home with the dear ones. Found a bright letter from Hal.

SUNDAY, 5. Read and rested, and wandered about the farm, drinking in the exquisite beauty of an almost perfect day. The autumn tints are at that point of highest beauty of blended colors which can last but a few days, and the air is balmn [balmy]. How I wish I could rest a week in the sweet seclusion of this very perfect home life! Dr. Robison came in the afternoon and we had a long, pleasant visit. Among other things we discussed the relative influences of dam and sire, mother and father, upon the character of offspring. The Doctor holds that the father communicates the more permanent characteristics, and makes two points. The scriptural one that "Isaac was in the loins of his father," etc., and also the fact that a calf got from a common cow, by a perfect shorthorn bull, when bred by a perfect bull for four generations, becomes thoroughbred and entitled to registry in the herd book of England. He suggested that in the human race, the father furnished the material, and the mother gave it the form, or make up. Read, wrote, and retired early.

MONDAY, 6. The men failed to awaken me in time for the 4.22 train. Jerry drove me down to the station for the 7.44 train, but missed it by half a minute. I telegraphed to the New London Committee and then [they] answered, Come by fast train.

Worked at my mail until noon when I took the train to Cleve-

[282]Edward S. Meyer of Cleveland, who entered the Union army in 1861 as a private, rose to the rank of major, and was breveted brigadier general in 1865, was now assistant U.S. attorney for the northern district of Ohio.

land, and thence by the 1.55 P.M. train on the 3 C's,[283] arriving at New London at 3.30.

Addressed an audience of 5,000 an hour and a half, and was taken into a carriage at 5 P.M. by Capt. Skelton [Skilton][284], and driven to Monroeville, 24 miles, arriving at 7.30.

Addressed 1,500 people at the woollen mill 2 1/4 hours, and spent the night with H. M. Roby,[285] one of the candidates for the state senate.

TUESDAY, 7. Took the morning train for Findlay. At Fostoria, C. W. Foster,[286] father of Hon. C. Foster, came on board and went with me to Findlay. I studied his face and general characteristics with great interest in view of the reflections I had with Dr. J. P. Robison last Sunday in reference to the relative force of father and mother in the propagation of the race. In the father I see the marked type which has been reproduced in C. W[F.]. He has received from his mother his eyes, hair and complexion, and doubtless many modifications of his mind and spirit, but the type is unmistakeably paternal.

Frye was on the train with me and he spoke first an hour and a quarter, in the court house yard to an audience of about 3,000. I followed an hour and a half and held the audience better than usual. At 5 took train to Fremont. Rode in the Director's Car of Mr. Shoemaker[287] of Cincinnati. His daughter was along, whom I have not seen since she was one of my travelling companions to the Yosemite. Visited the President and his family, who are

[283]The Cleveland, Columbus, Cincinnati & Indianapolis Railroad.

[284]Alva S. Skilton, a captain in the 57th Ohio Infantry Regiment during the Civil War, was a Monroeville merchant and grain dealer; he was the son-in-law of John S. Davis, a Monroeville banker and Republican of some prominence.

[285]Henry M. Roby, a malter of Monroeville, Ottawa County, was defeated in the fall election.

[286]Charles W. Foster (1800–1883), a native of Massachusetts, came to Ohio in 1826, where he became a wealthy merchant and banker in Fostoria, a town named for him. His son Charles was associated with him in business and owed his nickname, "Calico Charlie," to the family's large scale dry goods enterprise.

[287]Robert M. Shoemaker (1815–1885), who had a long and prominent career in railroading, was president of the Cincinnati, Hamilton and Dayton Railroad Company. Mary, the daughter Garfield refers to, was nicknamed Minnie.

now at their home in Fremont. On reaching the house the President said, "Mrs. Hayes has been gathering hickory-nuts, and is now <u>having</u> her feet washed. She will be down soon." After an hour's visit, went back to Shoemaker's car and retired for the night.

WEDNESDAY, 8.   Awoke in Toledo; took breakfast at the Boody House, and wrote letters and visited friends until near noon, when I took the train for the West and at 2 P.M. reached Stryker, where a large out-door audience was awaiting me, the train being nearly an hour late. I spoke fully two hours quite satisfactorily. Cousins William[288] and Amos Letcher and their wives and Louisa Letcher Learned were there. At half-past four, Cousin Wm. Letcher and I started in a buggy for Pioneer, 20 miles distant, and arrived at half-past 7.

Spoke an hour and a half in the Methodist Church, which was crowded. At 10, started for Bryan, 14 miles distant, and arrived at midnight.

An hour later took the train for the East and retired, to get what sleep I could in an upper berth.

THURSDAY, 9.   Breakfast in Cleveland Depot. Took the 8.20 train for Akron, and had Gen. Ewing as my seatmate in the car. He talked very freely of the outlook and thinks he will be elected by a small majority. Thinks I made a personal mistake in not accepting the Republican nomination for Governor, for our success would have made me the Presidential nominee, as he thinks it will him if he carries Ohio. I see clearly that he and Thurman are political enemies, and he and Pendleton are not friends.

Was met at the Akron Depot by Conger[289] and Krause

---

[288]William Letcher was the Williams County Republican candidate for the Ohio house of representatives. His success enabled him to support Garfield for U.S. senator. In 1881 Garfield appointed him register of the land office at Mitchell, Dakota Territory.

[289]Arthur L. Conger (1838–1899), a prominent Akron businessman (at this time vice president of the Whitman-Barnes Manufacturing Co., makers of reaper and mower knives) and an active Republican. He was for many years a member of the Summit County Republican committee and served also on state and national committees.

[Crouse]290. Stopped at the Empire House, bathed, slept an hour and a half, and after dinner visited the shops and mills.

While visiting the knife works, suggested that the machine now used to cut the serrations in the sickle might be so modified as to make files, which are now manufactured by hand.

In the evening addressed 3,000 people in South Akron—on the street. Carried my audience better than usual. In company with Capt. Henry spent the night at Capt. G. K. Pardee's.

FRIDAY, 10. Breakfast at 6.30, and at 7.15 took the Atlantic and Great Western train for Ravenna, where Halsey R. W. Hall met us (Capt. Henry and me) and I spent an hour with old Ravenna friends who came to see me, while I waited for the train south. Took the 10 A.M. train for Alliance, where I was met by the Republican Committee and driven to Mr. Amos Coates's. Slept 3/4 hour. Dined, and was driven to the Fair Grounds where I addressed 8,000 for 2 1/4 hours. Maj. McKinley followed me in a spirited speech. The town has made a great demonstration, and is much aroused. Took the 5 P.M. train for Cleveland, was met at the Depot by Hon. Amos Townsend who drove me to the Heights, where a meeting was in progress, to encourage the Committee, and thence to the residence of Edwin Cowles, where we visited an hour.

Then I took the train for the east and was let off at 11.30 at my lane gate and reached home 11.40.

SATURDAY, 11. Wrote letters, and made some studies of a new point I hope to make in my speech at Cleveland tonight.

In company with Crete and Irvin took the train to Cleveland, after telegraphing birthday congratulations to Harry. Spent the afternoon shopping with Crete, paying bills, and completing the study of the point referred to above. Supper at Dr. Boynton's. Foster and Grow came at 7.10 and at half-past seven we were on

---

290George Crouse was at this time chairman of the Summit County Republican committee. During this year he was associated with Arthur L. Conger in reorganizing the old Akron Steam Forge Co., of which he became president. See Vol. III, p. 373.

the stand at the public square. Foster spoke with great clearness and good sense for an hour and a quarter, Mr. Grow[291] followed in a spirited speech of 20 minutes.

I spoke an hour and a half, and made my new point, in a more effective way than I had expected.[292] The audience was very large, and I strained my voice more than I have done for a month. But I made them hear; there must have been 8,000 or 10,000 people present.

At 11.15 was serenaded at the Kennard House. Visited an hour with Foster, lunched at Richards'[293] with him, and joined Crete and Irvin at Dr. Boynton's an hour after midnight.

Very hoarse and tired.

SUNDAY, 12. Breakfast at 6.45. Took the train at 7.30, at 8.20 were let off at Mentor, and at 8.30 were at home. I am very hoarse and very tired. Slept a part of the forenoon.

At 2 P.M. Crete, Ellen Larabee, Mother and I went to Dr. Robison's and took Dinner. In the evening drove over the farm, and late[r] wrote for an hour and retired early.

Oh for the end of the struggle!

MONDAY, 13. Jerry sat up all night so as to be sure to awaken me. I rose at 3.45 and at 4.20 took the train to Cleveland. Breakfast at the Forest City House. Mahoning train at 7.10 for the east. Read the *Leader*'s short-hand report of my speech of Saturday evening. It is better than I thought. Arrived at Youngstown at 10 A.M. and stopped at the Tod House.

---

[291]Galusha A. Grow (1823–1907), lawyer and businessman, was a native of Connecticut who moved to Pennsylvania in 1834, graduated at Amherst College in 1844, and was a Democratic member of the U.S. House of Representatives from Pennsylvania, 1851–57, and a Republican member, 1857–63 and 1894–1903. He was Speaker of the House, 1861–63.

[292]In his Cleveland speech Garfield charged that the recent attacks by the Democrats on federal election laws were related to the presidential campaign of 1880. According to him, the Democrats, recognizing their need to carry New York and Ohio to win the presidency, sought to assure their success in New York City and Cincinnati by making it possible to carry these cities by corrupt methods at the polls.

[293]A restaurant operated by J. M. Richards & Co. in Cleveland's Public Square.

At 12, B. J[S]. Higley,[294] Thomas Wilson,[295] Walter Campbell and I started in a carriage, and went via Poland to Petersburg, 14 miles. Dinner at Dr. Petit's [G. W. Pettit's]. Addressed 2,000 people in the grove, speaking nearly two hours. Very hoarse; but by speaking slowly made myself heard.

Returned to Youngstown. Supper at the Tod House, and at eight P.M. went to the Opera House, which was crowded. Spoke two hours with an effectiveness enhanced by the fact that it was the end. Spent the night at Widow Wick's. Wilson, Higley and several others accompanied me there and took lunch. Did not retire until midnight. Very tired.

I found on Saturday last that I weighed 206 pounds, an increase of six pounds since July. It is unusual for me to gain weight in the summer and fall.

TUESDAY, 14.   Arose at seven, and after breakfast Nunkey Wick drove me to the Mahoning train, whereon at 7.50 A.M. I left for Cleveland. Made the connection with the Lake Shore train at 11.15, and at 12.19 was at Mentor Station. Drove to the Town Hall and voted and came home. It is a very perfect day, and we shall have a large vote. Now, at 3 P.M., while the election is going on, I note my expectations—

1.   That Foster will be elected by 15,000.
2.   That the Republicans will carry the legislature by a very small majority.
3.   That the Greenback vote will not exceed 15,000 in the whole State.

We may do better than the above—we may do worse—but I expect better rather than worse.[296]

---

[294]Brainard S. Higley, a Youngstown lawyer, was in 1879 an unsuccessful candidate for the office of county prosecutor. He was a member of the Mahoning County Republican committee, and in 1880, as secretary of that committee, he took a leading part in the presidential campaign in his county.

[295]Thomas H. Wilson, an employee of the banking house of Wick Brothers & Co. in Youngstown, was the district's Republican candidate for the state house of representatives; elected by a narrow margin, he served, 1880–81.

[296]In the election Foster won the governorship by about 17,000 votes. The Greenback vote for governor was about 9,600 and about 11,000 for other state

On the whole, I think I have done better work on the stump than ever before. I have seen numerous proofs that my reputation is growing, that it has been enhanced by the last session's work.

Two days Later.

Went to Cleveland soon after writing the above, and spent the night at The Forest City House with D. A. Pardee.

The election turned out better than my estimate, made above, especially the majority in the Legislature.

WEDNESDAY, 15. Spent the day in preparing to give Brother Joseph Rudolph and his new wife a reception on their arrival here this evening from Pittsburgh.[297] Crete and Mollie went yesterday to attend the wedding.

Spent some time dictating letters to Pomerene and bringing up my neglected correspondence.

In the evening at 7.45 I gave a supper and reception to Brother Jo and his wife. Present at table:

James Mason
Albert Mason
George Mason
Mrs. Mary Curtis
Mr. and Mrs. White
Mr. and Mrs. Putz
Mr. and Mrs. Sherwin
Mr. and Mrs. Henry
Mrs. Martha Rudolph
Mr. Short
Crete, Mollie and I

A very good supper, in the private dining room of the Forest City House. Our guests left us at 11 P.M. Night at F.C. House.

---

candidates. The Republicans won 22 of the 37 senate seats and 69 of the 114 house seats.

[297]Joseph Rudolph's first wife died in February, 1878. His second wife was Lida Mason, who died in 1926 in her 84th year. At Garfield's surprise reception were relatives and friends of the newlyweds and several of Rudolph's associates in the mail service.

THURSDAY, 16. Spent the forenoon shopping and dictating letters, and at noon went to Cousin James Mason's, where we took dinner.

In the afternoon, continued dictating letters to Pomerene, completing in all about 75 letters.

At 7 in the evening attended the wedding of Eugene Cowles and Miss Hale,[298] at the Episcopal Church on Euclid Avenue, and then a reception at the residence of the bride's father, where we remained until 9 P.M., when we went to Col. John Hay's and attended the reception which he gave to W. D. Howells and wife, a fine party. The President and Mrs. Hayes were present. We remained until eleven o'clock. Returned to James Mason's and spent the night.

FRIDAY, 17. Completed shopping and letters and in company with Martha Rudolph took the 11.15 A.M. train for Mentor and reached home for dinner. Mollie stayed over another day at Mr. Mason's. In the evening Lt. Harber came from Youngstown to make us a visit.

The reaction from the long strain of the campaign makes me feel disinclined to work, and the telegrams which assail me for speeches in Pa., N.Y., Mass., and Wisconsin I am leaving unanswered from sheer indisposition to work.

A pleasant evening of visit at home. I should have mentioned that at 7.00 this morning I went to the Depot to meet Gen. Irvin McDowell, who is en route to San Francisco, and telegraphed me that he would stop to visit me. I took him to Mr. Mason's to Breakfast, and he came home with us and spent the afternoon and night.

We went carefully over some of the leading points in the case of Fitz John Porter.

I should also [have] added that on our return home we found our old friend W. C. Howells, U.S. Consul at Toronto, awaiting us, and he remained until the evening train east.

SATURDAY, 18. Drove Gen. McDowell to Painesville in time for

---

[298] Alice M. Hale, daughter of Edwin B. Hale (1819–1891), a prominent Cleveland banker.

the 8.20 A.M. train to the east [west], and after a little shopping, came home.

Dawdled through the day doing but little. In the evening Pres. Hinsdale came, and we spent the evening in visiting and reviewing the character and results of the political campaign just closed. Burke is, as usual, disposed to take as gloomy a view as victory will permit. He has become very conservative, and shows evidence of being unduly influenced by the New York *Nation,* a paper that has turned much talent into the channel of cynicism and supercilious criticism.

SUNDAY, 19. Drove the family, including Hinsdale and Lt. Harber, to Willoughby, where we listened to a very thoughtful and powerful sermon by Hinsdale on the thought of Paul, "Woe is me, if I preach not the gospel." Home to dinner. Dr. and Mrs. J. P. Robison and Jimmie Robison with us.

In the evening I drove Burke again to Willoughby where he preached again.

Our evening talk, after returning from W., was more foodful than the second sermon.

MONDAY, 20. Took Burke to the train, and tried to make some use of the day in looking after farm and correspondence, but I am yet too tired and worn to do any thing, and so I let the day drift by in listless indolence, interspersed with Croquet and watching the work of digging potatoes, which is something akin to mining for the precious metals. Each hill has a possible surprise, and you are curious to know what the soil and seed have produced.

Many friends called during the day. Went to bed early—for if I can do nothing else I am just now quite capable of sleeping ten or eleven hours a night.

I should have added that in the afternoon I went to the Blacksmith's and had the mares shod all around. The quarter-cracks which two years ago threatened to ruin Kit, have almost disappeared, by careful handling.

TUESDAY, 21. Spent the forenoon between my library and the potato field without doing much in either.

In the afternoon took the grays and large carriage and drove the family to near Little Mountain, where we gathered chestnuts for two hours and had a pleasant time.

On our return Dr. Streator came to have a full talk with me on the senatorship.

If I were to act upon my own choice, without reference to influences outside of my preferences, I would remain in the House of Representatives. But I have resolved to be a candidate for the U. S. Senate for these reasons:

First. I am, and as leader of the House shall continue to be, too hard worked, and am likely to break down under its weight.

Second. There are many good men in my District who will think it selfish in me to keep them out of the House when I have a fair chance of promotion.

Third. I once gave way at the request of the President, and a few fellows of the baser sort said I was afraid to risk my strength in the larger field of the state. If I should decline now, I should lose still more in this direction.

Made an appointment to see Dr. Streator and other friends tomorrow. Drove him to Willoughby for the 6.22 evening train.

WEDNESDAY, 22. After an early breakfast Lt. Harber left us, Moses driving him to Painesville in time for the 8.40 train.

Spent the forenoon in assorting my telegrams and letters, and preparing for dictating a new batch when I reach Cleveland.

The recipe which Senator Hamlin gave me, a year ago, for preparing a field for potatoes, I tried this season, and the result is that I am now gathering in the best crop I know of in town. I think the recipe would have been better with less lime (It was 15 bushels ashes, 5 lime and 4 plaster to the acre), for I find occassionally a potatoe eaten by the lime. This, however, may have been the result of care[le]ss covering.

Crete, Abe and I took the noon train to Cleveland, and stopped at Dr. Robison's. I had a long interview with Henry, Sherwin and Streator *de re senatoris* [on the senatorial question]. In the evening we attended the wedding of S. T. Everett and Alice Wade. A very beautiful wedding—a thousand guests and many very rich presents. There [*sic*] display does not seem to me in good taste, e.g., a $10,000 check to the bride pinned up for public inspection is not to my notion of the *res sacrae Domi.*

Returned to Dr. Robison's at eleven P.M. and spent the night.

THURSDAY, 23. Spent the day in dictating 50 letters, shopping, and in holding conferences with friends on the subject of the senatorship.

A committee of three, Capt. Henry, W. S. Streator, and N. B. Sherwin have taken it in hand to find out the exact situation, by a reconnoissance of the field.

I feel greatly averse to doing anything about it myself. I feel that my services to the country should speak for themselves, rather than that I should speak for them or of them.

Perhaps the customs of the times will modify this so that I may be compelled to look after the matter myself; but I hope not. Made arrangement at the Bank for the payment of the note on my farm which falls due the 26th inst.

Took the evening train (Crete, Abe and I) amid a dash of snow, and reached home in time for supper. Read a large mail and retired at 8.30.

FRIDAY, 24. An almost wintry day, in strange contrast with the July weather we have had since the commencement of October. The potatoes, which have had such a charm for me, are all in the cellar at last, and I am losing my interest in them now that no mystery remains.

I made some success at resuming my work by doing some writing and beginning to put my library in order. I am still remiss about helping N. Y. and Pa., and feel like continuing so.

Have had the young trees mulched, and the strawberry vines covered for winter.

Have declined to deliver the oration at the unvailing of the Thomas Monument, 14th St. Circle, Washington, Nov. 19, because I know some of the Committee wanted Stanley Matthews to deliver it, and I don't want anything but unanimity on the subject.

Retired early.

SATURDAY, 25. After repeated solicitations from Wis., N.Y., Philadelphia and Boston, I have concluded to deliver three speeches in N.Y. next week and thus close my campaign for the season. At ten A.M. drove Crete and the children to Storrs and

Harrison's nursery and engaged some trees for the farm. Stopped at Painesville, paid bills, and returned home at 2.30. Several gentlemen called, among others a Mr. Prescott[299] of Derry, N.H., a member of the N.H. Legislature. He came here with his father-in-law, Dr. Beardslee[300] of Painesville. At 4 Crete, Mother and I started to make some calls on our neighbors. Called at Mrs. Dickey's, Bradly's [Emily Bradley's], and the two Mrs. Parmlees' [Parmeles'][301].

In the evening read Michelet's *Roman Republic.* [302] Brilliant and suggestive, but like most brilliant Frenchmen, never quite makes you sure you can trust his judgment.

The senatorial question stands in my mind thus: If I were to follow my own preference I would stay in the House, and run for the Speakership when we win, as I think we will next time. But three reasons determine me to run for the Senate:

1. I foresee that the heavy work which my leadership of the House imposes, and the frequent campaigns as a candidate, will soon make a break in my health. A seat in the Senate will delay the catastrophe.

2. It will be unkind to those friends at home who aspire to my present seat not to get out of their way, when an opportunity occurs for what is usually and almost universally regarded a promotion.

3. In March, 1877, I declined the Senatorial Candidacy when the place was plainly within my reach. To people of the better sort this was properly construed as an [act] of generous self-sacrifice. But by a large class of people it was

[299]Nathan B. Prescott, of Derry, Rockingham County, New Hampshire, who was engaged in the ice business in Boston and vicinity, was a member of the state house of representatives, 1879–83.

[300]Henry C. Beardslee (1807–1884), a native of Connecticut, who graduated at Yale College and also earned his medical degree at Yale, settled in Painesville in 1845, where he practiced medicine. He also became known as a botanist. He compiled *Selections from the Mosses of Ohio* (1871), and a *Catalogue of the Plants of Ohio . . .* (1874).

[301]Erastus Parmele and his wife Margaret and their widowed relative, Jane Lewis, who lived with them, were neighbors of Harriet Dickey.

[302]Jules Michelet, *Histoire Romaine, Première Partie: Republique,* 2 vols. (1831). An English translation was published in 1847.

construed as cowardice. They thought I had a pocket borough (the 19th District) which I could control, but that I feared to risk the chances of a larger field. If I should again give way, this impression would be deepened to an extent which would seriously injure me in the public estimation.

I shall therefore be a candidate, preferring to be defeated, rather than not make the race. But I do not think I shall be defeated. Nearly or quite 30 members-elect to the General Assembly have voluntarily during the late campaign tendered me their support, and several others have done so, since.

The Cincinnati end of the state will do what it can against me. Taft, Matthews, and perhaps Young and Eggleston[303] will be candidates. In the Center, my friend Gov. Dennison is a candidate. On personal grounds I regret this. In July last Sherman assured me he was not, and would not be, a candidate, and to that position I think he will adhere. Foster will keep his faith as my friend; and unless so[me] new phase presents itself I shall have no serious opposition. If money is to be used, if the Senatorship is to be bought, I am not a purchaser. But I do not believe it is for sale.

SUNDAY, 26. Spent a quiet day at home, writing, and riding over the farm until one P.M., when I took the family to Dr. Robison's to dine. Home in the evening and wrote a long letter to the boys. I wrote an older letter than I have ever before sent them to see if they will be interested in it.[304] Crete also wrote a long letter to Jimmie.

MONDAY, 27. Devoted the day pretty steadily to my mail, which, in spite of my best efforts, gains on me. The Senator question pushes itself vigorously to the front. I wish it would wait until the Legislature assembles. But our telegraphic age refuses to wait. I

[303]Benjamin Eggleston (1816–1888), a native of New York, moved to Ohio in 1831 and in 1845 settled in Cincinnati, where he became a merchant. He was a Republican member of the state senate, 1862–65, 1880–81, and of the U.S. House of Representatives, 1865–69.

[304]In a six-page letter devoted largely to politics, Garfield explained how tired campaigning had left him, how satisfied he was with the Republican victory in Ohio, and why he preferred the Senate to the House at this point in his career.

see there is danger that the Senatorship will get itself entangled with the Speakership, which ought not to be.

Have planned a cheap root house in which to store my beets, and tomorrow the men are to commence building it. I have not done much farm thinking this year, for which I feel reproachful regrets. Still, with the extra session it was well nigh impossible.

Wrote until ten P.M. and had 25 letters ready for the mail.

TUESDAY, 28.   Went to Cleveland by the 7.45 A.M. train to meet Gen. J. S. Robinson. Found that Capt. Henry had returned from Cincinnati with a favorable report from the chief camp of the opposition. He thinks my opponents have but small hope of success, but are holding together the better to take advantage of any fortunate accidents.

Dined at the club with Capt. F. H. Mason of the *Leader.* Called on Col. R. C. Parsons,[305] who has settled down into solid support for the Senatorship. At 3 P.M. Gen. Robinson came, and we went over the financial business of the State Central Committee and also the Senatorial question. He thinks I am safe against all opposition.

Came home on the 4.50 P.M. train. Found two good letters from the boys. Hal has been running in the "Hare and Hounds" race and was ahead till the last mile when he was seized with cramp in the legs, and stopped until three fellows passed him. Then went on, passed one, and came home third at the end of the 12 miles. Jimmie's letter for the first time has a little tinge of discouragement. But he had just had a boil lanced, and had not been in the race.

I brought home a new English book, Mallock's *New Republic,*[306] and read the first chapter to Crete, after we had retired.

---

[305]Richard C. Parsons (1826–1899), a native of Connecticut, who became a Cleveland lawyer and a prominent Republican, was a member of the Ohio legislature, 1858–61, collector of internal revenue for the Cleveland district, 1862–66, marshal of the U.S. Supreme Court, 1866–72, and a member of the U.S. House of Representatives, 1873–75. He was editor and part owner of the *Cleveland Herald,* 1877–80. There are references to him in Vols. I, II, and III.

[306]William H. Mallock, *The New Republic; or, Culture, Faith, and Philosophy in an English Country House . . .* (London, 1877).

WEDNESDAY, 29. Spent the day with letters and farm affairs. In the evening Brother Jo and his wife came and spent the night with us.

THURSDAY, 30. Jo and his wife and Crete went with me to Painesville, where I took the 8.20 A.M. train for the East. On the way had a long talk with Phin ——— of Buffalo.

Was met at the Buffalo Depot by the Republican Committee. After dinner at the Tifft House, went to the Hall (St. James) and spoke an hour and three quarters. A large audience, but not such enthusiasm as we had in Ohio. Dined with Senator Rogers,[307] and examined his fine English house. With him attended the Church Choir *Pinafore.* Fine music.

Night at the Tifft House.

FRIDAY, 31. Took the eight o'clock train to Lockport. Capt. Henry with me. Hon. Burt Van Horn,[308] former member of Congress, met me and drove me to his house. After dinner Hon. Richard Crowley[309] drove me to visit the Holly Water Works and also Holly's City Heating Works.[310] The latter will come

[307]Sherman S. Rogers (1830–1900), a prominent Buffalo lawyer, was a Republican member of the state senate, 1876, resigning to run unsuccessfully for lieutenant governor. A friend of George William Curtis, he was an advocate of civil service reform.

[308]Burt Van Horn (1823–1896), of Niagara County, New York, was a member of the state legislature before being elected as a Republican to the U.S. House of Representatives, in which he served, 1861–63, 1865–69. He was collector of internal revenue at Rochester from 1877 until his removal by President Arthur in March, 1882. There are numerous letters written by him to Garfield during 1880 and 1881 in the Garfield Papers.

[309]Richard Crowley (1836–1908), a lawyer of Lockport, New York, was a Republican member of the state senate, 1866–70, U.S. attorney for the northern district of New York, 1871–79, and a member of the U.S. House of Representatives, 1879–83.

[310]Birdsall Holly (1822–1894), a pump manufacturer in Lockport, New York, developed a system for pumping water under pressure into underground mains; more than two thousand cities and towns had adopted his system before his death. In 1877 he organized the Holly Steam Company to inaugurate in Lockport his system of distributing steam heat from central stations through underground pipes; during the winter preceding Garfield's visit more than a thousand consumers were thus supplied.

into general use I think. The former is likely to be superseded by Green's system of gangs of driven wells.[311]

In the evening spoke nearly two hours to a very large audience.

Passed the night at Van Horn's.

November

SATURDAY, 1.   Took the five A.M. train for the East. Breakfast at Rochester. Arrived at Auburn at 11 A.M. and was met by Hon. T. M. Pomeroy[312] and driven to his residence where I dined. At two o'clock attended a meeting in the Opera House, addressed by a Mr. Hicks[313] of Florida, who made a very able and striking speech on Southern affairs.

In the evening I spoke two hours to a very large audience.

Spent the night at Pomeroy's.

SUNDAY, 2.   At eleven A.M. attended the Disciple church and listened to a very good sermon by the Pastor, Mr. Aylesworth [Aylsworth][314]. Dined with classmate John T. Pingree[315] and his family.

[311]Nelson W. Green, a New York City businessman, specialized in driven wells and water supply systems for "cities, towns, manufactories, &c." His article, mentioned in the entry for November 3, is "Why Do Springs and Wells Overflow?" *Popular Science Monthly,* XVI (November, 1879), pp. 71–82.

[312]Theodore M. Pomeroy (1824–1905), a Republican member of the U.S. House of Representatives from New York, 1861–69, and Speaker for a day (March 3, 1869), was now a partner in the Banking House of Wm. H. Seward & Company. During the 1870's he was also mayor of Auburn and a member of the state senate. In a letter to Mrs. Garfield (November 2) Garfield called him "a noble fellow."

[313]William W. Hicks, of Dade County, Florida, was, during the reconstruction period, a member of the state legislature and an official in the Republican administration of Governor Marcellus L. Stearns, who was defeated in 1876. In 1880 Hicks was a Florida delegate to the Republican National Convention, and in 1881–82, as the Reverend Mr. Hicks, served as spiritual adviser to Charles Guiteau.

[314]N. J. Aylsworth wrote to Garfield on November 1, inviting him to a service.

[315]John T. Pingree (1835–1883) practiced law in Auburn most of the last twenty-five years of his life.

In the afternoon, went with Mr. Pomeroy and visited W. H. Seward,[316] who lives in the old family mansion. Spent two hours very pleasantly among the family pictures, library and curios—the fruit of Sec'y Seward's trip around the world.

At 7 P.M. took the train for the east. At Syracuse and after found several inches of snow.

MONDAY, 3.   Awoke on the Hudson, near N.Y. Arrived at the 5th Avenue Hotel at seven A.M. Made some calls and at 3 P.M. took the train with my classmate H. E. Knox and arrived at Springfield, Mass., at eight P.M. On the way read Col. Green's article in the *Popular Science Monthly* for November on the cause of lakes and springs on the tops of hills and mountains. The theory is new and, I think, true. Soon after supper was waited on by a Republican Committee, and invited to attend a meeting in the City Hall, which I did at 10, and at the conclusion of a speech by Gen. Hawley, I spoke half an hour, threat closing my campaign speaking for this year. Before going, I listened an hour to Col. Green on his water theory and his gang well patent.

Knox and I spent the night at the Massasoit House.

TUESDAY, 4.   In company with Col. Green and his son, Knox and I went to Holyoke and spent the forenoon visiting the several paper mills where the gang wells are at work. Their performance is wonderful, and seem[s] to verify Green's theory. At noon we took the train for Springfield. The conductor told us he had just left two feet of snow at Bellows Falls, Vt., and 19 inches at the Mass. line.

My classmate Dr. S. W. Bowles met us at Springfield, and took us to his house to dinner. He is an eminent physician.

Knox and I took the 1.25 P.M. train for New York. Took supper with Knox at his home on 69th St. Went thence to the 5th Avenue Hotel, where by 9 P.M. enough returns were in to indicate the success of the Republicans in all the northern states voting today.

---

[316]William H. Seward (1839–1910), son of Lincoln's secretary of state and brother of Frederick W. Seward (1830–1915), assistant secretary of state under Lincoln and Hayes, was a brigadier general in the Civil War and long the head of the Banking House of Wm. H. Seward & Co.

Took the 10 P.M. train for Washington.

WEDNESDAY, 5.   Awoke in sight of the Capitol. Went to our house and found the Tylers not up. Went to the Arlington and before I was dressed rec'd an invitation to take breakfast at Sec'y Sherman's in company with Foster, which I did.

The Dep'ts are closed on account of Senator Chandler's funeral,[317] and I did not accomplish much of the business which brought me here. Dined and spent the night with Col. Rockwell.

THURSDAY, 6.   Busy day, ordering cleaning of house, and arrangements for starting it up when family comes. Visited the President. Lunched with him. Went also to War, Interior and P.O. Dep'ts.

In conversation with Gen. Sherman, learned inferentially that there is a plan on foot to get some paying position, like R. R. Presidency, for Gen. Grant, to keep him from being a candidate for the Presidency. I doubt if this will suit him.

Gen. Sherman told me this curious anecdote. In 1867, when Grant was being talked of for President, he one day said: "Sherman, what are you going to choose for your hobby?" "What do you mean?" "I mean that you and I must have a hobby, something to keep people from always talking war and politics to us. I am going to choose the Horse." Sherman said that this was done deliberately, and it proved a great success.

Dined with Col. Rockwell. Spent evening with Gen. McCook making arrangements for the meeting of the Army of the Cumberland on the 19th and 20th inst.[318]

---

[317]Zachariah Chandler, one of the Republican party's most popular speakers, gave a campaign speech in Chicago on the evening of October 31. The next morning he was found dead in his bed in the Grand Pacific Hotel. The funeral was held in Detroit. On November 2 Garfield wrote to Mrs. Garfield from Auburn: "I thought as I was waking, of the sudden death that came to Senator Chandler, in his bed at Chicago yesterday morning—when he had just finished his campaign, and was to be awakened early to leave for home; and I thought that I did not want to die away from you."

[318]Garfield was chairman of the local executive committee of the Society of the Army of the Cumberland in charge of arrangements for the eleventh reunion of the Society, to be held in Washington on November 19 and 20. The other members of the committee were Thomas L. Young and Anson G. McCook; the

Spent the night with Foster at Sec'y Sherman's. F. and I were alone, Sherman having gone to N. Y. to meet his wife, who is to return from Europe tomorrow.

FRIDAY, 7. Foster and I took the 8.35 A.M. train, Baltimore and Ohio R. R., and spent the day in discussing the political situation, and especially the Senatorship. He is for me, and has agreed to see several of the members-elect whose attitude is as yet doubtful. He thinks I will be nominated on the first ballott.

We dined at Cumberland, Md., supped at Grafton and went to bed while we were crossing the Ohio at Bellaire.

SATURDAY, 8. Our train was belated, and we reached Shelby too late for the Cleveland connection. Went on, took breakfast at Chicago Junction, where I parted with Foster, and went on to Monroeville. Called on Capt. Skilton, dined at Mr. Roby's, where I had spent a night during the campaign, and took the noon train for Cleveland, arriving at 2.30.

Spent two hours with friends at the P.O. learning the news *de re senatoris,* and took the 4.50 P.M. train for Mentor and reached home for supper with the dear ones.

Very tired, and my head buzzing with 20 gr[s]. quinine taken since Friday morning. Retired early.

SUNDAY, 9. Spent the day at home, feeling the great reaction of my long campaign and hardly able to read my great mail.

I long for a fortnight of quiet on the farm but cannot get it. Much accumulated work must be undone.

Retired very early.

MONDAY, 10. A pretty full day's work, with letters and farm affairs. I am not satisfied with the condition of the farm. Though it has improved in some respects, I have not been able to give it the time I desired and must leave many things for the future.

TUESDAY, 11. Took the morning train to Cleveland to meet

---

secretary was Henry C. Corbin. When Garfield called the business meeting of the Society to order on November 19, he made this comment: "Although Chairman of the Committee, I have no credit for any work that has been done. General McCook and Colonel Corbin have done whatever has been done to make the preparations for this meeting."

A. L. Conger of Akron. He is inclined for Taft but is not decided. I did not feel sure of him, and so talked guardedly.

I dictated about 25 letters to Pomerene. Dined at the Forest City House with Sherwin and Capt. Henry. Was introduced to the Evangelist Moody, who said he hoped I would be elected Senator.

Crete and Mother came on the 1.30 train and with them I went to Solon at 2.40. Took Dinner with Sister Hitty and reviewed her buildings and repairs; left Mother there, and Crete and I went to Sister Mary's, where we spent the night.

This is the 21st anniversary of our marriage, a date most blessed, and always to be marked with a white stone.

WEDNESDAY, 12.   Crete and I took the 7.52 A.M. train for Hiram, driving from Garrettsville in a heavy shower. Stopped at Father Rudolph's. I went to the college and inspected the new boarding hall, and stone walks.

Dined at Father's, drove back to Garrettsville, and took the 12.45 train, reaching Cleveland at 2 P.M. Shopped, paid bills, signed letters, spent half an hour with political friends, and took the 4.50 P.M. train to Mentor. Capt. Henry came home with us.

A day of violent show[er]s and sunbursts.

Letters from Hal and Jim, and retired early.

THURSDAY, 13.   Capt. Henry and I spent most of the forenoon in sending copies of my tariff and extra session speeches to the members of the legislature to answer the attempt that is being made to make out that I am an enemy to a protective tariff.

Capt. H. left at noon for home. I spent the P.M. in writing letters, and putting my affairs here in order to be left for the winter.

In the evening Northcott came and we settled our accounts to date and made arrangements for the winter.

Hon. Thomas H. Wilson of Youngstown called and spent several hours, leaving at eleven P.M. He is strongly for me for the Senatorship.

FRIDAY, 14.   Spent the morning in packing my letters and documents for transportation, and in getting my Library in order to be left. Paid all bill[s] about town, wrote a few letters, received many calls, took dinner at half-past eleven, and at 12.31, having dismissed all our servants, including Moses, we took the train for Cleveland, where we were met by Sherwin and Capt. Henry.

At 1.45 P.M. we left for Pittsburgh, Capt. Henry accompanying [us] as far as East Liverpool. At Pittsburgh took the eight P.M. train for Washington. Our party consisted of Mother, Crete, Mollie, Irvin, Abram and myself, and Mr. Steele's man Henry, who goes to Washington under my protection.

SATURDAY, 15. Awoke in York, the train being an hour and a half late. Arrived at Washington 10.30 A.M. and at 11 took breakfast in the house which seems strange[ly] empty without our two boys.

Soon after breakfast Gen. McCook and Col. Corbin came and I worked with them several hours on the preparations for unveiling the Thomas Monument. In the evening called on the President and made arrangements with him to have the Dep'ts closed on the 19th, and to have the procession reviewed at the Executive Mansion.

The tide of office-seekers begins to flow already, and this greatest drawback to the pleasure of living in Washington threatens to be all the stronger because of our late successes at the elections.

Retired early, very tired.

SUNDAY, 16. Spent about three hours with the Committee, making preparations for the Thomas Celebration. We are pitching a tent 200 ft × 80 in the White Lot south of the Executive Mansion, and are decorating the Vt. and Mass. Avenue Circle for the unveiling ceremonies. Called on Gen. Schenck.

The remainder of the day I spent at home, resting, and getting my papers in hand. Rose came and I dictated a dozen letters. Many gentlemen called in the evening. Col. Rockwell stayed until 10.30 P.M.

MONDAY, 17. Spent the forenoon with McCook on the Reunion programme, and with Crete selecting carpets. At noon went to the Capitol, and met the Committee on Rules; all present except Alex. H. Stephens. Adjourned to meet on Thursday morning.

Spent the afternoon and evening working on my mail, and seeing people who called.

TUESDAY, 18. Working with the Local Executive Committee on preparations for the Reunion.

Brown came in the morning and I dictate[d] letters. In the evening Rose came and I did more of the same.

During the day I called on P. H. Watson, in reference to his patent case, and went to the Interior Dep't to get the hearing on interference postponed until Watson recovers from temporary illness.

A large number of friends called. At 6 1/2 P.M. dined at Mr. Justice Field's, on Capitol Hill, in company with Gen. Sherman, the Chief Justice, Judges Bradley and Swayne, Senator Conkling, Wm. Beach Lawrence and the French Minister[319]—a very pleasant party. Home at eleven.

WEDNESDAY, 19. My Birthday.

At 9 A.M. went to the Arlington and thence at 10, went to Willard's Hall to meet the Society of the Army of the Cumberland. At one P.M. the unveiling of the equestrian statue of Gen. Thomas (by Ward)[320] was witnessed by at least 20,000 people. I presided. Stanley Matthews made a noble oration, and the President received the statue in the name of the people. On the whole, I think it the finest of any equestrian statue in this country.

[319]Maxime Outrey was the French minister to the United States, 1877–82.

[320]John Quincy Adams Ward (1830–1910), a native of Ohio, maintained a studio in New York City for nearly half a century. He was present to unveil his statue of General George H. Thomas in Thomas Circle. Garfield first met the sculptor in 1861 in the office of Governor William Dennison in Columbus. Having introduced the two young men, the Governor is reported to have made this remark: "No doubt, Mr. Garfield, but that when you become a great statesman, Mr. Ward will be called upon to immortalize you in marble or in bronze." On May 12, 1887, Ward's bronze statue of Garfield was unveiled in the circle at First Street and Maryland Avenue, S.W., in the presence of President Grover Cleveland; it was erected by the Society of the Army of the Cumberland. See *Society of the Army of the Cumberland, Eighteenth Reunion, Washington, D.C., 1887* (1888). Governor Dennison's remark is quoted in the footnote on page 116. Other nineteenth century figures sculptured by Ward include Roscoe Conkling and Winfield S. Hancock.

There will probably be some difference of opinion as to the superiority of this to the Scott statue,[321] but I vote for this.

In the evening the Society met in the tent (200 × 80 ft) set up in the White Lot south of the Executive Mansion. I was forced to speak and was well received. I tried to do justice to Gen. Buell,[322] and I brought out for speeches, the President, Sec'y of War, Gen's McDowell and Van Vliet.

On the whole the evening was a very pleasant one. Home at eleven.

This, my 48th Birthday, finds my whiskers considerably sprinkled with gray, and little touches of rheumatism in my shoulders, to remind me that the years have been leaving their marks. I suppose I shall soon find it necessary to husband my fuel. I wonder if it is possible for consciousness and memory to act in harmony, and so justly as to enable me to compare my past with

[321]The equestrian statue of General Winfield S. Scott by Henry Kirke Brown (1814–1886) in Scott Circle, Washington, D.C. was unveiled in 1874. Ward began his career as a sculptor in Brown's studio in New York City.

[322]Don Carlos Buell (1818–1898), a native of Ohio, graduated at West Point in 1841 and served in the army for two decades before the Civil War. In 1861 he was appointed brigadier general of volunteers and given command of the Army of the Ohio (later to be called the Army of the Cumberland). Later in that year he became Garfield's commander. In October, 1862, three of his divisions engaged in a hard-fought battle with the forces of General Braxton Bragg at Perryville, Kentucky. Although neither side could claim victory, the Confederates withdrew. After following them slowly for four days, Buell gave up the pursuit. For this and for his failure to prevent Bragg's invasion of Kentucky, he was severely criticized. He was relieved of his command, investigated, and, in 1864, discharged from the Volunteers; he resigned his commission in the regular army at the same time, thus ending his military career. In his brief talk Garfield had this to say about Buell:

> But we were fortunate in having General Buell to be the great soldierly organizer of the Army of the Cumberland. He, like many other soldiers, has passed through the fires of criticism. With patient, capable, and enduring labor, he took the comparatively raw, undisciplined volunteers in hand, and largely laid the foundation of that splendid military discipline that made the Army of the Cumberland what it was to become.

For Garfield's speech see *Society of the Army of the Cumberland, Eleventh Reunion, Washington City, 1879* (1880), pp. 76–78.

my present and future self, and thus note the process of growing old.

THURSDAY, 20.   The Society of the Army of the Cumberland met at Willard's Hall,[323] at 9.30 A.M., and at 11 went on board the Steamer *Jane Mosel[e]y,* and thence to Mt. Vernon. The meeting was continued on board, and was a very happy one. I spoke a few moments in reply to an ex-rebel, Watkins,[324] who eulogized Thomas.

Returned at 4.30 P.M. and at 5 P.M. dined at Gen. Sherman's, in company with Gen. Hancock, Stanley Matthews and wife, Gen. Schofield and wife, and a few others.

At 7.30, in company with Crete and Miss Ransom[325] attended the President's Reception to the Army of the Cumberland, and at 9.30 the promenade concert at the Rotunda of the Capitol.[326] A very great crowd.

[323]The adjourned session of the Society was held in Willard's Hall because the huge tent on the White Lot behind the White House had blown down during the night.

[324]Lewis J. Watkins, of Ellicott City, Howard County, Maryland (he was at this time clerk of the county court), had served in the First Maryland Regiment of the Confederacy. His very brief speech included this statement: "I carry in my breast a bullet, evidently fired by a Federal soldier, but I recognize the fact that the period of strife has passed, and that we are brothers and citizens of a common country." In his response Garfield had this to say: "The Army of the Cumberland gives its hand to Mr. Watkins and wishes that there were a million Watkinses. Such hands as his the Army of the Cumberland would always grasp in fraternal welcome and love. Watkins carried a bullet of the Army of the Cumberland. He now carries its heart. The Army of the Cumberland sent its bullet to wound; it sent its heart to heal. I am glad the day of wounding is over, and that the day of healing has come." For the remarks of the two men see *Society of the Army of the Cumberland, Eleventh Reunion,* pp. 115–117.

[325]Through Garfield Caroline Ransom had extended an invitation to members of the Society of the Cumberland to visit her studio and view her ill-fated portrait of General George H. Thomas. Although Miss Ransom bequeathed the portrait to the government, the gift was not accepted; in 1977 it was still privately owned. See Vol. II, p. 399, n. 205, and Vol. III, p. 26, n. 44.

[326]"For the first time in the history of the country a ball was given in the Capitol of the Nation, and the marble halls that hitherto had resounded only to martial music, or to fevered eloquence, were to repeat the echoes of 'Lydian strains,' and the pattering of soft feet in the mazy measures of the dance." *Washington Post,* November 21, 1879.

The Reunion has been a great success, though the weather has been against us.

FRIDAY, 21. Calls on visiting comrades, letters and shopping filled the day. Many friends called in the evening.

In the evening in company with Col. and Mrs. Carter, Crete and I attended the Theatre, and heard Miss Neilson in *Twelfth Night.* I have never before heard it on the stage, and I wonder how such a charming play came to be dropped from the stage. I have heard but few plays equal to it in pleasant dramatic effects.

SATURDAY, 22. Spent the forenoon shopping with Crete, and completing the fitting up of our rooms for winter.

At noon, lunched with Col. Corbin, in company with the Sec'y of War, Gen. McCook, Maj. Bickham[327] and Dr. L. W. Bishop,[328] member-elect to the General Assembly from Clermont, O.

In the evening, Mr. Brown and Mr. Rose came, and we made considerable progress in working off my mail. Mr. Nichol of Racine came, and talked over the political situation for an hour or more.

SUNDAY, 23. Attended church with Mother and Crete, and heard a pretty good sermon from Mr. Power. During the afternoon, many friends called, among them Mr. Moulton[329] of Cincinnati

---

[327]William D. Bickham (1827–1894), a native of Cincinnati, attended Bethany College, entered journalism and worked on several newspapers in the 1850's. He was war correspondent for the *Cincinnati Commercial* and volunteer aide-de-camp on the staff of General Rosecrans, 1861–63. He was proprietor and editor of the *Dayton* (Ohio) *Journal,* 1863 to his death. The *National Republican* reported on November 29 that when Bickham, who had attended the reunion of the Army of the Cumberland, was asked who would succeed Thurman in the Senate, he responded, " 'General Garfield, of course.' " He was a delegate to the Republican national conventions of 1872, 1876 and 1880.

[328]Leonard W. Bishop, of Batavia, Clermont County, served one term in the Ohio senate, 1880–81.

[329]Charles W. Moulton (1830–1888), a native of Ohio, practiced law in Mansfield, Toledo, Cincinnati, and New York City. During the Civil War he achieved the rank of colonel in the Union army. His wife Frances was the sister of John and William T. Sherman. He was active in the movement to win the Republican presidential nomination for John Sherman in 1880. In April of that year he

(John Sherman's Brother-in-law) who came to tell me he will do what he can to secure my election to the U.S. Senate. He says he is quite sure of the vote of Fleischman[n][330] and Voight,[331] and perhaps two others of the Cincinnati delegation. I gave him to understand that my course towards Sherman's candidacy for the Presidency would depend in part upon his conduct towards me in the pending contest. Indeed, I had said this some time ago, and perhaps this visit is a result.

Moulton made several suggestions, and promised to write me after his return to Ohio.

At 4 P.M. Crete and I called at Col. Corbin's to see his family and Maj. Bickham and wife. Dr. Bishop of Clermont Co. came and took tea with us.

In the evening read and wrote.

MONDAY, 24. I resolved to devote most of this week to clearing up the neglected mass of letters which it was impossible for me to answer during the campaign. Nearly 500 must be answered before my decks will be cleared, and I must deny myself of all other pursuits until this is done. Late in the evening nearly 75 letters had been disposed of.

---

reorganized the Sherman campaign bureau in Washington, D.C., and in June attended the Republican National Convention. Three days after the convention ended he wrote a very long letter to Sherman about it. "I am not unaware," he wrote, "that very much has been said, and much will continue to be said, as to the unfaithfulness of alleged friends, but I do not think it wise for you to allow this impression to gain any foothold or make any impression upon you. Whoever may have been guilty of lukewarmness or bad faith, it is certain that General Garfield can not be charged with either. I consider him entitled to your full confidence and I took considerable pains to ascertain the facts before I arrived at my conclusions." Moulton to Sherman, June 11, 1880, John Sherman Papers, Library of Congress.

[330]Charles Fleischmann (1835–1897), a native of Hungary, in 1868 settled in Cincinnati, where he helped organize a company to engage in distilling and in the manufacture of yeast. Yeast made his name famous throughout the United States. Active in the Republican party, he was a member of the state senate, 1880–81, 1896–97, and a delegate to a number of Republican national conventions, including that of 1880.

[331] Lewis Voight, a Cincinnati merchant, was a member of the state legislature, 1880–81, 1898–99.

TUESDAY, 25.   A day devoted to correspondence, and to a meeting of the Committee on Rules. Brown, Simkins and Nichol all helped a portion of the day.

Our usual weekly letters from the dear boys came, to make a bright place in the otherwise dreary waste of correspondence. The brave fellows are doing excellently well. Jimmy stands no. 5 in a form of 25 boys. Poor Hal drops from 11 to 14, but is working hard.

WEDNESDAY, 26.   Another day devoted almost exclusively to correspondence. Not far from 60 letters were gotten off.

In the current mail, the Senatorship constitutes a leading topic of correspondence, and the letters I am compelled to write on that subject are specially irksome to me.

THURSDAY, 27.   Brown came early and took from my dictation until ten o'clock, when Simkins came and took until eleven. Then Nichol and I sat at the desk working at the mass of letters until far into the evening. Under the load of letters "I die daily."

FRIDAY, 28.   Again Brown and Simkins came for short-hand, and Nichol came to help by reading and answering, so that we got off very nearly 50 letters today, and reached nearer to the bottom of the pile than I have been before for six months.

The current mail is unusually heavy, and it is difficult to gain on the overplus. The whole day was devoted to it.

SATURDAY, 29.   Spent a part of the morning (after dictating several letters) shopping with Crete. At half-past ten A.M. went to the National Hotel, and met the Committee on Rules. But the Speaker not being present, we did but little business.

Departments in the afternoon, and letters in the evening. Major Swaim came.

SUNDAY, 30.   Read a very large mail, and at eleven A.M. attended church in company with Mother and Crete.

Swaim and T. M. Nichol took dinner with us. Several people called. Wrote and read a little, but felt too stupid to do any good work.

Many called in the evening.

December

MONDAY, 1. Struggled during the forenoon with the great flood of letters.

At noon Congress convened. In the House, the usual crowd, the usual ceremonies, and adjournment as soon as the message was read.

The rush of callers continued, and I retired late and weary.

TUESDAY, 2. I dictated about 30 letters, and met with the Committee on Rules before the House met.

An hour was spent in stately nothings, and then we adjourned. There is much commotion over the President's recommendation to retire the Greenbacks. The paper craze struck very deep into our people. They seem unwilling to let the Government pay a debt whenever it is in the form of paper notes.

In the evening, Crete, Swaim and I went to hear McCullough in *The Gladiator.* [332] The subject is distasteful to me, but it helps one to be reconciled to the fall of Rome.

The cordial reception I meet with from my fellow members of the House, and the earnest and hearty way in which the[y] express their regrets at the prospects of my leaving them, makes me reluctant to go to the Senate.

If the public opinion of three-quarters of a century had not decided that to go from the House to the Senate is a promotion, I would prefer to remain in the House, where my leadership is unquestioned, and the speakership is almost certain to come.

WEDNESDAY, 3. The story of yesterday forenoon repeated, except that I went to the Departments and thence to the Committee on Rules.

Nothing done in the House and done with a flourish.

In the evening, went with Irvin, Swaim, and J. K. Hamilton[333] of Toledo, to see McCullough in *Othello.* He gave a touch of

[332]Garfield saw this play on Monday, December 1. McCullough was at the National Theater throughout the week with a different offering each night and at the Wednesday matinee.

[333]James K. Hamilton (1839–1918), a Toledo lawyer who graduated at Kenyon College in 1859, held a number of local offices, including that of mayor. During

madness to the Moor which relieves his character [of] the appearance of innocent gullibility.

THURSDAY, 4.   Letters in the morning. War Dep't with Swaim at 10. Committee of Ways and Means at 11. House at 12—an hour's effort to do nothing and valorously adjourned at one.

P. O. and Census Bureau. Letters later in the afternoon. Crete, Swaim, Mollie and I went to the Theatre and heard McCullough in *Virginius*. It is his best acting so far as I have seen.

FRIDAY, 5.   Got off a large number of letters. At 10 A.M. went to the National Hotel and sat until 2 P.M. with the Committee on Rules. We finally committed our whole work to the Committee on Style—Frye and Blackburn.

Home and lunch at 2.30. Shopped with Crete. Called on John McCullough, and invited him to breakfast with me tomorrow.

In the evening wrote several letters to correspondents on the Senatorial question.

SATURDAY, 6.   At ten o'clock I gave a breakfast to John McCullough. Present, Gen. Sherman, Senator Allison, Amos Townsend, Gen. A. G. McCook, Col. Rockwell, Col. Swaim, T. M. Nichol and Gov. Foster. We sat until half-past one—a very pleasant party. McCullough recited with great effect "The Little Stow Away."[334]

Callers all day until six. At seven I went to a dinner party at Welcker's; several Senators and Representatives were present, and also ex-Senator Ramsey, the incoming Secretary of War.

At nine o'clock went to the Theatre and hear[d] McCullough in *Richard III*—a very fine performance.

---

the war he attained the rank of captain in the 113th Ohio Infantry Regiment, Army of the Cumberland.

[334]"The Little Stow-away" (of which there are versions in both prose and verse) is the tale of a small boy whose father stowed him away on a ship and who is saved from hanging by his steadfast adherence to the truth when the ship's captain, who has believed that he is lying, is persuaded of his truthfulness. See *The Speaker's Garland and Library Bouquet,* Vol. IV (1878), No. 14, pp. 141–145 (prose), and No. 13, pp. 68–71 (verse).

Home at half-past eleven.

SUNDAY, 7. Mother was not well and none of us attended Church.

Wrote letters, read and visited with friends who called.

At 6 P.M. Crete and I went to the Executive Mansion and dine[d] with the President in company with Mr. and Mrs. Key and two young ladies. There is a curious spirit of chaffing between the President and Mrs. Hayes and Webb. It is pleasant comradeship; but I should not be willing to have it exist between myself and family, except by ourselves.

MONDAY, 8. Letters until 12. House with usual wash day work.

At three called at the Treasury Dep't and attended [to] some items of business.

In the evening Rockwell came and stayed with Swaim and me until after eleven.

TUESDAY, 9. Not less than 40 letters were gotten off today, by the force of friends who are helping me.

Several calls on the Senatorship, more seeking office.

Three hours in the House and nothing done. Foster came late in the evening, and remained until an hour and a half past midnight. Talked over his future as Governor, and sundry political matters.

WEDNESDAY, 10. Today was a repetition of yesterday, except that I met the Committee on Rules at Mr. Stephens' room, and we reviewed a portion of the final revision.

THURSDAY, 11. The crush of letters continues—a large number of them relate to the Senatorship. Brown, Simkins, and Nichol helped me answer a large number. Departments at eleven. House at 12. Nothing done of consequence.

FRIDAY, 12. Worked a[t] desk until 10.30 when I attended a meeting of the Committee of Ways and Means.[335]

---

[335] According to the minutes of the committee the meeting was held on Thursday, December 11. At the meeting Garfield was directed to ask the Librarian of Congress "to buy at a price not exceeding $500 such works on finance and political economy" as might be selected by the committee to be kept in the committee room.

But little was done in the House except to pass the appropriation bills for pensions and fortifications.

Mr. Neal,[336] the member from Ironton, told me he was willing to aid me in the senatorial contest, and had written several letters to his District in my favor.

In the evening visited Gen. Schenck, who is steadily failing. I don't think he will live long. It is very sad.

I should have added above that Jonas R. Learned of Port Austin, Mich., took dinner with us.

SATURDAY, 13. Worked at my desk until ten A.M. when I went to Mr. Stephen's Room at the National Hotel, and worked with the Committee on Rules until 2 P.M.

In the evening wrote letters and received a large number of visiters, among them M. E[L]. Scudder of Chicago.

I should have added that Mrs. Thorne, Mrs. Davis and Mrs. Reddington of Cleveland dined with us.

SUNDAY, 14. A dreary, drizzly day. At half-past ten called on John Sherman in reference to the meeting of the National Republican Committee, in view of a dispatch I received this morning from Richmond, Va., signed by T. C. Platt[337] of N. Y. and

[336]Henry S. Neal (1828–1906), a graduate of Marietta College, was an Ironton, Ohio, lawyer who was a member of the state senate, 1862–65, a Republican member of the U.S. House of Representatives, 1877–83, and solicitor of the U.S. Treasury, 1884–85.

[337]Thomas C. Platt (1833–1910) had a long career in New York State politics. In 1870 he became a lieutenant of Senator Roscoe Conkling, and aided him in the subsequent overthrow of a rival faction in the Republican party. He was a member of the U.S. House of Representatives, 1875–79. In 1880 he was made president of the United States Express Company, and moved from Owego to New York City. Although a leading member of the Stalwart faction of his party, which sought the nomination of Grant for President in 1880, he contributed to the election of Garfield; he was at the time chairman of the Republican state committee and a member of the Republican national committee. In January, 1881, he was elected to the U.S. Senate, but he served only from March 4 to May 14, when he and Senator Conkling resigned their seats as a result of Conkling's struggle with President Garfield over appointments in their state. His failure to win reelection put him into a political eclipse for several years; from 1888, when he was a major influence in bringing about the nomination of Benjamin Harrison for President, until the turn of the century, he was the most powerful Republican in the state. He was again a member of the U.S. Senate, 1897–1909.

Dr. Jorgensen[338] of Va., asking me to meet them at Senator Hamlin's room at 10.30 tonight. Made some other calls. Knox of N. Y., my classmate, took dinner with us.

Several gentlemen called.

At half-past 10 P.M. went to the Hamilton House, and met Messrs. Sener[339] and Jorgensen of Va., who came to request Senator Hamlin and me to go to Richmond, Va., to urge the Republicans-elect to the Legislature to vote for a Republican for senator. They have now agreed to vote for Gen. Mahone,[340] the candidate of the Readjusters, alias repudiators, of the state debt.

I fear it is too late to make a change in the programme. I cannot go, but will join Hamlin in a letter to them. Home at half-past eleven.

MONDAY, 15. Letters until noon, when I went to the Capitol, but on my way stopped at the office of the District Collector and paid my taxes, and arranged for receiving drawbacks on old taxes levied in excess under the District Government of 1871.

In the House but little was done. Another meeting of the Committee on Rules. I think we are getting the agglomeration of rules—the growth of 90 years—into a much better shape.

Sent a draft of $30 to James Milner Coit to enable to [the] dear boys to come home on Friday next.

---

[338]Joseph Jorgensen (1844–1888), a native of Philadelphia and a graduate in medicine of the University of Pennsylvania, served for several years as a cadet surgeon and assistant surgeon in the U.S. Army. In Virginia he entered politics as a Republican. After serving in the state legislature and as postmaster of Petersburg, he was a member of the U.S. House of Representatives, 1877–83, a delegate to the Republican National Convention, 1880, and register of the land office at Walla Walla, Washington Territory, 1883–85.

[339]James B. Sener (1837–1903), a Fredericksburg, Virginia, lawyer, and editor for a number of years of the *Fredericksburg Ledger,* was a Republican member of the U.S. House of Representatives, 1873–75, and chief justice of Wyoming Territory, December 1879–83.

[340]William Mahone (1826–1895), a native of Virginia, graduated at the Virginia Military Institute in 1847 and, during the Civil War, attained the rank of major general in the Confederate army. An engineer, he was long engaged in railroading. He was a member of the Virginia senate, 1863–65, and of the U.S. Senate (he was elected as a Readjuster), 1881–87.

TUESDAY, 16. Letters until 10.30. Departments until noon. House, in which, again, not much was done.

The Republican National Committee are assembling for their meeting tomorrow, to determine the place of the nominating convention, and to elect officers. This brings many Ohio men here, and many callers to me.

Joyous letters from the boys on the near approach of their vacation, and coming home.

WEDNESDAY, 17. Not less than 30 letters dispatched. Meeting of the Committee on Rules, in which we settled all remaining questions of doubt and ordered the report presented for printing and recommittal.

Settled the drawback matter with the District Government.

House at one P.M. Several minor matters discussed, and House adjourned at 3, when I went to the President's with Butterworth and the two Crowells to ask for Capt. Crowell's appointment to a paymastership.

L. W. Heath of Grand Rapids dined with us. He was a student at Hiram 22 years ago. He is now a member of the National Republican Committee.

At 7 P.M. I dined at Hon. L. P. Morton's—a large company, and a fine dinner. They occupy the old Hooper house, corner 15th and H St., earlier still occupied by Gen. McClellan in the early years of the war.

THURSDAY, 18. Heavy mail, and work at desk with Brown and Simkins. In the House a long debate occurred on the removal of the Ute Indians of Colorado to a reservation.[341]

After the adjournment, played billiards with Rockwell and Swaim. In the evening Gen. Robinson and Gen. Grosvenor of

---

[341]Under a treaty with the United States the Utes were living on a reservation in Colorado bounded on the east by an imaginary line which the Indians did not observe. Neither did miners, who moved onto the reservation where, it was rumored, rich deposits could be found. Debate over the resolution, the purpose of which was to get the Indians out of the way of the miners, centered around the treaty obligations of the United States. Opponents of the resolution claimed that it violated the treaty rights of the Indians. Supporters argued that the goal was to negotiate, not for removal, but for such cessions of reservation land (for which the Indians would be compensated) as seemed necessary to preserve peace.

Ohio, called, and Crete, Swaim and I went with them and called on Senator and Mrs. Thurman, Gen. Schenck, Mrs. Frye, and Sec'y and Mrs. Sherman.

Home at 11 and retired.

FRIDAY, 19.   Worked in the usual way until 11 A.M. when I went to the Departments and thence to the Capitol. A few unimportant bills and resolutions were passed, and the House adjourned for the Holidays, to meet again Jan'y 6th.

On the whole, this session thus far has been the most meek and stupid of any I have known. The late elections have greatly subdued the spirit of the Democracy, and they have not yet determined what their plans for the future are to be.

This morning our boys leave St. Paul's for home, and the family is in eager and happy expectation.

In the evening I dined at the French Minister's, Mr. Outrey. Company, Chief Justice Waite, Judge Bradley, Senators Bayard and Allison, Admiral Temple,[342] and several members of the Foreign Legations in Washington. Madame Outrey is an American born lady of fine abilities and great social force.

Home at 10.30. As we retire, our boys are steaming up the Sound, and sleeping, I hope, in safety.

SATURDAY, 20.   Worked off a large number of letters, and at eleven went to Col. Rockwell's, to find a telegram that the boys had left Jersey City at 10.[0]5. Finished my work and reached home at 3. The whole household were putting themselves in readiness to meet the dear boys, even the little boys being dressed as for a holiday. Little Mollie had fixed herself up quite elaborately. Grandma dressed herself soon after noon as if for company.

At four-fifteen, Col. Rockwell drove our two and his own boy up to the door, and very soon the joy of our house was full.

---

[342]William G. Temple (1824–1894) began his long career in the Navy as a midshipman in 1840, attaining the rank of rear admiral in 1884 (he was a commodore when Garfield dined with him). He was a member of the Retiring Board, 1878–84. He has been described as "an officer of unusual ability and striking personality." *Dictionary of American Biography,* XVIII, p. 364.

I think I never saw happiness nearer perfect than that which beamed on every face and warmed every heart.

Swaim and Nichol dined with us, and at 7 both left us for the West.

The boys retired early, and at half-past eight I went to see Gen. Schenck and spent an hour. The noble old man is fading away into the weakness of disease.

SUNDAY, 21. A quiet and delightful breakfast with our whole family, and only them, the double pleasure of completeness and exclusiveness.

Mother, Crete and I went to church, and I endured rather than enjoyed the Sermon.

There is something radically wrong in the common methods and ideas of the clergy, so far are they removed from the real needs of the soul, and of daily life.

Mrs. Reed dined with us at 2 P.M. Spent the evening at home with the children, reading and visiting. Edwin Cowles and his son called and spent one or two hours in discussing the general political situation and specially the situation in Maine.[343]

[343]Maine was in political turmoil. In the state elections, held on September 8, Daniel F. Davis, the Republican candidate for governor, polled 68,766 votes; Alonzo Garcelon, the Democratic incumbent, 21,688; and Joseph L. Smith, the the National or Greenback-Labor candidate, 47,590. The Republicans claimed that they had won the senate, 19–12, and the house, 89–61, with one Republican vacancy by death. The state constitution required that the governor and his council examine the returns and summon the successful candidates to take seats in the new legislature. In early December the governor and council discharged that duty, but in doing so they ruled against a sufficient number of Republican candidates to gain control of the legislature for the Fusionists, a combination of Democrats and Nationals. The Republicans complained of irregularities and late in December asked for a ruling by the state supreme court. On January 3, 1880, the court handed down an opinion against the Fusionists, who ignored the court and on January 7 organized the legislature, claiming their president of the senate to be *ex officio* governor of the state until a successor was elected by the legislature. Five days later the Republicans organized the legislature, elected Davis governor, and asked the state supreme court for a ruling on their action. On January 16 the court upheld as legal the action of the Republicans, sealing the fate of the Fusionist bid for power. In March, an investigating committee established by the legislature reported that Governor Garcelon and his council must be held accountable for

MONDAY, 22. Worked at my mail with Brown and Simkins until half-past ten o'clock, when I went to the Departments. Went shopping with Hal and then to the President's. Then in company with Monroe and Burrows to the Attorney General's to solicit the appointment of Mr. Horr's brother in Washington Territory. Came home to lunch, when I went shopping with Jimmy, getting shoes for him and rubber boots for Irvin and Abram. Played billiards for an hour with Rockwell and came home to dinner. In the evening six or seven correspondents of the press came to see me in reference to an article in the *Star* of this evening, which alleged that I had consulted with the President and recommended the Republicans of Maine to resist by force the attempted usurpation. This of course was wholly false, but I gave the correspondents my opinion on the situation in Maine, which will be pretty generally published in the papers.[344] In the evening Rose and Brown came and I dictated the Journal and some letters. Harry, Jimmy and Mollie have gone to Mrs. Lander's to attend a Pound Party.[345]

TUESDAY, 23. My mail is sensibly decreasing in the absence of

---

illegal and fraudulent acts designed to secure for the Fusionists control of the legislature without regard for the expressed will of the people.

[344]The *New York Times* reported Garfield's views on December 23. According to the dispatch he denied having had any conversations with the President on the Maine proceedings. He said that he had talked with a number of Republican members of Congress, including those from Maine, and had advised that if the Republican legislators thrown out by the governor and council had law and equity on their side, they should make a contest. He added that he had no doubt the equities were with the Republicans and it was for the Maine Republicans to determine whether they had the law with them. If the governor and council had with them the technicalities of the law, he thought that "the Republicans should not proceed in a manner which would array them against the forms of law, but should contest the seats of those unjustly returned as members of the Legislature in the regular manner."

[345]Defined by Mitford M. Mathews, ed., *A Dictionary of Americanisms on Historical Principles* (Chicago, 1951), as "a social gathering at which each one in attendance brings a pound of something to be donated or used on the occasion"; according to Mathews the term originated in 1877. In reporting a pound party the *Washington Post* (March 7, 1878) said that "among the donations were eight sovereigns, besides pounds of nickels, silver, soap, coffee, tea, etc."

Congress, probably because many people suppose I am away from the City. Still I dictated a good many letters to Brown. Among others I dictated a long letter to R. D[F]. Queal[346] of Pensacola, Florida, on the history of the Garfield and Ballou family of Wooster [Worcester]. He is a Wooster [Worcester] man (of New York State) and has given me some valuable data concerning the history of my family in that town, sixty odd years ago. Commenced work on Judge Day's[347] brief in the Mahoning County Court House Case. I begin by recording my impression that the case is a hopeless one. The Supreme Court of Ohio was unanimous and the tendency is to waive all doubts on the construction of laws in favor of the authority of the Legislature. In the afternoon the children went to Rockwell's to dinner.

WEDNESDAY, 24.   Worked on my mail. Dictated many letters to Brown and then spent several hours with Crete and the boys getting Christmas things for the children and our friends. We took Harry and Jimmy into our confidence, for the [first] time, in selecting Christmas things. They are now old enough to share them with us, and do not need the surprises of the stocking. Spent some hours during the day in studying the Mahoning County Case, which I find requires a great deal more labor than I had

---

[346]Robert F. Queal, whose family lived in Evanston, Illinois, and who was connected with a lumber company, described himself as being kept in Florida by investments. He was a native of Worcester, New York, the birthplace of Garfield's father. When he visited the town in the summer of 1879 his attention was called to a letter addressed by Garfield to the postmaster there in the hope of obtaining from records left by a former doctor dates of births and deaths in the family of Thomas Garfield, Garfield's grandfather. On November 17, 1879, Queal wrote the first of six letters to Garfield, all but one of which were largely concerned with the Worcester of the past and its people. He attended the Republican National Convention in 1880 and was not surprised at the outcome—he had seen the same circumstances in 1860, "the leading candidates giving place to a generally acceptable compromise man." Queal to Garfield, June 30, 1880. Garfield's letter mentioned in this entry is dated December 24.

[347]Luther Day (1813–1885), a Ravenna lawyer and judge, was a member of the Ohio senate, 1864, and judge of the supreme court of Ohio, 1865–75; he was the father of William R. Day, a justice of the Supreme Court of the United States, 1903–22.

supposed. It is a difficult question in reference to the law of legislative contracts. Played with the children in the evening. Crete and I worked until nearly midnight in getting of [up] the the Christmas things.

THURSDAY, 25. Christmas morning filled the house with joy. For several hours the children were busy with their presents and Crete and I experienced even a greater pleasure than their own, in seeing their happiness. Read my mail, wrote a few letters, spent several hours playing billiards with Rockwell, and at four o'clock we ate our Christmas Dinner of Turkey with thanksgiving. Emily Reed was with us. In the evening Rose came and I dictated several letters and at half-past nine took the Limited Express train to New York.

FRIDAY, 26. Arrived in New York at seven o'clock and stopped at the Brevoort House. Called at General McCook's place of business to find the address of Major McKinley. Called on Drake DeKay at 115 Broadway on mining business. Made several other calls. Among others saw Mr. Sala.[348] Called at 345 West 34th Street where Major McKinley and his wife are stopping, but the Major was out. He came to me late in the afternoon and spent an hour or two talking over the political situation. Having concluded my shopping and other business I took the ten o'clock train for home.

SATURDAY, 27. Reached home a few minutes before seven o'clock. Worked on my mail and on the Mahoning County Case until two o'clock when I went to the Treasury Department and saw Secretary Sherman on business. At 3 o'clock, I returned at [and] worked on the case until evening. At half-past seven Crete and I went to Mrs. Lander's and attended the Literary Club.[349]

[348]George Augustus Sala (1828–1896), an English journalist, visited the United States from November 1863 to December 1864, November 1879 to March 1880, and during the early months of 1885. Among his many publications are *My Diary in America in the Midst of the War,* 2 vols. (1865), *America Revisited: from the Bay of New York to the Gulf of Mexico, and from Lake Michigan to the Pacific,* 2 vols. (1882) and *The Life and Adventures of George Augustus Sala,* 2 vols. (1895).

[349]At this meeting Garfield was elected president of the Society for the coming year.

SUNDAY, 28. [No entry]

MONDAY, 29. A busy day closing up business to leave for Ohio. Dictated a large number of letters in the forenoon. Went to the Capitol. Obtained books from Law Library on Mahoning County Case, made a few calls; among them called at General Beale's[350] (at the old Decatur House)[351] on General and Mrs. Grant. The General was out but I had a pleasant visit with Mrs. Grant. At 7.30 Hal and Jim went with me to the Baltimore and Ohio Depot, where I took the 7.40 train for the West via Point of Rocks and Pittsburgh. I go to Ohio to look after the Senatorship and farm affairs. It is my purpose after consulting with Cleveland friends and visiting Mentor, to go back to Washington and let the Senatorship take care of itself. I greatly dislike the bad custom which has sprung up in recent years, of placing that office in the arena to be scrambled for personally, but I will not decide this point finally until I see my Cleveland friends.

TUESDAY, 30. Awoke in Pittsburgh. Rode across the City in a street car. Took breakfast at the Union Depot. Sent a few tele-

[350]Edward F. Beale (1822–1893), graduated at the Naval School in 1842, served on detached duty with land forces during the Mexican War, and resigned from the navy in 1851. He was superintendent of Indian affairs in California and Nevada, 1852–55. He conducted surveys of far western lands, served as surveyor general of California and Nevada, 1861–65, and was appointed brigadier general of California militia in 1865. He owned an immense tract, the Rancho Tejon, near present Bakersfield, to which he retired in 1865. He was minister to Austria-Hungary, 1876–77. See following note.

[351]The Decatur House on Lafayette Square was designed by Benjamin H. Latrobe (1764–1820), America's first professional architect, and built in 1818–19 for Stephen Decatur (1779–1820), a naval officer noted for his successful exploits against pirates on the Barbary Coast. In 1820, following Decatur's tragic death in a duel, his widow left the house, never to return. The structure became the residence of a succession of famous people, including Henry Clay, Martin Van Buren, Edward Livingston, and George M. Dallas. In 1877, Mary (Edwards) Beale, wife of General Edward F. Beale, purchased the house, in which they resided about six months of each year. President Grant, a close friend, was a frequent visitor. The House remained in the family until 1956 when Mrs. Truxton Beale, widow of Edward's son, bequeathed it to the National Trust for Historic Preservation. In 1962 the Department of Interior designated the Decatur House a registered national historic landmark.

grams and left by Cleveland and Pittsburgh Road at 8 A.M. Worked on my law case on the way and stopped at Ravenna at one P.M., where I spent four hours with Judge Luther Day going over the chief points of his brief in our case. We have, I think, a sound constitutional foundation and strong equities, but the drift of modern tendencies is against us, and I doubt our success. Visited Halsey Hall. Several old friends called. Took tea with Mr. Horton[352] and family and took the late train for Cleveland. Went to Captain Henry's and after a two hours' visit, spent the night at his house.

WEDNESDAY, 31. At nine A.M. met several friends by appointment at the Post Office. Found that Dr. Streator had arranged to have a select party of Cleveland men go to Columbus on Friday next on his Director's car and reconnoitre the field. Spent several hours discussing the situation, comparing notes and deciding upon a policy to be pursued by my friends. I allowed rooms to be taken at the Neil House and cigars to be kept for visitors, but no liquors of any kind, no offer of offices nor any other thing to any member for his support. Called on Hon. R. C. Parsons and Amos Townsend. Many friends called on me, among them Thorp, Clement,[353] Carran,[354] Chapman,[355] of the General Assembly, who are en route to Columbus. Dined at Dr. Robison's in company with Dr. Streator and spent the afternoon at the Post Office receiving calls and writing letters. Took tea at six in company with General and Mrs. Sheldon at their relative's, Mr. Kelley on Case Avenue, where I spent the night.

[352]Joseph D. Horton, a native of Portage County, practiced law in Ravenna for many years. He was long a law partner of his cousin Ezra B. Taylor (Garfield's successor in the House) and of Luther Day.

[353]George W. Clement, a businessman of Willoughby, was a Republican member of the state house of representatives, 1880–81, 1886–87.

[354]Thomas J. Carran, a Cleveland lawyer, was a Republican member of the state senate, 1880–81.

[355]George T. Chapman, a Cleveland lawyer, was a Republican member of the state house of representatives, 1880–81, and of the senate, 1882–83.

1880

January

THURSDAY, 1.   Spent the forenoon with friends at the Post Office. Received a large mail from Washington. Dined at Dr. Robison's. Made a few calls and spent three hours of the afternoon at the Post Office, alone, answering letters. I am homesick as a boy to be with the dear ones at 1227 I Street today. In the evening at 6 1/2 Dr. Robison and I went to J. H. Wade's and with him to H. B. Payne's and spent a pleasant evening in visiting and Euchre. Returned home with Dr. Robison.

FRIDAY, 2.   Met a large number of friends at the Post Office and held a final consultation before their departure for Columbus. It is gratifying to know that the best citizens of all parties here are earnestly in my favor. Harmon Austin is here en route for Columbus. He dined with me at Dr. Robison's. At 2.40 P.M. I took the Mahoning train to Solon and went to Sister Mary's. My dog "Veto"[1] was in transports of delight at seeing me. When I would no longer let him leap up on me, he lay at my feet and licked my

[1]In the spring of 1879 Garfield proposed that a newly acquired dog that he was about to send from Washington to the Mentor farm be named Veto. Irvin, who was in Ohio with the other younger children, objected to this unilateral choice. Garfield promised that when the family were all together, they would hold a meeting to settle the question, "each man, woman and child to have a vote." Garfield to Abram (May 11) and to Irvin (May 17). When Garfield suggested the name, President Hayes had vetoed one appropriations bill during the special session and was preparing to veto another; Garfield was fully in accord with the vetoes.

boots. During my whole visit he followed me everywhere. There is something peculiarly touching in this affection of a brute. In the evening visited my niece Hattie Palmer in her new home. Spent the night at Sister Mary's. I am sorry to see that the work of life has left so many of my dear ones in the gossip ways of the world. I suppose that must follow when there is not enough culture to give resources in one's self. I shall try to give my children enough intellectual stores for rainy days and old age, that they may if possible learn how to consume their own smoke.

SATURDAY, 3.   Took the 6.22 A.M. train for Cleveland and found a[t] the Post Office a large mail awaiting me. Letters from home, with love messages from all the family, and letters from Columbus, telling me of the progress of the Senatorial contest. All looks well, and I think I shall be nominated on the first ballott. Indeed, there are signs that the opposition will wholly break down, though they yet talk loud.

Dinner at Dr. Robison's, and at 4.50 P.M. with him and his wife and their girl Josie, we took the train for Mentor and spent the evening and night at the Doctor's farm house. Thomas Northcott came and gave me a full account of my farm affairs.

The separate caucuses of the two Houses of the Legislature are to be held this evening. I sent word to my friends to have an early senatorial caucus.

SUNDAY, 4.   A very dreary rainy day. Remained in the house (Dr. J.P.R.'s) all the forenoon. The Sunday morning papers give the result of the last evening's caucus and say that the Senatorial Caucus is fixed for Tuesday evening next, an unusually early period, which was done on motion of my friends.

In the afternoon, we drove over my farm in the rain, and examined the stock and the field. I am having my woods cut down and already 450 cords of wood are ready for hauling. Not much work is being done except chores and wood-chopping, but the expenses are not great. In the evening, settled with Northcott the farm accounts for December.

Rec'd a telegram from Dr. Streator asking me to go into Cleveland in the morning. During the day have read most of Miss Sprague's charming book, *An Earnest Trifler.* [2]

Night at Dr. J.P.R.'s.

MONDAY, 5. Went into Cleveland on the 7.50 train with Dr. Robison and party, and found at the P.O. a great mail and many friend[s], anxious about the Senatorship. Dr. Streator has dispatches from Columbus telling him that powerful delegations are coming from Cincinnati to work for Taft and Matthews, and that there are signs of a combination of all my rivals against me. I don't think they can beat me if they do combine, but I have asked a number of friends from here to go down to Columbus this evening and look after the allies against me. [3] My orders are no liquor, no promises of office, or any other thing, no compromise, no delay of action, but a manly test of the question on its merits. I want the senatorship with absolute freedom, or not at all. The old motto of George Canning comes to me—"My road must be through character to power." At six P.M. dined at Mr. Edwards' on Prospect St. in company with 20 leading gentlemen—dinner given to Amos Townsend and me. Night at Dr. J.P.R.'s.

TUESDAY, 6. Spent most of the day at the Post Office answering letters and receiving friends. Several dispatches came during the day which inform me that many friends from distant parts of the state are at Columbus at work for me. The spontaneous opinion of the party seems to be so strong in my favor that I do not believe the political managers can resist it. At 3.50 P.M. I learned

[2] Mary A. Sprague (1849–1939), the daughter of a Newark, Ohio, lawyer, taught in Newark High School, published a number of articles in national periodicals, and was the author of *An Earnest Trifler* (1879). In an interview with George Alfred Townsend (*Cincinnati Commercial,* June 9, 1880), Garfield spoke about the book: "I have read it through. It is of simple materials, and has hardly any plot; but there is a maturity of thought about it which at once made it taking."

[3] The *New York Times,* which followed the contest closely, reported (January 5 and 6) that Stanley Matthews, Garfield's chief opponent, was working hard for the nomination with powerful backing from Cincinnati, that the iron and manufacturing interests opposed Garfield, and that friends of Matthews and Alphonso Taft claimed that if they could force a second ballot, Garfield's support would collapse. At the same time, the paper noted, Garfield's supporters held that their candidate had fifty-four votes, or eight more than needed to win the nomination.

that Gov. Dennison withdrew from the contest, and it is probable that Senator Matthews and Judge Taft would do likewise. I dined with Capt. Mason and had a pleasant time. Called at the Union Club and had a pleasant visit with several gentlemen and a game of billiard[s] with Capt. Mason. At 8.30 P.M. telegrams informing me that at the Legislative Caucus at Columbus, Dennison, Taft and Matthews withdrew, and I was nominated for U. S. Senator by acclamation.[4] The manner of it is more gratifying than the nomination itself. Telegraphed Crete, and the Chairman of the Caucus, Senator Pond. Night at J. P. Robison's.

WEDNESDAY, 7.   At eight A.M. Dr. Streator and Capt. Henry arrived from Columbus, and gave me full details of the proceedings in the Caucus, and of the great enthusiasm which prevailed. I believe the event of last evening is without parallel in the history of the state. It leave[s] me untrammelled by any commitments, or complications with any member of the Legislature. Many friends called and offered their congratulations. I have known by long experience that "it is more blessed to give than to receive," but I did not know until now the obverse of this truth that [it] is vastly more embarrassing to receive than to give. Dinner at Dr. Robison's. At 2.40 took the Mahoning train for Pittsburgh. At Warren, many old friends called at the Depot to welcome me as I passed through. Reached Pittsburgh at 8.30 and at 9 took the Baltimore and Ohio R.R. for Washington. Finished *The Earnest Trifler* and then slept.

THURSDAY, 8.   Reached home at 9 A.M. and found the dear ones well, and full of quiet sweet looks of congratulation. Found not less than 200 letters and telegrams awaiting me. Read mail until noon, when I went to the House, where I was very warmly welcomed by members of both parties. After the morning hour

---

[4]According to the *New York Times* (January 7), early in the morning of January 6 members of the Republican caucus were surging to Garfield, causing Taft, Dennison, and Matthews, in that order, to announce their intentions to withdraw from the race. In the caucus, however, Dennison's withdrawal statement was read, then Garfield was nominated in a "stirring speech" by Charles Townsend, after which the withdrawal statements of Matthews and Taft were read. The caucus then nominated Garfield by acclamation.

[the] House went into Committee of the Whole to discuss the new Rules. Reagan of Texas made a long speech against referring the River and Harbor Bill to the Committee on Appropriations. I replied in a speech of half an hour.[5]

Home at 5. At half-past seven, Crete and I attended a state dinner at the President's, a large and [*sic*] party, wet down with coffee and cold water. At ten we went to the marriage reception given to a daughter of the late Sec'y Edwin M. Stanton.[6] Home at eleven P.M.

FRIDAY, 9. Worked at my mail until near noon, but then was obliged to go to the Capitol, leaving at least seventy-five letters unread. In the House the day was devoted to private bills. I remained until about three o'clock, when I went to the Census Office on business. Home in the evening and dictated a large number of letters. Eighteen years ago tonite, I slept on the ground with my command on Abbott's Hill in Eastern Kentucky awaiting the morning to fight Humphrey Marshall.[7]

[5]Reagan urged that annual appropriations for rivers and harbors be reported, not by the Committee on Appropriations, but by the Committee on Commerce, which he believed to be the best qualified for the work. Garfield replied that if Reagan's reasoning prevailed, the Committee on Military Affairs would report the Army Appropriations Bill, the Committee on Naval Affairs would report the Naval Appropriations Bill, the Committee on Indian Affairs would report the Indian Appropriations Bill, and so on. Such a procedure would result in larger appropriations, he said, for each of those committees contested annually for larger sums for its area of special interest than the Committee on Appropriations recommended.

[6]Eleanore (Ella) A. Stanton, daughter of President Lincoln's Secretary of War, was married to James C. Bush of New Haven, Connecticut, in the Epiphany Church.

[7]Humphrey Marshall (1812–1872), a native of Kentucky, graduated at West Point in 1832, practiced law in Frankfort and Louisville, 1833–46, served as an officer in and helped develop the Kentucky militia, and fought in the Mexican War. He was a Whig member of the U.S. House of Representatives, 1849–52, a Know-Nothing member, 1855–59, and minister to China, 1852–54. He was a brigadier general in the Confederate army, 1861–63, and commanded the force that opposed Garfield's in the Sandy Valley campaign (see Vol. 1, p. xxxi). He was elected to the Confederate Congress in 1864. At his death he was practicing law in Louisville.

SATURDAY, 10. Devoted all the morning to correspondence and made good progress on the mail, though a large amount still remains unanswered. The usual work in the House, with some discussion of the Rules.[8] In the afternoon Crete and I attended a Kettledrum at Baird's on Massachusetts Avenue Terrace.[9] In the evening we attended the Literary Club at Judge Johns[t]on's on K Street. I presided. The subject of discussion was the relative merits of the poets and prose writers of America. With the exception of a paper by Mrs. Long the discussion was not very thorough. Home at eleven o'clock. This is the an[n]iversary of my battle at Middle Creek, fought eighteen years ago today. This an[n]iversary and my nomination to the Senate this week are pleasant events to remember in connection with each other.

SUNDAY, 11. Crete, Mother, Harry and I attended church, and listened to a sermon little better than usual, which is not saying much. Brown came and I dictated forty or fifty letters, a thing I seldom do, but it seemed necessary. I telegraphed Foster that I could not attend his inauguration tomorrow and should not go to Columbus until after my own election. Having staid away from the Capital during the contest, I decline to go until it is all over.

MONDAY, 12. Letters again all the forenoon. House at twelve. Crowds of callers. Ordinary Monday business. An attempt was made to repeal the duty on salt by a suspension of the rules but it failed. Indeed there was a majority of one against it. Home in the evening and worked on letters again. Two telegrams from Foster came late at night, saying that I must leave for Columbus

[8]The House did not meet on January 10.

[9]A kettledrum (sometimes simply called a drum) is commonly defined as an afternoon tea or a fashionable afternoon entertainment less formal than an evening party. Of the affair mentioned by Garfield, the *Washington Star* (January 12) reported that "Professor and Mrs. Baird entertained guests in their pleasant home on Massachusetts Avenue from 3 to 6 on Saturday afternoon, and many divided the afternoon between this and the White House reception. . . . When the Director of the Smithsonian is understood to be 'at home' to visitors with his family, the guests are sure to include a number of ladies and gentlemen whose busy lives, devoted mainly to intellectual pursuits, give them little time to indulge in the ordinary round of fashionable pleasures."

Wednesday evening to meet the Legislature after the election is over.

TUESDAY, 13. A busy day. Dictated a large number of letters until near noon. Called at the Departments on my way to the Capitol. In the House, I carried through a resolution to purchase $500 worth of books on political economy and finance for the use of the Committee on Ways and Means. Left the House at half-past three. Went to the Departments. Came home and read letters until half-past seven in the evening, when Harry and I went to the Baltimore and Ohio R. R. Depot and left on the 7.45 train for Columbus.

WEDNESDAY, 14. Awoke near the Ohio River. Took breakfast at Benwood. At Newark read the Cincinnati papers announcing my election on the day before by a majority of each House of the Legislature voting separately. We arrived at Columbus at twenty minutes after three and rode to Governor Foster's residence at the foot of Ninth Street. He sent for me to go to his room at the Capitol, which I did. Both Houses were in session, and several members called on me in the Governor's Room. Took supper with the Governor and his family and at half-past seven Senators Perkins, Hitchcock,[10] and Pringle[11] waited on me to go to the State House. On motion of a Democratic Senator the Senate Chamber had been tendered to me for a reception and Governor Foster was invited by a resolution to attend. Went to the Chamber which I had not entered before for eighteen years. About 1,200 to 1,500 people were present. Nearly all the members of both Houses. They were introduced to me by Governor Foster, being first introduced to him by Senator O'Hagan,[12] a Democrat, and Senator Richards,[13] a Republican. After the introductions were over, I was called on for a speech and spoke about fifteen

[10]Peter Hitchcock (1839–1906), for many years a leading manufacturer of iron and steel in Cleveland, was a member of the Ohio senate, 1880–81.

[11]Thomas J. Pringle, a Springfield lawyer who served seven years as a prosecuting attorney, was a member of the Ohio senate, 1880–81, 1886–87.

[12]Henry E. O'Hagan, of Erie County, was a Democratic member of the Ohio senate, 1880–81.

[13]Reese G. Richards, a Jefferson County lawyer, was a member of the Ohio house of representatives, 1874–77, and of the Ohio senate, 1878–81.

minutes,[14] after which others came in and the reception lasted until half-past ten. Then went to the Neil House with my Cousin, William Letcher. A few minutes after Foster came in and we remained there until eleven o'clock. Returned to Foster's and took a cup of tea and visited until half-past twelve. Harry and I went to the Depot and took the one o'clock train for Cleveland.

THURSDAY, 15. We were awakened at Berea and half an hour later were in Cleveland in time for the Mahoning train, which we took. There were a number of Cleveland friends on board [going] to Nellie Austin's wedding. Arrived at Warren at nine o'clock. Harmon Austin met us and Harry and I were driven to Judge Kinsman's house where we took breakfast. Then went to Mr. Parks's, a neighbor of Mr. Austin's, where a number of friends were assembled awaiting the hour of the wedding. Called at Mr. Freeman's[15] to see some Cleveland friends who were stopping there, at two o'clock went to Austin's house, where the wedding ceremony was performed by Dr. Thayer; a very large company was present. Miss Nellie Austin was married to W. C. Pendleton,[16] son of President Pendleton of Bethany College. At

---

[14]As reported in the *New York Times* (January 16), Garfield recalled that he was in the Capitol when he first heard of the fall of Fort Sumter, spoke briefly about Columbus and the Civil War, paid a warm tribute to his Democratic predecessor, Senator Allen G. Thurman, and then spoke about his own long service as a congressman from one district, whose approval he had always desired. But, he said, "without egotism he still more desired the approbation of one person, and his name was Garfield. Continuing after the laughter had subsided, he said: 'He is the only man I am compelled to sleep and eat with, and if I could not have his approbation, I should have bad companionship [laughter], and in the larger constituency, which has called me to represent them now, I can only do what is true to my best self, applying the same rule, and if I should be so unfortunate as to lose the confidence of this larger constituency, I must do what every other fair-minded man has to do—carry his political life in his hands and take the consequences.' He said a few words more and bade the Republicans and Democrats good night."

[15]Samuel L. Freeman, a Warren merchant and banker, was the only son of Judge Francis Freeman. In 1846 he married Charlotte L. Tod, a niece of Governor David Tod. His sister Laura married Charles Hickox (1810–1890), a Cleveland businessman and a member of the Little Mountain Club when Garfield belonged to it.

[16]Helen ("Nellie") King Austin (1853–1924), elder daughter of Harmon Austin, was married to William C. Pendleton (1849–1922). Pendleton, a graduate of

five o'clock Harry and I took the train for Pittsburgh via Youngstown. Arrived at 8.20 and took the Baltimore and Ohio train for Washington.

FRIDAY, 16.   Arrived at Washington at twenty minutes after eight. Found the family well and not less than two hundred letters awaiting me. After breakfast read about seventy-five letters and then went to the Capitol, thinking it was the morning of the meeting of the Committee on Ways and Means, but was mistaken, the meeting having been held yesterday. In the House the day was devoted to private bills. I spoke briefly on one of them reported from the Committee on Ways and Means.[17] At three o'clock went to Colonel Rockwell's and played billiards for an hour and a half. Home at five. Took an early dinner in the evening. Dictated letters in the evening to Brown, until eight o'clock, when about fifty children came to attend a party given by Mollie and the two older boys. A pleasant gathering with dancing and lunch which lasted until midnight. Fanny[18] and Scott

---

Bethany College, was the grandson of Alexander Campbell. At the time of his marriage he was employed in the office of the West Virginia state superintendent of schools (his father was then state superintendent as well as president of Bethany). Despite his desire for a career in railroading, in which he had had some experience, the young couple, as a result of Nellie's homesickness and the urging of Harmon Austin, soon moved to Warren, where William was employed in one of Austin's business enterprises, and where they spent the rest of their lives. The wedding gift of the Garfields was a set of the works of Sir Walter Scott.

[17]The bill provided for an appropriation of $5,850 for the relief of Charles Clinton of New Orleans, late United States assistant treasurer in that city, from whose office $5,850 had been stolen on May 1, 1871. Clinton had refunded the money. The central question of the debate was whether Clinton had exercised due diligence to protect the money. Garfield argued that he had and supported the appropriation, which was approved on March 2, 1881.

[18]Frances (Fanny) Hayes (1867–1950), the only daughter of Rutherford B. and Lucy Webb Hayes, was born in Cincinnati and attended Sarah Porter's school in Farmington, Connecticut, where her classmates included Mollie Garfield and Nellie Arthur, daughter of President Chester A. Arthur. She was a constant companion of her father. In 1897 she was married at the Hayes home in Fremont to Ensign Harry F. Smith of that town. They had one child. Following World War I she divorced Smith and resumed her maiden name. At her death she was living in Lewiston, Maine.

Hayes,[19] the President's children, were here and a very pleasant company of young people.

SATURDAY, 17. Spent all the day until four o'clock at my desk, reading letters and dictating answers. Got off over fifty. At four o'clock went with Crete and the Rockwells to Mrs. Hayes's Reception, and thence to the Reception of Mr. and Mrs. Ferdon,[20] on K Street. At half-past seven in the evening Crete and I attended a party at Secretary Sherman's. Returned home at half-past eleven o'clock.

SUNDAY, 18. Slept until nearly nine o'clock, making up arrears of the last week. Cousin Orrin Ballou came at nine to visit us. Crete, Jimmy, Mollie and I attended church, and invited Frank Green, the Preacher of the day and one of my old Hiram students, home with us to dinner. He spent the afternoon with us. Mrs. Reed was also here. In the evening Brown came and I dictated a large number of letters.

MONDAY, 19. Worked at my desk until quarter before eleven when I went to the Treasury Department on business and thence to the Capitol. The Committee on Rules had a brief meeting, as also had the Committee on Ways and Means. I attended both. In the House the day was spent in the usual Monday work until 11[2] o'clock, when the Committee on the District of Columbia was called for reports, which consumed the remainder of the day.[21] I went with the Sub-Committee on Ways and Means to the Congressional Library, to agree about the line of books to be purchased for the Committee on Ways and Means. Home in the

---

[19]Scott R. Hayes (1871–1923) was born in Columbus, Ohio, graduated at Cornell University in 1890, and engaged in banking and business enterprises in Ohio and New York. At his death he was vice president of the New York Air Brake Company.

[20]John W. Ferdon (1826–1884) was a Republican member of the House from New York, 1879–81.

[21]Under a House rule the Committee on the District of Columbia was entitled to the floor at two o'clock on this day. When that hour was reached (the session had begun at noon), the chairman of the committee claimed the floor. After a brief discussion of whether the vote then in progress should be completed or postponed, the Speaker turned the floor over to the committee.

evening; dictated letters until nine in the evening when Cousin Orrin Ballou, the two boys, Harry and Jimmy, Crete, Mr. and Mrs. Rockwell and their son Don, with myself, took the train for New York.

TUESDAY, 20. Awoke in Jersey City, and at seven o'clock reached the Astor House, where we took breakfast. Spent the day in shopping, and at four o'clock went on board the *Old Colony* Steamer with the boys and saw them safely in their stateroom. Bade them good bye and at nine o'clock in the evening we and the rest of our party left for Washington.

WEDNESDAY, 21. Reached Washington at 6.20 in the morning. Found all well at home. Found a very large mail awaiting me. Dictated some letters. Went to the Capitol at twelve. No business of special importance was accomplished. The Fitz John Porter case has been reported by the Committee on Military Affairs, with a minority report, which I shall probably support.[22] In the evening at seven o'clock, Amos Townsend of Cleveland and General Anson G. McCook of New York gave me a dinner at Wormley's. There were 22 people present. A very pleasant meeting. Speeches by General Sherman, Secretary Sherman, Governor Hawley, Mr. Clymer, Randolph Tucker and a number of other friends. Home at half-past eleven o'clock.

THURSDAY, 22. Dictated letters until half-past ten o'clock, when I went to the Committee on Ways and Means and spent two hours in the discussion of the bill for refunding the Public Debt.[23] I spoke about fifteen minutes enforcing the necessity of

[22]The majority of the committee reported a bill which provided for removing Porter's disqualifications and reinstating him as a colonel, or, if he preferred, retiring him as a major general with full pay, as arrears, which would amount to a sum between $50,000 and $60,000. The minority report declared that Porter had been justly tried and found guilty and opposed either reinstating him in the army or paying him any arrears. It did recommend restoring his rights of citizenship. Both reports are in the *Congressional Record,* 46 Cong., 2 Sess., pp. 492–500.

[23]A refunding bill had been referred to the Committee on Ways and Means after Fernando Wood, chairman of the committee, introduced it in the House on January 12. In committee debates on the measure William D. Kelley, who opposed long-term refunding plans advanced by Wood and Secretary of the Treasury John Sherman, proposed retiring outstanding government loans, redeemable at

immediate action and the wisdom of authorizing the refunding to continue under the old law, issuing the same bonds that the people are already familiar with, of which they have taken such large numbers. No very important business was transacted in the House. At eight o'clock, the members of the Ohio Republican Association, accompanied by about 2,000 persons, came and serenaded me. Judge Shellabarger made an address and I responded. Several Gentlemen followed. About 100 people came into the house and called on the family. The weather was unpleasant and at about ten o'clock a heavy rain set in.

FRIDAY, 23. Dictated letters until eleven, when I went to the Departments on business and to the House at twelve. The day was devoted to private bills. At eight o'clock in the evening Mr. Chittenden gave me a card reception at his house, in recognition of my election to the Senate. The President, several members of the Supreme Court, about 250 gentlemen in public life and prominent citizens of Washington were present. An elegant lunch was served and the company remained until eleven o'clock, when I went to Mr. Starin's[24] Party, where Crete was, and came home with her at half-past eleven.

---

government option between then and September 1, 1891 (the total of such loans was $1,031,840,900), by maintaining the sinking fund and making from it equal annual payments which would retire all 6 per cent bonds in six years, all 5 per cent bonds in the next thirteen years, and all 4 1/2 per cent bonds in the next six years. Kelley argued that in twenty-five years those loans would be paid off completely, with the interest amounting to approximately 2 1/4 per cent. (See entry for January 26.) Kelley's plan was debated and rejected by the committee, which presented to the House a substitute bill designed to retire outstanding bonds bearing 4 1/2 per cent interest by issuing bonds, redeemable in twenty years, bearing 3 1/2 per cent interest and maturing in forty years. After months of debate and several House and Senate amendments, Congress passed the Refunding Bill on March 1, 1881. Two days later President Hayes vetoed the measure. The House promptly tabled the veto message, thereby postponing until the next Congress further consideration of the question.

[24]John H. Starin (1825–1909), of New York, was active in various enterprises, including the drug and medicine business, river and harbor transportation, banking, railroading, agriculture, and stock raising. He was a Republican member of the House from New York, 1877–81.

SATURDAY 24. Cousin Orrin left us for home, having spent a week with us. Worked at my desk until 10 o'clock, when I spent nearly two hours at the Departments. At twelve o'clock attended the meeting of the Committee on Ways and Means. Two hours and a half were spent on the Funding Bill. No conclusion was reached. The House was not in session. At eight o'clock the Literary Society met at our house. About ninety people were in attendance. A translation from the German was read by Mrs. Coleman and a paper by Dr. Gallaudet on the poetry of the deaf. A very interesting essay. The party broke up at half-past eleven.

SUNDAY, 25. Spent the day at home. Dictated a large number of letters and made a valiant struggle to reduce the pile of unanswered letters. Among other things I wrote a letter to Senator R. A. Horr, who had asked my opinion on the Presidential nomination to be made at Chicago in June next. I expressed the opinion that the State of Ohio ought to support Sherman.[25]

MONDAY, 26. Before I had finished the reading of my mail, I was sent for to go with Townsend and McKinley to the President's and the Treasury on business. Went thence to the Capitol and attended the meeting of the Committee of Ways and Means, where the discussion of the Funding Bill was continued. Judge Kelley has now a new kink in his head to the effect that we ought not to refund the debt at all, but that if we pay it in accordance with the Sinking Fund, it will cost us about one and a half per cent interest.[26] I replied that if we should pay it all off tomorrow [end of entry]

TUESDAY, 27. Dictated a large number of letters and answered numerous calls until half-past ten o'clock, when I went to the Capitol and attended the Committee on Ways and Means. The room was filled with sugar men and Mr. Searles[27] of Connecticut

[25]Horr, who had worked for the election of Garfield to the Senate, released to the press Garfield's letter, which was written with that in mind.

[26]See n. 23, January 22, 1880.

[27]John E. Searles (1840-1908) began his career as a bookkeeper and clerk. In 1862 he became a partner in the West India shipping firm of L. W. & P. Armstrong of New Haven, Connecticut, which soon developed a large sugar business. He assisted in organizing the Havemeyer Sugar Refining Company in 1880 and the

made a speech favoring a uniform duty on the lower grades of sugar. In the House after the morning hour the day was devoted to a discussion of the codified rules and good progress was made. I came home at half-past four and dictated a large number of letters to Brown. Had not less than forty callers during the evening. Rose also came and I dictated to him for some time.

WEDNESDAY, 28. Dictated letters until ten o'clock, when I went to the Treasury Department with some iron men from Youngstown and Cleveland protesting against the ruling of the Department, which let in hoop iron cut to length, under the residuary clause, [at] 35 per [cent] ad valorem, instead of under the specific clause relating to hoop iron. Thence to the Committee on Ways and Means and listened for an hour to arguments on the sugar question. After the morning hour the House took up the report of the Committee on Rules. Mr. Tucker offered an amendment to enable the Speaker to count a quorum when members refused to vote. I made a speech in opposition and all the Republicans around me and some Democrats, among them Alexander Stephens, supported me.[28] Home in the evening. Dictated letters

---

Sugar Refineries Company in 1887. He became secretary, treasurer and chief executive officer of the latter organization, which was rechartered in 1891 as the American Sugar Refining Company.

[28]Tucker's amendment provided that "whenever a quorum fails to vote on any question, and objection is made for that cause, there shall be a call of the House, and the yeas and nays on the pending question shall at the same time be ordered. The Clerk shall call the roll, and each member as he answers to his name, or is brought before the House under the proceedings of the call of the House, shall vote on the pending question. If those voting on the question and those who are present and decline to vote shall together make a majority of the House, the Speaker shall declare that a quorum is constituted; and the pending question shall be decided as the majority of those voting shall appear." Garfield argued that the amendment gave excessive power to the Speaker and to the chairman of the Committee of the Whole, either of whom could declare that a quorum was present when in fact there was no quorum. The next day, Tucker withdrew his amendment, explaining that the opposition of Republicans and many Democrats, and his unwillingness to fight to alter a longstanding practice of the House, prompted his action, even though he believed that the amendment was a good one. In 1890, during the speakership of Thomas B. Reed, the Republican majority in the House adopted the procedure Garfield opposed.

until ten o'clock, when Crete and I attended Judge Strong's reception, returning at half-past eleven.

THURSDAY, 29. Worked at my desk until ten o'clock, when I went to the State Department with Mr. Whitney,[29] the Attorney of the New York Life Insurance Co., to ask the Secretary's intervention in some troubles the Company is having in France. Thence to the Capitol to attend the meeting of the Committee on Ways and Means. I tried an experiment which illustrates better than anything I have seen the frauds in the sugar tariff. I took some coarsely crystalised sugar of No. 7 Dutch standard in color and pulverised it, when it became at least No. 16 Dutch standard in color. In the House after the morning hour, the report of the Committee on Rules was resumed. Mr. Tucker withdrew his proposed amendments [amendment] of yesterday, authorizing the Speaker to count those who did not answer to their names and thus make up a quorum. An attempt was made to distribute the appropriation bills to several committees. I made a short speech in opposition.[30] Home in the evening; worked at my mail until a late hour.

FRIDAY, 30. Worked at correspondence until half-past ten o'clock, when I attended the Committee on Ways and Means. An hour and a half was devoted to the sugar question. Made a further discovery that moist sugar was about two grades lower in Dutch standard of color that [than] the same sugar thoroughly dried. A curious incident occurred in the Committee Room. The

[29]Charles C. Whitney (1832–1904) graduated at Williams College in 1853 and was for many years employed by the Western Union Telegraph Company. After the Civil War he entered life insurance and in 1876 joined the New York Life Insurance Company.

[30]Muldrow of Mississippi proposed that the Committee on Appropriations be limited to recommending appropriations for the executive, legislative, and judicial departments, the consular and diplomatic service, the sundry civil service, and general deficiencies. He further proposed that the committees on military affairs, naval affairs, foreign affairs, Indian affairs, post-offices and post-roads, commerce, agriculture, and Mississippi levees report appropriations for their respective departments. Garfield declared that the proposal would break down "all economy and good order and good management of our finances." He added that the efficiency of the Appropriations Committee could be greatly increased by disallowing riders to appropriations bills.

impudence and rascality of a man of the name of McKay. I put him under the fire of cross examination for a few moments and pretty thoroughly dissected him.[31] In the House the day was devoted to private bills. Home in the evening. Dictated letters until half-past nine, when Crete and I attended Mr. Moulton's reception.[32]

SATURDAY, 31. Worked at my desk dictating letters until half-past ten, when I went to the Capitol and attended the Committee on Ways and Means. We had a long session on the Sugar Question. An able argument by Mr. Havemeyer and others. The session continued until one o'clock; after the morning hour the House devoted the remainder of the session to eulogies on Rush Clark of Iowa and adjourned early.[33] I spent about two hours at the Departments settling Post Office questions and other similar matters. Played billiards for an hour and a half with Rockwell. At half-past eight, Crete and I called on General Schenck for half an hour and thence went to Mr. Evarts' and staid until half-past ten, when we came home.

[31]The incident, reported on the front page of the *New York Times* (January 31), occurred during testimony which showed how high grade sugar could be artificially colored to make it represent a low grade, thereby reducing considerably the duty the exporter had to pay when it entered the United States. An assistant secretary of the Treasury explained that the Treasury Department was investigating the matter, and quoted from a letter written by one Nathaniel McKay to Sir Michael Hicks-Beach, the English colonial secretary, in which McKay said that he had been given semi-official authority by the Committee on Ways and Means to determine whether artificial coloring was practiced in Demerara, British Guiana. Garfield's questioning revealed that McKay had never been concerned with the importation of sugar; had gone to Demerara not solely to investigate the sugar matter, but on business of his own; had no authorization from the committee to conduct an investigation; and had reported that coloring of sugar was not practiced in Demerara, a report that contradicted the findings of a commission appointed by colonial officials.

[32]It appears that Garfield's secretary erred in writing "Moulton," for on the evening of January 30 Representative Levi P. Morton of New York hosted a large party attended by many congressmen and other dignitaries.

[33]The House voted to dispense with the morning hour, and, after disposing of several minor items of business, devoted the rest of the session to a tribute to Rush Clark.

February

SUNDAY, 1. Brown came and I dictated a large number of letters. At 11 o'clock went with Crete and Mother to church and heard an old fashioned sermon on the action of baptism. General Robinson and Captain Frank Mason of Ohio dined with us at two. Towards evening read nearly half of Scudder's *Romance of the Great Dividable.*[34] At seven o'clock Crete and I went to Mrs. Johnson's to tea. Rockwell and his wife and Mrs. Myers [Myer], Secretary Schurz and Baron Schlözer called and we had a pleasant visit.

MONDAY, 2. My mail still continues to be very heavy. Calls, reading and dictating letters filled the morning until half-past ten when I went to the Committee on Ways and Means and took up the discussion on the Funding Bill. The House met at twelve o'clock and after the morning hour, went into Committee of the Whole on the rules and made considerable progress. The Committee on Appropriations was saved by a close vote from being divided and subsequently broken up by the distribution of its work to other Committees. At four o'clock went to Colonel Rockwell's and played billiards for a short time. Mr. and Mrs. Horace Steele dined with us at six. Letters [Later] in the evening Crete and I went with them to call on the President.

TUESDAY, 3. Worked at my Desk until half-past ten o'clock dictating letters, when I went to the Treasury Department and thence to the Capitol. Mr. H. V. Poor[35] spoke before the Committee on Ways and Means for an hour and a half on the tariff on steel rails. After the morning hour the House went into the Committee of the Whole on the new rules. A sharp debate sprang

---

[34]M[oses] L. Scudder, *Brief Honors; a Romance of the Great Dividable* (1877).

[35]Henry V. Poor (1812–1905) was an editor, author, and a recognized authority in economics. He published many works, including books on the tariff, currency and railroads. In 1867 he established with his son a firm to import rails and railway supplies, and in the following year they compiled and published the first *Manual of the Railroads of the United States,* which appeared annually under different titles for many years.

up on the distribution of the appropriations to the several Committees. I made a short speech against the wisdom of continuing the practice of riders on appropriation bills. Randall attacked me somewhat sharply and I replied to him, I think to the general satisfaction of the House. In the evening dictated a few letters to Brown, then went to dinner at Gardiner Hubbard's on K Street. Secretary Evarts, Chief Justice Waite, Judge Harlan, Senator Hill, Congressman [Congressmen] Frye and Reed. After dinner went home with Judge Harlan accompanied by Reed and Frye and played whist for an hour or two. Home at twelve.

WEDNESDAY, 4. Worked at my desk until half-past ten o'clock when I went to the Capitol. In the Committee the hearing on the duty on steel rails was continued. James F. Wilson[36] of Iowa addressed the Committee. In the House after the morning hour debate was resumed on the Rules. Swaim came in the morning. Played billiards with him and Rockwell in the afternoon. Home in the evening.[37]

THURSDAY, 5. Letters at desk until ten. Went to the Treasury Department on business. With the Committee on Ways and Means from eleven until half-past twelve. Hearing on steel rails continued. Brilliant speech before the Committee of Emory [Emery] Storrs of Chicago.[38] In the House after the morning

---

[36]James F. Wilson (1828–1895), a Republican member of the U.S. House of Representatives from Iowa, 1861–69, and of the Senate, 1883–95. He appeared before the Ways and Means Committee to urge, on behalf of several western railroad companies, a reduction of the tariff on steel rails. He was appointed a director of the Union Pacific Railroad by President Grant.

[37]Information belonging in the entry for February 11 was included in the entry for February 4 (the entry is in the hand of Garfield's secretary, George Rose). When the error was discovered the secretary wrote "Wednesday 11, 1880" above the first words of the erroneous part of the entry. On February 11, after the words "Governor Pound called" he wrote in parenthesis "see Wednesday 4, 1880." The February 11 portion of the entry for February 4 has been transferred to the entry for February 11, and the secretary's cross reference omitted.

[38]Emery A. Storrs (1835–1885), a Chicago lawyer and eloquent speaker, appeared in behalf of steel manufacturers, opposing any reduction of the duty on steel rails. An active Republican, he was a delegate to the national Republican

hour the usual humdrum on the rules. At five o'clock went to Fernando Wood's for a short talk in the evening. Crowd of callers after my return. Commenced work on the Fitz John Porter Case.

FRIDAY, 6.   Worked at my desk until half-past nine o'clock, when I went to the Agricultural Department in company with Major McKinley and Capt. Blackford to secure a place for the latter. Returned and worked at my desk until twelve, when I went to the Capitol. The day was devoted to private bills. I went to the Library and looked after some documents in the Fitz John Porter Case, which is coming up next week. In the evening Brown came and I dictated a number of letters. Swaim and I spent some time in studying the Porter Case.

SATURDAY, 7.   Worked at my mail all day until two o'clock, when I went to the Departments and then played billiards for an hour. At seven in the evening, I dined at Mr. Walter Wood's[39] on I Street with a large and pleasant company of Senators and members.

SUNDAY, 8.   Remained at home until eleven o'clock when Swaim and I went to McCook's and spent three hours listening to his speech on the Fitz John Porter case and making suggestions at various points. Home in the afternoon and worked on the case, for which I must prepare a speech.

MONDAY, 9.   Dictated letters until twelve o'clock when I went to the Capitol. A crowd of callers constantly interfering with my work. But little work was done in the House, except a discussion of the Hot Springs Reservation Bill.[40] Dictated a few letters

---

conventions of 1868, 1872, and 1880. In 1876–77 and 1880–81 he had some support for the office of U.S. attorney general.

[39]Walter A. Wood (1815–1892), inventor and manufacturer of agricultural implements, was a Republican member of the House from New York, 1879–83.

[40]In 1832 Congress reserved "for the future disposal of the United States" the hot springs in Arkansas Territory, "together with four sections of land including such springs, as near the center thereof as may be." Over the years the small city of Hot Springs grew up in the reserved area without authorization from the federal government; as a result, land titles there were under a shadow. The bill that became law on June 16, 1880, enabled claimants approved by a commission established by Congress in 1877 to buy the land claimed at forty per cent of the appraised value as determined by the commission. Lands were given to the town

in the evening and at seven o'clock Crete and I went to the President's to a dinner given in honor of Mrs. Astor.[41] There were present about twenty people, among them Secretary Evarts, Secretary Schurz, Judge Swayne, Senator Hoar and myself and ladies. A very pleasant dinner. Mrs. Astor was covered with diamonds, such a display of which I have never before seen. Rumor says that her outfit of diamonds is worth one million dollars. It is impossible for me to understand how a woman can make herself willing to become a show case to such an extent. At half-past nine o'clock we went to Zamacona's, the Mexican Minister, who had a great party.[42] His house was brilliantly illuminated and elaborately decorated.

TUESDAY, 10. Worked at my desk until half-past ten o'clock, when I attended the Committee on Ways and Means. Several private bills were acted upon, among them one for N. and G.

---

of Hot Springs and to a church there. The hot and warm springs area was "forever reserved from sale and dedicated to public use as parks. . . ." Remaining lands were to be sold at public auction, the receipts to go for a special fund to improve and care for the hot springs reservation.

[41]The party was in honor of John Jacob Astor (1822–1890) of New York, and his wife, Charlotte Augusta (Gibbes) Astor. Like Garfield, the Astors went from this party to one given by the Mexican minister to the United States. The next evening Mrs. Astor was in the "receiving party" at the White House reception for the diplomatic corps, and, according to "Miss Grundy" in a despatch to the *Philadelphia Times* (February 10), she wore diamonds estimated to be worth two million dollars, "and they were not the same jewels as last evening. It is said that she always has a body guard of policemen armed to the teeth on her carriage when she wears these precious stones. Her dress was pearl-colored satin brocade trimmed with rare lace. The neck was cut square and bordered with diamonds, as others would use glass beads. She had several strands of black pearls around her throat, falling below a black velvet ribbon studded with diamonds. The whole front of the waist was covered with diamonds; several ornaments of these jewels were worn in the hair and the diamond bracelets on the arms."

[42]Commenting on the party given by Manuel Marie de Zamacona (1826–1904), Mexican minister to the United States, 1878–82, the *Washington Star* (February 10) said that "Washington is indebted to the Minister from Mexico for an entertainment which combined more of the elements of good taste and magnificence than anything ever before devised for its enjoyment."

Taylor and Co. of Philadelphia,[43] in relation to the payment of customs duties. Not much was accomplished in the House and the adjournment was early. At six o'clock Crete and I went to J. B. Alley's[44] to dinner. Mr. Alley's residence is on the outskirts of the City. Quite a large party were present at dinner, among them Senators Ferry and Edmunds. At nine o'clock we returned and at half-past nine in company with Mrs. Dahlgren and Swaim attended the President's Reception, which was given to the Diplomatic Corp[s], and was one of the most brilliant I have ever seen in Washington.[45] This closes the social season. For the present people of all religions are Episcopalian, as Lent here in Washington relieves them of the necessity of social calls for a time.

WEDNESDAY, 11. Worked at my desk until half-past ten when I went to the Committee on Ways and Means. Secretary Sherman was before the Committee on the Funding Bill. We had a very interesting examination of his opinion. The Committee resolved to vote tomorrow on the various propositions connected with refunding. In the House after the morning hour, the rules were taken up and considerable progress made. Played billiards with Swaim and Rockwell a little while before supper. Home in the evening. My time was taken up until after ten o'clock with callers. I doubt if I have ever been so raided before, not less than 75 people having called on me on matters of business. Among others Governor Pound called on me for a serious talk on the Presidential question. He expressed the opinion that unless

[43]The company manufactured tin plate, and roofing tin which it produced covered many of the buildings at the centennial exposition.

[44]John B. Alley (1817–1896), of Massachusetts, a shoe manufacturer who was for a time active in state and local politics, was a Republican member of the U.S. House of Representatives, 1859–67, and was for many years affiliated with the Union Pacific Railroad Company. The party was given in honor of his newly wed son and daughter-in-law.

[45]In his diary for February 11, Hayes, who was much absorbed in his plan for an Isthmian waterway, wrote simply that "our diplomatic reception last evening was very successful. The Senators and Representatives quite generally attended." See T. Harry Williams, ed., *Hayes: the Diary of a President, 1875–1881*, p. 263.

Grant was nominated with substantial unanimity, he could not be elected and he believed neither Blaine nor Sherman could be. He furthermore expressed a belief that the Convention would be compelled to take up some other man and that I was likely to be its choice. He approved of the attitude I had taken on the subject, but wished me to hold myself free from any entanglements, so that should the contingency arise to which he referred I might be unfettered.

I told him that I had observed the course of comments in the public press and in numerous letters which I had received, but that I did not regard the subject as at all serious, especially as it related to me, nor did I believe that the matter would turn out as he expected; that whatever happenned, I should act in perfect good faith towards Mr. Sherman and do nothing that would in the slightest degree interfere with his chances for success; at the same time, I would consider such suggestions as he might make always within the limitations just mentioned.

THURSDAY, 12. Worked at my desk intending to go to the Capitol, but my watch ran down and I did not discover it until after eleven. Took a carriage and drove rapidly to the Capitol. The Committee had voted on several matters, but none had been taken on the Funding Bill. I had my vote recorded and at half-past twelve the Committee settled upon a bill—for 3 1/2 per [cent] 20–40 bonds and short time certificates at 4 per cent. I voted against the 3 1/2 per cent, not believing that it could be successful. On my motion the Third Section which relates to the reserve for resumption was separated from the bill. In the House the day was given to the Committee on Rules. In the evening worked on the Fitz John Porter case.

FRIDAY 13. Worked at my desk until 12 o'clock, when I went to the Capitol. After the morning hour Sparks of Illinois undertook to bring up the Fitz John Porter case. He was antagonized by Mr. Bright[46] in favor of going to the Private Calendar. A number of people were in the galleries expecting the Porter debate to come

[46]John W. Bright (1817–1911) was a Democratic member of the House from Tennessee, 1871–81.

off. Among them Porter himself, who I have never seen since I saw him in the room of the Court Martial seventeen years ago. He has grown very gray since then, and I pity him for the great misfortune which he brought on his own life. Really the political spirit of the McClellan Cabal in the Army of the Potomac is as guilty as Porter himself and probably was the cause of his crime. Sparks's motion was defeated by a decisive vote. I think some of the Democrats are beginning to be alarmed at the prospect of a fight over Porter and what may come of it. The day in the House was spent on private bills. At three o'clock I called on the venerable Joseph Holt, late Judge Advocate General in the Army.[47] I found him alone in his large house on New Jersey Avenue, where he seems to live in great seclusion. He greeted me with great cordial[ity] and we had a long and to me very interesting conversation. This historical part of it I note.

On my reference to the charge made by Porter's defenders that President Lincoln approved the finding of the Court without reading the record, reading only Holt's summary of the case, General Holt said: "I read my review of the law and the testimony in the Porter case to President Lincoln and Mr. Stanton. My interview with those two men was very impressive. I read my review slowly and carefully, Lincoln and Stanton frequently interrupting with questions and references to the testimony.

I was surprised to find how perfectly familiar the President was with the proceedings and the testimony and I expressed my astonishment that in the midst of his great cares, he had been able to read it all so carefully. He had followed the proceedings from day to day during the session. When I read that portion of the case which indicates that Porter must have known that Pope's Army was being driven from the sound of the artillery, Lincoln stopped me and said 'I distinctly heard that Battle from the southern windows of the War Department and I knew that the Army was retreating from the sound of the guns.' " Home in the evening. Dictated letters and did miscellaneous work. At nine

[47]As judge advocate general, Holt prosecuted the government's case against Porter in 1862.

o'clock, went to Secretary Sherman's, at his request, to consult with him on the political situation in Ohio.

SATURDAY, 14. No meeting of the House today.[48] I worked at my letters until eleven o'clock, when I took a carriage and drove to the several Departments and spent two hours in running around for my constituents and correspondents. Lunch at half-past one; wrote and received calls until three. Played billiards with Swaim an hour. At seven o'clock in the evening the Committee on Ways and Means gave a dinner to Messrs. Gibson and myself celebrating our election to the Senate.[49] It was a very beautiful dinner and the strongest expressions of kindness and friendship were given by several of the member[s]. Randolph Tucker of Virginia enlivened the evening by some of the wittiest and most effective anecdotes I have ever heard told. The story of the shooting stars in Virginia in 1833 was one of the most powerful pieces of acting I have ever seen.[50] Take him all in all he is a most remarkable man. Home at twelve o'clock.

SUNDAY, 15. Got as much sleep as I could before a late breakfast. Went with Swaim, Nichol, Mother and Crete to All Souls Church hoping to hear Dr. Collyer,[51] but found the church so crowded

[48]The House met on Saturday and by previous arrangement resolved itself into a Committee of the Whole on the State of the Union for the sole purpose of allowing members to debate on any subject they wished.

[49]On January 20, 1880, Randall Lee Gibson was elected to the United States Senate by the state legislature of Louisiana for a six year term to begin on March 4, 1883.

[50]Tucker, a Virginian, was nine years old at the time of the "star shower" of 1833, which began at approximately 11:00 P.M., November 12, when numerous meteors began falling through the sky over the American continent. Sailors far out on the Atlantic Ocean and trappers in the Rocky Mountains observed the phenomenon. Comparable only "to one grand and continued discharge of fireworks," the spectacle went on until daylight rendered it invisible. The bright flashes of light awakened people in their beds and caused many to fear that the end of the world was at hand. For eyewitness accounts of this event, see Denison Olmsted, "Observations on the Meteors of November 13th, 1833," in *The Americal Journal of Science and Arts,* Vol. XXV (January, 1834), pp. 363–411.

[51]Robert Collyer (1823–1912), a native of England, migrated to the United States in 1850 and settled in Shoemakertown, Pennsylvania, where he became a blacksmith and a Methodist lay preacher. In 1859 he entered the Unitarian minis-

that the ladies could not get in. Crete, Mother and I went on to the Disciple Church. At two o'clock Archibald Campbell and wife of West Virginia and C. Thompson of Louisville dined with us. After dinner several friends called. At half-past seven in the evening Crete, Mollie and I attended All Souls Church and heard a powerful sermon by Dr. Collyer from the text "I was in the spirit on the Lord's day." At my desk during the remainder of the evening. Retired at half-past eleven.

MONDAY, 16.   Brown came and I dictated letters until half-past 9, when Rose came and I continued until half-past ten when I went to the Capitol to attend the meeting of the Committee on Rules. Not a full attendance so the meeting was postponed. Shortly after the assembling of the House, I called the Republican Caucus Committee of Nine and consulted over the Fitz John Porter Case. I urged the importance of having debate on that question and the Committee resolved to aid in bringing up the question for consideration. After two o'clock the day was devoted to the District of Columbia. I came home at four and dictated a few letters and at half-past seven went to the National Hotel to attend a meeting of the Committee on Rules. Returned home at half-past ten and worked with Swaim on the Fitz John Porter case until half-past one.

TUESDAY, 17.   Worked at my desk until half-past ten o'clock, when I went to the Capitol to attend the meeting of the Committee on Ways and Means. We finished the Refunding Bill and ordered it to be reported to the House. I voted against [it] not believing the terms of the proposed bond are wise or likely to make it a success. In the House the day was devoted to the Committee on Rules. Had a continuous struggle for nearly two hours over the rule in relation to independent legislation on appropriation bills. The Democracy beat us by one vote after a close contest. They seem determined as a point of honor to maintain their rule. In the evening Judge Kinsman and Harmon

try and held a pastorate in the Unity Church, Chicago, 1859–79, and the Church of the Messiah, New York City, 1879–1903. Studious and hard-working, he was a self-made man who had great renown as an eloquent preacher and lecturer.

Austin came to visit us. I called on Secretary Sherman at his request to confer about the condition of his canvass in Cleveland. It appears that there is much opposition to him in Northern Ohio. I have agreed to assist him. On my return worked on the Fitz John Porter case until late in the evening.

WEDNESDAY, 18.   Worked at my desk until half-past ten o'clock, when I went to the Navy Department with Blackburn of Kentucky to recommend the promotion of Captain Jouatt [Jouett].[52] Thence to the Capitol and attended the meeting of the Committee on Ways and Means. In the House a large part of the day was consumed in hearing and discussing the report in reference to the behavior of J. M [H]. Acklen, a member from the State of Louisiana.[53] Had the case referred to the Committee on the Judiciary. Wharton Barker[54] of Harrisburg came to see [me] in reference to the proposed commercial union with Canada, and read me a letter which he intends to send to some parties in Canada. He

---

[52]James E. Jouett (1826–1902), a native of Kentucky, had a long and distinguished career in the United States navy. During the Civil War he served with the blockading squadron on the Gulf Coast and in the Battle of Mobile Bay received from David G. Farragut the historic command: "Damn the torpedoes. . . . Jouett, full speed!" His efforts in 1880 to secure promotion ahead of sixteen superior officers were unsuccessful, but they created much bad feeling. He was promoted to commodore in January, 1883, and to rear admiral three years later. He retired at the latter rank in 1890.

[53]Acklen had requested an investigation of a statement in the *Detroit Post and Tribune* (January 26) accusing him of violating established procedures of the House by asking for the printing of a report of the Committee on Foreign Affairs, a report which that Committee had never seen! Acklen explained that the controversy resulted from a misunderstanding that was no fault of his, and he denounced the paper's accusation as "perhaps one of the most willful and malicious perversions of fact on record." The matter was referred to the Judiciary Committee which subsequently submitted a report asking that the testimony in the case be printed for the Committee's own use. The House approved the request.

[54]Wharton Barker (1846–1921), of Philadelphia, Republican, financier and publicist, opposed a third term for Grant and was one of the first to propose and work for Garfield's nomination as Republican candidate for President. Years later Barker claimed that Garfield knew and approved of his plans to defeat Grant, Sherman, and Blaine, and to secure the nomination of Garfield. (See entry for April 24, 1880.)

gave me some interesting facts in regard to the relation of the Dominion with the United States. He also told me that they were organizing Young Republican Clubs in Pennsylvania; that they do not believe that either of the three candidates Grant, Blaine, or Sherman can be elected and he and his friends were in favor of nominating me. I told him I would not be a candidate and did not wish my name discussed in that connection, and if anything happenned to me in that connection, it would only be in case the Convention at Chicago should find that they could not nominate either of the candidates and I should do nothing to procure such a result; that I was working in good faith for Sherman and should continue to do so. Home in the evening, several friends called. Swaim and I worked until half-past twelve. I should have added in this connection, that Mr. Sherman said that in case he could not be nominated, he preferred me to any other man and that he would be entirely willing to have his strength transferred to me.

THURSDAY, 19. Worked at my desk until half-past ten, when I went to the Committee on Ways and Means, where several private bills were disposed of. In the House the day was consumed in a long struggle on the rules. We succeeded by a strong effort in gaining a victory and afterwards lost it by the indiscretion of Mr. Robeson who desired to strike out all the "rider" clause, in which the Democrats joined and thereby killed our former amendment, and of course when they get into the House will be able to beat us finally.[55] Home in the evening. Swaim and I

---

[55]Before Robeson presented his amendment, the Committee of the Whole, which was debating Rule XXI, had defeated several proposals authorizing riders to appropriations bills, and had approved an amendment by Adoniram J. Warner, a Democrat of Ohio, which placed stringent limitations on attaching riders to any general appropriations bill. Robeson's amendment nullified all this by striking out Warner's proposal and, as the chairman of the Committee of the Whole explained, "other matter which was reported by the Committee on Rules." Robeson's amendment was adopted, with the help of Democrats, who then approved a substitute clause authorizing riders to appropriations bills. The *New York Times* (February 20) attributed the Democratic victory to the blundering management of "Garfield, Robeson, and a few others on the Republican side who are ambitious for leadership." See n. 69, March 2, 1880.

worked on the Fitz John Porter case. Crete took Mother, Austin and Kinsman to the President's house and also to the Ebbitt House to call on President Pendleton and wife.

FRIDAY, 20. Worked at the desk until half-past ten when I went with Mr. ———— to call on the President and Secretary of State. Went thence to the Capitol, worked in the Library for half an hour. In the House after the morning hour the day was devoted to the rules and considerable progress was made. In the evening Mrs. Pendleton, Judge Black and his wife dined with us, and in the evening about 60 friends called. Crete held an informal reception. After the guests retired Swaim and I worked a while on the Fitz John Porter case. Retired about half-past twelve.

SATURDAY, 21. No meeting of the House; Brown and Rose came. I dictated letters steadily until half-past twelve [ten?] when I went to the Committee on Ways and Means. At half-past twelve o'clock went to the Department of the Interior, Post Office Department, Treasury Department and State Department on business. Played billiards for two hours later in the afternoon. In the evening at eight went to Kendall Green, to President Gallaudet's with Crete, and attended the meeting of the Literary Society. The hour was devoted to memories of Washington. Some interesting original memoranda were presented, and many valuable suggestions as to his life were made. Home at half-past eleven o'clock.

SUNDAY, 22. Crete, Mother and I attended church and listened to a sermon from President Pendleton of Bethany. At one o'clock Major Gardiner[56] of the Judge Advocate's Corps came and spent the afternoon and a good part of the evening going over the grounds of the Fitz John Porter case. Retired at 10 o'clock with a sharp headache.

MONDAY, 23. Brown came. I dictated a number of letters until half-past nine when Rose came and I continued until 11 o'clock, [when I] went to the Capitol to attend a meeting of the Committee on Ways and Means, which was devoted to private bills. In

[56]Asa Bird Gardiner (1839–1919), lawyer, army officer (he was awarded the congressional medal of honor for his service in the Gettysburg campaign), author, and authority on military law, was designated by President Hayes in 1878 to be the government's counsel in the Fitz John Porter case.

the House the usual bills were introduced during the morning hour, after which eulogies were pronounced on the late Mr. Lay from Missouri.[57] Adjourned early. Came home at two o'clock and worked at my desk for some time. Played billiards with Swaim and Rockwell later in the afternoon. In the evening called with Crete at Dr. Updegraff's and at half-past eight Swaim and I visited Amos Townsend.

TUESDAY, 24. Worked at my desk until half-past ten o'clock, when I went to the Committee on Ways and Means, where the sugar question was debated quite fully but no conclusion reached. At half past twelve o'clock went to the Interior Department with Horace Steele on business, but found the Secretary absent to Cabinet meeting. Adjourned to the Capitol. After the morning hour, which was devoted to the Judicial Bill, the House went into Committee of the Whole on the Rules. I took part in the debate against a rule offered by Mr. Turner[58] of Kentucky proposing that at the end of 30 days all bills referred to Committees by a majority of the House be taken from the Committee and put upon their passage. I resisted it as a disorganizing measure and it was defeated by a large vote. Left the House at half-past three with a leave of absence for three days. Came home and took Swaim, Mollie and Crete to visit the house of Mrs. Henry.[59] Rose came, dictated letters. At half-past seven Crete and I took the Baltimore and Ohio train West.

WEDNESDAY, 25. Awoke near Pittsburgh where we arrived a few minutes before seven. Went to the Monongahela House and crossed the bridge in time for the train on the Lake Shore Road. Reached Youngstown at 12 o'clock, where several friends found me on the train and called during my ten minutes' stop. Reached Cleveland at two o'clock, where Dr. Robison's carriage was waiting and took us to his house. Dr. Streator was waiting there to

[57]Alfred M. Lay (1836–1879) was a Democratic member of the House from Missouri, March 4, 1879, to his death on December 8.

[58]Oscar Turner (1825–1896) was a Democratic member of the House from Kentucky, 1879–85.

[59]Harriet (Alexander) Henry, widow of Joseph Henry.

see me. At 4.50 Dr. Robison, his wife and their household went with us to the Lake Shore Road Depot where we took the train for Mentor. We were delayed an hour by the wreck of a freight train. Reached the station at seven o'clock and found [Ira J.] Green awaiting us with our grays and the carriage and Northcott with the Doctor's Omnibus. We were driven to the Doctor's where we spent the night. I should have added that Mr. Judd, a Cleveland builder, went with us to Mentor.

THURSDAY, 26. After breakfast we all went to our house and spent the forenoon in making a careful examination of the frame of it and devising the best means for raising the upper story and making repairs. Found the horses, cattle and sheep in good condition and farm looking well. The change of the ram to a lower position in the field is being proceeded with. Dinner at the Doctor's and returned to our house, where we spent the afternoon in removing the furniture and crockery into the library, taking the piano over to Mrs. King's to be left until we returned. Spent the night at Dr. Robison's. Just as I was going to bed, General Fitch and Mr. Allen came from Madison, having seen in the newspapers that I was home on political business.

FRIDAY, 27. Took the morning train to Cleveland. At half-past nine o'clock Mr. Judd came and we completed our plans for the repair of the house. He will have a draft made and sent to us for approval. At twelve o'clock went to the Case building, where a dozen or fifteen men called to see me on the political situation. Mayor Erritt [Herrick][60] was elected as Chairman and Mr. McFarland[61] Secretary. At the request of these persons I spoke

[60]Rensselar R. Herrick (1826–1899), a native of New York, moved to Cleveland in 1836 and became a builder and contractor, retiring from that work in 1870. He was elected mayor of Cleveland in 1879, and re-elected in 1881. He was for a time president of the Dover Bay Grape and Wine Company, which he helped to organize. In 1890 he became president of the Produce Exchange Banking Company, which was organized in that year.

[61]William C. McFarland (1838–1904), a native of Pennsylvania and a Republican member of the Ohio house of representatives, 1872–73, was a Cleveland lawyer.

a few minutes, giving my reasons why Grant ought not to be nominated and expressing the opinion that Ohio ought to give its vote to Sherman in order that he and Blaine might have strength enough to prevent the nomination of Grant.[62] It is evident, however, that it will be very difficult to carry this part of Ohio for Sherman. Dinner at Dr. Robison's. At 2.40 Crete and I took the Mahoning train for the east. Saw Brother Joe and his two children at the depot. At Solon two of my nieces called at the train to see us. At Garrettsville, Brother Joe's wife joined us on the road to Pittsburgh. Several members of the Legislature were on the train. At Youngstown a number of friends called to see me. Reached Pittsburgh just in time for the eastern train. Retired early.

SATURDAY, 28.   Reached home at eight o'clock in time for breakfast and found not less than 250 letters awaiting me. Shortly afterwards Brown came and I dictated a large number of answers. No meeting of the House today. Spent the forenoon and until two o'clock reading the mail. Played billiards with Swaim a portion of the afternoon. In the evening a number of friends called. I retired at half-past ten.

SUNDAY, 29.   At home all day not feeling well. George Steele and wife of Painesville dined with us and spent the afternoon. At eight o'clock got at work on the new testimony in the Fitz John Porter case. Swaim and I worked continuously until half-past

[62]The meeting was Garfield's principal reason for being in Ohio at this time. On February 17, John Sherman had sent for him "to talk about an important matter." The matter (see Garfield's entry for that date) was the opposition to Sherman's presidential candidacy in northern Ohio. This was of grave concern to the secretary of the treasury, who well knew the importance of having the Ohio delegation solidly behind him at the national convention. Garfield was embarrassed and worried by the anti-Sherman sentiment, especially in his own district, since he knew that the Sherman people would blame him. Sherman, it was said, suggested the visit to Ohio. The mission did not have the result hoped for by Sherman; at the convention he commanded only 34 of the 44 votes of the Ohio delegation. Until the final ballot nine of Ohio's votes went to Blaine and one to George F. Edmunds. Garfield's friend, Lionel Sheldon of Lorain County, who was bitterly anti-Sherman, was a member of the delegation.

twelve. The testimony of White,[63] Stewart [Stuart][64], Long-street[65] and General Schenck[66] is exceedingly strong and clear and I cannot understand how the Board could ignore it.

March

MONDAY, 1. Worked at my desk until 11 o'clock when I went to the Interior Department with George Steele. Had an interview with Secretary Schurz in reference to the appointment of Government Directors for the Pacific Railroad.[67] Thence to the Capi-

[63]B. S. White, a major on General J. E. B. Stuart's staff during the Second Battle of Bull Run, testified in October, 1878, that late in the morning of August 29, 1862, Longstreet was not in a position, as Porter contended, to repulse an attack by Porter's corps. White admitted, however, that he relied on "memory simply" regarding the events of that morning.

[64]Reference is to the official report of General J. E. B. Stuart (1833–1864), Confederate cavalry commander, on the Second Battle of Bull Run. The report, dated February 28, 1863, six months after the battle, stated in part that on August 29, 1862, Longstreet's corps was not in a position to stop Porter's advance, that he (Stuart) had dragged brush on the Gainesville road along which Porter was advancing, and that Porter, believing that the dust clouds were caused by enemy troops, stopped his forward movement. The testimony of both Longstreet and Porter contravened Stuart's report.

[65]Garfield either misspoke or was misunderstood by his secretary. The testimony of General James Longstreet (1821–1904), a corps commander in the Confederate army, was very helpful to Porter. It was the testimony of John Landstreet, a Confederate chaplain who was with Stuart during the Second Battle of Bull Run, that was damaging to Porter.

[66]Schenck, a brigadier general in the Union army during the Second Battle of Bull Run, testified that at no time on August 29, 1862, were the Confederates in strength south of the Warrenton Pike, where Porter insisted that Longstreet's corps, much stronger than his own, was in position by about noon of that day.

[67]Since Congress in 1862 chartered the Union Pacific Railroad Company to build a western railroad, construction of which was heavily subsidized by the government, the board of the company had included five government directors or commissioners. They attended board meetings, made annual inspections of the railroad and its accounts and made reports to the secretary of the interior. George Steele (1824–1881), Garfield's old friend of Painesville, Ohio, was interested in a directorship; he was not appointed.

tol where the day was consumed in the usual Monday work. I went to the Senate and heard a portion of the speech of Senator Randolph[68] who opened the debate in favor of Fitz John Porter. It was a feeble speech but he found it necessary to denounce General McDowell and the late Capt. Douglass Pope[69] as perjurers. We shall see before this debate is through how many men are to be sacrificed to the vindication of Porter. At half-past seven I went to the Executive Mansion with George Steele but found the President absent. At nine o'clock went to Sumner's on Ninth Street to attend a party given in honor of Mr. Ballou's birthday. On my return stopped at Senator Logan's and consulted with him in regard to the Porter case, on which he is to make a speech tomorrow. Retired at half-past twelve.

TUESDAY, 2.   Worked at my desk until ten o'clock, when I went to the President's with George Steele and thence to the Capitol to attend the meeting of the Committee on Ways and Means and also the Committee on Rules. Was present part of the time with each Committee. In the Committee on Rules we determined to present to the House the Rules with several amendments and press them to a final action today. In the Committee on Ways and Means, the Sugar Bill and the Steel Rails Bill were indefinitely postponed; also a bill of Mr. Morrison's reducing all tariff duties; also, on my motion, Gibson's proposition to appoint a sub-committee of five to take up the general subject of the tariff, was laid on the table. In the House the day was devoted to the Rules, which were finally adopted. I made a short speech on one phase of the subject to settle a controversy between some members of our own side.[70] In the evening at seven o'clock went with Dr.

[68]Theodore F. Randolph (1826–1883) of New Jersey was a member of the state house of assembly, 1859, of the state senate, 1862 and 1863, governor of New Jersey, 1869–72, and Democratic member of the U.S. Senate, 1875–81. He was largely responsible for Hayes's decision to reinvestigate the Porter case.

[69]Douglass Pope, who died in February, 1880, was a nephew of General John Pope, commander of the Union army at the Second Battle of Bull Run. He was on his uncle's staff during that battle and his testimony was damaging to Porter.

[70]Some Republicans, like Conger of Michigan, wished to continue the struggle to eliminate riders to appropriations bills, while others, like Frye of Maine, preferred to accept defeat and not engage in further useless debate. Claiming a moral victory for the Republicans, Garfield opposed reopening the question. But he

Updegraff to see [William B.] Thompson, Superintendent of the Railway Mail Service. Thence to Mr. Chittenden's with Wilson of West Virginia, in reference to gold mining property in North Carolina. Thence went to Archibald Campbell. Home at half-past nine and read Randolph's speech on Fitz John Porter. Retired at eleven.

WEDNESDAY, 3.   Worked at my desk until half-past ten, when I went to the Census Office on business and thence to the Capitol to attend a meeting of the Committee on Ways and Means. Mr. Tyson and his Attorney, Mr. Archer of Maryland, addressed the Committee on the subject of bichromate of potash.[71] A good many curious facts in the history of that manufacture were presented to the Committee. In the House the Judiciary Bill was passed after several ineffectual attempts to amend it. I voted against it believing that it curtails the rights of citizens to enjoy their constitutional privilege of having their cases heard in the courts of the United States.[72] After the morning hour I went to the Senate and listened to the continuation of Logan's speech. He spoke three and one-quarter hours on the Fitz John Porter case and did not finish his speech. It was very powerful. Home in the evening.

THURSDAY, 4.   Worked at my desk in the forenoon until half-past ten. Met with the Committee on Ways and Means until 12. In the

---

reviewed certain aspects of the debate on the subject and accused the Democrats of exercising all the power of party discipline upon those among them who opposed riders. He also charged that the latter were promised that no political riders would be offered in the current session, if they would let the rule remain unchanged so that the Democrats might have "the appearance of victory to cover the reality of defeat."

[71]Stevenson Archer (1827–1898), a lawyer, was a Democratic member of the House from Maryland, 1867–75. His client, Jesse Tyson, was president of the Tyson Mining Company of Baltimore County, Maryland, which mined chrome and copper and was the only manufacturer of bichromate of potash in the United States. They opposed the abolition of the tariff on bichromate of potash.

[72]In 1875 Congress had passed legislation authorizing the removal of a variety of causes from state to federal courts. The bill mentioned by Garfield (it was actually an amendment to the law of 1875) limited the causes that citizens might remove from state to federal courts. The House approved the measure on March 4, with Garfield voting against it.

House nothing striking was accomplished. Logan continued his speech, being the third day. He devoted three hours to an examination of the testimony and made powerful points against Porter all through. I think the Democrats are becoming alarmed at the developements in the case, and I doubt if they will ever allow it to come to a vote. Home in the evening and worked on the Porter case.

FRIDAY, 5. Worked at my desk until half-past 11, went [when] I went to the War Department to get some documents in connection with the Porter case. Then went to the Capitol and after the House met, went to the Senate to listen to Logan's speech. He concluded about four o'clock having in all spoken over ten hours. It was a powerful presentation of the case and I think it has considerably disturbed the defenders of Porter. At half-past seven dined with Sec'y Robeson and a number of gentlemen. Returned at quarter-past nine. A number of visitors were present. Col. Wm. Letcher of the Ohio Legislature came and spent the night with us.

SATURDAY, 6. The House was not in session today. Worked at my desk during the forenoon, went to the Departments at noon and at half-past one o'clock went to the Senate and heard Carpenter's speech on the Fitz John Porter case. It was a very bright and able presentation of the law, disfigured at the end by an unnecessary and illogical though complimentary reference to General Grant.[73] Home in the evening. Rockwell came.

SUNDAY, 7. A gloomy, rainy day. Remained at home. Wrote letters and worked on the Porter case.

MONDAY, 8. Worked at my desk until ten o'clock when I went to the Pension Office with Cousin Letcher and thence to the Capitol. In the House the New Rules went into operation at twelve o'clock. A short contest arose in reference to the meaning of some portions of them in which I took part. In the Senate Mr.

[73]Carpenter closed his speech against Porter with the comment that the Democratic effort to reverse the decision against Porter might be necessary to convince the American people that they needed "in the White House once more the steady hand, the cool head, and the patriotic heart of U.S. Grant."

Bayard spoke on the Fitz John Porter case.[74] Home in the evening. Mr. Letcher left at half-past seven.

TUESDAY, 9.   Worked at my desk until half-past ten, when I went with Mr. Hatch[75] to the President in reference to the appointment of Mr. Chamberlain of Missouri, late a soldier from Ohio, to be a Postmaster in Hatch's District in Missouri.[76] Went thence to the Capitol to attend the meeting of the Committee on Ways and Means. Further hearing on bichromate of potash. Action on some private bills. In the House the morning hour was devoted under the New Rules to references from Committees for printing and references to the Calendar. The Rules works [*sic*] admirably in clearing the dockets of Committees of their accumulated work and putting their reports in print where they can be got at. After the morning hour the Civil Service Bill of Hostetler was taken up,[77] after which a violent and bitter speech was made by House of Tennessee, denouncing the Administration and the Republican Party.[78] In the Senate McDonald of Indiana made a speech on the Porter case.[79] In the evening at seven o'clock Crete and I dined at Judge Swayne's in company with Justice Waite, wife and daughter, Mr. and Mrs. Young of Toledo[80] and Amos Townsend of Cleveland. Home at half-

---

[74]Bayard spoke in defense of Porter.

[75]William H. Hatch (1833–1896) was a Democratic member of the House from Missouri, 1879–95.

[76]Wilbur F. Chamberlain, an officer in the 29th Ohio Infantry Regiment, 1862–65, was appointed postmaster, Hannibal, Missouri, on March 19, 1880.

[77]Hostetler's bill prohibited federal officers, claimants and contractors from making contributions for political purposes.

[78]John F. House (1827–1904), a Democratic member of the House from Tennessee, 1875–83, had the floor for one hour to debate Hostetler's bill. After he had devoted his entire hour to attacking the Hayes administration and the Republican party, a motion was made to extend his time. At that point J. C. Burrows drew laughter when he remarked: "I would like to inquire of the gentleman whether, if his time be extended, he proposes to speak on this bill?"

[79]Joseph E. McDonald spoke in defense of Porter.

[80]Samuel M. Young (1806–1897) was a Toledo, Ohio, banker and businessman. His daughter Helen was married to Francis B. Swayne, a lawyer, who was the son of Noah H. Swayne, justice of the U.S. Supreme Court.

past 9 not feeling fit for work and accomplished but little.

WEDNESDAY, 10. Worked at my desk until half-past ten, when I went to the National Hotel and attended a meeting of the Committee on Rules. We made some corrections in the new rules. Capitol at 1/4 past twelve. After the morning hour the day was consumed in a lively political debate on Hostetler's bill to prevent political contributions. Richardson of New York made a very brilliant speech and placed himself among our foremost speakers.[81] Crowley of New York made a long legal argument[82] and Ben Butterworth made a very effective attack on the bill. At home in the evening and worked on the Fitz John Porter case until eleven o'clock.

THURSDAY, 11. Worked at my desk until half-past ten, when I went to the Capitol to attend the meeting of the Committee on Ways and Means. The meeting was devoted to hearing arguments on the tariff on salt. Speeches were made by Hiscock of New York and Hoar [Horr] of Michigan. In the House after the morning hour the day was devoted to a struggle on Hostetler's Civil Service Bill. After an ineffectual attempt to get the previous question and prevent further debate, a motion was made by Aiken of South Carolina, which failed by a small vote, to pass the bill. It is substantially killed, and now marks another curious blunder of the Democracy.[83] In the Senate after a speech by Jones of Florida, the Fitz John Porter bill was virtually disposed of for the session.[84] I have devoted several weeks to preparation for arguing that case and shall probably have no

[81]The "very brilliant speech" of David P. Richardson (1833–1904), a Republican member of the House from New York, 1879–83, was as "violent and bitter" toward the Democrats as House's speech was toward the Republicans.

[82]Richard Crowley did speak against Hostetler's bill, but the long legal argument was presented by Philip C. Hayes (1833–1916), a Republican member of the House from Illinois, 1877–81.

[83]After Hostetler's failure "to get the previous question," Aiken moved to lay the bill and all amendments to it on the table. The motion failed, 121–112, and there the debate ended.

[84]After the speech by Charles W. Jones (1834–1897), a Democratic member of the Senate from Florida, 1875–87, the Senate voted to lay the bill for the relief of Porter on the table.

opportunity to speak this session if ever. Home in the evening.
FRIDAY, 12. Letters in the morning. Meeting of the Committee
on Ways and Means at half-past ten, and very interesting addresses were made by Erastus Brooks[85] of the *New York Express*
and Mr. Jones[86] of the *New York Times* and Messrs. ————
[William A. Russell][87] and Miller of the House Representatives
on the subject of wood pulp as used in the manufacture of paper.
Mr. Miller showed himself to be a man of very fine ability.[88] In
the House the Deficiency Bill was taken up and debated during
the day. Home in the evening. Dictated a large number of letters
and got my desk nearer cleared than it has been for a month. A
few persons called.

[85]Erastus Brooks (1815–1886), a native of Maine, attended Brown University,
entered journalism and worked for several papers before joining his brother James
in the editorial management of the *New York Express.* He was a founder and
sometime manager of the Associated Press. In 1877 when the *Express* changed
ownership, he retired to devote more time to public service. He served several
terms in the state legislature. As a representative of the newspapers, Brooks argued
for the repeal of the duty on wood pulp. He attributed the sharp rise in recent
months of the price of newsprint to a combination of American paper manufacturers. The elimination of the duty on wood pulp would reduce the cost of manufacturing paper.

[86]George Jones (1811–1891), a native of Vermont, founded the *New York Times*
with Henry J. Raymond and others (1851). He served as the business manager
of the paper, and soon after the death of Raymond in 1861 assumed direction of
the editorial policy. He was largely responsible for the successful fight against the
Tweed Ring in New York City. As did Brooks, he favored the removal of the duty
on wood pulp.

[87]William A. Russell (1831–1899), long a manufacturer of paper in Lawrence,
Massachusetts, and a Republican member of the House, 1879–85, denied that a
combination of paper manufacturers controlled the price of paper and opposed the
bill before the committee. Many Republican manufacturers of wool, paper and
other items supported tariffs on their raw materials as a means of winning support
for the maintenance of protective duties on competing manufactures of foreign
origin.

[88]Warner Miller (1838–1918), paper manufacturer of Herkimer, New York,
pioneer and leader in the manufacture of wood pulp, and president of the American Paper and Pulp Association, was a Republican member of the House from
New York, 1879–81, and of the Senate, 1881–87. He opposed the removal of
the duty on wood pulp.

SATURDAY, 13. Worked at my desk during the forenoon and at half-past ten went to the Capitol, where two hours and a half were devoted to a public hearing on the duty on paper and paper stock.[89] There being no meeting of the House I went to the Departments. Spent an hour or two in errands. Home in the evening; a number of friends called. Swaim took Crete and the children to the theatre to see Mary Anderson.[90] I worked at my desk and read Metternich.[91]

SUNDAY, 14. Attended church with Mother and Crete. In the forenoon Brown came and I dictated letters until in the evening when several friends called. At quarter before nine Swaim and I went to the Sixth Street Depot and after waiting an hour and a half took the train for New York.

MONDAY, 15. Arrived at New York at eight o'clock and went to the Sturtevant House. Spent the day in shopping. Concluded to change from Devlin to Brooks Bros. for my cloth[e]s. Had a long and interesting conversation with John Roach[92] on the subject of

[89]This was a continuation of the hearing before the Ways and Means Committee of March 12; Warner Miller, William A. Russell and Erastus Brooks were again among the speakers.

[90]Mary Anderson (1859–1940), an American actress of remarkable charm and beauty, made her stage debut as Juliet at the age of sixteen. She toured the United States for some years, acting various roles, one of her most famous being Rosalind. Garfield saw her at the National Theater as Parthenia in *Ingomar.*

[91]An English translation of Prince Richard Metternich's edition of the *Memoirs of Prince Metternich, 1773–1835,* appeared in five volumes (1880–1882). Mrs. Alexander (Robina) Napier translated Volumes I–IV and Gerard W. Smith translated Volume V. Volumes I and II appeared in 1880.

[92]John Roach was an active supporter of Garfield in the presidential campaign of 1880. Shortly before the October elections in Ohio and Indiana he contributed $2,000 for use in one of those states. He prepared a pamphlet that was widely circulated among workingmen on the stake of the workers in a protective tariff and Garfield's views on the subject as set forth in his letter of acceptance. A few days before the November election he presided at a meeting of workingmen in Chester, Pennsylvania, where his Delaware Iron Ship Building and Engine Works was located. It was his opinion that the emphasis in the campaign on Garfield's view of a protective tariff as a means of national defense brought about the Republican victory in New York—without which Garfield would not have been elected. As a ship builder, Roach was interested in the expansion of the U.S. merchant marine and the U.S. navy.

Eads's scheme for the Panama Railroad[93] and also for the general improvement of American commerce. He told me that on the occasion of Grant's late reception in Philadelphia, Roach promised to send his two thousand workmen up to town and found that only 50 of them were able to go, although he provided a special and free train to take them there and back. Their reason for refusal was that they did not believe in a third term and not until he paid their wages during the day's absence did they consent to go. Roach gave this as a reason for believing that the working men of the country would not support Grant. Major Gardiner and General McKibbin[94] called on us during the evening and at nine o'clock I left the hotel and at ten boarded the train for Washington. Swaim left New York for Fort Leavenworth.

TUESDAY, 16.   Arrived in Washington at half-past six o'clock and found a large mail awaiting me. Worked at my desk until half-past ten, when I called on the President in behalf of General B [D]. W. Lindsay [Lindsey][95] of Kentucky, who is seeking a Judgeship. I had recommended Samuel McKee and asked the President in regard to him when he informed me that he could not appoint McKee. Thereupon I recommended Lindsey. Went thence to the Committee on Ways and Means. Aldrich's bill for direct importation to interior ports, such as Chicago, Cleveland, Buffalo, etc., was passed. Home in the evening; worked at my

[93]After completing his projects on the Mississippi River (see Vol. III, p. 99), Eads devoted most of his remaining years to promoting a ship railway across the Isthmus of Tehuantepec (he opposed a canal across the Isthmus of Panama, which would result in a route some 2,000 miles longer than the Tehuantepec route), but his efforts to win the necessary support of Congress were in vain.

[94]David B. McKibbin (1831–1890), a native of Pennsylvania, was an officer in the army most of the time from 1855 to 1875, when he retired as major. During the Civil War, in which he was wounded several times, he was breveted colonel, brigadier general and major general of volunteers.

[95]Daniel W. Lindsey of Frankfort, Kentucky, commanded the 22nd Kentucky Volunteer Infantry Regiment in Garfield's Eighteenth Brigade during the Sandy Valley campaign. He served during most of the war in the western theater as a brigade commander, winning promotion to brigadier general late in the conflict. The President appointed John W. Barr of Louisville to the U.S. district judgeship in Kentucky vacated upon the death of William H. Hayes.

desk until nine o'clock, when I called with Nichol at John Hay's
and Amos Townsend's. Both of them were out. Then called at
Haskell's. Home at half-past ten. Retired at eleven.

WEDNESDAY, 17. Worked at my desk until half-past 10, when I
went to the Capitol to attend the meeting of the Committee on
Ways and Means. In the House the Deficiency Appropriation
Bill was taken up and I got the floor and made a speech of
twenty-five minutes on the Democratic attitude against obeying
the election laws. I made a strong presentation of the theme
"Obedience to law the duty of Congress as well as of the People." The speech was I think very effective. Twenty thousand
copies were subscribed for in a few moments and I learned
afterward, in the evening, that the Congressional Committee
ordered fifty thousand copies for distribution.[96] At home in the
evening and revised the notes of the speech.

THURSDAY, 18. The same story as yesterday both as to work at
home and in the Committee. Debate on the Deficiency bill continued under the five minute rule during the day. I find the
Democrats are a good deal disturbed with my speech.

FRIDAY, 19. Attending the meeting of the Committee on Ways
and Means in the morning and at twelve o'clock the Sub-Committee on Hoop Iron, consisting of Tucker, Carlisle[97] and myself,
listened to a long argument from R [J]. M. Wilson for the Iron

[96]On March 12, John A. McMahon introduced the Deficiency Bill with a speech
explaining that the measure contained no appropriation for special deputy marshals. "I doubt," said McMahon, "whether the democratic party ever will appropriate any money for such special deputies so long as the law stands in its present
shape." He also pointed out that the bill had no appropriation for the special
deputy marshals used in the recent California election. In his judgment those
marshals had already been paid by the Republican Central Committee. In a strong
reply Garfield declared that the Supreme Court, in a seven-to-two decision, had
recently upheld the constitutionality of the election laws, that the Democratic
position, as represented by McMahon, amounted to nullifying the law and thwart-
ing the collective will of the nation, and that "this cool, calm, deliberate assassination of the law will not be tolerated."

[97]John G. Carlisle (1835–1910), lieutenant governor of Kentucky, 1871–75,
was a Democratic member of the House, 1877–90 (he was Speaker, 1883–89),
and of the Senate, 1890–93. He was secretary of the treasury, 1893–97.

Manufacturers, and Scudder of New York, formerly a member of Congress, for the Importers.[98] Before the hearing was over I was sent for to come into the House, as a fierce controversy was going on in reference to my offer of two days ago to so amend the election laws as to appoint Deputy Marshals equally from the Republican and Democratic Parties.[99] Members generally had shown symptoms of returning to that proposition, which was yesterday defeated, and the fiery members of our party were opposing it because the Democrats favored it. I made a five minute speech declaring my purpose to suppose [support] the proposition if I stood alone. Although I did not vote for the proposition as a whole, my speech created a sensation.[100] I voted against the rider and against the bill because the rider was on it. I am satisfied that my independent position was the right one and that it will so prove.

SATURDAY, 20. Worked at my desk until a late hour. Went to the Departments and attended at the House for a short time. The date [day] was devoted to debate on the Funding Bill. In the evening J.H. Rhodes and Captain C.E. Henry and wife came to visit us.

[98]Secretary of the Treasury John Sherman had recently made a ruling that changed the way of assessing duty on imported hoop iron. Both Henry J. Scudder and Jeremiah M. Wilson protested the ruling, claiming that many dealers had made contracts under the old system and that some would be ruined if the new ruling was carried into effect. They wanted the Committee on Ways and Means to act on the matter.

[99]Garfield's amendment, which provided that special deputy marshals be appointed by the courts and equally from both political parties, was presented on March 18.

[100]Garfield maintained that his amendment responded to the valid complaint that the election law "had been used, or was capable of being used, to fill election precincts with men of one party whose time might be employed at the public expense for party electioneering purposes." He then pointed out that the Democrats, having defeated his bipartisan approach to preserving peace at the polls, offered a substitute proposal setting the number of marshals at no more than three in a precinct and limiting their use to three days, even though registration might lawfully continue longer, and a thousand rioters might attempt to break up an election. He voted as indicated in his entry, but the House passed the bill.

SUNDAY, 21. Attended the Unitarian Church with Rhodes and Henry. Took a long walk with them after church. After dinner Brown came and I dictated letters.

MONDAY, 22. Meeting of the Committee on Ways and Means, which was devoted to the duties on bichromate of potash. Several votes were taken. In the House under the New Rules, ordinary business was taken up so that we could get at the appropriation bills. The newspapers are fiercely discussing my speech and amendment, but on the whole they are approving it.[101] In the evening I went to hear the lecture of Joseph Cook on "Certainties in Religion." A very powerful and important subject.

TUESDAY, 23. Worked at my desk until half-past ten o'clock, then went to the Committee on Ways and Means and met until 12. In the House when the Journal was read this morning it was discovered that Townshend of Illinois had introduced a bill, whose title referred only to certain sections of the Revised Statutes, but which covered the whole subject of the tariff, and had it referred to the Committee on Revision of the Laws of which he is a member.[102] As no motion to reconsider the reference was in order, I made the unusual motion of amending the Journal, so as to show its reference to the Committee on Ways and Means, which amendment would carry the bill with it. I never had seen the motion made before but it occurred to me on the spur of

[101]Some papers were severely critical of Garfield's conduct. The *New York Times* (March 20 and 21) accused him of voting against a measure that was identical to his own amendment, and said that he had done so because leading Republicans opposed any compromise on the election laws. The paper further charged that he had lost courage and failed as a leader. "All Republicans agree that he blundered badly," said the *Times.* "Republicans and Democrats are unanimous in the opinion that he exhibited astonishing inconsistency, in view of his speeches, in voting against his own proposition." The paper held that if Garfield had maintained his position and voted for the measure, he would have carried with him a majority of his party.

[102]On March 23 Omar D. Conger of Michigan called the attention of the House to the fact that Townshend's bill to revise and amend certain Revised Statutes embraced all the tariff laws of the United States, and should have been referred to the Committee on Ways and Means rather than the Committee on the Revision of the Laws.

the moment as the only parliamentary way in which we could get the bill into the Committee on Ways and Means. After a long and angry talk, the Speaker ruled my motion in order and finally in the course of the debate, I charged that the House had been deceived by Mr. Townshend and owed it to itself to correct the proceedings and amend the journal. Townshend foamed and fretted with great vehemence and I answered, "After this indecent exposure of your person and your mind I have no more to say." Home in the evening. Crete and I went with Rhodes and wife and Henry and wife to call on the President and after that made a call on Mrs. Burnett.[103]

WEDNESDAY, 24.   Blackburn led about fifty men in fillibustering which consumed all the day and late in the night until 12 o'clock, to prevent action on McLane's resolution.[104] A wearisome profitless struggle in which the bluster and boasting of Blackburn, as to how long they would hold out, was very unbecoming, and which appears to be the certain prelude to his defeat. Got home half an hour after midnight and retired.

THURSDAY, 25.   Awoke tired from last night's long session. Desk until eleven. Ways and Means until twelve. Immediately after prayer the House resumed the contest of yesterday. Reed made

---

[103]In his book, *Captain Henry of Geauga,* p. 284, Frederick A. Henry discusses the visit of the three couples to the Burnett residence as a memorable part "of what was destined to be their last informal carefree, good time together." "At her home," Henry writes, "amid a lull in the conversation, Mr. Rhodes, who had been contemplating a beautiful marble which portrayed the poet Schiller with waving locks, suddenly and with great gravity inquired of Mrs. Burnett, 'Madam, is that your bust?' She laughingly undeceived him, and her callers soon afterwards departed. But they had scarce quitted her door when General Garfield demanded of Mr. Rhodes what he meant by such a question; and mimicked with sepulchral voice, 'Madam, is that your bust?' until poor Rhodes felt that he had really somehow insulted the lady."

[104]On March 23, following heated debate, interspersed with motions to adjourn, Robert M. McLane (1815–1898), a Democratic member of the House from Maryland, 1847–51, and 1879–83, moved, as a question of privilege, that Townshend's bill be reported back to the House by the Committee on the Revision of the Laws and be referred to the Committee on Ways and Means.

an offer of compromise which was objected to,[105] when Mr.
McLane modified his resolution, introduced as a question of
privilege, so as to have the Journal read and approved and a vote
to be taken on discharging the Committee on Revision of the
Laws from the further consideration of the Townshend bill and
referred it to the Committee on Ways and Means. This program
was adopted, separate votes taken on the two branches of the
resolution and on the preamble, and all carried by heavy majorities, thus completely vindicating the position I had taken and
overwhelming Townshend with defeat by a large majority of his
own political associates. I think it will be a long time before any
other man attempts to defraud the House as he did. Home in the
evening; letters and Metternich. Our friends Rhodes and Henry
and their wives left us this morning.

FRIDAY, 26. Sister Lida [Rudolph] left us this morning. Desk
until half-past 10. Departments until 11. Ways and Means Committee until 12. Private bills in the House during the day. Home
in the evening. Everywhere work.

SATURDAY, 27. Desk until eleven. Ways and Means Committee
next, but the Sub-Committee failed to get a quorum. In the
House the day was devoted to the Diplomatic Appropriation
Bill.

SUNDAY, 28. Crete, Mother and I attended church. Nichol dined
with us at two and at half-past four Crete and I attended the
Colored Catholic Church [St. Augustine] on 15th Street and
listened to their very fine Easter Music. Metternich in the evening. I read with special interest the ideas of a strong man who
was the embodyment of all the conservatism of Europe during
the first half of this century and who all his life regarded the
French Revolution as the great calamity of modern times.

MONDAY, 29. Worked at my desk until eleven o'clock, when I
went to the Capitol and met the Sub-Committee on the sugar
question. Tucker's proposition to abolish the grade between 10

[105]Fernando Wood of New York offered the compromise proposal. Conger of
Michigan objected to it, and he was sustained by the Speaker, who ruled that the
proposal required unanimous consent before it could be placed before the House.

and 13 Dutch standard and have but two grades of refining sugars, was adopted by the Sub-Committee as was also his plan to fix a specific rate on all the grades equal to fifty per cent ad valorem. This was done provisionally to let it go to the press to draw the fire of public opinion. In the House a long time was consumed in the introduction of bills and the rest of the day consumed by the Consular and Diplomatic bills. Home in the evening, working at my mail and reading Metternich.

TUESDAY, 30. Worked at my desk until quarter-past ten, when I went to the Navy Department on behalf of Mr. Varney.[106] Thence to the Capitol to attend the meeting of the Committee on Ways and Means. After debate against any movement touching the tariff, I took the position that it was due to the House that the Committee should send bills back approved or disapproved. Thereupon several amendments were made to the bichromate of potash bill, adding paper and other article[s]. In the House the morning hour was dispensed with and the Consular Bill finished and passed. The rest of day was consumed on the contested election case of Slemmens [Slemons] of Arkansas.[107] In the evening at eight o'clock Crete, Mollie and I spent the evening at Colonel Rockwell's.

WEDNESDAY, 31. Worked at my desk until half-past ten, when I went to the Capitol and attended the meeting of the Committee on Ways and Means. The whiskey men of Cincinnati were heard in regard to the proposed change in the Internal Revenue laws allowing leakage and waste on what is known as "time whiskey." This whiskey they are allowed to cure by time before removal from the bonded warehouse. No conclusions reached. In the

[106]William H. Varney, a native of New Hampshire, was a resident of Massachusetts in 1869 when he was appointed naval constructor with the relative rank of lieutenant. In 1875 he was not recommended for promotion by an examining board. He and his wife believed that he had been unjustly treated and Garfield seems to have agreed. On February 28, 1882, President Arthur promoted him to naval constructor with the relative rank of captain, retroactive to March 13, 1875.

[107]William F. Slemons (1830–1918), a Democratic member of the House from Arkansas, 1875–81. His election to the Forty-sixth Congress was unsuccessfully contested by John M. Bradley.

House the day was devoted to a discussion of the appropriations in the Deficiency Bill for the Star Service.[108] No conclusions reached. The Senate passed the other Deficiency Bill, including my amendment, in regard to the appointment of Special Deputy Marshals, Senator Edmunds making a speech against it. Home in the evening until half-past seven when I went with Mr. Frye to the National Hotel to visit Mr. Stephens. We played a game of whist and had a pleasant conversation with the old gentleman.

April

THURSDAY, 1. Worked at my desk until quarter-past ten when I went with Crete to settle some grocery bills. Thence to the Capi-

[108]Most of the mail transported in the United States arrived at its destination by rail or steamboat. To serve a large number of small, out of the way places not thus accessible, especially in the West, the Post Office Department established "star routes" over which mail was carried in buggies and carts, on horseback and on foot. Local pressures and pressures from men who would profit from a contract entered into the decision of the department to establish a new route. The decision having been made, the department accepted bids and awarded a contract for providing the service; the contract specified the route, the amount to be paid for the service, the frequency of the service, and the time allowed for a trip. The system lent itself to fraud as sharp-eyed men recognized that large profits could be made through the system of contracts and sub-contracts. Often a modest bid for a route would be accepted and the mail service begun. Soon petitions from people served by the route would reach the department asking that faster and more frequent service be given. Under a new contract, costs sky-rocketed. For example: the cost of carrying the mail from Phoenix to Prescott (140 miles) in Arizona Territory increased from $700 a year to more than $32,000. The profits went not to the mail carriers but to men who worked behind the scenes with the connivance of officials in the Post Office Department, particularly the second assistant postmaster general, who was in charge of star route contracts. As a consequence of the corruption Congress was regularly asked to make up by an additional appropriation deficiencies incurred in maintaining the star route service. Congress had looked into the problem but nothing had come of its investigations, and President Hayes took no action. Garfield, aware of the seriousness of the situation, entered upon his duties as President determined to root out the corruption at once—before it could have devastating consequences for his own administration.

tol to attend the meeting of the Committee on Ways and Means, where we had further discussion and action in relation to the internal revenue tax on whiskey. The [In] the House the morning hour and private bills were dispensed with. The day was devoted to the Deficiency Bill, the chief point of debate being the appropriation for the Star Service. It ended at half-past four o'clock by the House agreeing to the Senate amendments by a small majority.[109] Home in the evening. At eight o'clock a large number of friends came in to Crete's Reception. A very pleasant party and most of them remained until midnight.

FRIDAY, 2.   Worked at my desk until half-past ten when I attended the meeting of the Committee on Ways and Means. Hearing on whisky was concluding [concluded] after consuming all the morning. The discussion has been protracted on a proposed amendment granting to the manufacturers of bourbon or time whisky a rebate on account of leakage and waste during the time when the whisky is in bond. This is opposed by parties who make refined whisky by addition[al] distillation or re-distillation and who put their whiskey immediately on the market after rectifying it. In the House the day was devoted to the Deficiency Bill relating to the Star Service. At half-past four o'clock the Senate amendments were concurred in against the unanimous recommendation of the Committee on Appropriations, an unusual defeat for that Committee.

SATURDAY, 3.   At eight o'clock Martha Mays and Miss Alice Hanscom arrived from Dayton, Ohio, to visit us. The meeting of the House today is for debate only. Worked at my desk until ten o'clock, when I played billiards with Rockwell for two hours. Home in the evening until 8 o'clock, when I went with Crete and Miss Hanscom to the Literary Club, where Mrs. Chaflin [Claflin][110] presided. The subject for discussion was: "Does the

[109]Debate on the Deficiency Bill continued into the session of April 2, when the measure was passed with Senate amendments which increased by $130,000 the sum originally approved by the House.

[110]Mary B. (Davenport) Claflin was an author and second wife of William Claflin (1818–1905) of Massachusetts, businessman, banker, and politician, who served as governor of Massachusetts, 1869–71, and was a Republican member of

rapid progress of civilization produce injurious social effects?"

The discussion except Mrs. Long's paper was a weak one. I closed it with a few remarks on the increasing leizure of the working classes caused by civilization and the deteriorating social influence of great cities. At the end of the discussion Mrs. Woolson[111] of Concord, New Hampshire, read a paper written by Mrs. Claflin on the life and character of Whittier, the Poet.

SUNDAY, 4. The day very warm and uncomfortable to venture out in. Remained at home. Rested and slept. Read Hazlitt's *Napoleon*[112] with Crete and also finished first volume of Metternich and about one quarter of the second. In the evening at eight o'clock, went with General Young and Mr. Defrees to the President's to recommend the pardon of Judge Wright, who was lodged in jail under a sentence of $1,000 fine and 30 days imprisonment for assault on Columbus Delano.[113] The fine is just but the imprisonment is too much for a sick man of seventy years. On my return went to McMahon's[114] on K Street where Crete, Miss Mays and Miss Hanscom were calling. Returned at ten o'clock and retired at eleven.

MONDAY, 5.   Worked at desk until 11 o'clock, when I went to the Capitol expecting to meet the Sub-Committee on Hoop-iron, but

---

the U.S. House of Representatives, 1877–81. She married Claflin in 1845. They were close friends of eminent persons, including Henry Wilson, John Greenleaf Whittier, and Henry Ward Beecher, whose visits to the Claflin home are discussed in her books, *Brampton Sketches* (1890), *Real Happenings* (1890), *Personal Recollections of John Greenleaf Whittier* (1893), and *Under the Old Elms* (1895).

[111]Abba Louisa (Goold) Woolson (1838–1921), teacher, author, and lecturer, was a native of Maine. She graduated and taught at the high school in Portland, Maine, and married Moses Woolson, principal of the school. She did her first writing for the *New York Home Journal* and the *Portland Transcript*. Her works include *Women in American Society* (1873), *Browsing Among Books* (1881), and *George Eliot and Her Heroines* (1886).

[112]William Hazlitt, *Life of Napoleon Buonaparte,* 4 vols. (1828–1830).

[113]See Vol. III, pp. 219–220, n. 24.

[114]John A. McMahon (1833–1923) of Dayton, where Martha Mays and Alice Hanscom were teaching, was a Democratic member of the House from Ohio, 1875–81.

Tucker did not come. In the House, this being the first Monday
of the month, suspension of the rules was in order. Weaver[115] got
in his financial resolution, after his long struggle. I spoke
ten minutes denouncing it as a combination of centralization,
inflation and repudiation. The vote stood 85 [84] yeas and
117 nays, only two Republicans voting for it.[116] Several bills
were passed under a suspension of the rules. Home in the
evening.

TUESDAY, 6. Desk until half-past ten. Then Ways and Means.
The merchants of New York addressed the Committee on existing law and regulation concerning the appraisal of goods and
proposed the French and English plan of allowing the merchants
to appraise their own goods, let the Government accept the
appraisement and if it choose take the goods at the price named
and sell them at auction. A very interesting hearing. In the House
after the morning hour the Army Appropriation Bill was taken
up. The old rider of last year is to be offered.[117] The Republican
Caucus Committee of nine met and consulted on what they
would do. I insisted that we ought not to vote against the rider
on its merits, but only on account of its being made in order as
a rider. We came to a conclusion as far as an agreement could
be had. At four o'clock went to the Base Ball Grounds with
Rockwell, but the Baltimore Club not arriving the game did not
come off. At seven o'clock Crete and I went to Secretary Sherman's to dinner. There were present Senator Pendleton and

[115]James B. Weaver (1833–1912) was a Greenback member of the House from
Iowa, 1879–81. In 1880 he was the Greenback candidate for the presidency. The
resolution declared that the government should control the volume of all currency, metallic and paper, and that the interest-bearing national debt of $782,-
000,000, redeemable in 1881, "should not be refunded beyond the power of the
Government to call in said obligations and pay them at any time, but should be
paid as rapidly as possible, and according to contract. To enable the Government
to meet these obligations, the mints of the United States should be operated to
their full capacity in the coinage of standard silver dollars, and such other coinage
as the business interests of the country may require."

[116]Four Republicans—Nicholas Ford, Albert P. Forsythe, William D. Kelley,
and Daniel L. Russell—voted for the measure.

[117]See pp. 206–253 *passim*

wife, John Hay and wife, Mrs. Stone,[118] Baron Hegeman [Hègermann] and wife, Vice President Wheeler, Mrs. Sprague,[119] General Fearing.[120] At ten o'clock, we went to Mrs. Sprague's to see Miss Thursby,[121] the singer, who had returned from concert.

WEDNESDAY, 7. Worked at my desk until half-past ten when I went to the Committee on Ways and Means where the session was devoted to the usual discussion. In the House the day was devoted to the Army Appropriation Bill. In the evening [afternoon] at four o'clock went with Rockwell to the Ball Grounds

[118]Mrs. Amasa Stone of Cleveland, mother-in-law of John Hay.

[119]Katharine ("Kate") Chase Sprague (1840–1899) was the daughter of Salmon P. Chase and the wife of William Sprague of Rhode Island. Garfield became well acquainted with her during the fall of 1862 when he was a guest for several weeks in the Chase home in Washington. Unhappy in her marriage, she was in the later 1870's closely associated with Senator Roscoe Conkling. In August, 1879, this relationship brought about a private and public confrontation between Sprague and Conkling that titillated the country; the Spragues were divorced in 1882. Kate attended the Republican National Convention in 1880. During her last years she lived in poverty and isolation on the outskirts of Washington in a decaying house that her father had bought in 1869. See Thomas Graham Belden and Marva Robins Belden, *So Fell the Angels* (1956).

[120]Benjamin D. Fearing (1837–1881), of Ohio, graduated at Marietta College at the age of nineteen and served in the Civil War, 1861–65, entering as a private and rising to the rank of colonel in 1863. He served under Sherman in the Atlanta campaign and in "the march to the sea," and was breveted brigadier general "for gallant and meritorious services" in those campaigns. Twice wounded and unable to live an active life, he resided after the war in Marietta.

[121]Emma C. Thursby (1845–1931), of Brooklyn, made her debut as a concert singer in 1875 at the Belford Avenue Church in Brooklyn. A brilliant soprano, she made successful tours of Europe, Asia and the United States, appearing in concerts and oratorios. She was now singing in Ole Bull's concerts in Lincoln Hall (see April 21). On April 7, the *Washington Star* made this comment about the behavior of some members of the audience on the preceding evening: "A number of persons present seemed to regard the occasion as a sort of *conversazione,* where talking rather than listening was the order of the evening, and kept up an incessant buzzing and chattering, which interfered not only with the efforts of the performers, but also with the rights and enjoyment of the audience. The vacant space occupied by such ill-bred people would have been far more acceptable than their presence. . . ."

and saw a fine game between the Nationals and the Baltimores.[122] Home in the evening and worked on Census papers.

THURSDAY, 8. Worked at my desk until one-quarter past ten, when I went to the Departments and thence to the Capitol to attend the Committee on Ways and Means. The session was devoted to action on the Whiskey Bill, which was adopted after some debate, by a divided Committee.[123] In the House the day was devoted to the point of order raised on Sparks's amendment to the Army Bill,[124] on which I spoke for a short time insisting that under the New Rules it was not in order. The Chairman, Cox, overruled me and an appeal was taken, which was lost by a strictly party vote. In the evening went with Crete and the children, Martha Mays [and] Miss Hanscom to Ford's Theatre and heard the *Pirates of Penzance.* [125]

FRIDAY, 9. Worked at my desk until half-past ten when I went to the Treasury Department. Thence to the Committee on Ways and Means, where the Hoop Iron Question was taken up. Tucker's report providing for contracts made for cut hoops to 10th of March, was offered. I offered an amendment confining the relief to absolute contracts before the 12th of March. My

---

122The Nationals won, 8–6.

123See n. 153, April 28, 1880.

124The amendment by Sparks provided "that no money appropriated in this act is appropriated, or shall be paid, for the subsistence, equipment, transportation, or compensation of any portion of the Army of the United States to be used as a police force to keep the peace at the polls at any election held within any State." On April 13 the House passed the Army Appropriation Bill with an amendment to Sparks's amendment which provided "that nothing in this provision shall be construed to prevent the use of troops to protect against domestic violence in each of the States, on application of the Legislature thereof, or of the executive when the Legislature cannot be convened."

125The world premiere of *The Pirates of Penzance* (except for two or three private performances in England for copyright purposes) was at the Fifth Avenue Theatre in New York City on December 31, 1879; it continued there until March 6, 1880. See George C. D. Odell, *Annals of the New York Stage,* 15 vols. (1927–1949), XI, pp. 35–36. In Washington it opened at Ford's Opera House on April 5, remaining there for two weeks. Tickets for evening performances were seventy-five cents and one dollar.

motion prevailed 6 to 5. In the House the day was devoted to private bills. Went out to the Base Ball Grounds to witness a game between the Nationals and [the] Providence Club. Left before it was closed.[126]

Dictated letters and Journal to Rose, and at half-past seven o'clock, Crete, Mother and I took the Baltimore and Ohio train for Pittsburgh en route to Ohio.

SATURDAY, 10. Awoke near Pittsburgh. Took breakfast at the Monongahela House and the Lake Erie train at quarter before eight. A number of friends called at Youngstown, some at Warren. Reach[ed] Cleveland at two. Edwin Cowles met us at the Atlantic Depot and took us to his house for dinner. A number of friends called, among them James Mason, Capt. Henry and Sherwin. At four-fifty we went to the Lake Shore Depot, where we took the train for Mentor. Stopped at Reynolds' station, where Dr. Robison met us and took us to his house. Spent the night at Dr. Robison's.

SUNDAY, 11. Cold raw morning. After breakfast we drove up to our house and spent several hours in examining the progress of the work and making such changes as the situation required. We are both pleasantly surprised at its appearance. It is far more comely than we had expected and will really make a very beautiful farm cottage. Ordered an addition to the horsebarn for the accommodation of carriages. After dinner at the Doctor's at three drove again to the house in company with Horace and George Steele who had come up from Painesville to see us. Thence to the Depot to answer a telegram. Called on the Tylers and the Aldrichs, thence to the Doctor's where we spent the night.

MONDAY, 12. Train to Cleveland in company with the Doctor. Spent the forenoon in examining mantels and house fixtures. Purchased two stoves. Determined upon the color to be put on the house. Dined at the Doctor's. Took the Mahoning train at 2.40 for Pittsburgh. Mrs. Purdy[127] joined us en route to Wash-

---

[126]The game ended in a 4–4 tie.

[127]Wife of Thomas C. Purdy of Cleveland, brother-in-law of Eugene V. Smalley. Garfield helped Purdy obtain an appointment in the Census Office (see May 17),

ington. Captain Henry went with me as far as Warren. Thinks I ought to go on to Chicago as a Delegate. Near Beaver we found a freight engine across our track which detained us three hours, so that we lost the connection at Pittsburgh, where we arrived at eleven o'clock. Spent the night at the Monongahela House.

TUESDAY, 13.   Took the Baltimore and Ohio train at seven-forty and spent a hot uncomfortable day on the journey. Read two speeches of Bismarck of May last on the Tariff and found some striking passages. Read several chapters of the second volume of Hazlitt's *Napoleon.* Reached Washington at seven-ten and found the family well.

During my absence the Army Bill has passed, Republicans voting unanimously against the amendment which last year received their almost unanimous vote. I think they have bungled the whole business and given a construction which will trouble us in the future.

WEDNESDAY, 14.   Desk until half-past ten; then called on Judge Black at [the] Ebbitt House—went with him to the Sec'y of State to get him special passport to Europe. Capitol [at] eleven. Committee on Rules had adjourned. In House, day devoted to Indian Appropriation Bill. At 9.30 Crete and I went to Senator J.S. Morrill's to celebrate the 70th anniversary of his birth. Large party. President and Mrs. Hayes and most of Cabinet. Blaine met the President the first time for two years. He was offended at Hayes's appointment of an U.S. Marshal in Maine who was personally offensive to him (Blaine).[128] Talked half an hour with

---

where he was assigned to the section concerned with the statistics of railroad, transportation, express, and telegraph companies.

[128]Hayes regretted Blaine's feelings toward him and had long been willing to be friendly. As he once explained to William Walter Phelps, he knew of "no good reason" why he and Blaine "should not be on the best of terms with each other. . . . I have understood that he was offended by an appointment which I made in Maine. He was opposed to it. I thought it was my duty to make it. There was certainly not the least *intentional* disrespect to him in the act itself or in the manner of doing it. I sincerely regretted that he felt as he did about it." Hayes to Phelps, December 7, 1879, in T. Harry Williams, ed., *Hayes: The Diary of a President, 1875–1881,* p. 255.

Blaine on the Presidency. He is bitter towards Sherman, says the letter of the latter, which introduced Hayes as a candidate, was a blow at him, Blaine, and that now, Sherman prefers Grant to Blaine.[129] Blaine thinks Grant's nomination impossible—says that it is currently reported he was drunk on the way from Texas to New Orleans. On the whole, I think Blaine is now more confident of the nomination than I have ever known him. I like Blaine—always have—yet there is an element in him which I distrust.

THURSDAY, 15. Worked at my desk until half-past ten when I went to the Committee on Ways and Means. It was a stormy and unpleasant session, with a good deal of personal controversy between the Chairman and Mr. Conger, both gentlemen being in excessive heat. The whole Committee has made as complete a breakdown as any I have ever known and yet they pretty fairly represent the sentiment of the House. In the House the day was devoted to the Indian Appropriation Bill. I made a short speech in defense of the Sioux Treaty, for which the Committee on Appropriations had not recommended a sufficient amount of money.[130] In the evening worked at my desk and read.

FRIDAY, 16. Worked at home on my mail until half-past eleven o'clock, when I went to the Capitol. Another day was consumed

---

[129]In a long letter (January 21, 1876) to an Ohio state senator John Sherman urged Ohio Republicans to support Hayes for the presidency. "I believe the nomination of Governor Hayes," he wrote, "would give us the more strength, taking the whole country at large, than any other man." The widely published letter provided a needed boost for the Hayes movement, but Blaine took it personally.

[130]Garfield held that a three-year old agreement with the Sioux had placated 20,000 "wild Indians" who had been fighting American pioneers, and that it could not be properly executed with the proposed appropriation, which was $95,000 less than the preceding year's appropriation, all of which had been spent. He favored restoring $95,000 to the bill before the House, but a proposal to do so was defeated. In an agreement made in 1876 (and ratified by Congress in February, 1877) between the United States and "certain bands of the Sioux Nation of Indians" and other Indians, the Sioux had agreed to cede to the United States the Black Hills region and part of their reservation; the United States had committed itself to additional expenditures in behalf of the Indians.

on the Indian Bill, which was not completed and the House adjourned pending a motion to transfer the Indian Bureau to the War Department.[131] Early in the day, Hon. Robert C. Winthrop, once Speaker of the House of Representatives, was on the floor, and called my attention to the fact that the picture of General Jackson [Lafayette] by Aery Schaffer [Ary Scheffer] painted in 1824, is being ruined by blisters. I made a short speech on the subject. I introduced a resolution for its renovation which was unanimously adopted.[132] In the evening Crete and I attended a party at Governor Hawley's given to Charles Dudley Warner.[133] A very select and pleasant company were present. Home at half-past eleven.

SATURDAY, 17.   Worked at my desk until 10 o'clock, when I went to the War and Navy Departments and to the Treasury Department on business.[134] Thence to the Capitol. The Indian Bill was

[131]The transfer amendment was ruled out of order on the following day.

[132]The famous Dutch painter Ary Scheffer (1795–1858) painted the portrait in 1824 when Lafayette was in the United States. It hung to the left of the Speaker's desk. Garfield's resolution provided "that the Joint Committee on the Library be directed to inquire what steps are necessary to cause the portrait . . . to be renovated and protected from injury, and report what sum may be necessary for that purpose."

[133]Charles Dudley Warner (1829–1900), of Massachusetts, graduated at Hamilton College in 1851, received his law degree at the University of Pennsylvania in 1858, and practiced law, which he soon learned to dislike, for a short time in Chicago. In 1860 he became an assistant to his friend, Joseph R. Hawley, editor of the *Evening Press* in Hartford, Connecticut. He assumed the editorship of the paper when Hawley left to serve in the Union army. In 1867 the *Evening Press* consolidated with the *Hartford Courant,* which he edited to his death. He wrote several novels, but his popularity rested on his essays. He collaborated with Mark Twain in writing *The Gilded Age* (1873).

[134]With the Ohio Republican convention less than two weeks away, Garfield, under pressure to attend the Republican National Convention in Chicago, called at Sherman's office to discuss the matter. Although he was committed to Sherman, he had no desire to go to Chicago and manage his campaign. Nor did he wish to be elected a delegate from his district, for he had told other candidates for that position that he would not stand in their way. Sherman, of course, wanted Garfield to attend the Chicago convention, for his presence in Sherman's behalf would make it virtually impossible for his own name to be placed in nomination. Sherman also hoped that Garfield would go as the elected delegate of his district, thereby

passed and the Special Deficiency Bill taken up; pending which the House adjourned at three o'clock. Worked at my desk until half-past six when I went to dinner at George Bancroft's. There were present Robert C. Winthrop and wife of Massachusetts, Governor Anthony,[135] Secretary Evarts, Horace Davis[136] and Senator Edmunds. Very pleasant party. Home at 10 o'clock.

SUNDAY, 18. At home nearly all day. Made some preparations for discussing the Marshals clause of the Deficiency Bill. Read several chapters of Hazlitt's *Napoleon* closing with the Battle. Called on Gilfillan, who is still confined to his bed. Also, Crete and I called on Rockwell and General Schenck.

MONDAY, 19. Worked at my desk until ten o'clock, when I went to the Capitol to attend a meeting of the Sub-Committee on Ways and Means on the Hurd Bill in regard to the transportation of goods in bond.[137] The members did not assemble in time for a

---

securing the district for Sherman and strengthening his candidacy in northern Ohio, where Blaine had considerable support. In his *Recollections,* Vol. II, p. 771, Sherman, writing of the meeting at the Treasury Department, said that Garfield "expressed his earnest desire to secure my nomination and his wish to be a delegate at large, so that he might aid me effectively." Two days after the meeting Garfield wrote to Harmon Austin as follows: "I want my friends to prevent my name being presented to the Warren Convention, as a Delegate, for two reasons: First, if I go at all to the Chicago Convention, I ought to go as a Delegate at large and Mr. Sherman said to me on Saturday that he understood that that arrangement was to be made. In second place the fact that I am announced by friends for Sherman, would incline many of my good friends at the Warren Convention to vote against me and I will not allow any division of that sort to spring up in the old district that has so long been friendly to me. Please take this matter in hand and see to it that my name is not presented." Delegates at large were chosen at the state convention.

[135]Senator Henry B. Anthony of Rhode Island, who was elected governor of that state in 1849 and reelected in 1850.

[136]Horace Davis (1831–1916), a native of Massachusetts who attended Williams College and graduated at Harvard, 1849, was a Republican member of the House from California, 1877–81, a member of the Republican National Committee, 1880–88, and president of the University of California at Berkeley, 1888–90. He was a nephew of George Bancroft.

[137]On this day the House referred the Hurd bill to the Committee on Ways and Means.

meeting and so the subject was postponed. This being Suspension Day the House devoted its time after the morning hour to suspension of the rules. Some bills were passed and some rejected. I spent an hour and a half in the Senate listening to Blaine's reply to Carpenter and other Senators who had assaulted him. He made a very brilliant speech, attacking one after another his assailants. There was evidently a combination to overcome him, but he was more than a match for them all. It is not Blaine's forte to make a long consistent, methodical argument analysing and establishing affirmative propositions, but he is the readiest man with the current facts of political history I have ever known and uses them in running debate with tremendous force and effectiveness. On the whole he is the completest gladiator in debate I know of.[138] Home at half-past five. At half-past seven Crete and I called at Mr. Frye's and spent the evening.

TUESDAY, 20. Worked at my desk until 11 o'clock. For the first time in many months, I neglected to attend the meeting of the Committee on Ways and Means. At 11 o'clock called on John Selden, Attorney at Law, and placed in his hand the deed to Judge Black and myself of the Hunter land in Virginia to examine whether the title was encumbered. Reached the House at half-past twelve, where the day was spent in another useless struggle at fillibustering on the question whether an hour and a half should be granted for general debate on the Deficiency Bill.[139] This struggle of the two parties appeared very like the dancers described by Goldsmith in "The Deserted Village," where

> The dancing pair, who simply sought renown
> By holding out to dance each other down.

WEDNESDAY, 21. Worked at my desk until half-past eleven

---

[138]The debate was on the distribution of money awarded by the Geneva Tribunal in the *Alabama* Claims. Blaine's speech, a reply to Carpenter of Wisconsin, Thurman of Ohio, and Bayard of Delaware, was interspersed with sharp exchanges between him and them. Blaine was particularly critical of Carpenter's preferences regarding payments to insurance companies.

[139]The Republicans were willing to give the Democrats all the time they wished for debate on the bill, asking in return one hour for themselves.

o'clock, when I went to Lawyer Selden's Office to engage him to look after the title to the 43 acres of farm land belonging to Judge Black and myself near Alexandria, Va., which is threatened with sale in connection with the whole tract of Mr. Hunter, from whom we purchased it. Went to the Capitol at 11 o'clock, where after the morning hour the same foolish controversy of the day before was resumed and continued for three hours, when Mr. McMahon withdrew the Deficiency Bill. I called up the House bill that had come back from the Senate with an amendment to repair and extend the Cleveland Post Office.[140] Home. In the evening, Mollie, Brown, and I attended the concert of Ole Bull[141] [and] Miss Thursby, who are aided by Brignoli,[142] Ferranti[143] and Miss Annie Rock [Anna Bock].[144] I am not able to speak intelligently of musical performances, but this seemed to me very fine. Home at ten o'clock.

THURSDAY, 22. Worked at my desk until half-past ten when I went with Crete to the Alderney Dairy and thence to the Capitol to attend the meeting of the Committee on Ways and Means, where at the end of a long discussion the Sub-Committee on the Tariff was increased to seven members and the whole subject of the Tariff referred to them. After the Journal was read in the House I called attention to the poem, copyrighted, of fifteen

[140]The House passed the bill as amended by the Senate.

[141]Ole Bornemann Bull (1810–1880), violinist, was a native of Bergen, Norway. He made successful concert tours in Italy and England, and three in the United States, 1843–45, 1852–57, and 1879–80. Of the concert Garfield attended in Lincoln Hall, the *Washington Star* (April 22) said: "Ole Bull, always a great favorite in Washington, was greeted with tremendous applause. Those who remember him thirty-five years ago on his first visit to the country, a remarkably handsome young man, tall, black-haired, full-chested, slender-waisted, will recall much of his old manner in the present white-haired veteran of seventy."

[142]Pasquale Brignoli (1824–1884), tenor and pianist, was for many years a favorite of audiences in the New York Academy of Music. A native of Naples, Italy, he finally made his home in the United States.

[143]Pietro Ferranti was described by the *Washington Star* (April 20) as "a born buffo" who received applause almost equal to that of Emma Thursby "for his inimitable drolleries and his superb musical execution."

[144]Anna Bock, a young pianist.

pages inserted in the record of this morning by Mr. Downey, the Delegate from Wyoming Territory, under the privilege of leave to print a speech. I raised a question as to whether he had exceeded the privileges of the House in having it printed and after some debate carried my motion to refer it to the Committee on Rules.[145] A Message from the President was then read, transmitting from descendants of Thomas Jefferson in Massachusetts, the desk on which Jefferson wrote the Declaration of Independence. An excellent speech was made by Mr. Crapo of Massachusetts, followed by another from Mr. Tucker of Virginia, after which resolutions accepting the desk we [re]adopted.[146] The House then went into Committee of the Whole on the Naval Appropriation Bill, and in less than an hour and a half the bill was passed.

[145]On April 12, Stephen W. Downey (1839–1902), a Republican delegate to the House from the Territory of Wyoming, 1879–81, introduced a bill which provided that up to $500,000 be appropriated "to commemorate in suitable paintings by the great living artists of this century upon the walls of the National Capitol the birth, life, death and resurrection of our Saviour Jesus Christ, as told in the four gospels of Matthew, Mark, Luke and John." On the following day he had inserted in the *Congressional Record,* as an argument supporting his bill, a poem entitled "The Immortals," which he had written and copyrighted. On April 22, when the *Record* for April 13 appeared, Garfield raised the question whether "the privilege granted a Member or Delegate to print remarks" in the *Record* extended to copyrighted material. After a brief debate the House adopted his motion to refer the matter to the Committee on Rules. Downey's bill died in committee. The poem is in the *Congressional Record,* 46 Cong., 2 Sess., Pt. 5, Appendix, pp. 337–352. See April 26.

[146]The desk was constructed in Philadelphia in the spring of 1776 from a drawing made by Jefferson and, as he himself noted, "is the identical one on which he wrote the Declaration of Independence." It has been described as "a portable mahogany writing-desk, of thorough workmanship, about twelve inches wide, sixteen inches long, and four inches deep. At one end is a drawer, parted off for ink, pens, letters, and paper. Within is a convenient writing-desk, lined with velvet. . . ." Thomas Jefferson gave the desk to Joseph Coolidge (1798–1879), a Boston merchant who married Eleanora Wayles Randolph, granddaughter of Jefferson, in May, 1825. The heirs of Coolidge presented it, through Robert C. Winthrop, to the nation so that it might "henceforth have a place in the Department of State in connection with the immortal instrument which was written upon it in 1776." Massachusetts Historical Society, *Proceedings,* 3 (1855–1858), pp. 151–152; *House Executive Documents,* No. 75, 46 Cong., 2 Sess., Serial 1925.

Several other matters came up for consideration and then Mr. McMahon re-introduced his Deficiency Bill and acceded to the Republican demand for an hour and twenty minutes. Mr. Reed got the floor and spoke for half an hour, the House then taking a recess. In the evening had a pleasant dinner party at our house, given to Mr. Baker and his daughter of Racine. The Wisconsin Delegation and their wives were present. The party lasted until 10 o'clock.[147]

FRIDAY, 23. Worked at my desk until half-past ten o'clock, when I went to the Departments and thence to the Capitol, arriving about twelve, when I found that the Sub-Committee of Ways and Means had had a long meeting and were in session on the tariff, of which meeting I had not been notified. Sat with them two hours during the session of the House. In the House the debate on the little Deficiency Bill was concluded and the bill sent to the Senate. I got in a ten minute speech under the five minute rule and stated my ground for believing the principle of the amendment was right although it should not be passed as a rider.[148] There has been recently a marked increase of radical feeling on the part of Republicans and it has become in many respects unreasonable and dangerous. This is the second or third time this session that I have tried to check it and each time I find myself suspected of being unsound. Home in the evening and revised the notes of my speech.

SATURDAY, 24. Desk until 11, when I went with Crete, at the request of Harper Bros., and sat for a photograph at

[147]Both of Wisconsin's senators and five of its eight House members were Republicans. One of the House members, Thaddeus C. Pound, had already concluded that Garfield was likely to be the next Republican presidential candidate (see entry and note for February 11, 1880). For the guest of honor, Robert H. Baker, see entry and note for January 1, 1880. On June 8, 1880, at the Republican National Convention, Wisconsin started the movement to Garfield by casting for him on the thirty-fourth ballot sixteen of its twenty votes, votes that had hitherto gone to Blaine and other candidates.

[148]The House was considering Senate amendments to the Deficiency Bill, one of which defined the procedure for appointing special deputy marshals. See April 25 and May 4.

Walker's,[149] in the building south of the Treasury. Thence to the Capitol, where I spent three hours in sub-committee of Ways and Means, in devising a new tariff—a vain work. Dictated letters in the evening. At 8 P.M. Mr. Wharton Barker of Philadelphia came and made a long statement of the political situation, of which this is the substance. "The independent Republicans of Pa., headed by Wayne McVeagh [MacVeagh] and Barker, have secured McManes[150] and his associates, who have pledged a majority of the Pa. delegates to oppose Grant at Chicago. This will make his nomination impossible, and at first help Blaine. Then Mass. and nearly all of N.E., except Maine, will throw its weight with N.Y. against Blaine, and break him. Pierrepont says, after Grant, Conkling will favor Garfield. Barker today visited the President, who says Sherman is in the field to prevent the nomination of Grant or Blaine, that Garfield can carry Ohio solid, as Blaine cannot, and in case the other two are broken, Sherman will give way for Garfield." In short, Barker thinks this is likely to be the outcome. I do not. I should be greatly distressed if I thought otherwise. There is too much possible work in me to set so near an end to it all, as that would do.

SUNDAY, 25. Crete and I attended church. Spent the remainder of the day reading and writing. Wharton Barker called again and

---

[149]Lewis E. Walker (c. 1824–1880), a native of Massachusetts, had a long career in the Treasury Department as chief photographer in the Office of the Supervising Architect. During the Civil War he was involved in the preparation of military maps and other materials for the army, and in 1874 he was in charge of the twenty-six photographers who covered the transit of Venus for the U.S. government. Garfield's photograph may have been taken by one of the other photographers in the Treasury Department's studio/gallery. Laurie A. Baty, author of "Photographers of Washington, D.C., 1870–1885," an M.A. thesis, George Washington University, 1979, furnished information for this note.

[150]James McManes (1822–1899) emigrated from Ireland to the United States when eight years of age and became, in the years 1866–81, the most powerful man in Philadelphia politics. As a delegate at large to the Republican National Convention in 1880 he was a leader of the anti-Grant faction in the Pennsylvania delegation whose members reportedly signed a pledge to vote against Grant (*Washington Star,* June 2). At the Convention he and his faction cast 21 votes for Garfield on the final ballot.

insisted that he has additional reasons for believing that the programme he mentioned yesterday will be carried out. At seven o'clock Crete and I went to dinner at the President's in company with his family and the Vice President. A number of people called after dinner. The President approved of the speech I had made in regard to the Marshals, but he will veto the bill on the ground of its being a rider. The message is already written although the bill has not yet reached him.

MONDAY, 26.   Worked at my desk until half-past ten when I went to the National Hotel to attend a meeting of the Committee on Rules at Mr. Stephens' room, where we had a discussion of my resolution about the Downey poem. After some hesitation the Committee determined to exclude the poem from the permanent record, and change the rule so that the records proper shall contain nothing but the actual proceedings of the House and that leave to print or a speech withheld for revision more than a day shall go into the Appendix. This proposition we will offer to the House, but I presume we will be beaten by the younger members of the House, who are anxious to appear as having participated in the running debate, whether they do or not. In the House the day was devoted to the District of Columbia Bill. Spent two or three hours in the Committee on Ways and Means on Tucker's absurd project. I say absurd because no general tariff bill can pass.[151] Played billiards with Rockwell for an hour and a half. At nine o'clock Crete and I went to Senator Pendleton's. Home at 11 o'clock.

TUESDAY, 27.   Worked at my desk until twenty minutes after ten, when I went to consult Dr. Baxter on the condition of my stomach. He puts me on bread and milk and rare beefsteak cooked without grease. He prescribes this for the next ten days together with some medicine. Went to the Capitol at one-quarter before eleven, where the morning was devoted to Hurd's bill to prohibit the transportation of dutiable goods through Canada. A

---

[151]The Committee did not meet on this day. It did meet on April 27 and Garfield is recorded as present, but his entry for that date contains no mention of the meeting.

long and interesting discussion of the subject was had. The bill will probably be defeated. In the House the bill making appropriations for the District of Columbia was passed and also the Trade Mark Bill.[152] Home in the evening and so unwell that I retired at half-past nine.

WEDNESDAY, 28.   Worked at my desk until half-past ten when I went to the Census Office. Thence to the Capitol to attend a meeting of the Sub-Committee on Ways and Means. In the House the day was devoted to Carlisle's bill to amend the Internal Revenue laws in relation to whiskey. I spoke about twenty minutes on two features of the bill with which I disagreed.[153] Home in the evening not feeling well. Received a long dispatch from Foster in regard to the State Convention at Columbus. Sherman called bringing several dispatches which he had received. Dennison, Bateman,[154] Foster and I were elected as

[152]The bill provided for the registration and protection of trade marks used in commerce with foreign nations or with Indian tribes, providing the owners were domiciled in the United States or were located in a foreign country or in a tribe which afforded the same privilege to citizens of the United States, and providing such owners complied with the requirements specified in the bill. It passed the Senate without amendment and was signed by the President on March 3, 1881.

[153]Garfield praised the bill as an improvement of the internal revenue laws pertaining to whiskey, but he objected to the omission of a provision, written into law about two years earlier, authorizing manufacturers to keep whiskey in bond, beyond the date set by law for withdrawal, by paying "an interest on the tax after the time when it was due and up to the time of its payment." He also favored a tax on the whole amount of whiskey placed in bond with no allowance for leakage. He argued that since the manufacturers profited from the aging process, during which no tax was required, the federal government should collect a tax, when the liquor was withdrawn from storage, on the full amount put into bond. He explained that distillers passed the tax on to the consumer, that it was a voluntary tax which could be avoided by not drinking whiskey, and that a law making no allowance for leakage would tend to prevent watering of whiskey or any tampering with the barrels while in bond.

[154]Warner M. Bateman (1827–1897), a Cincinnati lawyer, was a member of the state senate, 1866–67, and U.S. attorney for the southern district of Ohio, 1869–77. He was a friend of John Sherman. The *Washington Star* (April 26) called him "the factotum of the Sherman literary bureau" in Washington. In April, 1881, he declined President Garfield's offer to appoint him solicitor of the Treasury.

Delegates at Large. The Convention was strongly in Sherman's favor. Rockwell came and spent two hours with me. Retired with a serious headache.

THURSDAY, 29. Worked at my desk until half-past ten when I went to the Capitol and attended a long and unpleasant meeting of the Committee on Ways and Means. There was a good deal of personal feeling exhibited between the Chairman and several members, who seemed inclined to charge him with bad faith in bringing in a report favorable to the Hurd Bill on Canadian transportation. Some votes were taken on the hoop iron question and it was determined by a majority of one to reduce the duty on cut hoop and hoop iron to 35 per cent ad valorem. In the House the day was consumed on Carlisle's bill, "whiskey," which was not completed.

FRIDAY, 30. Worked at my desk until half-past ten when I went to the Capitol to meet with the Committee on Ways and Means, thence to the House. The day was consumed on private bills. Home in the evening. I have been dieting this week and taking medicine for my stomach. Since Monday night I have taken nothing [but] toast and milk and steak cooked without grease.

May

SATURDAY, 1. Worked at my desk until half-past ten when I went to the Office of the Commissioner of Internal Revenue and met with the Joint Committee of the two Houses, of which Senator Kernan is Chairman, to examine the subject of beer and tobacco stamps and to determine what device if any should be adopted to ensure their cancellation.[155] House at twelve o'clock. The day

[155]The joint committee consisted of Francis Kernan and Daniel W. Voorhees of the Senate Finance Committee and Garfield, Randall Lee Gibson and John G. Carlisle of the House Ways and Means Committee. The charge to the five men was "to take into consideration the alleged losses of revenue arising from the evasion of the stamp-tax on cigars and other articles subject to excise duties," and to recommend any remedial legislation or action they deemed proper.

was devoted to Carlisle's whiskey bill. Late in the day and during the hour given for final discussion, Carlisle yielded to me and I spoke 6 or 8 minutes in relation to the attack which the newspapers are making upon me through the Advertizing Agency of Rowell and Company of New York in regard to the duty on wood paper pulp. I think I put that question pretty effectually to rest.[156] In the evening at seven o'clock dined at Secretary Evarts' at a dinner given to the Chinese Minister Yung Wing[157] and two of the Chinese [American] ambassadors [commissioners] to China, Prescott [Trescot][158] and Sweet

---

[156]"I think it will be interesting to the House," said Garfield, "to examine one of the methods by which news and public opinion are manufactured." He then read a statement which George P. Rowell & Co., an advertising firm, had sent, at the request of "publishers of several leading New York dailies" and "manufacturers of paper," to newspaper editors in many sections of the country for editorial presentation. The statement charged that Garfield's opposition to the tariff bill, being prepared by the Committee on Ways and Means and placing wood pulp on the free list, was preventing the bill from getting out of committee and into the House, and that meanwhile manufacturers of wood pulp were charging an exorbitant tax which newspaper publishers had to pay so that the monopolists could grow rich. Garfield simply explained that he did not have "the casting vote" on the subject, since he was one of five Republicans on the committee which had eight Democrats. In response to a query about his position on a tariff on paper, he stated that he favored reducing "the duty on paper and the materials of its manufacture" as much as possible "without destroying or crippling the industries with which it is connected."

[157]Yung Wing (1828–1912), a native of China, received some schooling in Hong Kong before being brought in 1847 to the United States, where he studied at Monson Academy, Massachusetts, and graduated at Yale College (1854)—the first Chinese student to graduate at an American college. He became a citizen of the United States. It was largely owing to his efforts as a member of a commission established by the Chinese government that 120 boys were sent to the United States to study, 1872–75. From 1878 to 1881 he was assistant Chinese minister to the United States. From 1883 to his death he was a resident of the United States except for a seven year period. He is the author of *My Life in China and America* (1909).

[158]William H. Trescot (1822–1898), historian, diplomat, and lawyer, served as assistant secretary of state, 1860–61, and was one of three commissioners (the other two were John F. Swift and James B. Angell) sent to China in 1880 to negotiate changes in the Burlingame Treaty (1868) on Chinese immigration. See entry and note for January 26 and entry for February 23, 1879.

[Swift],[159] who are about to leave for their stations. Cabinet officers, Senators, and Members, and Mrs. Evarts (the only lady present) attended.

SUNDAY, 2. Crete, Mollie and I attended All Souls Church and heard an interesting sermon on the New Birth. I was, however, too sleepy to be sufficiently alive to all its points. Home in the afternoon and evening. Slept, read, wrote, dictated letters, and retired at 10 o'clock.

MONDAY, 3. Worked at my desk until eleven o'clock. Went shopping with Crete to make some purchases for curtain stuff for windows at Mentor. Thence to the Capitol. At half-past twelve, after the morning hour was over, it was rumored that an attempt was to be made by the Democrats to get in, under a suspension of the rules, a Third Term resolution. The [To] prevent this a motion was made and carried to adjourn and so the House adjourned at half-past two o'clock. Home early and worked at my desk during the evening.

TUESDAY, 4. Worked at my desk until half-past ten when I went to the Committee on Ways and Means, where the morning hour was devoted to the report of the Sub-Committee on the Tariff; several votes were taken and but little progress was made. In the House the day was devoted to the Post Office Appropriation Bill and the old quarrel over the Star Service was resumed and consumed the day.[160] I should have added that the President sent in his message vetoing the General Deficiency Bill, on account of the rider attached to it. He did not discuss the merits of the rider but only referred to the fact that it was not the proper place for the subject matter.[161] Letters from the boys with very cheering

---

[159]John F. Swift (1829–1891), lawyer and diplomat, was appointed a commissioner in 1880 to negotiate changes in the Burlingame Treaty with China. He was minister to Japan, 1889–91.

[160]The bill was taken up, but there was no debate on the star route service until the following day, when several members opposed cuts in the service proposed in the bill.

[161]Hayes stated that he would have signed the bill had it not contained "provisions which materially change, and by implication repeal, important parts of the laws for the regulation of the United States elections." To attempt to modify those

news of their progress. Jim is now three in his division and Hal is tenth. They have begun Sallust and Homer. I had not advanced as far as these two boys, one sixteen and the other fourteen, until I was near twenty-one.

WEDNESDAY, 5. Desk until half-past ten. Committee of Ways and Means until twelve, still working on the Tariff Bill. Useless work, for nothing will be done in the House. In the House $200,000 [$250,000] were appropriated by unanimous consent for the immediate wants of printing, that appropriation having been in the vetoed bill. The remainder of the day was consumed on the Post Office Appropriation Bill. A general and concerted assault has been made upon me by means of a circular issued by George P. Rowell and Company, a New York Advertizing Agency, charging me with preventing action on the Wood Pulp Bill. The charge is utterly groundless and I think it is an effort of some interested parties to hurt me just now in view of some loose talk in the papers mentioning me as a dark horse. Home in the evening. My Cousin Nathan Cornish[162] and his friend Mr. Cunningham dined with us. Nathan and I were playfellows thirty-five years ago. I have scarcely seen him since. He has had a stirring career in California and Colorado and is a sturdy vigorous man. Perhaps he and I might easily have changed places, if we had changed situations in the beginning. He has made a pecuniary fortune, without fame, I some fame without pecuniary fortune. Each condition has its advantages. In the evening Crete and I called at General Schenck's, who is suffering somewhat from ill-health.

---

long-debated laws by general and permanent legislation attached to an appropriation bill, he said, was a questionable and dangerous practice.

[162]Nathan Cornish, whose residence was in Whitewater, Wisconsin, was the son of Betsy Garfield Cornish, sister of Garfield's father. In 1880 he was listed on a letterhead as superintendent of the Davenport Consolidated Mining and Smelting Company, his address being given as Mineral City, San Juan County, Colorado. In New York City, where he spent considerable time, he was engaged in selling "mining property." In 1878 he offered to let Garfield acquire a share in a silver lode that would, he said, make him (Garfield) a millionaire in a few years. His brother Henry is mentioned later in the diary.

THURSDAY, 6.   Worked at my desk until nearly half-past ten, when I went to the Capitol and continued work on the Tariff Bill in the Ways and Means Committee. It was nearly completed. In the House the day was consumed in another struggle on the Post Office Appropriation Bill, without reaching a final conclusion. Home in the evening until nine o'clock, when Crete and I attended the wedding reception of Judge Strong's daughter.[163]

FRIDAY, 7.   Worked at my desk until half-past ten o'clock, when I went to the Departments and thence to the Capitol and attended an adjourned meeting. The Post Office Appropriation Bill was taken up and voting continued until 12 when the House adjourned, the final vote on the bill being taken soon after the reading of the Journal.[164] The remainder of the day was devoted to private bills. In the evening Dr. Updegraff and wife dined with us and a number of friends called for our final Friday evening reception.

SATURDAY, 8.   Worked at my desk until 10 o'clock, when I went to the Ways and Means Committee. There was more of unpleasant display of temper between members of the Committee, than I have ever seen at any previous meeting. A long struggle was had over the sugar tariff, which was at last separated from the main bill and ordered to be reported by itself. The remainder of the bill was then ordered to be reported. At two o'clock in the House the Yocum Election Case was taken up and consumed the remainder of the day.[165] At half-past two I went to the Treasury Photographer's and gave him a sitting, thence went with Rockwell to witness the game of Baseball between the Nationals and

[163]Amelia Strong, daughter of William Strong, a justice of the United States Supreme Court, married Francis H. Slade on May 6 at 7:00 P.M.

[164]At the close of the session of May 6 the House had recessed to meet at 10:30 A.M. on May 7. This action was taken because several Fridays had been set aside for the Private Calendar. The Post Office Appropriation Bill was debated in the morning and passed early in the afternoon.

[165]Seth H. Yocum (1834–1895) was a Republican member of the House from Pennsylvania, 1879–81. His election was contested by Andrew G. Curtin (1817–1894), governor of Pennsylvania, 1861–67, minister to Russia, 1869–72, and a Democratic member of the House, 1881–87.

Albanies. The latter were victorious.[166] Dined at Rockwell's. Returned home at half-past seven. Crete and I called at Wormley's to see Hiester Clymer and his new wife. They were out. Called at Blaine's and had a long and interesting visit with Abby Dodge (Gail Hamilton) and Dr. Loring. Conversed with the Doctor on the problem of Jimmy's health. Called his attention to Dr. Updegraff's suggestion of last evening—that for a boy of fourteen to get so good a report as Jimmy had gotten for the last month, it must be that his health and intellectual strength would be permanently injured. Dr. Loring thinks not so long as the boy likes his studies and does not do it against his inclination. I wrote a letter to Dr. Coit this morning asking his opinion on the subject.[167]

SUNDAY, 9.   Did not attend church but worked on my mail and wrote a considerable portion of my minority report of the Ways and Means Committee on Hoop Iron. At my request Mr. Shellabarger prepared the draft of the report to save me time, but really his style is so unlike mine that I have been compelled to re-write nearly all of it, for I feel that I cannot adopt his somewhat verbose method of presenting a case.[168] At four o'clock took

[166]The score was 6–4. "It is evident," observed the *Washington Star* on May 10, "that the National nine needs strengthening. It would only be a matter of a few dollars to make it a much better team. As it now is there does not seem to be much chance for the nine to make a brilliant record."

[167]Garfield's anxiety about Jimmy's health had been aroused by a letter from him (April 26) complaining about headaches. "I do not see why I have them so much now," Jimmy wrote, "I was hoping that they had commenced to stop, but they seem to be getting more frequent." In response to Garfield's query, Coit wrote (May 15): "Your boys are well. Your son James is not overworking. He has no occasion to do so, as he acquires with remarkable facility. He has suffered somewhat from his catarrh, and that may have caused one or two headaches, but he is as well as you could wish, and so far as I can judge his school-life agrees with him. I may say the same of Harry also, who seems to me better than when he first came here."

[168]The Committee on Ways and Means had adopted a bill to relieve importers of cut hoops, band hoops and scroll iron who were hurt by the Treasury ruling of March 12 (see entry and note for March 19, 1880) and to set a new rate on these products. The minority report, signed by the five Republicans on the committee, approved of the relief provisions of the bill but objected to the proposed

Crete and the children in the carriage and drove to Brightwood and the Soldiers' Home. In the evening Rose came and I dictated a large number of letters and worked still further on my Minority Report.

MONDAY, 10. Worked at my desk until half-past ten when I went to the Capitol to attend a meeting of the Joint Committee of the two [Houses] on the subject of Internal Revenue Stamps. Nothing was accomplished except the discovery that probably no new legislation was needed. This is perhaps more successful that [than] legislation would be. In the House the day was devoted to the Yocum-Curtin contested election case. During the day I completed my minority report on cut hoops and hoop iron and the[n] read it to the Republican members of the Committee. All assented. On my way home spent an hour at Barlow's[169] examining some of his new photographos. Played billiards with Rockwell an hour. Home in the evening. Mr. Riddle's son Bert [Albert] came down and gave me an exhibition of his training in elocution. He desires to go upon the stage and at his father's request, I wrote a letter introducing him to John McCullough.

TUESDAY, 11. Brown has gone to Kansas for ten days. Rose came and I dictated letters until ten o'clock, when I went to the Departments. Thence to the Capitol to meet with the Committee on Ways and Means. Not much was accomplished in the House. The contested election case of Yocum vs. Curtin was settled in favor of Yocum, the sitting member. The Legislative Appropriation Bill was then taken up, and good progress made. I should have added that I presented to the House my Minority Report on the duty on Hoop Iron. In the evening the President and Will Howells called and we had a pleasant visit, talking on architecture, literature and Napoleon. The President has lost all interest

rate, which it considered too low in relation to the rates on other manufactures of iron. It contended that if this rate went into effect 15,000 persons would be thrown out of work, and foreign producers would profit at the expense of American manufacturers without any material reduction in the cost to American consumers of the finished products.

[169]Henry N. Barlow's Gallery of Fine Arts, which was at 1225 Pennsylvania Avenue, N.W.

in Napoleon and looks upon him as a selfish, brutal man and did not care to read anything further about him. Among the curiosities of his mind is the fact that he sees no fun in *Pickwick, Don Quixote* and *Gil Blas.*

WEDNESDAY, 12. Shortly after breakfast I rode with Colonel Rockwell to 6th Street and Louisiana Avenue to examine a second-hand Phaeton which was on sale. It was too large for my purpose. Returned and dictated letters to Rose until half-past ten o'clock when I went to the Departments and worked off a large budget of business that had accumulated. House at twelve. The Legislative Appropriation Bill was taken up. Slow progress made on account of the factious opposition of several Southern gentlemen, who seem to desire a long session. At four o'clock I went with Rockwell to the Base Ball Grounds where a very finely contested game was played, lasting three hours, between the Nationals and Albanys. The former were the victors.[170] At eight in the evening Crete and I called on Will Howells and his wife, who are guests at the Executive Mansion.[171]

THURSDAY, 13. Worked at my desk until half-past ten, when I went to the Capitol to attend a meeting of the Committee on Ways and Means. We had a long and stormy session on the question of adjournment and after numerous votes a resolution

[170]"The Nationals took a new departure yesterday," said the *Washington Post* (May 13), "winning a game from the Albanys by a score of five to one. It must have seemed rather funny to the boys to win a game once more."

[171]William Dean Howells and his wife, Eleanor Mead Howells (who was a second cousin of President Hayes), spent more than a week at the White House during May, 1880. Lucy Cook (1851–1902), a cousin of Mrs. Hayes who visited the White House often during the Hayes administration, wrote thus of the Howells in a letter to her mother on May 9 (R.B. Hayes Library): "They are both very agreeable people, he is not in the least literary or even intellectual looking; is short, fat, dark and wears his hair parted exactly in the middle with short *bangs* across his forehead and would be coarse looking if it were not for a very genial pleasant expression about his eyes. He is not a bit awe inspiring; you feel acquainted with him at once, he has a great many good jokes and is fond of hearing others jokes. The President seems to enjoy him very much. Mrs. Howells is short and as thin as any one could well be. You could take her for the intellectual member of the firm. She is very pleasant but I like her husband better."

was passed fixing the adjournment for the 31st instant. Only two Democrats voted for it. One Republican—Dunnell[172]—was absent. In the House the Legislative Bill was taken up, and considerable progress was made until it was interrupted by a personal explanation from Mr. Springer in reply to one from Orth of a few days ago. Orth developed the fact that Springer's first report of some years ago, on the Venezuela Claims, was published in the Western papers and contained matter injurious to Orth, but the report which was adopted by the Committee omitted all those passa[ges] reflecting upon Orth and the latter report was not made until after Orth had withdrawn from the contest in consequence of the charges against him. A wicked party action.[173]

FRIDAY, 14.   Worked at my desk until half-past ten when I went to the Treasury Department and Pension Office on business and

[172]Mark H. Dunnell (1823–1904) was a Republican member of the House from Minnesota, 1871–83, and 1889–91.

[173]In 1868 a mixed commission, which included one person from the United States, met in Caracas to adjudicate claims of United States citizens against Venezuela and awarded $1,250,000 to claimants. Godlove S. Orth (1817–1882), a Republican member of the House from Indiana, 1863–71, 1873–75, and 1879 to his death, served as a lawyer for one of the claimants. Subsequent to the award the Venezuelan government charged that the tribunal had been illegally constituted, and that many claims were "fraudulent, fictitious, and dishonest." Under the chairmanship of William M. Springer, a Democrat, the House Committee on Foreign Affairs investigated the matter and Springer, on his own, released to the *Chicago Times* a report which the paper published on August 7, 1876. The report contained damaging charges against Orth that did not appear in the committee's official report completed and adopted at a later date. On May 4, 1880, Orth explained on the floor of the House that the Forty-second Congress (1871–73), of which he was not a member, had declared the awards to be valid, and that secretaries of state W.H. Seward, E.B. Washburne, Hamilton Fish, and W.M. Evarts had insisted that Venezuela never established the validity of her charges against the tribunal or the claimants. Orth accused Springer of conducting an unauthorized investigation for partisan political purposes (Orth was a gubernatorial candidate in Indiana in 1876, but withdrew from the campaign because of the Springer accusations). On May 13 Springer defended his actions, arguing that the investigation was proper, and claiming that the *Times* had disregarded his orders not to publish the report until the full committee had modified and adopted it.

thence to the Capitol. From 11 to 12 o'clock, being the adjourned session of yesterday, good progress was made on the Legislative Appropriation Bill and in the House, after Thursday's journal was read, the morning hour and private bills were suspended and the Legislative Bill was finished by half-past three o'clock. Then Mr. Gibson reported the resolution from the Committee on Ways and Means for final adjournment on the 31st. It was resisted by a majority of the Democrats and an attempt was made to recommit it with instructions not to report it until a bill had been brought in to put salt and printing paper on the free list. This failed when Blackburn fillibustered until adjournment. Home in the evening. Several people called, among others the Sixth Auditor[174] and his two daughters, who sang and played very beautifully. Rockwell came and we played a few games of billiards.

SATURDAY, 15. Worked at my desk until 11 o'clock when I went with Crete to call on Gilfillan and thence to Boteler's to do some shopping.[175] Thence to the Capitol where the day was spent in passing the adjournment resolution. I made a brief speech de-

---

[174]Jacob McGrew, of Ohio, was appointed chief clerk of the Sixth Auditor's Office in the Treasury Department in 1864 and promoted to sixth auditor in 1875. As auditor he was head of the office responsible for examining and adjusting all accounts of the postal service. On June 1 or 2, 1881 (see entry for June 1; McGrew said that the event occurred on June 2), President Garfield reluctantly asked for his resignation on the recommendation of the attorney general and the postmaster general, who were investigating frauds in the star route service. McGrew later testified that Secretary of the Treasury Windom and the President had both promised him that if the investigations did not find him implicated in the irregularities, he would be appointed to a post better than the one he then held. He further testified: ". . . On Thursday, the 30th of June, the President sent for me and said that he had become convinced that he had done me a very great injustice; and that he intended to redeem the promise he had given to me, and intended to make my restoration conspicuous." Two days after this interview Garfield was shot. After leaving office McGrew practiced law in Washington. See *House Miscellaneous Reports,* No. 2165, Part 2, 48 Cong., 1 Session, Serial 2234, pp. 151–155.

[175]J.W. Boteler & Bro., importers of china, glass and crockery ware, conducted a china hall on Pennsylvania Avenue.

fending the adjournment. It was carried by a handsome majority, three-fourths of the Democrats however voting against it. At three o'clock, I went with Cols. Rockwell and Hodges[176] to witness the champion game of base ball between the Nationals and Albanys. The former were victorious. At eight o'clock, I went to Amos Townsend's and spent the evening with a number of gentlemen, among them Judge Cartter, who expressed the belief that Grant would be nominated. The perfidy of Washburne towards [Grant] is manifestly working in Grant's favor.[177]

SUNDAY, 16.   Crete and I attended church. Called at General Schenck's on our way home. The General has [been] manifestly improving in health and has now some hopes of recovery. During the afternoon I finished the last volume of Hazlitt's *Napoleon.* I doubt if I shall ever again read the life of Napoleon unless a new one is written by some abler historian than any who has yet attempted it.[178] I find this time, as frequently before, great difficulty in judging Napoleon severely. I suppose I ought to come to a conclusion very unfavorable to his character, but in spite of my reasoning to the contrary, I find myself indignant at the alliance which crushed him. With all his inconsistencies, he was the hammer that broke in pieces the Divine right of Kings.

MONDAY, 17.   Worked at my desk until ten o'clock when I went to the Navy Department to make inquiries about the conditions and possibilities for Hal and Bentley Warren to enter the Naval Academy. Found that there would be no opportunity for either of them until they were too old. Called on Dr. Baxter in refer-

---

[176]Henry C. Hodges, a native of Vermont and a graduate of West Point, was now a deputy quartermaster general with the rank of lieutenant colonel. He was commissioned colonel in 1888 and retired (1895) at that rank in his forty-eighth year in the service.

[177]In Cook County, Illinois, anti-Grant Republicans formed a James G. Blaine-Elihu Washburne coalition with the understanding that they would support the man who developed the greater strength in the state convention. This movement united Grant's supporters across the state and he carried the convention by a majority of 85 votes. Washburne, who had long been Grant's close friend and had served as minister to France during his administrations, received as many as forty votes, even though he openly supported his former chief. Grant believed that Washburne had been false to him and the two never met again.

[178]See entry for May 18.

ence to Hal's physical fitness to pay [pass] an examination. Found that also uncertain. Called on the Sec'y of the Interior in reference to the appointment of Mr. Purdy, Mr. Smalley's Brother-in-Law. Thence to the Capitol. The [House] meets today and for the balance of the session at eleven. This is Suspension Monday and several bills were passed, among others the River and Harbor Appropriation Bill by an overwhelming majority. Several bad measures were voted down, among them one to authorize the banks to loan money on real estate up to one-quarter of their capital [and surplus]. Home at half-past four to aid Crete off to Ohio. At one-quarter past seven drove with her and Irvin to the Baltimore and Ohio, where at 7.45 they took the train for Ohio by the way of Pittsburgh. Abram went with us to the train. Soon after my return to the House Messrs. Bateman and Butterworth called and I went with them to Secretary Sherman's, where we had a long conversation lasting until 11 o'clock—on the Presidential Question. Mr. Sherman believes he will [have] 116 votes on the first ballot,[179] as follows:

38 O.	5 Va.	5 N.J.	8 Miss.
15 N.C.	3 Ky.	5 Md.	1 D.C.
8 Geo.	6 Tex.	3 Wis.	2 W. Va.
6 S.C.	5 N.Y.	4 Ind.	114 Total

TUESDAY, 18. Worked at my desk until ten o'clock, when I went to the Capitol to attend a meeting of the Committee on Ways and Means which was devoted to private bills. The House met at eleven o'clock. Deficiency Bill of $9,000,000 passed. Agricultural [Appropriations] Bill was then taken up and occupied the remainder of the day. At half-past three played a few games of billiards with Rockwell. Home in the evening; read Lanfrey's *Napoleon,* [180] and Brunson's [Bronson's] Life of John Sherman.[181]

WEDNESDAY, 19. Worked at my desk until half-past ten when I went to the Capitol, stopping on the way to buy suits of clothes

---

[179]On the initial ballot Sherman received only 93 votes.

[180]Pierre Lanfrey (1828–1877) completed four volumes of a projected five-volume work, *Histoire de Napoléon Ier* (1868–1875). MacMillan and Company published an English translation (1871–1879).

[181]Sherlock A. Bronson, *John Sherman, What He Has Said and Done . . .* (1880).

for the boys. In the House, the Agricultural [Appropriations] Bill was finished and an attempt made to get up the Tariff Bill. It was antagonized by the Funding Bill, which was taken up, and I sought to get the floor to speak, when the Committee arose and the House adjourned.[182] At three o'clock went to Col. Rockwell's, and with him, Col. Hodges, Mrs. Rockwell, Mollie and Abe went to see the Hanlon-Courtney boat race. A miserable performance which I do not care to see repeated.[183] Home in the evening.

THURSDAY, 20. Worked at my desk until 10 o'clock, when I went to the Committee on Ways and Means. The session was devoted to private bills. In the House after a struggle on calling up the Funding Bill and the Interstate Commerce Bill, the day was devoted to the report of the Committee on Public Lands. Went to the evening session for a short time. During the day had the carpets taken up and cleaned and the work of packing continued. Gradually getting the house ready to leave.

FRIDAY, 21. Worked at my desk until nearly 11, when I went to the Capitol. The unfinished business of yesterday, that is, bills from the Committee on Public Lands, occupied three hours and

[182]Garfield attempted to make the point of order that the Funding Bill, not the Tariff Bill, was the first to be considered, but he failed to get the floor. After considerable wrangling the House voted to recess until 7:30 P.M.

[183]A crowd estimated at 100,000 gathered along the Potomac River to watch Edward Hanlon (1855–1908), Canadian oarsman and single-sculls champion of the world, 1880–84, and Charles E. Courtney (1849–1920), famous and successful rowing coach at Cornell University, 1883–1916, compete in a much-publicized rowing contest over a five-mile course. A prize of $6,000 awaited the winner. From the start of the race Courtney proved to be a miserable competitor, failing to row hard, stopping frequently to wet his handkerchief and apply it to his head, and making little effort even to steer his boat. Hanlon won the race in just under 37 minutes without having to exert himself. In fact, a third oarsman, James H. Riley, who was guaranteed $500 for being on hand to race, in the event either contestant failed to appear, rowed ahead of Hanlon all the way. Some, including the referee, said that Courtney was ill; others thought he lacked grit; and still others believed that he was in the hands of gamblers and threw the race. Whatever the case, the spectators were, like Garfield, thoroughly disgusted with the performance.

the remainder of the day was devoted to the private Calendar. At four o'clock I went with Rockwell and Hodges to see the game of base ball played by the Nationals in [against] Baltimore.[184] Home in the evening. The President called to consult with me in regard to the bill for the appointment of marshals which passed the Senate yesterday. I told him I should resist the bill and pointed out the grounds of my objection but was willing to offer a substitute that I could support. He said he had come in hopes that we could get together and was glad to find our views were in accord. He read me a rough draft of a veto which he had already prepared. I suggested some additional points which he adopted. I should have stated that I received a letter from Crete, who arrived in Mentor safely after a hot and uncomfortable journey. She found the house well advanced and is pleased with it. Retired at 12 o'clock.

SATURDAY, 22. Worked at my desk until nearly ten o'clock. Prepared a speech on the Refunding Bill. Then went to the Navy Department. Thence to the Capitol. The day had been set apart under a suspension of the rules on Monday last for the consideration of reports from the Committee on Public Lands [Buildings], and by a singular ruling of the Speaker pro-tem, it was decided that nothing was in order, that not even questions of consideration could be raised. As the Committee on Public Buildings had recommended the erection of 45 new buildings, at an aggregate cost of nine millions of dollars, action was resisted by dilatory motions and breaking up a quorum, until wearied with the useless struggle, the House adjourned a little after three. In the afternoon Brown returned from the West and called. I dictated quite a number of letters.

SUNDAY, 23. Did not attend church. Rose came and I dictated a Minority Report on the Tariff.[185] Devoted about four or five

---

[184]The Nationals won, 5–1.

[185]The minority report (signed by four of the five Republican members of the Ways and Means Committee) consisted of a statement of about four pages written by Garfield but based largely on material supplied by protectionist interests, and about nine pages of letters, the most important of which were given to Garfield by John Lord Hayes, secretary-lobbyist of the National Association of Wool Manu-

hours to the subject. Mrs. Reed and Mr. Rose took dinner with us. At four o'clock I called on Blaine and we took a long walk in the grounds of the Naval Observatory. B. spoke very freely of the political situation. Said he did not much expect the nomination at Chicago, and would not have become a candidate but for the belief that he could more effectually prevent the nomination of Gen. Grant than any one else. On the whole, he thought the nomination of Grant quite probable. Called at his house on our return, and had a pleasant visit with Mrs. B. and Abby Dodge.

Home in the evening, and lonesome without Crete.

MONDAY, 24. Busy at my desk, and the Dep'ts in putting my things in order for leaving for Mentor and Chicago.

In the House after the morning hour I presented the minority Report on the Tucker Tariff bill. It was signed by all my Republican associates on the Committee of Ways and Means except Dunnell.

The House then took up the Sundry Civil Appropriation Bill, and made good progress upon it. There is still some hope that the adjournment may be reached the first of June—though I think it hardly probable.

Spent the evening in putting home affairs in order to leave tomorrow.

TUESDAY, 25. Worked at my desk until 10 A.M. when I spent two hours paying bills, visiting the Dep'ts, etc.

---

facturers. The minority agreed that "in many respects the tariff should be amended," and favored a reduction of exorbitant rates "as rapidly and as far as the wants of the revenue and the prosperity of our great national industries" would permit. They took sharp issue, however, with the bill the Democrats had devised, which they believed exhibited "a spirit of hostility" to American industries and "a partial and unjust treatment" of the subjects it embraced. Singled out for discussion were the duties on wool and the manufactures of wool, iron and steel —the products of the leading protected industries. Since the bill had no chance in the House (it never came to a vote), the minority report was, in so far as legislation was concerned, of little significance. As a campaign document it was of some importance for the Republican party and its presidential candidate. During his last day in the House Garfield proofread the report (with John Lord Hayes at his side) and submitted it. In setting out for the Republican National Convention, he left behind documentary evidence of his devotion to the protectionist cause.

Called on Sec'y Sherman and had a final interview in reference to his interests in Chicago. I asked him to suggest frankly what he considered the strong points of his public life, that I might present him to the Convention in the strongest light. He said he left that wholly to my judgment, but suggested that the chief characteristic of his life, from boyhood up, had been courageous persistence in any course he had adopted. In the House at 12. Corrected the proofs of my minority report on the tariff. Took a brief part in debate on the Appropriation Bill.[186] Left the House at 4 P.M. and went home. Dictated many letters, got affairs in shape at home, and at 9 P.M. left for Baltimore and Ohio R.R. Depot with Mollie, Abe, Mary and Ella White,[187] and at 9.30 left for Ohio via Pittsburgh.

WEDNESDAY, 26. Awoke near Pittsburgh. Caught the 8.30 train, Pittsburgh and Lake Erie R.R. Youngstown at noon—many friends called. Cleveland at 2 P.M., found Crete at Vincent and Sturm's.[188] Shopped two hours, took 4.50 train East. Dr. Robison met us at Reynolds, and at six were in our new house. Supper in the hall. The house full of carpenters and painters. The improvement is better than I had expected. It will take two weeks to finish it.

Family all well, and happy to be reunited again. Letters from Hal and Jim awaiting me. They are doing well at St. Paul's.

THURSDAY, 27. Spent the day in ordering details of finishing house—agreed to have the roof painted with fire proof paint.

Reviewed condition of the farm. Work a good deal behind because of repairs of house which has called off farm hands.

Total cost of repairs will reach $4,000, perhaps a little more.

[186]Garfield supported an amendment to increase from $275,000 to $300,000 the appropriation for the Coast and Geodetic Survey, which was a part of the Sundry Civil Appropriation Bill.

[187]According to the Mentor, Ohio, census of 1880 Mary and Ella White were age 30 and 20 respectively, black, natives of Virginia, and domestic servants.

[188]Vincent, Sturm & Barstow was a wholesale and retail furniture establishment located on Water Street.

Spent several hours with Dr. Robison adjusting accounts.

FRIDAY, 28.   Devoted forenoon to house, farm and family. The morning papers indicate good progress of appropriation bills in Congress; but they will hardly get session ended before Chicago Convention. I was greatly in hopes I would not be obliged to go back to Washington, but I fear I shall be obliged to do so. At noon Crete and I went to Cleveland and spent four hours in making purchases, arranging for mantels, hearths, furniture, etc.

In the evening she returned to Mentor, and I took the 7.30 P.M. train for Chicago. I go with much reluctance, for I dislike the antagonisms and controversies which are likely to blaze out in the convention. R.C. Parsons was on the train with me.

SATURDAY, 29.   Arrived at Chicago early morning, and went to Grand Pacific Hotel. Room 108, adjoining and communicating with Foster's 110, was awaiting me. The city is full of Republicans, and intense activity is seen in all the hostile camps. Put myself in communication with Gov. Dennison, Bateman and Foster, my associate delegates at large, and before the day was over urged them to take a bold and aggressive stand in favor of District representation, and against the unit rule, and for this purpose that we unite with the friends of all candidates who take this view. The settlement of these principles is more important than the fate of any candidate. This view finally prevailed— and the Blaine men cooperate. Dined with Commercial Club in evening, and made a short speech on art, the topic of the evening.

SUNDAY 30.   An unpleasant rainy day. At eleven, went to the Disciple Church on Indiana Avenue and 25th St.—a very small audience and a moderate sermon by the pastor.

The remainder of the day was devoted to consultations and calls of friends.

Did not retire until long after midnight.

MONDAY, 31.   Fresh crowds arriving by every train, and the interest increasing every hour. Grant men and Blaine men very confident.

The Ohio delegation appears to be divided, 9 for Blaine, 35 for Sherman, possibly one for Edmunds, but all agreed on District representation, and resistance to unit rule.[189]

I am strongly urged to make a speech against the third term, at mass meeting tonight. I decline. The fight of delegates should be in the convention. I never fight mock battles.

A very fatiguing day, and no sleep till long after midnight.

June

TUESDAY, 1.   The active work of our delegation today was devoted to the subject of the temporary organization. There is danger that Cameron will apply the unit rule in the organization of the Convention, and thus assume its existence without the authority of the Convention. I called on Senator Conkling and suggested that a temporary Chairman might be agreed on by the opposing forces and thus avoid a contest before rules were reported. He did not appear willing to take much responsibility for his followers. We suggested Senator Hoar for temporary Chairman.[190] This was found later in the day to be unacceptable to the Grant men. A long and unpleasant controversy was had in the National Committee. Cameron refused to put some motions, or to allow an appeal from his decision. Much talk of displacing him. Ohio delegation elected Dennison

---

[189]Under the unit rule each state would vote as a block, with the vote of its entire delegation going to the candidate supported by its majority. It was common knowledge that Ulysses S. Grant, who did not have the support of a majority of the convention, might be nominated if the unit rule was established. Thus delegates like Garfield, who were against a third term for Grant, opposed the unit rule and favored district representation, by which each delegate voted individually for the candidate of his choice.

[190]Senator George F. Hoar of Massachusetts was made temporary chairman on the first day of the convention and permanent chairman on the second day. Garfield benefited from this selection, for when he rose on the 34th ballot to protest against delegates voting for him, Hoar ruled him out of order and directed him to take his seat. For Garfield's nomination, see Vol. I, pp. liv–lvii

its Chairman and voted 35 Sherman, 9 Blaine, 1 Edmunds.
[WEDNESDAY, June 2–FRIDAY, July 23.   No entries.]

July

SATURDAY, 24.   Worked on the mail.

SUNDAY, 25.   Capt. Henry came this morning in response to my
telegram; and at 2 P.M. I sent him and Mr. Fitch to Painesville
to take the Eastern Express.[191] Fitch to go home and the Captain
to go to N.Y. in answer to Gov. Jewell's request of yesterday.[192]
Sent by Capt. H. a long letter to Hinsdale on my notions of the

---

[191]See Vol. I, p. 362, n. 27. An article by Fitch, "James A. Garfield," appeared
in the *International Review,* IX, pp. 447–458 (October, 1880).

[192]On July 24 Marshall Jewell, chairman of the Republican National Committee, telegraphed Garfield to send Charles E. Henry to New York City as soon as
possible and to have him "ready for a trip of a week." Garfield promptly telegraphed Henry to come to Mentor and there discussed with him a decision he had
to make relating to party factionalism. In New York, Senator Roscoe Conkling and
his supporters (Stalwarts) smarted over Grant's defeat at the Chicago convention
and feared that Garfield, if elected, would favor the minority whose votes helped
nominate him. Several Republican leaders, notably Garfield's running mate, Chester A. Arthur, and the secretary of the Republican National Committee, Stephen
W. Dorsey (both Stalwarts), believed that Garfield could do much to mend the
rift by meeting with the committee and with Conkling. Garfield was hesitant about
going for fear he might offend liberal Republicans and Independents who were
upset by his statement on the civil service in his acceptance letter (see below,
n. 195), and who might interpret such a trip as a surrender to Conkling. Some
advisors opposed the trip and others were undecided. Accordingly Garfield asked
Henry to appraise the situation and give his opinion. On July 26, Henry wrote
from New York City advising Garfield to come. "Your friends," he stated, "who
were opposed to your coming, now think best for you to come. The Conkling men
have got the idea that you will continue Hayes's policy and let Sherman and Schurz
run New York. You can clear up any misunderstanding. Your friends can not do
it so well." Henry thought that Conkling wanted nothing unreasonable, that he
simply failed to understand and was jealous of his enemies, and that Garfield had
"little to fear from the Independents" so long as the announced purpose of his trip
was to see the National Committee. On the following day, however, Henry
informed Garfield that both sides were unreasonable, but that he could "see no
other way to cure the bellyache in these New York politicians" than for Garfield
to come.

426

proper method of reforming the Civil Service,[193] also some material for his book.[194]

Crete, Swaim and I took a walk in the Dille grove, and discussed the N.Y. situation. On our return we found Cousin Nathan Cornish and his wife here to visit us. He brings good news from the people he knows in New York. Had a long and pleasant visit with cousin and his wife. The children went to the lake in the evening.

Retired at about ten o'clock.

MONDAY, 26. Resumed the work again, and made some progress in reducing the surplus letters. Reports from California indicate

[193]Concerned about how Independents and liberal Republicans regarded his position on civil service reform, Garfield asked Hinsdale to set them straight "by a letter to the *Nation,* or better still by getting Godkin to take the view of the subject . . . which I do." The *Nation,* edited by E.L. Godkin, supported Garfield but had criticized as "a cruel disappointment" this statement in his letter accepting the presidential nomination: "To select wisely from our vast population those who are best fitted for the many offices to be filled, requires an acquaintance far beyond the range of any one man. The Executive, therefore, should seek and receive the information and assistance of those whose knowledge of the communities in which the duties are to be performed best qualifies them to aid in making the wisest choice." Reformers like Godkin interpreted the statement to mean that the Republican candidate intended to continue the spoils system. Garfield also asked Hinsdale to write an article, if he had time, embodying the following chief topics: cooperation between Congress and the President in preparing a civil service reform program; a fixed term for minor officials; carefully prepared specifications for removal of officials and protection against removal on other grounds (these protections "should not apply to Cabinet and Bureau officers who should be chosen with reference to the policy of the administration as well as to their personal fitness for the places they hold"); protection of the lawful rights of office-holders to participate in political caucuses and conventions; and consultation with congressmen before making appointments. Hinsdale replied (July 27) that it would be two or three days before he could "look after the *Nation* and the Civil Service." "I understand," he added, "that the Independents are disgusted, but they are going to stand on your record (not on your letter). Hence it is fortunate that the record is good!"

[194]B.A. Hinsdale, *The Republican Text-Book for the Campaign of 1880. A Full History of General James A. Garfield's Public Life, with other Political Information* (New York, 1880). Garfield received from Hinsdale through the mail a copy of the book on August 23.

that my letter of acceptance[195] has been well received there by the better class of citizens. Glad to know that the "hoodlums" do not like me.

I had intended to haul in the oats today; but on examination, found them not dry enough. Put the force of extra men into the corn and beets. Am having roofs of barns and outhouses treated with a mixture of coal tar and iron, put on hot.

Many callers—most of them brief calls.

TUESDAY, 27. Long and urgent telegram from Dorsey urging me to attend the meeting of Executive Committee on 5th prox.

Answered he must give me reasons. I wrote yesterday to W.E. Chandler on the same subject, who is to meet Gov. Jewell in Boston tomorrow, made the point that there was danger of alienation [of] our friends the Independents, who are already disappointed at that portion of my letter on Civil Service Reform, and if they shall now think I am in any way surrendering unduly to the N.Y. regulars, it will alienate them still more.[196]

---

[195]Garfield's letter accepting the nomination as the Republican presidential candidate was a carefully written political document aimed at harmonizing his divided party. It was issued under the date of July 10 and touched upon the following issues: pacification of the South and the right of Negroes to vote; popular education; national finances; the tariff; federal regulation of the Mississippi River; Chinese immigration; and the civil service. In tone and content Garfield's statement on the civil service suggests that he had concluded that he might displease liberal Republicans and Independents without losing their support, but had to placate the Stalwarts or lose their support and the election. The letter of acceptance is in Burke A. Hinsdale, *The Works of James A. Garfield,* II, pp. 782–787.

[196]In his letter to Chandler Garfield cited two additional objections. First, the trip would entail numerous occasions for speeches, "to be accepted or declined," and as one who had been "talking for twenty years" he could "hardly play dummy with self-respect," but would "have to run from saying something" to avoid upsetting a good many friends. Second, he preferred that Conkling come to Ohio, perhaps with Grant who was planning a visit on his return from the West. The three could meet in Mentor or any near point "without embarrassment, and thus avoid all misconstruction." He posed the question whether his going to New York would not do more harm than good by raising "all sorts of disquieting rumors in reference to the object for the journey." He also asked for reasons why he should go and closed with the statement that if he went "there should be a general gathering of state committees and leading members of the party." He did not want it to appear that he was going only to meet with Conkling.

In the afternoon rec'd long letter from Dorsey on the subject.[197] It contained more anxiety than reasons.

WEDNESDAY, 28.   Nichol returned from N.Y. with letters from McCook[198] and Hiscock[199]—all anxious for me to meet the Committee Aug. 5th. Dorsey writes it is now inevitable that there will

---

[197]From New York City Dorsey wrote Garfield (July 25) urging him to come "before operations begin" and meet on August 5 with the Republican National Committee, the Republican state committees, and the Republican Congressional Committee. "I am as certain as I can be of anything," he warned, "that a failure to have matters put in better shape in this state by August 5 means our defeat in November." He assured Garfield that the trip would in no way injure him for it would be made public beforehand that "you come in response to an invitation of the two national committees to meet and consult with eminent men of your own party from all parts of the country at the beginning of the campaign." Dorsey added that he intended to proceed with arrangements on the assumption that Garfield was coming. On the following day he explained in another letter to Garfield that the regular Republicans wanted to know and intended to know whether they were to be recognized as a portion of the state party or whether the "scratchers" and Independents and "featherheads" were to ride over the party as they had for the last four years. "Your presence," Dorsey insisted, "is a paramount duty that you owe to yourself and your party."

[198]Anson G. McCook wrote (July 26) that conversations with Nichol and Dorsey had confirmed that certain parties in New York intended to make their active support in the campaign conditional upon a "talk" with Garfield. Without expressing an opinion "about that style of Republicanism or that exhibition of party fealty," he urged Garfield to make the trip for the following reasons: (1) if the problem was now "a mere scramble for spoils," the sooner it was known the better; (2) Garfield would be sure of himself, say nothing harmful, make no bargain if any was asked, and "go home retaining the self-respect of a gentleman and the foremost man of a great party"; and (3) the worst should be known as soon as possible, and after Garfield's trip, they would know exactly where they were and what to expect.

[199]In a "strictly confidential" letter (July 24) Hiscock, who originally opposed the trip, now advised that until Garfield made it the campaign in New York would run itself and no money could be raised. He wrote that Conkling and his supporters believed that Garfield, if elected, would give the patronage to the anti-Grant men in the state, and that they sought, not a bargain, only "a little fraternization." With a politician's concern for the state's powerful railroad interests, he suggested that by going on the New York Central and returning on the Erie, Garfield would do great good. He reminded the presidential candidate that Conkling had complete control over the politics of New York City, that ten thousand votes were at stake, and that he had much to gain and nothing to lose by making the trip.

be serious trouble with Conkling and his friends if I do not go. Nichol says nearly all our friends think so.

I am very reluctant to go. It is an unreasonable demand that so much effort should be made to conciliate one man. But to resist the opinion of the whole Committee would be ungracious, and perhaps unwise. I await the result of Jewell's conference today with Blaine and Chandler.[200]

Drove Nichol to Painesville. Crete, Martha and Swaim went with me. Made some calls, sat to Tibbals[201] for photographs, and had the colts shod all around. Home at seven-fifty.

THURSDAY, 29. A very busy day. Worked off most of the private letters on my own desk. Telegrams indicate a general feeling that I should go to N.Y. Many calls from neighbors and friends. In the afternoon Townsend, Coon[202] and Edison[203] of Cleveland,

---

[200]After a long conference in Boston, Jewell, who was now convinced that Garfield should attend the meeting, wrote that "Blaine is decidedly against," but that "Chandler is I think inclined to agree with me" (Jewell to Garfield, July 28). On the same day Chandler, in a letter critical of Dorsey for forcing the meeting, wrote Garfield that he reluctantly concurred with Jewell.

[201]Horace W. Tibbals (c. 1845–1904) conducted a photographic studio in Painesville for a number of years. His photographs of Garfield received high praise. In Washington a committee asked to select the best photograph of Garfield for use in making a steel engraving by the Bureau of Engraving were unanimous in choosing a photograph by Tibbals over those by many other photographers, including Sarony and Bogardus of New York and Ryder of Cleveland. Another Tibbals photograph of Garfield was reproduced as an autotype by Bierstadt of New York and sold throughout the country. The head of a posthumous portrait of Garfield painted for the White House by Eliphalet F. Andrews was taken from a Bierstadt autotype. Mrs. Garfield sent one of the Tibbals photographs to Queen Victoria. Tibbals advertised that he would "furnish cabinet sized photographs of President Garfield for 30 cents each." He later moved to Jamestown, New York, where he opened a studio.

[202]John Coon (1822–1908), of New York, moved to the Western Reserve in 1837, graduated at Yale (1847) where he was a classmate of Chauncey Depew, and became one of Cleveland's leading lawyers. He was for a time joint-owner and publisher of the *Cleveland Herald*. He lived the last years of his life in Lyons, Michigan.

[203]Simeon O. Edison was an iron manufacturer in Cleveland, 1877–87. He moved to Syracuse, New York, in 1887.

McKinley of Canton and Gen. Grosvenor of Athens came. Townsend staid over night. At 9 P.M. I drove to Dr. Robison's and asked him to do what he can to allay the feeling in Cleveland over the Congressional nomination there. It is said that C.B. Lockwood is likely to accept the Bolter nomination.[204]

Mollie came from Little Mt. with the Mason girls and spent the day. All returned in the evening.

Mr. Henderson[205] of Cincinnati came to get some notes for Stanley Matthews to use in reply to Judge Hoadley [Hoadly] at Cincinnati.[206] Spent two hours with him.

FRIDAY, 30. Usual work in the office.[207] Northcott came to arrange for threshing, and I put a force of men in to dispose of the straw.

At four P.M. the wheat, barley and rye were threshed. Got 239

[204]At a convention in Cleveland on July 24 the Republicans nominated Amos Townsend, the incumbent, as their candidate for Congress from Ohio's Twentieth District. A minority walked out of the meeting, held one of their own (July 29), and nominated Charles B. Lockwood (1829–1919), a Cleveland businessman (See Vol. II, p. 68, n. 209). Under pressure from the "regular" Republicans, who argued that Lockwood's candidacy would result in a Democratic victory, he withdrew his name (August 5). Throughout the difficulty the "bolters" proclaimed their support of the Republican presidential ticket.

[205]Edwin Henderson, longtime city editor of the *Cincinnati Commercial,* was city clerk of Cincinnati.

[206]In a letter (July 28), which Henderson handed to Garfield, Matthews explained that Hoadly was scheduled to speak the next evening (July 30) in Clifton, and that he (Matthews) had agreed, at the request of Cincinnati Republicans, to reply at the same place on the following evening. He said that he was "in a strait for time to prepare necessary material," and needed the following information to reply to Hoadly's pending speech on "the Electoral fraud of 1876 and the connection of J.A. Garfield therewith": a true statement showing the outrages, violence, and intimidation in Louisiana in 1876, "a comparison of the votes by parishes to show the suppression of the votes by parishes," and anything relating to the count in New Orleans in 1876.

[207]On this day Garfield telegraphed Dorsey that he would go to New York. He also sent two telegrams to Blaine, the first asking him to be with him in New York on the "fifth proximo without fail." In the second, sent in response to a reply from Blaine that is not available, Garfield said: "Too late to change arrangements. Committee nearly or quite unanimous and urgent. You must not fail me. Chandler promised your presence and I rely on you."

bushels from 7 5/8 acres—nearly 33 bushels to the acre—said to be the best yield yet reported in this vicinity.

Many people called in the afternoon. Mr. Townsend, who stayed over night, left early for Cleveland by carriage.

SATURDAY, 31. Men continued threshing until noon. Had the oats hauled in from the field and threshed as they arrived. Result 475 bushels. No[t] so good a yield as last year. All spring grain seems to be lighter this year than the fall sown crops.

In the evening went to Dr. Robison[’s] and visited with J.H. Wade and S.F. Everett, who came to see us.[208]

C.B. Lockwood has accepted the bolters' nomination for Congress in the Cleveland District—whereat the Democrats rejoice. The result will not be so serious to us as they hope, but it will be bad enough. Home at eleven P.M.

August

SUNDAY, 1. Attended Church with Mother, Martha and Crete; a thoughtful sermon by Mr. Merill of Collamer. In the afternoon T.W. Phillips[209] of New Castle, Pa., came from New York.

---

[208]Sylvester T. Everett, who was chairman of the Finance Committee of the Cuyahoga County Republican Committee in 1880, had written to Garfield suggesting that Jeptha H. Wade, wealthy Cleveland business man, be invited to come to Mentor. Everett believed that an invitation was all that was needed to bring Wade to the public support of Garfield.

[209]Thomas W. Phillips (1835–1912) was one of four brothers (the others, Isaac, Charles and John are mentioned in the diary) who entered the petroleum industry in western Pennsylvania soon after oil was discovered there. They prospered for a dozen years and then suffered severe reverses (see Vol. III, p. 3, n. 1) from which they recovered after many years. At his death Thomas was president of the T.W. Phillips Gas and Oil Company, which owned hundreds of oil and gas wells, extensive pipe lines and leases on oil and gas lands. He was a member of the Disciples of Christ, contributing largely to the denomination by his writings, his support of the *Christian Standard* and his benefactions to Hiram and Bethany colleges and other schools. During the campaign of 1880, he devoted himself wholeheartedly to the interests of his longtime friend Garfield. He proposed the publication of the first Republican campaign text book and made it a reality by his

Later, Hon. J.T. Updegraff came. I sent them to Dr. Robison's to tea, and took Swaim and the children to Little Mt., and after a visit of an hour, came back bring[ing] the boys and Mollie, who have been staying there some days.

Visited evening with Updegraff, who spent the night.

MONDAY, 2.   A busy day, clearing up correspondence—for the N.Y. trip.

At noon Col. John Hay and his wife came and during the afternoon, we had a pleasant visit. The[y] left by 6.22 train at Willoughby.

Many telegrams in reference to the journey to N.Y.

Bentley Warren left for home at 2 P.M., Harry driving him to Painesville.

TUESDAY, 3.   Worked on mail until noon, and nearly cleared the decks. Made up a package of letters to take with me to N.Y. for the consideration of the National Republican Committee. At noon, Maj. Swaim and I took the train at Mentor, and found a special car tendered me by the Lake Shore Co. to take me to N.Y. Gen. Harrison and John C. New[210] of Indiana were on board. At one-40 we reached Geneva, O., and were received by a great concourse of people. Dined with the soldiers at the town hall. Thence went to the public square, and heard an address by S.A. Northway. Then I spoke about ten minutes, extemporaneously and rather effectively.[211] At 4.41 we took train east. We were

---

financial contribution and assistance in its preparation (B.A. Hinsdale, *The Republican Text-Book for the Campaign of 1880*). He was a Republican member of the U.S. House of Representatives from Pennsylvania, 1893–97, and in 1898 became a member of the Industrial Commission. See *Dictionary of American Biography.*

[210]John C. New (1831–1906), a native of Indiana, graduated at Bethany College in 1851 and was admitted to the bar in Indianapolis the following year. He was a Republican member of the Indiana senate, 1861–63, treasurer of the United States, 1875–76, assistant secretary of the treasury, 1882–84, and consul-general of the United States at London, 1889–93. He was a member of his party's National Committee, 1880–92. He was for many years the proprietor of the *Indianapolis Daily Journal.*

[211]The thrust of Garfield's brief talk at the dedication of the soldiers' monument at Geneva was that the ceremonies were being held, not to honor the dead, but to commemorate the immortality of the ideas for which they nobly fought.

433

received by great crowds at the stations. At Dunkirk Lt. Gov. Hoskins,[212] and several members of Gov. Cornell's staff met us, and a car load of leading citizens from Buffalo.[213] At Buffalo not less than 50,000 people received us. I spoke briefly, and retired, Palace Hotel, an hour after midnight.[214]

WEDNESDAY, 4. We were awakened at 5, took breakfast at 5.30, and at 6.15 were at the Depot, where a special train was waiting, and two coaches filled with invited guests. Train stopped at about 25 places on the way to N.Y. and great crowds of people at each. I made short address[es], say[ing] but little, beyond thanks and an occasional remark on the localities through which we passed. Many leading Republicans joined us en route. At Albany Gov. Cornell and Gen. C.A. Arthur[215] came on board. The former accompanied us to Hudson, the latter to N.Y. Chauncey M. Depew[216] also went with us to N.Y. At Garrison Hamilton Fish

[212]George G. Hoskins (1824–1893), a resident of Attica, New York, 1867 to his death, was a Republican member of the House from New York, 1873–77, lieutenant governor of New York, 1880–83, and a delegate to the Republican National Convention in Chicago, 1880.

[213]At Dunkirk, Hoskins, representing Governor Cornell, welcomed Garfield to the state of New York. Garfield acknowledged the welcome, introduced Benjamin Harrison (who spoke briefly), and reentered the train, which left for Buffalo after a ten-minute stop.

[214]An enormous crowd lined the two-mile route from the Exchange Street Station to the Palace Hotel, where Garfield mounted a platform and told about 10,000 people that he wished not to make a speech or to discuss politics, but to thank all for a great greeting. The reception was attended by spectacular illuminations and the periodic firing of artillery and fireworks.

[215]Chester A. Arthur (1830–1886), a native of Vermont, graduate of Union College (1848), lawyer, officer in the New York State militia, and collector of the port of New York, 1871–78, was now the Republican candidate for vice president of the United States. He assumed the presidency upon Garfield's death and served, 1881–85.

[216]Chauncey M. Depew (1834–1928), a native of New York, graduate of Yale (1856), and lawyer and executive of the New York Central Railroad, to which his political career was closely related. He was an unsuccessful Republican candidate for the U.S. Senate in 1881, a delegate at large to the Republican national conventions in 1888–1904, and a Republican member of the U.S. Senate, 1899–1911.

and wife met us at the station. The greetings on the way were cordial and enthusiastic. A vast assemblage met us at N.Y. Went to the 5th Avenue Hotel, and after dinner hundreds of callers until midnight.[217] I think no harm has been done.

THURSDAY, 5.   Breakfast at 8.30 and then came the stream of callers. At noon, the Conference was held in the hotel parlor, and speeches were made by Blaine, Logan, Sherman and many others. The absence of Senator Conkling gave rise to unpleasant surmises as to his attitude.[218] His friends were embarrassed and somewhat indignant. If he intends to take actively hold of the campaign, it is probably best that he does not call on me here. I think his friends are showing zeal and enthusiasm, and will work, whether he does or not. There shall neither be nor appear to be, if I can prevent it, any mortgaging of my future freedom. Nearly all the members of the Conference called. Had a long and friendly talk with Blaine. He is the prince of good fellows. Have asked L.P. Morton to take the Chairmanship of the Committee on finance. He will do it. Callers and conferences kept me up till past midnight. The officers of the Union League tendered me formally their support.

[217]With a police escort Garfield went directly from Grand Central Station to the Fifth Avenue Hotel, where Republican leaders from many states filled the lobby. After his arrival he spoke from a balcony to about 8,000 people, dined privately, met for a short time with several dignitaries, shook hands with reporters, and retired.

[218]Conkling, it was reported, was in the hotel while the meeting was going on and on one occasion, when asked about his absence, stated that he had not been invited. The *New York Times* (August 6) suggested caustically that Conkling's absence could doubtless be explained by his sincere desire for party harmony and not by lack of sympathy for the principles at stake or disapproval of the candidates. "The Senator," said the *Times,* "has somewhat of a talent for making enemies—a talent which he did not fail to improve at Chicago—and it is but natural that he should carefully avoid any occasion to reopen wounds inflicted on party rivals were it only by his reappearance as the leader of New York Republicans. This scrupulous regard for the feelings of others augurs well for the tact and self-sacrificing effort which Mr. Conkling is likely to carry into the canvass. Mr. Garfield will doubtless leave New York thoroughly impressed with the magnanimity of our senior Senator."

FRIDAY, 6.   After an early breakfast, Swaim and I went to Bogardus' photograph gallery and I sat for pictures.[219] There W.W. Phelps of N.J. met me and drove me to Whitelaw Reid's house, and Jay Gould came and we had a conversation on the campaign.[220] I think he will help. Thence to the hotel, where a crowd of callers was waiting. At noon went to Sarony's[221] and sat for pictures. Hotel again, lunch, and many callers. Had a pleasant visit with Thurlow Weed,[222] who is a remarkably wise and well preserved man. At eight P.M. went to the Republican Head Quarters, 241 Fifth Avenue, where the Boys in Blue gave me a

[219]Abraham Bogardus (1822–1908) opened a daguerreotype gallery in New York City in 1846. He later became a famous photographer and made numerous contributions to the technical development of photography. He was first president of the National Photographic Association, which he helped to found in 1868. In 1880 his gallery was at 872 Broadway. The *New York Times* reported (August 7) that Garfield "was in Bogardus' gallery at 8:30 sitting for his portrait."

[220]For personal and political reasons Reid wanted Garfield to meet with Gould, a stockholder of the *Tribune* who had helped Reid gain control of it with a loan of undisclosed size, and who influenced, if not controlled, the columns of the paper. Gould and other leading capitalists, aware of Garfield's speeches and voting record as a congressman, saw reasons to fear that he favored extensive federal regulation of monopolistic corporations, especially railroads. They were also angry over recent Supreme Court decisions upholding public control, and realized that Garfield, if elected, would likely make appointments to the Court. Gould therefore wished to learn the Republican candidate's views, and to extract from him satisfactory assurances as to the policies his administration would follow. The Republican campaign managers, of course, were eager to secure a large contribution from Gould.

[221]Napoleon Sarony (1821–1896), a native of Quebec, went to New York City in 1836. After a successful career as a lithographer, he turned to photography, opening a studio on Broadway in 1866; five years later he opened a larger studio at 37 Union Square, where Garfield sat for him. A popular photographer patronized by thousands, he is best known for his photographs of actors and actresses. See Ben L. Bassham, *The Theatrical Photographs of Napoleon Sarony* (1978).

[222]Thurlow Weed (1797–1882), long the leading supporter of William H. Seward, was the powerful and politically influential editor of the *Albany Evening Journal,* 1830–63, and a dominant figure in the Whig and Republican parties. In poor health for many years, he spoke briefly in a barely audible voice at the conference, praising the accomplishments of the Republican party and predicting victory in November.

serenade. Not less than 50,000 people in attendance. I spoke about 15 minutes—rather well—getting above the range of ordinary politics. Many other speakers followed.[223] Retired an hour past midnight.[224] Did not sleep well. Had in the P.M. a long interview with Morton, Crowley, Arthur and Platt.

SATURDAY, 7. Breakfast at 6.30 and at 7.30 took special train at Jersey City. Gen. Harrison, Messrs. Williams, Conger, Platt, Rhod[e]s, Murat Halstead,[225] Cowles, Keffer[226] and others met us. The crowds and enthusiasm along the line of the Erie R.R. were even greater than on the way to N.Y. I spoke at every station, somewhat more fully than on the way down, and, I think, made no serious mistake. I noticed that the working men are more markedly interested than they were at the beginning of the trip. I think their sympathy and enthusiasm are being kindled.

[223]When Garfield appeared the Seventh Regiment Band struck up "Hail to the Chief" and the crowd broke into cheers. The Boys in Blue bore lighted torches and the veterans carried a banner with the inscription "1861—Ever Ready—1866." Garfield spoke on patriotism, praising the work of Alexander Hamilton and treating the American Revolution and the Civil War as inspiring patriotic events. There were several other speeches, mostly of the "bloody shirt" variety, including one by Charles Guiteau.

[224]The *New York Times* (August 7) reported that after the speeches the Seventh Regiment Band escorted Garfield to the Fifth Avenue Hotel, "followed by a large and enthusiastic throng of people who hung about the hotel and cheered for the candidate long after he had disappeared from sight."

[225]Murat Halstead (1829–1908), a native of Ohio, was the editor and principal owner of the *Cincinnati Commercial,* whose staff he joined in 1853. A forceful, energetic, and influential Republican editor for many years, he was an inveterate and outspoken foe of "laxity and corruption in public life."

[226]John C. Keffer left his position as associate editor of the *Cleveland Leader* in 1880 to become chief editor of the *Cleveland Herald,* which had been acquired by Mark Hanna, John D. Rockefeller and others. He later owned and edited the *East End Signal* in Cleveland. Under his editorship the *Herald* was a Garfield organ in 1880. On July 23 of that year he wrote to Garfield: "I wanted to say that the columns of the *Herald* are always open to such use as you or your Secretary shall desire to make of them—and not only that, but that I think you can furnish many replies to matters which should be promptly answered, and which are likely to escape the notice of those who have not 'lived' a part of the legislative history of the country as you have." He went to Mentor to get Garfield's views on "the conduct of the paper" for the candidate's "best interests."

Dinner at Elmira. Supper at Salamanca. Westward of the latter place, torchlight processions and bonfires greeted us. Arrived at Jamestown 11.45, was escorted to the steamer by a great concourse of people, and at 2.30 A.M. Sunday arrived at Fair Point, where we accept[ed] the hospitality of the Chautauqua Assembly. At 3 retired at the Palace Hotel.

SUNDAY, 8.   Awoke at 9.30 and after breakfast attended the services in the great tabernacle. Listened to a fair sermon by a N.Y. preacher. After dinner attended the annual meeting of the Y.M.-C.A. but refused to speak. Seven thousand people gave me the Chautauqua salute,[227] to which I responded with a bow, but refused to speak. In the afternoon visited the model of Jerusalem and Palestine. In the evening was waited on by the Fisk Jubilee Singers,[228] and listened to several of their very beautiful songs. Dr. Vincent[229] called and explained to Mr. Halstead and me the work being done in an educational way at Chautauqua. I am delighted to know that so comprehensive a scheme of public culture is being wrought out. A day of peril, safely passed.

MONDAY, 9.   Breakfast at seven. At 7.45 not less than 5,000 people assembled in front of the Palace Hotel to greet me. I spoke about 15 minutes, mainly on the Chautauqua educational

[227]The salute, given on signal from the leader of the meeting, consisted of waving white handkerchiefs. It replaced applause, which the Chautauqua Assembly did not allow.

[228]The remarkable career of this group began in 1871 when George L. White, an instructor of vocal music at Fisk University, took a group of nine students on a concert tour to raise money for the school, which was in financial difficulty that threatened its existence. The singers won immediate popularity, here and in Europe, and raised over $90,000 for Fisk.

[229]John H. Vincent (1832–1920), a native of Alabama, was ordained deacon of the Methodist Episcopal Church in 1855 and elder in 1857 (New Jersey Conference). He held a number of pastorates and served as editor of Sunday School literature and corresponding secretary of the Sunday School Union, 1868–88. He was made a bishop and served, 1888–1904. He planned and directed the Chautauqua summer programs, 1878–88. It was his idea to start a national training institute and with his friend, Lewis Miller, he commenced the summer school which developed into the so-called Chautauqua movement, a system of popular education.

ideas, and I think, spoke well.[230] At the wharf, the Jubilee singers gave me two parting songs—a very striking spectacle. After crossing the lake to Lakeport [Lakewood], stopped a few minutes at Packard's Hotel,[231] then train to the West. Great crowds all along the way. Dinner at Meadville. Most gratifying demonstrations in the old 19th District. Reached Cleveland at 4.30 P.M. Swaim and I took the 4.50 train for Mentor and at 6.15 were at the table with the dear ones. Very weary but feeling that no serious mistake had been made and probably much good had been done. No trades, no shackles, and as well fitted for defeat or victory as ever.

TUESDAY, 10. Very tired and right hand badly swollen. But resumed work on my mail, which is also swollen by my absence. The crowd of callers very large, so that I have not been able to do very much with correspondence. Overhauled farm affairs somewhat, and had the men begin clearing up the debris of house building and harvest.

Received a good and cordial letter from Gen. Grant.[232]

[230]He closed his speech with a tribute to the Fisk Jubilee Singers: "I heard yesterday and last night the songs of those who were lately redeemed from slavery, and I felt that there, too, was done one of the great triumphs of the Republic. I believe in the efficiency of forces that come down from the ages behind us; and I wondered if the tropical sun had not distilled its sweetness, and if the sorrows of centuries of slavery had not distilled its sadness into voices which were touchingly sweet—voices to sing the songs of liberty as they sing them wherever they go. I thank that choir for the lesson they have taught me here." The singers presented Garfield with an inscribed copy of J.B.T. Marsh, *The Story of the Jubilee Singers; with Their Songs* (1880). The book is in the library at Lawnfield.

[231]The Lakeview House.

[232]Grant's letter (August 5) was in answer to an invitation from Garfield (July 26) to visit Mentor. "I neither sought nor desired the nomination," Garfield wrote, "but since it came to me, I am anxious to do my whole duty to the country. Certainly no American is so well able by an experience wholly unequalled in our history as you, to aid in bringing our people into harmony and assuring the success of our party." From Colorado, where he was traveling, Grant replied that he would be glad to see Garfield on his return east. He expected to leave for home about the first week of September, and invited Garfield to join him anywhere along the way or at his home in New York. "I feel a very deep interest in the success of the Republican ticket," Grant wrote in closing, "and have never failed

The newspapers and letters indicate that the perils of the trip were overcome, and much good was done by it.

They now begin to urge me to take the stump. I will pause awhile before I consent. Yet on many accounts I would be glad to do so. If it were the custom, it would insure better nominations.

WEDNESDAY, 11. Letters relating to the N.Y. trip begin to come in streams. I hardly find a criticism, and much approval, but perhaps the critics do not write. I shall assume that there is much more than I hear of. Mr. L.S. Coffin of Iowa came today.[233] He was a teacher at Chester when Crete and I were there and has retained much of his freshness and vivacity. He is anxious about my smoking and labors with me like a missionary. We had a pleasant visit with him.

Made good progress on the correspondence. At noon Father Rudolph, Hal, Jim and Mother left for Solon and Hiram. Croquet in the evening. Coffin spent the night with us. Crete is pleased with my N.Y. speeches.

THURSDAY, 12. A good day's work on correspondence. At noon, Mr. Coffin left. Soon after, Mr. Witt,[234] the artist, came to paint a bust portrait of me for the National Committee. He will not begin it until tomorrow. This day the 19th District Convention is held at Warren to nominate my successor in Congress. It seems strange to think of such a convention meeting to choose anyone but me. I can hardly realize the fact that for 18 years I have been

---

to say a word in favor of the party, and its candidate, when I felt that I could do any good. I shall not fail in the future.''

[233]See Vol. I, p. 15, n. 5.

[234]John H. Witt (1840–1901), a native of Indiana, settled in the early 1860's in Columbus, where he painted portraits and offered instruction; many portraits by him of Ohio public men are in the State House in Columbus. During the 1870's he spent some time in Washington, D.C. In 1880 he was under contract to paint for the Treasury Department a portrait of Ohian Thomas Corwin, who was secretary of the treasury, 1850–53. In 1879 he moved to New York City, where he spent the rest of his life. His portrait of Garfield was commissioned by the Republican National Committee and was hung in the committee's headquarters in New York City.

their only choice, and whatever may befal[l] me in the Presidential campaign, I part from the 19th District with regret—all the more so from the fact that I have met and overcome many difficulties. Late at night, I learn that after three sessions, the Convention nominated E.B. Taylor of Warren.[235]

FRIDAY, 13.   After an hour's work at the mail, I gave Mr. Witt a sitting, and he made rapid progress on the picture, sketching a full outline, without crayon lines—working rather with colors than with lines. I have never seen a more rapid artist. I should have mentioned that Cam and Nell and their two children were here when I returned from N.Y. and they are making us a pleasant visit. Good progress was made on the mail, and in the evening we played croquet, that is, Swaim and Brown, Judd[236] and I.

Have agreed to send my wheat, about 200 bushels of it, to Cleveland for sale at 90 cents per bushel.

SATURDAY, 14.   Witt's picture had not dried enough to go over again, and so he took another sketch in a different position which I like better. Sitting is very irksome to me; but it was relieved today by Crete, who read to me while the artist worked. We got off about 60 letters today, are [and] are gradually working down towards the bottom of the accumulated mass. Green hauled the wheat to the Station. We had a refreshing rain which was greatly needed.

Croquet in the evening till dark. Then work in the office, and visiting and singing in the parlor. I miss my dear old boys. Their vacation is rapidly passing, and soon they will leave us for their second year at St. Paul's.

SUNDAY, 15.   Worked on correspondence until nearly 11 A.M. when Nellie and Cam, Crete and I went to Church and listened to a thoughtful sermon by Mr. Merrick. After dinner the same party with the children and Swaim drove to Painesville, stopped

---

[235]See n. 360, November 30, 1880.

[236]Otis L. Judd, of Adrian, Lenawee County, Michigan, was telegrapher at Lawnfield during the campaign and in the White House during Garfield's administration.

a few moments at Geo. W. Steele's, and then home to Mentor, stopping half an hour at Father Clapp's and visiting with Eliza Glasier.[237] Home at 6, bringing a very large mail, on which we worked until ten, then in the parlor by the fire discussed the current theories of creation. I wish I had time to study these great questions.

The evening by the fire, politics forgotten, was a delightful one. I shall be sorry if any public event shuts me out from such evenings. Retired at 11 3/4 P.M.

MONDAY, 16.   Worked on mail until noon, when Cam and Nellie and children left us. Swaim and Brown and Mollie went to Cleveland. The *soi disant* "Prof." Zadeker [Zedaker] of Youngstown, Warren and Cleveland came and dined, and then gave us the most amazing exhibition of egotism I have ever seen.[238]

---

[237]Descendants of Orris Clapp (1770–1847), a native of New York who was an early settler of Mentor, Ohio, were longtime friends of Garfield, the friendships growing out of the association of the Clapps with the Disciples of Christ and with the Western Reserve Eclectic Institute. Three sons of Orris, Thomas (1806–1882), Matthew S. (1808–1879) and Henry (1812–1897) all lived in Mentor for many years. Matthew, who married a sister of Alexander Campbell, preached in Ohio, New York, Michigan, and elsewhere, and served a term in the Ohio legislature. Henry, a farmer, lived in Hiram for a number of years, during which his son William H. (1836–1905) and daughter Eliza attended the Eclectic, as did Harrison ("Harry") Glasier, whom Eliza married. William served as adjutant in the Forty-second Infantry Regiment, and with Garfield's support obtained a commission in the regular army after the war; he retired as a lieutenant-colonel in 1900. In 1880 he sent Garfield one hundred dollars as a contribution to his campaign expenses. All the persons mentioned here except Orris appear in the diary. Garfield himself erred (Vol. II, p. 361, entry for September 19, 1874) in referring to William and Eliza as children of Thomas, and the editors repeated the error (Vol. II, p. 13, n. 33).

[238]The *Cleveland Leader* (August 17) published a letter from the self-styled professor, giving an account of the trip of which this visit was a part. It began with a stop at Garrettsville (he spelled it "garitville"), followed by an overnight call at Little Mountain, where, as he put it, "I had the Pleasure of danceing upon the evening of my arrival." Departing by hack on the morning of August 16, he went to Lawnfield and presented to Garfield his "poem book." Zedaker noted that he and Garfield had never met, but that "each knowing other by fame before this," he was invited to dinner.

Gave Witt another sitting in the afternoon, and wrote some letters.

Swaim returned in the evening, but Brown remained over night in Cleveland.

TUESDAY, 17. Gave Witt a sitting in the forenoon. He is starting two pictures, working on one while the other is drying. Brown returned at noon. Capt. Henry and Don A. Pardee came and also Mr. John Coon of Cleveland.

Taylor and Perkins (members of the Labor party which met in Convention at Sharon, Pa., and endorsed my nomination) were here and agreed to go to Indiana and work with the lodges of their party in that state to help the Republicans at the October election.[239] Coon left via Willoughby at 6. The others, i.e. Pardee and Henry, staid over.

WEDNESDAY, 18. Correspondence and consultation. Pardee and Henry left on the noon train. Gave Witt another sitting, which however was a good deal interrupted by callers. He is doing very fine work, but I find sitting very irksome. I could hardly endure it if Crete did not read to me. In the afternoon dictated a large number of letters. Played Croquet and read some of the Biographies.[240]

[239]"The National Independent People's Labor Convention" met on July 29 to endorse candidates for President and Vice President of the United States. It was reported that more than two hundred delegates, representing fifteen states attended, each state being assigned fifteen votes. W.H. Taylor of Cleveland, described as chairman of the national committee, nominated Garfield for President, and the nomination was seconded by a Mr. Perkins of Ohio. Garfield received 125 of the 225 votes cast, after which the nomination was made unanimous. Arthur was nominated for Vice President. William H. Taylor is listed as proprietor of *The Labor Press* in a Cleveland directory for the year ending in June, 1881; he does not appear thereafter. See the *New York Tribune* (July 30) and the *Painesville Telegraph* (August 5).

[240]Never had a presidential candidate been the subject of so many biographies as was Garfield. Campaign biographies in book form include those by James S. Brisbin, Jonas M. Bundy, Charles C. Coffin, Russell H. Conwell, James R. Gilmore, Burke A. Hinsdale, James D. McCabe, and Albert G. Riddle. Some of them are still of value. Hinsdale and Riddle knew Garfield intimately. Bundy paid visits to Lawnfield during the weeks following Garfield's nomination. His book has a

Also worked on the evening mail until a late hour.

I should have mentioned that a delegation from Toledo came to invite me to attend the Tri-State fair in September.

THURSDAY, 19. Judge Taylor of Warren (just nominated as my successor in the House) came and spent two hours—to get a full understanding of my position on the Tariff. I reviewed it with him quite fully.

Gave Witt another sitting, and dictated over 50 letters. We are slowly working down towards the bottom of the pile which accumulated while I was away in N.Y.

Callers as usual. Worked until 10 1/2 on mail.

Harry came home at noon, but Jimmy and Mollie remained at Cleveland at James Mason's.

FRIDAY, 20. Gave Mr. Witt another sitting and he finished one of the pictures. It is, I think, the best portrait that has ever been made of me, really a fine piece of work, very quickly done, for the sittings have been very few, and much interrupted.

Hal resumed his study of Greek, and is to recite to Prof. Gist[241] at Willoughby.

Capt. Henry and his boy Freddie[242] came at noon and spent the afternoon and night with us.

---

number of letters concerning Garfield's college days written by contemporaries at Williams. Gilmore, whose acquaintance with Garfield dated from the Civil War, consulted with the candidate and submitted chapters of the biography to him; he received information concerning Garfield's canal days from Amos Letcher, captain of the boat on which Garfield worked. Some of the volumes were updated after Garfield's death.

[241]William W. Gist (1849–1923) went to Willoughby after graduating at Ohio University in 1872. During the next eight years, except for a period spent at the Union Theological Seminary in New York City, he was associated most of the time with the Willoughby schools but also did some preaching. After leaving Willoughby in 1880, he settled in Iowa, where he had a long career as a minister and as a teacher at Coe College and the Iowa State Normal School (Cedar Rapids). In 1920 he was elected national chaplain of the Grand Army of the Republic.

[242]Frederick A. Henry (1867–1948) graduated at Hiram College in 1888, earned a Master of Arts and a law degree at the University of Michigan, practiced law for 57 years in Cleveland, and was judge of the circuit court, 1905–12. See Vol. II, p. 216, n. 140.

Col. W.F. Sanders of Helena, Montana, called in the P.M. and many others.

Got off 60 letters, played Croquet, and on the whole had a delightful day.

SATURDAY, 21. Made good progress with the letters. Several people called. Jimmie and Mollie came on the evening train.

At 6 P.M. Crete and I, in company with Dr. Robison and his wife, drove to Little Mountain, and spent the evening with Mr. Wade and Mr. Everett and their families. Had a pleasant visit, and a few games of euchre. At 11 P.M. drove down home in the quiet and clear moonlight.

SUNDAY, 22. Did not attend church today. Gen. H.N. Eldridge of Chicago (my college classmate) and N.B. Sherwin came by the morning train, and spent the day with us. J.H. Wade and wife came down from the Mountain and took dinner with us—also Dr. Robison and wife. At 5 P.M. Crete, Swaim and I drove Eldridge and Sherwin to Willoughby.

It has been a delight[ful] day at Lawnfield—as the papers insist on calling our place. The moonrise was unusually brilliant.

MONDAY, 23. Made special exertion to finish the back work, and very nearly cleared the decks.

Witt gave the 3/4 view picture a few finishing touches and left us at noon. He has made an excellent portrait, and he says it is the best piece of work on a man's face he has done.

Ordered two new stalls put up in the east end of the horse barn. Many visitors came. In the evening Pres. O.A. Burgess of Indianapolis came and spent the night. Drove him to Dr. Robison's where we visited an hour early in the evening.

TUESDAY, 24. Worked on mail during the day and got ready to leave for Ashland to attend the meeting of the 42nd Regiment. Harry went to Cleveland to make some purchases preparatory to going back to school. Jimmy, Swaim and I drove to Willoughby and took the 6.20 train for Cleveland. We were met by a number of friends and driven to the Forest City House. The Garfield and Arthur Glee Club serenaded us. A great crowd of callers thronged the rooms until midnight. Harry and Jimmy spent the night at James Mason's. Swaim and I spent the night at the Forest City House.

WEDNESDAY, 25.   Breakfast at the Forest City House. At half-past eight took Dr. Streator's special car,[243] which was well filled with a company of Cleveland friends. Harry, Jimmy and Major Swaim were with me. We went to Ashland. At every station we met the usual crowd of people and were greeted with much enthusiasm. Arrived at Ashland at half-past nine. The village was crowded in every part with a press of people far exceeding anything known in that place. From 12 to 15 thousand people were present. After dining at the hotel and receiving many callers, and many members of the 42d O.V.I., about 150 to 160 assembled in the Court House for their Annual Meeting. After transacting the usual business, went to the stand in front of the Court House, where the public exercises were held for at least three hours. I made a speech of about twenty minutes.[244] At half-past four took the train and returned to Cleveland. Spent the night at the Forest City House. Harry and Jimmy staid at Mr. James Mason's.

THURSDAY, 26.   Remained at Forest City House until ten, when after a little shopping with Swaim and the boys, I took the 11 o'clock train for Mentor. Found a great mass of mail awaiting me and devoted the afternoon to answering the most important letters.

FRIDAY, 27.   We made good progress today in clearing up arrea[ra]ges of work accumulated during my absence to the 42d Reunion. A single day of absence makes it hard to clear the docket.

SATURDAY, 28.   Busy day with correspondents and callers. An unusual number of people called and occupied a large share of

[243]See Vol. II, p. 15, n. 44.

[244]The speech, a tribute to the regiment and to the nation, was interrupted twice by collapses of the platform. In the second mishap Garfield and two or three reporters fell to the ground. No one was hurt, and Garfield quipped that "a military reunion without some excitement and accident would be altogether too monotonous and tame to be interesting." A crowd estimated at from eight thousand to ten thousand attended the afternoon ceremonies.

my time during the day. Rose began cataloguing the Library today,[245] having arrived this morning. At noon President Hinsdale and wife came and spent the night with us. There was printed today in the Cleveland papers a letter from President Hinsdale in answer to the assaults made upon me by the Temperance People.[246] It may have been a mistake to notice the matter for nothing short of the full doctrine of prohibition will satisfy so unreasonable a people.

SUNDAY, 29. Attended church in the forenoon and listened to a sermon by Mr. Hendricks.[247] Dictated some letters in the afternoon and evening.

MONDAY, 30. Worked at the mail as usual. The first suggestion that the Democratic assaults upon me are beginning to make

[245]This catalogue of Garfield's library, now on the second floor of his Mentor home, Lawnfield, is in the Library of Congress.

[246]In 1869 a national prohibition party was founded and participated in presidential elections regularly thereafter; state parties also came into existence. In 1874 an old temperance organization was reorganized as the National Woman's Christian Temperance Union; five years later Frances Willard became its national president. Temperance supporters hailed the stand taken by President and Mrs. Hayes against serving spirituous liquors at White House functions, and Mrs. Hayes became the heroine of the movement, although she was not a member of the National Woman's Christian Temperance Union. In 1880 much interest was expressed in Garfield's drinking habits, and the Hayes policy was urged upon him. Hinsdale's letter was an effort to counteract misinformation. Reporting a conversation with an "Eastern gentleman" who had heard that Garfield was not a temperance man and that Mrs. Garfield had said that her husband believed in the use of wine and preferred to use it on his table, Hinsdale wrote: "I told him that General Garfield *was* a temperance man, and always had been . . . that I had spent much time the last twenty years in Garfield's house, and had been at his table hundreds of times; that I had never seen wines or other liquor on his table; that I had never seen liquors drank at his table or in his house; that I had never heard of such a thing, that it could not be true; and that General Garfield is temperate in his own habits. I added, that he is not a prohibitionist and probably would not sign a pledge *never* to use spirituous liquors; but that his principles and his practices are, and always have been, such as to command the confidence and respect of sensible temperance people who know what they are." *Cleveland Herald,* August 28, 1880. See also n. 282, October 31, 1878.

[247]Warren B. Hendricks (his last name usually was spelled Hendrix or Hendryx) was pastor of the Disciple church in Mentor, 1880 and 1881–83.

inroads upon our strength comes today in a letter from Governor Jewell. He thinks more notice should be taken of the charges, especially those relating to the De Golyer Pavement. I have written him that while I am ready to receive and answer any assaults that they can make, it is evident that they are not satisfied with the issues, the Solid South and the business interests of the Country, and are trying by these personal assaults to divert the people from the great national questions on which the campaign depends. Still it grieves me to know that our people are being disturbed by the Democratic tactics.[248] I am discussing with some anxiety the question of going to the Canton Reunion.[249] On most accounts I would prefer not to go; but I missed the Columbus Meeting and perhaps ought to go. Hinsdale and wife left this evening.

TUESDAY, 31. Worked at the mail until noon, when Major Swaim, Jim Robison, Crete and I took the train for Cleveland. Went to the Kennard House and at 3 o'clock the President, Mrs. Hayes and their son Rutherford came and took dinner with us. At four o'clock and thirty minutes we went to his special car on the Valley R.R.,[250] lately completed, and went to Canton. Our

[248]During the campaign the Democrats made much of the charges of corruption brought against Garfield, particularly in connection with the DeGolyer Pavement and the Credit Mobilier affairs (see Vol. II, pp. 63–64, n. 198 and pp. 88–90, n. 249). Charles A. Dana's *New York Sun,* which had attacked Garfield as a corrupt man during the congressional campaign of 1874 (see Vol. II, p. 370, n. 159), kept up a bombardment during the campaign of 1880. Shortly before the election, the "329 mania" swept through the country; the number 329, representing the amount that Garfield was alleged to have received in dividends on Credit Mobilier stock, appeared on pavements, fences, doorsteps, envelopes, and in many other places. Although Garfield made no public statements concerning the charges, he saw to it that supporters (many of whom were deeply concerned) received material that would enable them to respond to the attacks.

[249]A national reunion of former Union soldiers and sailors organized by the citizens of Canton, under the auspices of the 23rd Ohio Volunteer Infantry Regiment, and attended by a crowd estimated at between forty and fifty thousand.

[250]The recently completed Cleveland and Canton Railroad, a section of a projected road to Wheeling, West Virginia, the primary purpose of which was to get coal to Cleveland.

route lay [a]long the Ohio canal. I had not been along that line since I left the canal 32 years ago.[251] Large crowds greeted us on the way and at Canton an immense mass of people were already assembled. We were driven to Major McKinley's. A large number of prominent soldiers and citizens greeted us. Spent the night at Major McKinley's.

September

WEDNESDAY, 1.   Before breakfast was over at Major McKinley's a great crowd had gathered in front of his house. During the morning President Hayes and I were repeatedly called out to shake hands with the crowd or acknowledge their compliments. At 11 o'clock the President, Swaim, and General Crook were driven to Mr. Altman's [Aultman's][252] where we met Gen'l Sherman; thence to the Opera House where the 23d Reunion was to be held. I did not remain but returned to Major McKinley's. At twelve o'clock joined the procession to the Fair Grounds, immense multitudes of people thronging the streets and the public squares, and making their way to the Fair Grounds. Tables were set for 40 or 50 thousand people and dinner was served to the soldiers. After dinner addresses were made by several people. One by the President, which was already in print, was a valuable statement of the business situation of the country.[253] I followed in a speech of ten minutes, defending the Soldiers' Reunion

[251]See Vol. I, pp. xv–xvi.

[252]Cornelius Aultman (1827–1884), a native of Canton, was an eminently successful manufacturer of mowing machines. A philanthropist, he contributed generously to schools and churches and was a founder of the Canton library. The Aultman hospital was a gift to Canton from his wife and daughter.

[253]Besides speaking about the sound economic condition of the country, Hayes pointed out that in 1878 approximately half of the school-age whites and Negroes in the late slaveholding states were not enrolled in any school, and that over 200,000 Indians, as well as the immigrants pouring into the country, needed an education. He called for universal suffrage based on universal education as the best means to strengthen the nation, and urged everyone to guard the truths men fought for—civil and religious liberty.

against the charge of Sectionalism.[254] Speeches were going on at both sides of the Grand Stand and I spoke at each front.

Returned to Major McKinley's at half-past three and at 4 o'clock Crete, Swaim, J.T. Robison, and myself with a dozen invited guests took a special car and went to Cleveland by the Valley Road. Arrived at half-past seven o'clock. Took supper with Hon. Amos Townsend at the Kennard House, after which Crete and I visited Dr. Boynton's. Major Swaim left for Fort Leavenworth. At half-past ten Crete and I took the train for Mentor being an half hour late. Arrived home at midnight.

THURSDAY, 2.   Slept until 8 o'clock, but the weather is too warm for comfortable sleep and I do not get enough rest. Found a large number of letters awaiting me and a vast mass of newspapers. Made some progress in reducing the piles. The afternoon mail brought me important letters from New York, Chicago and Indianapolis, in answer to which I wrote some strong letters to Jewell, Reid and Dorsey, urging the concentration of all our forces upon Indiana, assuming that Maine is safe. If we carry Indiana the rest will be easy.[255] Retired at 11 o'clock. Though we have had a heavy shower, yet the weather is intensely warm. I should have added that a number of people called during the day, among them Judge Clark [Clarke][256] of Mississippi, late of

[254]Garfield spoke of how the Civil War had brought together people who otherwise would have never met, giving as an example his meeting President Hayes, William Tecumseh Sherman, and others, whose war service he praised. He closed with a reminder that the veterans had fought for the whole Union against sectionalism and that their reunions, as national as anything in the republic, revitalized that nationalism.

[255]Garfield was particularly disturbed by reports about Conkling's saying that Indiana could not be won, that not much campaign money should be put into that state, and that New York was the real battle ground and would decide the election. Garfield told Reid to impress upon Arthur, Morton and all friends in New York the great danger of undervaluing the fight in Indiana, adding that detailed information in his hands led him to believe that if Republican workers in Indiana were supported, the state could be won.

[256]Charles W. Clarke, a native of Ohio, attended the Western Reserve Eclectic Institute before the Civil War. After serving in the Union army, he settled in Greenville, Mississippi, where he became a lawyer. Over the years he was judge

the 42d Regiment, and Mr. Hayes [Hays][257], Post Master of St. Louis. The latter came to urge me to attend the St. Louis Fair in October.

FRIDAY, 3. Worked on mail. I am still wrestling with the New York Finance Committee on the question of giving adequate aid to Indiana. Napoleon won the siege of Toulon, by announcing that Toulon was not in the city, but on the point of land projecting in the bay. He planted a battery there that compelled the abandonment of the city by his enemy.[258] So now the Republicans ought to see that, politically speaking, New York is in Indiana and the capture of the latter state in October, ensures New York in November. Haskell[259] and Southwick[260] from Ashtabula came to see Governor Foster, but he is not to be here until Monday.

SATURDAY, 4. Worked on mail until near noon, when a company of 95 ladies and gentlemen from Indiana arrived by special train,

---

of probate court, district attorney, and member of the legislature. After Garfield's election to the U.S. Senate, Clarke wrote to him (January 16, 1880): "Nothing gives a <u>Hiramite</u> or a member of the old 42nd more pleasure than the elevation of their chief." He was a member of the Mississippi delegation to the Republican National Convention in 1880.

[257]Samuel Hays was postmaster of St. Louis, 1878–84.

[258]On the night of August 27–28, 1793, Toulon revolted against the republican government of France and admitted an English fleet. The success of the government depended upon the fate of the Mediterranean seaport. In September, Napoleon Bonaparte joined the republican army besieging Toulon as commander of artillery. He saw at once that capturing the city required forcing the English fleet out of the inner harbor, and that the key to victory was the tip of the western promontory of Caire. On December 18 the republican army overran that position, set up a battery there, drove the fleet from the harbor, and on the following day captured Toulon. Thus Garfield likened Indiana to the tip of the promontory and New York to Toulon.

[259]David W. Haskell, a native of Ashtabula, had a lumber business and extensive interests in real estate. His first wife, who died in 1862, was the daughter of Henry Fassett. His father, John W. Haskell (1810–1885), a native of Vermont who settled in Ashtabula, engaged in banking, shipping trade on the Great Lakes, and railroad building.

[260]Amos A. Southwick was for a time cashier of the Ashtabula Loan Association, of which he was a founder in 1872.

having walked to the house from the railroad, by way of the lane. Their Chairman made a handsome address, to which I responded in a short speech, getting in [a] few sentences in praise of resumption.[261] After spending an hour about the house and grounds, they took the train for the West. Mr. Riddle and his daughter, Mrs. Knowlton, came and spent the afternoon and night with us. In the evening Mr. Riddle spoke at Mentor Village.

SUNDAY, 5. Remained at home during the day, visited with Mr. Riddle and his daughter, Mrs. Knowlton, drove them to Willoughby at six o'clock, where they took the train for Cleveland. Spent some hours during the day in clearing up the letter and paper mail.

MONDAY, 6. Chauncey L[I]. Filley[262] of St. Louis came early in the morning. Senator Plumb[263] of Kansas, and Messrs. Southwick and Haskell of Ashtabula came at noon. Governor Foster came at 4 o'clock and Townsend of Cleveland at six. Spent several hours with Filley in carefully going over the situation in Indiana. Subject resumed when Senator Plumb arrived and special points discussed with Governor Foster and Townsend after their arrival. Filley left at 6. Governor Foster and Townsend remained over night.

TUESDAY, 7. Governor Foster and Amos Townsend left by the morning train. Judge West of Bellefontaine and Mr. Tinker of Painesville called. At ten o'clock I drove with Hinsdale to Paines-

---

[261]He spoke of the vastness and importance of internal trade and of labor, citing the advances of the last eighty-four years on the Western Reserve. He congratulated his visitors that their government had "at last restored to its people the ancient standard of value," a move which made it possible to develop a sound and prosperous economy. At the close of his speech each member of the group was presented to Garfield and his wife and mother.

[262]Chauncey I. Filley was postmaster in St. Louis from 1873 to 1878, when he was dismissed for high-handed administrative practices and mistreatment of his subordinates. In 1880 he was a member of the Republican National Committee, chairman of the Republican State Committee of Missouri, and a delegate at large from Missouri to the Republican National Convention. After Garfield's election as President he hoped to be appointed postmaster general.

[263]Preston B. Plumb (1837–1891), newspaper publisher, lawyer, and politician, was a delegate from Kansas to the Republican National Convention of 1880 and a Republican member of the U.S. Senate, 1877 to his death.

ville and had the colts shod. Sat at Tibbals' Gallery for photographs. Dined at the Stockwell House with Judge West and son. Home at two o'clock. Hinsdale completed the revision of the Address of the Committee of the 19th District. Worked off a considerable amount of mail. T.W. Phillips came by evening train. The situation in Indiana was fully discussed. Appointments were made for Hinsdale in Ohio from the 10th to the 20th and in Indiana for the week after the 20th.[264] Drafted a plan of appointments for Blaine commencing in Ohio on the 25th of September and in Indiana on the 5th of October. Rained heavily in the evening.

WEDNESDAY, 8.   Hinsdale and Phillips left by the morning train. Worked on the mail and during the forenoon, nearly cleared the decks. Hon. J. Hubbell and wife of Michigan came at ten o'clock and remained until two. He is en route to New York to attend the meeting of the National Executive Committee tomorrow. In the forenoon received a dispatch from Vermont that the Republicans have 25,000 majority.[265] This is a very good indication. Hinsdale came in the evening.

THURSDAY, 9.   When [Went] to Glenville on the morning train and visited the Northern Ohio Fair. Dined at the Headquarters and made a short speech on the relation of city to country life.[266]

---

[264]Hinsdale's special mission in Indiana was to capture for Garfield the vote of the Disciples of Christ. On October 5 he wrote to Garfield from Miami County that he expected a Republican majority of 5,000 to 10,000, and added the following: "I have seen enough to convince me that Indiana politics is deplorably degenerate and corrupt. Nor, I am sorry to say, is the corruption all on one side." Four days later he informed Garfield that he had made sixteen speeches in the fifteen working days that he was in Indiana, that it was commonly understood that there were "30,000 merchantable votes in the State," that the Republicans planned to compete for them, and that gains were being made every day. See Mary L. Hinsdale, *Garfield-Hinsdale Letters,* pp. 459–460.

[265]On September 7 Vermont elected its state officials and U.S. representatives. Republicans won the governorship by a majority of 26,603, the three congressional seats, all of the state senatorships, and 217 of 236 seats in the state house of representatives.

[266]John P. Robison, president of the Fair Association, introduced Garfield while holding a napkin formed into the shape of a canal boat. Garfield spoke of the American migration to cities, saying that "a careful study of the men who have

Express train stopped for me at two o'clock and I reached Mentor at half-past three. A large mail awaiting me. Answered letters in the evening.

FRIDAY, 10. Over 60 letters came today. Most of them were answered. Commenced getting in wheat on the upland north of the young apple orchard, and sowing "blue stem" and putting with it 250 pounds of Detroit Phosphate to the acre.

SATURDAY, 11. A very busy day and an unusual number of callers. At ten o'clock Major Swaim, Mrs. Swaim and Mamie arrived, also, Hon. J.N. Tyner and wife, and at noon General Stewart L. Woodford[267] and wife of New York. In the afternoon my old Chester Classmate, Israel B. Curtis, and his wife called, also Messrs. Amidon[268] and Fenton[269] of Painesville and Mr. Balch of Sedalia. In the evening Lieut. Harber came. No one but he and the Swaims remained with us over night. Had a full consultation with Tyner on the situation in Indiana. At six o'clock drove to Willoughby with Mr. and Mrs. Woodford. Finished getting in the wheat.

---

won distinction in every field of activity, public and private, professional and commercial, will show that a large majority of them were born and bred in the country." He declared that the evils of the trend towards urbanization could be mitigated only by creating closer bonds of sympathy between country and city. The fair, he suggested, exemplified the interdependence of rural and urban areas, and by exposing people from the country to products of the cities, was most advantageous to residents of cities.

[267]Stewart L. Woodford, who was breveted brigadier general in 1865, was in Ohio during the week of September 6 campaigning for the Republicans. He spoke in Cleveland on the tenth.

[268]Andrew A. Amidon, a Painesville lawyer, was a student at the Western Reserve Eclectic Institute when Garfield was its head. During the campaign of 1880 he was president of the Hancock and English Club of Painesville. The day after the election he wrote a congratulatory note to Garfield, assuring him that he had opposed him solely on political grounds and had denounced the slanders against him.

[269]Arthur E. Fenton (1843–1902), a native of Ohio, had a farm on the Mentor Road in Painesville, 1877–81. In 1881 he went to the Red River Valley in North Dakota, where he bought land, farming it during the summer months and spending his winters in Painesville. In 1893 he left the Republican party and became a Populist.

SUNDAY, 12. At twelve o'clock attended church in company with Crete and Mother, Abram and Lieut. Harber. In the afternoon answered a large number of letters. The boys and Swaim and wife went to the Lake. In the evening a heavy rain storm came on and the night was cold.

MONDAY, 13. A heavy mail and large number of callers. The Maine election is going forward. I am led to expect about 5,000 majority, but shall be content with 3,000. This I noted in the afternoon before any news came. About 9 o'clock in the evening the telegrams began to arrive. First from the large cities, Portland, Bangor, etc., which showed heavy fusion gains with the probability of Republican defeat. At eleven o'clock it seemed quite certain that we had lost Reed in the Portland District, had not gained the Bangor and Rockland Districts and had probably lost the Governor. I noticed that we lost in the shipping towns and gained in the manufacturing towns. If we lose Maine at this election, it will throw additional uncertainty into the future of the campaign, but is by no means decisive of the result.[270] Retired at half-past 11 finding that no definite result could be reached tonight. I should have mentioned that I went by train to Collinwood, where George Blish met me and drove me to Collamer to attend the funeral of A.S. Hayden. It was a memorial service and several gentlemen spoke. I spoke a short time in reference to the life and character of Mr. Hayden.[271] Drove home with Dr. Robison.

TUESDAY, 14. Fuller details of the Maine election appear in the papers this morning, which indicate that we hold our own on

[270]In the election the Fusionists (Democrats and Greenbackers) won the governorship (see n. 276, September 18), two of the five congressional seats, nine of thirty-one seats in the state senate, and sixty-seven of 151 seats in the house of representatives. Reed was reelected, and continued Republican control of the state legislature resulted in the election of Eugene Hale and William Frye to the U.S. Senate, the latter to replace Blaine, who became Garfield's secretary of state.

[271]At the services for Hayden, long the preacher in the Disciple church in Collamer, Garfield recalled that he was a boy when he met Hayden, and spoke of Hayden's part in founding and serving as head of the school that had become Hiram College.

Congressmen and gain both Houses. The fusionists seem to have carried the Governor. At four o'clock in the afternoon received a long dispatch from Blaine saying that their canvass on Wednesday last indicated about 6,000 majority, but that a large sum of money, $70,000 to $100,000 dollars, was sent into Maine four days before the election and used by the Democrats as money never was used before. The fact is our people have claimed too much for Maine and the moral effect of their disappointment will be against us, at least for awhile. I did not expect a large majority but I did expect a decisive one. This will make the contest close and bitter throughout the North. It may turn the scale against us but I think not. Many callers during the day, among them Chauncey M. Depew of New York and a Mr. Spencer.[272] Depew is strong in the belief that we shall carry the election in November. They dined with us and left on the 3.30 train. Swaim left for Indiana to attend the Club Convention and look over the field.[273]

WEDNESDAY, 15. Large mail and a great many callers. The news from Maine today is a little better than yesterday, indicating that the fight was much closer than at first reported and the result still uncertain. I think our people are showing more determination in consequence of the backset. When the first shock of surprise is worn off they will get down to work with renewed energy. The flagging stone[274] came today and my men hauled most of it from the Depot. I had the grass seed sown on the wood and ram lots. Ploughing down below the railroad. The wood hauling is still going on. Played croquet just before

[272]In Chauncey M. Depew, *My Memories of Eighty Years* (1922), the visit to Mentor is discussed, pp. 108–110, but Spencer is not mentioned.

[273]About 300 delegates, representing nineteen states, attended the national convention of Republican clubs held on September 15 in Indianapolis. The purpose of the meeting was to appoint a national executive committee and establish an organization that could work effectively in the campaign and make Republican clubs throughout the country a permanent educational force and political power.

[274]The flagstones and the workmen to lay them were supplied by the Austin Flagstone Company of Warren, owned by Harmon Austin. On September 23 Garfield wrote to Austin: "I want you to let your 4 men know that I think they did better work and more of it while they were here than any other 4 men I have ever seen. They did the steps and walk exceedingly well."

supper and answered a large number of letters in the evening.

THURSDAY, 16. At noon today four men came from Warren, and commenced work on the steps and flagging. There [They] are very skillful and rapid workmen.

Callers and letters fill the day.

FRIDAY, 17. John Gawn[e] of Cleveland came to build cistern for cesspool and lay pipes for the escape of the roof water.

Flagging stone and steps going down with great rapidity.

Grant agrees to come to Warren and preside at Conkling's meeting to be held on the 28th. The people build a wigwam.[275]

SATURDAY, 18. It is becoming evident that Plaisted[276] is elected in Maine by a small plurality.

Besides the use of money with which the Democracy ambushed our people, it is evident that there was mingled in the contest an element of rebellion against Blaine and his autocracy.

At noon, the flagstones were all down and John Gawne had finished his work. I have never seen better or more rapid work of the kind. In the evening, Maj. and Mrs. Swaim, Crete and I, went down to Painesville and called at the Lake Erie Seminary and had a pleasant visit. I made a short speech to the Students. Home at 9, bring[ing] Mollie and Mamie.

SUNDAY, 19. Did not attend church, but made a tour over the

[275]In a letter (September 12) Chester A. Arthur informed Garfield of Conkling's inability to speak at an outdoor meeting and said that he did not see how the meeting could be held in Warren unless a wigwam was built. On September 19 Harmon Austin wrote Garfield that a wigwam 100 feet by 175 feet was under way and that thirty to forty men would be at work on it the following day; 50,000 feet of lumber had been ordered from Cleveland. "Wigwam" was often used to designate a large building (usually temporary) constructed to house political gatherings. In 1860 Abraham Lincoln was nominated for President in Chicago in the Wigwam built for the Republican National Convention.

[276]Harris M. Plaisted (1828–1898) graduated at Waterville (now Colby) College in 1853, was a Union officer in the Civil War, 1861–65, a member of the state legislature, 1867 and 1868, attorney general of Maine, 1873–75, and a Republican member of the U.S. House of Representatives, 1875–77. In 1880 he was elected governor of Maine (the vote was 73,713 to 73,544) as the candidate of the Democrats and Greenbackers. From 1883 to his death he published and edited *The New Age,* an Augusta newspaper which opposed Blaine and supported bimetallism.

farm, inspecting the cattle and crops. Also cleared up the accummulation of mail which had gained on us during the week. In the afternoon Geo. A. Baker called and gave me his views of the situation from the intelligence he had gathered from Democrats. He thinks Ohio is gravely threatened by an ambush like that in Maine. His brother from Chicago was with him.

Hinsdale came at noon, and reported good meetings during the week. In the evening Hon. E.W. Stoughton of N.Y. came, and reported from his meetings in Indiana. Both spent the night with us.

MONDAY, 20. Mr. Stoughton left at 7 A.M., Hinsdale at noon. The rush of letters and callers recommenced, and we had a busy day both in the house and office. A letter from Jimmie came last evening telling us that the boys reached St. Paul's School safely, and were getting settled in their new quarters at Miller's Cottage —they and Don Rockwell being roommates.

I should have added last week that Irvin and Abram commenced attending the District school at Mentor. This is their first experience at School away from their mother.

Pastel portrait artist came and I gave him a sitting.

TUESDAY, 21. Have been troubled by a question of discretion and propriety. The Republican Committee at Warren think that hospitality and courtesey demand that I meet Gen. Grant and Senator Conkling at Warren on the 28th. I think I ought not to go unless I am ready to take the stump, and have so written them. At noon Col. Rockwell and wife came.

Hard afternoon's work on mail—continued until late at night.

WEDNESDAY, 22. Swaim, Rockwell, Brown and I took the 5.46 A.M. train to Cleveland and after breakfast took Dr. Streator's special car for Toledo where we arrived 11.45 A.M. Were met by a Committee of soldiers, and driven to the Sangerfest Hall to attend the reunion of the Army of the Cumberland. Dinner at Boody House. At 3 attended Reunion of the 1st Ohio Battery in U.S. Court Room. At 5 P.M. attended a private Business Men's Republican meeting, where the state of the campaign was discussed. I spoke a few minutes. At 7 1/2 attended A.C. Reunion at Sangerfest hall. Gen. Harrison delivered the Annual Address.

I followed in [a] 15 minutes' speech—just fair one.[277] Two hours at Boody House with Dorsey, on Political Situation, then at midnight went to bed on special car, to leave for Cleveland at 3 A.M. During P.M. visited Cousin Geo. Garfield and saw relative[s]—Letcher and Harriet Fisher.[278]

THURSDAY, 23. Arrived in Cleveland at 7.30, Col. Rockwell having left us at Toledo for the West. We took breakfast at Union Depot. Thence to Kennard House. At 8.45 Crete, Mrs. Rockwell, Mrs. Swaim and Mamie and Mollie came, and went shopping. Townsend called. I went to Col. Hay's and saw Whitelaw Reid and Mr. A. Stone. At 11.15 Brown, Reid and I went to Mentor. Spent the afternoon with Reid and my mail. Went quite fully over the situation of the campaign, and made some suggestions in reference to its drift and outlook. Mrs. Rockwell, Crete and Mollie returned in evening. The Swaims left for Fort Leavenworth. I drove Reid to Willoughby in time for the 6.22 Express to Cleveland. Worked two hours in evening on mail.

FRIDAY, 24. All hand[s] in the office buckled down to the letters and telegrams. Green and Pete getting in anthracite coal, of which a car load came today.

Hon. S. Shellabarger visited for an hour this forenoon. He is to speak at Painesville tonight. J.B. Burrows was with him. Also Hon. W.H. Upson of Akron visited me. During the afternoon and evening very nearly caught up with the mail.

I find much criticism of Senator Conkling's speech at Cooper

---

[277]Garfield referred touchingly to General Thomas and recounted the achievements of the Army of the Cumberland, which he viewed as an instrument that reconciled and united professionals of West Point like Thomas and Sheridan, who were experts in war, with "the magnificent body of cultivated, thinking, independent private citizens" who volunteered to save their country. Praising each group, he complimented the Army of the Cumberland for always recognizing generously "both arms of our great service."

[278]Harriet (Letcher) Fisher, sister of William Letcher, was the daughter of Polly Garfield (1795–1859), sister of Abram (Garfield's father) and Thomas Garfield. She was married to Benjamin H. Fisher, a lawyer with small practice in Wichita, Kansas. One of their sons, Jonathan, a Wichita cattle dealer, is mentioned in the diary (February 22, 1881).

Institute. He did not help to enlarge the spirit of our northern Republicans, but said too much that was irritating to those whose help is necessary.[279]

SATURDAY, 25.   Green hauling in potatoes, after he finished housing coal. Large mail—showing much anxiety about Ohio. At 10 A.M. President Chadbourne[280] of Williams College came from Painesville, with Judge Wilcox.[281] Pleasant visit with them.

During the P.M. we very nearly cleared our docket of mail, and the young men sent off a large mass of Documents. Croquet before tea. At the table, we reached the letter S in our review of the little Dictionary of 3,000 words which are usually mispronounced. I want to keep my household from being so ab-

[279]At the Academy of Music in New York City, on September 17, Senator Conkling spoke to an audience that filled the Hall and corridors and ran onto the sidewalks and streets. Arguing that the general issues before the electorate were party and sectional, not personal, he presented numerous statistics to support his view that the nation had prospered under Republican administrations. He declared that the Democratic party was controlled by a politically corrupt southern wing whose purposes endangered the judiciary, especially the Supreme Court, and threatened the financial integrity of the nation. His handsome tribute to Chester A. Arthur depicted the vice presidential candidate as a "high-souled, honorable man" who could be trusted in every relation of life. Of Garfield, who fared less well, Conkling said: "That he has the intelligence, experience, and habits of mind which fit a man for the Presidential office, I think, I know. . . . That he is competent to the duties before him, there seems to me no reason to doubt." The *New York Times* (September 18) regarded the speech as "a substantial contribution to the success of the Republican cause" and agreed that the question before the country was one of parties, not of persons or even particular policies. But the paper thought that Conkling was ungracious to speak of persons who "first secure elevation at the hands of party, and then, in the hope of winning pretentious, non-partisan applause, affect a superior sanctity."

[280]Paul A. Chadbourne, a Republican presidential elector in Massachusetts in 1880, campaigned in Ohio for his party during the week following his visit to Lawnfield.

[281]Aaron Wilcox (1814–1881), a native of Connecticut, moved as a boy to Painesville, where he became a successful merchant. In 1865 he left the mercantile trade and purchased the Lake County Bank, which became Aaron Wilcox & Company. He was a founder and for many years a trustee and secretary-treasurer of the Lake Erie Female Seminary. He served several terms as mayor of Painesville.

sorbed in politics, as to have no other life. This is a diversion and a help towards a purer speech. We have kept it up nearly two months. I have declined to go to the Warren meeting, though strongly urged by our friends. Unless I were ready to take the stump I ought not to go.

SUNDAY, 26. Read an hour before breakfast in *The Sisters*[282] by George Ebers—an Egyptian Romance, which promises well. It is written from the stand point of an archeological scholar, and is full of suggestiveness. I must keep myself from being too much absorbed in the contest. If I could take the stump and bear a fighting share in the campaign I should feel happier. Soon after breakfast a Mr. Alexander and his mother (who is a sister of the late John Healy of Newburgh, O.) called to see us. Dr. Robison came and we drove over the farm inspecting crops and cattle. Did not attend church.

MONDAY, 27. Swaim returned from Indianapolis about 8.30, bringing with him Senator Allison and ex-Senator Simon Cameron, also a gentleman from Lancaster, Pa. Soon after their arrival Hon. L.P. Morton of N.Y. and Major ——— [John M. Francis],[283] an editor from Troy came. Had a full conversation with the parties on the political situation in Indiana. Senator Cameron and his Lancaster friend left in the afternoon to go to Cleveland to meet General Grant and thence to the Warren meeting. Allison and Morton spent the night with us and the situation of the campaign was quite fully discussed.

TUESDAY, 28. Mr. Morton, Swaim and Allison left at seven o'clock for Painesville, Morton to go thence to Warren and the others to New York. The day opened with rain threatening disaster to the Warren Meeting, but the science of Old Probabilities was vindicated, for before nine o'clock the sun burst out and

---

[282]George Ebers [Georg Moritz Ebers], *The Sisters, a Romance* (1880).

[283]John M. Francis (1823–1897), a native of New York, entered the newspaper business as a typesetter, became a writer and in 1851 established the *Troy Daily Times,* which he owned and edited for many years. He was U.S. minister to Greece, 1871–74, and to Spain and Austria, 1884–85. Garfield considered appointing him minister to Belgium.

the day was fair. About 11 o'clock, I received a telegram from Simon Cameron that General Grant would spend the night with me. A later dispatch informed me that a larger party was coming and would call en route to Cleveland. At half-past seven in the evening his special train came. Sent carriage to the Mentor Station for the party who arrived at the house about eight. The party consisted of General Grant, Senators Conkling and Logan, Congressman Morton and about fifteen gentlemen from Cleveland. Some 200 citizens came to the house and were introduced to General Grant. Crete gave them a lunch and coffee in the dining room. After remaining an hour the party were driven again to the station and their train took them thence to Cleveland. I had no private conversation with the party, but the call was a pleasant and cordial one all around.[284]

WEDNESDAY, 29. A rainy, drizzly morning. Isaac Errett reached Painesville at 8.20. Jimmy Robison drove down for him. I telegraph[ed] to the Doctor to return from Cleveland on the noon train and he did. In the evening we took tea at the Doctor's with the old members of the Quintinkle Society formed in 1861.[285] In the office the day was full of telegrams and letters. Conkling's

[284]The visitors arrived about 8:30 P.M. at the Mentor Station, where Grant, Conkling, Logan, and Morton entered Garfield's carriage, and the rest of the party, along with members of the press, boarded a "hack-like vehicle." They were escorted on the mile-and-a-half ride to Lawnfield by two mounted squadrons of Garfield Guards, whose hats bore torches that provided considerable light. Garfield waited on the porch of his home and greeted each guest with a handshake and words of welcome. (Conkling's greeting to Garfield was: "General, I am very glad to see you in your home.") In the house Garfield presented his wife, mother, and others, and following informal conversation a stand-up lunch was served. Grant received guests in the parlor, as many wished to shake his hand. Garfield then escorted him, Conkling, and Logan to the porch and introduced each to the crowd of about two hundred outside the house. Each made a courteous remark, but no speech. A violent rain and hail storm delayed for a few minutes the visitors' departure, which took place at 9:25 P.M. There is no evidence that Garfield and Conkling conferred privately; nevertheless, rumor soon had it that they had struck a bargain, and there were references to the "treaty of Mentor." See the *Cleveland Leader* and the *New York Times* (September 29) and the *Painesville Telegraph* (September 30).

[285]See Vol. II, p. 68, n. 208.

speech at Warren was an event of considerable importance.[286]
THURSDAY, 30.   Telegrams increasing as the Campaign advances.
At half-past nine the Jubilee Singers of Fisk University came from
Painesville. We gave them a cup of coffee and some fruit. They
sang some of their finest pieces. At the conclusion I made a few
remarks to them on the relation of their work to the education
of their race and Loudin their leader responded.[287] He was a
pupil of Crete's twenty-five years ago at Ravenna. He made a
very creditable speech. At noon the Rockwells left for Washington. Harrison Garfield[288] and wife of Lee, Massachusetts, came
and spent the afternoon. Col. Loveland[289] of New York came

[286]The meeting at Warren, attended by about 40,000 people, opened with a
short talk by Grant, at the end of which he introduced Conkling. The senator
"spoke fully two hours," reported the *New York Times* (September 29), "mostly
upon the election and census frauds in the South, the attitude of the Democratic
party upon the tariff question, and the foolishness of the Democratic demand for
a change." That the meeting contributed significantly to the Republican campaign
is beyond question, but Garfield resented Conkling's "manifest effort . . . to avoid
mentioning the head of the ticket in any generous way" (Garfield to Harmon
Austin, October 6). In fact, neither Grant nor Conkling so much as mentioned
Garfield's name.

[287]Garfield's secretary, Joseph Stanley-Brown, left a memoir of this visit (see
American Heritage (August, 1971), pp. 49–53, 100–101). He recalled that Garfield, having listened to the repertoire of "vibrant but mournful spirituals," each
of which deeply touched the living room audience of family and a few neighbors,
began to speak in low conversational tones, explaining to the singers "his understanding of the needs and aspirations of a race out of place." He closed his speech
with this statement, delivered in "ringing tones": " 'And I tell you now, in the
closing days of this campaign, that I would rather be with you and defeated than
against you and victorious.' " Frederick J. Loudin, a native of Portage County,
Ohio, learned the printer's trade, but racial prejudices prevented his entering it.
Following the Civil War he went to Tennessee, where in 1875 he joined the
Jubilee Singers just before their second visit to Great Britain.

[288]Harrison Garfield, manufacturer and banker, owned and operated paper
mills, served in both branches of the Massachusetts legislature, and was now
president of two banks in Lee. The *Gazetteer of Berkshire County, Massachusetts*
(1725–1885) describes him in the latter year as the oldest active maker of business
paper in the county.

[289]Frank C. Loveland, a native of Ohio, served in the Civil War, rising from first
lieutenant (1863) to colonel and commanding officer of the 6th Ohio Volunteer

from Indiana, where he has been spending two months in the campaign, and visited me until two o'clock. S.S. Warner of Wellington came and spent some hours. He and the Garfields went to Willoughby to take the six o'clock train. Isaac Errett, Dr. Robison and wife, members of the Quintinkle, took supper with us and spent the evening.

October

FRIDAY, 1.   Isaac Errett remained and I visited with him during the forenoon. He went in the evening to Willoughby. At noon Uncle Thomas Garfield, Cousin Harriet Fisher and her daughter came to visit us. In the afternoon I went with Uncle over the farm. Many callers and telegrams during the day. Mr. Hurd of Cleveland called in the evening before making a speech at Mentor.

SATURDAY, 2.   Uncle Thomas Garfield and party of relatives, who came yesterday, left us on the morning train. Did not feel well in the forenoon and slept an hour. Did not have sufficient rest during the night. At noon dictated some letters. Started with Crete for Cleveland. Telegraphed Swaim to meet me there on his way from New York. When I was half way to Willoughby I found that John Q. Smith and wife from Montreal had stopped at Mentor. I left our train at Willoughby and was driven home. Spent the afternoon with Smith visiting. Crete, Swaim, and Judd returned in the evening.

SUNDAY, 3.   Went to church with Crete, Abe and Mary White. After dinner went over the farm. Then dictated some letters. Read up the papers and at five o'clock drove Mother over the farm. At half-past five Crete and I drove Major Swaim to Willoughby where he took the train for Columbus. Letters and Newspapers in the evening.

Cavalry Regiment (1865). He was for many years a pension agent in New York and a member of various organizations, including the Union League and Republican clubs. He died in Suffern, New York, in 1916.

MONDAY, 4. Large number of callers during the day and heavy correspondence. In the afternoon I drove to Painesville Station and met Blaine, rode with him to the Mentor Station whence he came home with me and spent the night. Had a long and interesting conversation on the general situation. He believes that Grant and his associates are specially busy in running the campaign of 1884. This it seems to me is rather too far in advance to lay plans.

TUESDAY, 5. Blaine took the morning train for Cleveland whence he is to be taken by special train for Sandusky. A great many callers in the forenoon. Went to the noon train and saw Governor Foster. He was on his way to Painesville. Swaim returned from Columbus bringing good reports of the situation. At four o'clock Foster came from his Painesville meeting and spent an hour with us. He gives a good account of the state of the fight and says we have gained rapidly within the last ten days.

WEDNESDAY, 6. Began to receive returns from my letters of the fourth asking the situation in the different counties. At noon Swaim started for Indiana to review the progress of the fight there. Have nearly cleared the deck of letters during the afternoon and evening. They are coming at the rate of seventy-five or a hundred every day. My telegraphic correspondence is also increasing. The campaign on the Democratic side has become also one of exclusively personal assault. They have evidently become alarmed at the progress of the contest on the doctrines of the two parties and take this mode of diverting the public mind from the real issue.

THURSDAY, 7. Whitelaw Reid came before I was up. I spent several hours with him going over the situation very fully. He took the noon train for Cleveland. A large mail came today. Many answers from my letters of inquiry to the different counties. About 25 or 30 visitors came in the afternoon. The boys got off a large number of documents and I ran through the mail. About seventy letters came to hand. Old Father Barnes has been closing up the wood house opening to keep out the cold when winter comes. Green has finished hauling in the clover.

FRIDAY, 8. Day full of work. Some progress made on the letters in the forenoon. Mr. W.C. Howells and his daughter from Montreal came to see us. At noon Captain Henry and Dr. Streator came. At three o'clock the Young Men's First Voters Garfield and Arthur Club of Cleveland, four hundred in all, came by special train and spent an hour here. I spoke to them a little while.[290] It was a pleasant call. A number of other callers later in the afternoon and evening. James Mason and his little girl came and spent the night.

SATURDAY, 9. A busy day in sending final messages and directions to various parts of the field, preparatory to the battle of Tuesday next. Received from Indiana the final report which will test the thoroughness and faithfulness of our organization. It admits twenty-four thousand odd hundred Democratic majorities, but claims twenty-nine thousand majorities in Indiana, a net Republican majority of 5,350.[291] We shall see.

SUNDAY, 10. At ten o'clock, Crete, Mollie and I, with the black colts and carriage, started for Solon, going by the way of Kirtland, Chester, Russell, Chagrin Falls. Arrived at Sister Mary's at two and spent the afternoon there and at her daughter Hattie's. Called at Sister Hitty's, but she was away from home. In the evening drove to Orange and spent the night at Cousin Henry Boynton's by the old birthplace. Walked out under the cold starlight and tried to recall the old sensations of boyhood. Here I first learned the constel[l]ations and their places in the heavens.

---

[290]To the First Voters' Garfield and Arthur Battalion of Cleveland, who arrived on a special train of six cars, Garfield spoke briefly of the magnificence of the United States and of the delusion of many Americans that one must go abroad to find glory and greatness. "Right here in this yard," Garfield assured his audience, "is a splendid specimen of American sovereignty, the roof and crown of the world of sovereignty. Enlarge it into the millions of men who vote and you have the grand, august sovereign of this last and best-born of time, the American Republic."

[291]The source for this puzzling statement (it may have resulted from a misunderstanding by Garfield's secretary) was not found. *The Annual Cyclopedia* (1880) reports the following election results: Republican candidate for governor, 231,405; Democratic candidate, 224,452; Greenback candidate, 14,881; Republican plurality, 6,953. The Republicans controlled the state house of representatives with a majority of six, but the Democrats had a majority of two in the senate. The congressional delegation had eight Republicans and five Democrats.

It is my Greenwich, where all the world is exactly in its right place. Every other place shows variation more or less.

MONDAY, 11. Breakfasted at seven. Went with Crete and Cousin Henry and his wife into Mother's old orchard and gathered some apples from the trees which my father planted. At a quarter before nine we started along the road leading towards Bentley-ville, on which I do not remember to have traveled for more than thirty-five years. I drove slowly—for every spot was crowded with childhood memories—by the old places of Smith, Frazer [Frazier], Willey, Rathbone, Hoyt, Bentley. All gone, nearly all dead. Turning back from Bentleyville, we went down the river by the Old Widow Fisher place, Burnett's, Gates Mills on the road to Willoughby and thence home. It was a perfect autumn day and the foliage was just at the point of perfect coloring. Reached home at half-past twelve, just as the family were at dinner. But few telegrams and letters came during my absence. It is the lull before the battle of tomorrow.

TUESDAY, 12. A cloudy morning, threatening rain, but before eight o'clock the sky cleared and the sun came out bright. Excellent day for election. At ten o'clock went to the polls and cast the 94th vote of the morning. At home in the afternoon. Played croquet for an hour or two. Cleared the decks of letters. At six o'clock Mr. [H.W.] Jeffers, a Telegraph Operator, came from Cleveland to assist Judd. Early dispatches showed a very heavy vote and a quiet, orderly election both in Indiana and Ohio. Messrs. Everett and Howe came out from Cleveland and spent the evening. Fifteen or twenty neighbors gathered to hear the news and staid with us until after midnight. Retired at half-past three with the news of certain and large Republican gains in both states. We have probably carried Indiana.

WEDNESDAY, 13. Rose at eight. Family breakfasted at nine. Morning papers brought fuller details, but nothing much fuller than our news of last night. Our plurality in Ohio will be about 20,000. Losses in some parts of the state. Gains in other parts. The most gratifying fact in connection with the campaign to me, is that the 19th District has increased the vote of last [election]

1,600.[292] The day has been crowded with callers and telegrams. By noon the magnitude of the victory had increased. By night it was certain that we had carried Indiana by over five thousand, had gained two Congressmen and had probably captured the Legislature.

THURSDAY, 14.   On the farm, the following: Four teams at work hauling wheat. Green and Bailey preparing an acre south of the railroad for wheat. Pete and Hauer sodding the back yard. Apple pickers at work in the orchard. In the Office an unusual number of joyful Republicans gathering the latest news from Tuesday's election. Telegrams and letters from all sides. The effect in Indiana and Ohio has been overwhelming. An aggregate gain of at least eight Republican Congressmen and a Republican Legislature who will let their first bolt fall upon McDonald, who was my first prominent slanderer in this blackguard campaign of the Democracy.[293]

FRIDAY, 15.   Letters and telegrams of congratulation are pouring in so rapidly that I am compelled to abandon the purpose of answering them except a few of the most important. About fifty ladies came from Painesville in the forenoon. Some missionary society was in session, which brought a large number of ladies from other parts of the state. An unusual number of gentlemen also called. Major Swaim left for New York in the afternoon, with my letters to the Committee suggesting what the future course of the campaign should be. Col. Dudley[294] of Indiana,

[292]Garfield's statement was based on incomplete returns. In the election of October 12, 1880, the total vote in Ohio's Nineteenth Congressional District was 32,910; in 1878 it was 27,867. In the 1880 election Taylor received 22,794 votes; in 1878, Garfield got 17,166 votes. The district of 1880 was not exactly the same as that of 1878; Portage County had replaced Mahoning County.

[293]Joseph E. McDonald (see Vol. III, p. 439–440, n. 60), of Indiana, was the Democratic candidate to succeed himself in the U.S. Senate. But the election gave the Republicans control of the legislature and they elected Benjamin Harrison as his successor.

[294]William W. Dudley (1842–1909), a native of Vermont, moved to Indiana in 1860, was a Union officer in the Civil War, 1861–65, and was breveted brigadier general for meritorious service at Gettysburg, where he lost a leg. He was a clerk of courts, 1866–74, bank cashier, 1875–79, and U.S. marshal for the district of Indiana, 1879–81. He was a member of county and state Republican

who has been spending the day with me, took the evening train for Willoughby. At three o'clock a thousand business men of Cleveland came on a special train of thirteen cars. Mr. Ely delivered an address to which I replied in a short speech.[295] In the evening made some progress on the accumulated mail.

SATURDAY, 16. One hundred and five letters came by the first mail, nearly 200 during the day. The papers speak kindly of my speech to the business men of Cleveland. Smalley of the *New York Tribune* came in the morning and remained during the day. He left during the afternoon, as did also Mrs. Reed. Crete, Mollie and I went to Dr. Robison's to take dinner [in] company with Dr. Streator and wife and two or three other friends. After dinner the party came here and spent some time with us. On the farm, the men finished getting in the acre of wheat on the south side of the road. Two wagon loads of apples were taken to the cider mill. The work of sodding the back yard is progressing slowly.

SUNDAY, 17. Remained at home all day a good deal tired with the over-work of the week. Went carefully over the paper and letter mail that came today. Sent Mr. Brown to Cleveland to make some inquiries in regard to the German Delegation which is to visit me tomorrow. Crete, Mollie and I called at Mr. Aldrich's a few minutes in the evening.

MONDAY, 18. Worked on correspondence during the forenoon. Many callers came. In the afternoon at three o'clock, seven cars loaded with Germans came from Cleveland. Mr. Kaufmann, Editor of the *Anzeiger,* delivered the address in German. The translation had been sent to me in advance and I replied to its leading

---

committees and took a prominent part in the presidential elections of 1880 and 1884. He was appointed by Garfield commissioner of pensions and served, 1881–85, resigning to practice law in Washington.

[295]In his response to George H. Ely, president of the Cleveland Republican Businessmen's Club, Garfield said that businessmen could get no insurance policy guaranteeing them prosperity during the next four years, but that a great political organization could protect them against the evils of "bad legislation" and "bad finance." He praised the accomplishments of capital and labor and told his listeners, including "the blacks" in the group, that the country held them the equal of any man, anywhere.

points, closing with a brief quotation from the poem of No-valis.[296] They remained about an hour having had a pleasant visit. Mrs. Mary Curtis also visited Crete and spent the night.

TUESDAY, 19. Like yesterday the day has been very cold but without snow, of which we had a little yesterday. At half-past ten o'clock 500 members of the Lincoln Club of Indianapolis came on a special train. They wore linen dusters and three-cornered straw hats. An address was delivered to which I replied.[297] Capt. Farrar of Cambridge, Ohio, and Mr. D [T]. M. Johnson[298] of

[296]In response to William Kaufmann's remarks, Garfield praised the contributions over the centuries of the Germanic people and said that the best elements of their race and other races everywhere were coming to America and making her a stronger nation. He referred to the recent completion of the Cathedral of Cologne, which was under construction for 630 years and which Kaiser Wilhelm dedicated "to peace and the glorious memories of Germany." Garfield then expressed his belief that his listeners had come to the United States to erect a grander temple, not a Gothic building made from the quarries of the Rhine, but from the hearts, minds, aspirations and hopes of all who came to this country to build institutions that should be free, under continuing construction, and ex-periencing improvement. "To all such people," he concluded, "the genius of America speaks the language of . . . the great Novalis:"

> Gib traulich mir die Hände,
> Sei Bruder mir und wende
> Den Blick vor Deinem Ende
> Nicht wieder weg von mir.
>
> Ein Tempel—wo wir Knieen—
> Ein Ort—wohin wir ziehen,
> Ein Glück—für das wir glühen
> Ein Himmel—mir und Dir.

[297]The delegates, whose costumes were "a burlesque on the rich costumes of the Jefferson Club of Indianapolis," were led by a band through the lane from the railroad to the house. Chairman M. G. McLain spoke for the group, praising the Republican party and saying that he brought news of victory from Indiana. In reply Garfield told the delegates that their hats represented the Revolution and their badges represented Lincoln, whose views were in accord with the doctrines of 1776. His closing remarks on the conquest of George Rogers Clark and on Indiana's glorious contribution to the Civil War, were followed by three cheers, the firing of a cannon, handshaking, and the departure of the delegation.

[298]Thomas M. Johnson, who was cashier of the Quaker City National Bank, 1872–84, had previously been postmaster, treasurer of Guernsey County, and agent for the Baltimore and Ohio Railroad.

Quaker City, came early in the morning and spent the day. General Hancock's recent deliverance[s] on the tariff have I think been unfortunate for him.[299] They show him to be unfamiliar with the topics of which he treats and is evidently between two conflicting opinions in his own party. In the evening dictated letters and made some progress in gradually clearing up the mail.
WEDNESDAY, 20.   Working on mail as usual. During the day I received a telegram from Simonton,[300] Agent of the Associated Press, and one of the proprietors of a newspaper in San Francisco, a telegram asking if a letter purporting to be written by me on the Chinese question was genuine. I answered requesting that a copy be sent me, which later in the day Simonton did by wire. I answered him that it was a forgery, that I had written no such a letter. It is evidently the purpose of the Democracy in their desperation to seek by this means to take the Pacific Coast from us at the coming election.[301]

[299]Since the Democratic platform supported a tariff for revenue only, and since Winfield Hancock said nothing about the tariff in his acceptance speech, the *Paterson* (New Jersey) *Daily Guardian* sent a reporter early in October to interview him on the subject. Hancock's statement on that occasion was particularly controversial, for he insisted that the outcome of the presidential election could not affect the tariff in the least. He said that the tariff was a local question, that the federal government seldom cared to interfere with it, and that nothing was likely to be done to interfere with the industries of the country.

[300]James W. Simonton (1823–1882), a native of New York, was a reporter for the *Morning Courier and New-York Enquirer* for several years before becoming one of the original owners of the *New York Times* (1851), whose Washington correspondent he became. He lived for several years in San Francisco, where he was part owner of the *Evening Bulletin* and the *Morning Call.* He was general agent of the Associated Press in New York City, 1867–81, a position of power. He died on an estate he had acquired in California.

[301]On October 20, *Truth,* a penny newspaper that began publication in New York City in 1879, published in type a letter purported to have been written by Garfield. Two days later it published a facsimile of the letter. The letter, written on a House of Representatives letterhead, is dated January 23, 1880; the words "Personal and Confidential" appear at the top of the sheet. The facsimile reads as follows:
Dear Sir:
    Yours in relation to the Chinese problem came duly to hand.
    I take it that the question of employees is only a question of private and

THURSDAY, 21.   A copy of the New York *Truth* came this morning containing my alleged letter to H. L. Morey, of Lynn, Mass. I never heard of such a man and the sentiment of the letter is one I never expressed. I can hardly believe that a rational and just-minded public will be influenced by such a wicked device. We worked at the mail as usual and are gradually clearing our decks for the November struggle.

FRIDAY, 22.   At about one o'clock this morning, I was awakened by a messenger from the Station bringing a telegram from James Gordon Bennett saying that Abram S. Hewitt had said last night that he had seen the original of the Morey letter and believed the letter to be genuine. Bennett reports great excitement in New York and desiring me to answer. I made no answer, not wishing to be a newspaper correspondent in my own behalf. During the day the evidence multiplied by telegram and letter that a serious attempt is being made to circulate the forged letter to my prejudice. Neither I nor any of the clerks remember any letter from Morey. Concluded to send Rose to Washington to search our files, which had been carefully indexed, and see if they contained any such letter. He left on the noon train. In the evening [telegraphed] Gov. Jewell, authorizing him to denounce the letter as a forgery, but not to publish my telegram. I did this last because I still hope to get through the campaign without appearing in my own defense against any of the charges.

---

corporate economy, and individuals or companys have the right to buy labor where they can get it cheapest.

We have a treaty with the Chinese government, which should be relegiously kept until its provisions are abrogated by the action of the general government, and I am not prepared to say that it should be abrogated, until our great manufacturing and corporate interests are conserved in the matter of labor.

Very truly yours,
J A Garfield

H. L. Morey
  Employers Union
    Lynn, Mass.

For details concerning the Morey letter and for facsimiles of the letter see John I. Davenport, *History of the Morey Letter,* a paperback volume published by the author in 1884. For Davenport see n. 347, November 20, 1880.

SATURDAY, 23. The morning mail brought us a lithographic facsimile of the forged Morey letter. It relieved my mind of the only oppression I had, the fear that there might have been a letter from Morey and that Nichol might have answered it without my seeing the letter or answer.[302] The facsimile settled all that. It is not in the hand writing of any person whom I know, but is a manifestly bungling attempt to copy my hand and signature. During the day, also, I received a telegram from Jewell that the City was ablaze with excitement and that it was necessary for me to deny the forgery over my own signature. I therefore telegraphed him authorizing him to print my telegram of the night before.[303] I regret to do this, for I hoped to answer all my accusers by silence. We shall see whether this last device of a desperate party will avail them before the people. It may lose us the Pacific States and possibly some others, but I do not

[302]On Garfield's return to Washington on January 16, 1880, after his trip to Ohio to attend the reception given him in Columbus following his election as senator, he found "not less than two hundred letters" awaiting him. During the days that followed the flood continued, most of the letters being congratulatory. In answering them, Garfield received help from George Rose, Joseph Brown, Thomas Nichol, and perhaps others. Thus he could not be sure until he had seen the facsimile that one of his aides had not written the Morey letter, which was dated January 23, 1880.

[303]The telegram: "Your telegram of this afternoon is received. Publish my dispatch of last evening if you think best. Within the last hour, the mail has brought me the lithographic copy of the forged letter. It is the work of some clumsy villain, who cannot spell—nor write English—nor imitate my hand-writing. Every honest and manly Democrat in America who is familiar with my hand-writing, will denounce the forgery at sight. Put the case in the hands of able detectives at once, and hunt the rascals down." For a facsimile of the telegram in Garfield's hand see Davenport, *History of the Morey Letter,* p. 61. In a letter to Jewell dated October 23 but written on October 24, Garfield expressed himself more forcefully: "In my dispatch of yesterday and this evening (which are also sent you by mail) I have denounced the Morey letter as a base forgery. Its stupid and brutal sentiments I never expressed nor entertained. The lithographic copy shows a very clumsy attempt to imitate my penmanship and signature. Any one who is familiar with my handwriting will instantly see that the letter is spurious." This letter was published in facsimile in the *New York Herald* on October 26.

think it can turn the current that now sweeps so strongly in our favor.[304]

SUNDAY, 24. Attended church and afterwards made a clearing up of correspondence and newspapers.

Rec'd telegram from Rose that he finds no letter from Morey in our files, and no memorandum of an[y] letter to him.

The enemy cannot conceal their desperation. Perhaps the old motto will become "Memento Morey."

MONDAY, 25. The only doubt I have had in reference to the Morey letter was solved today by the appearance of the lithographic copy in *Truth*. I had thought it barely possible that Nichol may have found a letter on the subject, and answered it without my seeing it. The penmanship is not his, nor any I have ever before seen.

In the afternoon, Stephen Burnett [Burnet][305] of Vincennes, formerly of Orange, came with 14 other Indianians, and made us a pleasant visit. Even so small a company could not dispense with an address.

Swaim returned in the evening.

TUESDAY, 26. I find by N.Y. papers of yesterday that Hon. S. B. Chittenden of N.Y. has offered a reward of $5,000 for the arrest and conviction of the forger of the Morey letter. I think will [this] will lead to his detection.

About one o'clock a delegation of 300 people from Warren, and the neighboring townships of Trumbull County, came. Hon. E. B. Taylor spoke for them, and I replied. I took occasion to speak specially of that large number of citizens of this District

---

[304]The Morey letter appears to have been a factor of some importance in determining election results in Nevada and New Jersey, which Garfield lost, and in California, where he lost five of the six electoral votes.

[305]Stephen S. Burnet, a native of Ohio, moved to Vincennes, Indiana, where he lived, 1852–58. In the next decade he moved from Indiana to Missouri, Tennessee, and Kentucky. Returning to Vincennes in 1868, he became a successful businessman, engaging in the manufacture of tobacco boxes and in the planing mill business.

who had supported me so many years with no selfish end in view, never having asked for office for themselves.[306]

It began to rain while they were here, and wound up with a heavy rain-storm in the evening.

WEDNESDAY, 27. Very large mail. *New York Herald* of yesterday has lighthograph [lithograph] of my letter of the 23rd to Jewell on Morey letter. Lowery day, with unpleasant prospect for the visit of ladies of Cleveland, which is set for this afternoon. Prepared an affidavit to be used in case the forger of Morey letter is arrested.[307]

At 3.30 about 900 ladies of Cleveland and neighboring towns came and I made a brief address setting forth the relation of women to American public life.[308] They were all presented to Crete and Mother. It was a curiously impressive scene. At 6.22 P.M. Maj. Swaim and I took the train at Willoughby and went to Cleveland. Mr. Wade, Commissioner of N.Y., met me at the

---

[306]Deeply moved by this visit of longtime friends, Garfield also spoke of the value, responsibilities and durability of friendships, and expressed his desire to shake hands with every member of the delegation.

[307]Garfield took this step after Edwin W. Stoughton, John I. Davenport, Henry Knox, and Almon F. Rockwell, who were investigating the Morey letter in New York in behalf of Garfield and the Republican party, had telegraphed him (October 26) asking that he do so. In his affidavit Garfield asserted that the Morey letter was a forgery both in the body and in the signature and that to the best of his recollection he had never known or heard of such a person as Henry L. Morey until the publication of the letter.

[308]Garfield told the ladies that such a visit could occur only in our democratic nation where those who govern remain at home, sending servants off to govern. In the Civil War, he explained, there were three forces at work: the army that fought; those who paid and supplied the army; and those at home, mostly patriotic women who labored and loved and inspired the nation in its hour of peril. In all great public work, he declared, "the will of the Nation resides in the hearts and homes and by the firesides of fifty millions of people, and there by the hearthstone nearest to the heart of our sovereign, the people, it is woman's great and beneficent power to impress itself upon the national will. I greet you for having brought the spirit of home to my home," for showing by this visit "the growing power of home upon American public life, and for it and all that it means, I thank you with all my heart."

P.O. and witnessed my deposition that the Morey letter is a forgery. Started home on 10.30 train, but were delayed by freight wreck at Wickliffe, and did not reach home until nearly two hours after midnight.

THURSDAY, 28. Our detectives have arrested a Mr. Philp,[309] one of the editors of *Truth* on the charge of forging the "Morey" letter. The evidence is claimed to be conclusive. Whoever the actual scribe may be, Barnum[310] is the chief criminal, by his conduct in peddling the forgery.

[309]Kenward Philp, a native of London, age 33, came in 1865 to the United States, where he was associated with the *Brooklyn Eagle* and other papers. He was a regular contributor to *Truth,* which on October 22 carried an editorial by him entitled "Lying and Sticking With It," in which Garfield was charged with lying about the Morey letter. Republican investigators reached the conclusion that Philp was also the author of the Morey letter. The Republicans, desirous of court hearings before the election, arranged to have a complaint brought against Philp, charging him with criminal libel in the editorial. Arrested on October 27, he was brought on the same day before Judge Noah Davis of the New York supreme court for examination. The examination, which lasted several days, enabled the Republicans to present evidence concerning the Morey letter—evidence which, in the opinion of John I. Davenport, saved the election for the Republicans. Philp was held for action by a grand jury, which indicted him for writing the editorial and the three top men associated with *Truth* for publishing it. Davenport wrote (*History of the Morey Letter,* p. 23) that he "became satisfied" soon after the indictment that Philp was not the author of the Morey letter; the district attorney postponed action on the indictment. On January 9, 1881, Joseph Hart, publisher of *Truth,* declared in a letter to Garfield that the results of his investigations had "conclusively satisfied" him that the Morey letter was a forgery; on January 4, 1881, *Truth* published an open letter to Garfield with a similar acknowledgment. On May 19, the district attorney entered a *nolle prosequi* in the matter of the indictments for libel against Philp and the other men. On April 2, Philp was in Washington, hopeful of seeing the man who, next to himself, had been "the sufferer by a forgery." Philp to Garfield, April 2, 1881. *Truth,* which had started out well, suffered as a result of the Morey episode; it ceased publication in 1884.

[310]William H. Barnum (1818–1889), a Connecticut iron manufacturer, was a Democratic member of the state legislature, 1851–52, the U.S. House of Representatives, 1867–76, the U.S. Senate, 1876–79, and chairman of the Democratic National Committee, 1876–89. As soon as the Morey letter was published he declared that it was authentic and in Garfield's handwriting. The Democrats subsequently circulated thousands of facsimiles of the letter and facsimile plates for the use of newspapers.

Shortly after noon, a special train brought 200 people from Portage County. Judge Luther Day made the address, a very touching and beautiful one. I responded and asked the whole party into the house.[311] There were so many old neighbors and friends that Crete had her first cry in public while receiving them. The indications are that our friends in Indiana are recovering from their scare of last week, and are again hopeful that they will maintain the ground they gained on the 12th inst.[312]

FRIDAY, 29. This is the only day since Sunday last, on which we have not had large delegations, though many callers came. We made some progress in bring[ing] up back work of mail. The forgery trial[313] made good progress and Philp appears to be guilty of writing the letter. I may be in error, but I confidently believe this forgery will injure the party in whose interest it has been concocted and circulated. Moreover, it is a confession that the Democrats cannot hope to win on the merits of their doctrines and practices.

SATURDAY, 30. The proceedings before Judge Davis[314] in N.Y. yesterday disclosed the fact that [the] envelope of the Morey

[311]Garfield spoke of the memories that filled his mind as he saw in the crowd former classmates, former pupils, and men who started him in politics twenty-one years earlier. He recalled that in 1861 he and Judge Day recruited young men in the old church in Hiram, laying the base for the 42nd Ohio Infantry Regiment. Assuring his callers that the memories of their loyal support were more precious than a jewel, he said that all the doors of his house were open to them, and that the hand of every member of his family was outstretched to them.

[312]In Indiana certain Democrats challenged the constitutionality of the state election and plotted to secure control of the state legislature. The man who would have benefited most by the success of those efforts, Senator Joseph E. McDonald, promptly and publicly repudiated them.

[313]Garfield is incorrect in referring to the court proceedings against Kenward Philp as "the forgery trial." See n. 309, above.

[314]Noah Davis (1822–1908), a native of New Hampshire, was a lawyer in New York State for many years before serving as judge of the supreme court of the state for the eighth judicial district, 1857–68. He was a Republican member of the U.S. House of Representatives, 1869–70, U.S. attorney for the southern district of New York, 1870–72, and judge of the New York supreme court, 1873–87. In 1873 he presided at the trial of William Marcy ("Boss") Tweed.

letter was sent from Washington to N.Y. and has since been altered by erasures and additions.

Large mail and many callers. At 12 M. 329 citizens of Youngstown came.[315] At 3, 500 from West Salem, with the glee club of that place, also people from Ashland and Wayne Counties. Also 100 iron men from Cleveland.[316]

At 4 P.M. about 1,500 members of Clubs came from all the towns of Lake Co. and from several towns of Ashtabula, Geauga and Cuyahoga. Shortly after noon it began to rain, and the storm grew in violence into the night. But the clubs, cavalry and foot, paraded in the field south of the road until after dark.[317]

In the evening I read Ingersoll's speech before the business men of Wall St.[318] I should have added that Maj. Swaim left at noon for Indianapolis to look after the situation there.

SUNDAY, 31.   The week comes in clear and cold, with promise of

[315]The group, numbering about 150, wore badges with "329" on their hats, symbolizing Garfield's three years in the army, two in the Ohio senate, and nine terms in Congress. Garfield told them that man was the only animal that made tools for his own use, and that while tool-making was not the whole business of a civilization, the tools a people used were probably as good an index of their intelligence and civilization as any that could be found. He reminded them that they were largely engaged in tool-making, in making products for the defense, independence, and well-being of their country, which he called "a great, material, and patriotic work which the Government should protect and defend for the good of all."

[316]The spokesman for this delegation from the Britton Iron and Steel Works of Cleveland let Garfield know that they wanted a protectionist at the head of the government. In response, Garfield reminded his visitors that he knew "something about the iron works of Cleveland," suggested that Bismarck's motto, Iron and Blood, was "pretty strong," and expressed the motto of the United States as "Iron, together with all the other industries, and liberty." He closed by expressing the hope that whatever his visitors did would "tell in the direction of justice."

[317]At about 6:00 P.M. this body of "guards," consisting of infantry and cavalry, formed two columns in the meadow opposite the house, and Garfield, in a carriage, reviewed them. The street was crowded with vehicles and a large crowd, whose enthusiasm was not dampened by the steady rain, watched the proceedings.

[318]Robert G. Ingersoll spoke on the afternoon of October 26 in front of the Sub-Treasury. His long speech, punctuated frequently by applause and laughter, contains this famous statement: "Every man that tried to destroy the Government, everyman that shot at the holy flag—was a Democrat."

fair weather for Tuesday. The morning paper brings news of Gov. Jewell's first serious mistake in managing the campaign, viz., in holding any parley with the forger-rascals. Still he did no wrong, and in no way committed me, but he gave the adversary a chance to deceive him.[319] Crete, Mother and I attended church. In the P.M. and evening I worked off a large number of letters. Judd went home to Mich. last evening, and this morning Mr. Jeffers came to relieve him.

Retired at eleven.

November

MONDAY, 1. A lull along the whole line of battle. Only a few callers. Many letters and some telegrams, announcing the readi-

[319]Abram G. Dittenhoefer, a New York lawyer who was counsel to *Truth,* represented to Jewell that there were misgivings in the office of the paper concerning the authenticity of the Morey letter and that the paper was willing "to come out and say so plainly"—with the understanding that the only "consideration" for the action would be "consideration" for Dittenhoefer, that is, that Garfield and Jewell would know and recognize it as his doing. "It is their proposition and I have accepted it," Jewell wrote jubilantly to Garfield on October 26. Jewell also talked with Joseph Hart, publisher of *Truth,* who had sent Dittenhoefer to him. The approach to Jewell turned out to be a ruse on the part of *Truth.* Dittenhoefer, who claimed that he had been deceived and betrayed, said that he had concluded that Hart had been using him to extract a paper from Jewell that would appear to be an attempt to bribe the newspaper to make a retraction in regard to the Morey letter. In the lead editorial of October 28, *Truth* said that it had acted as it had to prevent Republicans (whose investigators were in hot pursuit of the paper) from taking action against it before it could publish proofs of the authenticity of the Morey letter. "An offer," it said, "was made by *Truth* to Chairman Jewell to suppress the proofs—an offer at which he jumped like a trout for a fly. In less than two hours the fact that *Truth* had sold out was discussed in all prominent Republican circles in the city. And it was owing to that offer and its acceptance that the readers of *Truth* were able to read the damning evidence which we published yesterday." Jewell telegraphed Garfield on October 27 that by listening to Dittenhoefer he had got himself "into a ridiculous scrape." See Jewell to Garfield, October 26, and Dittenhoefer to Garfield, October 27 and 28; the editorial from *Truth* was enclosed in Dittenhoefer's second letter. Dittenhoefer's letter of October 27 is indexed under "A. Hart" in the Library of Congress, *Index to the James A. Garfield Papers*—the signature or the initialing on the letter is illegible.

ness of our friends for the contest, and their confidence of success. On the farm, the men are gathering and hauling in beets. The turfing in the front yard is nearly completed. At 3 P.M. drove to Painesville, with Crete and Capt. Foote,[320] Crete to do shopping, I to get Kittie shod, and a bolt in the spring wagon.

In the evening answered a large number of letters.

Retired at ten.

TUESDAY, 2. The day opened clear and bright with indications here, and in the weather reports, of a fair day throughout the country. Very quiet in the office—few callers and few telegrams in the forenoon. Dictated and wrote many letters. Arranged for plowing and seeding garden east of house, and starting a new one in rear of engine house. At 2 P.M. went to town hall and voted for Republican electors. On return stopped at cheese house and settled dairy accounts. During afternoon telegrams indicated peaceful election and heavy vote. At 6 returns began to come in, Judd and Jeffers taking dispatches. Some reporters, and friends from Cleveland came. Later in evening many neighbors came in. By 11 P.M. it became evident that we had carried N.Y. At 12 P.M. we gave supper to about 25 friends. At 3 A.M. we closed the office, secure in all the northern states except N.J. and the Pacific states, which are yet in doubt.[321]

---

[320]Morris J. Foote, a native of Ashtabula County, Ohio, served in a New York regiment during the Civil War, attaining the rank of captain and losing a leg as a result of a shot in the knee. After the war he served for four years as treasurer of Ashtabula County. In 1874 he went to Washington, where he studied law and worked for a time in the Treasury Department. He was a member of the Washington bar into the 20th century. In 1880 he spent several weeks in Indiana campaigning for Garfield, and had now come home from Washington to vote.

[321]Some of the flavor of the evening at Lawnfield has been preserved in a round robin written to the absent Hal and Jim by Martha Mays and members of the household between 11:00 P.M. of November 2 and 3:00 A.M. of November 3. At 11 o'clock Martha Mays tells of sitting with Mrs. Garfield before a blazing fire in the living room while Abram, "a splendid little Mercury," brings the latest returns to them from the little office building behind the house. Joe Brown gives the boys a picture of the office "filled with vile men smoking and spitting all over our nice floor," and describes himself as "uproariously enthusiastic, but decidedly stuffy." Martha Mays returns with a note about the midnight supper at which she

WEDNESDAY, 3. Arose at eight; breakfast at 9. The news of 3 A.M. is fully justified by the morning papers and by the fifty telegrams that were awaiting me after breakfast. We appear to have lost N.J. and Nevada by a small margin, due I think to the influence of the forgery, and [it is] possible California is against us. It is very close. We have at least 212 electoral votes, a small majority in the House and the Senate nearly or quite a tie. About 500 telegrams of congratulation came during the day, and many friends and neighbors called. At 3 P.M. the President, Faculty and 70 students of Oberlin College called, having come by special train. Pres. Fairchild made a brief address and I responded.[322] Many neighbors called. Mother went to Warren with Harmon Austin.

THURSDAY, 4. More than 500 letters, and about 150 telegrams and cablegrams came. Many callers. About noon, several Cleveland gentlemen, and with Mr. Cave,[323] a member of the British Parliament, and his son called. At 4.30 P.M. the President and Mrs. Hayes came. We had a pleasant visit of two or three hours with them. The President is very happy over the result of the

---

and Mrs. Garfield sat with twenty-two men. "The candles which have graced the mantel all summer were lighted in honor of Victory." Joe Brown speaks gloatingly of the "jolly feed—canvasbacks—oysters—ham in champagne." Mollie and Mrs. Garfield make short comments. In the middle of the third page Garfield writes one of his favorite mottoes: *"Esse quam videri"*—better to be than to seem. See Lucretia Comer, *Strands from the Weaving* (1959), pp. 15 and 16.

[322]Speaking for the delegation, variously estimated at between 500 and 700, President Fairchild said that the faculty and students had started the day in the usual way, but as the good news continued to arrive, they gave up everything to rejoicing, engaged a special train, and, as he said, "here we are." Garfield replied that a spontaneous visit was better than a prepared one, and praised Oberlin for maintaining an active interest in politics and for shunning a cloistered scholarship. "I am glad," Garfield said in closing, "to be greeted here today by the active, live scholarship of Ohio, and I know of no place where scholarship has touched upon the nerve center of public intelligence so effectively as at Oberlin. For this reason I am specially grateful for this greeting."

[323]Thomas Cave was a member of parliament, 1865–1880. He was the father of five sons, the second of whom, George (1856–1928), was a lawyer and statesman.

election.[324] Whatever his critics may say he has given the country a very clean administration and his party has not been handicapped in the late contest by any scandals caused by him. Father Thorpe[325] of the Catholic Cathedral came during the P.M. and presented me a cane which had been voted to me at a fair. I replied.

Father Rudolph came and spent the night.

Molly went to Warren with Lt. Harber.

FRIDAY, 5.   The mail increases. Two or three thousand letters have now accumulated, and the flood seems to be rising.

The Democrats are quarrelling among themselves in reference to the causes of the defeat.

At noon, Maj. Swaim, Father Rudolph, Crete and I went to Cleveland. As we reached the Union Depot, the President's train was just pulling out. We greeted him good-by.

Spent the P.M. in shopping. Called a few moments at Dr. Boynton's, where we met Mrs. James Mason and arranged [to] have Mollie go to school and board with the Masons.[326] Home by the 6 P.M. train. Mr. Bridg[e]land[327] of Indiana, now in the consular service, called with his friend. Also later, Mr. Thomas[328] of Maine, who wants the Swedish mission.

[324]"General Garfield's nomination at Chicago was the best that was possible. It was altogether good," President Hayes wrote in his diary on June 11. The President did not, however, take any public part in the campaign. On September 1, he and Mrs. Hayes, with a party of friends, started on a trip to California and the Pacific Northwest; he returned to Fremont the day before the election.

[325]Thomas P. Thorpe, a priest in the Cleveland diocese, was the first editor of the *Catholic Universe,* 1874–77. A leading educator, he spoke frequently on parochial and public school education. The gold-headed cane which he formally presented had been voted to Garfield, as the most popular presidential candidate, at a Roman Catholic fair in Cathedral Hall, Cleveland.

[326]Augusta Mittleberger conducted a private school "on fashionable Prospect Avenue" in Cleveland, 1878–1908. Mollie Garfield attended it for the few months before the family's departure for Washington, D.C., where she was enrolled in Madame Burr's School on New York Avenue.

[327]John A. Bridgeland was U.S. consul in Le Havre, France, 1873–81. Garfield recalled him and named John A. Glover to that position.

[328]William W. Thomas (1839–1927), lawyer and diplomat, graduated at Bowdoin College in 1860, earned the degree of Master of Arts there and was admitted

SATURDAY, 6. The mail increases but telegrams are falling off. We made some progress in answering the most important, but the great mass must remain unanswered.

At noon the Republican State Central Committee, and some other Indianians came, and also Maj. McKinley, Mr. Aultman and several friends from Canton, together with Hon. Amos Townsend of Cleveland, in all, about 40 people, who remained two hours. Later Mr. and Mrs. Gansevoort of Bath came to pay us a visit and stay over Sunday.

In the evening a heavy storm of wind, rain and snow came on and raged through the night. The Democratic managers are trying to raise a row in N.Y. and threaten to throw out the vote of that state. They cannot do it.

SUNDAY, 7. A very blustering day. Remained at home. Over 400 letters came. Made some progress in answering the most important. In the evening reviewed the telegrams and answered many of them. Mr. and Mrs. Gansevoort remained with us.

I commenced to read *A Sailor's Sweetheart*[329] by the author of *The Wreck of the Grosvenor.* Am also reading the volume of letters published in 1823 [1832] by H. Lee, son of Light Horse Harry Lee, on the character of Thomas Jefferson.[330] I am fully persuaded that the time will come when the character of Jefferson will be analysed and presented to the world in a very different light than that in which it is now seen.

MONDAY, 8. At last we have a bright morning. The day is clear

---

to the Maine bar in 1866. He served in both branches of the Maine legislature, and was a delegate to the Republican National Convention in 1880. He was U.S. consul in Gothenburg, Sweden, 1862–65; promoted the settlement of Swedes in Maine and founded in 1870 the colony of New Sweden in northern Maine; was minister to Sweden and Norway, 1883–85, and minister to Sweden, 1889–94, 1897–1905. He was the author of *Sweden and the Swedes* (1892), which appeared in both Swedish and English. He received an honorary LL.D. degree from Bethany College in 1901 and from Bowdoin College in 1913.

[329]William Clark Russell, *A Sailor's Sweetheart. An Account of the Wreck of the Sailing Ship 'Waldershare' from the Narrative of Mr. William Lee, Second Mate* (1880).

[330]Henry Lee, *Observations on the Writings of Thomas Jefferson* . . . (1832).

and beautiful. Worked on our letters until a little after noon, when Miss Evans,[331] her teachers and one hundred pupils from the Lake Erie Seminary came in carriages and made us a call of two hours. Mr. and Mrs. Gansevoort left at noon.

TUESDAY, 9. Some progress was made on the vast volume of letters, which still shows little sign of diminution. Father Barnes is slowly pushing the building of the engine house, but at the present rate the snow will strike us before he finishes it.

WEDNESDAY, 10. We are making decided progress on the mail. Rose and Brown both at work. Number of letters has dropped to about 250 per day and will probably go much lower. At noon Gov.-elect Porter[332] of Indiana came and dined with us. He makes special meritorious mention of McKay[333] and J. W. Gordon,[334] for services during the campaign.

[331]Mary A. Evans (1841–1921), a native of Philadelphia, and a graduate of Mount Holyoke College, 1860, was principal of Lake Erie Female Seminary (renamed Lake Erie College in 1898), 1868–1909. Her career was closely associated with that of Luella Bentley, the assistant principal, 1868–1909. Of these two educators the following has been written: "Gracious, always ladylike, with twinkling eyes, they managed trustees, faculty, janitors, girls (and their beaus) with intelligent ease."

[332]Albert G. Porter (1824–1897), a native of Indiana, was city attorney of Indianapolis, 1851–53, reporter of the Indiana supreme court, 1853–57, city councilman, 1857–59, a Republican member of the U.S. House of Representatives, 1859–63, first comptroller of the treasury, 1878–80, governor of Indiana, 1881–85, and U.S. minister to Italy (appointed by President Harrison), 1889–92.

[333]Horace McKay (1841–1914), a native of Ohio, attended Wittenburg College, served in the Union army, 1862–65, and in the latter year moved to Indianapolis where he was long prominent in civic and cultural activities. He was for many years a member of the city council. In 1882 President Arthur appointed him collector of internal revenue for the sixth district of Indiana.

[334]Jonathan W. Gordon (1820–1887), a native of Pennsylvania, attended Hanover College for one year (he was a classmate of Porter), studied law and was admitted to the bar in Indiana, where he became a prominent attorney and served two terms in the state legislature (the second as Speaker of the House). He defended L. P. Milligan, whose life he saved by persuading Governor Morton to stay his execution. He prepared a brief used by Garfield in *Ex parte Milligan* before the Supreme Court. He became postmaster in Auburn in December, 1881. In the following year he was widely criticized for writing to the U.S. attorney general a public letter arguing that on purely legal grounds Charles Guiteau was insane

Mr. and Mrs. Francis of Troy, N.Y., came and spent several hours. Mr. F. seems specially anxious to make me know that Conkling is peculiar though great, that I ought not to be surprised. He left about 8 P.M. Hon. C. Davis[335] of Cincinnati and Swift of the *Cleveland Leader* came in the evening.

THURSDAY, 11. Crete went to Cleveland in the morning train. I worked on the mail until noon when Swaim and I went to Cleveland. Met two gentlemen at the Depot who were en route to visit me, but who returned on the same train. One was Mr. George Antisdale[336] of Michigan and the other B. S. Higley of Youngstown. We were met at the railway station and driven to the Forest City House. Spent the afternoon with Crete shopping. At four o'clock Governor Foster, Mrs. Foster and their daughter came and we attended the wedding of D. P. Eels's[337] daughter to Prof. Newcomb's [Newberry's] son in the church near Euclid Street. The wedding and its appointments were very beautiful.[338] Re-

---

and should not be executed for assassinating Garfield. Governor Porter appointed him clerk of the Indiana supreme court.

[335]Charles C. Davis, a Cincinnati lawyer, was a member of the Ohio house of representatives, 1880–82.

[336]S. G. Antisdale was born in 1830 in Geauga County, Ohio, moved to Michigan in 1870 and settled in Benton Harbor, where he farmed, engaged in merchandising, and served four terms as mayor. In 1881 he informed Garfield that if an appointment to the office of postmaster of Benton Harbor was to be made, he wanted it. His parents, George W. Antisdale and Sallie (Greeley) Antisdale (she was a cousin of Horace Greeley), were longtime residents of Geauga County and old friends of Garfield.

[337]Dan P. Eels, who was born in New York in 1825, studied at Hamilton College before going in 1846 to Cleveland, where he engaged in banking and other business pursuits; in 1880 he was president of the Ohio Central Rail Road Company and the Ohio Central Coal Company. Shortly after Garfield's nomination at Chicago, Eels sent him a check for $1,000 for the campaign. He made reservations for the Garfields at the Forest City House, where they were to be his guests when they came for the wedding. Charles Foster wanted Garfield to attend the ceremony. Of Eels, Foster wrote (November 8): "He is certainly one of the best men I ever knew, and he is the kind of man that we ought to cultivate and oblige whenever we can."

[338]Emma Eels married Arthur St. John Newberry (1853–1912), a Cleveland lawyer. The bridegroom was the son of John S. Newberry (1822–1892), a native

turned to the Forest City House and took Crete with us and in company with Mr. Townsend went to the reception at Mr. Eels's. Very brilliant company. Remained until 11 o'clock. Visited with Foster until twelve. Retired not feeling well.

FRIDAY, 12. Spent part of the forenoon with Foster. I told him I could take no part whatever in the Senatorial contest in Ohio. He has been announced as a candidate, as are also Sherman and Matthews. Foster and Family left at twelve o'clock. Shopped with Crete until 4.50 when we came home. A large mass of letters awaiting me. Mother, Mollie and Aunt [Alpha] Boynton came home.

SATURDAY, 13. The window-strip man finished his work, and the electric bell man his. He put in a front door bell, and one from my library upstairs to the office. Battery in the cellar.

Had four apple trees in the young orchard removed to fill vacant spaces, and leave room for grape vines. We are moving our garden from the east side of the house (which is to become a part of the lawn) to the rear of the engine house.

Visitors numerous. The great mails dropping off a little.

SUNDAY, 14. C. D. Wilber and wife came early this morning. Indeed, they arrived at the Mentor Station about 2 hours after midnight and stayed at the hotel till morning. About 10 A.M. my classmate H. E. Knox and his son Harry came to talk over the prosecution of the forgers in N.Y.

Wilber and wife, Aunt Alpha, Mother, Crete and I went to church, and heard a very good sermon by Hendricks. In the afternoon, Dr. Robison, Albert Allen,[339] Mess[rs.] Durham and

---

of Connecticut who was brought as a child to Ohio, where he graduated at Western Reserve College, 1846, and the Cleveland Medical School, 1848. After studying geology and medicine in Paris, he practiced medicine in Cleveland in the early 1850's. He was professor of geology and paleontology in the School of Mines of Columbia University, 1866–92, and state geologist of Ohio, 1869–74. The bride's uncle, Dr. James Eels, president of Lane Theological Seminary, performed the ceremony.

[339]Albert Allen (1827–1888), of Akron, an ardent Republican and zealous member of the Disciples of Christ, amassed considerable wealth in flour and stone milling. He willed generous sums to religious and educational institutions, including about $10,000 to Hiram College.

Comstock called and spent an hour. Knox and son stayed till ten and then went to Painesville. Swaim was driven to Willoughby to take the train for Leavenworth, to be gone a week.

MONDAY, 15. Six inches of snow on the ground. At 7.41 Crete took Mollie to Cleveland to put her into Mrs. Middleburger [Miss Mittleberger's] School. She is to stay at James Mason's. This is the beginning of her absence from home and of course marks one of the turning points in her life. At eight o'clock the President[340] and other officers of the Pennsylvania Company came by special train, stopping at the lane and wading up through the snow to make a brief call. Mark Hanna of Cleveland was with them. The volume of incoming letters is rapidly diminishing and we made good progress on accumulations. Wilber and I visited during the day. Crete returned at noon and a carpenter came with the vestibule doors which we found necessary. Several correspondents came during the day, Robertson and Kennedy[341] among the number. Late in the evening received a telegram that Sister Mary's daughter Hattie Palmer died last night. Her life makes me feel exceedingly old. She has been married four year[s], taught 12 terms of school before, yet I had taught my first winter's school before she was married [born].

TUESDAY, 16. Spent some time with Wilber, looking over the farm. At noon Edwin Cowles of Cleveland and Joseph Medill of [the] *Chicago Tribune* came. Had two hours' conversation with Medill or rather he talked to me nearly all that time his views on some phases of the policy of the incoming administration. He is very anxious that the greenbacks shall not be retired. He thinks that a currency panic is not possible so long as the Government controls. He is anxious that neither John Sherman nor any Wall

---

[340]George B. Roberts (1833–1897) was president of the Pennsylvania Railroad Company, 1880 to his death, succeeding Thomas A. Scott, who resigned on June 1 because of poor health.

[341]Charles E. Kennedy was a reporter on the *Cleveland Herald.* His brother, James H. (1849–1934), worked on several Cleveland papers during the 1870's and 1880's; at this time he was associate editor of the *Herald.* He was the author of *A History of the City of Cleveland* (1896) and several other books.

Street man shall continue in charge of the finances. I listened and occasionally propounded a question, but gave no indication of my purpose on any subject to which he referred. Capt. Henry came. Mr. Robertson, Mr. and Mrs. Wilber were driven to Willoughby to take the train. Dictated a large number of letters in the evening.

J. Medill of Chicago came today, and this is the substance of our conference:[342]

1. Gen. Logan and he have late become friends, and in their conversation Logan says he does not want, and would not accept a place in the Cabinet. He doesn't think the 306 people wish to be a faction, but to be treated like other staunch Republicans.[343]

   They will not give their opinion to G. unless it is asked. Medill thinks Logan is in good cordial state of feeling.

[342]On November 16 and 27 and December 8, Garfield made notes in a small notebook of conversations with Joseph Medill (November 16), Levi P. Morton and John Sherman (November 27) and of his reflections on the senatorship (December 8). In his regular diary he made entries for these dates (recorded by George Rose) in which he mentioned the talks with Medill and Morton but omitted information recorded by him in the small notebook, and did not mention at all his talk with Sherman or his thoughts about the senatorship. The pages on which Garfield made his notes were removed from the small notebook by Joseph Stanley-Brown and inserted in the regular diary as a unit between the entries in Rose's hand for November 15 and November 16. The editors have incorporated Garfield's notes in the regular diary under the dates indicated. In each instance they follow the regular entry in Rose's hand and are separated from it by double spacing.

[343]On the 36th and last ballot at the Republican National Convention in Chicago, 306 delegates supported Grant. Some months after the convention Chauncey I. Filley caused medals to be struck for those delegates. "The obverse includes a portrait of Grant and a listing of the votes cast for him on each of the thirty-six ballots. The reverse has this inscription: 'Commemorative of the 36 ballots of the Old Guard for Ulysses S. Grant for President. Republican National Convention Chicago June 1880.' " Below the inscription appears the name of the delegate for whom the medal had been struck. See Margaret Leech and Harry J. Brown, *The Garfield Orbit: The Life of President James A. Garfield* (1978), pp. 353–354, n. 21.

> To this I replied that I wanted all Republicans including the 306 to consider themselves in full fellowship.

2. He labored long to show that the retention of the green-backs as a fixed part of our currency was necessary. Hence neither Sherman, nor any Eastern man, would do for Sec'y of the Treasury.

> He wanted a Western man, e.g., Allison. To all this I was only a listener.

3. He thinks Davis of Illinois would resign and go back to the Supreme Court if he could.

4. Thinks the Senate can be secured.

WEDNESDAY, 17. Crete and I took the 7.41 train for Cleveland, where Captain Henry met us. We spent an hour or two shopping and then drove to the Atlantic and Great Western Depot, where a special train was in waiting to take us to Solon. Arrived in Solon a little before twelve o'clock. We were driven to Sister Mary's to attend the funeral of her daughter Hattie M. Palmer. The funeral was at one o'clock at Hattie's house. She was buried in her mother's dooryard under the fruit trees. A large number of old acquaintances of Solon and Orange were present. At half-past three o'clock took the special train and at a little before four arrived in Cleveland. Drove to the stove store and bought some stoves. Came home on the evening train in the midst of a heavy snow storm. More than 200 letters came during the day, among others a belated letter from Hal. Retired at half-past nine.

THURSDAY, 18. Heavy day's work on the mail. Frank Leslie's artist came to draw sketches,[344] but the weather was too boister-ous for outdoor work. A number of people came during the day. Brown went to Cleveland at noon, to bring Mollie and the Mason girls to meet us at Painesville. At five in the afternoon Crete and

---

[344]The popularity of *Frank Leslie's Illustrated Newspaper,* a weekly journal, was the result of its lavish use of engravings made from drawings by staff artists. Frank Leslie (1821–January 10, 1880) was succeeded in the management of the publishing concern by his widow, who legally assumed the name of "Frank Leslie" in 1882. She is said to have made $50,000 in July, 1881, when she broke up forms that were about to go to press and substituted illustrations and news reports of Garfield's assassination.

the two boys and I, Mr. Rose and Mr. Judd drove to Lake Erie Seminary, arriving at six, where I was tendered a reception by the Trustees, faculty and students, a very pleasant company, the house beautifully decorated. After tea the young ladies entertained us with some music and pleasing gymnastic exercises in the chapel. Left at nine o'clock, Brown, Mollie, [and] the Mason girls returning with us. Very cold.

FRIDAY, 19. At eight-thirty Senator Dorsey and Mr. Clint. Wheeler,[345] Police Commissioner of New York, and, also, Governor Jewell, T. W. Phillips from New Castle and Alanson Wilcox[346] of Cleveland [came, and I] spent the forenoon in consultation with different gentlemen. All went away at noon except Governor Jewell who remained over. Mother, Aunt Alpha Boynton, Crete and I took the train at noon for Cleveland. We were met by John Hofste who drove us to Uncle Thomas Garfield's at the edge of Warrenton, ten miles from Cleveland, where a family party of [for] Uncle Thomas and myself, he 79 and I 49, our birthday, was held. A pleasant family dinner party and visit. At half-past five, we were driven to Newburgh. Stopped at John Hofste's house, where I had a reception for an hour and a half. A large number of visitors called; thence to Cleveland, leaving Mother and Aunt Alpha Boynton at Dr. Boynton's. Crete and I came home on the 11 o'clock train, reaching the house at midnight.

SATURDAY, 20. John I. Davenport[347] arrived from New York

[345]Dewitt C. Wheeler, a sometime dry goods merchant, was a member of the New York City Board of Police Commissioners, 1876 to December 22, 1879, when he was forced to resign because of charges of misfeasance and malfeasance. By July 31, 1879, when the *New York Times* accused him of specific gross wrongdoings, he was regarded as a political liability to New York Republicans.

[346]Alanson Wilcox (1832–1924), who was for several years pastor of the Franklin Avenue Church of the Disciples of Christ in Cleveland, campaigned in Indiana and Kentucky to secure the Disciple vote for Garfield in 1880. He also kept Garfield informed about Disciple support in those and other states. He was the author of *A History of the Disciples of Christ in Ohio* (1918).

[347]John I. Davenport (c. 1845–1903), a native of Connecticut, attended public schools, worked for his father, a realtor, did some newspaper work, served as an "unattached member" of the staff of General Benjamin F. Butler, and, in 1866,

early in the morning and he and Governor Jewell spent the
forenoon with me reviewing very carefully the course of the
forgery trial in New York. I refused peremptorily to go to New
York as a witness but recommend that the[y] reserve Philp until
near the end of the struggle, first trying the forgers and other
parties implicated. Jewell and Davenport left at noon. Reverend
Jabez Hall of East Cleveland and L. E. Holden[348] called and took
dinner with us. In the afternoon Mrs. Shaw[349] and her son,

---

was admitted to the bar. Soon after the passage by Congress in 1871 of a law
authorizing U.S. circuit judges to appoint supervisors of elections, he was appointed chief supervisor of elections for the district of southern New York (which
included New York City); he was also a U.S. commissioner for the same district.
As chief supervisor, said the *New York Times* at his death (obituary, August 28),
he "wielded a power that few men of his day possessed, and in such a way as to
warrant the charge that he was not only tyrannical, but made his office serve the
political ends of his friends." He was at all times a Republican partisan. In 1878,
as a result of complaints of his highhanded tactics, a subcommittee of the House
Committee on the Judiciary investigated the charges against him; in its report the
committee wrote: "Your committee believes that the power conferred upon the
supervisors of elections, as it has been exercised in New York City, is destructive
of the rights of the citizen, and instead of promoting purity of elections, has been
made use of by partisans for purely personal purposes." See *House Miscellaneous
Documents,* No. 23, 45 Cong., 3 Sess., Serial 1862, and *House Reports,* No. 135,
45 Cong., 3 Sess., Serial 1866. Davenport continued as chief supervisor until his
office was abolished by law in 1893. He was indefatigable in his investigation of
the Morey letter, the "master spirit in the whole thing," A.F. Rockwell wrote
Garfield from New York City (October 26, 1880). He continued his investigation
after Garfield's death. For his conclusions see his curious book, *History of the Morey
Letter* (1884). He was also the author of another partisan study, *The Election Frauds
of New York City and Their Prevention,* Vol. I (1881); Vol. II never appeared.
Davenport's last days were clouded by mental illness.

[348]Liberty E. Holden (1833–1913), a native of Maine, graduated at the Univer-
sity of Michigan, 1858, where he earned the degree of Master of Arts in 1861.
A Unitarian and a Democrat, he engaged in teaching, law, real estate, mining and
journalism. He was a founder of the Salt Lake Academy in Utah, served as
president of its board of trustees for twelve years, and was also a trustee of Western
Reserve University, to which he left a part of his estate. In 1884 he bought the
Cleveland Plain Dealer. In 1860 he married Delia E. Buckley, daughter of Henry
G. Buckley, a professor of mathematics at Williams College. He died in Mentor.

[349]Alpha J. Benson, who married D. R. Shaw in 1856, was the great granddaughter of Seth Ballou, older brother of James Ballou, father of Eliza Garfield.

second cousins of Mother's, from Coshocton, came to see us. In the evening Mother, Mollie and Sister Mary came. Brown went to Cleveland at twelve and did not return. I dictated about one hundred letters to Rose in the afternoon and evening and retired at eleven.

SUNDAY, 21. A very blustering day. General McDowell and wife and Major Keeler,[350] his aide-de-camp, came on the morning express, arriving here at half-past six. We were all shut up in the house during the day by the storm. Had a long conversation with General McDowell on several phases of the political situation. Worked off a part of the accumulated mail which has been gaining on me for some days.

MONDAY, 22. Worked on the mail in the forenoon and gave directions for farm matters. At twelve o'clock, General and Mrs. McDowell, Major Keeler, Rose, Crete, and I, went to the Mentor Station, where a special car was awaiting us and took us to Cleveland. Spent the afternoon in shopping with Crete; thence to Mr. Mason's. I dined at Mark Hanna's with Lawrence Barrett and Amos Townsend. Drove to Mr. Mason's at eight o'clock and took the train at Euclid Street Station, Mr. Townsend and Kennedy having joined us. Just before leaving I telegraphed to Rockwell, requesting him to prevent the public demonstration being prepared at Washington for my arrival—38 guns, torchlight, etc.

TUESDAY, 23. Awoke on the mountains, half an hour before reaching Altoona. Breakfast in the car. We are out of the region of snow, though it is very cold and the streams are frozen. Reached Harrisburg at one o'clock. Senator Cameron met us and Townsend, Mrs. Garfield and I went to the house and took lunch. Had a frank conversation with him in the presence of Mr. Townsend on the political situation. I commenced it by asking him to

---

She was thus Eliza's first cousin twice removed. Her husband was a dealer in glassware and queen's-ware in Coshocton, Ohio. Three of their children were living at this time: Emma, William and Benjamin.

[350]Birney B. Keeler, a native of New York, served as an officer in the Civil War, 1862–65. He entered the regular army in 1866 and served to his death in 1886.

tell me how much 306 means. He thinks it will not be maintained as a separate faction inside of the party, certainly not if a proper career is afforded to General Grant and he suggested a novel one. On the whole his conversation was frank and manly and I do not think it will be a matter of very serious difficulty to harmonize the wishes of both wings of the Pennsylvania Republicans. Left Harrisburg at four o'clock and arrived in Washington at eight. A few hundred people were waiting at the Depot, but the reception was altogether informal. Rockwell met us and drove us to our house on Thirteenth and I, where after an hour's chat we retired.

WEDNESDAY, 24.   Swaim arrived at nine o'clock. A great crowd of callers in the morning. I find myself comparitively useless in the way of helping Crete with her packing. The rush was so great that I escaped it by driving out at one o'clock to Bell's the Photographer and sitting for portraits for the Treasury Department; thence we drove to the President's and spent two hours. A long interview on retirements and appointments, also on the person[n]el of the persons employed at the White House. In the meantime Crete had a pleasant conversation with Mrs. Hayes. Returned to the house and received company for an hour or two. Dictated some letters to Rose. At half-past four o'clock called at Secretary Sherman's. At five o'clock drove to Rockwell's and dined and visited until half-past seven. Brought Crete home and I in company with Rockwell called on [Hayward M.] Hutchinson on Massachusetts Avenue.

THURSDAY, 25.   Awoke at eight o'clock. Interviews with Butterworth and several other persons who called. At nine o'clock Swaim, Crete and I called at Col. Ingersoll's and had breakfast. A very pleasant family party. At eleven o'clock went to the Disciple Church on Vermont Avenue and listened to a Thanksgiving sermon. At the conclusion was pleasantly greeted by the members of the church. Came home, looked over letters, dictated answers and then called with Crete at Mrs. Sumner's. Took her with us to call on poor Mrs. Smalley, who is failing very fast; thence to Gilfillan's where we made a short call; thence home. On our return a large number of people called. Dictated letters and journal. At half-past five Swaim, Crete and I went to Secretary Sherman's to dinner. There were present Mr. and Mrs. Sherman, Amos Townsend, Ben Butterworth, a young naval officer and Major Swaim. Home at half-past nine o'clock. Later called on Ben Holladay with Major Swaim.

FRIDAY, 26. Dictated a few letters in the morning. Callers commenced again early. Came in crowds, the majority of all seeking to impress me with some special views of the political situation and what should be done for the future. At noon I went to General Schenck's breakfast. There were present Sir Edward Thornton, the French and Swedish Ministers, Dr. Crane[351] of the Army, Secretary Ramsey, J. Bancroft Davis, Levi P. Morton, Count Lewenhaupt,[352] Admiral Porter. A very pleasant breakfast. At half-past two drove Crete to the Bureau of Engraving and Printing and sat a few moments to the artist preparing a portrait for an engraving. In the afternoon callers continued in great numbers, among them Hubbell of Michigan, [and] Tucker of Virginia, who was anxious to warn me against an alliance with Mahone on the ground that he is a repudiator. Blaine came and spent an hour. At seven in the evening Crete and I dined at Senator Edmunds'. There were present, beside the Senator and his wife and daughter, Senator Morrill and wife of Vermont, Secretary Evarts and wife, George Bancroft, Mr. and Mrs. Morton of New York. Home at half-past ten. Wrote a letter to the boys agreeing to their plan to study the last half of the year under a tutor. Advised Hal not to make haste to join the Episcopal Church.[353]

---

[351]Charles H. Crane (1825–1883), a native of Rhode Island, entered the U.S. army in 1848 as assistant surgeon. He served in the Civil War, 1861–65, and was breveted brigadier general in the latter year. He was colonel and assistant surgeon general, 1866–82, and brigadier general and surgeon general, 1882 to his death.

[352]Count Carl Lewenhaupt (1835–1906) was educated in Lund, and served for many years in the diplomatic corps of the United Kingdom of Sweden and Norway. He was minister to the United States, 1876–82, minister of foreign affairs, 1889–95, and minister to Great Britain, 1895–1902.

[353]On November 21, Hal, who had turned seventeen a month earlier, informed his father of his decision to be confirmed. "I have thought it all over," he wrote,

SATURDAY, 27. A few callers before 8 o'clock. Went to Blaine's and took a light breakfast, then visited for an hour. On my return, many callers. At twelve Swaim, Crete and I took breakfast with Hon. L. P. Morton, a large company present, then made calls on several cabinet officers. At six dined at the President's. About twenty-four covers. A pleasant party. Left at 9 o'clock for home. A number of people called. Retired at 11, exceedingly tired. I am annoyed very much at a misunderstanding between Mr. Morton and myself, in regard to a conversation had in New York in August.

Conference[354] with L. P. Morton, whom I find under misapprehension, that Secretary of Treasury is promised to N.Y. This was not my understanding and seems wholly inadmissible. It would be a congestion of financial power—at money centre—and would create great jealousy at the West.

Collection and management of revenue should be kept as far apart as possible.

Satisfactory talk with Sherman. Asked him if he would feel wholly cordial, if he were not retained. Responded affirmatively, and I think earnestly.

"and think it will do me good. I like the services and have no special objection to the creed." "Now Hal," Garfield responded, "I say again you must be perfectly free to decide for yourself in all matters relating to religion. Neither Mamma nor I desire to control your choice. And certainly no body else should. Do not permit yourself to be persuaded or influenced to act hastily. I greatly prefer that you take no preliminary step, or binding obligation, until after the holidays, for I have some suggestions to make which I think will aid you. Remember that all the influences now around you are in one direction, and you may be a broader man for having looked on all sides before acting. Please do not forget that the ministers of almost every church are drumming up recruits for their own sect. I do not mean this in a bad sense; but I mean that it often amounts to undue influence. I have never asked you to join my church and I don't want any other man to take away your liberty. You are still very young. Your heart is fresh and pure, and I think the long experience of mama and papa, who love you as no stranger can, may be of service to you."

[354]See n. 342, November 16, 1880.

When [Went] to Blaine's house and took an early breakfast with him alone.[355] *Inter alia* I said, "Blaine, I have not made a single final decision in reference to my cabinet, and shall not until February. But let us talk provisionally. If I should ask you to take a place in my cabinet, what would be your probable response, and before you answer, please tell me whether you are, or will be, a candidate for the presidency in 1884. I ask this because I do not purpose for myself, nor to allow anyone else to use the next four years as the camping ground for fighting the next presidential battle."[356] He replied that [he] would not again seek

[355]Garfield made this record of his conference with Blaine in a volume bearing the words "Memorandum Diary." The entry was not copied into the regular diary nor inserted in it. The "Memorandum Diary" also includes copies of letters, 1868–81.

[356]Everything Garfield wrote in this entry appears to be true, but he was less precise and complete than he might have been. Why? He probably wanted a record that would help him later to reconstruct the conversation in greater detail, and that he could show friends without revealing his offer of the State Department to Blaine. Perhaps he also thought of protecting the secrecy of his cabinet-making activities in case the statement was seen by anyone who might disclose its contents. At any rate, letters and diary entries written in December, 1880, show that during his conversation with Blaine, Garfield invited him to become his secretary of state and urged him to accept the invitation. On December 12 and 15 Garfield told his diary that Blaine seemed to favor a place in the cabinet, and in the entry for December 23 appears the cryptic but suggestive notation, "Important letter from Blaine today—may have marked influence on his future and mine." The comment about Blaine in the entry for December 12 was prompted by letters from Blaine and Whitelaw Reid, each written on December 10. "The more I think of the State Department," Blaine confessed, "the more I am inclined thereto. . . ." Whitelaw Reid stated that Blaine was thinking seriously of "withdrawing from active politics in Maine for a while," was pleased "that you had spoken to me about it in such a way that he could feel free to talk with me," and "left on my mind the impression that he could be induced to take it, although I don't think his mind is yet clearly made up." The phrase "to take it" is a reference to a specific cabinet position known to both Reid and Garfield. The entry for December 15 was made after Garfield read a letter from Blaine (December 13) who was upset because Hayes's secretary of state, William Evarts, was "undertaking to delve into" Canadian-American relations under the Treaty of Washington. Blaine made clear that he had definite ideas concerning that realm of diplomacy and hoped that Garfield would write Hayes suggesting that "the whole question of a readjustment of Cana-

for a nomination. Indeed he thought he could not get it by seeking, that if he ever should be nominated, it would be because it came to him unsought.

He then asked me if I really wanted him in my cabinet. I answered, that if I should find it possible to make a cast of a cabinet in which he would be a harmonious factor, it would be personally very agreeable to have him with me. But as I would make no final decisions until February, we could canvass the subject freely in the mean time.

At first he spoke as though he could not exchange his place in the Senate for one in the cabinet. I pointed out the career which executive work offered, and told him, I thought it would be better for his fame, and for the health of his party in Maine if he would resign the leadership for a time; that the backset in his state was, in part, due to a rebellion against his rule, and he would be better liked if he withdrew his hand from the helm for a time. We both agreed that only the Treasury or State Dep't would be desirable for him. Nothing was concluded, except an agreement for a free correspondence on the subject. The same day I talked with Whitelaw Reid, and asked him to sound Blaine's mind, before he left the city, and let me know the result.

SUNDAY, 28. Slept poorly through the night. Tired and jaded this morning. Took a bath and a very light breakfast. At one o'clock

---

dian matters should be left without embarrassment to your administration."

The "important letter" mentioned in the diary for December 23 was written by Blaine on December 20, three weeks and two days after the conversation of November 27, and sent with a letter to Garfield's wife in an envelope addressed to her. "I send it under cover to you," he explained, "because I wish no eye but yours and the General's to see it. Its conclusion need not be made public until after Inauguration." In the enclosed letter to Garfield, Blaine wrote: "Your generous invitation to enter your cabinet, as Secretary of State, has been under consideration for more than three weeks. The thought had never once occurred to my mind until you presented it with such cogent arguments in its favor, and with such warmth of personal friendship in aid of your kind offer. I know that an early answer is desirable and I have waited only long enough to make up my mind definitely and conclusively. I therefore say to you, in the same cordial spirit in which you invited me, that I accept the position." In a warm acknowledgment (December 23) Garfield expressed his delight with Blaine's decision.

called at Judge Cartter's, where I found Mr. Morton, and stated to Judge Cartter the difference of understanding that had sprung up between us. Concluded the consultation with following points. First. I will not make and declare any particular choice of Cabinet Minister for a month or two yet. Second. I will not tolerate, nor act upon any understanding that anything has been pledged to any party, state or person. Governor Sprague of Rhode Island called and make a striking suggestion. Whitelaw Reid also came and many others. At six o'clock Crete and I dined at Secretary Evarts' and family. A very pleasant party. Shortly after dinner was over John Hay and Whitelaw Reid called and sat at the table. Mr. Evarts was very bright. Gave some interesting views on the estimation in which the people hold the Presidential Office. Returned home at ten and found Nichol and Rockwell there. Marshall Jewell soon came and I gave him my views of the situation of Tennessee and Virginia. Retired at 11 o'clock with a severe headache.

MONDAY, 29. Crowd of callers commenced early and continued until the hour of leaving. I drove to the Interior Department for a short time. At 10 o'clock drove to the 6th Street Depot. Mr. Pugh's[357] special car was in waiting. Messrs. Townsend, Richard Smith and Nichol joined us. Left at half-past ten. I laid down to sleep near Baltimore and did not awake until one o'clock. On the whole the trip to Washington has been very exhausting. We have partially dismantled the house by sending home a considerable portion of the furniture, books and pictures. I did not know how strongly I had become attached to the little Washington home. I have probably taken my final leave of it as a home. I cannot expect as much happiness in any other house in Washington.[358] There was snow all the way on our journey. We dined

[357]Charles E. Pugh (1841–1913), a native of Pennsylvania, was associated with the Pennsylvania Railroad Company, 1859–1911, beginning as an agent and advancing to first vice president. He was general superintendent of the railroad, 1879–82.

[358]Mrs. Garfield retained ownership of the Garfield house at the corner of 13th and I streets in Washington until 1895, when she sold it to Senator Redfield Proctor of Vermont. It was soon bought by a builder who added two bays and a fourth story and made other changes. It then became an apartment house; in the

and supped on board the car and went to sleep on the heights of the Alleghenies.

TUESDAY, 30. Was awakened half an hour before reaching Cleveland. Arrived at half-past six. Our car was attached to the half-past seven train. We reached Mentor a little before 9. Sleighing still good. Spent the day in overhauling the accumulated mail and worked off a large number of letters. Senator Paddock[359] and wife of Nebraska called and spent an hour. He is anxious to secure the appointment of the late Senator Hitchcock [as] a member of the Cabinet. I told him I could give no sign on that subject, at least until February, but would willingly receive suggestions from all quarters. At five o'clock drove to the Town Hall and voted for E. B. Taylor as my successor in the 19th District for the short term.[360] In the evening dictated a large number of letters. Retired at half-past 9.

December

WEDNESDAY, 1. *Presidential Election Day.* Worked on the mail and with callers during the forenoon. It is remarkable how little

city directory of 1903 it is listed as "The Garfield." In 1942 it became the Atlantic Hotel. In 1964 it was demolished to enable the owner to expand his parking lot. "Thus passes, 'unhonored and unsung,' " wrote Carlton J. Corliss, "another landmark which in nearly any other city in America would have been marked and preserved as an historic shrine." The quotation and the information in this note is from Carlton J. Corliss, "Another Washington Landmark Passes" (1964), an unpublished paper, a copy of which was given to the editors by the author.

[359]Algernon S. Paddock (1830–1897) was a Republican member of the U.S. Senate, 1875–81, 1887–93.

[360]In the state election in Ohio, October 12, 1880, Ezra Booth Taylor, Republican, was elected to the U.S. House of Representatives from the Nineteenth District as reorganized by the state legislature in February, 1880 (Mahoning County was replaced by Portage County) for the 47th Congress, which began on March 4, 1881. On November 8, 1880, Garfield resigned his seat in the 46th Congress, which expired on March 4, 1881. A controversy arose over whether his successor for the remainder of the 46th Congress should be chosen by the old or new district; the decision was in favor of the old. On November 30, Taylor was elected for the short session by a very large majority.

attention the people [pay] to this day's business in the several states. At noon today the law requires the Electors to meet at the Capitol of each state and the real presidential election takes place. About three o'clock I received the first return from Indiana stating that the 15 Electoral Votes had been thrown for Garfield and Arthur. Then followed dispatches from Ohio, Illinois, Massachusetts, Wisconsin. We had no dispatches from the other states. My successor was elected to Congress from the Nineteenth District, and I am a private citizen for the first time in twenty-one years. Worked off a large number of letters in the afternoon and met many people who called.

THURSDAY, 2. Heavy snow fell during the night and sleighing is still excellent. A large mail came in the morning and callers began to drop in soon after breakfast. Worked on mail and saw visitors until noon when Governor Foster and the Ohio Electoral College and several other gentlemen, in all about thirty-five, stopped at the foot of the lane and called on me. Chairman Grosvenor made a short address and I replied. I took the occasion to refer to the majesty of the body of voters. I think I presented a somewhat new view of the case. I wanted to lay a foundation for making our political God an honest and intelligent one.[361] Our guests left about two o'clock, except Governor Foster and T. M. Nichol, who spent the night with us. Had a long conversation with Foster on the general political situation. While I shall remain neutral in regard to the Senatorial contest, it would

---

[361]On December 1 Ohio's twenty-two presidential electors met in Columbus and cast their votes for Garfield and Arthur. Their visit to Mentor in company with the governor was a courtesy call. In his response to Charles Grosvenor's address, Garfield emphasized "the august sovereign of the Republic," the American people, whose November fiat had been carried out by the electors, and whose command every man must obey. "In that presence, therefore, I stand and am awed by the majesty and authority of such a command." He went on to say: "In so far as I can interpret the best aspirations and purposes of our august sovereign, I shall seek to realize them. You and I, and those who have acted with us, in the years past, believe that our sovereign loves liberty, and desires for all the inhabitants of the Republic peace and prosperity under the sway of just and equal laws."

be a great deal better I think for the politics of Ohio and for the Administration if Sherman should be elected.

FRIDAY, 3. Callers increased during the day to such an extent as to become a positive hindrance to work and I am beginning to despair of making any fit preparation for my work unless I can be more let alone. Major Bundy and his mother came at noon and spent the afternoon and night with us. Elliot F. Shepherd [Shepard][362] from New York called and spent a short time. Many persons of less consequence came. Still I made some progress with the mail. We were disappointed in the evening in not seeing Mollie come home from Cleveland.

SATURDAY, 4. The morning was spent mainly in conversation with Bundy,[363] Nichol and others who called, when I went to the depot to meet Mollie. Nichol left for Washington. General

[362]Elliott F. Shepard (1833–1893), lawyer and banker, practiced law for over twenty-five years, established a number of banks, and founded in 1876 the New York Bar Association, of which he later became president. In 1868 he married Margaret Louise Vanderbilt, daughter of William H. Vanderbilt. Late in 1880 he sought the position of U.S. attorney for the southern district of New York. On December 20, Whitelaw Reid wrote to Garfield that Vanderbilt had called to support his son-in-law for the position, and two days later Garfield replied that he had written to Hayes in reference to Shepard and that Reid might let Vanderbilt know it. President Hayes, however, reappointed the incumbent, Stewart L. Woodford. Shepard gave up the law in 1884, traveled to Europe, Asia, Africa and Alaska, and in 1888 bought the *New York Mail and Express.*

[363]Jonas M. Bundy (1835–1891), a native of New Hampshire, was taken as a child to Wisconsin, where he graduated at Beloit College (1853) and became a journalist in Milwaukee. He served in the Union army during the Civil War, attaining the rank of major. After the war he settled in New York City, where he became a drama, musical and literary critic on the *Evening Post.* In 1868 he helped to found the *New York Evening Mail,* becoming the paper's editor-in-chief, a post he held to his death. Cyrus W. Field bought the paper in 1879 and in 1881 combined it with the *New York Evening Express,* which he had just acquired. In 1888 Elliott F. Shepard bought the paper. Immediately after Garfield's nomination at Chicago, Bundy was asked by a New York publisher to write a campaign biography of the Republican candidate. With Garfield's consent Bundy undertook the task. He made two visits to Lawnfield—in June and July—to gather materials for his book, which was published on August 3, 1880, under the title *The Life of James A. Garfield.* An expanded edition was brought out in 1881 after Garfield's death.

Bates[364] of Illinois and Mr. Blossom[365] of Cleveland came. Also Mr. Shepard of New York. Spent two or three hours with Major Bundy. He and his mother left at three o'clock. Dictated a large number of letters in the forenoon and made some progress on arrears of work. Swaim and I walked to the Post Office in the evening and brought the mail home through a rain.

SUNDAY, 5.　At sunrise the snow had almost entirely disappeared. We passed in a single night from excellent sleighing to bare roads and fields. Remained at home all day and dictated a large number of letters and nearly closed up my desk. I am determined to answer fewer letters in the future, otherwise I shall have no time for study and reflection. Determined also to reduce my number of interviews with people who call. I could let myself be eaten up before the fourth of March. If I save myself for work before me, it must be by denying myself to many. Shall bend my energies now to clearing up and putting in order, all the correspondence, old letters, [and] documents that I want to lay safely away until the Presidential term is over. I must be found fault with at any rate. I prefer to be found fault with by the few, than by the many who look forward to a good public service.

MONDAY, 6.　A very busy day and unusually free from callers. It was stormy and blustering and we devoted the time to opening our Washington goods. In the afternoon Healey [Healy] the artist came desiring to paint my picture for the Paris Exposition, but I declined to give him the time and he went on by the evening train. Went to bed at ten o'clock with a good physically tired feeling which I ought to have oftener for health.

TUESDAY, 7.　Continued yesterday's work hanging pictures and

---

[364]Erastus N. Bates, a native of Massachusetts, moved to Illinois and was an officer in the 80th Illinois Volunteer Infantry Regiment, 1862–65. He was breveted brigadier general in 1865. He was for some time associated with the firm of William T. Allen & Company, wholesale grocers in Chicago. In 1881 he encouraged Garfield in his stand against Conkling, writing that the people were almost unanimously behind him and were saying that if Conkling was to rule the country, they wanted to know it.

[365]Henry C. Blossom (1822–1883), a hardware merchant and one of the most prosperous businessmen in Cleveland.

arranging furniture. Devoted most of the afternoon to the mail. In the afternoon Mrs. Morton and lady friends from Quincy, Illinois, came asking for the Post Office at that place for Mrs. Morton. Ex-Governor Pierpont[366] [and] Mr. Sturgis[s][367] from West Virginia came urging the appointment of A.W. Campbell of Wheeling to the Cabinet. During the past ten days I have been dieting, carefully abstaining from tobacco, tea, coffee, potatoes, butter and grease of any kind. I am beginning to feel the beneficial results in my digestion which has been endangered by overwork. Capt. Henry came and in the evening went to Painesville.

WEDNESDAY, 8. Stormy and blustering. Weather I think colder than it has been during the Winter. Pipe leading from my ram to the tank is frozen and the water supply cut off. Made good progress on my mail clearing up old scores. The old pile of congratulatory letters is all disposed of. At noon my cousins Henry and Nathan Cornish of Wisconsin came to make us a visit. They spent the night. I retired at half-past ten.

The Ohio Senatorship annoys me.[368]

1. It is perilous for me to interfere *inter partes.*
2. The defeat of Sherman leaves him where he can hardly accept anything else, and out of office he creates a dissatisfaction in Ohio, dangerous to the party peace.
3. If F[oster] would withdraw it would heal all.

[366]Francis H. Pierpont (1814–1899), lawyer and businessman, was a native of Virginia and a graduate of Allegheny College (1839). When Virginia seceded from the Union he took a leading part in establishing at Wheeling a government, backed by Unionists, which claimed to be the legitimate government of Virginia and which was responsible for the creation of West Virginia. Though he headed that government, was later the governor of the "restored" state of Virginia (it consisted of areas under Union control), and was governor of all of Virginia from the end of the Civil War to 1868, he was never governor of West Virginia.

[367]George C. Sturgiss (1842–1925) was a native of Ohio. He settled in West Virginia where he practiced law, was a state legislator, 1872–80, unsuccessful Republican candidate for governor, 1880, a member of the U.S. House of Representatives, 1907–11, and judge of the circuit court, 1912–20.

[368]See n. 342, November 16, 1880.

4. Where can I find his equal for the Treasury?

5. His app't has numerous serious resulting embarrassments.

THURSDAY, 9. Storm still continues with unabated force. Worked off a considerable mail and spent some time in visiting with my Cousins, who left at noon. After they left Capt. Henry and Dr. and Mrs. Pomerene came.[369] The Captain spent the night. The Doctor and his wife left about six o'clock.

FRIDAY, 10. Crete and Major Swaim went to Cleveland on the morning train. I had intended to go, but could not well leave. General Kilpatrick came about nine o'clock and staid nearly two hours, so that I got but little work done. Wrote a long letter to Rockwell requesting him to assist Rose in getting my letters, notes of letters, together in some fireproof place.

At noon Rose left for Washington to do some work for me, and to be at home during the impending illness of his wife.[370]

In the evening Major Swaim, Crete and Mollie [came]. I had been raided on by a great number of people—Speaker Cowgill,[371] Ohio House of Representatives and Mr. Ray[372] of the Senate [House] to urge me to put Gov. Foster in the cabinet, and thus save the contest in Ohio between him and Sherman for the Senatorship. I deplore the contest, and see peril in it, but refuse

[369]Joel Pomerene (1825–1881), a native of Millersburg, Ohio, graduated at Jefferson Medical College in Philadelphia and practiced medicine in Middletown, Ohio, until 1861. He was the surgeon in Garfield's 42nd Ohio Infantry Regiment. In 1863 illness forced his retirement from the army and plagued him thereafter. In 1864 he returned to Millersburg, where he spent the remainder of his life.

[370]Lucretia ("Crete") Rose was born in the Garfield house in Washington, D.C., on January 12, 1881, the only daughter in George Rose's large family. She never married but remained at home, devoting herself to her family until her father's death in the 1930's. In the early 1960's she was living alone at her home in Lanham, Maryland; she then remembered many things she had heard about the Garfields and possessed a small collection of Garfield memorabilia.

[371]Thomas A. Cowgill, a native of Champaign County, was a Union officer in the Civil War, 1862–64, and served for ten years as a trustee of Ohio State University. He was a member of the Ohio house of representatives, 1876–81, 1886–87 (he was Speaker, 1880–81), and of the Ohio senate, 1888–89.

[372]Daniel G. Ray (1833–1881), a Cincinnati lawyer, was a Republican member of the Ohio house of representatives, 1880–81.

to interfere. Aunt Phebe Ballou and Cousin Orrin came, and spent the night. Several other people called.

SATURDAY, 11. Made some progress in clearing up arrears of mail. Capt. Henry stayed and helped file letters. In the evening Capt. Henry left and Burke Hinsdale came and spent the night. Had a long talk with him on the general situation. He sees the difficulties in my way very strongly. We spent some time in discussing the Civil Service. The ideas of the reformers are very vague, and mainly impracticable. This he sees, but still thinks they aim at good things and ought to be encouraged.

The personal aspects of the presidency are far from pleasant. I shall be compelled to live in great social isolation; almost every one who comes to me wants something which he thinks I can and ought to give him, and this embitters the pleasure of friendship. I must confront the problem of trying to survive the Presidency, or as is said of criminals, live it down.

SUNDAY, 12. Drove to Church with Crete, Mother, Aunt Phebe Ballou, Martha Mays, Mary White and Burke. On our return went to Dr. Robison's and made a short visit. Gave him the result of my recent readings on ensilage, and expressed my regret that I could not be here next August to try the experiment on my farm.

Home to dinner. Letters from Whitelaw Reid[373] and Blaine.[374] The latter I think is inclined to take a place in the Cabinet if it should be offered. On many accounts he would be a brilliant Sec'y of State. Other adjustments might be more difficult.

The downfall of Kelley [Kelly][375] in N.Y. is the marked politi-

---

[373]See n. 356, November 27, 1880.

[374]See n. 356, November 27, 1880.

[375]John Kelly (1822–1886), a Democratic political leader in New York City for three decades, was head of Tammany Hall from the early 1870's to his death. He was a member of the U.S. House of Representatives, 1855–58, sheriff of the city and county of New York, 1859–62 and 1865–67, comptroller of New York City, 1876–80, and a delegate to Democratic national conventions, 1864–84. In 1880 dissension between Tammany Hall and opposing Democrats in Irving Hall contributed to the election of Alonzo B. Cornell, Republican candidate for governor.

cal event of the past week. I am not sure it was a wise thing for our Republicans to aid in accomplishing.

Retired at 9.30 P.M.

MONDAY, 13. The day quite full of work and callers. In the evening Senator Dorsey came with Swaim, who went to Cleveland to meet him. At 7 P.M. Gov. Cornell, Hon. Richard Crowley and a Mr. Payne [Payn][376] of New York, came to see me. They came from Senator Conkling and Mr. Morton, to urge the appointment of the latter to the Sec'yship of the Treasury. The[y] said that M. had understood from me, in N.Y. in August, that that was one of several places he could elect to have, and the fact of his supposed permission to choose had probably lost him the Senatorship. I answered that I did not give him the option, and by no implication tendered him the Treasury. That he is ineligible by statute for that place,[377] and it would be most unwise in

In December Edward Cooper, who was elected mayor in 1879 as the fusionist candidate of Republicans and anti-Tammany Democrats, did not reappoint Kelly as comptroller, and the mayor was supported (December 10) by a combination of Irving Hall Democrats and Republicans on the board of aldermen. In a letter to Garfield (December 10), Whitelaw Reid attributed this result to Senator Conkling and Vice President-elect Arthur, explaining that Conkling thought that he could thus gain strength in the coming struggle to elect a new United States senator. He also said that Conkling's and Arthur's arrangements had been made through William C. Whitney, a Democrat who was the son-in-law of Ohioan Henry B. Payne. Kelly's "downfall" was limited; he continued as head of Tammany Hall and in 1882 succeeded in electing his candidate for mayor. At about 2:00 A.M. on September 20, 1881, in New York City, he administered to Chester A. Arthur the oath of office as President of the United States.

[376]Louis F. Payn (1835–1923), a native of New York and supporter of Conkling and Platt, was U.S. marshal for the southern district of New York, 1877–81. On Conkling's recommendation Garfield nominated him for another term in that office in 1881 but withdrew his name, along with others (see entry for May 5, 1881), and never resubmitted it. Payn, who was active in New York politics for fifty years, was a delegate from his congressional district to every Republican National Convention, 1868–1920.

[377]Section 8 of an act to establish the Treasury Department, approved September 2, 1789, provided that "no person appointed to any office instituted by this act, shall directly or indirectly be concerned or interested in carrying on the business of trade or commerce, or be . . . concerned in the purchase or disposal of any public securities of any State, or of the United States. . . ." This legislation

a party sense to give the place to N.Y. City. Furthermore, I would not intervene pending the senatorial elections, but would postpone the choice of a cabinet until after senatorships were decided. They left at 10 P.M., evidently disappointed. Crowley said Conkling hoped to sustain my administration, and give me a second term. I answered I would not permit this four years to be used to secure the next for any body.

TUESDAY, 14. Senator Dorsey left early in the morning for Painesville, to take the train east. He is a man of great ability, and with strong and decisive views of the merits of men. He thinks the N.Y. proposition altogeth[er] inadmissible, doubts the wisdom of appointing any southern man to the cabinet, for the reasons they are difficult to [find] and when chosen it will not conciliate the Southern people.

The Steeles and Joel Tiffany[378] called in the late afternoon, Chain[379] of Philadelphia at noon. Dr. Bronson Alcott[380] with Mrs. Rickoff[381] and Mrs. Geo. A. Baker came early and spent half a day. Dr. Alcott is 81 years old and remarkably well preserved, a man of fresh strong ideas, who has gone far into liberalism, but is coming back toward his earlier views, as is frequently the case with very old men.

---

applied to top officials in the Treasury Department and remained operative as part of the revised statutes.

[378]Joel Tiffany (1811–1893), a native of Connecticut, lived for more than twenty years in Ohio (part of the time in Painesville), where he was a lawyer, writer and lecturer. After leaving Ohio in the late 1850's he lived in the East and in Chicago, lecturing widely on abolition, spiritualism and temperance. He was the author of a number of works, including *A Treatise on Government* (1867). A debate with Isaac Errett at Warren, Ohio, was published under the title *Modern Spiritualism Compared with Christianity . . .* (1855). A copy of this book is in the Garfield library at Lawnfield.

[379]Joseph I. Chain, a provisions dealer in Philadelphia, was seeking appointment as inspector of Indian agencies in the Bureau of Indian Affairs.

[380]Amos Bronson Alcott (1799–1888), author, educator, mystic, and father of Louisa May Alcott.

[381]Rebecca Rickoff, daughter of William M. S. Davis of Cincinnati, was the wife of Andrew J. Rickoff, superintendent of Cleveland public schools, 1867–82. Rickoff, with the help of his wife, wrote a number of textbooks and readers.

Nichol left for Washington on Swaim's affairs.

WEDNESDAY, 15. Had Northcott come with his separator and thrash my buckwheat. The ground is again bare except in fence corners, but the air is icy and the water and soil is strongly frozen. I still diet and am trying to take a little horseback exercise but I get only a little time for it.

Another letter from Blaine which strengthens my impression of his tendency.[382]

Have finally closed with Dr. Hawkes[383] of Helena, Montana, to teach Hal, Jim and Don 6 months, beginning Jan'y 15, at $100 per month, we paying his traveling expenses to Washington.

The crowd of callers less large and imminent than usual.

THURSDAY, 16. Made some progress with the mail and gave the remainder of the day to callers. At noon thirteen men came from Indiana, Pa., headed by a Judge from Westmoreland Co., asking me to appoint Gen. Harry White to a place in the Cabinet.

---

[382]See n. 356, November 27, 1880.

[383]William H. Hawkes (1845–1904), a native of Connecticut, graduated at Brown University, 1867, and in medicine at the University of Pennsylvania, 1874. He taught at Philips Academy, Andover, 1867–71, and at Rugby Academy, Philadelphia, 1872–74. He practiced medicine in Philadelphia, 1874–79, and in Helena, Montana, 1879–81. Edward Clarence Smith, founder and head of Rugby Academy and Williams College classmate of Garfield and Rockwell, recommended Hawkes to them. Before the inauguration, classes were held in the home of Rockwell, where Harry and James were staying. After the Garfields moved into the White House, classes were held there, with Dr. Hawkes giving some instruction to Irvin and Abram also. Early in September he accompanied Harry, James and Don to Williams College, where the boys began their freshman year. Dr. Hawkes devoted the rest of his life to medicine—as acting assistant surgeon in the U.S. army, 1881–83, attending or consulting physician in Garfield Memorial, Providence and Emergency hospitals in Washington, D.C., and professor of medicine at Georgetown University. He was a contributor to medical journals. On February 9, 1881, James wrote thus to his father: "We like Dr. Hawkes very much he is the best teacher I have ever had. He knows how to teach and to educate. He never tells us any thing but draws it out and thus makes us remember it better. He is a very pleasant gentleman and does not get out of patience with us if we do not understand a thing quickly. . . . We are reading Xenophon now, and also writing an english dictation every day. I like staying here very much indeed; it is a great deal better than going to St. Paul's. We get letters frequently from Treadwell who keeps us informed about the 'Old Hole.'"

After they had gone, I was worried by a life insurance agent, who did not disclose his business until I had wasted some time on him. At the same time a lady from Covington, Ky., came to plead for a P.O. for her husband. Four old friends came, to whom I told, in a talk of 15 minutes, how my time was being consumed by thoughtless friends—and none of them saw the point.

In the evening Hon. Henry B. Perkins and Harmon Austin came and spent the night. Had a long talk with them on the condition of state politics. Gen. Grosvenor came, also Edwin Cowles.

FRIDAY, 17. Messrs. Perkins and Austin remained with us until noon, when they took the train—Judd, Crete and I going by same train to Cleveland. While there, I had a deed executed to T. W. Phillips of the West Va. lands he sold to me in 1875, he having paid me the full amount of debt secured by said deed.[384]

Did some shopping, and came home on evening train. Found James Atkins[385] of Georgia at the Depot. He had called to see me during the afternoon. Mr. Underwood[386] of Ravenna and a Mr. Hurley of Columbus called in the evening.

Papers today say that Akerman[387] of Georgia has been appointed Circuit Judge *vice* Woods of Georgia—promoted to the Supreme bench.

SATURDAY, 18. Last night was an unfavorable one for sleep.

---

[384]See Vol. III, p. 3, n. 1

[385]See Vol. III, pp. 148–149, n. 253.

[386]Albert Underwood (1811?–1881), a native of Massachusetts, was a Portage County farmer who moved late in life from Brimfield to Ravenna.

[387]Amos T. Akerman (1821–1880), a native of New Hampshire and a graduate of Dartmouth (1842), settled in Georgia in the 1840's, where he became a lawyer. Although he served the Confederacy during the Civil War, he became a Republican in the reconstruction period and remained one thereafter. He was U.S. district attorney for Georgia for a short time before he held the office of attorney general of the United States, 1870–71. Garfield's interest in the judgeship of the Fifth U.S. Judicial Circuit resulted from the desire of his old friend Don Pardee (then a state judge in Louisiana) to be appointed to fill the vacancy. Akerman, who had not been nominated by President Hayes, died on December 21. On March 14, 1881, President Garfield appointed Pardee to the post; he was confirmed in May and served to his death in 1919 (from 1891 he was a judge of the circuit court of appeals of the Fifth District).

Nearly every member of the household reported his sleep disturbed by unknown causes. I awoke at 4 A.M. and could not sleep again. Even Irvin, who is a good sleeper, was awake and dressed before I awoke. There must be some force, electric, nervous or spiritual which operates in such cases.

After the usual forenoon's work I slept half an hour. Many calls.

At 4.25 went horseback riding. Rode nearly seven miles in an hour. Dictated letters in the evening and retired at eleven o'clock.

SUNDAY, 19.   Staid at home during the day and brought up some private letters, which I must needs answer myself. At one P.M. Swaim left for Fort Leavenworth. I expect every day to hear of his promotion to the head of his corps, in which case he will soon go to Washington.

After dinner I went to Dr. Robison's and closed our long account of housebuilding.[388] He and Betsey came back home with me, and spent some time. Important letter from N.Y. indicating that Mr. Conkling is really desirous of sustaining my administration.[389] It ought to be true—I will try to make it so,

---

[388]After the Garfields bought the farm in Mentor, they considered building a new house on land to be acquired adjacent to their property. By early 1880, however, they had decided to renovate and enlarge the totally inadequate farm house into which they had moved. Since Garfield could not be in Mentor to supervise the project, he enlisted the aid of Dr. John P. Robison, whose own farm was near that of the Garfields. The supervisory task was much to the doctor's liking, and he threw himself into it with vigor and enthusiasm. He had his own ideas about the design of the house, but was brought reluctantly to accept the plans of Mrs. Garfield, whose will was at least as strong as his own. It was not long before the doctor was announcing that the new home would be "a mag-*nif*icent house." Work on the house proceeded with great rapidity during the spring.

[389]Reference is to Dorsey's "strictly confidential" letter (December 16) addressed to Swaim at Mentor, which discussed at length a full afternoon of conversation he had just had with Conkling. Among other things Conkling stated that Garfield, during his August visit, had promised the Treasury Department to New York, saying that if four names of good, respectable men representing the dominant wing of the Republican party were presented, and Morton's name was among them, he would appoint Morton. Conkling, said Dorsey, revealed "in words and in manner of unmistakable sincerity" his strong desire "to support the General's

without surrendering the proper control of any function I should hold.

Retired at eleven, after dictating many letters.

MONDAY, 20. Made the first actual study for inaugural by commencing to read those of my predecessors. Read and made notes on the two Inaugurals of Washington. This was done however in intervals of interruptions. Hon. D. J. Morrell,[390] and several with him called and spent several hours. The[y] do not think Harry White the choice of Pa. Rec'd a letter from the President saying he would make Swaim Judge Advocate Gen'l in January, also that if I knew who would be my Sec'y of the Navy he would appoint him now to fill vacancy left by Thompson's resignation. I have

---

administration as he had supported General Grant's." Conkling declared that if Garfield's intentions were not to give the Treasury to New York, he should say so now, for Conkling and his friends would then know better what to do. He hoped that Garfield would give some place in his cabinet to the man who had been offered the Treasury and thus "consolidate the party in New York." Dorsey was certain that Conkling wanted two things: Platt or Morton in the cabinet along with such other recognition as a Republican senator would naturally expect in local appointments, and to support the new administration. Dorsey said that Conkling, who spoke of Garfield as "one of the ablest men the country had produced," realized that he, Grant, and Blaine were out of the race and was "anxious to be in with those" who were not out. Five days later, in response to a query from Garfield, Reid wrote a letter expressing his belief that the story about a change in Conkling's feelings lacked a word of truth, and labeling it as "pretence, the object being to gain something from" Garfield. On January 1, 1881, Reid informed Garfield that there was no change in the feeling of Conkling or that of his people. "They mean to confront you," Reid said, "with the two Senators from the state, and to demand the entire patronage of the state. In a word they mean to be your masters, and when you submit they will like you well enough. But they don't trust you. Even their common mode of alluding to you shows their feeling. It is always 'This man Garfield.' "

[390]Daniel J. Morrell (1821–1885), manufacturer, banker, and a leading protectionist, was a native of Maine of Quaker descent. He moved to Pennsylvania and in 1855 established in Johnstown, with C. S. Wood, the firm of Wood, Morrell & Co., which became the largest manufacturer of railroad iron in the country, and was one of the first to substitute Bessemer steel for iron in the manufacture of rails. He was a Republican member of the U.S. House of Representatives, 1867–71, president of the American Iron and Steel Association, 1879–84, and president of the First National Bank of Johnstown, 1863–84.

written to Dorsey to find out whether that would not suit Morton and the N.Y. muddle.[391] In the evening, Crete, Mollie and I went to Mr. Aldrich's and took tea. Home at 8. Dictated letters and read the papers. Gov. Foster has published a letter withdrawing from the contest for Senator. It will bring harmony to the Republican party in Ohio. Retired at eleven.

TUESDAY, 21.   Crete and the children went to Cleveland to shop for the Holidays. I was nearer alone than on any other day for many months. Read John Adams' inaugural address and made notes. Far more vigorous in ideas than Washington's. His next to the last sentence contains more than 700 words. Strong but too cumbrous.

Very nearly cleared my desk of letters. At noon Harry Rhodes came. He read aloud Jefferson's inaugural. Stronger than Washington's, more ornate than Adams'. All apologetic, and unnecessary self-depreciating.

In the evening rode horseback a few miles, coming back in time to escort Crete and the children from the station.

Retired at 11 P.M. and read a few chapters of Beaconsfield's *Endymion*[392] before going to sleep. My Lord appears to have made a great hit, at least among the book sellers. As to the rest, we shall see.

WEDNESDAY, 22.   This has been one of the quietest days I have had since the nomination. Worked off the usual number of letters, and in company with Rhodes and Crete, read the Inaugurals of Jefferson, Madison and Monroe. Curious tone of self-depreciation runs through them all—which I cannot quite believe was genuine. Madison's speeches were not quite up to my expectations. Monroe's first was rather above. Since John Adams he was the first to review the experiment of Independence and the Constitution, in an inaugural address.

Hal and Jim leave Concord today, go to Boston and thence by

---

[391]Having received no definite answer to his query, Garfield suggested that Hayes offer Morton the Navy Department (January 5, 1881). Morton, with his eye fixed on the Treasury, declined Hayes's offer.

[392]Benjamin Disraeli, Earl of Beaconsfield, *Endymion,* 3 vols. (1880).

Fall River to N.Y. and home via the Erie and Lake Shore. Had Green sow 20 bushels of fresh elm wood ashes to the acre on half the meadow by the barns. I try the experiment on the snow. Will put bone dust on other half. Harry Rhodes remained over night. We sang old songs in the evening.

THURSDAY, 23.   Rhodes left by the A.M. 7.41 train. Worked off large mail in the forenoon. Several people came at noon, among them Judge Don A. Pardee of New Orleans. Had a long conversation with him in reference to the political situation of the South. In the evening Gen. Sheldon came, and we three field officers of the 42nd O.V.I. had a long and pleasant visit. The first real let-up I have had (last evening and this) for many months. Southern men very fully discussed.

Retired at eleven. The family retired earlier, so as to greet the two older boys at their early coming tomorrow morning. Important letter from Blaine today—may have marked influence on his future and mine.[393]

FRIDAY, 24.   Irvin and Mollie wakened us a little after five. Judd was called down from the attic to find, by wire, whether the Eastern Express was on time. It was found to be but 20 minutes late (would reach Mentor at 6.[o]5 A.M.). Brown and Irvin went to the train with Peter, Grandma was neatly dressed—in short the whole family was ready at six-ten to meet the dear boys, who bounded in at 6.15 joyful and joy giving. Jimmy has grown a full inch in height since Sept. Hal has the pubescent outline of side whiskers. Sheldon and Pardee left us at noon. Senator Saunders[394] of Nebraska came and spent two hours. I rode to Willoughby and back in 50 minutes. Nichol came in the evening and gave me important facts in reference to affairs at Washington.

SATURDAY, 25.   The day was mainly devoted to Christmas festivities, playing bagatelle with the children, answering a few of the most important letters, and reading a few chapters of *Endymion*. I have not been feeling well for some days, and today have

---

[393]See n. 356, November 27, 1880.

[394]Alvin Saunders (1817–1899) was governor of the Territory of Nebraska, 1861–67, and a Republican member of the U.S. Senate, 1877–83.

suffered from catarrhal cold and head-ache. Mr. Nichol left this evening. He goes to Mr. Stone of Cleveland, to smooth the way for Col. Hay's taking the place of Private Sec'y to the President —a position that I am more anxious to have well filled than some of the cabinet officers. I have offered it to John Hay, and I think one of the obstacles to his acceptance may be the desire of his father-in-law to have him at home.[395] Retired at eleven.

SUNDAY, 26. Slept late, but arose as I retired, with a dull head-ache. This is unusual for me, and I do not understand it. Mother, Aunt Phebe [Ballou], Crete and I attended the Methodist church, and heard a very good Christmas Sermon from the Pastor, Mr. Stedman. After dinner, read some of the early inaugural messages, wrote a synopsis of Jefferson's first, which is more ornate and elaborate than any which preceded it. In the evening, the three boys, Crete and I attended the Disciple Church and heard the last half of a Christmas sermon. Home at eight. Read the proof of my speech at Chicago, in June last, when I nominated Sherman for the Presidency. The Re-

---

[395]Garfield had written (December 20) to Hay, then assistant secretary of state, that with "the help of another mind, a trained, independent, friendly mind," he would feel that his "strength was doubled." He stressed the importance of the position, saying that "the Secretary of the President ought to rank with any of the seven members of the Cabinet. In a thousand ways the President needs a trusted and capable friend at hand, one who can see the moves on the chessboard more clearly than the players can. Does it lie within the possibilities of the situation," Garfield asked, "that you can help me in that way?" Hay responded (December 25) that after long and serious consideration of "the important and honorable duty" he had been offered, he must say how sorry he was that he could not "see the way clear to doing it." The prospect of working with Garfield and his wife, he wrote, had tempted him to accept, but "the other half of the work, the contact with the greed and selfishness of office seekers and bull dozing congressmen is unspeakably repulsive to me. . . . The constant contact with envy, meanness, ignorance, and the swinish selfishness which ignorance breeds, needs a stronger heart and a more obedient nervous system than I can boast." He also noted a promise to his family and to the man taking care of his personal affairs that he would come home on March 4, 1881, and he confessed that he looked to that date as his "day of deliverance." After trying without success to get Hay to change his mind, Garfield wrote to him (January 4, 1881), saying that he would try to think that Hay was right not to accept.

port of the Convention has not yet been published in pamphlet.

Took a nasal douche for a catarrhal cold I have, and retired at 10.30.

MONDAY, 27. A cold stormy day. Several callers. At noon Mother and Aunt Phebe Ballou went to Cleveland. At one P.M. Crete, Harry, Irvin and [I] drove to Willoughby to take Miss Mays to Mr. Hanscom's. Worked on my mail in the afternoon. Letter from Blaine favoring Allison for the Treasury.[396] In the evening Cousin William Letcher came to visit us. His son Orlando has been robbed of $9,500 by a burglar.[397] Made but little progress in my studies. I see but little chance to do what reading I ought to do. I have suffered now four days from a continuous dull head-ache, the cause of which I do not know. Retired at ten, after reading a few chapters of *Endymion.*

TUESDAY, 28. Mail and usual work. Cousin William Letcher went at noon. In the afternoon, Senator P. Hitchcock and wife and Mrs. W. J. Ford made us a visit. Mrs. F. spent the night. The day has been very cold. The thermometer has been down to zero a good share of the day.

In the evening Hon. Amos Townsend and Hon. Wm. McKinley came and spent the night. We had a long conversation on the state of public affairs as seen from Washington whence they have

[396]"Your Secretary of the Treasury," Blaine began his letter of December 24, 1880, "should be taken from the West." He noted that John Sherman "thought Allison better posted in financial capitalism than any in Congress *except Garfield and Blaine.*" He then justified his choice: "Allison is known to you thoroughly . . . . He is true, kind, reasonable, fair, honest and good. He is methodical, industrious, and intelligent, and would be a splendid man to sail along with smoothly and nicely and peacefully. He would always hearken to your views. In the whole U.S. I do not believe you could do as well." Blaine added that in Allison, Garfield would have "a perfectly staunch friend in the Treasury."

[397]Orlando Letcher, a dealer in stock, grain, butter, eggs and other commodities in Bryan, Ohio, sold a large lot of hogs and cheese in Chicago for $9,500, receiving payment in cash. He returned home on the midnight train. About two hours later a burglar bored or cut a hole through the door to enable him to unlock it, entered the house and held a revolver close to Orlando's head, threatening to kill him unless he handed over the money within one minute. Orlando handed it over; he was still confined to bed under a doctor's care several days later.

just come. The[y] favor Blaine for the State Dep't, Allison for the Treasury, and think there will be more unity in the party than is apparent on its face. Sat with them until near midnight.

WEDNESDAY, 29. Townsend and McKinley went at noon. D. L. King[398] of Akron came and spent part of the forenoon—wants Goodhue[399] to have some place. At noon, Hon. Mr. Cannon of Illinois, and two other gentlemen came for a short visit. At two P.M. Senator Cameron, Messrs. Gorham,[400] Smith and Burt[401]

---

[398]David L. King (1825–1902), son of anti-slavery crusader Leicester King, was born in Warren but lived during most of his adult years in Akron. He graduated at Harvard in 1846 and practiced law for many years before abandoning it for business in 1867. He was active in public affairs.

[399]Nathaniel W. Goodhue (1818–1883), an Ohio lawyer, held several public offices before serving as a state senator for Summit and Portage counties, 1874–75. In 1880 he was president of the Ohio Electoral College. He was probate judge of Summit County, 1881 to his death.

[400]George Gorham (1832–1909), a native of New York, went to school in Connecticut before going to California in 1849. During the next eighteen years he was associated with a number of California newspapers, entered politics (he was the Union candidate for governor in 1867), and was clerk of the U.S. Circuit Court serving California, Oregon and Nevada, presided over by Supreme Court Justice Stephen J. Field. In 1868, aided by Senator John Conness of California, he was elected secretary of the U.S. Senate, a position he held until 1879. He was California's representative on the Republican National Committee, 1868–80. After the election of his friend William Mahone of Virginia to the Senate in 1880, he sought to win for the Republicans Mahone's vote in organizing the Senate. One of the terms offered to the Republicans by Mahone was Gorham's restoration to the secretaryship of the Senate. After Thomas J. Brady secured control of the *National Republican* in 1880, Gorham became its editor. At first friendly to President Garfield, the paper turned virulently against him as a result of Garfield's struggle with Conkling and Brady's forced retirement from the Post Office Department. Gorham did not again become secretary of the Senate. When the Republicans were once more in control of that body in 1883, Gorham was defeated by Garfield's friend Anson McCook. In the letter to Dawes (Dawes Papers, Library of Congress) mentioned in the diary, May 2, 1881, Garfield wrote: ". . . I will not aid any arrangement, which includes in it, the advancement to a post of political honor, a man who as Editor in Chief of a newspaper is daily assailing me and my administration."

[401]Probably Frank A. Burr (1843–1894), who was associated with the *Philadelphia Press,* an organ of the Camerons. In October, 1880, he and F. C. Loveland were in Virginia as representatives of the Republican National Committee in

came by special train. They brought 57 pages of manuscript written by Mahone of Va. giving his views of the debt question of Va. They say he intends to act with the administration, and they want the Republicans of Va. to offer no state ticket next year. I answered, that I must regard his statement as *ex parte,* but I wanted to hear the other side and see what Republicans said of it. I stated that a bankrupt state could be asked only to run the government economically, sustain its schools and apply all the remnant of its revenues as the maximum of reasonable taxation to its debts. If that is Mahone's position, followed up in good faith, it is defensible. If he acts with administration senators he shall be treated like them, but he must take the first step. Long talk with Cameron. He inclines to be pleased with the suggestion of MacVeagh for Att'y-Gen. and suggest[ed] Robert Lincoln for the cabinet.[402]

THURSDAY, 30.   Weather very cold. Gentleman from N.Y., who spent last night in Painesville, froze his ear in coming here and reported the thermometer at 13 below zero. Several callers,

---

behalf of the Readjuster ticket. (See their letter in the *Richmond Whig,* November 9.) In February, 1881, when he visited Richmond with Simon Cameron, he was identified (*Richmond Whig,* February 3) as Cameron's private secretary. His writings include a biography of U. S. Grant (1885). The Smith who was in the quartet mentioned by Garfield may have been John Ambler Smith (1847–1892), who was a Republican member of the U.S. House of Representatives from Virginia, 1873–75, and a lawyer in Washington after his term expired. In June, 1881, he was a member of a group described (*Alexandria Gazette,* June 24) as a delegation of Republicans who had deserted their party "and gone over to Mahone" and who expected to see the President and advise him "to give all the federal patronage to Mahonites."

[402]Robert Todd Lincoln (1843–1926), son of Abraham Lincoln, graduated at Harvard, 1864, and served on Grant's staff during the last months of the Civil War. He studied law in Chicago and practiced there, principally as a corporation lawyer with railroads. Several leading Republicans, in particular John A. Logan of Illinois, supported him for a cabinet position, and on February 28, 1881, Garfield offered him the War Department. Lincoln accepted the offer on March 2, and served, 1881–85. He was minister to Great Britain, 1889–93, and president of the Pullman Company, 1897–1911. His wife Mary was the daughter of James Harlan (1820–1899), a member of the U.S. Senate from Iowa, 1855–65, 1867–73.

among them Senator Kirkwood of Iowa.[403] He recommends J. F. Wilson for a place in the Cabinet. Thinks perhaps Allison would like the Treasury, but no other place. Fears Allison would not be approved by eastern Republicans on account of his views on silver.

Brown of Toledo came and wanted to be a government contractor. I told him I should have nothing to do with awards. Hon. Geo. W. Williams,[404] colored member of the Ohio Legislature, came to report his visit to New Mexico. His Exodus scheme for that territory seems to have failed, at least for the present. He is able, but too full of himself. Cousin Phebe and Lizzie came, also Mrs. Cutting[405] of Cal., and John Ryder, wife and boy and spent the night.

FRIDAY, 31. Worked off considerable correspondence. Harry,

[403]Samuel J. Kirkwood (1813–1894), a native of Maryland, lived in Ohio (where he became a lawyer) for twenty years before moving to Iowa in 1855. In the new state he quickly rose to leadership in the Republican party; he was a member of the state senate, 1856–59, governor, 1860–64, 1876–77, and a member of the U.S. Senate, 1866–67, 1877–81. Desiring a westerner as secretary of the interior, Garfield was still undecided whether to name Kirkwood or William B. Allison, of the same state, to the post when he left Mentor for his inauguration. On March 5 he appointed Kirkwood, who served until he resigned in April, 1882.

[404]George W. Williams (1849–1891), a native of Maryland of white and Negro blood, served in the Union army, 1862–65, attended Howard University, graduated at the Newton Theological Institution in Massachusetts, and was ordained as a Baptist minister. In 1876 he settled in Cincinnati, where he started a weekly newspaper and was admitted to the bar after reading law in the office of Alphonso Taft. President Hayes appointed him to a post in the internal revenue service. He was a member of the state legislature, 1880–81, and U.S. minister to Haiti, 1885–86. He died in England while in the employ of the Belgian government. He was the author of *History of the Negro Race in America from 1619 to 1880*, 2 vols. (1883) and *A History of the Negro Troops in the War of the Rebellion* (1888). Dissatisfaction among the Negroes over their lot in the South led in 1879 to their migration (known as the "Exodus") in considerable numbers beyond the Mississippi in quest of a better life.

[405]Ella (Martin) Cutting was the daughter of Garfield's cousin, Ezra Martin of Columbus, Ohio (see Vol. I, pp. 88, 240, 245). She married John T. Cutting of San Francisco. In 1881 he sought a position in the United States mint in that city, but the director, he claimed, objected because of his wife's relationship to President Garfield.

Jimmy and Mollie went to Cleveland, morning train. Wrote brief of Jefferson's second inaugural, which has less self-depreciation than the first. Rev. Geo. H. Ball[406] of Buffalo, Capt. J. C. Hill[407] and several others called. Also Mr. Steelee [Steele?], and two friends.

Finished *Endymion*. It is a bold venture, an autobiographical novel, covering in its plot thirty years of British politics closing with about 1857. He evidently despises Dickens and Thackeray. Lampoons the latter unmercifully. Treats Gladstone (Hortensius) rather kindly. Makes his own success depend mainly upon the influence of women and hard work. It shows adroitness, great reserve on dangerous questions, with enough frankness on other question[s] to make a show of boldness. Retired at 11.40.

I regret that I am too much occupied to review the impressions which the year has brought. In regard to the principal political event of my life, I have to say that my chief gratification arises from the fact that the office came to me without any violation of the law of my life, viz., never to ask for an office. I came to that resolution in October, 1849, (after a four days' fruitless search for a school) and I have followed [it] ever since, until I have come to believe that should I violate that law, I would fail. It may be a whim. I would not impose the rule on others: for each shall have and obey his own law of life. I close the year with a sad conviction that I am bidding good-by to the freedom of private life, and to a long series of happy years, which I fear terminate with 1880.

[406]George H. Ball (1819–1907) held pastorates in Buffalo, 1850–55, 1857–71, and 1877–90. He was editor of the *Baptist Union,* New York, 1871–77, and wrote several books on religion. He was a delegate to the first Republican National Convention in 1856 and an invited guest to the Republican National Convention in 1900. See Vol. I, p. 16, n. 7.

[407]Joseph C. Hill served in the 5th Kentucky Cavalry Regiment before joining the staff of General William S. Rosecrans as a volunteer captain. After the war he moved from place to place—the Territory of New Mexico, Nebraska, and Iowa —and in 1880 was practicing law in Montevideo, Minnesota. On December 20 of that year he wrote to Garfield that he was going east to see the "loveliest lady in the land" (she was Charlotte C. Caryl of Massachusetts whom Hill hoped to marry), and asked permission to call at Lawnfield on his way home.

1881

January

SATURDAY, 1. The New Year comes in with clear and very cold weather. Worked on the mail until noon when Cousin Phebe Clapp and her daughter Lizzie and Crete and I went to Cleveland. Called at Dr. Boynton's and at Col. Sheldon's. At 4.25 Crete and I took the Mahoning train and went to Solon. Drove to Sister Hittie's, where we found Mother, Mary and Hittie and Brother Thomas and his wife and had a family reunion, the first for 14 years.

We spent the night at Sister Hittie's.

SUNDAY, 2. Attended church at Solon with the family. Mr. Moore[1] read a sermon on the Lord's Supper. We dined at Sister Mary's. Henry Boynton and his family with us. Aunt Phebe Ballou and Thomas and his wife went to Orange with Cousin Henry.

At 6.19 P.M. Crete and I took the train to Cleveland. Went to Dr. Boynton's and spent the night.

MONDAY, 3. After breakfast, went to the Dentist's (Dr. [Joseph C.] Merritt) and had one tooth filled and a wisdom tooth drawn, the first for 32 years, the second in all. The first was drawn by Dr. [Ira] Lyman in Chester. In this case I took laughing gas and felt but little pain, though the Doctor made three attempts before the tooth came out. Crete and I went home by the noon train.

[1]W. C. Moore was pastor of the Disciple of Christ church in Solon.

Jesse Spaulding[2] and Mr. Eaton[3] of Chicago came. In the evening Mrs. Mary Patterson (née Buckingham)[4] and Brother Joseph Rudolph came, and spent the night.

TUESDAY, 4. Face very sore and a dull head-ache. Worked off large amount of mail. Read Madison's inaugural. Five miles tramp à cheval. Nichol came from Washington bring[ing] letter from Col. Hay who declines the Private Sec'yship.[5] On many accounts I regret this; for I have seen the evil of inefficient officers in that place.

WEDNESDAY, 5. Sold five head of cattle—two cows not very valuable, and three yearlings—for $130. Nichol helped on current work in the office.

Rode five miles on horseback to work off the sluggishness which so much office work brings. Mr. W. W. MacFarland came and remained until the 11 P.M. train for N.Y. He has announced his entrance into the Republican party, having always hitherto been a Democrat. Long visit with him in reference to N.Y. affairs.

THURSDAY, 6. Worked on mail till noon, when Hal, Crete and I drove the colts and sleigh to Willoughby, where we meet [met] Cousin Henry Boynton and wife, and Brother Thomas and wife,

[2]Jesse Spaulding (1837–1904) established a lumbering business in Chicago which became the Spaulding Lumber Company in 1882; he owned thousands of acres of timber land in Wisconsin, invested much money in the Chicago and North Western Railway and in Chicago street railways, was a director of several banks, and left an estate estimated at $10,000,000. He was appointed collector of customs for the district of Chicago in December, 1881.

[3]Probably Thomas W. Eaton (1839–1910), a native of Vermont, who moved to Chicago in 1871 and became a successful manufacturer of elevators.

[4]Mary Buckingham Patterson attended the Western Reserve Eclectic Institute when Garfield was principal and where she was a contemporary of Charles E. Henry. After graduating at Oberlin, she taught at Kansas State University and elsewhere. She married John L. Patterson, a lawyer in Lawrence, Kansas. She later returned to Hiram to live in her old home; she had a daughter Esther.

[5]Hay wrote (December 31) that he had given the matter careful and constant consideration, and that even Nichol, whose campaign of persuasion was as "faithful" as any Hay had seen, concurred with the decision. See n. 398, December 25, 1880.

en route to Mentor. We returned in advance, taking Brother Thomas with us.

In the evening, Mother, Sisters Mary and Hittie and Mollie came and completed our family gathering.

In the evening I suffered greatly from pain in my face.

FRIDAY, 7. Spent most of the day in visiting with the brother and sisters. Many callers, and letters. On the whole, a very busy day. Henry Boynton and wife left us at noon for Cleveland. Weather still very cold. Caught cold in my face, on the trip to Willoughby yesterday, and have suffered much pain from it.

SATURDAY, 8. An unusually large number of callers, among them Baker of Racine, Wis. In the evening Harry Jones of Mt. Union came and spent the night. A large sleigh load of friends from Newburgh came. Moses I. Richar[d]s[6] and the Cahoon family[7] called and spent an hour. Capt. Henry was also here. Sent two loads of friends to Willoughby to take the evening train to Cleveland.

SUNDAY, 9. Took a large sled load to Church. Harry Jones preached. In the afternoon Col. Hay and Nichol came from Cleveland and spent the night. Had a long conversation with Hay on political questions. He is very bright and able. I more and more regret that I cannot have him for my private secretary.

The question of wine at the Executive dinners is taking on proportions of importance. The whole discussion is an impertinence, but it may have important political bearings.

MONDAY, 10. Col. Hay remained during the forenoon. At noon, he and Thomas and wife, Mary and Hittie and Ellen Larabee left

---

[6]Moses I. Richards was a resident of Solon while a student at the Eclectic during the late 1850's. Now a resident of Cleveland, he had more than once sought Congressman Garfield's help in securing a government position, the last request of record (January 12, 1880) being for assistance in getting a job in the mail service. When in 1889 a fellow-student at the Eclectic saw him in Cleveland, "Old Mose," with "not a gray hair nor whisker, with boyish teeth unworn and unsullied by cigars and tobacco, and not a day older than . . . [he was thirty years ago]," was a postal clerk on the Lake Shore Railroad.

[7]The Cahoon family of Cleveland consisted of Ida M. and Lydia E., who were school principals, Laura E. and Martha W., who were teachers, and D. K. Cahoon whose occupation was not discovered. They were neighbors of Moses I. Richards.

for Cleveland. Before Sister Hittie left, I settled with her in full for the money she deposited with me from her pension.

In the afternoon a Colorado delegation, consisting of Senators Teller[8] and Hill,[9] Representative Belford[10] and Mr. Ward[11] now of Colorado, but lately M.C. from Illinois, came to urge the appointment of Gov. Routt[12] as P.M. Gen'l. D.C. Forney[13] of Washington came on behalf of Harmer[14] for same place. He

---

[8]Henry M. Teller (1830–1914), a native of New York who moved to Illinois in 1858 and to Colorado in 1861, was a member of the U.S. Senate from Colorado, 1876–82, 1885–1909, serving as a Republican, 1876–82 and 1885–97, as an Independent Silver Republican, 1897–1903, and as a Democrat, 1903–09. He resigned from the Senate to serve in President Arthur's cabinet as secretary of the interior, 1882–85.

[9]Nathaniel P. Hill (1832–1900), a native of New York who graduated at Brown University in 1856 and taught chemistry there, 1860–64, became a resident of Colorado in 1867 and was a Republican member of the U.S. Senate, 1879–85.

[10]James B. Belford (1837–1910) was a Republican member of the U.S. House of Representatives from Colorado, 1876–77, and 1879–85.

[11]Jasper D. Ward (1829–1902), a native of New York, practiced law in Chicago for several years before the Civil War, served in the Illinois senate, 1862–70, and was a Republican member of the U.S. House of Representatives from Illinois, 1873–75. In 1877 he moved to Colorado, where he was judge of the state's fifth judicial district, 1881–82, and practiced law, 1882 to his death.

[12]John L. Routt (1826–1907), a native of Kentucky, moved to Bloomington, Illinois, in 1836, and was an officer in the Union army, 1862–65. His valuable service in the Vicksburg campaign helped him to secure from President Grant an appointment as U.S. marshal for the southern district of Illinois, 1869, as second assistant postmaster general, 1871, and as governor of Colorado Territory, 1875. He was elected first governor of the state of Colorado, later reelected for a second term, and served, 1876–79, 1891–93. He made a fortune in mining ventures in the Leadville area and invested much money in Colorado farms, ranches, and mines. He received no appointment to office from Garfield.

[13]Daniel C. Forney (1827–1897), a native of Pennsylvania, was long associated with *Forney's Sunday Chronicle,* which was established in Washington, D.C. by his cousin John W. Forney in 1861; a daily edition of the newspaper was published, 1862–77. At the time of his visit to Garfield, Daniel was proprietor and editor.

[14]In letters to Garfield (January 3 and 5, 1881), Forney contended that Alfred C. Harmer (1825–1900), a businessman of Germantown, Pennsylvania, and a Republican member of the U.S. House of Representatives, 1871–75, and 1877 to his death, had worked assiduously to bring about more harmonious relations

brings apology from Randall for the part he took in Morey letter business.[15] I answered R.'s apology must be as public as his offense. Hal, Jim and I went on freight train to Cleveland, arriving at 7.45 and attended banquet of Williams College Alumni. I spoke briefly. Night at Forest City House.

TUESDAY, 11. Callers until 10 A.M. when I went to the Dentist's, Dr. Merritt, who worked on my teeth three hours. Much pain from scraping and filling. At 2.30 P.M. went to Wm. Edwards'[16] on Prospect St., where I met Gov. Foster and spent the afternoon with him. Colored delegation from Alabama came and made speeches. I replied.[17] Reporter of the *Cleveland Herald* was

---

among feuding Republican factions in his state, and urged Garfield to give him a cabinet position.

[15]Immediately after the Morey letter was published in *Truth*, the editor of that journal brought the original of the letter to the headquarters of the Democratic National Committee for inspection by William H. Barnum, Samuel J. Randall, Abram Hewitt, and other prominent Democrats. On the following day *Truth* announced that the men named above and others who were familiar with Garfield's handwriting and mode of expression had pronounced the letter "absolutely genuine." Randall made no further public comments about the letter. Hewitt on several occasions indicated his belief that the signature on the letter was Garfield's. In February, 1881, Marshall Jewell, in a letter published in a New York paper, appealed for contributions of one hundred dollars or less for the prosecution of the inquiry into the Morey letter. Hewitt responded promptly (letter to Jewell, February 7, 1881, copy, Garfield Papers), sending Jewell a check for one hundred dollars and indicating his willingness to match funds with him if the appeal did not yield sufficient means to pursue the inquiry.

[16]William Edwards (c. 1831–1898), a wholesale grocer in Cleveland since the early 1830's, was a partner of Charles Foster.

[17]Speaking for the delegation, G. G. W. Baxdell and L. P. Wilkins said that they came, not in the interests of any man, but in the interests of their race and of the South, and they asked Garfield to aid in advancing the education and material prosperity of all Negroes and all Southerners. In response, Garfield said that he most cordially concurred with all their efforts to "enlighten and elevate and strengthen" Negroes. The friends who stood by the Negroes during and since the war, he said, "have always had to meet on the part of their antagonists this thought: You have thrown upon us a great mass of ignorant voters, wholly unacquainted with the wants of the people and the management of affairs, and you have done us a great injustice in compelling that class to be our equals in voting." He declared that there was "a great deal of force" in that argument and that Negroes

present. In the evening dined at Edwards', 30 guests, a very elegant dinner. Party did not break up until after one o'clock. Foster and I staid at Edwards', Hal and Jim at James Mason's.

WEDNESDAY, 12. Late breakfast at Edwards' and long talk with Foster. At eleven went again to the Dentist's and had two front teeth filled. Shopped. Called at Dr. Robison's. Dined at James Mason's and came home to Mentor by the 3 P.M. Express. Dictated large number of letters and made good progress on back work.

Prof. O. C. Hill of Oregon, Mo., and his little boy spent the night with us.

During my absence Nichol has nearly finished the summary of previous inaugural addresses, and Crete had entered most of them in book.

THURSDAY, 13. Not a very satisfactory day. The questions of persons, and the value which each places upon his own merits as compared with the estimate which others place upon him, is the chief evil of choosing men for service.

Several people called during the day. Capt. Henry came, and took the boys with him to Painesville, where he is to lecture this evening at the Lake Erie Seminary. Hon. J. A. Hubbell of Michigan came and spent the night. A long talk on the state of public affairs.

A continuous thaw until evening when it turned cold again. Boys returned from Painesville at 10.30 P.M.

FRIDAY, 14. Jimmie went with Capt. Henry on the 7.41 train. Harry remained until noon, when he and Crete went to Cleveland in company with Jay A. Hubbell. Hal and Jim and Hubbell took the 1.45 P.M. train for Washington. The boys go to Col.

---

must make a sustained effort so to improve themselves that one day that argument could not be made. "When that day comes," he said, "I do not see any argument that any human being can make against the fair right of all men to equal privileges under the law." He promised to do what he could to help them remove "the last obstacle that confronts us in adjusting the troublesome question which your race and its late condition have given to this country," urged them to do all that they could to achieve that purpose, and told them to let nobody abuse them because they were black, nor to expect praise because they were black.

Rockwell's to begin their studies under the tutorship of Dr. Hawkes. Crete came back in the evening bring[ing] Mollie and May Mason.[18] Martha and Addie Rudolph came also and spent the night. During the afternoon many callers came, among them a delegation of 12 colored people from the Gulf States, headed by Gen. Elliott[19] of South Carolina, who made a long address concerning the Negroes. I replied briefly and not very satisfactorily to myself.

Worked off many letters. Wrote to Rose.

SATURDAY, 15. Devoted the forenoon to unpacking the books which have come from our house at Washington, and in arranging them and the others here. Swaim came at noon. At 4 P.M. Sec'y Sherman came, also T. W. Phillips. The latter has hopes of the Pa. Senatorship. After supper I spent three hours with Sec'y Sherman alone. Went over the political situation fully. His suggestion for Sec'y of Treasury was 1. Windom, 2. Allison. I asked him what he though[t] of John J. Knox for the position. It appeared to strike him favorably. We went quite fully over the ground and he made many valuable suggestions. I am more than ever impressed with his good judgment. He sees our chief financial trouble in the future of the silver question. Thinks the green-

[18]Mary Laura Mason, daughter of James Mason of Cleveland, and sister of Belle, who married Harry Garfield in 1888. Mary was about the same age as Mollie Garfield.

[19]Robert B. Elliott (see Vol. II, p. 274) was assistant adjutant general of South Carolina, 1869–71; he worked throughout his life to improve conditions for Negroes in the United States. As spokesman for the Negro delegation from the Gulf states, he told Garfield that the prayer of all Negroes was that he might "be guided by the Divine wisdom in securing all American citizens the blessings of equal laws and just administration." He said that many Negroes were deprived of their political rights and that in some localities a white minority oppressed a Negro majority. He declared that Negro children lacked adequate educational facilities and called for a national system of education for the toiling masses. In reply Garfield seized upon Elliott's statement about a minority oppressing a majority, and, attributing that state of affairs solely to training, explained that one trained man was the equal of two or three untrained men. He agreed that education was the key to solving the problem and that government ought to do everything it could properly do, but he insisted that government alone could not do the job. The solution, he believed, was to lay a "firm foundation for racial advancement" through parental cultivation of every child's "thirst and hunger," and hard work.

backs should be let alone for the present. Curious fact in regard to the appearance of a large amount of old fractional silver. Retired at 10.45.

SUNDAY, 16. While we were at breakfast Senator Allison came. He and Sherman sat with me in the library an hour. Then Sherman went by Mrs. G.'s request to talk over the wine question. Later had further conference with Sherman on financial question and on Cabinet. He is more and more pleased with suggestion of Knox's name. He left on the 3 P.M. Express for Cleveland.

Long conference with Allison. He favors Wilson or Kirkwood for Interior. I asked him what he thought of these four objections to himself for Treasury. Unsound 1st on the Silver question, 2nd Currency, 3 Tariff and 4, not ready for a rugged fight vs. the machine. He acknowledge[d] the force of some of them. Said he was ready to stop the coinage of silver, and was now sound on the Tariff. Thought the last point not well taken. He will be satisfied if Iowa has Wilson or Kirkwood. I drove him to Willoughby to take evening Express. If I were compelled to make a cabinet today, it would read State Dep., Blaine, N.Y. or James[20] Morton, Pa., MacVeagh, Ind., Harrison, Ills., Lincoln. Treas. Knox or Allison, South Phillips[21] or Morgan.[22]

[20]Thomas L. James (1831–1916), a native of New York, was an official in the customs house at the port of New York, 1861–73, and postmaster of New York City, 1873–81. On March 5, 1881, Garfield appointed him postmaster general, a post he held until January 1882. He was chairman of the board of directors of the Lincoln National Bank, New York City, 1882 to his death.

[21]Samuel F. Phillips, who was born in New York City, was taken as an infant to North Carolina, where he received his education and was admitted to the bar. A Unionist during the war, he became an active Republican and received from President Grant appointment as solicitor general of the United States. See Vol. II, p. 123, n. 301.

[22]Philip H. Morgan (1825–1900), was a native of Louisiana, where he practiced law and served as a state judge before the Civil War. A Unionist, he is thought to have spent the war years in England. He was U. S. district attorney for Louisiana, 1869–73, a judge of the state supreme court, 1873–76, a judge of the

MONDAY, 17. Worked off mail in the forenoon. Mollie and Addie Rudolph left on the early morning train, one for Cleveland, the other for Collingwood. At noon, Crete went to Cleveland and at 2:55 took the train, with Mrs. Sheldon, for N.Y. where she goes as quietly as possible, to do shopping.[23] Martha Rudolph left at noon. At 3:30 rec'd telegram from Gen. Sheldon that Crete and Mrs. S. had gone on time. Many callers. The newspapers announce the death of Warren Belden [Alfred Belding], in Bryan, Mich., the man with whom Mother made an unfortunate marriage 36 [38] years ago. The[y] separated in less than two years. After this long silence, ended in death, it is hard for me to think of the man without indignation.[24]

international court in Egypt, 1877–79, and U. S. minister to Mexico, 1880–85. After returning from Mexico he lived in New York City, where he practiced law. Garfield expected to follow President Hayes's example and appoint one southerner to his cabinet. On January 24, he wrote in a letter to James G. Blaine: "The southern member still eludes me—as Creusa's image eluded Aeneas. One by one the southern roses fade. Do you know of a magnolia blossom that will stand our northern climate?"

[23]Traveling incognita as "Mrs. Greenfield," Garfield's wife went to New York City to acquire wearing apparel. She also planned to get information about recent political developments and pass it on to Garfield. She and Mrs. Sheldon were the house guests of Whitelaw Reid for a few more days than originally intended because the dressmakers required more fittings than anticipated. The curious, unsettling effect on Garfield of his wife's prolonged absence is revealed in a ten-page letter begun at four A.M., Monday, January 31, for her to read when she returned. The subject was his "experience of the past week." That experience included sleepless nights, desolate loneliness, an urge to wring the necks of all dressmakers in New York, frustration from lack of needed information about New York politics, and inordinate weariness, out of which, he lamented, "I sing with Milton [Tennyson], 'Strong Son of God, Immortal Love,' as though it were written for us."

[24]Alfred Belding died in Byron, Michigan, on the night of January 14. In reporting his death the newspapers of Grand Rapids called him "William Belden." On January 18 the *Grand Rapids Daily Eagle* corrected the error. The census of 1880 lists him as a retired farmer, age 80, living in the household of a grandchild. The Grand Rapids newspapers reported him to be 70 years of age and identified him as the stepfather of Garfield. This revelation seems to have excited no national interest. Eliza Garfield's secret was preserved until publication of Vol. I of the *Diary* in 1967 (see p. xiv).

The house is very empty without Crete. I must begin special preparations for the inaugural. I have half a mind to make none. Those of the past except Lincoln's, are dreary reading. Doubtless mine will be also.

Dr. Gray and Wife and three members of Indian Committee of Presbyterian Church called on Indian affairs.[25] This call was Wednesday.

TUESDAY, 18. Even the hard work and numerous calls have [not] kept away the loneliness which Crete's absence has brought upon the house. Sam. Robinson[26] and his daughter Lucy from Chagrin Falls called. In the evening Col. G. W. Carter of La. came and spent several hours.[27] The Committee of the Presbyterian

---

[25]In May, 1880, the General Assembly of the Presbyterian Church in the United States of America adopted a resolution on the welfare of American Indians and set up a committee to act on the resolution "and urge upon the Government of the United States such action as will, on the whole, best promote the welfare of the Indians." In January, 1881, the committee met in Washington, D.C., where they interviewed President Hayes, Secretary of Interior Schurz and members of the House and Senate committees on Indian affairs. The report of the committee, presented in 1881, includes this statement:

The Western members of your Committee were delegated to call upon the President-elect at his home in Mentor, Ohio, which they did; finding him, amid the multiplicity of the cares and labors of preparing for his great trust, to be less furnished, with clearly defined plans for the benefit of the Indians, than were the President and Secretary of the Interior, who had been considering and laboring upon the subject for years. But President Garfield, your Committee are glad to say, may be relied on to give his influence for any just measure of reform.

The Dr. Gray accompanying the committee may have been William C. Gray (1830–1901), a native of Ohio who was associated with a number of Ohio newspapers, 1851–71, and was editor, 1871 to his death, of *The Interior,* a Presbyterian weekly paper published in Chicago. See Presbyterian Church in the United States of America, General Assembly, *Minutes* (1880), pp. 75–76, and (1881), pp. 565–568.

[26]Samuel Robinson was an elderly farmer in Chagrin Falls; his unmarried daughter Lucy lived at home.

[27]Much interested in the condition and needs of Negroes, Carter was now urging Garfield to appoint Senator Blanche K. Bruce of Mississippi as a member of his cabinet or to some other high office in his administration. Carter himself desired to be appointed assistant attorney general for the Post Office Department.

Church, five in number, called to ask me to consider favorably the bill now pending in the House of Representatives in reference to allowing Indians to hold land in severalty, also to express the hope that I would appoint a Sec'y of the Interior who had sympathy for the missionary work among the Indians. Some of the names of the callers are mentioned on the preceeding page.

Capt. Henry came and spent the night. In the late evening read in *Anecdotes in Parliament.* [28]

WEDNESDAY, 19. The monotony interruption continues. Capt. Henry stayed during the day and helped with letters. A large delegation from Texas came, headed by a Mr. Glenn. They urge the appointment of ex-Gov. Davis to a place in the Cabinet.[29] Had an interesting conversation on the future of Texas and the South. The delegation took dinner with us. The winter is wonderfully beautiful, with its perfect sleighing, and the morning displays of hoar frost. I regret that I have so little time to feed myself on the beauties which the Season spreads over the world.

I must shut myself up to the study of man's estimate of himself as contrasted with my own estimate of him.

THURSDAY, 20. After breakfast walked to Mentor P.O. and caught the wonderful glory of the frost. Called at Mrs. Tyler's to inquire after Mrs. Aldrich, who has fallen and broken her hip. Home and read mail. Letter from Crete and one from Harry,

[28]George Henry Jennings, comp., *An Anecdotal History of the British Parliament, from the Earliest Periods to the Present Time, with Notices of Eminent Parliamentary Men, and Examples of Their Oratory* (1880). This is a revised edition of *A Book of Parliamentary Anecdote* (1872) compiled by Jennings and William S. Johnstone.

[29]John W. Glenn, a civil engineer for several years in Austin, Texas, and mayor of Austin, 1871–72, is listed in the city directory for 1881 as supervising architect of the U.S. custom house and post office. He was appointed mayor by Edmund J. Davis (1827–1883), lawyer, Union officer, 1861–65, and governor of Texas, 1870–74, whose dictatorial rule and support of unpopular causes, including disfranchisement of former Confederates, unrestricted Negro suffrage, and the division of Texas into three states, created considerable turmoil and gained him many enemies. Although soundly defeated for reelection in 1873, Davis attempted without success to stay on as governor, and in 1880 was again defeated as the Republican candidate for that office.

who is just started into his studies at Col. Rockwell's. These letters bring light into the house.

At a quarter before seven, Maj. Swaim and I drove to Willoughby and took the evening express (which [was] about one hour late) to Cleveland. Gen. Sheldon met us at the Depot and drove us to his house in Wil[l]son Avenue, where we spent the night.[30] I came with a view of seeing Judge Baxter of Tennessee, but a letter rec'd before leaving, and read on the way, leads me to postpone an interview.

FRIDAY, 21. Spent the day at Gen. Sheldon's, reading and visiting. Five hours of heavy snowfall. Had a full discussion with S. concerning Morgan and Pitkin[31] of La. Played casino, took a bath, had an interview with Gen. Edw[ard] McCook, who is en route for Colorado. Evident[ly] wants something; but I did not encourage his mentioning it. At 4.20 P.M. drove to James Mason's and took Mollie to the Depot, where we took the 4.50

[30]On January 21 Garfield made this record of a dream of the preceding night:

Last night I dreamed that General Arthur, Major Swaim and I were on an excursion to attend some great ceremonial. We were on a canal packet during the night. A heavy rain came on, and in the gray of the morning Swaim and I awoke just as the packet was passing a point to enter a deep broad basin. We leaped ashore, and in looking back saw that the packet was sinking. Just as it was sinking I noticed General Arthur lying on a couch very pale, and apparently very ill. In an instant more, the packet sank with all on board. I started to plunge into the water to save Arthur, but Swaim held me, and said he cannot be saved, and you will perish if you attempt it. It appeared that we were naked and alone in the wild storm, and that the country was hostile. I felt that nakedness was a disguise which would avoid identification. In this dream, for the first time in a dream, I knew I was President-elect. After a long journey, we somehow found a few yards of calico each for partial coverings. After a long and tangled journey we entered a house, and an old negro woman took me into her arms and nursed me as though I were a sick child. At this point I awoke.

[31]John R. G. Pitkin (1841–1901), a native of Louisiana, graduated at the University of Louisiana in 1861, was a public school principal in New Orleans, 1861–63, and practiced law most of his remaining years. He was U.S. marshal for Louisiana, 1876–77, 1882–85, and minister to Argentina, 1888–92.

train for home. Singular interview with Aella Green[32] of Springfield, Mass.

Dictated letters and read accumulated mail. Snow still falling, mails delayed and no letter from Crete. The "days go on," but very slowly when she is away.

SATURDAY, 22. The snow has fallen with constant accretion of depth for nearly 48 hours. The trains and mails have been blocked and deranged.

Gen. Benj. Harrison of Ind. came on the noon train and spent the afternoon and night. He brought a letter from the Ind. Congressmen asking an interview with me. They wish to urge me to choose a cabinet officer from that state; but I understand they are not agreed upon any one. Harrison gave me his estimate of Gresham,[33] Taylor,[34] Tyner, Dudley and several others who have been talked of. I told him, that if I took one from Ind., it would probably be himself.[35] He is in doubt whether he ought to leave the Senate. I like him. Gen. Stewart L. Woodford and Pres. Hinsdale came and spent the night. Woodford wants to be reappointed as District Att'y for southern N.Y.

SUNDAY, 23. All day at home. Continued snowfall. Gen. Woodford left at 7 A.M. for Painesville and the East. A good deal of conversation with Harrison and Hinsdale, on public questions. Harrison left at 2.45. He thinks he ought to stay in the Senate —but a place in the Cabinet was neither refused nor tendered. Geo. A. Baker came and spent two hours. Hinsdale read me a

[32]Aella Greene (1838–1903), journalist and author, published a number of books, including *Rhymes of Yankee Land* (1872), *Culminations* (1892), and *Reminiscent Sketches* (1902).

[33]Walter Q. Gresham (1832–1895), a native of Indiana, was an officer in the Union army, 1861–65, U.S. district judge, 1869–83, postmaster general, 1883–84, secretary of the treasury, 1884, and secretary of state, 1893–95.

[34]Robert S. Taylor (1838–1918), a native of Ohio, moved to Indiana, studied law in Fort Wayne and was admitted to the bar in 1860. He was judge of the court of common pleas, 1869–70, member of the state legislature, 1871–72, and unsuccessful Republican candidate for the U.S. House of Representatives, 1874 and 1880. He was appointed by Garfield to succeed Benjamin Harrison on the Mississippi River Commission, and served, 1881–1914.

[35]See entry for March 3, 1881. No Indiana man served in Garfield's cabinet.

strong paper on the wine question. I find myself getting angry and [at] the impertinence of the temperance people, and in some danger of acting on that anger. Hinsdale's paper is a strong one. He remained over night. In the evening rec'd a letter from Crete. No date fixed for her return yet. Mollie has brightened the home since Friday evening.

MONDAY, 24. I arose at seven to see Mollie and Hinsdale off. They left at 7.30. I did not sleep last night a[s] soundly as I ought to, and this is becoming habitual. I don't see how I am to correct the evil, with the amount of work that presses upon me.

At noon Hon. Edwards Pierrepont of N.Y. came and spent three hours. He had a long talk with Conkling on the 17th. C. was full of apprehension that Robertson[36] was to be appointed. He wanted Morton in the Treasury as N.Y.'s reply to Blaine in the State Dep't. Pierrepont told him that would not do. Both the law and public sentiment were against it. Mr. P. stated quite fully the history of recent N.Y. affairs and Conkling's relations to them. Said that Platt was wholly devoted to Conkling but that something less than C's demand would satisfy, and ought to

---

[36]William H. Robertson (1823–1898), a lawyer in Westchester, New York, was a member of the state assembly, 1849–50, and of the state senate, 1854–55, 1872–81 (president pro tempore, 1874–81), 1888–89, county judge, 1855–67, a Republican member of the U.S. House of Representatives, 1867–69, and collector of customs of the port of New York, 1881–85. In 1880 he led the revolt against Conkling's efforts to force all New York delegates to the Republican National Convention to support Grant. Robertson and most of the other dissidents voted for Blaine on every ballot except the last, when all of them (20) swung to Garfield. As the Republican boss of New York, Conkling did not wish to see Robertson or any other rebel appointed to important posts in the state. Blaine and his friend Whitelaw Reid of the *Tribune,* both of whom were eager to destroy Conkling, wanted Garfield to give prominent recognition to the Robertson group. Garfield did so when he appointed Robertson to the most important federal office in New York State—the collectorship of customs of the port of New York. A prolonged confrontation between the President and the senator ensued; the President won; Conkling resigned, was defeated for re-election, and retired from politics. Robertson served a full term of four years. Charles Guiteau's decision to "remove" the President was a direct result of his distress over the internecine struggle in the Republican party.

satisfy, the just demands of the state. Thinks the Att'y Gen'lship would be enough.

Pres. O. A. Burgess came and spent the night. F. M. Green and a Mr. Smiley[37] of the Indian Commission called. Maj. Swaim was today appointed Brigadier General.

TUESDAY, 25. At the foot of my calendar for this day stand these verses from Coleridge—

Habitual evils change not on a sudden,
But many days must pass and many sorrows.

This might be applied to the southern question. Time is the only healer, with justice and wisdom at work.

Pres. Burgess went on the 5.45 A.M. train. Many callers, and some work done. Wrote Blaine, declining to go to Washington now as he suggests. I think it will only cause and not heal, heart burnings. Crete does not come, nor set a time for coming. Hon. N. W. Goodhue of Akron dined with us. I must soon begin the inaugural address. I am quite seriously discussing the propriety of omitting it. Most of them are dreary reading, although they may have served their day. I suppose I must conform to the custom, but I think the address should be short. I am painfully impressed with the fact that I am getting but little growth out of these weeks.

WEDNESDAY, 26. Mail in the forenoon. At noon Judges Baxter and Welker came and remained until the evening train. The former gave me his views of the state of affairs in Tennessee. On some accounts he would be a good man in the Cabinet. While he was here, I received a telegram informing me of Jackson's[38] election to the Senate from Tenn. Our friends had not the strength of unity, or they might have prevented that result. Sent the Judges to Willoughby at 5.30.

[37]Albert K. Smiley (1826–1912), educator and humanitarian, was a native of Maine whose numerous and varied interests included the welfare of Indians. He was appointed by Hayes to the board of Indian commissioners, and served, 1879 to his death. He spent his last years in Redlands, California, where the Albert K. Smiley Library and the public park are testimonials to his generosity.

[38]Howell E. Jackson (1832–1895) was a Democratic member of the U.S. Senate, 1881–86, U.S. circuit judge for the sixth federal circuit, 1886–93, and associate justice of the U.S. Supreme Court, 1894 to his death.

Profs. C. D. Wilber and Aughey[39] of Nebraska came at noon, and spent the night. Ellen Larabee also came. I have no word from Crete since Monday. I sat up too late with Wilber for my health.

THURSDAY, 27. Wilber and Aughey went to the train before I arose. A bitter cold day and freer from callers than any this month. I commenced the first draft of the Inaugural. I feel but little freedom in its composition. There are so many limitations.

The general plan I have formed is 1st a brief introduction, 2nd a summary of recent topics that ought to be treated as settled, 3rd a summary of those that ought to occupy the public attention, 4th a direct appeal to the people to stand by me in an independent and vigorous execution of the laws. In the afternoon drove to the depot for an airing. Not having heard from Crete, I telegraphed to Reid, who answered she would leave N.Y. Friday evening at six. Retired at 10.40—not well.

FRIDAY, 28. In my great anxiety to hear from Crete, I telegraphed Reid, and he answered she would leave for home on the Friday evening train. I greatly hope this will be so, for I want to learn what she has learned of N.Y. matters, before the arrival of Gov. Cornell, who is to be here tomorrow afternoon. I made some progress in my inaugural, but do not satisfy myself. The fact is I ought to have done it sooner before I became so jaded.

The day has been very severely cold, and freer from callers

[39]Samuel H. Aughey (1831–1912), a member of the faculty of the University of Nebraska from its opening in 1871 to his resignation in 1883, taught various sciences and devoted much time to acquainting Nebraskans with the physical nature of the state. His publications include *Sketches of the Physical Geography and Geology of Nebraska* (1880) and, with Charles D. Wilber, a pamphlet entitled *Agriculture Beyond the 100th Meridian; or, A Review of the United States Public Land Commission* (1880). Of these two publications the historian of the university remarks: "The pamphlet and his book identified Samuel Aughey as the foremost proponent of the immediate settlement of the plains." After complaints by the regents of the university that he was "spending more time in Wyoming investigating coal deposits . . . than in the classroom," Aughey left Nebraska to settle in Wyoming. See Robert N. Manley, *Centennial History of the University of Nebraska, I, Frontier University, 1869–1919* (1969), pp. 41–44, and 74.

than any other for a month. The N.Y. people seem to be greatly stirred up at the prospect of having Blaine in the Cabinet. They want [?] a Conkling foil for his influence. If I could find a large, true man from N.Y. for the Treasury I would take him. Perhaps Judge Folger[40] will do.

SATURDAY, 29.   I did not sleep as I ought, last night—and this fact notifies me that I must take more exercise. Rec'd a letter from Crete dated the 26th. The mails have been greatly delayed. Reid telegraphs that they have postponed starting until Saturday (this evening). At seven, Gov. Cornell and Senator Platt came, and spent three hours, urging Morton for the Treasury. I told them it was inadmissible. In answer to their inquiry if I had ruled N.Y. out from that place, I said not N.Y. but Wall Street. I asked them what they thought of Conkling and Blaine for the two first places. They thought C. could not be spared from the Senate. I asked them to suggest some names. They had none to offer but Morton. I asked what they thought of Judge Folger for the Att'y Gen. or Treasury. They said he was a good man, but could not safely be spared. Letter from Grant on N.Y. question.[41]

[40]Charles J. Folger (1818–1884), of New York, graduated at Geneva (now Hobart) College, 1836, studied law, and was admitted to the bar in 1839. He was for several years a judge in Ontario County, a member of the state senate, 1861–69, and assistant treasurer of the United States in New York City, 1869–70. In 1870 he was elected associate justice of the New York court of appeals and in 1880, upon the death of the chief justice, he was appointed by Governor Cornell to that office. He was elected chief justice in 1880, lost to Grover Cleveland in the New York gubernatorial election of 1882, and was secretary of the treasury under Arthur, 1881 to his death. He declined the position of attorney general in Garfield's cabinet.

[41]In a letter of January 26 Grant expressed his dislike of Blaine but advised Garfield not to ignore the man for that reason, adding that if Blaine was to be appointed secretary of state, Levi P. Morton or "someone friendly to Senator Conkling should take the Treasury." Garfield replied (January 31) that while he had the "strongest desire" to preserve party harmony and to satisfy New York Republican leaders, the appointment of Morton as secretary of the treasury would violate the law, and would be regarded by many as a violation of the spirit of the law even if Morton left his banking business. He said that he had never considered appointing to his cabinet anyone from New York who was hostile to Conkling, that he had invited Conkling to Mentor to discuss the New York matter and hoped

SUNDAY, 30.   One half a sleep. The morning mail brought a letter from Crete, date 28th, that she could not leave until Sunday evening. Henry E. Knox came and spent the day. He thinks the solution of the N.Y. question is to put Judge Folger into the Treasury. I asked him to find some trustworthy, independent man who knows Judge F. well, to have an interview with him on the general situation and then have Knox report to me. This he will do. Gov. Cox came and spent five hours. Had a long and strengthening visit with him *de omnibus.* He went at 3 P.M., Knox at eight. Mollie had a hard struggle to conquer her disappointment at not seeing Mamma. At first she said she could not go back to school without seeing her. But finally her courage rose and she went bravely at her lessons.

No telegram from Crete. Retired at 9.30.

MONDAY, 31.   I slept less last night than usual—not more than four hours. The prolonged absence of Crete, when I so greatly need to consult her on several subject[s] about which she will bring me intelligence, is a part of the cause of this insomnia. I have no doubt I have grown morbid over her long absence. Swaim went to Cleveland with Mollie in the morn[ing]. About 9 A.M. Reid telegraphed me that Crete and Mrs. Sheldon left N.Y. last evening at six, and will go directly through to Cleveland. I found that her train was an hour late. I rode down the lane and caught a sight of her face as her train passed. At six she came with Major Swaim, and my joy was full. She has kept her *incognita* very successfully. Wrote to Senator Conkling inviting him to visit me for consultation. Retired at 10 P.M.

February

TUESDAY, 1.   In spite of all my efforts, got less than five hours sleep last night. Except the writing of two or three letters, laid

---

that he would come. He also reminded Grant that while he would try to avoid antagonisms, as far as he could, he had to select men who would work with him in the administration.

off and did no work. Lay down two hours in the afternoon but could not sleep—though I got some rest while Crete read to me from Trevelyan's life of Fox.[42] It has been a very wild cold day. Victoria Howells[43] remained. Crete set her sewing in order. Her work is much nearer ready for the 4th of March than mine. Only a few callers came, and I got some rest by giving up all attempts at work. I should have mentioned yesterday that 30 Indianians came and courteously suggested the importance of giving Indiana a place in the Cabinet.[44]

WEDNESDAY, 2. This day has been greatly broken up by visitors, and though I rested better last night than the night before I did not sleep well, nor enough. Among the callers were Amzi Rudolph of Georgia, Alanson Wilcox of Cleveland, and a Mrs. Bernhart [Barnhart][45] of Illinois.

Wrote a number of important letters, among them one to Sec'y Schurz, suggesting Mr. Nichol for Commissioner of Indian Affairs. Rec'd a long letter from H.E. Knox detailing Senator Harris'[46] interview with Judge Folger, and thinking he is the

[42]George Otto Trevelyan, *The Early History of Charles James Fox* (1880).

[43]Victoria Howells (1838–1886), oldest daughter of William C. Howells and favorite sister of William Dean Howells, stayed at home and cared for her mentally retarded brother Henry (b. 1852) for thirty years. On December 18, 1880, she wrote to Garfield from Toronto (where her father was U.S. consul): "Henry and I have been for the past month staying with Anne in Ottawa, whither we went for a change, for our poor afflicted one, and now we are come home, again for a change for him. . . ." She went on to say that she would be in Jefferson in January on business for her father, and would like to spend half a day with the Garfields. "I can be gone," she wrote, "but a short time from Toronto." See Kenneth S. Lynn, *William Dean Howells: An American Life* (1971).

[44]Headed by Senator-elect Benjamin Harrison, the visitors candidly told the press the purpose of their call, pointing out that Indiana had contributed much to the Republican victory. They spoke of the meeting at Lawnfield as informal and private, and of Garfield's response as cordial and non-committal.

[45]Sarah Barnhart, of Putnam County, Illinois, had recently written to Garfield to say that she was a blood relative of his. Her father, she explained, was part Ballou, and her mother was Elizabeth Ballou, a native of Rhode Island.

[46]Hamilton Harris (1820–1900), younger brother of Ira Harris, was born in Cortland County, graduated at Union College in 1841, and was long active in law and politics in New York. He was a founder of the Republican party, the chairman

N.Y. man for the Cabinet.[47] The same mail bring[ing] two others on the other side.

THURSDAY, 3.   A day nearly wasted by callers. I slept better last night [than] any night for four weeks. But nearly 20 people came. Senator Grady[48] came from Harrisburg—wanting me to appoint Grew [Grow] to the Cabinet, and thus end the Senatorial fight. I refused to take any part. A Cleveland delegation wanted me to help Matthews' confirmation as Associate Justice. I refused to write. A Michigan delegation, Duffield[49] and Heath, want Bagley[50] for the Cabinet, and Heath for an office. No promise. At six 22 Crete and I went to Cleveland, en route to Hiram.

---

of its state central committee, 1864–70, a delegate to its national convention in 1868, and a member of the state senate, 1875–79.

[47]Following a lengthy conference with New York state senator Hamilton Harris, Knox wrote Garfield (January 31) that Folger was "the man of all others" in New York to consider for the Treasury Department. His appointment, Knox believed, would please all factions in the state and "do more than anything else to solidify and harmonize the party."

[48]John C. Grady was born in Maine in 1847, moved to Philadelphia, studied law, and in 1871 was admitted to the bar. He served five successive terms in the Pennsylvania senate, and was president of that body, 1887–89. In 1881 he was selected by Republican leaders in his state to present to Garfield Pennsylvania's claims for a cabinet post. His candidate, Galusha A. Grow, was supported for the U.S. Senate by Republican "bolters" who opposed Henry W. Oliver, the nominee of the Republican caucus. The senatorial contest in Pennsylvania continued until February 23, when a compromise in which Grady took a key part was reached. In 1881 Grady declined Garfield's offer to appoint him surveyor of the port of Philadelphia.

[49]Henry M. Duffield (1842–1912), a native of Detroit, graduated at Williams College in 1861 and served in the Union army, 1862–65. Following the Battle of Chickamauga, in which he was wounded, he was provost-marshal general of the Army of the Cumberland, 1863–65. After the war he studied law, became a leading Detroit attorney, and was prominent in Republican politics. He commanded the Second Army Corps in Cuba during the Spanish-American war.

[50]John J. Bagley (1832–1881), a native of New York, moved to Michigan with his parents when he was eight years of age. He became a successful businessman in Detroit, where he engaged in manufacturing, banking, and mining. He held various public offices in Detroit and was governor of Michigan, 1873–77. In 1881 he came within one vote of being nominated by the Republican caucus as candidate for the U.S. Senate. He received no appointment from Garfield.

Spent the night at Col. Sheldon's, 838 Wilson [Willson] Avenue.
FRIDAY, 4.   Took the 7.10 A.M. train for Garrettsville, and drove thence to Hiram. Stopped at Father Rudolph's. At eleven o'clock attended the funeral of Aunt Emeline Raymond, the sister of Mother Rudolph. Burke preached the Sermon. We took dinner at Burke's. At 4 P.M. I went to the college, and made a short address to the students, and bade them and Hiram good-bye. It seems more final than any leave taking I have yet had.[51] We drove to Garrettsville, and took the 5.10 train for Cleveland and spent the night at Gen. Sheldon's. Before retiring, had a long talk with him on political affairs. I find he is not willing to be private secretary, but wants a position that has more pay, or larger political opportunities.

SATURDAY, 5.   Went to the Dentist's at eleven o'clock and he worked on my teeth nearly three hours. Crete went to her dressmaker's to have some fitting done. I got the 2.55 Express to stop and leave us at Mentor, but her work was not done in time, and I came on alone. Ex-Senator Lewis,[52] Mr. Hamlett and a colored man of the name of Pleasants[53] were awaiting me. Had an hour's

[51]To an assembly in the college chapel made up largely of students, Garfield spoke nostalgically of his days at Hiram and of how "completely" he now seemed to be leaving the place. He urged the students to conduct themselves wisely and reminded them that their college experiences were the foundation of their future life. At the end of his talk he asked everyone to sing "Ho! Reapers of Life's Harvest," joined in the singing "with evident pleasure," greeted individual members of the audience, and departed. See also Vol. I, p. lxi.

[52]John F. Lewis (1818–1895) was a Republican member of the U.S. Senate from Virginia, 1870–75, U.S. marshal for the western district of Virginia, 1878–81, and lieutenant governor of Virginia, 1882–85, having been elected by the Republican-Readjuster coalition (led by Mahone) that he had helped to organize. At the time of his visit to Garfield he was chairman of the Republican state central committee. A statement by Lewis on the meeting at Lawnfield, reported in the *Alexandria Gazette* (February 7), includes these words: "He [Garfield] seemed perfectly familiar with Virginia affairs, and the real gist of the interview was his approval of a coalition of the Republican party in Virginia with the Mahonites."

[53]William H. Pleasants, of Danville, Virginia, said to have been "one of the most indefatigable workers" in his congressional district, was a delegate to the Republican National Convention in 1880. During the presidential campaign he

talk on Va. matters. They favor combining with Mahone in next year's state issues, to secure protection and justice for the blacks, and I think they are right, if they can secure the good they seek without endorsing repudiation in any way. Several other callers, among them Robbins of the *Inter Ocean.*

SUNDAY, 6.   I had a good sleep last night, and arose this morning intending to begin the abandoned work on the inaugural, but letters and callers filled the day. I do not yet hear from Conkling or Logan. Brown and Mother went to Cleveland at noon. Gen. John Miller[54] of Cal. with his wife and daughter called. Had a long talk with him on people of the Coast. Told him I might want to call him to the Cabinet. The Harmons and Cannons of Aurora came. In the evening Marenus Larabee and his brother William came, also Ben Butterworth of Cincinnati, who staid three hours. At noon Capt. Henry came and spent the night.[55] Answered a few letters in the evening. Martha Mays came for two hours. Geo. and Horace Steele and wives came for a visit. Retired at 10.15 P.M.

MONDAY, 7.   Many callers, Capt. C. E. Henry among them. Near noon, Marenus G. Larabee and his brother William came and spent the night.

I have vainly tried to get at the inaugural but the day has been taken away from me piece meal. Still I am getting some sleep and with it more strength against the day of greater need.

TUESDAY, 8.   A warm rain came in with the dawn, and the great body of snow began to melt. Among the callers were Judge Clark[e] of Miss., Sec'y of State Morgan[56] of Wyoming, and Capt. Charles Garfield of Bryan, Ohio. The latter is in great grief

---

advised Garfield to take certain steps that would make the "Solid South . . . a thing of the past." He urged Garfield to appoint Samuel M. Yost of Virginia postmaster general.

[54]John F. Miller (1831–1886), a native of Indiana, served in the Union army, 1861–65, settled in California after the war and was a Republican member of the U.S. Senate from California, 1881 to his death.

[55]See the reference to Henry and the Larabee brothers in the next entry.

[56]Elliott S. N. Morgan, of Pennsylvania, was secretary of Wyoming Territory, 1880–87.

of his son Lewis, who is in prison. I could give no help, in the way of his release.

I find myself strangely disinclined to work on the inaugural. In fact I strongly incline to make none, yet I suppose I must. Telegram came in the evening announcing the death of Hattie Palmer's babe. Dr. Streator and C. B. Lockwood came and spent the night, after an evening's visit. Henry went at noon.

WEDNESDAY, 9. Rained nearly all day. The snow rapidly disappearing.

Olive Logan Sykes [Sikes][57] came and spent two hours. James Paine[58] also. Mr. Gibbs of California, one of the Commissioners who framed the Chinese treaty,[59] called and spent a few hours. Cooper the tailor came and tried on the new suits which I ordered on Saturday.

Brown and Judd went to Painesville. At 2.40 P.M. received a dispatch from Hal and Jim, that the count was successfully concluded and I was announced elected. The count appears to have been made without a jar.[60]

Worked a little on the inaugural in the evening.

THURSDAY, 10. Made some progress on the inaugural; but still

[57]Olive Logan Sikes (1839–1909), actress, journalist, lecturer, and author, made her stage debut in 1854 and retired from acting in 1868. She devoted most of her professional life to lecturing on women's rights and other political and social subjects, and to writing plays, news articles, and books. The second of her three husbands was William Wirt Sikes (1836–1883), a journalist and author whom she married in 1871.

[58]James H. Paine (1831–1910), a descendant of Edward Paine, the founder of Painesville, was a lawyer, a Union soldier, a naval officer, and chief clerk in the U.S. Department of Agriculture. In consequence of his poor management of his personal finances he died virtually penniless.

[59]This is an error. The treaties of 1880 between the United States and China were negotiated by commissioners James B. Angell, John F. Swift and William H. Trescot.

[60]"We all went to the Electoral Count yesterday," Jim wrote to his father (February 9), "and saw you duly elected. It was a very dry proceeding as far as the reports of the different states were concerned, but of great interest to me as being a Garfield. Mr. Blaine was not there and Mr. Conkling came in after the rest of the Senate had all taken their seats. He stood quite a while in the main entrance and then in a very dignified manner walked down the main isle and took the front seat of the House."

feel unusual repugnance to writing. At noon, Senator [-elect] Sawyer and Mr. Nichol came from Wisconsin. The Senator strongly recommends ex-Senator Howe for a place in the Cabinet. The suggestion strikes me favorably, and it may aid me in solving the Treasury question. It is strange that I have not thought of him before. He remained over night. Kennedy and Robertson of Cleveland came to see if there were anything I had to say, now that the count is over. I answered that I would speak officially when the time came.

Retired at 10.30 P.M.

FRIDAY, 11. Sawyer and Nichol remained until noon. About ten A.M. Senator Logan came in answering [answer to] my invitation. Had a long and pleasant consultation with him, and I think it will be productive of good. I incline to think favorably of Rob't Lincoln.

Received a note from Senator Conkling, accepting my invitation to visit me. Committee from Pittsburgh, asking me to ask Senator Cameron to end the Senatorial conflict.

Gen. Casement and ladies from Painesville called.

In the evening Mother and Mollie, and Mrs. J. H. Rhodes and her two children came. They and Gen. Logan passed the night.

SATURDAY, 12. Senator Logan remained until noon when he went to Cleveland en route for Washington. I took a horseback ride of an hour before dinner. The widow of Hon. Rush Clarke [Clark] of Iowa came to secure promotion for her brother. Several other people called during the day. In the afternoon I was drowsy for the first time (day) in a month, and went to bed and slept two hours.

In the evening Harry Rhodes came and spent the night. I retired at 10.20.

SUNDAY, 13. A very stormy day. Remained at home, and tried to do some work on the inaugural, but with poor success. Gov. Cullom[61] of Illinois came and spent an hour and a half.

[61]Shelby M. Cullom (1829–1914), was a Republican member of the U.S. House of Representatives from Illinois, 1865–71, governor of Illinois, 1877–83, U.S. senator, 1883–1913, and regent of the Smithsonian Institution, 1885–1913. In his

Rhodes and family remained during the day and night. In the evening, we sang the old childhood hymns for half an hour. Retired at 10.30.

MONDAY, 14. A busy day. Made the first fair start on the inaugural; but was greatly interrupted by callers.

At one P.M. Senator Dorsey came, and I spent most of the afternoon and evening with him. He is strongly of the opinion that the appointment of Judge Folger to the Treasury [is advisable].[62] He says Conkling is opposed to him because he is too independent. I am somewhat puzzled with this case.

Word came from Morton that Conkling was to leave Washington via N.Y. for Mentor.

Dorsey left on the 11.20 P.M. train; and Capt. Henry took the mail car on the same train.

Retired at eleven.

TUESDAY, 15. Got my first satisfactory start on the inaugural. It is difficult to understand the singular repugnance I feel in regard to doing this work. Henry telegraphed from Rochester "no interview," and later in the day the same from Albany.[63] I hear nothing from Conkling. His delay is annoying. A letter from B. F. M.[64] throws grave doubts on Folger, and yet I can hardly think

---

book, *Fifty Years of Public Service: Personal Recollections* . . . (1911), pp. 124–125, he wrote that he went to Mentor to recommend a cabinet appointment for Robert T. Lincoln, whose selection would honor Illinois and strengthen Garfield's administration. He remembered reaching Garfield's house after walking from the train "through banks of snow," and stating immediately the purpose of his visit. At the end of "quite a long talk," Cullom recalled, Garfield "announced that he would appoint Mr. Lincoln his Secretary of War."

[62]The bracketed words completing Garfield's unfinished sentence are consistent with Dorsey's view, expressed before and after his visit to Mentor, that Folger was "the most respectable and by all odds the ablest man" that Garfield could appoint as secretary of the treasury (Dorsey to Garfield, January 20 and February 24).

[63]The editors have not found the telegrams mentioned in this entry nor the specific purpose of Henry's mission in New York.

[64]Benjamin F. Manierre, a founder and member of the board of directors of the Equitable Life Assurance Society, was long involved in Republican politics in New York City. In 1880 he was chairman of the committee to conduct the campaign of the Republican Central Club in that city. In his letter to Garfield (February 12)

the reflections are just. Callers as usual. At 4 P.M. Swaim and I drove to Mr. Tanner's up the Chagrin River road, to look at a lot of leached ashes and barnyard manure which I am trying to purchase for the farm. On our return found Maj. Bradley[65] of Washington, who comes to show me that J. J. Noah[66] of the War Dep't is the writer of the Morey letter. The Major stayed over night.

WEDNESDAY, 16. Callers more numerous than usual. Uncle Thomas, Amasa Garfield and Jonathan Fisher among them. At 3 P.M. Senator Conkling came and remained until eleven-thirty P.M. I had a full conversation on the Cabinet and kindred subjects. His knowledge of men was fuller and more accurate than I had expected, and in the main his judgment was sound. He appeared frank and friendly. Urged the importance of recognizing N.Y. and thought Morton would do well in the Treasury. I told him I thought the objections insuperable. I asked his opinion of Folger, and he spoke highly of him, but thought it we [would] be dangerous to the party in N.Y. to take him from the Chief Justiceship. I told him I wanted his friendship, and believed we could work together with indepen[den]t and mutual respect, but I could not give Morton more than the War or Navy. He went at 11.30.

THURSDAY, 17. Made pretty fair progress on the inaugural,

---

he questioned Folger's fitness for a cabinet position on the ground that as a member of the state senate he had joined with Tammany Democrats to prevent the confirmation of appointments made by the Republican governor. Manierre also claimed that when Folger ran for associate justice of the state court of appeals in 1870 he lost heavily in rural areas and had been elected only because of Tammany support in New York City.

[65]Thomas H. Bradley served in the Union army, 1861–65, rising from private to major; he remained in the army at reduced rank and was on duty in the War Department, 1868–82. He retired in 1892, eleven years before his death.

[66]Jacob J. Noah, a native of New York, lived for many years in Washington, D.C., where he was a lawyer, an employee in various departments of government, and a journalist. During the period of the excitement over the Morey letter he was the Washington correspondent of *Truth* (see n. 301, October 20, 1880). No evidence connecting him with the writing or publication of the Morey letter was ever brought to public attention.

though much interrupted. Telegraphed Judge Folger inviting him to visit me. Everything waits on the N.Y. tangle. Letter from Knox still strongly favoring Judge Folger. The only doubt I have is as to his independence of faction and the machine. The Dorsey dinner was a curious affair whose whole significance I do not yet understand.[67] Retired at ten.

P.S.

Sold the mare Fanny for $150.

FRIDAY, 18. Made some progress in writing but interruptions continue. The name of E. B. Wight has been suggested for Private Sec'y, also that of Edward McPherson. There may be light in one or the other direction.

In the afternoon Wm. Penn Nixon[68] of the Chicago *Inter Ocean* came, also Rev. S. D. Bates of Marion, O., my old schoolmate

---

[67]According to the *New York Times* (February 12), the dinner, held at Delmonico's on February 11, was given by prominent members of the Union League Club to honor Dorsey for his successful work in Indiana during the campaign of 1880. The Committee of Invitation included John Jacob Astor, J. Pierpont Morgan, John A. Stewart, Levi P. Morton, and Thurlow Weed. President Grant, who was master of ceremonies, arrived early and attracted so much attention that Dorsey's entrance went unnoticed. Grant delivered a handsome tribute to the guest of honor, saying that he had done more than any man to bring about the Republican victory. The gathering, estimated at approximately two hundred, heard speeches by Chester A. Arthur, Henry Ward Beecher, William Windom, Whitelaw Reid, and others. In a letter urging Garfield to attend (January 15), Dorsey wrote that the dinner would have "no political or factional significance," invited the President-elect to set for the affair a date in February, and expressed his understanding that the dinner would be "in many respects the greatest thing of the kind ever held in this city," adding that he expected about two hundred of the most prominent men in the country to attend. The chief promoter of the Dorsey dinner, according to some observers, was Stephen W. Dorsey.

[68]William Penn Nixon (1833–1912), a native of Indiana and a graduate in law at the University of Pennsylvania, 1857, practiced law in Cincinnati for several years and was a member of the Ohio state legislature, 1865–68, before turning to journalism, first in Cincinnati and then in Chicago. He was associated with the Chicago *Inter Ocean,* 1872–97, from 1875 as general manager and editor. He made it a strongly Republican paper and a vigorous advocate of protection for American industries. President McKinley appointed him collector of customs for the district of Chicago in 1897, a post he held for several years.

at Chester. In the evening Mollie came and also Col. Rockwell. Visited in the evening and retired at 10.30 P.M.

I should have added that Swaim was today confirmed as Judge Advocate General.

SATURDAY, 19.   Crete went to Cleveland this morning with Gen. Swaim and the two little boys. Rockwell spent the forenoon in conversation *de multibus*. At 3 P.M. Judge Folger came. I had a long and frank talk with him on the situation in N.Y. I was greatly please[d] with his spirit and his manifest great ability. I broached the question of his going into the cabinet. He gave me two reasons why I should not take him. One was the assault upon him in reference to his first election.[69] The other was his suit now in the Supreme Court for a large claim on the Treasury.[70] I answered that the last might embarrass him for the Treasury but would not for the Att'y Gen'lship, which I offered him. He said he could not answer until he reached home, but would answer Tuesday next. He left at 11.20 P.M.

SUNDAY, 20.   At home all day. Just as I was about leaving for Church, Dr. Robison came with Mr. J. H. Wade and S. T. Everett of Cleveland who remained about two hours, talking mainly on

[69]Reference is to his first election as associate justice of the New York Court of Appeals (1870), when, because he had been the candidate of both the Democratic and Republican parties, opponents accused him of a corrupt alliance with Tammany.

[70]In late 1869 and early 1870 Folger served as assistant treasurer of the United States in New York City. During that service he sold and distributed internal revenue stamps valued at nearly $3,675,000. That sum included in stamps the commissions to purchasers authorized by law. When Folger retired from office he settled his accounts without asserting any right to commissions to himself and without deriving any financial benefit from the sales. Five years later (May, 1875) he brought legal action to recover approximately $185,000 as commissions for selling the stamps. The Court of Claims ruled that the law contained no provision for compensation to government officials who performed such services. He appealed the ruling, and in a majority decision, announced on February 28, 1881, the Supreme Court of the United States affirmed the ruling of the Court of Claims. Since by that time it was generally known that Folger might become secretary of the treasury, his opponents were citing his suit against the federal government to show that he was unfit for the office. See *Folger v. the United States* (13 U.S. 168).

the funding bill. I have rec'd a dispatch from Gen. Grant urging that the pending bill will bring great business disaster, and should be resisted. I cannot interfere with the President. He must take the responsibility. In the afternoon and evening I made some progress on the inaugural, but it drags heavily and does not please me.

Some more callers in the P.M. Scovel[71] of N.J. and a Col. Shoemaker of Philadelphia.[72]

Retired at 10.30.

MONDAY, 21.   Swaim and Rockwell left for Washington at noon. The delay of the N.Y. adjustment is crowding me into a close corner and may be embarrassing. It seems nearly impossible to do any work on the inaugural for the pressure of callers. In the afternoon Crete went to Painesville, and many callers came. Among them Dr. Jorgensen and Defendorf [Dezendorf][73] of Va. They are strongly oppose[d] to Mahone.

TUESDAY, 22.   Nichol came from Washington with messages from Blaine, who is distressed at the fear of Folger's appointment to the Treasury.

A whirl of callers all day, among them, Wm. H. Smith[74] of

[71]James M. Scovel was a U.S. commissioner to London and a New Jersey state senator during the Civil War. In 1872 he was state chairman of the Liberal Republican party. He returned to the Republican party and was appointed special agent of the Treasury Department by President Arthur. He again fell out with his party and became a Democrat. He died in 1904 at the age of seventy-five.

[72]"Samuel B. Shoemaker," said the *Cleveland Leader* (February 21), "is a fine young man, of one of the old Quaker families of Philadelphia, and is secretary of the Philadelphia Republican Central committee." He urged Garfield to appoint a Pennsylvanian to his cabinet, preferring Henry W. Oliver, the candidate of his close friend Senator James D. Cameron.

[73]John F. Dezendorf (1834–1894), a native of New York, resided for over a decade in Ohio, where he studied and engaged in architecture and civil engineering. He moved to Norfolk, Virginia, in 1863, worked in the shipping business, and held municipal and federal offices. He was an alternate delegate to the Republican National Convention in 1880 and a Republican member of the U.S. House of Representatives from Virginia, 1881–83.

[74]William H. Smith (1833–1896), a native of New York who was brought to Ohio as a child, devoted much of his life to journalism. During the 1860's he was associated with several Cincinnati papers, and was Ohio's secretary of state, 1864–

Chicago, to arrange about sending a press agent with me to Washington. Nichol went in the evening. Miss Mays and Miss Evans came to tea.

Retired at 11.15 P.M.

WEDNESDAY, 23. Letter from Folger.[75]

THURSDAY, 24. Delegation of Chicago men who want Storrs.

FRIDAY, 25. Gen. Sharpe of N.Y.[76]

SATURDAY, 26. Sent letter to L. P. M[orton] offering him the Sec'y-ship of the Navy, and requiring an answer by Monday next ten A.M., and gave him cipher.[77]

Worked on inaugural in the midst of great discouragement—or rather, interruption, from callers. Swaim came in the evening and brings me news of the state of the Washington mind.

SUNDAY, 27. At church. J. H. Jones preached. After the com-

---

66. In 1870 he became manager of the Western Associated Press in Chicago. President Hayes, whose intimate friend he was, appointed him collector of customs for the district of Chicago, a post he held, 1877–81, while continuing to perform his duties for his press association. For a decade after the Western Associated Press and the New York Associated Press set up a Joint Executive Committee in 1882 he was general manager of the joint organization. He wrote or edited a number of books on American history.

[75]In a letter (February 21) Folger reviewed the discussion they had had in Mentor, noting that Garfield had invited him to be attorney general of the United States, and had intimated that "in the happening of a contingency" the offer might be changed to secretary of the treasury. Recalling that he did not ask and Garfield did not state what the contingency was, Folger wrote that to accept the offer would hold him and his state "to the acceptance of the place of law officer of the government." In his judgment this would not meet the expectations of the people of his state or of the foremost men in its Republican party.

[76]George H. Sharpe (1828–1900), a native of Kingston, New York, was a graduate of Rutgers College and of the Yale School of Law. After practicing law for several years in New York City and Kingston, he served in the Civil War, 1861–65. He was on the staffs of Generals Hooker, Meade, and Grant, rose from captain to colonel, and was breveted brigadier general in 1864 and major general in 1865. President Grant appointed him U.S. marshal for the southern district of New York, 1870–73, and surveyor of the port of New York, 1873–78. He served in the New York assembly, 1879–83 (as Speaker, 1880 and 1881), and was a member of the Board of United States General Appraisers, 1890–99.

[77]On the morning of February 28, Morton telegraphed his acceptance, using the code words "your suggestion approved."

munion, in the farewell prayer he made a very touching and friendly allusion to me by name, and to the family. The members crowded around us and gave us good bye.

The afternoon and evening were devoted to packing and general preparation.

The newspaper men are gathering in force for the final break-up tomorrow.

I am greatly dissatisfied with the inaugural, which is still incomplete.

This is the slate I carry to Washington, which will not be much changed. 1. Blaine, State. 2. Windom, Treasury. 3. Lincoln. 4. Morton, Navy. 5. Wayne MacVeagh, Att'y Gen. 6. Hunt or Pardee, P.M.G.[78]

MONDAY, 28. Wrote a few pages on the inaugural in the early morning. Wrote Lincoln, tendering War Dep't. Breakfast at 9.30. The forenoon devoted to giving final orders about the management of the farm, and to disposing of books and papers. The crowd of callers increased. At 10 Morton accepted by telegraph. At 12.15 the last load left the house—Crete, Grandma, Mollie, Abe, Irvin and I, with Swaim, Brown and Judd. Several hundred people at the Depot. A. L. Tinker made a speech to me, and I said a [few] farewell words to my neighbors.[79] Our family

---

[78]In a small pocket notebook in which he made notes during January and February, 1881, Garfield wrote this entry on February 27:

This is the cast with which I leave Mentor. It will be but little changed.

1. Blaine	State
2. Windom	Treasury
3. Kirkwood or Allison	Interior
4. Lincoln	War
5. Morton	Navy
6. MacVeagh	Atty Gen
7. Hunt or Pardee	P.O. Dept

[79]In chilly weather and intermittent snow squalls Garfield spoke to approximately 350 people, many of whom were neighbors and longtime friends. After praising the beauty of northern Ohio and her people's selfless patriotism and devotion to the nation, he said: "What awaits me I cannot now speak of; but I shall carry to the discharge of the duties that lie before me, to the problems and dangers

as named above with Gen. Sheldon and wife and Capt. Henry took two directors' cars and gave a sleeping car to the press.[80] At 1 P.M. we left for the East. Speeches to the people at Ashtabula, Warren, and Youngstown. At Warren Mrs. Harmon Austin came aboard and rode to Youngstown. There T. W. Phillips came on and rode to Pittsburgh.[81] At Rochester Wharton Barker came. Snow fell heavily all day. Retired at 10 P.M.

March

TUESDAY, 1. Reached Washington at 9 A.M. and were driven to the Riggs House. Mother and Abram, with Mary McGrath, went to the Executive Mansion as the guest[s] of Mrs. Hayes and the President. Mollie went to Rockwell's.

The rush and swirl of callers was too much to be remembered without discomfort. Interviews with Blaine and several leading men. Slate generally approved, but Allison pressed in place of Windom. Morton pleased with his new place but his N.Y. friends not.

Late at night I looked over the inaugural, and became so much dissatisfied with it that I have resolved to rewrite it and made a

---

I may meet, a sense of your confidence and your love, which will always be answered by my gratitude. Neighbors, friends, constituents, farewell."

[80]Of the several invitations from railroad companies for free transportation to Washington, Garfield accepted that of the Pennsylvania Railroad Company, whose general manager, J. D. Leaying, offered Garfield "as many private cars as may be necessary to carry him, his family and friends to Washington, and furnish for them transportation without expense or trouble to him." The train that carried Garfield and his party consisted of two Pullman cars, one of which newspapermen occupied, one palace car and one baggage car.

[81]The *New York Times* (March 1), reported that at Pittsburgh, in response to repeated calls from a large and enthusiastic crowd, Garfield appeared on the rear platform of the train to bow and acknowledge greetings. Following a five-minute stop the journey resumed and Garfield, who was in great good humor, visited the newspaper correspondents in their car, shook hands, sat and chatted a while, then returned to his own car and retired.

beginning though very weary. The tonic of Washington life is good for my mind. Retired at 2 A.M.

WEDNESDAY, 2.   Only 4 hours of sleep last night. Morton broke down on my hands under the pressure of his N.Y. friends, who called him out of bed at 4 this morning to prevent his taking the Navy Dep't. I told him he must ask to be released if he wanted to go, which he did by letter in the afternoon. The N.Y. delegation are in a great row because I do not give the Treasury to that state. The rush of callers was continuous and heavy. I made fair progress, between calls, on my redraft of the inaugural, which amounts almost to a reconstruction of it. It seems important to get a volunteer soldier into the cast if possible, and I am discussing Judge Gresham of Indiana, and that would require a change in the Treasury, Allison instead of Windom. On some accounts this change will be more agreeable. I had James of N.Y. telegraphed for; I want to measure him for P.M.G. Drove to Judge Hunt's and asked him to Cabinet.

THURSDAY, 3.   Got but three hours of sleep last night, but made some progress on the new draft of inaugural. During the forenoon T. L. James of N.Y. called, and I asked him if he was so connected with any person that he would be embarrassed in giving his full and first support to me in any contest about matters of administration and policy. He seemed free and earnest. Later, Conkling, Arthur, and Platt came, the former full of apprehension that he had been or was to be cheated. Plead for Howe for Sec'y of the Treasury. In the evening I offered the Treasury to Allison, and he accepted it. I have been ready to appoint Harrison or Porter of Ind. to the Cabinet, or possibly Gresham, but the two first can't accept, and the last is objected to. Dinner at the President's, with his Cabinet. Thence to Wormley's where I found 16 of my classmates at dinner. I spoke.[82] Hotel at 11. Worked on inaugural 2 1/2 hours, and wrote last sentence at 2 1/2 o'clock A.M. March 4.

FRIDAY, 4.   At 8.30 A.M. Allison broke down on my hands and absolutely declined the Treasury, partly for family reasons, but

[82]See Vol. I, p. lxi.

mainly from unwillingness to face the opposition of certain forces. Though this disconcerts me, the break had better come now than later. The day opened with snow and sleet, but towards noon the sky began to clear. At 10.30 President Hayes called at my room, and [at] the Riggs, and we drove to the Executive Mansion, and then with the Committee, Senators Bayard and Anthony, along the Avenue to the Capitol. The crowd of people was very great. Reached President's chamber in the Senate wing at 11.30; at 11.55 went to the Senate, and witnessed the inauguration of the Vice President. Thence to the east portico of the rotunda, and read my inaugural—slowly and fairly well—though I grew somewhat hoarse towards the close. Returning to the Executive Mansion, lunched with the family[83] and then two and a half hours on the reviewing stand.

Inauguration reception at Museum building in the evening.[84] Home at eleven. Met Windom by appointment, and after a full hour's talk, offered him the Treasury. Retired at 12.30. Very weary. On the day of his inauguration Polk was 49 y[r]s. and 4 mos., Garfield, 49 yrs., 4 mos. and 15 days. Pierce was 48, 2 mos. and 15 days. Grant was 47, 10 mos. and 23 days. The latter 1 year and 22 d. old[er] than Pierce and 1 yr., 4 mos., 22 days older than [?] Grant.[85]

SATURDAY, 5. Four hours' sleep only. The crowd of callers commence[d] early and continued in great force. The pleasant event of the day was the call of the Williams College Alumni, and the speech of Dr. Hopkins, to which I replied briefly. Received Cleveland Troop and Grays,[86] also several other military organi-

[83]The lunch was given by President and Mrs. Hayes.

[84]The "Inaugural Reception and Promenade Concert" was the first event held in the Smithsonian Institution's new National Museum. The concert and reception ended at 11 o'clock; the President with his wife and mother left as the dancing began.

[85]The sentences relating to the age of presidents, which may have been written by Garfield at a later date, are crowded in at the bottom of the page for March 4 and are difficult to read. The computations of exact ages are inaccurate.

[86]The Cleveland Grays, organized in 1837 as an independent infantry company and later a unit in the National Guard, won fame as a ceremonial company. On

zations. At 10 Windom accepted. Sent him and Blaine out to enquire about Gresham, Hunt and Kirkwood for the Interior. They returned to me at 1.30 and both agreed with me that Kirkwood was the safest suggestion, and so, at 2.30 I had signed and sent to the Senate the exact cast with which I left Mentor, except that in N.Y. Morton for the Navy was replaced by James, for P.O. At 6.05 P.M. Mr. [Henry E.] Peyton, executive clerk of the Senate, brought me the message that the whole cabinet had been unanimously confirmed.[87] The result is better than I expected. Though not an ideal cabinet, it is a good combination of *esse et videri* [to be and to seem].

SUNDAY, 6. Slept six hours, which is much better than I have done of late. The inaugural and cabinet seem to be well received. Some soreness over the latter, but it will soon disappear, except in a very few cases.

Attended Church with Mother, Crete and Mrs. Sheldon. A great and annoying crowd. In the evening had Hinsdale, Henry, Rhodes, Austin, Kent and Phillips and his wife to dinner with us.

The drift of public comment on the inaugural and Cabinet is far better than I expected they would be, especially in the South and among leading Democrats.

I retired at 10.20 weary to the bone.

MONDAY, 7. At 10.30 A.M. all the members of the Cabinet except Lincoln were sworn in. Judge D. K. Cartter administered the oath. The members of the old Cabinet were present, and each took his successor and introduced him to the Department.

The rush of callers was very great—so many were visitors to

February 15, 1861, it served as a bodyguard for Lincoln when he stopped in Cleveland on his way to his inauguration as President. A drive to raise money to send the Grays to Washington for Garfield's inauguration got off to a good start when Garfield's friend Dan P. Eels contributed one thousand dollars. The First Cleveland Troop, organized in 1877, also became a unit in the National Guard. As a ceremonial troop it was associated with a number of presidents, including Hayes, Garfield and McKinley.

[87]In accordance with custom the Senate met in special session at the beginning of a new administration to vote on presidential nominations. The Senate also had on its agenda pending treaties with China and Japan.

the inauguration, that I went to the East room four or five times during the day to meet delegations. The core of these crowds is the indurated office seeker who pursues his prey with the grip of death. This page is quite insufficient for any adequate summary of the groups and wants which the day brought to me.

TUESDAY, 8.   The fountains of the population seem to have over-flowed and Washington is inundated. It is said that no day in 12 years has witnessed such a jam of callers at each Executive Dep't. Again and again we were compelled to shut the doors, with the files of people extending to the avenue. I received several thousand in the East room. This was the easiest part of the day's work, for these callers were pleasant kind people who wished to see me and shake hands, before going home. But the Spartan band of disciplined office hunters who drew paper on me as highway men draw pistols were the men with whom I had to wrestle like a Greek, and the night brings me great weariness.

WEDNESDAY, 9.   This day, though very rainy and dreary without, was crowded with a whirl of people, who were emergent and strenuous beyond anything yet. I kept my temper, without flaw, except once, when a southern Republican demanded to know whether it was to be a stalwart administration, whether Democrats were to be preferred, etc. I told him I declined to be lectured or to have my Republicanism questioned, and he left rather sooner than he intended to. Neither yesterday nor today have I stepped out of the house, but have played a game or two of billiards in the basement.

THURSDAY, 10.   McCook, Miller and Hiscock breakfasted with us, and then discussed N.Y. affairs. The crowd today was less ceremonial and more fiercely place hunting than on any previous day. I wrestled with them until one when I shut the doors, and went to lunch. Lincoln came while we were at lunch, and joined us. Soon after, he took the oath of office in the Library. At two P.M. in company with the old and new Cabinets, we received the Diplomatic Corps in the East room. For a formality, it was very pleasant. Crete grows up to every new emergency with fine tact and faultless taste. At 3.30 we (she and I) took a long drive, and rested. Returning, played billiards with Jimmy until dinner.

Senators Hoar and Dawes dined with us. Many callers in the evening. Retired at 11.

FRIDAY, 11.   Senator Dawes and Hoar breakfasted with us and I spent half an hour with them on the situation in N.Y. At half-past ten the rush of callers commenced, and was checked only by the meeting of the Cabinet at 12. I stated to the full Cabinet that it was vital to our harmony that the head of a Department should not intermeddle with other Departments. If any suggestion was to be made across the lines of Departments it should be to me. Settled the question of re-issue of withdrawn bank notes, adversely to the banks.[88] Set next Cabinet day for discussing extra session.

Appointed Maj. Powell Geologist *vice* Clarence King. Drove with Crete from 3 1/2 to 5 1/2 P.M. Soldiers' Home. At eight P.M. held a reception to the officers of the army and navy. We stood in the blue room and allowed the other rooms on that floor, and the conservatory, to be used as a promenade. The array was brilliant. The cabinet developes fine social qualities. Mrs. Lincoln has arrived. Retired at 10.30.

SATURDAY, 12.   I made perhaps twenty-five appointments, mostly

---

[88]In the period February 19–March 11, various national banks deposited in the United States Treasury about $18,000,000 of legal tenders (greenbacks) to retire that amount of their circulating notes, and received from the Treasury government bonds which had secured that amount. When one of those banks sought to redeposit the bonds it had received in return for the greenbacks it had deposited, the secretary of the treasury had to make a ruling. That ruling, announced on the afternoon of March 11, disallowed the recovery of greenbacks in that manner, but did permit the banks to deposit the identical bonds withdrawn as security for circulating bank notes. The effect of the ruling was to require banks desiring to increase circulation to follow the established practice of depositing bonds in the Treasury as security for new circulating bank notes. It should be added, however, that the banks benefited from the decision permitting them to redeposit the identical bonds withdrawn, for most of those securities, as the *New York Times* (March 12) observed, "were 5 per cent funded bonds . . . redeemable after May 1." In redeeming those bonds, the *Times* explained, the law required "that the highest numbers be first called for payment. Had the banks been required to obtain new bonds for deposit the bonds thus obtained would have been the first called for payment, which would have reduced to some degree their value."

Postmasters. The crowd of callers was very great. The Senate not being in session made the Senatorial calls more than usually numerous. At four P.M. to 6 we held the first general reception, a very large attendance. Several friends dined with us, and special calls for business and congratulations kept us up until after eleven. Retired at 11.30 very weary.

SUNDAY, 13.   Wakened at 6 and sought [caught?] but little sleep afterwards. Breakfasted with the family, Gov. Foster and Carl Schurz. A long talk with the latter, who seems to feel well about our start. Mother, Crete and I went to Church—another crowd outside and in. On my return stopped at Gen. Schenck's, who is quite ill. Home at 1.30 and found a dispatch from St. Petersburg informing me of the assassination of the Czar at 3.30 P.M. St. Petersburg time. Ordered a dispatch of condolence.[89] Many calls in the evening. I should have added that I took a long drive with Blaine in the afternoon, and discussed *varia.* Evarts called and talked over Monetary Conference.[90] Retired at 10.30.

MONDAY, 14.   Sent in a great many nominations of Postmasters. Also Stanley Matthews for the Supreme Court, and Don A. Pardee for the 5th Circuit. Cut off the stream of callers at three 30, and drove with Crete to the book store to buy school books for the children, and thence to the Congressional library to get books

[89]Secretary of State James G. Blaine sent the following dispatch to the U.S. minister to Russia: "Express to Minister of Foreign Affairs the sentiments of sorrow with which the President and the people of the United States have heard of the terrible crime of which the Emperor has been the victim, and their profound sympathy with the imperial family and the Russian people in their great affliction."

[90]In March, 1880, the governments of France and the United States invited other governments to participate in a conference in Paris "to consider and adopt for presentation to the governments so represented for their acceptance a plan and system for the establishment by international convention of the use of gold and silver as bi-metallic money at a fixed relative value between those two metals." After a number of meetings between April 19 and July 8, 1881, the conference adjourned to April 12, 1882. Although the British delegates at the conference favored the double standard, their government was not prepared at that time to adopt it. On his return from Paris in July, 1881, Timothy Howe, a member of the United States delegation, made this comment: "The attitude of Great Britain was the principal obstacle we had to contend with." See April 3, 1881.

for Crete on House decoration. She is to study up the repairs of the Executive Mansion. Home via Smithsonian and Monument.

I must resist a very strong tendency to be dejected and unhappy at the prospect which is offered by the work before me. The contest between personal interests is very hateful to me. I love to deal with doctrines and events. The contests of men about men I greatly dislike. Perhaps I shall feel better by and by. I would rather have Mahone's chance of today than my work.[91]

TUESDAY, 15. The event of yesterday—the declaration of Senator Mahone that he would not act with the Southern Bourbons —may be the open door to larger consequences in the South. The moral power of the movement is somewhat marred by the apparent advantages to him and to the Republicans which his

[91]Virginia emerged from the Civil War with a large debt and a greatly reduced tax-paying capacity. Yet the post-war governments, determined to uphold the state's fiscal integrity, took the position that the debt, with its interest, must be paid, and adopted funding legislation to accomplish that purpose. By 1874 the state was bankrupt and her debt was increasing at a rate of one million dollars a year. This financial dilemma produced a movement whose members called for a readjustment of the debt. In 1879, William Mahone, a leader of the movement, was elected to the United States Senate by a legislature comprised mostly of Readjusters. Although Mahone had not supported Garfield in 1880, he realized that to defeat the Bourbon Democracy in the state election of 1881, the Readjusters would need the help of Virginia Republicans and the friendly cooperation of the national Republican party. Mahone got a remarkable chance to aid his cause soon after the Senate convened in March, 1881, for that body had 37 Republicans, 37 Democrats, one Independent who had announced his intention to vote with the Democrats, and Mahone, who had not said how he would vote. Since the Republican Vice President could cast a tie-breaking vote, Mahone would determine which party would organize the Senate. On March 14, in a dramatic exchange with Democratic Senator Benjamin H. Hill of Georgia, who spoke for the purpose of "smoking out" the Virginian, Mahone declared that he was not elected to the Senate by the national Democratic party, would not be run by the Democratic caucus, but would vote to represent the people of Virginia and not "that Bourbonism which has done so much injury to my section of the country." He said in effect that he would vote with the Republicans, which he subsequently did, but only after a prolonged deadlock in the Senate, during which he used his position to secure from them important concessions (see n. 92). The *Washington Star* (March 14) reported that George Gorham had "piloted General Mahone in and out" of the White House that day.

affilliation brings. The situation makes my policy towards the Republicans of Va. unusually difficult.[92] Cabinet meeting at 12. Called attention to the recent habit of Cabinets allowing substance of proceedings to go into papers. After meeting spent half an hour with the Sec'y of the Treasury and P.M. General in making appointments. Rode with Crete from 3.45 to 5, then with Blaine until 6.10. Many callers in the evening—200 Wisconsin people in one party. Retired at 10.30 after reading a letter from Rose which greatly distresses me.[93]

WEDNESDAY, 16. Got on fairly well through the day, with the usual rush; the numbers smaller, but the appetite for office apparently keener. It will cost me some struggle to keep from despising the office seeker. Worked off many minor appointments, and some of importance.

Drove out as usual, and got a little rest; but I do not take kindly to this sort of life. Determined to retire at 10, when Gen. Logan came and showed me the intensity of the contest in Ills. over Long Jones for Marshall.[94] When he left, I went to bed by [but]

[92]These observations reveal Garfield's awareness of the implications of the balance of power held by Mahone, who had made clear that he wanted Republican "recognition" in return for his vote. Garfield was prepared to make certain concessions, but he opposed a Republican-Readjuster alliance which would taint "our party with the flavor of repudiation," and though he was prepared to remove Bourbon Democrats from offices in Virginia, he was unwilling to remove Republicans to make room for Mahone men.

[93]Upset because Garfield, upon assuming the Presidency, had not appointed him his private secretary, George U. Rose (see Vol. II, p. 40, n. 144) wrote (March 14) emotionally of their long relationship and of his unfailing loyalty and devotion, notwithstanding the modest wages Garfield had paid him. He said that he had believed, despite warnings from friends, that Garfield would keep his promises to help him and to improve his pay if he were ever in a position to do so. "I am indignant. I am hurt," Rose declared, closing his letter with these lines: "God grant that your administration may be a glorious success. I am of small account compared to that, and shall quietly but with a broken spirit, plod along."

[94]Alfred M. ("Long") Jones was recommended by Logan for the position of U.S. marshal for the northern district of Illinois to put an end to a bitter contest for that office between the incumbent, Jesse S. Hildrup, and his chief deputy, John Stilwell. Garfield appointed Jones, who served, 1881–84. In 1881 Jones and three other men, James W. Scott, Frank W. Palmer and Daniel Shepard, founded the

could not sleep until far past midnight. More sense of annoyance and worry than I have yet experience[d]. Vexed with the thought that I am wholly unfit for this sort of work.

It was probably two hours past midnight before I slept.

THURSDAY, 17. The morning drizzles without and is gloomy within. Mr. Monroe and Cousin Ellis Ballou took breakfast with us. I went to my work jaded by the restless hours [?] of last night. Had a long tussel with the Ills. questions. After lunch, reviewed the Irish Societies which march[ed] through the port-cochere, celebrating St. Patrick's day. At eight and a half, gave a reception in the blue parlor to the Supreme Court and members of the Senate and House, and their families. It was a very pleasant occasion, not too crowded for comfort.

Retired at 10.30 but could not sleep. At half an hour past midnight, arose and walked vigorously for half an hour, and applied the flesh brush.

FRIDAY, 18. Awoke at 6 A.M., having slept not quite five hours. This must be changed, if I know any way to change it. Walked with Crete to the stables before breakfast and looked at the new Baltimore cow. Soon after breakfast the crowd came. Gen. Logan, at the end of a long conference, agreed to withdraw Jones from the candidacy for the Marshalship. Senator Rogers of Buffalo and Edwards Pierrepont of N.Y. took lunch with us. Spent some time with each, on N.Y. politics. At 3.30 drove with Crete to Arlington, returning at 5.45.

Many ladies and gentlemen called during the evening. Crete has taken Tuesday and Friday evening, rather than allow herself to be called on every evening.

Business kept me at work until 10.45.

SATURDAY, 19. Beginning immediately after breakfast, I was kept constantly engaged until ten at night, with emergent people. Some on matters of great importance and others merely hungry.

Finding that Sec'y Blaine was confined to his house by illness,

---

Chicago Herald to support Logan Republicanism, but the paper encountered financial difficulty and Jones sold out in 1883. He was chairman of the Illinois Republican Committee in 1880.

I drove over to see him, in reference to the part we should take in the Czar's funeral. After consultation it seemed best to send no special ambassador, but to write a strong dispatch of sympathy and condolence, making allusion to our own loss in the death of Lincoln. A long call from Senator Logan and Col. Jones of Chicago. Sec'y Windom called with Mr. Norvel [Norvell][95] of N.Y. to discuss the question of funding the debt and the necessity or not of an extra session.

SUNDAY, 20.   Attended church with Mother and Crete. The usual crowd outside and in. It gives me a sorry view of human nature, to see a little church filled to double its usual attendance by the accident of one of its frequenters having been elected to a high office. A few friends dropped in during the afternoon. At 3 Senator Conkling called, and spent 2 1/2 hours reviewing the N.Y. situation. I adopted many of his suggestions; but told him I must recognize some of the men who supported me at Chicago. He wanted me to give them foreign appointments. I said they did not deserve exile, but rather a place in the affairs of their own state.

I will go as far as I can to keep the peace; but I will not abandon the N.Y. protestants.

MONDAY, 21.   Made a new rule, that I would see only members of the government and Congress until 12, then the general public until one.

This gave me some relief from the crowd of last week. But still the pressure is great, and will be until the appointments are sent in. Senators Plumb and Ingalls took lunch with us.

TUESDAY, 22.   About noon, sent in a large number of appointment[s], including most of the N.Y. vacancies.[96] Cabinet at 12.

[95]Caleb C. Norvell (1813–1891) was associated with the *New York Commercial Advertiser,* a Republican paper, of which Hugh Hastings was editor. A special dispatch from Washington on the President and the finances and the position on financial questions of Treasury officials appeared on the front page of the *Commercial Advertiser* on March 21.

[96]Garfield sent to the Senate the names of fifteen men whom he nominated to office and of two army officers whom he nominated to higher rank. Seven nominations were for positions in New York State. Two of them were postmasterships.

Two hours was spent in discussing the propriety and necessity of an extra session. No conclusion reached.

Mother is quite ill and very weak. I fear she may not recover. Two letters of hers to her Cousin, Mrs. Flint, appeared this morning in the papers, greatly to the annoyance of us all.[97]

In the evening, while we were at dinner, Blaine came, and expressed great distress at the N.Y. appointments. In one of them, I think I have made a mistake, and will try to correct it. Many called in the evening. At 8.30 walked with Swaim to Senator Sherman's and thence to Sec'y Windom's, and talked over extra session. At 10.30 Blaine came, and stayed until near 12.

WEDNESDAY, 23. Foreseeing the difficulties which attend the affairs of N.Y. and determined not to be classed as the friend of one faction only, I carried out a plan which I discussed with Judge Folger when he was in Mentor, and which he approved. Instead of waiting for the long two years' contest over the N.Y. Collectorship, which will attend the remainder of Gen. Merritt's[98]

The other five New York nominations were reappointments of Conkling supporters whose terms in offices to which they had been appointed by President Grant had recently expired. The men and the offices to which they were being named were: John Tyler, collector of customs for the district of Buffalo Creek; Asa W. Tenney, U.S. attorney for the eastern district of New York; Stewart L. Woodford, U.S. attorney for the southern district of New York; Clinton D. McDougall, U.S. marshal for the northern district of New York, and Lewis F. Payn, U.S. marshal for the southern district of New York.

[97]In letters to her cousin Mary Flint (the first was written on September 17, 1880, at Mentor, and the second on March 7, 1881, at the White House), Eliza recalled their girlhood association, commented innocuously about longtime mutual friends and relatives, and spoke of Garfield's career and of her pride in him. The Garfields were probably more annoyed by the release of the letters for public consumption than by what they contained.

[98]Edwin Atkins Merritt (1828–1916), a native of Vermont who settled in St. Lawrence County, New York, in 1841, was a Union officer in the Civil War, 1861–64, quartermaster general of the state of New York, 1865–69, naval officer of the port of New York, 1869–70, surveyor of the port of New York, 1877–78, collector of the port of New York, 1878–81 (he replaced Chester A. Arthur), and consul general at London, 1881–85. He was for several years a trustee of St. Lawrence University.

term, I appointed Merritt Consul General to London, and Judge Robertson Collector of N.Y. This brings the contest to an early close, and fully recognizes the minority element. The change of Badeau[99] from London to Copenhagen may not be pleasing to Gen. Grant; but the transfer of Kramer [Cramer][100] to Switzerland will be.

The sensation produced by the above nomination was very great but I think the Senate will approve. I nominate[d] Lew Wallace for Paraguay and Gen. Sheldon for New Mexico.

THURSDAY, 24.   A large number of minor nominations were sent in today and a great many people were seen. Secretaries Windom, James, Lincoln and Blaine came during the day. I closed the doors at one P.M. and did not see the general public after that hour. At four P.M. Gen. Swaim, Crete and I drove to the Soldiers' Home and examined the house in which the President and his family spend the summer. Dinner at six, Gen. Swaim with us, after which played billiards an hour, received a few business calls, and then wrote a summary of the arguments for an[d] against the extra session. At Cabinet tomorrow will decide against it. Went into Hal's room and heard him play *Fra Diavalo.* Retired at eleven.

FRIDAY, 25.   The unanimous resolution of the N.Y. Senate yester-

[99]Adam Badeau (1831–1895), a native of New York, served on the staffs of three Union generals: W. T. Sherman, 1861–62, Q. A. Gillmore, 1862–64, and U. S. Grant, 1864–69. He was secretary of the U.S. legation at London, 1869–70, and consul general at London, 1870–81. Grant wrote to Garfield (March 16) that Badeau wished to be retained at his post in London or be made naval officer of the port of New York. Garfield appointed him chargé d'affaires at Copenhagen, but withdrew his name at Badeau's request. Badeau was the author of *Military History of Ulysses S. Grant,* 3 vols. (1868, 1881), and *Grant in Peace* (1887).

[100]Michael Cramer (1835–1898), a native of Switzerland, was brought as a boy to the United States, where he graduated at Wesleyan University in 1859, and became a Methodist minister. In 1863 while a pastor of a church in Cincinnati, he married Mary Frances Grant, sister of Ulysses S. Grant. He was U.S. consul at Leipzig, 1867–71, minister to Denmark, 1871–81, and minister resident and consul-general in Switzerland (to which he had asked, for reasons of health, to be assigned), 1881–85. He was the author of *Conversations and Unpublished Letters of Ulysses S. Grant* (1897).

day, favoring the nomination and confirmation of Judge Robertson, has given new strength to the position I have taken in
reference to N.Y. affairs, although I am confident, that there will
be a severe contest growing out [of] the Custom house appointment. Cabinet meeting at noon. Blaine ill and absent. At 3 P.M.
James and MacVeagh came for a confidential talk. James protested against the appointment of Robertson, and said he was
regretfully compelled to resign in order to make his friends
understand that he was not a party to the appointment. Mac-
Veagh considered my appointment of Chandler as compelling his
resignation after what he had formerly said to me against it. I
gave them both to understand that I had meant no discourtesey,
but had intended to use my own discretion. At 8 1/2 talked with
Chandler. An appointment for Vice President, Conkling and
Platt but they failed to come.[101] Crete had many callers. Sheldon
left for Ohio. Mrs. S. remains.

SATURDAY, 26. After mature deliberation and consideration of
the arguments on both sides, I decided against calling an extra
session of Congress, preferring the certainties of partial refunding to the uncertainties of the session. Lincoln called on Mac-
Veagh and found him determined to resign if Chandler is made
Solicitor General. I called on Blaine, who is in bed with inflam-

[101]After the nomination of William H. Robertson reached the Senate, Conkling
urged James to call on Garfield about the matter, and to discuss it first with Wayne
MacVeagh, who was himself upset over the President's appointment of William
E. Chandler, without MacVeagh's approval, to the office of solicitor general in the
Justice Department. After James met with MacVeagh, both men went to the White
House. Garfield dissuaded them from resigning, and told them to have Conkling
call in the evening, when the cabinet would be present, to try and settle the
Robertson matter. James and MacVeagh found Conkling in his room with Platt,
who joined the two cabinet members in urging Conkling to call on Garfield.
According to James, Conkling was about to consent when he received from
Governor Cornell of New York a telegram advising him to abandon his opposition to the Robertson appointment for the reason that too few people in the state
supported it. "Angry, Conkling threw down the telegram and refused to budge,
saying that he was no place hunter." See Leech and Brown, *The Garfield Orbit*, pp.
230–231.

matory rheumatism, and he agreed to have Chandler decline, after he is confirmed. In this way I hope to tide over a catastrophe. I do not know that I shall ever become reconciled to this office. I see few signs that I shall. The prospect is a long struggle with personal wishes, and a painful series [?] of deciding between men. In some way the civil service must be regulated by law, or the President can never devote his time to administration. If I am right in my plan of adjusting N.Y. affairs, I may conquer a peace. Retired at 10.25 after seeing many callers.

SUNDAY, 27.   Attended church with Crete only. Mother has been quite ill for some days, and was not able to go. On our return we called at Blaine's half an hour. He is still in bed with rheumatism.

Probably I have made a mistake in the Buffalo Collectorship, for since Tyler's[102] name went to the Senate, Windom has found a report (made against his moral character) of a very serious kind. The appointment of Robertson is likely to be the *casus belli.* Senator Allison was here, and gave me the substance of a long interview with Senator Conkling. It appears that the gravamen of my offense was that I did not consult him about Robertson's appointment.

The President is authorized to nominate, and did so. A senator considers it a personal affront that he was not previously told of the purpose. I stand joyfully on that issue—let who will, fight me.

MONDAY, 28.   Senator Platt called, and we had a full conversation on the N.Y. appointments. I see no mistake in what I have done in re Robertson, unless it be in not having talked with the two

---

[102]John Tyler was appointed collector of customs for the district of Buffalo at the end of Grant's administration. His four year term having expired on March 2, 1881, Garfield reappointed him on March 22 on Senator Conkling's recommendation. Subsequently Garfield received numerous objections to the nomination. On May 5 (see entry for that date) Garfield withdrew from the Senate the nominations of five New Yorkers recommended by Conkling, Tyler's among them. After Garfield's victory over Conkling, he resubmitted the nominations of three of the five New Yorkers; Tyler's was not among them. As Tyler's successor Garfield named Charles A. Gould—to the great distress of Blaine.

senators beforehand. But that would have made no difference in the result. I sent in Dr. Craig[103] for P.M. at Albany. The day was full as usual of calls and demands; but the crowd is thinning out a little. Edw. Cowles and Dr. Streator of Cleveland were here. In the evening Judge Strong called to express the hope that there was no truth in the N.Y. story that Robertson was to be withdrawn. He highly approved the nomination. Senator Dorsey called, and said I had made a mistake in nominating Tyler for Buffalo. I retired at eleven o'clock.

TUESDAY, 29. I sent in another batch of minor appointments. Saw the usual though perhaps somewhat lessened crowd, and at noon met the Cabinet. The meeting was devoted mainly to refunding. It was agreed that the Sec'y of the Treasury and the Att'y Gen'l should go to N.Y. soon, and consult with bankers and brokers, and lay the result of their consultations before the Cabinet a week from today. The Senate has now spent nearly a week in a struggle to change its officers. I doubt if they can succeed the parties being equally balanced.

At 3.45 rode out with Sec'y Windom, and had a pleasant visit [of] two hours. In the evening saw Sec'y Kirkwood and the Att'y Gen. on business, and spent some time with Crete's visitors in the parlors. Billiards with Swaim till 10.30.

WEDNESDAY, 30. Drizzle rain and snow, with lucid intervals of sunshine. After I got started into the work of seeing people, there was no let up except for lunch, until six in the evening. Sec'ys Windom and McVeagh came before leaving for N.Y. to negotiate with bankers and report. James came on P.O. business and for a leave of absence, Blaine and Evarts in reference to the silver conference, and Schurz for a general visit.

In the evening played billiards with Swaim and Rockwell. I have had the billiard room in the basement fitted up so as to have a chance for exercise. Some servant has leaked about the callers here, for Mr. Conkling is reported to have said that Mr. Blaine called at the White House at 10 P.M. The next leaker leaves. Bed 11.30.

[103]William H. Craig was postmaster in Albany, New York, 1877–85.

THURSDAY, 31. Late last evening I wrote to Sec. Windom, urging him to keep in view a popular loan and not to be diverted from it.[104] This morning I wrote him to see Gen. Merritt and get from him a letter expressing his willingness to accept the London Consulate so as to make the fight easier in the Senate. The usual rush of callers, though perhaps a little diminished in numbers. I think the current of fight is setting in my favor in the N.Y. matter. The legislature at Albany has not rescinded the resolution in favor of Robertson and I think will not do so. Sheldon returned and brings good news from Ohio. Retired at 10.30.

April

FRIDAY, 1. Gave an audience to the retiring and new minister from Chili.[105] Cabinet meeting at 12—only four members present, Windom, MacVeagh and James being absent in N.Y. After regular business was over, I stated to the members present the condition of the N.Y. fight, and received their generous support of my position.

At 2 P.M. Geo. W. Jones of the *Times* called and talked over N.Y. affairs. He talks like a supported [supporter], but write[s] *tout au contraire.* Pardee at dinner. Billiards with him and Swaim and Rockwell. In the evening spent some time in the parlor with Crete's company. There are some evidences that Conkling is being disturbed by rumors that Cornell is not standing by him, and that Platt agreed, at Albany when he was elected Senator, to help Robertson if nominated.

[104]Garfield explained to Windom that a popular loan would eliminate "all chance of encountering the popular prejudice which syndicates encounter, and would give your administration of the Treasury a most handsome send-off. If some of the leading capitalists would help the movement at the start, the popular tide would be likely to set in with additional strength. Probably the bankers and brokers may try to discourage this view, but if they see it is to be vigorously tried they may see that it is safest to join it."

[105]Señor Don Marcial Martinez succeeded Señor Don Francisco Solona Asta-Buruaga as Chile's minister to the United States.

SATURDAY, 2. I commenced, in bed, and finished half an hour after breakfast Mrs. Burnett's new novel *Louisiana,* [106] a bright and tender little book full of pathos. Having received, last night, pretty full details of Mr. Conkling's plan of attack upon my nomination of Robertson, I have taken occasion, during the day, to let several senators know that the vote on R.'s confirmation was a test of friendship or hostility to the administration; and I find a good deal of strong and hearty support among senators who have long be[en] restive under the arrogant domination of the N.Y. Senator. If he assails me, he will find it no rosewater war. We gave a dinner to Dr. Hopkins of Williams College. Present, his wife, Judge Nott and Doctor's daughter, Senators Hoar and Dawes and their wives, and Dr. Hawkes. A very pleasant party and a good dinner *sine vino.* I drew the party into a discussion of the female element in the Catholic worship and its lack in Protestant churches. I retired at midnight.

SUNDAY, 3. Arose at seven and wrote my journal of yesterday in the little dressing room off our chamber. The long light shadows are traced upon the lawn like the outlines of a picture. It is almost the first time I have been able to look at the earth or sky since I came here.

Did not attend church today. Mollie was ill and Crete stayed with her. At three P.M. had a long ride with Senator Sherman, and reviewed the political situation. He agrees to take charge of the fight in the Senate on the N.Y. nomination of Collector. Thinks we can confirm Robertson. Home at 5.15. Senator Howe and S. D. Horton [107] dined with us at six. They sail in a few days for Europe to attend the Monetary Conference. I don't expect much to result from it. England is in the way. H. E. Knox of N.Y.

[106] Frances Hodgson Burnett, *Louisiana* (1880).

[107] Samuel Dana Horton (1844–1895), a native of Ohio and the son of Valentine B. Horton, graduated at Harvard University, 1864, and the Harvard Law School, 1868. After studying law in Berlin, he was admitted to the bar and practiced in Ohio until 1885. From 1875 he was a leading advocate of bimetallism, writing many treatises on the subject. He was secretary of the International Monetary Conference in Paris, 1878. Garfield appointed him a delegate to the second Paris Monetary Conference, 1881.

came and gave me the situation of the Robertson fight there. Read Gilmore's harmony of the Gospels.[108]

MONDAY, 4. Republican caucus of Senators resolved to hold on until Mahone should be satisfied. This will continue the deadlock indefinitely. I sent in no appointments today, preferring to hear what the Senate will do. Rode out with Crete at 4 P.M., after having Bateman of Ohio at lunch. Rockwell took dinner with us. The P.M. General returned from N.Y. this morning, Windom and MacVeagh this evening. The last two called at half-past seven and remained two hours. The visit to the bankers has been pleasant and instructive, and results in the belief that we can sell the remaining four per cent bonds by popular sale; also, that we can get in the 6's and 5's partly by purchase and partly by our agreement with their holders to take three and a half per cent interest. If this last could prevail it would be a very brilliant feat of financiering. Retired at 11 P.M.

TUESDAY, 5. Cabinet meeting for two hours, having a full discussion of the funding scheme mentioned yesterday. The prospects for its success are good. Directed the Sec'y of the Treasury to discuss the plan with several experts of both parties and report to me as soon as possible. Crete had a large company of visitors in the evening to whom I gave some time.

Senator Platt called at 8.30 and discussed the N.Y. situation. He wants me to withdraw all the N.Y. nominations, and then appoint Robertson in place of Woodford to the District Att'y-ship. I refused to take the initiative or make any suggestion to change to Robertson. I should add that Hale and Frye were here this morning—the latter thinks Conkling makes a very strong case and wishes Robertson would withdraw.

Retired at 11 P.M.

---

[108]Reference is to James R. Gilmore and Lyman Abbott, *The Gospel History: Being a Complete Connected Account of the Life of Our Lord, Woven from the Text of the Four Evangelists* . . . (1881). The phrase "harmony of the Gospels" is used to describe such an arrangement of the first four books of the New Testament. Gilmore makes this statement in the preface: "It may be said in brief that the writer edited the book in manuscript and Dr. Abbott re-edited it in proof-sheets. . . ."

WEDNESDAY, 6. The rush of visitors was greater today than usual. I sent in some nominations of marshalls [marshals] and postmasters. In the evening Gen. and Mrs. Logan dined with us, and after dinner, I had a long conversation with the General *de rebus certaminis inter Senatores meque* [about certain matters between the Senators and me]. Conkling alleges that Robertson is his bitter personal enemy.

I summed up the case in reply to allegation. 1. The Robertson appointment is mine not another's. 2. The office is national, not local. 3. Having given all the other places to Conkling's friends, he is neither magnanimous nor just, in opposing this one friend of mine. 4. He has raised a question of veracity with me and it shall be tried—by the Senate. Senator Ferry and Representative Pound called. The only exercise I had today was billiards and casino. Retired at 11 P.M.

THURSDAY, 7. Among the callers today was Judge Tourgee,[109] author of *A Fool's Errand,* who convinced me I had made a mistake in sending in Gov. Holden[110] for Post Master. I with-

---

[109]Albion W. Tourgée (1838–1905), a native of Ohio and a student at the University of Rochester at the outbreak of the Civil War, served in the Union army, was admitted to the bar, 1864, and in 1865 moved to North Carolina with his wife, where they lived until 1879. Editor, writer, lawyer, and Republican politician, he became a well known figure in the state; he was a judge of the superior court, 1868–74. In 1881 he bought a country home in western New York, although it was several years before the family settled there. He campaigned widely for Garfield in 1880, and would no doubt have been rewarded by an appointment to office had the President lived. He was consul at Bordeaux, 1897–1905. Tourgée was a foe of racial segregation and an enthusiastic advocate of federal aid to education, which he considered basic to progress in the South; his educational views were well known and may have been influential in moulding the views of Garfield, 1880–81. Today his fame rests chiefly on two of his novels —*A Fool's Errand by One of the Fools* (1879) and *Bricks Without Straw* (1880). These books and three of his short stories "constitute," according to his most recent biographer, "the invaluable testament of a carpetbagger and provide a panoramic view and an astute analysis of the Reconstruction South." See Otto H. Olsen, *Carpetbagger's Crusade: the Life of Albion Winegar Tourgée* (1965).

[110]William W. Holden, journalist and politician, was a native of North Carolina who wrote for the *Raleigh Star,* 1837–43, and owned and edited the *Raleigh Standard,* 1843–68. He was provisional governor of North Carolina, 1865, and governor, 1868–71. Impeached in 1870 for high crimes and misdemeanors, he

drew it, and sent in a name he recommended—Mr. Nichols.[111] The Judge was greatly moved. W. M. A. [W. A. M.] Grier[112] took lunch with us. He is the Pa. delegate to Chicago who cast the first lone vote for me. In the afternoon Crete and I drove out to the Soldiers' Home. On the way, stopped at our house cor[ner] 13th and I. The dear old nest is deserted now. It almost made me homesick to leave it, or rather to see it. At nine P.M. Mr. and Mrs. Sheldon and Miss [Josie] Mason left for Cleveland. They have been with us since we came, and have been very pleasant guests.

Retired at eleven.

FRIDAY, 8.   At breakfast we had only our own family, the first time this has happened at any meal for 15 months. After breakfast, Harry and I drove to Morrison's bookstore, where I bought

---

was convicted and dismissed from office in 1871. Following a move to Washington, D.C., where he was for a time editor of the *National Republican,* he returned home and was postmaster of Raleigh, 1873–81. See Vol. III, pp. 215–216, n. 18.

111John Nichols (1834–1917), a native of North Carolina, was trained as a printer and engaged in the printing and publishing business for a time. He was principal of the North Carolina Institute for the Deaf and Dumb and Blind, 1873–77, revenue stamp agent in Durham, 1879–81, postmaster of Raleigh, 1881–85, an Independent member of the U.S. House of Representatives, 1887–89, an employee of the Treasury Department, 1889–93, and U.S. commissioner for the eastern district of North Carolina, 1897 to his death.

112William A. M. Grier was a banker in Hazelton, Pennsylvania, and the president of a textile manufacturing company whose office was in New York City; he was the nephew of Robert C. Grier (1794–1870), associate justice of the U.S. Supreme Court, 1846–70. As an anti-Grant delegate to the Republican National Convention in 1880, he voted for Garfield on the second ballot and on all but five of the succeeding ballots. His votes for Garfield were prompted by Wharton Barker and were conceived as a means of keeping the name of Garfield, who had not been placed in nomination, before the convention. Grier's nomination as third assistant postmaster general was an embarrassment both to him and to Garfield. The President nominated him after having been assured by Attorney General MacVeagh (also a Pennsylvanian) that he would accept the post. According to Grier, he never had any intention of accepting it and had so informed MacVeagh before the nomination was made. The nomination was withdrawn from the Senate on May 9. Following a request by Grier on June 20 for an interview at Elberon, New Jersey, where Garfield was vacationing, Garfield agreed to meet with him on June 22. Nothing has been found concerning the reason for the meeting.

Kent's *Commentaries*[113] for him. He wants to begin the study of law. I do not expect him to do much now, but will let him try. In the evening, he came to me with the names of the writers on International law which are mentioned in the first chapter, desiring to know their pronunciation. I found he had well comprehended the chapter. Cabinet meeting two hours. Blaine read first draft of instructions to the Monetary Commissioners. Refunding of 6 per cents agreed to.

Billiards in the afternoon. Gen. Swaim and Judge Pardee dined with us. In the evening assisted Crete to receive her friends in the parlor. Retire 10.30.

SATURDAY, 9. The Senate not having been in session since Thursday, I have had less to do in the way of Senatorial calls, because many of them have left the city. In the afternoon, Crete and I drove out, taking Abram to his music lesson (he is just beginning the piano) and thence went to the Congressional Library—or as Bryant preferred, Library of Congress—to get some books and to ask Mr. Spofford to look into the history of the White House and its contents of which very little seems to be known. We went through the House of Representatives wing, and I felt more regret that [than] I expected, at being separated from my old associations at the Capitol. In the evening the P.M. Gen. and Special Agent Lockwood [Woodward][114] came and reported what they had discovered concerning the star contract service.

---

[113]James Kent, *Commentaries on American Law,* 4 vols. (1826–1830).

[114]P. H. Woodward was an employee of the Post Office Department, 1865–76; as chief special agent he was instrumental in putting a stop to one type of fraudulent bidding on star route contracts. In March, 1881, Postmaster General James, knowing Woodward as "a man of character and integrity," asked him to act as his confidential agent in the star route investigations, and appointed him postal inspector. On the evening of April 9 Woodward showed James a comparative tabulation of "the most corruptly manipulated routes." James, "amazed at the revelation," hurried Woodward to the White House, where the President "shared in the astonishment of the Postmaster General," and instructed the men to cut the ulcer out no matter whom it hurt. See *House Miscellaneous Reports,* No. 2165, Part 2, 48 Cong., 1 Sess. (Serial 2234), "Testimony Relating to the Star-Route Cases," pp. 2–4, 333–335. Woodward is the author of *Guarding the Mails; or, the Secret Service of the Post Office Department* (1876).

Great frauds have been practiced, and I will clear out the Contract office.

SUNDAY, 10.   Spring has made more decisive advances today than before. Indeed it is the first really spring-like day we have had. Crete, Mother and I attended Church. After lunch, they and the children drove out; Swaim and I took a long walk. During the day Crete and I read up the genealogy of the Mason family, and found this the line—1. Maj. John Mason of Pequot fame, 2. Capt. Jno. Mason, 3. John Mason, 4. Peleg Sanford Mason, 5. Elijah Mason, 6. Arabella [Mason], 7. Lucretia Rudolph. Senator Cameron came at 8 and we had a long conference. Later Maj. Bundy and J. B. Bowman,[115] and still later Swaim.

Read the first few chapters of *Ben Hur* by Lew Wallace.[116] Retired at eleven.

MONDAY, 11.   Not many Senators called today. The dead-lock has drizzled to a game of give-away. So many have paired and gone home, that there were but 39 senators, a bare quorum, in attendance today. At 2 P.M. Crete and I drove to the Navy Yard, in company with Sec'y and Mrs. Hunt. Spent two hours in visiting various points of interest. Saw the ammonia engine of Prof. Gamgee,[117] also the air engine of Briton

---

[115]According to the *Washington Star* (March 8) John B. Bowman had aspired to a cabinet position and was now seeking an appointment as commissioner of internal revenue. He received no appointment from Garfield.

[116]See Vol. III, pp. 383–384, n. 397.

[117]John Gamgee (1831–1894), a member of a British family distinguished for its work in veterinary science and education, had made his own substantial contributions in the field before his first visit to the United States in the late 1860's. During this visit he pursued at the request of the commissioner of agriculture an investigation of diseases in American cattle; his reports were published by the government. He was back in the United States, 1878–85. Yellow fever being epidemic in the South during the late 1870's, he investigated the problem and devised plans for a refrigerating and disinfecting ship (see n. 108, April 15, 1879), but the government did not act on its decision to construct such a ship. In 1879 he published *Yellow Fever: A Nautical Disease. Its Origins and Prevention* (Garfield's presentation copy is in the library at Lawnfield). In the spring of 1881 he received an American patent for a thermodynamic engine that would use "a liquefiable gas or vapor at low temperature as a motor fluid"; at the exhaust the gas or vapor

[Brayton],[118] which starts in full motion 15 seconds after the petroleum is lighted. Home at half-past four.

Swaim and Rockwell dined with us in the evening. Several people called, among them Gen. Le Duc and Col. John Hay, who is about to leave official life, having resigned the Ass't Sec'yship of State.

Retired at 11.

TUESDAY, 12. Our plan of refunding promises to work well. The six per cent bonds have risen from 1/2 to 3/4 of a cent in consequence of the offer to let the holders retain them at 3 1/2 per cent interest, and the 4's, [of] which we have not [now] offered the surplus to the market, have fallen as much; this shows that capitalists are buying in the sixes to prepare for the exchange. The Sec'y of the Treasury tells me he had sixteen hundred thousand of the sixes offered today for exchange.

At Cabinet the dead-lock in the Senate was discussed and it was suggested that a message should be sent calling attention to the need of confirming officers and the Chinese treaty.

WEDNESDAY, 13. The calls and appeals for office continue with-

---

would return "in great measure" to its liquid state and a new cycle would begin. Simon Newcomb declared that it might be "pronounced a chimera with as much safety and certainty" as they called perpetual motion machines by that name. The biographer of the Gamgee family, speaking of John, echoes the scientist: "Perpetual motion was a chimera he was to pursue to the end of his life." At his death *The Veterinary Record* (quoted in Ruth D'Arcy Thompson, *The Remarkable Gamgees: A Story of Achievement,* 1974) said of him: "He had as clear and practical a brain as any man and seldom proposed or started anything which was not afterwards perfected by someone else. He was twenty years in advance of his age. . . ." For his engine see *Scientific American,* Vol. 11, May 21, 1881, pp. 4477–4479.

[118]George B. Brayton (1830–1892) developed (1872) the first successful internal combustion engine in the United States; it was superseded by the more efficient Otto and Langen engine, developed in Germany and patented in the United States in 1877. "The President," reported the *National Republican* (April 12), "witnessed with much interest a trial of the launch mystery, propelled by Brayton's petroleum engine, by which she goes through the water about nine knots an hour. This engine consists of two small cylinders, one for air and the other for generating the motive power, all enclosed in a fore-and-aft box, with nothing visible above the water-line to show how she is propelled through the water, not even a smoke-stack."

out much abatement. The success of refunding is still more promising.

In the evening Crete and I dined at Att'y Gen. MacVeagh's in company with Mr. and Mrs. Blaine and Abby Dodge, Mr. and Mrs. Windom and P.M. Gen. James. A very pleasant party. Our first dinner out of the House since we came. After dinner the members of the Cabinet present had a long conference over the corruptions being disclosed in the Star Service. The situation will require the removal of several prominent officers. I shall wait a few days, for fuller knowledge of the facts. It was a pleasant release from the monotony of the White House to get out for an evening. Home at eleven. Retired soon after and read *Ben Hur* until 2 A.M. Thursday.

THURSDAY, 14. Lt. Harber is with us—on a brief leave from his ship.

Before noon, Post Master General James and the Att'y Gen., in company with a Special Agent and ex-Senator Spencer[119] [came] with further developements in reference to the Star routes. The corruption and wrong doing has been of a very gross and extensive kind. I am surprised that it could have so long escaped the notice of Pres. Hayes's Administration. Cabinet meeting 12 to 2. Question of Indian policy so far as the relation

[119]George E. Spencer (1836–1893), a native of New York State, practiced law in Iowa before the Civil War, served in the Union army (he was breveted brigadier general), and after the war practiced law in Alabama. He was a Republican member of the U.S. Senate from Alabama, 1868–79. After leaving the Senate he went to Nevada, where he had a ranch, engaged in mining, and learned something of the frauds in the star route service. He told Postmaster General James what he knew, receiving from James, he said, a pledge that information furnished by him would be "strictly confidential." He also claimed that President Garfield gave him a similar assurance. Subpoenaed as a witness in the first star route trial, he left Washington before his presence in court was required. In New York City Roscoe Conkling advised him that the subpoena was illegal; Spencer returned to Nevada. He did not appear as a witness in the star route proceedings at any time. In 1883 he was arrested for his failure to obey the subpoena; in Washington the case was dismissed on the ground that the subpoena was illegal. See *House Miscellaneous Reports,* No. 2165, Part 2, 48 Cong., 1 Sess., Serial 2234, "Testimony Relating to the Star-Route Cases," pp. 7, 13–15, and 53–65.

of appointment of agents on recommendation of churches is concerned quite fully discussed. I concluded to ask general cooperation of the churches, but not to let them control appointments. It brings sectarian strife into the government.[120] Hal and Jim went to Hampton Roads with Harber. In the evening Vice President Arthur called. Long and earnest talk on N.Y. appointments.

FRIDAY, 15.   Awoke with a dull pain near the cervical cord at the base of the brain, which, all day, gave me a feeling as if I had been struck a light blow with a hammer. The crowd was not so pressing as usual, perhaps because of Cabinet meeting. All the members present except Lincoln and Hunt.

After lunch, I took some time with *Ben Hur,* which keeps up in dignity and interest.

Received an enigmatical note from Knox, saying my interview with Robertson [Arthur] had done great good.[121] I can hardly believe, after what he [Arthur] said, that he (T.P.) can come into the cordial support of Robertson.

It being the Good Friday of the Anglican Church, the evening was comparatively quiet.

[120]In an effort to secure better federal Indian agents on reservations, President Grant inaugurated a policy of appointing agents chosen by religious denominations. This policy was not a notable success, and during the 1870's there was much discussion of transferring the Bureau of Indian Affairs to the War Department, from which it had been removed when the Interior Department was created in 1849; many believed that the use of army officers as agents would improve the Indian service. Although Garfield had concluded that it was better to leave the Bureau in the Interior Department, it is clear that he proposed to lessen church influence in the choice of agents.

[121]In a note dated April 15, written in the reception room at the White House, Henry Knox told Garfield that he and E. M. Stoughton had just left Arthur and were calling to request an appointment for Arthur that evening. The next morning Knox sent the "enigmatical note" dated April 16 to Garfield after having been present at an interview of MacVeagh with Arthur. If Knox's dates are correct, Garfield errs in respect to the dates of his interview with Arthur and the receipt of the note from Knox mentioned in this entry. The President was less sanguine than Knox; he did not believe that, in the context of New York politics as described by Arthur, Senator Platt was in a position to vote for Robertson's confirmation. The Library of Congress, *Index to the Papers of James A. Garfield,* errs in dating the second Knox note April 11.

SATURDAY, 16. The day has been a hard one. My headache has not wholly disappeared, and the crowd of callers was unusually persistent. Towards evening I got forty minutes of ride with Crete, and this was my only recreation except an hour of billiards. In the evening callers and *Ben Hur* kept me, until bed time. I should have added that yesterday Hal and Jim, and Don Rockwell, went to Fort Monroe with Lt. Harber to visit his Ship, the *Tennessee.* [122]

SUNDAY, 17. Gens. Pope and Swaim took breakfast with us. Had a pleasant visit with them concerning army matters and politics generally. At eleven Swaim, Mother, Crete and I went to Church. On our return I stopped half an hour at Gen. Schenck's, who is quite ill. In the afternoon saw a few callers, but spent most of the time with *Ben Hur.* The plot of the story is powerfully sketched and its tone is admirably sustained. I am inclined to send its author (Lew Wallace) to Constantinople, where he may draw inspiration from the modern East for future literary work.

At seven, Mollie, Crete and I went to Blaine's to tea, with their family and Gov. Jewell, and Geo. M. Robeson. Stayed until ten. A pleasant evening. Curious stories of Gen. Grant's recent visit to Cuba and Mexico.

MONDAY, 18. Breakfast at 8.15. At 9.30 Crete started for N.Y. with Col. and Mrs. Rockwell and Miss Ransom. I went with her to the Station. On my return, stopped at Dr. White['s], the chiropodist,[123] and had my corns overhauled.

Emory [Emery] Storrs of Chicago lunched with me, and we had a long talk on the political situation in Ills. and N.Y.

---

[122]See entry for April 14. According to William T. Crump, the White House steward who kept a record of callers at the Executive Mansion, Harber arrived in the evening of April 13, had three meals with the Garfields on April 14, and departed after breakfast the next day.

[123]An advertisement in the *Washington City Directory* (1881) reads:
Dr. White's Establishment, 1416 Pennsylvania Avenue, opposite Willard's Hotel, is patronized by thousands of well-known personages, among them the highest Medical, Judicial, Political, Military and Naval dignitaries of this and leading foreign countries. Foot surgery, Corns, Bad Nails, etc. Fee, $1 per visit.

The lawn in the south front was crowded with little children, during most of the day (Easter Monday), rolling eggs down the green slopes.

The children (ours) went to the Barnum Show—circus, etc., and the house was quite deserted, except my never failing seekers for place. At four P.M. the Att'y Gen. came for an hour's business. After nine, I read *Ben Hur* for an hour and a half and then retired. Crete's absence changes the face of the home world.

TUESDAY, 19.   Awoke at half-past five, and finished *Ben Hur* in bed. It is a book of great power. Wallace surprises me with his delicacy and penetration, as well as his breadth of culture. I think Constantinople would give him opportunities for yet greater success, and I will try to give him that Mission.

At the Cabinet meeting a discussion of a few general topics and then business with the individual members. I insisted on the immediate action of the P.O. Dep't in reference to the Star Service. After some discussion James and MacVeagh came at 3 P.M. and we agreed upon names for the 1st [2nd] and 2nd [3rd] Ass't P.M. Gen. I prefer to remove Brady[124] than to receive his resignation but James and MacVeagh want him to resign. I arranged to go to N.Y. but business prevented. Drove an hour with Blaine.

WEDNESDAY, 20.   Made out the appointments for the P.O. Dep't. Thompson[125] for 1st Ass't [Postmaster General], Grier

---

[124]Thomas J. Brady (1839–1904) was second assistant postmaster general and an owner of the *National Republican* (Washington, D.C.). A native of Indiana, he was a Union officer, 1861–65, commissioner of internal revenue for Indiana and Ohio, 1875–76, and for a time chairman of the Indiana Republican State Committee. As second assistant postmaster general, 1876–81, he was the head of the Bureau of Contracts with responsibility for letting out contracts for the delivery of mail over the various postal routes. The investigation by James and MacVeagh of the star routes (n. 108, March 31, 1880) revealed that Brady was deeply implicated in a conspiracy to defraud the government. He was permitted to resign, but it was public knowledge that Garfield had forced him to do so (see, for example, the *New York Times,* April 21 and 22, 1881).

[125]William B. Thompson was at this time superintendent of the railway mail service and later treasurer of the Republican National Committee. Garfield was proposing to appoint Thompson second assistant postmaster general and Grier

for 2nd, and Hazen[126] for Ass't Att'y Gen. for Post Office Department. An hour later Woodward came to say that Thompson was possibly in intimate relations to Brady. James proposed Elmer,[127] and I consented. Also at his request, instead of removing Brady, demanded and received his resignation. At 11 1/2 Knox came, suggesting that Platt was behind Elmer and had much to do with Star Contracts. I sent for James and had Knox talk with him, but he (James) said he would vouch for Elmer. I sent in the list.

Baltimore has been on my back all day with its factions pushing for the control of the Post Office, which Gen. Tyler has resigned at my request since the verdict of the jury against him.[128] Finally, I sent in Col. Adreon.[129] Retired at 11 P.M., not well.

THURSDAY, 21. After breakfast took a horseback ride with Jimmie. Callers until one P.M. Simon Cameron came and spent half an hour. Spoke during the day with many Senators concerning the necessity of early action on the nominations. The violent speeches of some of our friends recently have aroused the Democrats to possible hostility to the administration and nominations.

I have been very lonely during the past three days, without Crete. She came at four P.M. and brought light and joy into the house. At 9 P.M. we received the members of the Academy of

---

third assistant postmaster general; the first assistant postmaster generalship was not open, James N. Tyner having been carried over from the Hayes administration.

[126]When W. A. M. Grier rejected the post of third assistant postmaster general, Garfield withdrew the nomination of Abraham Hazen as assistant attorney general for the Post Office Department and left him in the post of third assistant postmaster general from which he was to have been moved to make way for Grier.

[127]Richard A. Elmer, of New York, was confirmed as second assistant postmaster general on May 16.

[128]See n. 190, July 23, 1878.

[129]Harrison Adreon, a native of Baltimore, served in the Union army and was breveted colonel for gallantry at Hatcher's Run. Returning to Baltimore at the end of the war, he studied law and was admitted to the bar, 1866. He was U.S. pension agent for Maryland, 1869–77. He took an active part in the Republican campaign in 1880 as commander of the Boys in Blue in his state and as an organizer of a great mass meeting in his city. He was postmaster of Baltimore, 1881–85.

Science,[130] and their ladies. The Blaines, Windoms and Hunts were with us, a very pleasant party. At ten I met ex-Senator Spencer and had a full review of the Star Service and the New York row. Retired at 11 1/2.

FRIDAY, 22. The usual crowd until noon, when the Cabinet met, all present, and remained two hours with miscellaneous business.

After the meeting, lunch, and then the P.M. Gen. came and we made further examination of the Star Service. Knox was with him, and thought the investigation, if pushed, would involve several Senators, and possibly would change the politics of that body. I said, no matter, but let the work go on. At 2 1/2 P.M. Crete and I went to the Vestry of All Souls' Church and attended the closing session of the Academy of Science.

Helped Crete in the evening receive her friends in the parlor. Hon. Rob't C. Winthrop gave me the history of the picture of Hamden [Hampden] in the Ex[ecutive Mansion] librar[y].[131]

SATURDAY, 23. A weary day, closing a hard week's work. Much miscellany. Many calls. Rode on horseback an hour with C. O. Rockwell of St. Louis, and gave Brady a few sittings for photographs.

At 4 P.M. Mrs. Farragut[132] came to be our guest during the

[130]The National Academy of Sciences met in Washington, April 19–22. The President and Mrs. Garfield attended the final session. The last paper presented was entitled "The Auriferous Gravels of California."

[131]John MacGregor (1797–1857), British statistician, historian and member of Parliament, bought the portrait of John Hampden (1594–1643), English statesman and opponent of Charles I, and in 1856 presented it to the United States through James Buchanan, U.S. minister to Great Britain. The gift, accepted by Congress in 1857, was framed and placed in the Executive Mansion. Winthrop first saw it there in 1861 and was responsible for Hampden's name being affixed to it. Under President Hayes "a somewhat more detailed description was substituted." Winthrop promised Garfield that he would put the portrait's history "into a shape in which it could be no longer in danger of being forgotten or misunderstood." See Winthrop's paper on the portrait delivered in June, 1881, Massachusetts Historical Society, *Proceedings*, 18 (1880–81), pp. 436–444. Information was also supplied by the office of the curator of the White House (1979).

[132]Virginia Loyall Farragut, of Norfolk, Virginia, was the second wife of David G. Farragut (1801–1870), first admiral of the U.S. navy. She died in 1884 in her sixty-first year.

ceremonies of unveiling the Statue of her husband, the late Admiral Farragut.

In the evening C. O. Rockwell left us for home. He has been here several days. The Star Service has stirred up a great deal of feeling and much apprehension among the people who have been concerned in that business. In the evening several people called.

SUNDAY, 24.   Just as we were about leaving for Church, I received a note from Gilfillan, informing me that Dr. Hopkins would preach at the Congregational Church in G St., and though Mrs. Farragut had expressed a wish to go with us to our own church, she cheerfully consented to go with us to hear the good Doctor and we went. The Doctor exhibited his usual thoughtfulness; but he has lost much of his old fire; and I felt also, that he has not broadened in liberal thinking quite so much as I had hoped he might have done. At 3 P.M. I rode with Senator Sherman to Arlington and back. Talked over the situation. In the evening, had about ten guests at tea to meet Mrs. Farragut. The Secs. of State and Navy and their wives, Admirals Porter and Rogers [Rodgers], Mr. Farragut fils[133] and wife, and Mr. Maynard.[134]

Several naval people called after tea. Retired at 10.30 after reading Carlyle's *Miscellany.*[135]

MONDAY, 25.   Departments closed in honor of the Farragut ceremonies. I am down on the programme for a short speech, accepting the Statue of the great Admiral.[136] Thought a little, what to

---

[133]Loyall Farragut was a secretary to his father at the beginning of the Civil War and served for a time on the flagship *Hartford.* He graduated at West Point in 1868 and in the following year married Gertrude, daughter of Dr. John J. Metcalf of New York City. He resigned from the army in 1872 and entered the offices of the Central Railroad of New Jersey, of which his wife's uncle was president. He wrote *The Life of David Glasgow Farragut, First Admiral of the United States Navy* (1879). He had been a widower for about twenty years when he died at age seventy-two in 1916.

[134]Congressman Horace Maynard of Tennessee, Farragut's native state.

[135]Thomas Carlyle, *Critical and Miscellaneous Essays,* 4 vols. (1839).

[136]In accepting for the nation the heroic bronze statue, sculpted by Vinnie Ream Hoxie (1847–1914), and erected in Farragut Square, Garfield paid a tribute to the admiral's remarkable career, spoke of the singular province of art in breaking

say, but concluded not to write. A few callers in the forenoon. At 11 to 12 Cabinet and Naval Committee assembled here, and at 12.30 moved out to Farragut Square at the head of a fine naval and army procession. After the unvailing [unveiling], I spoke about two minutes—fairly well—Crete says very 'well. Maynard and Voorhees[137] followed. On return, reviewed the troop[s] from the front of the White House. About 20 people lunched with us. After dinner drove with Mrs. Farragut, Crete and Jimmie to look at the Statue. It is very fair. From eight to ten, gave a reception to the Army and Navy officers, for Mrs. Farragut.

TUESDAY, 26. Mrs. Farragut left us this A.M. All the Heads of Dep'ts present at Cabinet meeting except the Sec'y of State, who has gone to New York. The refunding going on favorably. We have sent an agent to London to effect the transfer of the bonds from 6 to 3 1/2 per cent. I have taken hold of the dead-lock question and talked with about 20 Senators. I think the caucus will soon take it up and give me some Executive Sessions.[138] Then will come the test of the strength of the administration against the bosses. Rumors reach me this evening that a Caucus Committee is to call on me with a view of harmonizing differences. We shall see whether they will venture to dictate my discretion in reference to nominations. Helped Crete at her reception in the evening. Mrs. Hawley here.

WEDNESDAY, 27. A very busy day. Not many Senators called, because the Caucus occupied their forenoon. But an unusual

---

down the limitations which separate generations, and called attention to the growing number of statues of war heroes in Washington, characterizing them as permanent guardians of the country's glory.

[137]The speech of Senator Daniel W. Voorhees of Indiana, an able orator, is in Harriet Cecilia Voorhees, et al., eds., *Forty Years of Oratory: Daniel Wolsey Voorhees, Lectures, Addresses and Speeches,* 2 vols. (1898), II, pp. 686–705.

[138]The Senate goes into executive session to consider nominations to office made by the President and treaties submitted by him. The deadlock of the Senate kept the body from completing its organization and postponed the holding of executive sessions. Thus it was essential that the deadlock be ended and the Senate settle down to the work which it had been called into special session to accomplish.

amount of work was done by heads of Dep'ts. The Att'y General came, and we agreed upon several nominations in his Dep't. After dinner I spent nearly two hours with Brown in overhauling my mail—that part of it which has been reserved for my personal inspection. At the Caucus this morning, and later session in the afternoon, it is said that the majority seems to be in favor of executive sessions, but a committee was appointed to report to another session on Saturday or Monday.

John D. Defrees called and spent an hour. Several other callers consumed most of the evening. Retired at 10.30.

THURSDAY, 28. The spring is bursting into sudden bloom, with heat quite enervating. Took a horseback ride of an hour, immediately after breakfast—went up F St. to the river, and thence down its margin to the public grounds below the President's House.

The Senate adjourned until Monday, leaving their questions in the hands of their Caucus Committee of seven.[139]

The day passed much like its fellows, so far as work in the office is concerned.

FRIDAY, 29. The Senate not being in session, I received an unusual number of calls from their [its] members.

At Cabinet meeting I asked the opinion of my associates on the Mahone question. There was a strong feeling of distrust of the outcome of the Mahone alliance and a desire to go very slow.

In the evening at 8.30 the Senate Caucus Committee came to consult upon three topics. 1st, Va. problem; 2nd, The importance to the Administration of executive session[s]; and 3rd, The possibility of harmony [?] in the Senate over the N.Y. nominations. On the first I expressed my willingness to aid an alliance between the Va. Republicans and [the] Mahone party, but not the abandonment of the Republican organization. 2nd, That the adminis-

[139]The Republican caucus in the Senate, distressed by the struggle between the President and Senator Conkling, established a committee of five headed by Henry L. Dawes of Massachusetts to effect a peace. The committee (called the Committee of Conciliation by Dawes) invited Conkling to present his side of the controversy, and he did so on April 29 in a speech of two and a half hours. On the evening of the same day, the Dawes committee met with Garfield for three hours. See entry for that day.

tration needs the 300 vacancies filled. 3rd, That the N.Y. nominations are my best judgment and will not be withdrawn. Conference ended at eleven P.M. The Committee had been bulldozed by Senator Conkling.

SATURDAY, 30. Crete and Mrs. Hawley went to Mt. Vernon in company with Mrs. Gen. Barnes.[140] I was kept very busy with callers all day. At 12 the Sec'y of State came and presented the new Spanish Minister, Signor Barca,[141] who made his speech to me in Spanish, and delivered his letter from King Alphonso.

In the evening Senator Dawes called again from the Caucus Committee, and remained two hours. I told him there could be no peace by evading the N.Y. contest. I wanted it known soon, whether I was the registering Clerk of the Senate or the Executive of the government. He left me at ten. Retired at 10.30.

May

SUNDAY, 1. A very perfect day, in which Spring revels and rejoices. Mother, Mrs. Hawley, Crete and I attended church and listened to a very good sermon from Mr. Power—better than he usually preaches. In the afternoon read a little book by Gail Hamilton, *What Think Ye of Christ?,* a thoughtful essay on a theme which has often been badly handled.[142] Read also a part of Carlyle on Edward Irving, in his late volume (posthumous) of reminiscences.[143]

[140]Mary (Fauntleroy) Barnes was the wife of Joseph K. Barnes (1817–1883), surgeon general of the U.S. army, 1864–82, who attended both Lincoln and Garfield after they had been shot.

[141]Señor Don Francisco Barca (1831–1883), politician and writer, was minister of Spain to the United States, 1881 to his death by suicide in New York.

[142]Gail Hamilton [Mary Abigail Dodge], *What Think Ye of Christ: the Testimony of the English Bible* (1877).

[143]Thomas Carlyle, *Reminiscences,* edited by James Anthony Froude (1881). On the first blank page of his copy Garfield wrote: "Washington, May 22, 1881. Finished reading this book this morning. If it be not the result of crabbed and cynical old age, it shows Carlyle to have been a selfish, churlish and unjust mind. And yet the book has much fascination for me. I shall look for his correspondence with more interest than I did for this. J. A. G."

Walked an hour with Swaim, and half an hour in the grounds with Crete. In the evening at 7 Mrs. Hawley, Crete and I took tea at Blaine's in company with Mr. McCormick and wife and Wm. Walter Phelps. Mr. Bancroft called. A pleasant visit.

Home at 10.10. Retired at 10.30. No sleep for nearly 4 hours. Don't know why.

MONDAY, 2. Most of the Cabinet went to Mt. Vernon with the Duke of Newcastle [Sutherland][144] and his party. I did not go. Declined on account of the official limitations which custom has imposed upon the office. Some one should write out a code of etiquette for various ceremonial occasions relating to the President and his wife. During the day I wrote to Mr. Dawes, Chairman, Senate Caucus, that I would not be a party to any scheme which included George Gorham[145] as a beneficiary. At 7.30 Crete and I dine[d] at Blaine's—din[ner] to Duke of Sutherland. Present, Gen. Sherman, Sir Edward Thornton and wife, Senator Hale, W. W. Phelps, Sec'y and Mrs. Hunt and two English friends of the Duke, Russell,[146] the correspondent, and [Solicitor] Gen. Phillips, plus [?] his son the Marquis,[147] and a Scotch-American. Home at ten and spent two hours with Dawes and J. R. Hawley. Retired at 12.

TUESDAY, 3. At Cabinet meeting, after routine business was

[144]George Granville William Sutherland Leveson-Gower (1828–1892), third Duke of Sutherland, sportsman, traveller, and member of Parliament, 1852–61, had large investments in land and railroads. The main reason for his visit to the United States was to investigate American railroads with a view to improving those in which he was interested. He arrived in New York on April 25 accompanied by his eldest son, Cromartie, and several executives of the London and Northwestern Railroad, of which he was a principal stockholder.

[145]See n. 400, December 29, 1880.

[146]William Howard Russell (1820–1907) became famous for his reporting of the Crimean War. During the Civil War he served in the United States, 1861–63, as a war correspondent for the *Times* (London). He became known as "Bull Run" Russell, some said because of his reporting of the First Battle of Bull Run, and others because of his flight from that battlefield.

[147]Cromartie (1851–1913), who carried the title Marquis of Stafford and became the fourth Duke of Sutherland, was a member of Parliament, 1874–86, and reportedly Europe's largest private landholder, next to the Czar of Russia, owning over a million and a half acres at his death.

finished, I reviewed the conduct of the Senate towards the nominations, and the behaviour of Senator Conkling as developed by the Caucus Committee, mentioning his threat to disclose my letter to Hubbell asking him to get Brady's help about the Campaign.[148] I detailed to them my interview with the Caucus Committee, and said I wanted the aid of the Cabinet to resist the encroachments of the Senate, and to secure the confirmation of Robertson. There was a general hearty approval of my course.

In the evening, helped Crete in receiving her friends in the red parlor. Poor Crete, she is not well—malaria, almost a chill this morning. Retired at 11.15.

WEDNESDAY, 4. The Senate met as usual, but the dead-lock was broken by the prevalence of the motion to go into Executive Session.[149] The caucus has agreed to consider first, treaties, 2nd,

---

[148]The deadlock in the Senate prevented action on Garfield's appointments and delayed resolution of his struggle with Conkling. During a session of the Republican caucus committee (see n. 139, April 28, 1881), held to hear Conkling's side of the controversy, the New York senator delivered a long, devastating attack on Garfield and Robertson, remarking at the end that he had in his pocket an autograph letter which, if made public, would make the President "bite the dust." In the letter, written during the presidential campaign to Jay Hubbell, chairman of the Republican Congressional Committee, Garfield said: "Please say to Brady that I hope he will give us all the assistance he can. I think he can help effectively. Please tell me how the Departments generally are doing." Garfield wrote the letter to prod Hubbell's efforts to secure campaign contributions from government employees, including those in Second Assistant Postmaster General Thomas J. Brady's department. To be sure, Brady had recently resigned as a result of his involvement in the star route frauds (see n. 124, April 19, 1881), and civil service reformers would object to government workers being hounded for campaign funds, but the letter contained nothing scandalous, criminal, or even extraordinary. Garfield himself was willing to make it public, but on advice from Blaine did not. Conkling released the letter for publication and on May 4 and 5 it appeared in the leading newspapers without creating anything like the sensation he had predicted. Indeed, Conkling's machinations hurt him more than Garfield.

[149]The deadlock over the election of the Senate's officers was broken by a vote of 53–0 on the motion of Henry L. Dawes of Massachusetts that the Senate "now proceed to the consideration of executive business." Immediately after passing the resolution the Senate adjourned, but began holding executive sessions on the following day.

uncontested nominations, 3rd, before any further business is done an Executive Session shall be called. It may be possible for Mr. Conkling to have all his N.Y. friends confirmed, and let the Senate adjourn without acting on Robertson's case. If I find that is likely to occur, I will withdraw all the N.Y. nominat[ions] except Robertson's, and await action on that.

Crete has been quite ill all day with something like chill fever. She has been too hard worked during the past two months. Callers increased in consequence of the broken dead-lock.

THURSDAY, 5. I found, this morning, that one of the N.Y. nominations was confirmed yesterday, and under the caucus order the Senate is likely to confirm all the others and let Robertson go over without action. This will leave me no chance to make any adjustment which will recognize the minority of the Republicans of N.Y. To prevent such a result, I withdrew five of the N.Y. appointments.[150] This will bring the Robertson nomination to an issue. It may end in his defeat; but it will protect me against being finessed out of a test. In the evening nine senators called, most of them to deplore the contest, and express the hope that I would do something to avoid it. I told them my reasons for the withdrawal, and expressed the hope that action would be had on Robertson's case. Several telegrams came during the evening approving my course. Crete has been in bed all day with a bad fever. I slept in the guest chamber, retiring at 10.

FRIDAY, 6. The dear wife is still ill, but is better than yesterday. I fear that I have not been thoughtful enough about her work during the last three months. She has had very many cares and activities which with malaria have given her this illness.

The withdrawals of the N.Y. appointments of yesterday have brought me vigorous responses from many quarters, and I think show that the public do not desire the continuance of boss rule in the Senate. It may have lessened the chances of Robertson's confirmation, though I think not. Long discussion in Cabinet on

[150]The names withdrawn were those listed in n. 96, March 22, 1881. James G. Blaine had suggested this action to the President some weeks earlier, and on May 5 urged him to send his withdrawal message at once.

our treaty with Columbia [Colombia], and its relation to De Lesseps' canal scheme.[151] Rode an hour in the afternoon with MacVeagh. Still Crete is ill, and I slept in the guest chamber, retiring at half-past 12, after a long reading of Carlyle's *Reminiscences.*

SATURDAY, 7. The dear one passed a painful night, and looked worn and very weary this morning. I arranged to have her doctor, Miss Edson, stay with her as nurse, and we kept the room very quiet, so that she had a better day than yesterday, and gives us hopes of a speedy recovery.

The calls were unusually numerous. The breaking of the deadlock and the withdrawal of the N.Y. appointments have brought back many people who had left the city.

We have arrested some people in Philadelphia who were connected with Post Office frauds. This, I think, will show our determination to go through the Dep't and see the bottom of its troubles.

Remained with Crete until near midnight. Slept in guest chamber.

SUNDAY, 8. Did not attend church, but spent most of the day with poor Crete, who is still very ill, and suffered a great deal of pain —great nervous prostration. My anxiety for her dominates all my thoughts, and makes me feel that I am fit for nothing.

Many friends called to inquire after [her], and many to see me. At 4 P.M. rode out with Senator Sherman, and had a long conversation on the situation in the Senate.

Callers continued until far into the evening.

Retired at 10 1/2.

---

[151]By a treaty concluded in the late 1840's with New Granada (later Colombia), the United States obtained transit rights in the Isthmus of Panama, and in return guaranteed the neutrality of that region to assure that "free transit of traffic might not be interrupted." When in 1879 Ferdinand de Lesseps, the head of a private French company, began a serious effort to build a canal across Panama, the United States became somewhat alarmed. In 1880, President Hayes notified Congress that the nation's policy was "a canal under American control," and Congress responded by protesting against a canal built or controlled by foreigners. Garfield's administration inherited and had to deal with this problem.

MONDAY, 9.   Crete rested more last night than recently; but she still suffers great pain in the head. I wanted the judgment of a fresh mind on her situation, and sent for Dr. Baxter and had Miss Edson state the case fully. He agrees that it is the result of malaria and overwork, but fears there may be danger of cerebrospinal meningitis. I telegraphed to Dr. Boynton to come, but receive answer that he has gone from Cleveland to Kansas. At 11 P.M. had Dr. Pope come. He confirms Miss Edson's views of Crete— malaria and nervous exhaustion. Republican Senators in Caucus five hours this afternoon. Edmunds moved to postpone action on Robertson till December. Conkling supported motion in a long speech. Sherman, Hawley and Conger *obstantes* [opposing]. I sat up with Crete until midnight.

TUESDAY, 10.   Crete had a very hard night. We removed her to the room on the north side of the house, to get her further from the river air. She made a gallant effort of will to master her nervous fancies and partially succeeded. The Doctors assure me she is not in danger, but I am distressed and anxious about her pain and weakness.

Cabinet meeting with only four members—Windom and James in N.Y. and Kirkwood sick.

At the Caucus of the Republican Senators Edmunds' resolution was withdrawn to avoid defeat, and a resolution unanimously adopted delaying action temporarily in hopes an adjustment can be made. I sat up with Crete until four hours past midnight. It was a sweet privilege to watch her and serve her in her great trial. My heart is very full of anxiety.

WEDNESDAY, 11.   Retired at 4.15 A.M. and slept until 8.15. The dear one slept an hour and a half after I left her. The Doctor says she is better, and I was made tearfully proud by the fact that she told the Doctor I was much the best nurse she had had.

Gov. Foster was at breakfast with us, and reviewed the political situation. At 10 1/2 A.M. I took a bath and went to be[d] hoping to get some sleep. Arose at four, having slept but little. The dear one has still a threatening fever—temperature at 104 1/10. Talked with Dr. Baxter, then went to Dr. Pope's office and brought him. He gave her fever powders, and bathed her with alcohol and ice water. I refused to see people on business. All my thoughts center in her, in comparison with whom all else fades into insignificance. At seven Pope and Baxter came again. For her sake, more than my own, I retired at 10.30.

THURSDAY, 12. I awoke this morning, and found my precious one a little better, but very weak. Her temperature was 103 1/2 and pulse at 90. This still shows too much fever.

I went through the duties of the office, very anxiously getting away every few moments to see her. About noon, she felt so markedly better that she ate a few strawberries with relish.

I have no heart to think of the contest going on at the other end of the avenue against me. Nor until near evening, did I get time to read the ugly assault upon me in the N.Y. *Herald* written by Gorham, and evidently inspired by Conkling. At eleven P.M. Dr. Boynton came, having travelled from Wichita, Kansas. Earlier in the evening Mrs. Sheldon came, to our great relief.

FRIDAY, 13. The hope of our house is still clouded. I have become satisfied that her illness is more serious than either Dr. Edson or Pope believes, and that their remeinedies [remedies] are not of sufficient potency. I there[fore] put the case absolutely in Dr. Boynton's hands, who has burst the narrow barriers of Homoeopathy, and gives heroic doses whenever the case requires it. Her temperature is up to 104, and pulse at 100. This will burn her out if not arrested.

Cabinet meeting from 12 until 2. Hard to think of business with any shadow of doubt hanging over the life of my life, but forced myself to think of other things. The conversions of 6's and 5's into 3 1/2 promised to be a great success. Remarkable letter from Gen. Grant, April 24, which I must answer in self-defense.[152] New saddle horse, "Denmark," dapple-gray, came from Dr. Updegraff. Retired at 11.

[152]The letter, written in the "City of Mexico" (April 24) was sent through Senator John P. Jones of Nevada, who handed it to Garfield on May 13. "I write," Grant said, "as an earnest well wisher of my country and of you individually. I believe sincerely that with such an administration as you can give, and have the opportunity of giving, you will have no competitor for the nomination in [18]84, and that your reelection will be much easier than your election. But this cannot

SATURDAY, 14.   A gleam of hope comes [to] the household from the record of the thermometer. Her temperature this morning was 101°, against 103° yesterday morning, and at 4 this P.M. 102° against 104° 24 hours ago. Dr. Boynton has been giving medicine of nearly or quite full allopathic potency. The abatement of the fever leaves her very weak, and its disappearance will be the great trial of her strength. A day or two more will be

---

be by giving the administration over to the settlement of other people's private grievances, nor by recognizing factions as the party. When I saw the batch of appointments made correcting what I believed a grievous mistake of your immediate predecessor, I felt that you had struck the key note of success. When the appointments of the next day went in, I was saddened and thought it would have been better, or rather not half so bad, if you had continued the policy of Mr. Hayes in recognizing disgruntled factions, who support the party only when they are made the leaders of it, as the party. It is always the fair thing to recognize the representatives chosen by the people. The Senators from New York were chosen against all the power an administration of their own party could bring to bear. It is fair to suppose that those senators represent at least their party within the state. To nominate a man to the most influential position within the gift of the President in their state without consulting them, would be an undeserved slight. To select the most obnoxious man to them in the state is more than a slight. Mr. Robertson did not support the nominee of the Republican party in 1872—I think he did not—when that nominee received the unanimous vote of his party [the nominee was Grant]. He gave indications at the convention which nominated you that if the nominee of 1872 were nominated in [18]80 he would not support the ticket although he went as a delegate to that convention pledged to support the candidate. I am disposed, so far as I am concerned, to ignore, if I cannot forget, all wrongs perpetrated against me personally, for the general good. But insults and wrongs against others for the crime of having supported me, I do feel and will resent all that is in my power to resent. I gave you a hearty and strong support, in the presence of an assembled crowd, the moment your nomination was sent over the wires. I continued that support up to the night preceding the election. I claim no credit for this for it was my duty. I had been honored as no other man had by the republican party and by the nation. It was my duty to serve both. But I do claim that I ought not to be humiliated by seeing my personal friends punished for no other offence than their friendship and support. I do hope and trust that you may see this matter in the same light I do, and if you do not, believe at least that I have no other object in writing to you at this time than to serve you, the party, and the nation you represent. The republican party has gone through four years of trials hard to bear, and it may not be able to withstand four years more. I sincerely trust it may not be put to the test."

necessary to show whether the betterment is temporary or permanent.

The public are very considerate and tenderly solicitous for <u>her</u> safety. Many called to inquire. I was kept up until midnight by business connected with Dorsey's trouble.[153] I have great sympathy with him and some doubts. Retired at 12.30—after seeing the dear one. It seems almost neglectful to sleep or be well, while she is so ill.

SUNDAY, 15.   Our hope almost reached triumph when we learned this morning that the thermometer announce[d] but 100 1/2°. At breakfast we had the first laugh since <u>she</u> left the table. The little ones have been very brave but very still, the waiting days. The house has been very still. Gov. Foster was with us and spent most of the day. Lt. Harber left us last evening—on his way to N.Y. to take command of his first ship, the *Alarm.*

The external heat has abated, the very birds seem kind [to] her, in fact the whole world seems anxious to help her back on shore. I must think that God will be merciful to us and let her

[153]As U.S. senator from Arkansas (1873–79) and after his departure from the Senate, Stephen W. Dorsey was associated with his brother John and others in securing star route contracts (see n. 108, March 31, 1880). The investigation into star route frauds begun by Postmaster General James and Attorney General Mac-Veagh was a staggering blow to Dorsey, presaging as it did the end of his high hopes of a lucrative relationship with the Garfield administration, the loss of reputation and the probability of criminal indictment. Thirty-nine years of age, with a wife and children, he was thoroughly demoralized. The situation was embarrassing to Garfield since Dorsey, as secretary of the Republican National Committee during the campaign, had worked tirelessly for his election. As a member of the "Dorsey combination" Dorsey was twice tried on a charge of conspiracy to defraud the government. In the first trial (June 1–September 11, 1882), the jury was unable to reach a verdict in his case; in the second trial (December 4, 1882–June 14, 1883) he was acquitted. Dorsey maintained his innocence, blaming his troubles largely on MacVeagh and James, one of whom he characterized as "a cold blooded scheming villain," and the other as "a pretentious political mountebank." See Dorsey to President Arthur, September 26, 1881, Chester A. Arthur Papers, Library of Congress; see also Dorsey to Garfield, May, 1881 (a ten page letter).

stay. In the evening, nearly all the members of the Cabinet called to inquire after <u>her</u>, MacVeagh and James to talk of Star route frauds and Dorsey's connection with them, Windom to counsel caution in listening to accusations. I gave order that no prosecutions should be begun with[out] my order. Capt. Henry came to take Marshalship.[154]

MONDAY, 16. We were depressed by a worse day for <u>her</u>, not knowing whether it indicates relapse, or a remittent phase of the fever. She had a hard day of weakness and flightiness.

At 12 Senators Conkling and Platt tendered their resignations as senators, a very weak attemp[t] at the heroic. If I do not mistake, it will be received with guffaws of laughter. They appeal to a legislature which they think is already secured. Even in this they may fail. The[y] have wounded the self love of their brother Senators, and will lose by it. Late at night the Associated Press sent me their letter to Gov. Cornell, giving their reasons for resigning.[155] It is a weak attempt at masquerading as injured innocents and Civil Service reformers. They are neither. I go on without disturbance. Having done all I fairly could to avoid a fight, I now fight to the end. Retired at midnight.

TUESDAY, 17. The precious one is better again, showing her fever remittent, and we take new hope. Long Cabinet meeting. Excellent feeling. The N.Y. thunderbolt a *brutem fulmen* [a harmless thunderbolt]. The Senate now turns its wrath upon the two

[154]Charles E. Henry was nominated U.S. marshal for the District of Columbia on May 13 and confirmed by the Senate on May 16. Henry made this entry in his diary (Hiram College Library) for May 15: "Arrived in Washington at night. Saw President Garfield. He told me of illness of Mrs. Garfield—how anxious he felt. How small and insignificant was the presidency compared with her life. She is removed from danger but still sick. I spent an hour with him. During which time he often went to her bedside to see if she had wakened."

[155]Conkling and Platt resigned from the Senate because they realized that they had lost their fight with Garfield over the appointment of Robertson. They believed, moreover, that the New York legislature would vindicate them by re-electing them. Following the session in which the resignations were announced, the Republican senators held a caucus and decided to consider without delay all pending appointments and any sent in during the week.

members who have abandoned them. My nominations will go through soon. But I await the confirmation of Robertson before sending many more.

I have answered a very remarkable letter from Gen. Grant.[156] Rumors are in the paper that his will be published. If so, my reply

[156]"I am in hearty accord," Garfield wrote, "with every expression in your letter touching the welfare of the country, and the success of the Republican party. You are, however, under serious misapprehension in reference to my motives and purposes concerning the New York appointments. . . .

You say that success cannot be achieved by 'giving the administration over to the settlement of other people's private grievances.' You do me great injustice to suppose that I am capable of permitting such use of the power entrusted to me. It has not been done nor will it be. I have no thought of making any appointment to injure you.

While I heartily agree with you when you say that you 'ought not to be humiliated by seeing my (your) personal friends punished for no other offence than their friendship and support,' I am sure you will agree with me that worthy and competent men should not be excluded from recognition because they opposed your nomination at Chicago.

That I had no purpose to proscribe your friends in N.Y., but every disposition to deal justly and at the same time cultivate their friendly feelings toward my administration, appears from the fact that I selected for a very important cabinet position one of your warm supporters, and gave ten other important positions to your friends in N.Y., most of whom had been strongly recommended by one or both of the Senators and by other friends of yours. In making a selection of a Collector of the Port of N.Y., an office more national than local, I sought to secure the services of a gentleman of eminent ability, and, at the same time, to give just recognition to that large and intelligent element of N.Y. Republicans who were in accord with the majority of the Chicago Convention. For this I am assailed by some of your indiscreet friends. As I said in the Chicago Convention, it needed all grades and shades of Republicans to carry the election. So it needs the support of all good Republicans to make the administration successful.

In this connection, let me correct two errors of fact into which you have inadvertently fallen. Judge Robertson did not, as you suppose, oppose your election in 1872, nor did he declare in the Chicago Convention that he would not support you if nominated. He was elected State Senator in 1872, running on the same ticket with you. At Chicago, on the roll-call, before any nominations had been made, he voted to support the nominee of the convention whoever he might be.

Now while I agree substantially with you that 'it is always the fair thing to recognize the representatives chosen by the people,' I am not willing to allow the power of the Executive in selecting persons for nomination to be restricted to the consideration of those only who may be suggested by the Senators from the State

shall appear.[157] He seems to have forgotten that he is only one

from which the selection is to be made. I feel bound, as you did when President, to see to it that local quarrels for leadership shall not exclude from recognition men who represent any valuable element in the Republican party. It is my purpose to be just to all; and while I am incapable of discriminating against any Republican because he supported you, I am sure you will agree with me that I ought not to permit any one to be proscribed because he did not support you.

Before Judge Robertson's nomination I had reason to know that it was the wish of both N.Y. Senators that the Collector should be changed. I knew that in Senator Platt's recent election, he had received the support of Judge Robertson both in the caucus and in the Senate, and I had reason to believe, and did believe that the nomination would be satisfactory to him, and to the Governor of the State (both of whom were your warm supporters), and that it would be eminently satisfactory to a large body of N.Y. Republicans. I had no reason to suppose that Mr. Robertson was regarded as a personal enemy by Senator Conkling—Judge Robertson had twice voted for Mr. Conkling for U.S. Senator, and had supported him for the Presidency at Cincinnati, so long as the N.Y. delegation presented his name. He occupied a leading and distinguished position in his state and party. His fitness for the collectorship had not been, and is not questioned. Notwithstanding all this, when, on the day after the nomination, I heard that it was objected to by Senator Conkling, I made an appointment for a conference with him, Senator Platt and the Vice President, on the subject, and waited an hour and a half beyond the time they had fixed. They did not call—nor has Senator Conkling called to see me since. The course of subsequent events has placed the question far beyond the personal fate of Judge Robertson as a nominee. The issue now is, whether the President in making nominations to office shall act in obedience to the dictation of the Senators from the State where the office is to be exercised. I regard this assumption as at war with the Constitution, and destructive of the true principles of administration.

To submit to this view would be to renounce the trust I have undertaken.

My dear General, I can never forget your great services during the late campaign. They were given ungrudgingly and as whole heartedly as I always gave you mine, when our positions were reversed before the people. You supported me without condition or attempted stipulation, and my heart warms generously in response to any request or desire of yours. In this connection, I may say that I shall be glad if I find myself able to carry out your wish in reference to Gen. Badeau.

Be assured that whatever concerns your happiness and prosperity will always be a matter of sincere interest to me." The text of this letter is from a careful copy in the Garfield Papers.

[157]Neither letter was published, but Grant did release to the public, through Senator John P. Jones, a statement of what his letter contained. Disgusted by this action, Garfield wrote to Jacob D. Cox (May 22) that "the unmanly course of Grant in writing a letter to me and then giving its substance to the public in a letter

citizen—and hence is unconsciously insolent. I have not answered him sharply, but plainly, and I think conclusively. Many callers in the evening. Sat with Crete [until] about midnight and then retired.

WEDNESDAY, 18. A slight betterment in her condition. The closed gates, and the two bulletins per day show how ill she is and how tenderly anxious her friends are.

Great pressure of work in the office. Robertson confirmed without a roll-call. This leaves Conkling's attitude ridiculous. His row is with the Senate equally with me. In the afternoon I rode the new horse "Denmark" ten or twelve miles in company with Jim, Don Rockwell, and Brown.

In the evening, many callers and much business. Senate Committee asks if I have any further communications, as they are nearly ready to adjourn.

Retired at near midnight. Crete sleeping fairly well.

THURSDAY, 19. The busiest day yet. Sent for Gen. Le Duc and asked for his resignation.[158] Ordered the retirement of the Surgeon Gen'l and Paymaster General, and the appointment of Baxter[159] and McClure.[160] But just as we were about to send them in, some facts appeared about an old case of McClure [which] led me to recall the order. Cabinet meeting (special) from eleven to two. Sent in old N.Y. nominations except Payn and Tyler, thus maintaining the consistency of the administration.

Much feeling because I did not send all anti-Conkling men in. Blaine and MacVeagh here in evening. Crete rested better during the day.

---

to Jones, so as to keep from the public his letter to me, and my answer, is so unworthy that I will not further attempt to characterize it."

[158]See n. 80, March 23, 1878.

[159]See Vol. II, p. 275, n. 4.

[160]Daniel W. McClure, a native of Indiana, graduated at West Point in 1849. After resigning from the army in 1850, he reenlisted and served, 1858–88. He was assistant paymaster general with the rank of colonel, 1866–88. As a result of Garfield's decision not to appoint him paymaster general, the incumbent, Brigadier General Nathan W. Brown, retained the office to his resignation in 1882.

Retired at eleven

FRIDAY, 20. The dear one slept better last night than heretofore during her illness, and our hope grows. But she is still very very weak. Cabinet meeting to clear up odds and ends of executive work. Committee came from the Senate, and I told them I would send in a few important things at once, and then would have no further communication.

The Senate sat about 5 1/2 hours and adjourned *sine die.* This is a great relief. All the N.Y. nominations have been confirmed, and the war of Conkling vs. the administration has passed the first state successfully for me. It was not of my seeking, but I think he sees by this time that he has undertaken too difficult a task. I believe I have been strengthened in the public judgment and support. Senator Sawyer and T. M. Nichol took tea with us. I retired at 11.45.

SATURDAY, 21. Her disease appears to be of a two-fold nature— fever, resulting from some malarial or other poison, and nervous prostration. The remedies which ally [allay] the fever seem to aggravate the nervous prostration.

This makes the management of her case very difficult. The Doctor has been giving her nerve remedies for the past three days. Meantime, the temperature has risen and the pulse increased; the former to 102, the latter to 100. But her nervous condition is better. Many senators called this forenoon to take leave before going home.

The children and Mother went down the river on the Revenue cutter with the Cabinet and their families. I was to have gone, but special anxiety for Crete kept me from going. Had a very quiet afternoon, the public supposing I had gone.

The weather is perfect—and for the last four days has been graciously cool to the great blessing of our dear one.

Read nearly the last of Carlyle's *Reminiscences.* Retired at 11.

SUNDAY, 22. The fever was up to 102 1/2 this morning, and a little below 102 this afternoon. But the nervous condition is better, and the pulse is stronger and more rapid, being nearer in harmony with her temperature. Mother and Mrs. Sheldon attended church at eleven. I remained with Crete, and wrote some letters. At 5 P.M. Senator Sherman came and I rode with him. Called at the Soldiers' Home to look after the condition of the house <u>she</u> is to occupy. It will be a week or ten days before the smell of paint will have disappeared, and I fear it will be longer before she will be strong enough to go. Home at seven. Don and Jim with us at tea. The day has been very beautiful—graciously cool for her.

In the evening Albert Daggett[161] of Brooklyn called and talked over N.Y. matters. He goes to Albany, and think[s] Conkling and Platt can not be elected. Read Freeman's Historical Atlas and text.[162] Retired at 11 P.M.

MONDAY, 23. The elements still favor her—with cool weather—and the vital forces of her dear body seem to be in league with our hopes. But the movement is very very slow.

The lingering senators keep a busy scene in the office, closing up arrearages of work, and I have been nearly as much thronged today as at any time for a month. The Refunding has been a complete success. More than a month before the option expires for converting the registered 5's into 3 1/2's we have received the full amount invited—250 millions—and several millions in addition. The secretary will give notice in the papers tomorrow

---

[161]Albert Daggett (1845–1903), a native of Troy, New York, worked in Washington in the office of Secretary of State William H. Seward for several years before settling in 1869 in Brooklyn, where he became active in the inner circles of the Republican party. He was sheriff of Kings County, 1876–78. A Sherman delegate to the Republican National Convention in 1880, he swung to Garfield on the last ballot, and in the presidential campaign contributed largely to his election. After Conkling and Platt resigned their seats in the U.S. Senate on May 16, Daggett worked in Albany to prevent their reelection by the state legislature. "Mr. Daggett," said the *National Republican* (May 30) in reporting a conference of Daggett with the President on May 28, "is the lieutenant-general of the Bread-and-Butter forces at the New York capital, Robertson, of course, being the general in command." After being elected chairman of the state Republican committee in 1881 and serving a term in the state senate, 1884–85, his fortunes waned, both politically and financially; he then engaged in a number of business pursuits without success. During his last years he was a U.S. postal contractor. At the time of his death he was living in Maine.

[162]Edward Augustus Freeman, *The Historical Geography of Europe,* 2 vols. (1881).

morning that no more can be received. The N.Y. fight is raging with increased fury. Conkling and Pratt [Platt] are now making the sturdiest efforts to recover the Commission they lately threw away.

TUESDAY, 24. Cousin Anna Boynton, the Doctor's wife, came this morning—to stay with Crete, as Mrs. Sheldon must go soon. The precious one has made [a] bound towards recovery during the last 24 hours, and we now feel great assurance that she is coming back to us. This fact has made the day sing with joy.

At Cabinet meeting only three members were present—Windom, James and Kirkwood. The rest are out of town, Lincoln gone to Ft. Leavenworth, Blaine and Hunt to N.Y. The few nominations that went over without action I am re-appointing. Only one of my whole lot (Chandler) was rejected. At six-thirty I rode out on my new saddle horse, "Denmark," reaching home [at] 7 1/4. The improvement of the dear one has steadily continued all day. In evening read up back news, and examined new revision of New Testament.[163]

WEDNESDAY, 25. Her condition is so nearly unchanged from day to day, since the checking of the fever, as nearly to discourage any soul less brave than hers. But the Doctor say[s] every day brings a little gain.

I am sorry Blaine has gone to N.Y. just now. It gives occasion for a faction there to transfer the controversy to Conkling and Blaine.[164]

[163]A revision of the authorized version of the New Testament, prepared by committees of English and American scholars who labored for over a decade, was published simultaneously in England and the United States on May 20, 1881. So great was the public demand that on the date of publication there were orders in the two countries for about 2,250,000 copies. Although the revision was generally recognized as a valuable contribution, it was unfavorably received by reviewers and church groups, "owing to many irritating and apparently unnecessary alterations of familiar passages." See Sir Paul Harvey, comp. and ed., *The Oxford Companion to English Literature* (1946), p. 87.

[164]The departure of Blaine for New York City on May 24, a week before the New York state legislature was to begin balloting on successors to Senators Conkling and Platt, led to rumors that he had gone to participate in the struggle. That same day Conkling went to Albany to take charge of his campaign for re-election.

I have fought the assumption of Mr. Conkling against my authority, but I do not think it best to carry the war into N.Y. except to see that my enemies are not armed against me, by my own administration. Rode an hour and a half with Brown, Jim and Don. At 9 1/2 Mrs. Sheldon left us for Cleveland. She has been a great blessing to Crete during the last fortnight.

Swaim returned.

THURSDAY, 26. Her betterment is very slow—to the eyes of our love hardly a change; but the Doctor says the movement is all along the line, and that her forces are on the march. The day was a crowded one for me, and gave me a gloomy prospect for future rest from office hunters.

The news from Albany shows that the seceeded senators are to have a more and more difficult task in their efforts to get back.

At 3.30 I drove to the Navy Yard in company with Swaim, Brown and Dr. Boynton, and took a trip on Prof. Baird's steamer to a seine haul, a few miles below Mt. Vernon. Saw the mystery of fecundating shad eggs artificially. Returned at 8.30. Found Crete anxious for my non-return. Jones of the N.Y. *Times,* Blaine, Windom, and James called and stayed until 11.30. Retired at 12.

FRIDAY, 27. She is brighter in spirits, clearer in mind, but so very weak. It fills me with tears to see how wasted and weary she looks. But I bless God every hour for the soft sound of her returning footsteps. Harry and Jim wanted to go to Fortress Monroe with the Rockwells but I found Crete would feel a little happier to know they were at home. She said, "I wish you had let them go and not told me of it." So the good boys stay, perhaps

---

During the day several men "in the interest of the administration" called on Garfield to protest Blaine's trip. Garfield said that he did not know that Blaine had gone and he rejected the notion that the trip was for the purpose suggested. In New York Blaine claimed that he had come solely on Treasury Department matters. It was noted, however, that during his stay in New York he was visited by several anti-Conkling men, some of whom left for Albany on the morning of May 25. Blaine left for Washington on the same morning. *Washington Post,* May 25 and 26, 1881.

to go quietly a day later. Cabinet meeting with two members, Lincoln and Kirkwood, away.

At five o'clock Swaim, Windom and I went down below Glymont on Peters'[165] little boat and had a quiet, restful time, returning at 10 P.M. Found the dear one sleeping well.

SATURDAY, 28. The dear one sleeps long and peacefully, and seems to get restful help. She was anxious to [be] lifted into a lounge chair. I got one and put her in it, nearly in lounge shape, but it tired her very much. Her weakness is most pitiful.

Much business in the office. Let Hal and Jim go to Fortress Monroe, but kept it from Crete. In the evening Irvin, while attempting to scale the iron fence near the house, caught his foot between the pickets and fell forward badly spraining his ankle. This also we keep from her, that she may not worry.

Daggett came from Albany with news from the N.Y. battle, in which I am only an interested spectator.

SUNDAY, 29. Attended church with Mother. First time to church since Crete's illness. (The house is full of joy at her increasing strength.) The preacher reviewed the new translation (or revision) of the New Testament. American sales first day were a quarter of a million.

On my return from church, found that Crete had a chill, followed by fever—which gives me great anxiety. It may be a relapse; but we hope it is the clearing up storm. The fever was followed by several hours of perspiration, a good indication. Retired late and found it difficult to think of sleep, with the uncertainty which this new phase of her illness brings.

MONDAY, 30. She comes through the night with the fever apparently all gone—temperature 98 3/4°, almost normal—and gives us strong hopes that yesterday['s] change was the fluttering sob of the fever.

At 10 A.M. I went with Windom, Hunt and James to the Soldiers' Home and attended Decoration Day services there;

[165]Ensign George H. Peters was in the office of Professor Simon Newcomb, superintendent, Nautical Almanac.

oration by District Att'y Corkhill.[166] Thence to Arlington, and listened to a long dull poem, in which the poet used "learn" as a transitive verb, and the orator, Dunnell, went out of his way to strike Windom a back-handed blow.[167]

On our return stopped at Fort Myers and lunched with Capt. Strong.[168] Home at 5 and found the light of the house brighter than when I left, and hopeful of speedy recovery. Read, rested, rejoiced and retired.

TUESDAY, 31.   At last, on the 28th day of her illness, the Doctor says with emphasis, it is ended. She now needs only care and strength, and, in spite of all other cares and besetments, a deep strong current of happy peace flows through every heart in the household.

Cabinet meeting at 12 and much miscellaneous business was done. Conkling received just one-third of the Republican votes

[166]George Corkhill, lawyer and journalist (he was at one time editor of the Washington *Sunday Chronicle*) was appointed U.S. attorney for the District of Columbia by President Hayes in January, 1880. After the star route investigations had begun he asked for the appointment of a special assistant district attorney to take charge of the cases in the District. Although this was done, Attorney General MacVeagh and others were of the opinion that Corkhill himself should be replaced since he was said to be "in friendly, cordial, sympathetic relations with the parties who were involved" in the star route frauds. Garfield accepted this view, and on the night before he was shot, he authorized MacVeagh to offer Corkhill's position to Albert Gallatin Riddle; the shooting prevented the carrying out of Garfield's purpose. Pressed to remove Corkhill, President Arthur concluded that he should be left in office until the Guiteau trial ended (Corkhill had secured the indictment of Guiteau). Corkhill was retained until the end of his term (1884), and was involved in the trial of Guiteau and in both star route trials, in all of which he was overshadowed by more experienced lawyers who were associated with him. See *House Miscellaneous Reports,* No. 2165, Part 2, 48 Cong., 1 Sess. (Serial 2234), pp. 32–34.

[167]Apparently a reference to Mark H. Dunnell's statement attributing the success of the recent and present administrations in managing and reducing the national debt largely to legislation ordained by the people, rather than to any action by secretaries of the treasury. Both Dunnell and Secretary of the Treasury Windom were Minnesota men. See the *Washington Star,* May 30.

[168]Richard P. Strong, a native of New York, was an officer in the Union army, 1862–65. He was breveted captain and major in 1865. He remained in the service, retiring in 1902 as a lieutenant colonel.

of the two Houses at Albany, Platt 29—six less than Conkling. And this is the "vindication" he appealed for. I do not pursue him to N.Y. but I will resist the spirit of Bossism whenever it assails me.

Am reading Riddle's delightful tales, the *House of Ross,* etc.[169]

June

WEDNESDAY, 1. Her improvement continues, appetite comes, and strength begins to return, but she is very very weak. At her thoughtful suggestion I send Brown to London on business to give him a rest after the long strain of the past year.[170]

Demanded the resignation of McGrew and his Deputy of the 6th Auditor's office—this on the report and request of MacVeagh and James. I am very sorry for McGrew, and hope he may still prove himself innocent of wrong.

In the evening I went with Brown to attend the Commencement Exercises at the Law Dep't of Howard University. I delivered the Diplomas to the graduates; one of them (Chas. H. Lemos) is my barber.[171] On our return Brown drove to the train, en route for N.Y. [and] London.

Retired at 11.30.

THURSDAY, 2. Today she talks about what shall be done the best to aid her restoration by a change of air, and she shows a great desire to sit up. Took her first taste of beef steak this morning.

The crowd of callers very great, especially from Maryland.

The ballotting at Albany shows a small decrease in the strength of the two resigned senators, and an increasing indication that two friends of the administration will be chosen.

Capt. George Garfield is here, and took dinner with us. Also

[169]Albert G. Riddle, *The House of Ross, and Other Tales* (1881).

[170]Joseph Stanley Brown, the President's secretary, who needed a vacation, was detailed by Garfield, at Mrs. Garfield's suggestion, to carry $6,000,000 in U.S. bonds to London. He was accompanied on the trip by Secretary of the Treasury Windom's brother-in-law, and returned to Washington on July 1.

[171]Charles H. Lemos, of Fredericksburg, Virginia, was employed in the Treasury Department for many years after his graduation at Howard University.

ex-Gov. Davis of Texas, who is a man [of] considera[b]l[e] culture and vigor. Retired at 11.45. Harry slept with me.

FRIDAY, 3. A very busy day. Cabinet meeting—Windom and Kirkwood out of the city and Blaine ill.

Soon after adjournment learned some things about the employment of Gibson[172] and Cook[173] by the Att'y Gen. in connection with Post Office investigation which trouble me. The latter [former] has long been my defamer, the former [latter] has an unsavory reputation. Called on Blaine and found [him] unable to go to Ft. Monroe with us. Crete is rapidly recovering, and

[172]Albert M. Gibson, formerly the Washington correspondent of the *New York Sun,* was at this time a lawyer in New York City; he usually spent his winters in Washington. During the 1870's he devoted considerable time to the study of star route contracts. Postmaster General James, hearing of his study of star routes, invited him to come to Washington, where, after he had talked with James and MacVeagh, he was employed (April 22, 1881) as special counsel in the star route investigations; he was associated with the investigations until January, 1882. The tabulation of star routes shown to Garfield on April 9 (see n. 114) was chiefly indebted to an earlier tabulation of 93 routes made by Gibson. In testifying before a congressional committee in 1884, Gibson said that it was "a little remarkable that it should have excited so much surprise on the President's part, because I have a distinct recollection of showing him the same table in 1880." See pp. 65–67 of the volume cited in n. 166, May 30, 1881. Garfield's objections to Gibson were the result of Gibson's activities as a journalist. See Vol. III, p. 485. Gibson was the author of *A Political Crime; the History of the Great Fraud* (1885), an account of the election of 1876 and its aftermath from the Democratic point of view.

[173]William A. Cook, a leading criminal lawyer in Washington, D.C., began to practice law in 1847. He was attorney for the city, 1868–70, and for the District of Columbia, 1871–74. On June 1, 1881, Attorney General MacVeagh appointed him special assistant U.S. attorney for the District of Columbia to aid in the star route prosecutions; his association with the investigations continued until March 1, 1882. Although he testified that he thought he had had four interviews with President Garfield, it is probable that he had only one—on Wednesday, June 28, in the company of the postmaster general and P. H. Woodward. On that occasion, as he was leaving, he cautioned the President to be careful of his movements in view of the bitterness growing out of the star route investigations. Garfield had been given an unfavorable view of Cook by journalist Henry Van Ness Boynton and perhaps by a justice of the Supreme Court of the District of Columbia. See pp. 7, 93–99, 336–337, 805–807, 808–809, 845–846 of the volume cited in n. 166, May 30, 1881.

commands me to go—so, at 3.50 I reached the Navy Yard, and in company with Hal, Jim and Mollie went on board the *Dispatch,* and joining Sec'y and Mrs. Hunt, their two sons, and Col. Rockwell, Lulu and Don, started down the river. A pleasant trip in prospect, if only Crete were with us.

Retired at 11.45.

SATURDAY, 4.   Arrived at Ft. Monroe at 8 A.M. The yards of three men of war (one of them the German ship *Nymphe*) were manned, and salutes of 21 guns were fired. The officers of these ships called on me soon after we anchored. After an hour's delay we went to Norfolk, but arriving in a pouring rain, did not go ashore. Many officers came on board, and a few citizens, among them Mr. Dezendorf, M.C. The storm not abating we steamed back to Ft. Monroe, and took rooms at the Hygeia Hotel, where we passed the night. Many people called in the evening.

Retired at 11.30—after receiving telegram assuring me that Crete was still improving. I would not have come on this trip but for her order.

SUNDAY, 5.   Breakfast at 8.30, then visited the fort and Gen. Getty,[174] the Commandant, thence went by carriages to the Soldiers' Home, where 750 veterans marched in review, thence to Hampton and heard the last 15 minutes of a vigorous and sensible sermon by the chaplain. At the close, and after dismission, I made a few remarks on the labor problem and its two phases as seen in the Indian and Negro races there represented.[175] We

---

[174]George W. Getty (1819–1901) graduated at West Point, 1840, fought in the Mexican War and the Civil War, rising to the rank of brevet major general in 1865. He served on the board which reinvestigated the Fitz John Porter case (1878–79) and reversed the decision of 1863 reached by the court martial of which Garfield had been a member. He commanded troops along the Baltimore and Ohio Railroad during the railroad strike and riots of 1877, and for six years commanded the post and the artillery school at Fort Monroe. He retired from the army in 1883.

[175]The principal of Hampton Institute, Samuel C. Armstrong, invited Garfield (April 15) to the school's anniversary exercises on May 19, to lay the cornerstone for "a large new building for the education of Indian Girls," and to speak, but Garfield declined the invitation. He therefore made it a point during this trip to visit nearby Hampton, on whose board of trustees he served, 1870–75.

then visited the buildings, heard the singers, and returned to the Hygeia at 2 P.M. Soon afterwards our party visited the *Portsmouth* and [*Saratoga*], U.S. war ships, and saw the maneuvres of the apprentice boys. I then returned to the *Dispatch* while Sec'y Hunt and Admiral Porter visited the *Nymphe,* tradition not allowing the President to go on board a foreign man-of-war. I do not know the origin of this custom.[176] At 5.30 we steamed around the three ships, who manned their yards and cheered us. The fort fired a salute of 21 guns and we left for Washington.

MONDAY, 6. Reached the Navy Yard at 9 A.M., after taking breakfast on board. Home 30 minutes later, and found the dear one much better than when we left. At noon I helped her walk to a chair, and she sat for nearly an hour. The light grows stronger in our family circle and we can hardly know trouble since she is safe. The stream of callers, which was dammed up by my absence, became a torrent and swept away my day. In the evening I sent for Mr. Woodward, Post Office inspector, to find what was being done in the Star route investigation and to know why Gibson and Cook had been employed. I am not pleased with these men. The first has been a vile calumniator of public men and the second appears to have an unsavory reputation. I find there is much feeling among my friends that such men should have been employed without first consulting me.

TUESDAY, 7. After breakfast spent an hour and a half overhauling the mail and dictating answers. I miss Brown (who is today in midocean) for his anticipating thoughtfulness in reference to office work.

Cabinet meeting with Windom, MacVeagh and Kirkwood absent. Interesting conversation on the sad condition of Peru, and our duty to prevent her destruction.[177] I called up the importance

---

[176]The editors have found no evidence of such a custom, and authorities at the United States Naval Academy, and at the Navy Yard, Washington, D.C., maintain that there never was one.

[177]Early in 1881 Peru suffered catastrophic reversals in her war with Chile. In January, a Chilean army launched a campaign which culminated in the destruction of the Peruvian army, the capture of Lima, and the flight to the mountains of the Peruvian dictator Don Nicholás de Piérola. In March, leading men of Lima held a council and established under García Calderón a provisional government which

of the Sandwich Islands in relation to the future commerce of the Pacific, and the Isthmus canal or railway. In the evening attended the Law Commencement of Columbia[n] College at the National Theatre. Address by Judge Wm. Lawrence, prizes awarded by Solicitor General Phillips.

Crete is rapidly gaining in appetite and strength. Retired at 11 P.M.

WEDNESDAY, 8. The dear one, the first time since her illness began, put on a morning dress, and sat up several hours. Her recovery promises to be rapid at least in its first stages, but the full restoration of strength will, I fear, be slow. She made a special point of being dressed to celebrate this day, the anniversary of my nomination at Chicago. It was the beginning of an active year. The friends of the administration at Albany made some progress towards concentrating on Depew. They gave him 51 votes. My day in the office were [was] very like its predecessors. Once or twice, I felt like crying out in the agony of my soul against the greed for office, and its consumption of my time. My services ought to be worth more to the government than to be thus spent. Horseback at 6. National Law College Commencement at Congregational Church evening. Retired at 10.30. Slept with Crete first since illness.

THURSDAY, 9. The dear one is daily improving in strength and cheerfulness of hope, and every other sorrow fades in the light of the joy her recovery brings.

The crowd of callers was very great. I miss Brown, whose tact saved me from many people who now elude the skill of Pruden.[178]

---

the United States formally recognized. The *New York Times* (June 7) reported that its latest news from Peru, dated May 28, indicated that the Chilean invader might organize a government backed by the army, and that business was "exceedingly depressed, and poverty and distress" prevailed everywhere. Unfortunately for the Peruvians their condition under Chilean domination continued to deteriorate as the year progressed. The United States attempted without success to bring about a peaceful settlement of the conflict, but not until October, 1883, did Chile and Peru conclude a treaty of peace.

[178]Octavius L. Pruden was a clerk in the Bureau of Military Justice before being transferred in 1873 to the White House, where he became an executive clerk.

The Ohio State Republican Convention has spoken wisely, endorsing me very strongly, but not referring to N.Y affairs in the platform, although the several speakers spoke with great directness about the "boss" system. The Albany fight goes on with signs of Bribery accompaniment.[179]

Conkling, who has always inclined to think some one was trying to "humiliate" him, has succeeded in inflicting measureless humiliation on himself. Suicide is the chief mode of political death after all.

FRIDAY, 10.   After breakfast Gen. Swaim, Dr. and Mrs. Boynton and I drove to the Baltimore and Ohio Depot, and took a special train for Annapolis, where we attended the graduation of the Class of 1881, in the Naval Academy. I was specially interested in Schock[180] of Pa., who not only graduated at the head of his class, but with higher marks than any cadet has made in many years.

Lunched with the Superintendent, Admiral Balch,[181] and dined at 6, at the "Board" House. Took the train at eight-fifteen, and reached home about ten P.M. Found that Crete had kept on

President Hayes promoted him to assistant private secretary, a post that he retained until his death in 1902. He "earned the sobriquet of 'the Sphinx of the White House' because of his extraordinary reticence concerning all matters pertaining to official business." See Kenneth E. Davison, *The Presidency of Rutherford B. Hayes* (1972).

[179]On June 9 a member of the New York state assembly who had been supporting Conkling and Platt for reelection, declared that on the previous evening he had been given $2,000 by a state senator with the understanding that he would vote for Chauncey Depew for senator; the assemblyman further stated that he had reported the incident to the Speaker, George H. Sharpe, and handed over the money to him. The Speaker acknowledged that the assemblyman had told him the same story and that he now had the $2,000 in bills in his pocket. The legislature voted to set up a committee to investigate the matter. Some believed that the bribery charge was contrived for the purpose of injuring Depew. Other stories were afloat concerning efforts to influence votes by the use of money.

[180]John L. Schock was an assistant naval constructor at his death in Greenwich, England, in 1885.

[181]Rear Admiral George B. Balch (1821–1908), a native of Tennessee who served in the U.S. navy, 1837–83, was superintendent of the Naval Academy, 1879–81.

her upward course of improvement. The speech I made at the Academy was a pretty good one, but was dreadfully botched in the report, which was long hand and stupid.

Retired at eleven.

SATURDAY, 11. The crowd was kept away more effectually by the private secretaries than usual. Spent some time with Crete. Our dear Harry is having the first wild dream of love, is dead in love with Lulu Rockwell,[182] so much so, as to be an absorbing disturbance in both their lives. His mother had a long talk with him today, counseling him to avoid such absorption. I have never known such frankness in any lad of his age. Later in the day I talked with him. He feels powerless to draw back from the passion which involves him. It is a most innocent and intense passion, which, of course, at his age, cannot last.

The Marine band gave its first Concert for the season on the President's grounds this evening. Retired at eleven.

SUNDAY, 12. Went to church with Dr. Boynton and his wife— a very stupid sermon on a very great subject—a dull young man, with a loud voice, trying to pound noise into the question "What think ye of Christ?"[183]

---

[182]Lulu Rockwell married a Frenchman, by whom she had one son. In the 1920's she was living in Switzerland at Ouchy on Lake Geneva. She was then visited by Ruth (the daughter of Mollie Garfield) and her husband, Herbert Feis. Mrs. Feis recalled the visit nearly four decades later: Lulu "gave us a charming lunch and was very soignée in black silk, and I could see she had been quite a gal!"

[183]Charles Guiteau (1842–1882), self-styled "lawyer and theologian," was a hanger-on at Republican national and state committee rooms in New York City during the campaign of 1880. He arrived in Washington on March 6, hoping to secure an appointment as a consul. As weeks passed he grew increasingly disturbed by the struggle between the President and Senator Conkling, fearing that it would ruin the Republican party. Considering himself a Stalwart, he at length determined to "remove" the President in the interest of party harmony. About June 8 he bought a .44 calibre revolver. On Saturday, June 11, he test-fired it on the Potomac flats. The next day he was at the Disciple church when the President and the Boyntons were there. After the White House party had left, Guiteau looked from the outside through a window near the Garfield pew to discover whether it would be possible to shoot into the pew from that location.

At two P.M. Harry and [I] made a chair of our hands and arms and carried Crete down to the dining room—so she sat at her place the first time for 36 days. The joy was visible on every face at the table. At 5 P.M. took Dr. Boynton and wife and Mollie and the two little boys to the Soldiers' Home and inspected the President's House. Met Mr. and Mrs. Blaine on the ground and had a pleasant visit. At 7, Hal and I took Crete to the dining room to tea.

Retired at 10.30.

MONDAY, 13. I am feeling greatly dissatisfied with my lack of opportunity for study. My day is frittered away by the personal seeking of people, when it ought to be given to the great problems which concern the whole country. Four years of this kind of intellectual dissipation may cripple me for the remainder of my life. What might not a vigorous thinker do, if he could be allowed to use the opportunities of a Presidential term in vital, useful activity? Some civil service reform will come by necessity, after the wearisome years of wasted Presidents have paved the way for it. In the evening took Crete out on the south porch to see the sun set. Blaine came and read draft of instructions to our Minister to Chili. Retired at 12.

TUESDAY, 14. The dear one improves slowly, and begins to feel the imprisonment of her room. She is promised a ride tomorrow if the day is fair.

Cabinet full today for the first time for two weeks. Blaine read an important identic note to several of our leading Ministers in Europe on the neutrality of the South American Isthmus, holding that the U.S. has guaranteed its neutrality and denies the right of other, especially European powers, to take any part in the guarantee. Many callers. A long session in the evening with Sec'y Kirkwood on business which has accumulated during his absence. The children, except Irv and Abe, went down the river, and were delayed by an accident to the launch till near midnight. I had a broken night.

WEDNESDAY, 15. On the whole, about the hardest day for two weeks or a month. Not only an unusual number of people called,

610

but some trying work—among other things to ask Bentley[184] to resign the Commissionership of Pensions. On some accounts he has been an admirable officer, but there are irritations without and within the office which will, at least for a time, disappear with a new man.

The event of the day at home was that Crete rode out, and christened the new carriage which we have kept waiting for her more than a month. The air and sunlight were kind to her, and I could see the joy of convalescence shining in her face. But she realized her weakness when she attempted to step up into the carriage.

THURSDAY, 16. Appointed Col. Dudley, of Ind., Commissioner of Pensions, Judge N. C. McFarland,[185] Commissioner of the General Land Office.

Crete rode out again, a little longer trip than yesterday. We have concluded to take her to the sea shore for its bracing air. Will go to Long Branch on Saturday next.

In the evening I attended the graduating exercises of the Normal School at the Congregational Church. A very long address by Dr. Gregory[186] of Illinois, a marked case of an

---

[184]John A. Bentley was born in 1836 in New York, studied law and was admitted to the bar in 1857. He moved to Milwaukee, Wisconsin, where in 1859 he opened a law office. He served in the state senate and was U.S. commissioner of pensions, 1876–81. He moved to Colorado in 1881, practiced law, and, after serving as judge of the district court of Denver, 1891–95, turned to mining and milling precious ores.

[185]Noah C. McFarland (1822–1897), a native of Pennsylvania, attended Washington College (in which James G. Blaine was a fellow student) before going to Ohio, where he studied and practiced law and served a term in the state senate. In 1870 he moved to Topeka, Kansas, where he continued to practice law; he also served in the state senate. He held the office of commissioner of the general land office, to which Garfield appointed him, until 1885, when he returned to Topeka. He received two appointments as a regent of the University of Kansas.

[186]John M. Gregory (1822–1898), a native of New York, graduated at Union College in 1846, became a Baptist minister and an educator in Detroit, where he helped establish the *Michigan Journal of Education.* He was editor of that journal, 1855–70. He was president of Kalamazoo College, 1865–67, and of the Illinois

able man disgusting his audience by not knowing when to stop.
Home at 10.30. Retired at 11.45.

FRIDAY, 17. Crete again took a short ride and proved that she is able to make the contemplated journey to the sea shore.

Cabinet meeting fully attended. The crowd of callers before and after Cabinet specially large in view of my intended absence.

In the evening attended the exercises of Madame Burr's School, at the house of R. T. Merrick[187] in F St. Mollie took a part in the French play and did well.

The day has been the warmest of the season thus far.
Retired at 11.30.

SATURDAY, 18. At 9.30 took the limited train[188] (special car) with Crete, Mollie, Irvin and Abram, and Dr. Boynton and wife and Col. Rockwell for [New Jersey] and at 6.20 P.M. reached the Elberon station (Long Branch) and were driven to the Elberon House. Crete stood the journey very well, and the cool sea air promises to revive and restore her.

Many people called, and I saw a few. We have pleasant rooms in the east wing, which overlooks the sea.

SUNDAY, 19. Passed a restful day, with manifest betterment in her strength. Attended church at the little chapel near the hotel, in company with Dr. and Mrs. Boynton, and Col. Rockwell.

Industrial University (now the University of Illinois), 1867–80. He was the author of several books and articles, and devoted considerable time to public speaking.

[187]Richard T. Merrick (1828–1885), prominent Washington lawyer, had five daughters attending Madame Burr's School on New York Avenue. The school was small (having about thirty pupils) and exclusive (attended largely by children of the prominent). Madame Burr, who was born in Paris, came to the United States as a girl, married an American, and conducted her school for several decades. By 1881 her daughters had "assumed the more active duties of the school." On the evening of Garfield's attendance three French plays were presented; Mollie appeared in *La Loterie de Frankfort,* Lulu Rockwell in *L'Incognito.* See the *National Republican,* June 18, 1881.

[188]Charles Guiteau was at the station with loaded revolver when the Garfields arrived. But he could not bring himself to shoot: ". . . Mrs. Garfield," he wrote, "looked so thin, and clung so tenderly to the President's arm, my heart failed me to part them, and I decided to take him alone."

The worry and work of Washington seems very far away, and I rest in the large silence of the sea air.

I have always felt that the ocean was my friend, and the sight of it brings rest and peace. A few friends came during the day.

MONDAY, 20.   Remained in-doors nearly all day. Several people came on business, and for a social call—Amos Townsend, Horace Porter, Senator Miller, and several others. In the evening Secretary Lincoln came, bringing several matters of business.

In the late afternoon Crete walked with me to the beach, and sat for half an hour, and by my help walked up the stairs to her room. She is manifestly improving in strength.

I have denied myself to many people who called.

Retired about 12 [P.]M.

TUESDAY, 21.   Took a long drive with Crete and Dr. Boynton and wife. She is gaining strength every hour and I am getting rest.

Knox came with latest news from Albany, which is not decisive. It appears that Gen. Grant received my letter of May 15 before he left Mexico, and that he is now preparing a reply. He has permitted himself to drift into a violent prejudice against Blaine, and unjustly attributes Conkling's rage to Blaine. It is now evident (what I had not supposed) that Grant had his heart fully set on the nomination at Chicago, and was deeply hurt at his failure. He is talking wildly and very unjustly.

Retired at 12.

WEDNESDAY, 22.   Disposed of the New England invitation[189] and answered the accumulated mail. At 5.45 P.M. Dr. Boynton and wife, and Crete and I rode to Ocean Grove and back, a very pleasant trip. Secretaries Windom, Hunt and James, with their families, came in the evening, and at nine P.M. we held a Cabinet

[189]Garfield might have intended to write "invitations," for he was invited to be the guest of individuals, organizations and institutions in every New England state. Among the letters from Massachusetts was one from Mark Hopkins, who wanted to know whether Mrs. Garfield and the boys would make the trip, who and how many would stay at his home, and where Garfield planned to be on the Sabbath, the first day of Commencement, which he hoped the President would spend on the campus. Hopkins' letter reached the White House on June 20 and was immediately forwarded to Garfield at Long Branch.

meeting. Among other things the question of Gen. Grant's behavior was talked of, and Sec'y Hunt suggested that they ought not to call on him, unless he calls on me. The General arrived this evening and is stopping at his son's cottage opposite the Elberon.[190]

While the Cabinet was in session telegrams came informing me that my Uncle Thomas Garfield was killed by the cars, and Mrs. Arnold (Dr. Boynton's sister) had her skull fractured.[191] The Doctor leaves by first train. I offered him a cheque for $1,000 for his services in Crete's sickness, but he altogether refused. Retired at 12 midnight.

THURSDAY, 23. Rested, wrote, read, rode, and answered dispatches. Dr. Boynton left at 6.40 this morning to catch the 9 A.M. train on the Erie R.R.

At 1 P.M. I reviewed the 7th N.Y. veteran Reg't from the steps of the Elberon.[192] At 1.30 drove to the Ocean House and received the Pa. editors and their wives to the number of about 600. The members of the Cabinet present attended the banquet of the 7th Reg't at the West End Hotel. I did not go on account of the death of Uncle. Dispatches from Ohio that Cordelia['s]

[190]While Garfield was riding to Ocean Grove and back, Grant reached Long Branch, where he stayed at the cottage of his son Jesse because his own was not ready. He visited the hotel while Garfield was eating dinner, but he did not seek an interview. "As yet," said the *New York Times* (June 23), "they have not met."

[191]On the afternoon of June 22 an eastbound train on the New York, Pennsylvania and Ohio Railroad struck a buggy carrying Cordelia (Boynton) Arnold and Thomas Garfield. Mrs. Arnold suffered a badly fractured skull; Uncle Thomas was killed instantly. On receiving news of the tragedy, the *New York Times* (June 23) reported, "the President retired to his room."

[192]The occasion was the anniversary of the regiment, which appeared with nearly eight hundred members and a full regimental band. After passing in review before Garfield they marched to the West End Hotel for dinner and speeches. The first of several toasts was to the President, to which Secretary of the Treasury Windom responded. He praised Garfield for the financial condition of the country, which "was never more sound," and declared that he himself was "a good deal more of a civil service reformer" than when he joined the administration three and a half months earlier. "In the last 100 days," he noted, "a few thousand men in search of office have taken nine-tenths of the time of the President and his Cabinet advisors. This time is due to the 50,000,000 people rather than to the office-seekers."

case is very critical, though not altogether hopeless. At 6, Crete, Anna, Rockwell and I took a pleasant drive back into the country.

Retired at 11.

FRIDAY, 24. Windom and his daughter left for Washington after dinner. The Post Master General went to N.Y. and returned in the evening. Many callers during the day, but only a few received. At 6 P.M. drove out with Crete, Anna and Col. Rockwell. Gen. Grant was standing in front of his son Jesse's cottage, and bowed, lifting his hat. This is his only courtesy to me since he came four days ago. I do not think he can afford to show feeling in this way. I am quite certain he injures himself more than he does me. It is evident that the third term passion had entered very deeply into his heart, and that he does not bear himself as becomes a citizen. He has no right to consider the appointment of Robertson a personal affront. He appointed a postmaster in my county against my consent when I was a Representative in Congress.[193]

Retired at 11.30.

SATURDAY, 25. Crete is not so well as she was yesterday. Perhaps she is eating too much for her strength. The absence of Dr. Boynton leaves her without the counsel she has had hitherto. At 11.30 Crete, Mollie and I drove far out into the country, making a drive of two hours and a half. This rested Crete more than sitting in the house. At 5.30 P.M. I held a reception in the parlor of the Elberon, seeing the cottagers near here. A very pleasant company. Gen. Grant came in and remained two [or] three minutes—a tardy recognition of the respect due to the office he once held. He has been here four or five days.[194] Played whist

[193]In the early weeks of his first administration Grant disregarded Garfield's recommendation for the post office in Ravenna and nominated one of his father's acquaintances for the position. Although this action contravened the custom whereby a president consulted pro-administration congressmen about their preferences for postmasters in their districts, Garfield failed to get Grant to change his mind and resentfully gave way.

[194]The informal reception was held at Garfield's request and intended only for Elberon cottagers, but, said the *New York Times* (June 26), "guests of hotels, cottages, and cottagers above the West End also hastened to pay their respects to

at Judge Hunt's cottage with him and Mrs. Hunt and Mrs. James. Retired at 11.50.

SUNDAY, 26. Attend[ed] St. James Church near the Ocean House at the invitation of Gen. Webb,[195] President of the College of New York. Home to the Elberon and read aloud to Crete from *Holland and Its People,* by De Amicis.[196] Lieut. Harber came and spent part of the day.

At six P.M. drove with Crete to Mr. Hooey's [Hoey's][197] place, she and Anna returning, while Rockwell and I remained to an elegant dinner. Present with us, Hugh Hastings,[198] McMi-

the Chief Executive." Garfield received guests for an hour or more, and "at the last moment Gen. Grant . . . entered the reception room. There was a buzz of excitement as the General, with hat in hand and bowed head, approached Mr. Garfield and extended his hand, which was heartily shaken by the President. A moment of whispered conversation ensued between them, when Gen. Grant stepped back and, walking out to the platform, entered his carriage. . . . Three minutes did not elapse from the time of Gen. Grant's entrance until his departure."

[195]Alexander S. Webb (1835–1911), graduated at West Point in 1855, fought in Florida against the Seminoles, taught at West Point, and was a Union officer in the Civil War, winning the Congressional Medal of Honor (awarded in 1891) for "distinguished personal gallantry in the Battle of Gettysburg." Following his military career he was president of the College of the City of New York, 1869–1902. The *New York Times* (June 27) reported that while Garfield and his wife attended the church of St. James in East Long Branch, Grant and his wife worshipped in the St. James Chapel near the Elberon Hotel.

[196]Edmondo de Amicis, *Holland and Its People,* translated from the Italian by Caroline Tilton (1881).

[197]John Hoey (1825–1892), a native of Ireland, migrated in boyhood to the United States, peddled papers, entered the express business and made a fortune. He was general manager of the Adams Express Company, 1854–88, and president, 1888–91. In Elberon he owned the Hollywood estate, which he transformed into Hollywood Park. Opened in 1882 and admired over the years by thousands of visitors, the park had a magnificent house, English lawn, conservatory, beautiful gardens, swimming tank, luxurious hotel, and costly cottages. His wife, Josephine Shaw, an English actress, retired upon marrying Hoey, but returned to her profession for about fourteen years following Laura Keene's departure from Wallack's theater in 1853.

[198]Hugh J. Hastings (1820–1883), a native of Ireland, migrated with his family to the United States in 1831 and settled in Albany, New York. He reported for

cha[e]l[199] of Philadelphia, William Garrison,[200] Thos. Murphy,[201] Sec'ys Hunt and James and Mr. Jameson. Returned at 9 P.M. Mr. Ballou called and visited half an hour. Retired at 10.15.

MONDAY, 27.   Left by Special at 9.30 in company with Rockwell, Sec'y Hunt and family and Sec'y James, and arrived at Washington at 4 P.M.[202]

Heavy storm afternoon and evening. Much back work to bring up. Many callers in the evening.

Retired at 11 P.M.

TUESDAY, 28.   A very hard day. The flood which had accumulated in my absence burst forth with resistless force and I was borne along by it till the Cabinet met. We sat three hours—all present but MacVeagh.

Mrs. Rockwell went to Long Branch today to stay with Crete who telegraphs me this morning that she is improving. I fear the sea air is too strong for her—thought it greatly helped her the first four or five days. Gov. Foster is here. In the evening while he (F.) was with me, Dorsey and Ingersoll[203] came, and read an

---

the *Albany Atlas,* 1840–43, and in 1844 established the *Albany Knickerbocker.* He became the editor of the *New York Commercial Advertiser* in 1868 and its proprietor in 1875. Active in state and national politics, he was a strong supporter of Grant.

[199]William McMichael (1841–1893), a native of Philadelphia, was a lawyer, a Union officer, 1861–65, U.S. minister to Santo Domingo and U.S. attorney for the eastern district of Pennsylvania. Garfield appointed him to the Board of Indian Commissioners.

[200]William R. T. Garrison (1834–1882), a native of Goderich, Ontario, graduated at Palmyra College in 1852, entered the bank in San Francisco of which his father was a proprietor, and made a fortune in banking, shipping, and railroad development. He moved to New York in 1864 and lived there to his death in a railroad accident in Elberon.

[201]Thomas Murphy (see Vol. III, pp. 32–33, n. 58) had an imposing residence at Long Branch.

[202]Charles Guiteau was among those who witnessed the arrival at the station of the President and his party.

[203]Robert G. Ingersoll was acting as counsel for Stephen W. Dorsey in connection with the star route investigations. He was chief counsel for the defendants in the two trials of the "Dorsey combination" for conspiracy to defraud the government.

affidavit of Reedell [Rerdell][204] recounting his pretended revelations to James and MacVeagh. I told them R. confessed himself a liar and scoundrel, and I did not believe a word of his stuff as against James and MacVeagh. Retired at 11.30.

WEDNESDAY, 29.   Telegram from Crete says she is still improving, and Mrs. Rockwell is with her. Long discussion of the Yorktown Centennial Celebration Commission, and urging to greater activity in preparing for it. Delegation from Mobile in reference to the Post Office at that place. General rush as usual. Had a long talk with General Dent[205] in reference to the District Commissionership. Doubt the wisdom of removing now, yet possibly a change ought to be made.

Drove at 6—8 with Harry and Capt. Henry.[206]

[204]Montfort C. Rerdell, as secretary and agent of Stephen W. Dorsey during Dorsey's years in the Senate (1873–79) and afterwards, was deeply involved in the business of star route contracts (see n. 108, March 31, 1880). In early June, 1881, apparently alarmed by the course of the investigation of star route frauds then in progress, he decided to make "a clean breast" of his activities in relation to star routes, and did so to Postmaster General James and soon after to Attorney General MacVeagh. Before the authorities could obtain documentary evidence in his possession, however, Rerdell, under heavy pressure from a distraught Dorsey, who considered him a squealer and traitor, recanted his statements in an affidavit to James and MacVeagh. In the first star route trial of the "Dorsey combination" Rerdell was prosecuted with seven others (including Dorsey and Thomas J. Brady) for conspiring to defraud the government. Rerdell and another underling were the only ones convicted; two defendants were acquitted; on four (including Dorsey and Brady) the jury was unable to reach a verdict. The judge set aside the verdict in the case of the two men convicted. In the second trial Rerdell pleaded guilty and became a government witness—not that his testimony was worth much at that point. The jury having brought in a verdict of not guilty for all the defendants, the judge discharged Rerdell also, recognizing that it took more than one person to conspire.

[205]Josiah Dent was one of three commissioners of the District of Columbia from 1878 to 1882, when President Arthur appointed Joseph R. West to succeed him. At the time of this entry he was president of the commissioners. Julia Dent Grant, wife of President Grant, once referred to Josiah Dent as "an old and esteemed friend of my family." See John Y. Simon, ed., *The Personal Memoirs of Julia Dent Grant* (1975), p. 325.

[206]From a bench in Lafayette Park, across from the White House, Charles Guiteau, armed with his revolver, watched the departure of the carriage. It was

Telegram from Brown who has reached America.
Retired at 12.

THURSDAY, 30. A very busy day, closing up the fiscal year. Nearly all the members of the Cabinet called on business. Telegram from Dr. Boynton that Cordelia is unconscious and fast sinking. Telegram from Crete that she is improving. Wants Rockwell or me there Friday to see the little boys off for Ohio. Swaim goes tonight. In the evening dined at Sec'y Hunt's with Rockwell, Lincoln and James. Home at eleven, retired at 12.

July

FRIDAY, 1. This opening of the Fiscal Year, and day before my trip to New England, has been very full of work. Appointed very nearly 25 ministers and consuls. Dismissed French,[207] the R. R. Commissioner, in consequence of his sending an official letter to the President of the Pacific R.R. instead of his superior officer. Also called for the resignation of the Register of Wills. Appointed Walker Blaine 3rd Ass't Sec'y of State. He is a bright and able young man and I wanted to compliment both him and his

a "very warm" evening, and when half an hour had passed and the carriage had not returned, he "let the matter drop for that night."

[207]Theophilus French, of Ohio, held the office of commissioner of railroads in the Department of the Interior, to which he had been appointed by President Hayes in 1878. His office was concerned solely with western railroads to which the government had made land grants or loans. One of his duties was "to examine the books, accounts, and property" of those roads. In the spring of 1881 he spent several weeks on the Pacific coast, during which he took it upon himself to inform in writing the president of the Central Pacific Railroad that he would deem it his duty "at an early date to communicate with the Attorney-General of the United States with a view to a discontinuance of" a suit brought by the government against the railroad in the U.S. Circuit Court for the southern district of New York. See editorial in the *New York Times* (June 24). According to the *Alexandria Gazette* (June 29) the departing commissioner would "step into the lucrative position of agent of the Central Pacific Railroad."

father. Brown returned today, greatly refreshed by his European trip. Cousin Cordelia died today, of the R.R. injuries rec'd when Uncle Thomas was killed. Retired at 12.[208]

---

[208]In the late afternoon of this day Garfield walked to the home of James G. Blaine on Fifteenth Street. Charles Guiteau, armed with his revolver, was sitting in Lafayette Park when the President came out of the White House. He followed him on the opposite side of the street, and, after Garfield had entered the Blaine house, watched from the nearby Wormley Hotel. Garfield gave Mrs. Blaine a bound copy of his inaugural address and chatted with her until her husband's return. Soon after the arrival of the secretary, the two men emerged from the house, arm in arm. Guiteau waited until they had passed him, then followed them as they walked through the park. He made no effort to shoot. The next morning Blaine came to the White House in a State Department carriage to escort the President to the Baltimore and Potomac Railroad station, where the presidential party was to begin its trip to New England. Guiteau was lurking in the Ladies' Waiting Room when the President and the Secretary of State entered it. This time he fired, and at close range.

ACKNOWLEDGMENTS

In Volume I we acknowledged our indebtedness to many individuals and institutions for their assistance with the first two volumes. To many then named we owe our thanks for continuing aid.

We are also grateful to individuals, not listed in Volume I, who have contributed to the last two volumes and in some instances to the first two. They include Thorn Pendleton of Warren, Ohio, great grandson of Harmon Austin, Professors Fritz Herzog, Justin Kestenbaum and Edward Nordhaus of Michigan State University, Richard A. Baker, historian of the U.S. Senate, James Ketchum, curator of the U. S. Senate, Harriet Scofield, C.G., of Cleveland, Laurie A. Baty, George Eastman House, Rochester, New York, Frances Slack, former administrative secretary, Lake County Historical Society, and the late Constance McLaughlin Green.

Institutions not listed in Volume I whose collections and staffs have contributed to the completion of the last two volumes and to which we are grateful, include in Ohio: the Lake County Historical Society (Eric J. Cardinal, administrator, Mrs. Laine Mull, and other staff members), the Andrews School (George A. Kleinfeld), the Ashtabula County District Library, the Caldwell Public Library, the Carnegie Public Library (Conneaut), the Cincinnati Historical Society, the Public Library of Cincinnati and Hamilton County, the Dawes Memorial Library (Marietta College), the Logan County District Library (Bellefontaine), the London Public Library, the Morley Library (Painesville), the Ohio Wesleyan University Archives, the Pomeroy Public Library, the Reed Memorial Library (Ravenna), the Sandusky Public Library, the Steubenville Public Library, the Warren Public Library, the Way Public Library (Perrysburg), and the Public Library of Youngstown and Mahoning County. Institutions outside Ohio include the Austin Public Library, the Butler Library (Columbia University), the Department of Archives and History (Jackson, Mississippi, and Raleigh, North Carolina), the Grand Rapids Public Library, the Hotsprings Public

Library (South Dakota), the Joint Free Public Library (Morristown, New Jersey), the Memphis Public Library, the Nimitz Library (U. S. Naval Academy), the National Portrait Gallery, the New Orleans Public Library, the Topeka Public Library, the Warren Library Association (Pennsylvania), the Public Library of Washington, D. C., and the Withers Public Library (Bloomington, Illinois).

We owe special debts of gratitude to Lyle Blair, director of the Michigan State University Press, for his help since the beginning of our project; to Russell Smith, microfilm specialist, Manuscript Division of the Library of Congress; to Susan McMahon for her skillful typing and cheerful disposition; and to Michigan State University for leaves and grants that have made it possible for us to complete our work.

APPENDIX

Listed below are the parts of the diary for the years 1878, 1879, 1880, and 1881 which are in Garfield's hand (with the exception of an occasional correction made by him).

1878

January 7	Second paragraph.
January 18–19	Entire.
January 24	Second paragraph.
January 25–March 4	Entire.
March 9–10	Entire.
March 12–24	Entire.
April 4	Second paragraph.
June 16	Second paragraph.
June 17–18	Entire.
June 21	Second and third paragraphs.
June 22–November 25	Entire.
December 7–13	Entire.
December 14	Second paragraph.
December 15	Entire.
December 18–19	Entire.

1879

February 23	Entire.
March 19	Second Paragraph.
June 19	Second paragraph.
July 2	Second paragraph.
July 3–27	Entire.
July 28	First two sentences.
August 21–December 20	Entire.
December 21	Except for last two sentences.

1880

January 3–8	Entire.
April 14	Entire.
April 24	Entire.
May 24	From "in the grounds of the Naval Observatory" to end of entry.
May 25–June 1	Entire.
July 24–August 23	Entire.
September 16–25	Entire.
September 26	Except for last two sentences.
October 24–November 7	Entire.
November 10	Entire.
November 13–14	Entire.
November 16	From "J. Medill of Chicago came today" to end of entry.
November 27	From "Conference with L. P. Morton" to end of entry.
December 8	From "The Ohio Senatorship annoys me" to end of entry.
December 10	Second paragraph.
December 11–31	Entire.

1881

January 1–July 1	Entire.

The Diary of Lucretia Rudolph Garfield
March 1–April 20, 1881

Between 1854 and 1856 Lucretia Rudolph kept a diary intermittently. After a lapse of a quarter of a century, stimulated by inaugural preparations, she began once more to keep a personal record. The record extends over a period of fifty-one days. Two weeks after her last entry she came down with a serious illness diagnosed as malaria and "nervous exhaustion." She was still convalescing on the New Jersey coast when President Garfield was shot. Most of the names of persons mentioned by Mrs. Garfield appear in the Garfield *Diary.* The reader is referred to the indexes to locate earlier identifications.

March

MARCH 1. At nine A.M. arrived in Washington at the Baltimore and Potomac Depot. As we stepped from the cars we were met by the Committee, who had been waiting for several hours—appointed to welcome the President elect. They conducted us quickly through the great crowd of people who were in waiting. Mr. Webb Hayes the President's son took especial charge of Mother, and drove with her immediately to the President's House—also Abram and Mary McGrath. The remainder of our party were driven to the Riggs House where we remain until after the Inauguration. It was a strange coming back to Washington—so many years our home; and as we drove through Pennsylvania Avenue—the sun shining a warm welcome, banners and flags fluttering out a "Hail to the Chief" from every street corner and almost from every house top—the tears would tell of the strange excitement that had touched my heart. The last eight or nine months have been so like a dream and yet so intensely real. The beginning of June found me at our farm home in Mentor wholly absorbed in the rebuilding and refitting our house and

625

during the days of excitement before and during the Chicago Convention I gave myself no personal anxiety in regard to it. I knew General Garfield did not desire the nomination for the Presidency and knowing that I did not believe he would receive it, and when the telegram came telling me that it had been done, I did not know whether to be sad or rejoice. But I was given no time to reflect over it. From all quarters congratulations were poured in by visitors by telegrams and by letters. Then came the triumphant return home, by way of our old first home where we met. The carriage that brought my darling precious husband was met by our own—which had brought me across the old nine-teenth district—at the corner of the College grounds (another of those strange coincidences which marked the first days of the nomination). From that time on through the summer, through the campaign, past the elections—each period filled with exciting events—we scarcely knew a quiet moment. Then—the struggle over—the winter was passed in waiting and preparation for our return here.

MARCH 4.   At three o'clock in the morning I awoke to hear the storm raging, and thought of the dreadful day that was coming with dispiriting cold and drizzle to make so uncomfortable the immense crowd that had gathered here. We rose early, took a hurried breakfast and prepared for the coming ceremonies. At half-past nine my party—a few chosen friends—Mrs. General Sheldon, Mrs. Colonel Rockwell with her children, Mrs. James Mason of Cleveland and her three daughters, Harry's friend Bentley Warren, and our children, met at the President's House by invitation of Mrs. Hayes, who with her party went with us directly to the Capitol, and were taken immediately to the gallery of Diplomatic Corps where we watched the closing hours of the Senate. Long before eleven o'clock the galleries were all crowded and over all hung the suspense of expectation. Grandma sat at the head of our seat—the most observed of all—Mrs. Hayes graciously having granted to her the seat of honor. Before twelve the floor of the Senate had become the centre of curiosity. The Diplomatic Corps in their glittering court uniforms, the Supreme Judges in their gowns and many of the Army and Navy officers in uniform made very brilliant the Chamber ordinarily so sombre in appearance. General Hancock lent his magnificent presence and was greeted with an outburst of applause. As the time drew near for the Inaugural ceremonies my heart grew stiller and stiller, when the rustle in the galleries and the standing up of the whole body of people in the chamber below told the approach of the two Presidents, I only saw them as they came in sight. I heard nothing and could not now tell from my own consciousness whether they were received with applause or with absolute silence. I am told there was applause, but I feel that silence would have been a higher tribute. After the inauguration of the Vice President and the opening of the new Senate an adjournment was made to the platform in front of the Rotunda. We were taken through the Rotunda and as we passed out upon the platform, the vast concourse of people massed in solid phalanx covering all the vast space in front of the Capitol was the grandest human spectacle I have ever seen. I have once or twice seen as large a number of people gathered in a moving swirling crowd, but this was grand in its unity. The eyes of all that vast assembly were centered on the one majestic figure that now stood before them —the President elect—waiting to witness the simple ceremony of taking the oath of office which should make him the head of this great nation. Again I heard no sound. I remember only a sublime silence. After a short pause the President elect stood out before the people and with the inspiration of the time and the occasion lifting him up into his fullest grandeur he became in the magnificence with which he pronounced his Inaugural almost superhuman. The ceremony ended, we all returned to the President's House where Mrs. Hayes presided for the last time at luncheon. After luncheon we all sat for two hours on the platform built for the President to review the troops. It was cold but the rain had ceased early in the day and the sunshine had conquered in its struggle with the clouds. At the first burst of sunshine just as we were starting for the Capitol, Mrs. Hayes exclaimed in her enthusiastic manner, "There! all is right now. I have no more anxiety," and we all hailed it as an omen of good to the new Administration. Were at the Inaugural Reception from 9 'till 11 in the evening. The new Museum Building was beautifully decorated for the occasion, and the whole entertainment was managed most charmingly.

MARCH 5. Slept too soundly, after all the fatigue of the past few days, to remember any dream; and so our first night among the shadows of the last eighty years gave no forecast of our future. All the morning was full of delegations and to the President full of weariness; but before night an immense load was lifted. The Cabinet was formed after all the weeks of struggle over it, and within three hours from the time the names were announced in the Senate, a Committee brought back word to the President that the confirmation of the whole number had been made.

MARCH 8. Evening—the Old and New Cabinet called to pay their respects.

MARCH 10. At two P.M. the Diplomatic Corps were formally presented. Mr. Evarts, the former Secretary of State, presented the Foreign Ministers and their wives to Mr. Blaine, the Secretary of the new Administration. He presented them to the President. Mrs. Blaine and Mrs. Evarts assisted me in the reception. It was all very brilliant, and I hope satisfactory. General Schenck —our former Minister to England and a very dear old friend of ours—came with his eldest daughter Lilly by special request. The General was not feeling well, but as always full of bright spirit and cheer.

MARCH 11. Evening—received the Army and Navy Officers and their families. For the first time we had the Marine Band. The House was beautifully decorated with flowers and plants from the Conservatory, and in the full blaze of light that can be turned on was really brilliant in spite of all its shabbiness.

MARCH 12. Held our first morning Reception for all the great roaring world. For two hours we took the hands of the passing crowd without a moment's intermission. Before the first hour was over I was aching in every joint, and thought how can I ever last through the next long sixty minutes. But the crowd soon made me forget myself, and though nearly paralyzed the last hour passed more quickly than the first.

MARCH 17. Was greatly surprised this morning to receive a letter which the following is a verbatim copy.

Thursday March 17, '81

1349 L st.

Mrs. Garfield

Madam,

I called last evening wishing to see you for a moment, to ask you if you desired to make any changes, regarding the social official etiquette of Washington Life. I am requested to bring out a fifth edition of my *Etiquette,* and before giving the order to the publisher it was my desire to have some conversation with you on the subject. To my surprise, however, the Flunkey at the door absolutely refused to take you my card, or make known to you in any way that I had called. Never having before in my life experienced a similar refusal, and being naturally unwilling to subject myself a second time to its possible recurrence, by again being sent away, I write, dear Madam, to ask you if you wish to see me about this matter, and if so kindly to mention what time will be agreeable to you.

I am Madam

Very Respectfully Yours

Madeleine Vinton Dahlgren.

To which I made the following reply—

Mrs. Dahlgren

Dear Madam

I regret that you were subjected to embarrassment at the door of the President's House last evening. It was through no fault of the usher, however, and unless he were disrespectful in manner he was only acting under orders. I had set apart two evenings of each week to be at home to all who should desire to call—reserving the others for special appointments in order that I might see my friends more socially than would be possible were all the evenings given up to promiscuous visiting. I may have blundered in my

629

method of getting this to be understood; but this custom once inaugurated I should have presumed upon your approval. If agreeable I will expect the pleasure of seeing you on Saturday evening next at eight o'clock, as this evening and tomorrow are for more public occasions.

Respectfully Yours

Lucretia R. Garfield

Very soon the following was received—

Mrs. Garfield

Dear Madam

I will do myself the honor on Saturday evening at eight o'clock to meet the "Special appointment" indicated by your favor just received. I am Madam with sentiments of the most distinguished consideration

Yours Very Respectfully &c &c

Madeleine Vinton Dahlgren

March 17th 1881

And this is the beginning of the petty criticism which might worry me, if I would let it. It is very evident to my mind that it all grew out of pique on the part of Mrs. Dahlgren because her card was refused.

MARCH 18. Very many persons called in the evening and among them I was glad to observe several of those who had left cards the same evening that Mrs. Dahlgren had been refused, and by a few indirect questions I was convinced that they had taken no offense, on the contrary had quite approved of my plan.

MARCH 19. This evening Mrs. Dahlgren came by appointment and we discussed at some length the innovation upon an old custom which she insisted I had made. She was sure the Democrats who are so afraid of "Republican Imperialism" would comment very unkindly on being refused to send in their cards, at the same time she was more severe than I had presumed to be on the character of the visiting that had been allowed during the last Administration. The whole affair only shows what sticklers we all are for our own opinions. Mrs. Dahlgren and I had the same result to be obtained at heart, namely to restore the dignity of the President's House; but she wished it to be done in her way and evidently thought me wax in her hands. I have never forgiven her for her attempt at intimidation which her first note indicated, nor do I think she by it gave evidence that she is the lady she assumes to be. I will give her credit however for kind feeling and with no desire to break with the present Administration.

On looking out this morning I discovered the newly made beds in the conservatory grounds and the yellow crocuses beginning to show their color. The birds were singing and the breath of the on-coming Spring came in through the open window. It made me reconciled that for the present, we were not among the still lingering snowbanks of our Mentor home.

MARCH 20. This afternoon General Schenck and Sallie called. The dear old General was looking very well again. The General insists that I am quite justified in my small change of the custom, and moreover does not think Mrs. Dahlgren is authority in regard to the unchangeableness of the rule.

MARCH 21. Today and yesterday received letters from home. It was like a breath of free, pure air to hear from the dear old home. I wonder if the time can come when we should be sorry to go back to it. Sent for Mrs. Blaine today to learn her opinion of Mrs. Dahlgren's criticism. She regards it altogether unjust. In the evening Mrs. James called, with the Post-Master General. She has only just arrived and this was her first visit. She is very agreeable and I think will be a pleasant addition to our political family. She was anxious to know what etiquette required in regard to visiting among the Cabinet Ladies.

MARCH 22. Sent letters this morning to Mrs. Ex-Secretary Evarts and to Mrs. Blaine to learn the rule in regard to Cabinet visiting. Mrs. Evarts answered that the custom of the last Administration was for the latest arrival to make the first visit to the others. Mrs. Blaine answered that she regarded any rule unnecessary as all were supposed to be on terms of friendly familiarity, but to avoid any embarrassment she would assume the responsibility of making the first visit. Since her position as wife of the Secretary of State puts her at the head her decision is very gracious, and comme[n]dable.

631

While at dinner today one of the ushers brought a card to the President saying that Secretary Blaine desired to see him for one moment only. He left the table, and after staying away through two or three courses came back looking very pale, but composed. A hush fell on all at the table and no one had quite the courage to ask why; nor did the President yield to the inquisitive eyes that were centered upon him from all sides. After we had gone to our room he said to me, "I have broken Blaine's heart with the appointments I have made today. He regards me as having surrendered to Conkling. I have not but I don't know but that I have acted too hastily. Perhaps I ought to have consulted Blaine before sending in some of those New York appointments."

The General was in real distress over Mr. Blaine's feelings and could not sleep. He had decided, on account of the Secretary's anxiety, to send in another batch of appointments tomorrow which will very thoroughly antidote the first. These the President did not intend to send so soon, but urged by Mr. Blaine has concluded that *now* is the time.

MARCH 23.   The new list was sent in and the two New York factions stood looking into each others eyes astonished and enraged, but feeling themselves thoroughly fettered and outwitted. The Conkling faction may make a struggle yet, but before the country they are powerless.

MARCH 25.   This morning little Miss Bryan called to see me again in regard to her Father's prospects. She came to me soon after the inauguration to ask me to learn from the President whether there were any hope that her Father could have the Mission at Berlin in case Mr. [Andrew D.] White came home. She had said nothing to him about it but with the consent of her Mother had come in her artless girlhood to make the request of me. I am afraid the President will not think best to give it to her Father, but I really had not the courage to crush out her hope until it should be definitely determined. Last evening the President gave to Mrs. Sheldon and me the profound State secret that there would be no extra session called, and just now he gave to me another, namely that two of the

Cabinet officers had come to him with their resignation[s]—the Post Master General and the Attorney General—the first because of Mr. Robertson's appointment to the Collectorship in New York, and the second on account of Mr. Chandler's appointment as Solicitor General. The President was much less disturbed with this than with the first outbreak on Tuesday last.

Yesterday the 24th we with General Swaim drove out to Soldiers' Home and went through the President's House there. It looks very bare and desolate now, but I think has in it very pleasant possibilities.

Many persons called during the evening, among them Ex-Senator Thurman and wife. I was very glad to see them, and from the long ramble through the house I think they were very glad to come here again having banished themselves during the last Administration on the political belief of the Senator that Mr. Hayes had not been elected. The old Senator is very greatly gratified with the appointment the President has given him as one of the Commissioners to the "Money Conference" to meet in Paris. Mrs. Thurman goes with him and they both looked very happy last evening. We have always been good friends notwithstanding political differences, and when the President made this appointment, he sent to the Senator this message quoting from an old speech—"This is one of the flowers that grow over the party walls in Politics." Mrs. Blaine and Mrs. Hunt were here and were both very cordial. I hope we may be able to establish a delightful "Social family."

MARCH 26. This morning the ground was again covered with snow, and it continued to sift down for several hours until we began to feel that Venner's storm spirit was abroad again.[1] Toward noon it cleared. At two o'clock Mollie had ten little girls to lunch with her. I am delighted with the sense and tact of the child. She, like her Father, seems to know intuitively just what to do. Fanny Hayes was one of the party and in giving Mollie some instruction in regard to seating them at table I

[1]See Oliver Wendell Holmes, *Elsie Venner* (1861). The tale began appearing in the *Atlantic Monthly* (December, 1859) under the title "The Professor's Story."

forgot to mention to her that Fanny should be considered the chief guest. But to my surprise I discovered that Mollie had comprehended her position and had taken Fanny out and seated her at her own right.

In the evening Col. and Mrs. Rockwell called with Mrs. Johnson. Mrs. Johnson was as elegant and charming as ever. She is to me a sort of enigma, and the Madam Merle of Aldrich's [James's] new story, *The Portrait of a Lady*,[2] is her facsimile.

MARCH 29.   Mrs. Evarts called this morning to say good bye before starting with her husband and daughters for Paris. When I last saw her she was in doubt whether to go or stay, but has finally decided to go with two of her daughters. Miss Bessie's fiancé is private secretary to Mr. Evarts and will be of the party. Also Miss Rachel Sherman, a bright daughter of General Sherman's. She came on Sunday evening with her Father to bid us good bye, as bright and happy as a bird over the prospect of such a delightful trip.

During the evening as many persons called as on previous Tuesdays and Fridays. I have run into so many entanglements over my plans that I should not have been surprised had there been a marked falling off. Mrs. Blaine and Abby Dodge stayed until all were gone. I shall grow to be fond of Mrs. Blaine as well as admire her. I have always been just a little afraid of her, and am glad to find it was without reason; for while she criticizes sharply she can be kind. Secretary and Mrs. Kirkwood also came, and helped to entertain very agreeably. Attorney General MacVeagh made an especial effort I imagined to be gracious. Evidently he is worried with the position he has taken in regard to Mr. Chandler, and hopes he may find some solution which will not take him out of the Cabinet. He brought me the following message from Mrs. MacVeagh. "I am coming on Monday next to take possession of the house we have rented, and am going to *stay.*" The New York muddle thick-

[2]See Henry James, *The Portrait of a Lady* (1881). Beginning in 1880 this novel appeared simultaneously in the *Atlantic Monthly* and *Macmillan's Magazine.*

ens. It begins to look as though the General's dream had a meaning.[3] I am sorry that it will probably alienate Vice President Arthur altogether. So far as Mr. Conkling is concerned I am indifferent—perhaps the truth is, I am glad of it. His whole course since the President's nomination has been contemptible, and I am glad that he rushes to take a position which will not require me to pretend politeness to him. I have despised him ever since I have known of his relations with Mrs. [Kate Chase] Sprague. However innocent he may be of crime, he is guilty of most selfishly compromising the reputation of Mrs. Sprague and of appearing cruelly neglectful of his own wife. Whatever may be said of his power it is only used to gratify his own vanity and selfishness, and to bolster up his hates. There is no true loyalty to Right, nor patriotism in him, and history will write him down for just what he is—*a peacock.*

April

APRIL 1. The last days of March have been cold and blustering. The snow and wind storms predicted by Venner do come, and his prognostications are making us almost superstitious. This morning dawned in a quiet spring-like fashion but the afternoon grew sullen, and forbade any enjoyment outside the house. At eleven o'clock this morning Mrs. Pound of Wisconsin called by an appointment made at her request. She told me the story of her first marriage, and of circumstances which had led to rumors detrimental to her character as a true woman. Her story convinced me that she has been cruelly wronged, although it has not changed my mind in regard to her fitness to be the wife of a Cabinet officer.

This evening there were fewer visitors than on any preceeding evening; due perhaps to the storm and in part doubtless to a more general understanding of my expectation for these evenings. The company was also more select. Mrs. Mahone,

[3]See n. 30, January 20, 1881.

the wife of the new Virginia Senator whose independent position in regard to party has given him just now so much notoriety, and her son spent nearly the whole evening. She is bright and I judge interesting, although I had little opportunity for conversation with her. Evidently she is a politician from the brisk determined way in which she called Senator Don Cameron of Pennsylvania to an account for failure to deliver some paper she had intrusted to him to the proper person. Among the visitors were Mrs. Senator Morrill of Vermont and her sister Miss Swan, Mrs. Dahlgren and Mr. Dana Horton, and Mr. Hoffman of the Congressional Law Library who said to me on entering the room, "This is the first time I have been in this house since 1860. I then attended the reception given to the Prince of Wales by Mr. Buchanan." And he related some of the incidents of that Reception.

APRIL 2. This morning Miss Withington, a news paper correspondent, came at eleven by appointment. She is sentimental and visionary. The sum of her talk was that from whisperings which came to her ears, she didn't know—she was afraid the President was too much influenced by his advisors, and finally it simmered down to this, that she did not quite trust Mr. Blaine, Secretary of State. I made her understand I think that the President knew not only the men around him but also knows what he is about, and I took occasion to make her know that I regard Mr. Blaine not only a brilliant fascinating man, but a man full of good impulses and of great magnanimity, and sterling worth withal. At half-past eleven Mrs. [Sara Andrews] Spencer called. She is the same erratic creature, and yet that is not the expression to use. Better call her a *genuine fanatic* although she would deny such a charge stoutly. She gave me one idea on the Temperance question which I confess new to my mind. In reply to my remark that drinking wine at a respectable dinner was so small a factor in bringing about the intemperance of the country that I felt there was great inconsistancy in giving it so much prominence, she said "Yes but all reforms must come from the better classes. You cannot expect the degraded man to give up his whisky when the rich and cultured sip wine at their own tables." This evening we gave a dinner to Doctor and Mrs. Hopkins. It was only a small informal dinner. The Chief Justice and Mrs. Waite, the two Massachusetts Senators and their wives, Judge Nott and Miss Susie Hopkins and Dr. Hawkes were the only guests beside our regular family. General and Mrs. Sheldon and Josie Mason are still here. After dinner I took occasion to talk with Dr. Hopkins on the wine question. The dear old man is broad and generous in all his views and has no sympathy with fanatics, but after looking at it on all sides he consented that if the hospitality of the Nation can be maintained with respectability he should be glad to have all alcoholic drinks banished from the President's table. About nine o'clock P.M. Mrs. Senator Hawley of Connecticut and Miss Olive Risley Seward, an adopted daughter of Secretary Seward, called. Miss Seward is an interesting woman, and expressed very great interest in the new administration. We sat in the red parlor, and she remarked, "I was sitting in this room with Mrs. Lincoln the night that the news came of the fall of Richmond. I remember the excitement that prevailed. Mr. Lincoln was away but many of the foreign ministers called to express their congratulations to Mrs. Lincoln." They could not see the dark pall that would so soon rest down not only on this House but on the Nation. These little scraps of reminiscence that I gather up now and then lend to this old place a weird charm that I fancy might grow into a solemn silence with me, did not my live boys go tumbling through it with their hand-springs and somersaults.

APRIL 3.   Did not attend church. Mollie was ill in bed with a cold and sore throat. Read one of Mrs. Burnett's stories, *Louisiana,* the first one of her stories I ever read. It is bright and picturesque in description, but knowing her as I do, I discovered her tastes and ideas controling her heroine in a way that shows how self-appreciative the author is. Perhaps that is natural. We all have our ideals of perfect dress, and I suppose as we would try to adopt it for ourselves, we would also put it on the heroine of our story.

APRIL 5.   This evening many persons called. Mrs. Senator

Davis among them. She is queer! I was really afraid she would provoke Mrs. Blaine to a cutting retort upon her, and I confess I am surprised at Mrs. Blaine's forbearance. It seems Mr. Davis is in some way responsible for continuing the dead-lock in the Senate, and Mrs. Blaine took occasion to ask why Mr. Pendleton's proposition to the Senate to go on with the executive work and discuss the organization or rather the election of the officers afterward, was not a good and reasonable one. Mrs. Davis with her grotesque grimaces and motions shook her finger at Mrs. Blaine, saying of course it could not be listened to coming from a Democrat, and is it possible that you Mrs. Blaine with your great intellect can ask such a question, and turning to some one she said Mrs. Blaine was a good Republican in the Senate but now her husband is in the Cabinet she would be glad to compel the Senate to do any thing to please the Democrats, &c, &c. Of course it was all intended to be pleasantry but there was both in what she said, and in her manner such a display of vulgarity, that I was surprised that Mrs. Blaine could withstand the impulse she must have felt to give her a sharp rebuke.

APRIL 7.   This evening General and Mrs. Sheldon and Josie Mason started for Ohio and we all have a sense of being abandoned. Mrs. Sheldon is without exception one of the most lovely characters among my acquaintance. Her face has always been to me most attractive. Her clear blue eye is the open window to a soul so bright and pure that you almost feel it angelic. Each year has added to my fondness for her, and this winter in New York and here with us this Spring I have grown to love her almost too well. So well that to be without her makes me really sad. She has fascinated every person who has had the good fortune to meet her. I fancy the celebrated Madam Récamier[4] may have been like her, I am sure she could not have been more charming. I so wish her husband could have been retained here. But the President felt that he must

---

[4]Madame Récamier (1777–1849), French society beauty and wit whose salon attracted the notables of the period of the Consulate and Empire.

not give him the only place he was willing to take; and now they are to go so far away that I shall almost feel she is lost to me. The children too miss her as much as I do. Josie too is bright and winsome and were she in good health would be most excellent assistance. But the poor child was suffering all the while she was here and could not be natural. Doctor and Mrs. Hopkins called with several friends, also Mrs. Dahlgren and Mr. and Mrs. Merrick.

APRIL 8.   The evening was very stormy and the visiting was quiet; not more than two or three parties being here together.

APRIL 10.   Yesterday we drove to the Capitol and ordered from the Library several books of the New England genealogies, and this morning we hunted through them for the record of the Mason family. To my surprise I found my mother's family descended directly from Major John Mason of Pequot fame. This afternoon rode with Mother and the younger children.

APRIL 11.   This P.M. the Secretary of the Navy and Mrs. Hunt drove with us to the Navy Yard. We visited the workshops, examined the new method of obtaining steam power by the evaporation of ammonia. The inventor—an Englishman—is most enthusiastic. It was very wonderful to see a piece of machinery run by *cold* instead of *heat.* The temperature was so low that parts of the engine were covered thick with snow. Went down to the wharf and saw the little boat in which they have just introduced an engine run by petroleum. The engine lies in the bottom of the boat wholly concealed and as there is no smoke nor steam pipe to indicate an engine and no oars, the spectator might imagine it a boat bewitched as he watches it scudding along indeed like "some *thing* of life."

APRIL 12.   A large number came this evening. Dr. Loring presented a company of Unitarians from Massachusetts; all interesting people. On the whole the company was much more select than at first. The Secretary and Mrs. Hunt came in to help me entertain, and the President gave us nearly the whole evening.

APRIL 13.   Dined this evening at Attorney General MacVeagh's—the first meal we have taken away from the White

House since the 4th of March. The dinner and all its appointments were very elegant. The MacVeaghs had just gotten fairly settled in their house and desired to have the whole Cabinet present, but succeeded in getting only the Secretary of State and Mrs. Blaine. The Secretary of the Treasury and Mrs. Windom. The Post Master General and Miss Dodge—with the President and myself. It was a very genial and con-genial party. After the ladies had returned to the parlor we dropped into a talk which I think would have satisfied the intellectual tastes of a "Corinne."[5] In the course of our talk Mrs. Windom suggested a theory concerning the transmission of intellectual tastes and talents which was new to me. She said that among her acquaintances were a husband and wife of fine intellect and eager for culture, but their circumstances did not allow them more than the most meagre gratification of them. They had several children who like themselves hungered and thirsted for knowledge. Finally they grew able to gratify their desires and before the birth of their last child they gave themselves up to the most thorough enjoyment of reading and study and to their surprise this child had no love for study whatever —was in fact the dullest of all the children. The question then was whether the child were not more affected by the un-gratified wants of the parent than by the positive qualities belonging to either Father or Mother, and whether that does not in part at least account for the utter distaste that the children of very intellectual parents have for study, and the strong desire they often exhibit for the most active life.

APRIL 15.   Good Friday and I decided to see only a few friends with whom I had an appointment. Mr. and Mrs. Nordhoff came with Mr. Joseph Harper and daughter.[6] We sat down to a good rattling talk over the dilapidated condition of this old White House, and I think I have enlisted both Mr. Nordhoff

---

[5]See Madame De Staël, *Corinne; or Italy* (1807). The heroine of this novel, one of the loveliest women of Rome, was an accomplished literary and artistic figure.

[6]The White House steward recorded these visitors as Mr. Jas. W. Harper, Jr., and Miss Josephine Harper.

and Mr. Harper to support me or rather the President in making a plea to Congress to rebuild during the summer following this. With much less money than a new house would cost this might be made a magnificent house.

APRIL 18.   Went to New York with Colonel and Mrs. Rockwell and Miss Ransom. Stopped at the Fifth Avenue Hotel. Went in the evening to visit the electric baths with reference to the advantage they might be to the President, and the possibility of introducing one in the White House.[7]

APRIL 19.   My forty ninth birthday. Spent all the morning in Sloane's carpet store studying designs suitable for the parlors of the President's Home. Selected at Scribner's a beautiful set of books for Mr. Whitelaw Reid as a wedding gift. He is to be married on the 26th.

APRIL 20.   Blundered! Allowed Miss Ransom to take us to the City Hall to see Alexander Hamilton's portrait, and she, poor woman! committed the mistake of presenting me to some of the officials, and the penalty is that this P.M. I am announced as having called on the Mayor at City Hall. I wonder if I shall ever learn that I have a position to guard! Spent the rest of the day shopping.

---

[7]An electric bath was, or was supposed to be, a remedial agent for individuals suffering with lame limbs, stiff necks, or rheumatic troubles. The bather entered a zinc-lined tub filled with water slightly above body temperature and equipped with wires that extended along its sides and connected to a battery. An inflated rubber pillow was placed under the neck of the bather, whose feet had to be pressed against the lower end of the tub. The operator turned on the current which sent, as a reporter for the *New York Times* (November 13, 1881) put it, "a pleasant sensation through the body. Its strength is gradually increased," the reporter noted, "until the muscles begin to twitch. Lie at full length in the tub and the current goes easily through the body without interruption, but bend a leg and such a current is instantly felt at the knee as sends the victim out of the water with a flop like a fish." The operator observed the bather closely during the forty-minute ordeal, which was followed by "a rubbing with bay rum."

Index